CIVILIZATION IN THE WEST

20°E 40°E 60°E 80°E 100°E 120°E 140°E 160°E

ARCTIC OCEAN

Barents Sea

Laptev Sea

SCANDINAVIA

SIBERIA

URAL MTS.

NORTH EUROPEAN PLAIN

Volga R.

Ob R.

Yenisey R.

Lena R.

Amur R.

Sea of Okhotsk

EUROPE

Aral Sea

ASIA

Baikal

ALPS

Danube R.

CAUCASUS MTS.

Black Sea

Caspian Sea

GOBI (DESERT)

Huang He R.

JAPAN

Sea of Japan

ZAGROS MTS.

Tigris R.

TIBETAN PLATEAU

HIMALAYA MTS.

Chiang Jiang

East China Sea

Mediterranean Sea

Euphrates R.

Indus R.

Ganges R.

Tropic of Cancer

AHARA ESERT)

Nile R.

Red Sea

ARABIAN DESERT

THAR DESERT

DECCAN PLATEAU

Persian Gulf

Mekong R.

South China Sea

PHILIPPINES

PACIFIC OCEAN

SUDAN

Arabian Sea

Bay of Bengal

AFRICA

ETHIOPIAN HIGHLANDS

SUMATRA

BORNEO

INDONESIA

NEW GUINEA

Zaire R.

Congo

CONGO BASIN

Victoria

JAVA

INDIAN OCEAN

Zambezi R.

MADAGASCAR

GREAT SANDY DESERT

KALAHARI DESERT

Tropic of Capricorn

AUSTRALIA

GREAT VICTORIA DESERT

Darling R.

Cape of Good Hope

NEW ZEALAND

CONTEMPORARY WORLD

Land Elevation

Feet		Meters
13,123		4,000
6,562		2,000
3,281		1,000
1,640		500
0		0
Below sea level		Below sea level

Ice-covered

0   1,000   2,000 mi.

0   1,000   2,000 km

Robinson Projection

ANTARCTICA

CIVILIZATION IN THE WEST

Seventh Edition

Volume C: Since 1789

Mark Kishlansky
Harvard University

Patrick Geary
University of California, Los Angeles

Patricia O'Brien
University of California, Los Angeles

PEARSON
Longman

New York   San Francisco   Boston
London   Toronto   Sydney   Tokyo   Singapore   Madrid
Mexico City   Munich   Paris   Cape Town   Hong Kong   Montreal

Senior Acquisitions Editor: Janet Lanphier
Assistant Development Manager: David Kear
Development Editor: Barbara Conover
Executive Marketing Manager: Sue Westmoreland
Supplements Editor: Brian Belardi
Media Editor: Melissa Edwards
Production Manager: Donna DeBenedictis
Project Coordination, Text Design, and Electronic Page Makeup: Elm Street Publishing Services, Inc.
Cover Designer/Manager: John Callahan
Cover Image: Getty Images, Inc./The Bridgeman Art Library
Photo Researcher: Vivette Porges
Manufacturing Buyer: Lucy Hebard
Printer and Binder: Quebecor World/Dubuque
Cover Printer: Phoenix Color Corporation

For permission to use copyrighted material, grateful acknowledgment is made to the copyright holders on pp. C-1–C-3, which are hereby made part of this copyright page.

Library of Congress Cataloging-in-Publication Data
Kishlansky, Mark A.
    Civilization in the West/Mark Kishlansky, Patrick Geary, Patricia O'Brien.—7ed.
        p. cm.
    Includes bibliographical references and index.
    ISBN 978–0–205–55684–7 (single v. ed.)—ISBN 978–0–205–55685–4 (v. I)—ISBN 978–0–205–55686–1 (v. II)—ISBN 978–0–205–55687–8 (v. A)—ISBN 978–0–205–55688–5 (v. B)—ISBN 978–0–205–55689–2 (v. C)
    1. Civilization, Western—History—Textbooks. I. Geary, Patrick J., 1948-II. O'Brien, Patricia, 1945-III.Title.

CB245.K546 2008
909'.09821—dc22

Please visit us at http://www.ablongman.com/kishlansky

ISBN-13: 978–0–205–55684–7   ISBN-10: 0–205–55684–1 (Combined Volume)
ISBN-13: 978–0–205–55685–4   ISBN-10: 0–205–55685–X (Volume I)
ISBN-13: 978–0–205–55686–1   ISBN-10: 0–205–55686–8 (Volume II)
ISBN-13: 978–0–205–55687–8   ISBN-10: 0–205–55687–6 (Volume A)
ISBN-13: 978–0–205–55688–5   ISBN-10: 0–205–55688–4 (Volume B)
ISBN-13: 978–0–205–55689–2   ISBN-10: 0–205–55689–2 (Volume C)
ISBN-13: 978–0–13–600706–7   ISBN-10: 0–13–600706–6 (Advanced Placement* Edition, Since 1300)

*Advanced Placement Program and AP are registered trademarks of The College Board, which was not involved in the production of, and does not endorse, this book.

2 3 4 5 6 7 8 9 10—QWD—10 09 08

BRIEF CONTENTS

DETAILED CONTENTS

Note: Each chapter ends with Questions for Review, Key Terms, Discovering Western Civilization Online, and Suggestions for Further Reading.

DOCUMENTS

MAPS

CHRONOLOGIES, GENEALOGIES, AND FIGURES

PREFACE

In planning *Civilization in the West,* our aim was to write a book that students would *want* to read. Throughout our years of planning, writing, revising, rewriting, and meeting together, this was our constant overriding concern. Would students read our book? Would it be effective in conveying information while stimulating the imagination? Would it work for a variety of Western civilization courses with different levels and formats? It was not easy to keep this concern in the forefront throughout the long months of composition, but it was easy to receive the reactions of scores of reviewers to this simple question: "Would students *want* to read these chapters?" Whenever we received a resounding "No!" we began again—not just rewriting but rethinking how to present material that might be too complex in argument or detail or that might simply seem too remote to engage the contemporary student. Although all three of us were putting in long hours in front of computers, we quickly learned that we were engaged in a teaching rather than a writing exercise. And though the work was demanding, it was not unrewarding. We hope that you will recognize and come to share with us the excitement and enthusiasm we felt in creating this text. We have enjoyed writing it, and we want students to enjoy reading it.

From the reactions to our first six editions, they have. We have received literally hundreds of cards and letters from adopters and users of *Civilization in the West.* The response has been both overwhelming and gratifying. It has also been constructive. Along with praise, we have received significant suggestions for making each subsequent edition stronger. Topics such as the Crusades, the Enlightenment, and imperialism have been reorganized to present them more clearly. Subjects such as the ancient Hebrews, Napoleon, and German unification have been given more space and emphasis. New features have been added to freshen the book and keep abreast of current scholarship, and more than 100 excerpts from primary sources are presented to give students a feel for the concreteness of the past. We believe that the seventh edition of *Civilization in the West* not only preserves the much-praised quality of its predecessors but also enhances it.

APPROACH

We made a number of decisions early in the project that we believed contributed to our goal. First, we were *not* writing an encyclopedia on Western civilization. Information was not to be included in a chapter unless it related to the themes of that chapter. There was to be no information for information's sake, and each of us was called upon to defend the inclusion of names, dates, and events whenever we met to critique one another's chapters. We found, to our surprise, that by adhering to the principle that information included must contribute to or illustrate a particular point or dominating theme, we provided as much, if not more, material than books that habitually list names, places, and dates without any other context.

Second, we were committed to integrating the history of ordinary men and women into our narrative. We believe that isolated sections, placed at the end of chapters, that deal with the experiences of women or minority groups in a particular era profoundly distort historical experience. We called this technique *caboosing,* and whenever we found ourselves segregating women or families or the masses, we stepped back and asked how we might recast our treatment of historical events to account for a diversity of actors. How did ordinary men, women, and children affect the course of historical events? How did historical events affect the fabric of daily life for men, women, and children from all walks of life? We tried to rethink critical historical problems of civilization as gendered phenomena. To assist us in the endeavor, we engaged two reviewers whose sole responsibility was to evaluate our chapters for the integration of those social groups into our discussion.

We took the same approach to the coverage of central and eastern Europe that we did to women and minorities. Even before the epochal events of 1989 that returned this region to the forefront of international attention, we realized that in too many textbooks the Slavic world was treated as marginal to the history of Western civilization. Thus, with the help of a specialist reviewer, we worked to integrate more of the history of eastern Europe into our text than is found in most others, and to do so in a way that presented the regions, their cultures, and their institutions as integral rather than peripheral to Western civilization.

To construct a book that students would *want* to read, we needed to develop fresh ideas about how to involve them with the material, how to transform them from passive recipients to active participants. We borrowed from computer science the concept of being "user-friendly." We wanted to find ways to stimulate the imagination of the student, and the more we experimented with different techniques, the more we realized that the most effective way to do this was visually. It is not true that contemporary students cannot be taught effectively by the written word; it is only true that they cannot be taught as effectively as they can by the combination of words and images. From the beginning, we realized that a text produced in full color was essential to the features we most wanted to use: the pictorial chapter openers; the large number of maps; the geographical tours of Europe at certain times in history; and the two-page special feature essays, each with its own illustration.

FEATURES

It is hard to have a new idea when writing a textbook. So many authors have come before, each attempting to do something more effective, more innovative than his or her predecessor. However, we feel that the following features enhance students' understanding of Western civilization.

The Visual Record: Pictorial Chapter Openers

It is probably the case that somewhere there has been a text that has used a chapter-opening feature similar to the one we use here. What we can say with certainty is that nothing else we experimented with, no other technique we attempted, has had such an immediate and positive impact on our readers or has so fulfilled our goal of involving the students in learning as *The Visual Record* pictorial chapter openers.

An illustration—a painting, a photograph, a picture, an artifact, an edifice—appears at the beginning of each chapter, accompanied by text through which we explore the picture, guiding students across a canvas or helping them see in an artifact or a piece of architecture details that are not immediately apparent. It is the direct combination of text and image that allows us to achieve this effect, to "unfold" both an illustration and a theme. In some chapters we highlight details, pulling out a section of the original picture to take a closer look. In others we attempt to shock the viewer into the recognition of horror or of beauty. Some chapter-opening images are de-

CHAPTER 21

INDUSTRIAL EUROPE

PORTRAIT OF AN AGE
THE RAILROAD

The Normandy train has reached Paris. The coast and the capital are once again connected. Passengers in their city finery disembark and are greeted by others who have awaited their scheduled arrival. Workmen stand ready to unload freight, porters to carry luggage. Steam billows forth from the resting engine, which is the object of [...] engine stares as enigmatically as [...] Renaissance portrait. Yet the train that [...] *Saint-Lazare* by Clau [...] is as much the cent[...]

THE VISUAL RECORD trait of the industria [...] ual in portraits of ag[...] The train's iron [...] around it. Indeed, i[...] are in view. The r[...] massive frame of the station, no less [...] all formed from iron—pliable, durabl[...] miracle product of industrialization. [...] glass panels became as central a featur[...] cities as stone cathedrals were in the M[...] tions changed the shape of urban [...] travel changed the lives of millions of [...]

There had never been anything [...] Romans had hitched four horses to th[...] century Europeans hitched four horse[...] The technology of overland trans[...] changed in 2000 years. Coach journey[...] able, and expensive, and they were go[...] and muddy, rutted roads that caused [...] horses with alarming regularity. Firs[...] inside, where they were jostled aga[...] breathed the dust that the horses kick[...] Second-class passengers rode on top [...] and risking life and limb in an accider[...]

Railway travel was a quantum lea[...] cheaper, and safer. Overnight it cl[...] time, space, and, above all, speed. P[...] what once were distant places in a [...]

came trips, and the travel holiday was born. Commerce was transformed, as was the way in which it was conducted. Large quantities of goods could be shipped quickly from place to place; orders could instantly be filled. The whole notion of locality changed, as salesmen could board a morn[...]

Arrival of the Normandy Train, Gare Saint-Lazare, 1877

[...]859) in his obituary for the passing of horse [...]d our speed, we saw it, we felt it. This speed [...]duct of blind, insensate agencies, that had no [...]re, but was incarnated in the fiery eyeballs of [...]ng brutes."

[...] the railways, like the fruits of industrializa- [...]ll sweet. As the nineteenth century progressed, [...]o doubt that, year by year, one way of life was [...]y another. More and more laborers were leav-

groups, and even whole societies. It was an engine racing down a track that only occasionally ended as placidly as did the Normandy train at the Gare Saint-Lazarre.

LOOKING AHEAD

As this chapter will discuss, industrialization began in Great Britain, spurred by its mineral wealth and entrepreneurial skill. It

618

signed to transport students back in time, to make them ask the question, "What was it like to be there?" All of the opening images have been chosen to illustrate a dominant theme within the chapter, and the dramatic and lingering impression they make helps reinforce that theme. A *Looking Ahead* section provides a brief overview of chapter coverage and further strengthens the connection between the subject of the opener and the major topics and themes of the chapter.

NEW! Image Discovery

Our commitment to using visual materials to enhance learning is seen throughout the book and is reinforced in the seventh edition with a new feature, *Image Discovery.* In *Image Discovery,* students are asked to approach an image as if it were a text. Appearing in each chapter, *Image Discoveries* guide students through suggestive questions to interrogate the image, understand its context, and unpack its multiple meanings.

Map Program

We have taken a similar image-based approach to our *presentation of geography.* When teachers of Western civilization courses are surveyed, no single area of need is cited more often than that of geographical knowledge. Students simply have no mental image of Europe, no familiarity with those geophysical features that are a fundamental part of the geopolitical realities of Western history. We realized that maps, carefully planned and skillfully executed, would be an important component of our text.

Map Discovery

To complement the standard map program of the text, we have two additional map-based features. The first is *Map Discovery.* This feature, which appears two to three times per chapter, offers specially designed maps with supporting caption information and questions designed to engage students in analyzing the map data and making larger connections to chapter discussions. We have found that focusing students' attention on the details of what a map shows and asking them to consider why that information is important is an effective way to strengthen critical thinking skills as well as to expand geographical knowledge.

Geographical Tours of Europe

The second map feature is the *Geographical Tours of Europe.* Six times in the book, we pause in the narrative to take a tour of Europe. Sometimes we follow an emperor as he tours his realm; sometimes we examine the impact of a peace treaty; sometimes we follow the travels of a merchant. Whatever the thematic occasion, our intention is to guide the student around the changing contours of the geography of Western history. In order to do this effectively, we worked with our cartographer to develop small, detailed maps to complement the overview map that appears at the beginning of each tour section. We know that only the most motivated students will turn back several pages to locate on a map a place mentioned in the text. Using small maps allows us to integrate maps directly into the relevant text, thus relieving students of the sometimes frustrating experience of attempting to locate not only a specific place on a map but perhaps even the relevant map itself. We have also added labels to all the tour maps and have included in-text references to direct students to relevant maps at specific points in the narrative of the tour. The great number of maps throughout the text, the specially designed geo-

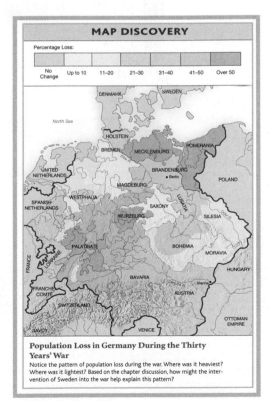

IMAGE DISCOVERY

Living with the Bomb.
This photo from the early 1950s shows an American family installed in their fallout shelter, intended to protect them from a nuclear blast. These shelters were built below ground or in basements. Note the supplies on hand. From your knowledge of the effects of atomic bombs on Japan, how realistic were people's hopes that radioactive fallout could be avoided? Why were photos like this one common in the 1950s in the United States? Why is this family smiling?

MAP DISCOVERY

Population Loss in Germany During the Thirty Years' War
Notice the pattern of population loss during the war. Where was it heaviest? Where was it lightest? Based on the chapter discussion, how might the intervention of Sweden into the war help explain this pattern?

THE STAINLESS STAR OF WISDOM'S DISCIPLINE

Public philosophers were prized citizens of every ancient city. The austere teachers, distinguished by their black robes, were courted by the wealthy as tutors of their sons and by the powerful for the benefit of their wisdom. But in the early fifth century, Alexandria, long famed for its great museum and rival schools, boasted a philosopher with a difference: Hypatia (ca. 370–415), a woman famed for her wisdom and described by one supporter as "mother, sister, teacher, benefactress in all things." Her controversial career and terrible death summarize the complexity and factionalism of late antiquity.

As was the case with many other professional philosophers, Hypatia's father had ren phi bef spe ast ma div and Neoplatonic philosoph wrote commentaries on ma and astronomical treatises

est praise—and her greatest criticism—for her practice of philosophy. Popular teachers are often controversial, and as a pagan, as a woman, and as a philosopher in the turbulent world of late antiquity, Hypatia was the center of more than her share. But philosophers were more than teachers in antiquity. Because of their deep learning, their detachment from the concerns of daily life, and their eloquence, they were allowed to play a public role, advising, admonishing, and rec-

A CLOSER LOOK

WORLD TRADE CENTERS

Trade is older than civilization, and almost as old are specialized buildings where trade is carried on. When the World Trade Centers in New York City were destroyed on September 11, 2001, the terrorist attack was aimed at a symbol of American economic power. But like other trade centers throughout the centuries, these buildings contained a truly international community: citizens of eighty countries were among the victims. The tragedy struck at the United States but wounded a global community of business, finance, trade, and civilization.

Specialized buildings for international trade were well established in Asia, Europe, and Africa by the thirteenth century.

Merchants needed protection from bandits, judicial organizations

■ The Twin Towers of the World Trade Center.

to settl nizatic partne locatic mercha cilitate of Ch constr the Ti was u ground and its for me at Pri Berger chants row of old wh

Eur similar special throug the Isla offered chants their ness. V Polo tr first t

THE WEST AND THE WIDER WORLD

■ The Tithe Grange at Provins, France.

■ Merchant houses on the old wharf of Be

THE TREATY OF VERSAILLES

Of the various treaties negotiating the peace at the end of World War I, the Treaty of Versailles, signed in 1919, was the most important. This treaty dealt with Germany as a defeated nation and was signed in the great Versailles palace outside of Paris in the same location where in 1871 Germany as victor signed a treaty with its defeated enemy, France, at the close of the short Franco-Prussian War (see pp. 694). In the 1919 treaty, the Allies, represented by President Woodrow Wilson of the United States, Prime Minister David Lloyd George of Great Britain, Prime Minister Georges Clemenceau of France, and Prime Minister Vittorio Orlando of Italy, imposed sole blame for the war on Germany and its expansionist aims. According to the treaty, the war was Germany's fault, and Germany must pay reparations for all the destruction of Allied property by its military. Germany lost territories and suffered a greatly reduced military capability. Especially burdensome was article 231 of the treaty, which came to be known as the War Guilt Clause, which spelled out Germany's responsibility and the basis for the need to make restitution.

Focus Questions

In article 42, for whose benefit were the left and right banks of the Rhine demilitarized? How many different forms of reparation can you identify in the articles cited here? For whose benefit was the German navy scaled back? Examine carefully article 231—the War Guilt Clause. What is your judgment of its validity in light of what you know about the causes of the war?

Part III. Political Clauses for Europe
Article 42. Germany is forbidden to maintain or construct any fortifications either on the left bank of the Rhine or on the right bank to the west of a line drawn 50 kilometers to the east of the Rhine....

Article 45. As compensation for the destruction of the coal-mines in the north of France and as part payment towards the total reparation due from Germany for the damage resulting from the war, Germany cedes to France in full and absolute possession, with exclusive rights of exploita-

Article 89. Poland undertakes to accord freedom of transit to persons, goods, vessels, carriages, wagons, and mails in transit between East Prussia and the rest of Germany over Polish territory, including territorial waters, and to treat them at least as favorably as the persons, goods, vessels, carriages, wagons, and mails respectively of Polish or of any other more favored nationality, origin, importation, starting-point, or ownership as regards facilities, restrictions and all other matters.[1]...

Part IV. German Rights and Interests Outside Germany
Article 119. Germany renounces in favor of the Principal Allied and Associated Powers all her rights and titles over her overseas possessions. (This renunciation includes Germany's concessions in China.)...

Part V. Military, Naval, and Air Claims
Article 159. The German military forces shall be demobilized and reduced as prescribed hereinafter.
Article 160. (1) By a date which must not be later than

---

graphical tour of Europe feature, and the ancillary programs of map transparencies and workbook exercises combine to provide the strongest possible program for teaching historical geography.

A Closer Look

Another technique we have employed to engage students with historical subjects is the two-page *A Closer Look* special feature that appears in many chapters. *A Closer Look* focuses on an event, phenomenon, or personality chosen to enhance the student's sense that history is something that is real and alive. The features are written more dramatically and sympathetically, with a greater sense of wonder than would be appropriate in the body of the text. The prose style and the accompanying illustration are designed to captivate the reader. To help the student relate personally and directly to a historical event, we have highlighted figures such as Hypatia of Alexandria, Isabella of Castile, and Sigmund Freud.

The West and the Wider World

To engage students with historical subjects, two-page *The West and the Wider World* essays that appear 11 times in the book. These essays focus on instances of dynamic cultural encounters and exchanges between the West and the non-West at different points in history. The topics for this feature were chosen to enhance the student's sense of connections among the events, phenomena, politics, and products of the West and the wider world. At the end of each feature, we have included questions to spark class discussion and to reinforce such connections.

Documents

Civilization in the West contains selections from primary sources designed to stimulate students' interest in history by allowing them to hear the past speak in its own voice. We have tried to provide a mixture of "canonical" texts along with those illustrating the lives of ordinary people in order to demonstrate the variety of materials that form the building blocks of historical narrative. Each selection is accompanied by an explanatory headnote that identifies the author and work and provides the necessary historical context. Following the headnote are two to three *Focus Questions* to guide students' reading and to spark critical thinking. Most of the extracts relate directly to the discussion within the chapter, thus providing the student with a fuller understanding of a significant thinker or event.

Discovering Western Civilization Online

Discovering Western Civilization Online encourages students to further explore Western civilization. These end-of-chapter Website resources link students to documents, images, and cultural sites currently not included in the text.

Questions for Review

Although a standard feature in many texts, the *Questions for Review* in *Civilization in the West* nonetheless are worth noting. They do not provide just a factual review of the chapter. Instead, they prompt students to think critically about the major topics in the chapter and to pull together for themselves some conclusions about the events and peoples of the time.

CHANGES IN THE NEW EDITION

In the seventh edition, we have made significant changes in content and coverage.

NEW! Image Discovery

Appearing in every chapter, new *Image Discovery* features ask students to approach an image as if it were a text. The feature challenges readers to move from a passive mode of information absorption to an active analysis of the visual and material evidence of the past. Through suggestive questions, *Image Discoveries* guide students to interrogate the image, understand its context, and unpack its multiple meanings. Examples include "A Revolution in Warfare" in Chapter 2, which uses a Corinthian vase depicting hoplites to explore questions of training and warfare; the painting *The Milch Cow* in Chapter 14, which allows for an examination of the politics surrounding the Netherlands in the late sixteenth century; and a photograph in Chapter 28 of Nazi soldiers seizing Jews in Warsaw, which speaks to the experience and expectations of the captured.

Content Updates

The past may not change, but both our understanding of the past and the questions we need to ask about it change constantly. We have taken the opportunity of a new edition to project our history back in time as well as to explore more closely the entangled nature of human history. In the first chapter, a new *The West and the Wider World* feature, confronts the growing consensus that history begins not with Sumer but with the Paleolithic. Here we explore the exciting frontiers of history, genetics, and archaeology that attempt to understand the complex waves of migrations out of Africa that ultimately populated the planet. Elsewhere we explore those extraordinary crossroads of cultural and economic exchange that were trade centers where merchants from Europe, Asia, and Africa have sought the safety and peace necessary to tie together the great civilizations of the world.

Throughout the early chapters we have pruned, eliminating unnecessary and potentially distracting detail while fine tuning content in response to the input from readers and users of previous editions. The addition of the *Image Discovery* feature has provided the opportunity for a broad range of analysis. In some, as in Chapter 3, we ask readers to compare a Hellenistic statue with a classical one; in Chapter 7 we ask them to reflect on how the profession of faith inscribed on Jerusalem's Haram al-Sharif or The Dome of the Rock might be understood as challenging Christian belief. In others, we encourage readers to make use of what they have learned in the text to interpret the images with which they are confronted.

In the middle chapters of the book the authors have continued their efforts to expand the boundaries of Europe and to relate its experiences to those of the wider world. A new feature on the Columbian Exchange highlights the interactive nature of the European encounter with Atlantic populations. It emphasizes the biological and economic impact of discoveries, the disastrous consequences of interchanged diseases, and the enhancements of new products and tools. Pigs and cattle were brought to the new world, potatoes and tomatoes to the old.

Europe's encounters with non-Europeans in the early modern period were not limited to discoveries. The centuries-old struggle between the Ottoman and Holy Roman empires continued deep into the seventeenth century. It reached its apex with the siege of Vienna in 1676—an event that might have transformed European history had it turned out differently. Throughout this section the text has been updated to reflect new historical discoveries and to account for reinterpretations of familiar events. A special effort has been made to enhance sections on the biological sciences.

In the modern chapters, beginning with Chapter 20, attention has been given to updating coverage and information and incorporating the latest bibliographic information. The new *Image Discovery* feature for these chapters (Chapters 20 through 30) includes political cartoons and caricature in understanding how visual images and symbols are a central feature of modern political life beginning in the late eighteenth century. *Image Discovery* has also allowed the authors to interrogate the role of photography in shaping modern consciousness.

One of the great challenges has been the proper inclusion of the United States in the story of *Civilization in the West* from the French Revolution to the war on terrorism. Greater attention to the United States in the story of *Civilization in the West* recognizes the expanding concept of the West as an idea rather than a place. There is expanded treatment of the U.S. role especially in the post–World War II period with the Cold War and the subsequent decline of the Soviet Union. The global context of political, religious, intellectual, and social changes has resulted in increased coverage of Afghanistan, China, South Africa, and India to understand the phenomenon of change in the West. For example, the return of the Taliban changes earlier interpretations about the gains of democratic government in Afghanistan. And the work of Mahatma Gandhi is included in a new way here (in *The West and the Wider World*) to show the influences of ideas in Asia on political discourse in other nations.

The changing nature of ethnicity and nationalism in the contemporary world has required not only updating information but also reconsidering interpretations of the rapid historic changes of the post–Cold War world. Contemporary events such as the trial and death of Saddam Hussein and the civil war in Iraq require new perspectives on the war on terrorism in the final chapter. The chapters that cover the modern period in general are influenced by the weight of contemporary events that continually require reframing and revisiting conclusions.

New West and the Wider World

Two-page *The West and the Wider World* essays explore instances of dynamic cultural encounters and exchanges between the West and the non-West at different points in history. Understanding the importance of viewing the West within this larger context, we have added in this edition six new essays throughout the text: Chapter 1, "The First European Immigrants"; Chapter 10, "World Trade Centers"; Chapter 12, "The Columbian Exchange"; Chapter 16, "The Siege of Vienna"; Chapter 25, "Babylon Discovered"; and Chapter 29, "Mahatma Gandhi's Legacy."

Key Terms and Glossary

In each chapter, key terms are highlighted in boldface type to alert students to principal concepts and events discussed in the chapter. A page-referenced list of the key terms is included at the end of the chapter to help students review the main ideas and events covered in the chapter. A glossary at the end of the book provides definitions for the key terms. In this edition, we have added over 60 new terms.

New Documents

Nine new documents have been added in this edition as well. Chapter 3 now includes an excerpt from Plato's "The Apology" that presents Socrates in his summation to the Athenian jury; Chapter 7 includes Usamah ibn Munqidh's observations in "An Arab in Crusader Jerusalem"; in Chapter 8, Gregory of Tours describes a conflict between two families from Tournai that ultimately destroyed them both; in Chapter 14, in "The Heart and Stomach of a King," Queen Elizabeth rallies her subjects to oppose the invasion of England by the Spanish Armada; Chapter 19 now contains excerpts from Voltaire's great comic novel, *Candide*; the *Treaty of Versailles* is excerpted in Chapter 26; and Chapter 30 now includes both Václav Havel's address to Czechoslovakia from 1 January 1990 and a press release from London Mayor Ken Livingstone regarding his commitment, and that of 21 other mayors from major cities around the world, to reducing greenhouse gases.

New Visual Record Essays

Six new *The Visual Record* pictorial essays were developed for the seventh edition as well. Chapter 3: Classical and Hellenistic Greece, 500–100 B.C.E. opens with a pictorial essay on the Parthenon and Pericles, the man responsible for its construction; Chapter 9: The High Middle Ages, 900–1300 begins with an essay on a portion of the Bayeux tapestry that may well subvert the story of the Battle of Hastings as told by the victors; Chapter 11: The Italian Renaissance opens with an exploration of Leonardo da Vinci's *Last Supper*; Chapter 20: The French Revolution and the Napoleonic Era, 1789–1815 begins with an essay on Jacques-Louis David's *The Oath of the Tennis Court*, which captures the spirit of a key moment in the history of democracy; Chapter 21: Industrial Europe begins with an examination of the transformative power of the railroad as alluded to in Claude Monet's *La Gare Saint-Lazarre*; and Chapter 23: State Building and Social Change in Europe, 1850–1871 opens with an examination of the construction and meaning of London's extraordinary Crystal Palace of 1851.

ACKNOWLEDGMENTS

We want to thank the many conscientious historians who gave generously of their time and knowledge to review our manuscript. We would like to thank the reviewers of the first six editions as well as those of the current edition. Their valuable critiques and suggestions have contributed greatly to the final product. We are grateful to the following:

Achilles Aavraamides, *Iowa State University;* Meredith L. Adams, *Southwest Missouri State University;* Joseph Aieta, III, *Lasell College;* Ken Albala, *University of the Pacific;* Patricia Ali, *Morris College;* Gerald D. Anderson, *North Dakota State University;* Arthur H. Auten, *University of Hartford;* Suzanne Balch-Lindsay, *Eastern New Mexico University;* Sharon Bannister, *University of Findlay;* John W. Barker, *University of Wisconsin;* Patrick Bass, *Mount Union College;* William H. Beik, *Northern Illinois University;* Jean K. Berger, *University of Wisconsin, Fox Valley;* Patrice Berger, *University of Nebraska;* Lenard R. Berlanstein, *University of Virginia;* Raymond Birn, *University of Oregon;* Donna Bohanan, *Auburn University;* Werner Braatz, *University of Wisconsin, Oshkosh;* Thomas A. Brady, Jr., *University of Oregon;* Anthony M. Brescia, *Nassau Community College;* Elaine G. Breslaw, *Morgan State University;* Ronald S. Brockway, *Regis University;* April Brooks, *South Dakota State University;* Daniel Patrick Brown, *Moorpark College;* Ronald A. Brown, *Charles County Community College;* Blaine T. Browne, *Broward Community College;* Susan Carrafiello, *Wright State University;* Kathleen S. Carter, *High Point University;* Robert Carver, *University of Missouri, Rolla;* Edward J. Champlin, *Princeton University;* Stephanie Evans Christelow, *Western Washington University;* Sister Dorita Clifford, BVM, *University of San Francisco;* Gary B. Cohen, *University of Oklahoma;* Robert Cole, *Utah State University;* Jan M. Copes, *Cleveland State University;* John J. Contreni, *Purdue University;* Tim Crain, *University of Wisconsin, Stout;* Norman Delaney, *Del Mar College;* Samuel E. Dicks, *Emporia State University;* Andrew Donson, *University of Massachusetts, Amherst;* Frederick Dotolo, *St. John Fisher College;* Frederick Dumin, *Washington State University;* Janusz Duzinkiewicz, *Purdue University;* Laird Easton, *California State University, Chico;* Brian Elsesser, *Saint Louis University;* Dianne E. Farrell, *Moorhead State University;* Margot C. Finn, *Emory University;* Allan W. Fletcher, *Boise State University;* Luci Fortunato De Lisle, *Bridgewater State College;* Elizabeth L. Furdell, *University of North Florida;* Thomas W. Gallant, *University of Florida;* Bryan Ganaway, *University of Illinois;* Frank Garosi, *California State University, Sacramento;* Lorne E. Glaim, *Pacific Union College;* Joseph J. Godson, *Hudson Valley Community College;* Sue Helder Goliber, *Mount St. Mary's College;* Manuel G. Gonzales, *Diablo Valley College;* David Graf, *University of Miami;* Louis Haas, *Duquesne University;* Eric Haines, *Bellevue Community College;* David Halahmy, *Cypress College;* Paul Halliday, *University of Virginia;* Margaretta S. Handke, *Mankato State University;* David A. Harnett, *University of San Francisco;* Paul B. Harvey, Jr., *Pennsylvania State University;* Benjamin Hett, *Hunter College;* Neil Heyman, *San Diego State University;* Daniel W. Hollis, *Jacksonville State University;* Kenneth G. Holum, *University of Maryland;* Patricia Howe, *University of St. Thomas;* David Hudson, *California State University, Fresno;* Mark M. Hull, *Saint Louis University;* John Hymes, *Horry-Georgetown Technical College;* Charles Ingrao, *Purdue University;* George F. Jewsbury, *Oklahoma State University;* Cynthia Jones, *University of Missouri—Kansas City;* Donald G. Jones, *University of Central Arkansas;* William R. Jones, *University of New Hampshire;* Richard W. Kaeuper, *University of Rochester;* David Kaiser, *Carnegie-Mellon University;* Jeff Kaufmann, *Muscatine Community College;* Carolyn Kay, *Trent University;* John S. Kemp, *Truckee Meadows Community College;* William R. Keylor, *Boston University;* Joseph Kicklighter, *Auburn University;* Charles L. Killinger, III, *Valencia Community College;* Alan M. Kirshner, *Ohlone College;* Charlene Kiser, *Milligan College;* Barbara Klemm, *Broward Community College;* Janilyn M. Kocher, *Richland Community*

College; Alexandra Korros, *Xavier University;* Cynthia Kosso, *Northern Arizona University;* Lara Kriegel, *Florida International University;* Lisa M. Lane, *Mira Costa College;* Lawrence Langer, *University of Connecticut;* David C. Large, *Montana State University;* Catherine Lawrence, *Messiah College;* Bryan LeBeau, *Creighton University;* Erik Lindseth, *Indiana University–Purdue University Indianapolis;* Robert B. Luehrs, *Fort Hays State University;* Donna J. Maier, *University of Northern Iowa;* Margaret Malamud, *New Mexico State University;* Roberta T. Manning, *Boston College;* Lyle McAlister, *University of Florida;* Therese M. McBride, *College of the Holy Cross;* David K. McQuilkin, *Bridgewater College;* Victor V. Minasian, *College of Marin;* David B. Mock, *Tallahassee Community College;* Don Mohr, *University of Alaska–Anchorage,* Robert Moeller, *University of California, Irvine;* Elise Moentmann, *University of Portland;* R. Scott Moore, *University of Dayton;* Ann E. Moyer, *University of Pennsylvania;* Pierce C. Mullen, *Montana State University;* John A. Nichols, *Slippery Rock University;* Thomas F. X. Noble, *University of Virginia;* J. Ronald Oakley, *Davidson County Community College;* Bruce K. O'Brien, *Mary Washington College;* Dennis H. O'Brien, *West Virginia University;* Maura O'Connor, *University of Cincinnati;* Richard A. Oehling, *Assumption College;* James H. Overfield, *University of Vermont;* Catherine Patterson, *University of Houston;* Sue Patrick, *University of Wisconsin, Barron County;* Peter C. Piccillo, *Rhode Island College;* Peter O'M. Pierson, *Santa Clara University;* Alisa Plant, *Tulane University;* Theophilus Prousis, *University of North Florida;* Marlette Rebhorn, *Austin Community College;* Kimberly D. S. Reiter, *Stetson University;* Jack B. Ridley, *University of Missouri, Rolla;* Salvador Rivera, *State University of New York Cobleskill;* Thomas Robisheaux, *Duke University;* Constance M. Rousseau, *Providence College;* Thomas J. Runyan, *Cleveland State University;* John P. Ryan, *Kansas City Community College;* Geraldine Ryder, *Ocean County College;* Joanne Schneider, *Rhode Island College;* Steven Schroeder, *Indiana University of Pennsylvania;* Steven C. Seyer, *Lehigh County Community College;* Lixin Shao, *University of Minnesota, Duluth;* George H. Shriver, *Georgia Southern University;* Ellen J. Skinner, *Pace University;* Bonnie Smith, *University of Rochester;* Patrick Smith, *Broward Community College;* James Smither, *Grand Valley State University;* Sherill Spaar, *East Central University;* Ilicia Sprey, *Saint Joseph's College;* Charles R. Sullivan, *University of Dallas;* Peter N. Stearns, *Carnegie-Mellon University;* Saulius Suziedelis, *Millersville University;* Darryl B. Sycher, *Columbus State Community College;* Roger Tate, *Somerset Community College;* Janet A. Thompson, *Tallahassee Community College;* Anne-Marie Thornton, *Bilkent University;* Donna L. Van Raaphorst, *Cuyahoga Community College;* James Vanstone, *John Abbot College;* George S. Vascik, *Miami University, Hamilton;* Steven Vincent, *North Carolina State University;* Richard A. Voeltz, *Cameron University;* Faith Wallis, *McGill University;* Sydney Watts, *University of Richmond;* Eric Weissman, *Golden West College;* Christine White, *Pennsylvania State University;* Vance Youmans, *Spokane Falls Community College;* William Harry Zee, *Gloucester County College.*

Each author also received invaluable assistance and encouragement from many colleagues, friends, and family members over the years of research, reflection, writing, and revising that went into the making of this text.

Mark Kishlansky thanks Ann Adams, Robert Bartlett, Ray Birn, David Buisseret, Ted Cook, Frank Conaway, Constantine Fasolt, James Hankins, Katherine Haskins, Richard Hellie, Matthew Kishlansky, Donna Marder, Mary Beth Rose, Victor Stater, Jeanne Thiel, and the staffs of the Joseph Regenstein Library, the Newberry Library, and the Widener and Lamont Libraries at Harvard.

Patrick Geary thanks Mary, Catherine, and Anne Geary for their patience, support, and encouragement; he also thanks Anne Picard, Dale Schofield, Hans Hummer, Jared Poley, and Richard Mowrer for their able assistance throughout the project.

Patricia O'Brien thanks Elizabeth Sagias for her encouragement and enthusiasm throughout the project and Robert Moeller for his keen eye for organization and his suggestions for writing a gendered history. She is especially grateful to her assistants Susan Beals and Carolyn Drago for keeping her on track throughout the project.

All the authors thank Janet Lanphier, senior acquisitions editor, Barbara Conover, development editor, and Heather Johnson, project editor at Elm Street Publishing Services, Inc., for producing a beautiful book. Thanks are also due to Melissa Edwards, for her work in producing the media supplements that accompany this volume, and Brian Belardi who worked on the print supplements.

Mark Kishlansky
Patrick Geary
Patricia O'Brien

SUPPLEMENTS

For Qualified College Adopters

- **Instructor's Manual** This thorough instructor's manual includes an introductory essay on teaching Western civilization and a bibliographic essay on the use of primary sources for class discussion and analytical thinking. Each chapter contains a chapter summary, key terms and important geographic locations, discussion questions, and an annotated list of films (not supplied by Longman).
- **Test Bank** This supplement contains more than 1,200 multiple-choice, true/false, and essay questions. Multiple-choice and true/false questions are referenced by topic and text page number.
- **Computerized Test Bank** This flexible, easy-to-master assessment program includes all of the items in the printed test bank and allows instructors to select specific questions, edit them, and add their own items to create exams.
- **Instructor Resource Center (IRC) (www.ablongman.com/irc)** Through the Instructor Resource Center, instructors can log into premium online products, browse and download book-specific instructor resources, and receive immediate access and instructions to installing course management content.
- **Research Navigator and Research Navigator Guide** Research Navigator is a comprehensive website offering EBSCO's ContentSelect Academic Journal & Abstract Database, the *New York Times* Search-by-Subject Archive, *Financial Times* Article Archive and Company Financials, and "Best of the Web" Link Library. The Research Navigator Guide provides your students with access to the Website and includes reference material and hints about conducting online research.
- **Study Card for Western Civilization** Colorful, affordable, and packed with useful information, Longman's Study Cards make studying easier, more efficient, and more enjoyable.
- **Digital Transparency Masters** A set of full-color transparency masters drawn from *Civilization in the West*, Seventh Edition. Available exclusively on the IRC.

- **History Video Program** A list of more than 100 videos from which qualified college adopters can choose. Restrictions apply.
- **History Digital Media Archive CD-ROM** This CD-ROM contains electronic images and interactive and static maps, along with media elements such as video. It is fully customizable and ready for classroom presentation. All images and maps are available in PowerPoint™ as well.
- **Interpretations of the Western World** General Editor Mark Kishlansky has prepared a customizable database of secondary source readings. Selections are grouped topically so that instructors can assign readings that illustrate different points of view about a given historical debate.

For Students

- **Study Guide** Available in two volumes, each chapter in the study guide includes a summary; a timeline activity; map and geography questions; key terms, people, and events; and identification, multiple-choice, and critical-thinking questions.
- **Western Civilization Map Workbook** These two volumes test and reinforce basic geography literacy while building critical-thinking skills.
- **Longman Atlas of Western Civilization** This 52-page atlas features carefully selected historical maps that provide comprehensive coverage for the major historical periods.
- **A Short Guide to Writing About History, Sixth Edition** Written by Richard Marius, late of Harvard University, and Melvin E. Page, Eastern Tennessee State University, and Melvin E. Page, Eastern Tennessee State University, this engaging and practical text helps students get beyond merely compiling dates and facts. Covering both brief essays and the documented resource paper, the text explores the writing and researching processes, identifies different modes of historical writing, including argument, and concludes with guidelines for improving style.

MyHistoryLab (www.myhistorylab.com)

MyHistoryLab provides students with an online package complete with the electronic textbook and numerous study aids. With several hundred primary sources, many of which are assignable and link to a gradebook, pre- and post-tests that link to a gradebook and result in individualized study plans, videos and images, as well as map activities with gradable quizzes, the site offers students a unique, interactive experience that brings history to life. The comprehensive site also includes a History Bookshelf with fifty of the most commonly assigned books in history classes and a History Toolkit with tutorials and helpful links. Other features include gradable assignments and chapter review materials; a Test Bank; and Research Navigator.

MyHistoryKit (www.myhistorykit.com)

MyHistoryKit for Western Civilization is an access-code-protected course-based website that contains a sampling of Longman's premium history content. This website includes practice tests to challenge students' knowledge of the material, flashcards that aid in studying, and media and primary source activities (documents, maps, video and audio clips, and more) that report to an online gradebook. Also included in MyHistoryKit are Research Navigator and Writing About History, both of which provide assistance with and access to powerful and reliable research material.

The Western Civilization Study Site (www.longmanwesterncivilization.com)

Students can take advantage of this open-access online course companion that includes practice tests, Web links, and flash cards that cover the scope of topics covered in a typical Western civilization class.

Longman Library of World Biography Series

Pocket-sized and brief, each biography in the Library of World Biography series relates the life of its subject to the broader themes and developments of the time. Series titles include: *Ahmad al-Mansur: Islamic Visionary* by Richard Smith (Ferrum College); *Alexander the Great: Legacy of a Conqueror* by Winthrop Lindsay Adams (University of Utah); *Benito Mussolini: The First Fascist* by Anthony L. Cardoza (Loyola University); *Fukuzawa Yūkichi: From Samurai to Capitalist* by Helen M. Hopper (University of Pittsburgh); *Ignatius of Loyola: Founder of the Jesuits* by John Patrick Donnelly (Marquette University); *Jacques Coeur: Entrepreneur and King's Bursar* by Kathryn L. Reyerson (University of Minnesota); *Katô Shidzue: A Japanese Feminist* by Helen M. Hopper (University of Pittsburgh); *Simón Bolívar: Liberation and Disappointment* by David Bushnell (University of Florida); *Vasco da Gama: Renaissance Crusader* by Glenn J. Ames (University of Toledo); and *Zheng He: China and the Oceans in the Early Ming, 1405–1433* by Edward Dreyer (University of Miami).

Penguin-Longman Partnership

The partnership between Penguin Books and Longman Publishers offers a discount on a wide range of titles when bundled with any Longman history survey textbook. Visit www.ablongman.com/penguin for more information.

ABOUT THE AUTHORS

MARK KISHLANSKY   Mark Kishlansky is Frank B. Baird, Jr., Professor of English and European History at Harvard University, where he has taught Western Civilization and courses in the CORE program for general education. He has also been awarded Harvard's Hoopes Prize for undergraduate teaching. Professor Kishlansky served as Associate Dean of the Faculty from 1999–2001. Before joining the Harvard faculty he taught for sixteen years at the University of Chicago where he was a member of the Committee on Social Thought. Professor Kishlansky is a specialist on seventeenth-century English political history and has written, among other works, *A Monarchy Transformed, The Rise of the New Model Army,* and *Parliamentary Selection: Social and Political Choice in Early Modern England.* From 1984–1991 he was editor of the *Journal of British Studies.* He is currently writing a history of the reign of Charles I entitled *The Death of Kings.* He is the General Editor of Pearson Custom Publishing's primary source databases for Western and World Civilization.

PATRICK GEARY   Holding a Ph.D. in Medieval Studies from Yale University, Patrick Geary has broad experience in interdisciplinary approaches to European history and civilization. He has served as the director of the Medieval Institute at the University of Notre Dame as well as director for the Center for Medieval and Renaissance Studies at UCLA where he is currently professor of history. He has also held positions at the University of Florida and Princeton University and has taught at the École des Hautes Études en Sciences Sociales in Paris, at the University of Vienna, and at the Central European University in Budapest. He has coordinated and participated in programs for history teachers in Pennsylvania, Florida, and California, and has co-authored a television series on medieval knights. His many publications include *Readings in Medieval History; Before France and Germany: The Creation and Transformation of the Merovingian World; Furta Sacra: Thefts of Relics in the Central Middle Ages;* and *The Myth of Nations: The Medieval Origins of Europe.*

PATRICIA O'BRIEN   Between 1995 and 1999, Patricia O'Brien worked to foster collaborative interdisciplinary research in the humanities as director of the University of California Humanities Research Institute. Between 1999 and 2004, she held the position of Dean of the College of Humanities, Arts, and Social Sciences at the University of California, Riverside. She has also held appointments at the University of California, Irvine, Yale University, and at the École des Hautes Études en Sciences Sociales in Paris. Currently Professor O'Brien is the Executive Dean of the UCLA College of Letters and Sciences. Professor O'Brien is a specialist in modern French cultural and social history and has published widely on the history of crime, punishment, cultural theory, urban history, and gender issues. Representative publications include *The Promise of Punishment: Prisons in Nineteenth-Century France;* "The Kleptomania Diagnosis: Bourgeois Women and Theft in Late Nineteenth-Century France" in *Expanding the Past: A Reader in Social History;* and "Michel Foucault's History of Culture" in *The New Cultural History,* edited by Lynn Hunt. Professor O'Brien's commitment to this textbook grew out of her own teaching experiences in large, introductory Western Civilization courses. She has benefited from the contributions of her students and fellow instructors in her approach to the study of Western Civilization in the modern period.

CIVILIZATION IN
THE WEST

INTRODUCTION
THE IDEA OF WESTERN CIVILIZATION

The West is an idea. It is not visible from space. An astronaut viewing the blue-and-white terrestrial sphere can make out the form of Africa, bounded by the Atlantic, the Indian Ocean, the Red Sea, and the Mediterranean. Australia, the Americas, and even Antarctica are distinct patches of blue-green in the darker waters that surround them. But nothing comparable separates Europe from Asia, East from West. Viewed from 100 miles up, the West itself is invisible. Although astronauts can see the great Eurasian landmass curving around the Northern Hemisphere, the Ural Mountains—the theoretical boundary between East and West—appear but faintly from space. Certainly they are less impressive than the towering Himalayas, the Alps, or even the Caucasus. People, not geology, determined that the Urals should be the arbitrary boundary between Europe and Asia.

Even this determination took centuries. Originally, Europe was a name that referred only to central Greece. Gradually, Greeks extended it to include the whole Greek mainland and then the landmass to the north. Later, Roman explorers and soldiers carried Europe north and west to its modern boundaries. Asia too grew with time. Initially, Asia was only that small portion of what is today Turkey inland from the Aegean Sea. Gradually, as Greek explorers came to know of lands farther east, north, and south, they expanded their understanding of Asia to include everything east of the Don River to the north and the Red Sea to the south.

Western civilization is as much an idea as the West itself. Under the right conditions, astronauts can see the Great Wall of China snaking its way from the edge of the Himalayas to the Yellow Sea. No comparable physical legacy of the West is so massive that its details can be discerned from space. Nor are Western achievements rooted forever in one corner of the world. What we call Western civilization belongs to no particular place. Its location has changed since the origins of civilization, that is, the cultural and social traditions characteristic of the *civitas*, or city. "Western" cities appeared first outside what Europeans and Americans arbitrarily term *the West*, in the Tigris and Euphrates river basins in present-day Iraq and Iran, a region we today call the Middle East. These areas have never lost their urban traditions, but in time other cities in North Africa, Greece, and Italy adapted and expanded this heritage in different ways. If we focus on this peculiar adaptation and expansion in this book, it is not because of some intrinsic superiority but only because the developments in Europe after the birth of Jesus become more significant than those of Egypt and Mesopotamia for understanding our contemporary culture.

Until the sixteenth century C.E., the western end of the Eurasian landmass—what we think of as western Europe—was the crucible in which disparate cultural and intellectual traditions of the Near East, the Mediterranean, and the north were smelted into a new and powerful alloy. Then "the West" expanded beyond the confines of Europe, carried by the ships of merchants and adventurers to India, Africa, China, and the Americas.

Western technology for harnessing nature, Western forms of economic and political organization, Western styles of art and music are—for good or ill—dominant influences in world civilization. Japan is a leading power in the Western traditions of capitalist commerce and technology. China, the most populous country in the world, adheres to Marxist so-

North America seeking a better life but often find poverty, hostility, and racism instead. Finally, the advances of Western civilization endanger our very existence. Technology pollutes the world's air, water, and soil, and nuclear arms threaten the destruction of all civilization. And yet these are the same advances that allow us to lengthen life expectancy, harness the forces of nature, and conquer disease. It is the same technology that allows us to view our world from outer space.

cialist principles—a European political tradition. Millions of people in Africa, Asia, and the Americas follow the religions of Islam and Christianity. Both are monotheistic faiths that developed from Judaism in the cradle of Western civilization.

Many of today's most pressing problems are also part of the legacy of the Western tradition. The remnants of European colonialism have left deep hostilities throughout the world. The integration of developing nations into the world economy keeps much of humanity in a seemingly hopeless cycle of poverty as the wealth of poor countries goes to pay interest on loans from Europe and America. Western material goods lure millions of people from their traditional worlds into the sprawl of third-world cities. Hatred of Western civilization is a central, ideological tenet that inspired the attacks on symbols of American economic and military strength on September 11, 2001, and that fuels anti-Western terrorism around the world. The West itself faces a crisis. Impoverished citizens of former colonies flock to Europe and

How did we get here? In this book we attempt to answer that question. The history of Western civilization is not simply the triumphal story of progress, the creation of a better world. Even in areas in which we can see development—such as technology, communications, and social complexity—change is not always for the better. It would be equally inaccurate, however, to view the course of Western civilization as a progressive decline from a mythical golden age of the human race. The roughly 300 generations since the origins of civilization have bequeathed a rich and contradictory heritage to the present. Inherited political and social institutions, cultural forms, and religious and philosophical traditions form the framework within which the future must be created. The past does not determine the future, but it is the raw material from which the future will be made. To use this legacy properly, we must first understand it, not because the past is the key to the future, but because understanding yesterday frees us to create tomorrow.

3

20 THE FRENCH REVOLUTION AND THE NAPOLEONIC ERA, 1789–1815

THE TENNIS COURT OATH: THE BEGINNING OF THE FRENCH REVOLUTION

Imagine the world of Jacques-Louis David (1748–1825), who was an influential painter in the royal court in France during the 1780s. A leading artist who studied in France and Italy and perfected his own neoclassical style that bestowed dignity on his historical paintings and portraits alike, he was considered a leader of his generation by the liberal and aristocratic elite of the late eighteenth century.

And then the world changed. Beginning in 1789 a decade of political transformation and turmoil, beginning with the French Revolution, swept across Europe. In June of that year King Louis XVI summoned representatives of his subjects to meet at the royal residence at Versailles to deal with the fiscal crisis facing France.

THE VISUAL RECORD

Although he was not at Versailles, David has provided us with a strong visual record and interpretation of an event of particular significance that transpired there on 20 June 1789. Look at the warm sepia tones of David's *The Tennis Court Oath*, in which he captures the spirit of an important moment in the history of democracy. This scene depicts commoners, accompanied by some clergy (the three figures forming a circle in the middle foreground), taking an oath "never to separate, and to meet whenever circumstances demand until a constitution of the kingdom is established and affirmed on solid foundations." It is a jubilant scene—one of energy and camaraderie. It is a scene of hope.

How these men came to be standing together in an indoor tennis court at Versailles, the seat of the French monarchy, is a story rooted in the travails of the French king. It is also a story rooted in the optimism of the Enlightenment. Three days earlier, on 17 June 1789, the group pictured here—577 strong—declared themselves to be deputies of the **National Assembly** (see p. 595). On 20 June, finding that they were locked out of their regular meeting room by the king's guard and outraged by this insult, they moved to a nearby indoor tennis court whose high walls and high windows add drama to this scene.

The winds of change blow in from the windows on the upper left of the painting, and the common people, including women and children, crowd the windows in witness to the scene. Standing in the middle of the tableau, but by no means dominating it, and facing the viewer with his arm upraised is the deputies' president Jean-Sylvain Bailly (1736–1793), who leads the assembled in the recitation of the "oath." Many deputies indicate their enthusiastic assent with upraised arms. Despite the sense of unity that the composition and its warm tones convey, the viewer can find many different stories captured in the moment. In the lower left, see the old man being carried in on a chair. Look for those who are carrying on their own discussions with their neighbors or are caught up in their own worlds. To the right of the speaker one person grabs his chest with emotion, while another in the lower right corner sits cross-armed, perhaps the sole deputy who did not sign the oath. As well as the promise of political progress that a constitution would bring, David shows us the seeds of political dissension and in this dramatization of an event that spelled the end of absolute monarchy and the beginning of a new concept of state power that resided in the people. The revolution had begun.

■ *The Tennis Court Oath* By Jacques-Louis David, 1791.

LOOKING AHEAD

The revolution that took place in France in 1789 was not the first political upheaval of that era, but it proved to be the most violent. Six years earlier the American War of Independence against Great Britain ended. Other European countries were engaged in battles for liberty. All of these revolutions shared elements in common, including an awareness of the same Enlightenment philosophers and intellectuals on both sides of the Atlantic whose works questioned existing institutions and

traditions and endorsed democracy, liberty, and equality. To understand the revolution in France, one must understand the distinctive nature of French society, economy, and politics in the 50 years preceding 1789 and the crisis in the Old Regime. In their revolution, the French experimented with parliamentary government and representative and participatory democracy, all the while contending with internal violence and foreign wars. The French Revolution ended with the coming to power of Napoleon, who was both the heir of the revolution and its destroyer.

THE FRENCH REVOLUTION AND THE FALL OF THE MONARCHY

Those who lived through it were sure that there had never been a time like it before. The French Revolution, or the Great Revolution, as it was known to people alive at the time, was a period of creation and discovery. The ten years from 1789 to 1799 were punctuated by genuine euphoria and democratic transformations. But the French Revolution was also a time of violence and destruction. From the privileged elites who initiated the overthrow of the existing order to the peasants and workers, men and women, who railed against tyranny, the revolution touched every segment of society.

The revolution achieved most in the area of politics. The overthrow of absolutist monarchy brought with it new social theories, new symbols, and new behavior. The excitement of anarchy was matched by the terror of repression. In the search for a new order, competing political forms followed one after the other in rapid succession: constitutional monarchy, republic, oligarchy, and dictatorship.

At the end of the eighteenth century France was a state in trouble, but it was not alone. Revolutionary incidents flared up throughout Europe in the second half of the eighteenth century in the Netherlands, Belgium, and Ireland. Absolute authority was challenged and sometimes modified. Across the Atlantic, American colonists concerned with the principle of self-rule had thrown off the yoke of the British in the War of Independence. But none of the events, including the American Revolution, was so violent in breaking with the old order, so extensive in involving millions of men and women in political action, and so consequential for the political futures of other European states as was the French Revolution. The triumphs and contradictions of the revolutionary experiment in democracy mark the end of the old order and the beginning of modern history. Politics would never be the same again.

The Political and Fiscal Crisis of Eighteenth-Century France

The French monarchy was in a state of perpetual financial crisis across the eighteenth century. Louis XV, like his great-grandfather Louis XIV, ruled as an absolute monarch; but he lacked sufficient funds to run the state. He sought loans to meet his needs as well as to pay the interest on existing debts. Borrowing at high rates required the government to pay out huge sums in interest and service fees on the loans that were keeping it afloat. The outlays in turn piled the state's indebtedness ever higher, requiring more loans, and threatening to topple the whole financial structure of the state and the regime itself. The monarchy tried to reduce expenditures, but such attempts were limited by the necessity of maintaining an effective and costly army and navy because of wars on both the Continent and in the colonies.

The nadir of Louis XV's reign came in 1763, with the French defeat in the Seven Years' War. The defeat not only left France barren of funds, it also promoted further expenditures for strengthening the French navy against the superior British fleet. The king saw taxation as the only way out of the financial trap in which he now found himself.

But raising taxes was far from an easy undertaking, and it was one that required the support of the aristocracy. The heightened tensions between the monarch and the aristocracy found expression in various institutions, especially the parlements, which were the 13 sovereign courts in the French judicial system, with their seats in Paris and a dozen provincial centers. The magistrates of each parlement were members of the aristocracy, some of them nobles of recent origin and others of long standing, depending on the locale. Following the costly Seven Years' War, the parlements chose to exercise the power of refusal by blocking a proportional tax to be imposed on nobles and commoners alike. The magistrates resisted taxation, arguing that the king was attacking the liberty of his subjects by attempting to tax those who were exempt by virtue of their privileged status.

The parlements claimed that they represented the nation; the king said the nation was himself. The king repeatedly attempted to neutralize the power of the parlements by relying instead on his own state bureaucracy, which was too weak for the task. The king's agents in the provinces, the intendants, were accountable directly to the central government. The intendants, as the king's men, and the magistrates who presided in the parlements represented contradictory claims to power. As the king's needs increased in the second half of the eighteenth century, the situation was becoming intolerable for those exercising power and those aspiring to rule in the name and for the good of the nation. The financial crisis provided the elite of notables, made up of both aristocrats and bourgeois, with the basis for asserting their own ascendancy to political power. Louis XV, who is often remembered for his cavalier prediction, "*Après moi, la déluge*" ("After me comes the

DOCUMENT

Madame de Staël
on the Ancient
Regime

flood"), indeed left a debt that swamped his grandson and successor Louis XVI. This tension between a growing debt that was undermining the monarchy and the increased ascendancy of an elite of nobles and bourgeois came to characterize the **Old Regime** in France.

When Louis XVI assumed the French throne in 1774, he was only 20 years old. He inherited a monarchy in a state of perpetual financial crisis. Not only did he inherit a trouble-ridden fiscal structure, but Louis XVI also made his own contributions to it, increasing the debt greatly by his involvement in the War of American Independence (1775–1783). Following the advice of a series of ministers, Louis sought structural solutions to the debt through a reformed fiscal policy, taxation, and other new sources of revenue, but each set of reforms offended different established interests. In the end he resorted to an unusual but available step—the convening of the **Estates-General**—as a means of achieving reforms and providing financial stability for the state.

Historically, the Estates-General was the representative body of the three "estates," or social groups, of France—the clergy (the First Estate), the nobility (the Second Estate), and the commoners (the Third Estate). The **Third Estate** was composed of all those members of the realm who enjoyed no special privilege—28 million French people. The Estates-General had not been convened since 1614. Through this body and its duly chosen representatives, Louis XVI sought the consent of the nation to levy taxes. In the political organizing that took place in the winter of 1788–1789 the seeds of revolution were sown.

Convening the Estates-General

When Louis XVI announced in August 1788 that the Estates-General would meet at Versailles in May 1789, people from all walks of life hoped for some redress of their miseries. The king hoped that the clergy, nobility, and commoners would solve his fiscal problems. Every social group, from the nobles to the poorest laborers, had its own agenda and its own ideas about justice, social status, and economic well-being.

One in four nobles had moved from the bourgeoisie to the aristocratic ranks in the eighteenth century; two out of every three had been ennobled during the seventeenth or eighteenth centuries. Nobles had succeeded in expanding their economic and social power and they now sought to preserve it. Furthermore, a growing segment of the nobility, influenced by Enlightenment ideas and the example of English institutions, was intent on increasing the political dominance of the aristocracy.

Members of the Third Estate, traditionally excluded from political and social power, were presented with the opportunity of expressing their opinions on the state of government and society. As commoners in the Third Estate, the bourgeoisie embraced within it a variety of professions, from bankers and financiers to businessmen, merchants, entrepreneurs, lawyers, shopkeepers, and artisans. Those who could

■ This cartoon depicts the plight of the French peasants. An old farmer is bowed down under the weight of the privileged aristocracy and clergy while birds and rabbits, protected by unfair game laws, eat his crops.

not read stood in marketplaces and city squares or sat around evening fires and had the political literature read to them. Farmhands and urban laborers realized that they were participating in the same process as their social betters, and they believed they had a right to speak and be heard.

It was a time of great hope, especially for workers and peasants who had been buffeted by the rise in prices, decline in real wages, and the hunger that followed crop failures and poor harvests. There was new promise of a respite and a solution. Taxes could be discussed and changed, the state bureaucracy could be reformed—or better, abolished. Intellectuals discussed political alternatives in the salons of the wealthy. Nobles and bourgeois met in philosophical societies dedicated to enlightened thought. Commoners gathered in cafes to drink and debate. Although the poor often fell outside the network of communication, they were not immune to the ideas that emerged. In the end, people of all classes had opinions and were more certain than ever of their right to express their ideas. Absolutism was in trouble, though Louis XVI did not know it, as people began to forge a collectively shared idea of politics. People now had a forum—the Estates-General—and a focus—the politics of taxation.

"If Only the King Knew." In conjunction with the political activity and in scheduled meetings, members of all three estates drew up lists of their problems. This process took place in a variety of forums, including guilds and village and town meetings. The people of France drew up grievance lists—known as *cahiers de doléances*—that were then carried to Versailles by the deputies elected to the Estates-General. The grievance lists contained the collective outpouring of problems of each estate and are important for two major reasons. First, they made clear the similarity of grievances shared throughout France. Second, they indicated the extent to which a common political culture, based on a concern with political reform, had permeated different levels of French society. Both the privileged and the nonprivileged identified a common enemy in the system of state bureaucracy to which the monarch was so strongly tied. Although the king was still addressed with respect, new concerns with liberty, equality, property, and the rule of law were voiced.

"If only the king knew!" In that phrase, French men and women had for generations expressed their belief in the inevitability of their fate and the benevolence of their king. They saw the king as a loving and wise father who would not tolerate the injustices visited on his subjects if only he knew what was really happening. In 1789, peasants and workers were questioning why their lives could not be better, but they continued to express their trust in the king. Combined with their old faith was a new hope. The peasants in the little town of Saintes recorded their newly formed expectations:

> Our king, the best of kings and father of a great and wise family, will soon know everything. All vices will be destroyed. All the great virtues of industriousness, honesty, modesty, honor, patriotism, meekness, friendliness, equality, concord, pity, and thrift will prevail and wisdom will rule supreme.

The elected deputies arrived at Versailles at the beginning of May 1789 carrying in their valises and trunks the grievances of their estates. The opening session of the Estates-General took place in a great hall especially constructed for the event. The 1248 deputies presented a grand spectacle as they filed to their assigned places to hear speeches by the king and his ministers. Contrasts among the participants were immediately apparent. Seated on a raised throne under a canopy at one end of the hall, Louis XVI was vested in full kingly regalia. On his right sat the archbishops and cardinals of the First Estate, strikingly clad in the pinks and purples of their offices. On his left were the richly and decorously attired nobility of the Second Estate. Facing the stage sat the 648 deputies of the Third Estate, dressed in plain black suits, stark against the colorful and costly costumes of the privileged. Members of the Third Estate had announced beforehand that they would not follow the ancient custom for commoners of kneeling at the king's entrance. Fired by the hope of equal treatment and an equal share of power, they had come to Versailles to make a constitution. The opening ceremony degenerated into a moment of confusion over whether members of the Third Estate should be able to wear their hats in the presence of the king. Many saw in the politics of clothing a tense beginning to their task.

The Crisis in Voting by Estate. The tension between commoners and the privileged was aggravated by the unresolved issue of how the voting was to proceed. Traditionally, each of the three orders was equally weighted. The arrangement favored the nobility, who controlled the first two estates, since the clergy themselves were often noble.

The Third Estate was adamant in its demand for vote by head. The privileged orders were equally firm in insisting on vote by order. Paralysis set in, as days dragged into weeks and

■ "Abuses to Suppress." This cartoon depicts the Third Estate—represented here by the peasant following the carriage, the worker leading the horses, and the merchant driving—delivering a petition of "abuses" to be remedied by the National Assembly.

"WHAT IS THE THIRD ESTATE?"

As an ambitious clergyman from Chartres, Abbé Emmanuel Joseph Sieyès was a member of the First Estate. Yet Sieyès was elected deputy to the Estates-General for the Third Estate on the basis of his attacks on aristocratic privilege. He participated in the writing and editing of the great documents of the early revolution: the Oath of the Tennis Court and the Declaration of the Rights of Man and Citizen. The pamphlet for which he is immortalized in revolutionary lore was his daring "What Is the Third Estate?" Written in January 1789, it boldly confronted the bankruptcy of the system of privilege of the Old Regime and threw down the gauntlet to those who ruled France. In this document the revolution found its rallying point.

Focus Questions

Why does Sieyès claim that nothing in the nation can "progress" without the Third Estate? When he states that "the nobility does not belong to the social organization at all," what point is he making about the social utility of privilege?

1st. What is the Third Estate? Everything.

2nd. What has it been heretofore in the political order? Nothing.

3rd. What does it demand? To become something therein. . . .

Who, then, would dare to say that the Third Estate has not within itself all that is necessary to constitute a complete nation? It is the strong and robust man whose one arm remains enchained. If the privileged order were abolished, the nation would not be something less but something more. Thus, what is the Third Estate? Everything; but an everything shackled and oppressed. What would it be without the privileged order? Everything; but an everything free and flourishing. Nothing can progress without it; everything would proceed infinitely better without the others. It is not sufficient to have demonstrated that the privileged classes, far from being useful to the nation, can only enfeeble and injure it; it is necessary, moreover, to prove that the nobility does not belong to the social organization at all; that, indeed, it may be a *burden* upon the nation, but that it would not know how to constitute a part thereof.

The Third Estate, then, comprises everything appertaining to the nation; and whatever is not the Third Estate may not be regarded as being of the nation. What is the Third Estate? Everything!

---

the Estates were unable to act. The body that was to save France from fiscal collapse was hopelessly deadlocked.

Abbé Emmanuel Joseph Sieyès (1748–1836), a member of the clergy, emerged as the critical leader of the Third Estate. Sieyès had already established his reputation as a firebrand reformer with his eloquent pamphlet, "What Is the Third Estate?" published in January 1789. (See the document above.) He understood that although eighteenth-century French society continued to be divided by law and custom into a pyramid of three tiers, these orders or estates were obsolete in representing social realities. The base of the pyramid was formed by the largest of the three estates, those who worked—the bourgeoisie, the peasantry, and urban and rural workers—and produced the nation's wealth. He argued that so long as the First and Second Estates did not share their privileges and rights, they were not a part of the French nation.

Under the influence of Sieyès and the reformist consensus that characterized their ranks, the delegates of the Third Estate decided to proceed with their own meetings. On 17 June 1789, joined by some sympathetic clergy, the Third Estate changed its name to the National Assembly as an assertion of its true representation of the French nation. They dedicated themselves to the primary task of writing a constitution and thereby ending absolute rule of the king. (See The Visual Record, pp. 590–591.)

The Importance of Public Opinion. The drama of Versailles, a staged play of gestures, manners, oaths, and attire, also marked the beginning of a far-reaching political revolution. Although it was a drama that took place behind closed doors, it was not one unknown to the general public. Throughout May and June 1789, Parisians trekked to Versailles to watch the deliberations and then brought the news back to the capital. Deputies wrote home to their constituents to keep them abreast of events. Newspapers that reported daily on the wranglings and pamphleteers who analyzed them spread the news throughout the nation. Information, often conflicting, stirred up anxiety; news of conflict encouraged action.

The frustration and stalemate of the Estates-General threatened to put the spark to the kindling of urban unrest. The people of Paris had suffered through a harsh winter and spring under the burdens of high prices (especially of bread), limited supplies, and relentless tax demands. The rioting of the spring had for the moment ceased as people waited for their problems to be solved by the deputies of the Estates-General. The suffering of the urban poor was not new, but their ability to connect economic hardships with the politics at Versailles and to blame the government was. As hopes began to dim with the news of political stalemate, news broke of the creation of the National Assembly. It was greeted with new anticipation.

The Outbreak of Revolutionary Action in 1789

The king, who had temporarily withdrawn from sight following the death of his son at the beginning of June, reemerged to meet with the representatives of each of the three estates and propose reforms, including a constitutional monarchy. But Louis XVI refused to accept the now popularly supported National Assembly as a legitimate body, insisting instead that he must rely on the three estates for advice. He simply did not understand that the choice was no longer his to make. He summoned troops to Versailles and began concentrating soldiers in Paris. Civilians continually clashed with members of the military, whom they jostled and jeered. The urban crowds recognized the threat of repression that the troops represented. People decided to meet force with force. To do so, they needed arms themselves—and they knew where to get them.

The Storming of the Bastille.

On 14 July 1789, the irate citizens of Paris stormed the Bastille, a royal armory that also served as a prison for a handful of debtors. The storming of the Bastille became the great symbol in the revolutionary legend of the overthrow of the tyranny and oppression of the Old Regime. But it is significant for another reason. It was an expression of the power of the people to take politics into their own hands. Parisians were following the lead of their deputies in Versailles. They had formed a citizen militia known as the National Guard, and they were prepared to defend their concept of justice and law.

The people who stormed the Bastille were not the poor, the unemployed, the criminals, or the urban rabble, as their detractors portrayed them. They were petty tradesmen, shopkeepers, and wage-earners, who considered it their right to seize arms in order to protect their interests. The Marquis de Lafayette (1757–1834), a noble beloved of the people because of his participation in the American Revolution, helped organize the National Guard. Under his direction, the militia adopted the tricolor flag as its standard. The tricolor combined the red and blue colors of the city of Paris with the white of the Bourbon royal family. It became the flag of the revolution, replacing the fleur-de-lis of the Bourbons. It is the national flag of France today.

The king could no longer dictate the terms of the constitution. By their actions, the people in arms had ratified the National Assembly. Louis XVI was forced to yield. The events in Paris set off similar uprisings in cities and towns throughout France. National guards in provincial cities modeled themselves after the Parisian militia. Government officials fled their posts and abandoned their responsibilities. Commoners stood ready to fill the power vacuum. But the revolution was not just an urban phenomenon: the peasantry had their own grievances and their own way of making a revolution.

Peasant Fear of an Aristocratic Plot.

The precariousness of rural life and the increase in population in the countryside contributed to the permanent displacement and destitution of a growing sector of rural society. Without savings and destroyed by poor harvests, impoverished rural inhabitants wandered the countryside looking for odd jobs and eventually begging to survive. All peasants endured common obligations placed on them by the crown and the privileged classes. A bewildering array of taxes afflicted peasants: they owed the tithe to the Church, land taxes to the state, and seigneurial dues and rents to the landlord. In some areas, peasants repaired roads

■ This lively amateur painting of the fall of the Bastille is by Claude Cholat, one of the attackers. Tradition has it that Cholat is manning the cannon in the background. The inscription proclaims that the painting is by one of the "conquerors of the Bastille."

MAP DISCOVERY

Boundaries, 1789
★ **Revolutionary centers**
Areas of the Great Fear, July – Aug. 1789
French boundaries, 1793
Counter-revolutionary activity
• **Centers of counter-revolutionary activity**
Areas of insurrection

Revolutionary France

The French Revolution was not merely a Parisian phenomenon, as this map shows. Locate the revolutionary centers on the map. What feature is common to all of these centers? How do you explain their distribution throughout France? Pockets of insurrection and counter-revolution were scattered for the most part in the southeast and west. What did they have in common? What territories did France gain between 1789 and 1793 and why did it expand?

and drew lots for military service. Dues affected almost every aspect of rural life. The labor of women was essential to the survival of the rural family. Peasant women sought employment in towns and cities as seamstresses and servants in order to send money back home to struggling relatives. Children, too, added their earnings to the family pot. In spite of various strategies for survival, the lives of more and more peasant families were disrupted by the end of the eighteenth century as they were displaced from the land.

News of the events of Versailles and then of the revolutionary action in Paris did not reassure rural inhabitants. By the end of June the hope of deliverance from crippling taxes and dues was rapidly fading. The news of the Oath of the Tennis Court and the storming of the Bastille terrified country folk, who saw the actions as evidence of an aristocratic plot that threatened sorely needed reforms. As information moved along postal routes in letters from delegates to their supporters, and as news was repeated in the Sunday market gatherings, distortions and exaggerations crept in. It seemed to rural inhabitants that their world was falling apart. Some peasants believed that Paris was in the hands of brigands and that the king and the Estates-General were victims of an aristocratic plot. Rural vision, fueled by empty stomachs, was apocalyptic.

That state of affairs was aggravated as increasing numbers of peasants were pushed off the land to seek employment as transient farm laborers, moving from one area to another with the cycles of sowing and harvesting. Throughout the 1780s, the number of peasants without land was increasing steadily.

Starving men, women, and children, filthy and poorly dressed, were frightening figures to villagers who feared that the same fate would befall them with the next bad harvest. As one landowner lamented, "We cannot lie down without fear, the nighttime paupers have tormented us greatly, to say nothing of the daytime ones, whose numbers are considerable."

Most peasants had lived in the same place for generations and knew only the confines of their own villages. They were uneasy about what existed beyond the horizon. Transients, often speaking strange dialects, disrupted and threatened the social universe of the village. In order to survive, wanderers often resorted to petty theft, stealing fruit from trees or food from unwatched hearths. Often traveling in groups, hordes of vagabonds struck fear into the hearts of farm workers, trampling crops and sleeping in open fields. Peasants were sure that the unfortunate souls were brigands paid by the local aristocracy to persecute a peasantry already stretched to the breaking point.

The Peasant Revolt. Hope gave way to fear. Beginning on 20 July 1789, peasants in different areas of France reacted collectively throughout France, spreading false rumors of a great conspiracy. Fear gripped whole villages and in some areas spawned revolt. Just as urban workers had connected their economic hardships to politics, so too did desperate peasants see their plight in political terms. Historians describe this period of collective panic as the **Great Fear**. Peasants banded together and marched to the residences of the local nobility, breaking into chateaux with a single mission in mind: to destroy all legal documents by which nobles claimed payments, dues, and services from local peasants. They drove out the lords and in some cases burned their chateaux, putting an end to the tyranny of the privileged over the countryside. The peasants had taken matters into their own hands. They intended to consign the last vestiges of aristocratic privilege to the bonfires of aristocratic documents.

The overthrow of privileges rooted in a feudal past was not so easy. Members of the National Assembly were aghast at the eruption of rural violence. They knew that to stay in power they had to maintain peace. They also knew that to be credible they had to protect property. Peasant destruction of seigneurial claims posed a real dilemma for the bourgeois deputies directing the revolution. If they gave in to peasant demands, they risked losing aristocratic support and undermining their own ability to control events. If they gave in to the aristocracy, they risked a social revolution in the countryside, which they could not police or repress. Liberal members of the aristocracy cooperated with the bourgeois leaders in finding a solution.

■ A contemporary print of the women of Paris advancing on Versailles. The determined marchers are shown waving pikes and dragging an artillery piece. The women were hailed as heroines of the revolution.

Depart des Heroines de Paris pour Versailles le 5 Octobre 1789.

In a dramatic meeting that lasted through the night of 4 August 1789, the National Assembly agreed to abolish the principle of privilege. The peasants had won—or thought they had. In the weeks and months ahead, rural people learned that they had lost their own prerogatives—the rights to common grazing and gathering—and were expected to buy their way out of their feudal services. In the meantime, parliamentary action had saved the day: the deputies stabilized the situation through legislating compromise.

Women on the March.   Women participated with men in both urban and rural revolutionary actions. Acting on their own, women were responsible for one of the most dramatic events of the early years of the revolution: in October 1789 they forced the king and the royal family to leave Versailles for Paris to deal in person with the problems of bread supply, high prices, and starvation. Women milling about in the marketplaces of Paris on the morning of 5 October were complaining bitterly about the high cost and shortages of bread. The National Assembly was in session, and the National Guards were patrolling the streets of Paris. But the trappings of political change had no impact on the brutal realities of the marketplace.

Women were in charge of buying the food for their families. Every morning they stood in lines with their neighbors reenacting the familiar ritual. Some mornings they were turned away, told by the baker or his assistants that there was no bread. On other days they did not have enough coins in their purses to buy the staple of their diet. Women responsible for managing the consumption of the household were most directly in touch with the state of provisioning the capital. When they were unable to feed their families, the situation became intolerable.

So it was, on the morning of 5 October 1789, that 6000 Parisian women marched out of the city and toward Versailles. They were taking their problem to the king with the demand that he solve it. Later in the day, Lafayette led the Parisian National Guard to Versailles to mediate events. The women were armed with pikes, the simple weapon available to the poorest defender of the revolution, and they were prepared to use them. The battle came early the next morning, when the women, now accompanied by revolutionary men, tired and cold from waiting all night at the gates of the palace, invaded the royal apartments and chased Marie Antoinette from her bedroom. Several members of the royal guards, hated by the people of Paris for alleged insults against the tricolor cockade, were killed by the angry crowd, who decapitated them and mounted their heads on pikes. A shocked Louis XVI agreed to return with the crowd to Paris. The crowd cheered Louis's decision, which briefly reestablished his personal popularity. But as monarch, he had been humiliated at the hands of women of the capital. Reduced to the roles of "the baker, the baker's wife, and the baker's son" by jeering crowds, the royal family was forced to return to Paris that very day. Louis XVI was now captive to the revolution, whose efforts to form a constitutional monarchy he purported to support.

Declaring Political Rights

"Liberty consists in the ability to do whatever does not harm another." So wrote the revolutionary deputies of 1789. Sounding a refrain similar to that of the American Declaration of Independence, the Declaration of the Rights of Man and Citizen appeared on 26 August 1789. The document amalgamated a variety of Enlightenment ideas drawn from the works of political philosophy, including those of Locke and Montesquieu. "Men are born and remain free and equal in rights. Social distinctions may be based only on common utility." Perhaps most significant of all was the attention given to property, which was declared a "sacred and inviolable," "natural," and "imprescriptible" right of man.

In the year of tranquility that followed the violent summer of 1789, the new politicians set themselves the task of creating institutions based on the principle of liberty and others embodied in the Declaration of the Rights of Man and Citizen. The result was the Constitution of 1791, a statement of faith in a progressive constitutional monarchy. A king accountable to an elected parliamentary body would lead France into a prosperous and just age. The constitution acknowledged the people's sovereignty as the source of political power. It also enshrined the principle of property by making voting rights dependent on property ownership. All men might be equal before the law, but by the Constitution of 1791 only wealthy men had the right to vote for representatives and hold office.

Civil Liberties.   All titles of nobility were abolished. In the early period of the revolution, civil liberties were extended to Protestants and Jews, who had been persecuted under the Old Regime. Previously excluded groups were granted freedom of thought, worship, and full civil liberties. More reluctantly, deputies outlawed slavery in the colonies in 1794. Slave unrest in Saint Domingue (modern-day Haiti) had coincided with the political conflicts of the revolution and exploded in rebellion in 1791, driving the revolutionaries in Paris to support black independence although it was at odds with French colonial interests. Led by Toussaint L'Ouverture (1743–1803), black rebels worked to found an independent Haitian state, which was declared in 1804. But the concept of equality with regard to race remained incompletely integrated with revolutionary principles, and slavery was reestablished in the French colonies in 1802.

Women's Rights.   Men were the subject of the newly defined rights. No references to women or their rights appear in the constitutions or the official Declarations of Rights. Women's organizations agitated for an equitable divorce law, and divorce was legalized in September 1792. Women were critical actors in the revolution from its very inception, and their presence shaped and directed the outcome of events, as the women's march to Versailles in 1789 made clear. The Marquis de Condorcet (1743–1794), elected to the Legislative Assembly in 1791, was one of the first to chastise the revolutionaries for overlooking the political rights of women who,

DECLARATION OF THE RIGHTS OF MAN AND CITIZEN

Sounding a refrain similar to that of the American Declaration of Independence (1776), the Declaration of the Rights of Man and Citizen was adopted by the French National Assembly on 26 August 1789. The document amalgamated a variety of Enlightenment ideas, including those of Locke and Montesquieu. The attention to property, which was defined as "sacred and inviolable," rivaled that given to liberty as a "natural" and "imprescriptible" right of man.

Focus Questions

How are individual rights defined in relation to the rights of "society" and the "nation"? What is the role of law in protecting rights?

1. Men are born and remain free and equal in rights. Social distinctions may be founded only upon the general good.

2. The aim of all political association is the preservation of the natural and imprescriptible rights of man. These rights are liberty, property, security, and resistance to oppression.

3. The principle of all sovereignty resides essentially in the nation. No body nor individual may exercise any authority which does not proceed directly from the nation.

4. Liberty consists in the freedom to do everything which injures no one else; hence the exercise of the natural rights of each man has no limits except those which assure to the other members of the society the enjoyment of the same rights. These limits can only be determined by law.

5. Law can only prohibit such actions as are hurtful to society. Nothing may be prevented which is not forbidden by law, and no one may be forced to do anything not provided for by law.

6. Law is the expression of the general will. Every citizen has a right to participate personally, or through his representative, in its formation. It must be the same for all, whether it protects or punishes. All citizens, being equal in the eyes of the law, are equally eligible to all dignities and to all public positions and occupations, according to their abilities, and without distinction except that of their virtues and talents.

7. No person shall be accused, arrested, or imprisoned except in the cases and according to the forms prescribed by law. Any one soliciting, transmitting, executing, or causing to be executed, any arbitrary order, shall be punished. But any citizen summoned or arrested in virtue of the law shall submit without delay, as resistance constitutes an offense.

8. The law shall provide for such punishments only as are strictly and obviously necessary. . . .

9. As all persons are held innocent until they shall have been declared guilty, if arrest shall be deemed indispensable, all harshness not essential to the securing of the prisoner's person shall be severely repressed by law.

10. No one shall be disquieted on account of his opinions, including his religious views, provided their manifestation does not disturb the public order established by law.

11. The free communication of ideas and opinions is one of the most precious of the rights of man. Every citizen may, accordingly, speak, write, and print with freedom, but shall be responsible for such abuses of this freedom as shall be defined by law.

12. The security of the rights of man and of the citizen requires public military forces. These forces are, therefore, established for the good of all and not for the personal advantage of those to whom they shall be entrusted.

13. A common contribution is essential for the maintenance of the public forces and for the cost of administration. This should be equitably distributed among all the citizens in proportion to their means.

14. All the citizens have a right to decide, either personally or by their representatives, as to the necessity of the public contribution; to grant this freely; to know to what uses it is put; and to fix the proportion, the mode of assessment and of collection and the duration of the taxes.

15. Society has the right to require of every public agent an account of his administration.

16. A society in which the observance of the law is not assured, nor the separation of powers defined, has no constitution at all.

17. Since property is an inviolable and sacred right, no one shall be deprived thereof except where public necessity, legally determined, shall clearly demand it, and then only on condition that the owner shall have been previously and equitably indemnified.

DECLARATION OF THE RIGHTS OF WOMAN AND CITIZEN

"Woman, wake up!" Thus did Olympe de Gouges (d. 1793), a self-educated playwright, address French women in 1791. Aware that women were being denied the new rights of liberty and property extended to all men by the Declaration of the Rights of Man and Citizen, Gouges composed her own Declaration of the Rights of Woman and Citizen, modeled on the 1789 document. Persecuted for her political beliefs, she foreshadowed her own demise at the hands of revolutionary justice in Article 10 of her declaration. The Declaration of the Rights of Woman and Citizen became an important document in women's demands for political rights in the nineteenth century, and Gouges herself became a feminist hero.

Focus Questions

Why was a separate declaration of rights necessary for women? How does this declaration differ from the "Declaration of the Rights of Man and Citizen"?

Article I Woman is born free and lives equal to man in her rights. Social distinctions can be based only on the common utility.

Article II The purpose of any political association is the conservation of the natural and imprescriptible rights of woman and man; these rights are liberty, property, security, and especially resistance to oppression.

Article III The principle of all sovereignty rests essentially with the nation, which is nothing but the union of woman and man; no body and no individual can exercise any authority which does not come expressly from it [the nation].

Article IV Liberty and justice consist of restoring all that belongs to others; thus, the only limits on the exercise of the natural rights of woman are perpetual male tyranny; these limits are to be reformed by the laws of nature and reason.

Article V Laws of nature and reason proscribe all acts harmful to society; everything which is not prohibited by these wise and divine laws cannot be prevented, and no one can be constrained to do what they do not command.

Article VI The law must be the expression of the general will; all female and male citizens must contribute either personally or through their representatives to its formation; it must be the same for all: male and female citizens, being equal in the eyes of the law, must be equally admitted to all honors, positions, and public employment according to their capacity and without other distinctions besides those of their virtues and talents.

Article VII No woman is an exception; she is accused, arrested, and detained in cases determined by law. Women, like men, obey this rigorous law.

Article VIII The law must establish only those penalties that are strictly and obviously necessary. . . .

Article IX Once any woman is declared guilty, complete rigor is [to be] exercised by the law.

Article X No one is to be disquieted for his very basic opinions; woman has the right to mount the scaffold; she must equally have the right to mount the rostrum, provided that her demonstrations do not disturb the legally established public order.

Article XI The free communication of thoughts and opinions is one of the most precious rights of woman, since that liberty assures the recognition of children by their fathers. Any female citizen thus may say freely, I am the mother of a child which belongs to you, without being forced by a barbarous prejudice to hide the truth; [an exception may be made] to respond to the abuse of this liberty in cases determined by the law.

Article XII The guarantee of the rights of woman and the female citizen implies a major benefit; this guarantee must be instituted for the advantage of all, and not for the particular benefit of those to whom it is entrusted.

Article XIII For the support of the public force and the expenses of administration, the contributions of woman and man are equal; she shares all the duties [*corvées*] and all the painful tasks; therefore, she must have the same share in the distribution of positions, employment, offices, honors and jobs [*industrie*].

Article XIV Female and male citizens have the right to verify, either by themselves or through their representatives, the necessity of the public contribution. This can only apply to women if they are granted an equal share, not only of wealth, but also of public administration, and in the determination of the proportion, the base, the collection, and the duration of the tax.

Article XV The collectivity of women, joined for tax purposes to the aggregate of men, has the right to demand an accounting of his administration from any public agent.

Article XVI No society has a constitution without the guarantee of rights and the separation of powers: the constitution is null if the majority of individuals comprising the nation have not cooperated in drafting it.

Article XVII Property belongs to both sexes whether united or separate; for each it is an inviolable and sacred right; no one can be deprived of it, since it is the true patrimony of nature, unless the legally determined public need obviously dictates it, and then only with a just and prior indemnity.

■ Slaves revolting against the French in Saint Domingue in 1791. Napoleon sent an army to restore colonial rule in 1799, but yellow fever decimated the French soldiers, and the rebels defeated the weakened French army in 1803.

he pointedly observed, were half of the human race. "Either no individual of the human race has genuine rights, or else all have the same; and he who votes against the right of another, whatever the religion, color, or sex of that other, has henceforth abjured his own." Condorcet argued forcefully but unsuccessfully for the right of women to be educated.

The revolutionaries had declared that liberty was a natural and inalienable right, a universal right that was extended to all with the overthrow of a despotic monarch and a privileged elite. The principle triumphed in religious toleration. Yet the revolutionary concept of liberty foundered on the divergent claims of excluded groups—workers, women, and slaves—who demanded full participation in the world of politics. In 1792, revolutionaries confronted the contradictions inherent in their political beliefs of liberty and equality that were being challenged in the midst of social upheaval and foreign war. In response, the revolution turned to more radical measures to survive.

The Trials of Constitutional Monarchy

The disciplined deliberations of committees intent on fashioning a constitutional monarchy replaced the passion and fervor of revolutionary oratory. The National, or Constituent, Assembly divided France into new administrative units—*départements*—for the purpose of establishing better control over municipal governments. Along with new administrative trappings, the government promoted its own rituals. On 14 July 1790, militias from each of the newly created 83 départements of France came together in Paris to celebrate the first

anniversary of the storming of the Bastille. A new national holiday was born and with it a sense of devotion and patriotism for the new France liberated by the revolution. In spite of the unifying elements, however, the newly achieved revolutionary consensus began to show signs of breaking down.

The Counterrevolution.   In February 1790, legislation dissolved all monasteries and convents, except for those that provided aid to the poor or that served as educational institutions. As the French church was stripped of its lands, Pope Pius VI (1775–1799) denounced the principles of the revolution. In July 1790, the government approved the Civil Constitution of the Clergy: priests now became the equivalent of paid agents of the state. By requiring an oath of loyalty to the state from all practicing priests, the National Assembly created a new arena for dissent. Catholics were forced to choose to embrace or reject the revolution. Many "nonjuring" priests who refused to take the oath went into hiding. The wedge driven between the Catholic Church and revolutionary France allowed a mass-based counterrevolution to emerge. Aristocratic émigrés who had fled the country because of their opposition to the revolution were languishing for lack of a popular base. From his headquarters in Turin, the king's younger brother, the comte d'Artois, was attempting to incite a civil war in France. When the revolutionaries decided to attack the Church not just as a landed and privileged institution but also as a religious one, the counterrevolution rapidly expanded.

Late one night in June 1791, Louis XVI, Marie Antoinette, and their children disguised themselves as commoners, crept out of the royal apartments in the Tuileries Palace, and fled Paris. Louis intended to leave France to join royalist forces opposing the revolution at Metz. He got as far as Varennes, where he was captured by soldiers of the National Guard and brought back to a shocked Paris. The king had abandoned the revolution. Although he was not put to death for another year and a half, he was more than ever a prisoner of the revolution.

The Fiscal Crisis. The defection of the king was certainly serious, but it was not the only problem facing the revolutionaries. Other problems plagued the revolutionary government, notably foreign war and the fiscal crisis, coupled with inflation. In order to establish its seriousness and legitimacy, the National Assembly had been willing in 1789 to absorb the debts of the Old Regime. The new government could not sell titles and offices, as the king had done to deal with financial problems, but it did confiscate Church property. In addition, it issued treasury bonds in the form of assignats in order to raise money. The assignats soon assumed the status of bank notes, and by the spring of 1790 they had become compulsory legal tender. Initially they were to be backed by land confiscated from the Church and sold by the state. But the need for money soon outran the value of the land available, and the government continued to print assignats according to its needs. Depreciation of French currency in international markets and inflation at home resulted. The revolutionary government found itself in a situation which in certain respects was worse than that experienced by Louis XVI before the calling of the Estates-General. Assignat-induced inflation produced a sharp decline in the fortunes of bourgeois investors living on fixed incomes. Rising prices meant increased misery for workers and peasants.

New counterrevolutionary groups were becoming frustrated with revolutionary policies. Throughout the winter and spring of 1791–1792, people rioted and demanded that prices be fixed, while the assignat dropped to less than half its face value. Peasants refused to sell crops for the worthless paper. Hoarding further drove up prices. Angry crowds turned to pillaging, rioting, and murder, which became more frequent as the value of the currency declined and prices rose.

Foreign war beginning in the fall of 1791 also challenged stability. Some moderate political leaders welcomed war as a blessing in disguise, since it could divert the attention of the masses away from problems at home and promote loyalty to the revolution. Others envisioned war as a great crusade to bring revolutionary principles to oppressed peoples throughout Europe. The king and queen, trapped by the revolution, saw war as their only hope of liberation. Louis XVI could be rightfully restored as the leader of a France defeated by the sovereigns of Europe. Some who opposed the war believed it would destabilize the revolution. France must solve its problems at home, they argued, before fighting a foreign enemy. Louis, however, encouraged those ministers and advisers eager for battle. In April 1792, France declared war against Austria.

Individuals, events, economic realities, and the nature of politics conspired against the success of the first constitutional experiment. The king's attempt to flee France in the summer of 1791 seriously wounded the attempt at compromise. Many feared that the goals of the revolution could not be preserved in a country at war and with a king of dubious loyalties.

EXPERIMENTING WITH DEMOCRACY, 1792–1799

The Revolution was a school for the French nation. A political universe populated by individual citizens replaced the eighteenth-century world of subjects loyal to their king. The new construction of politics, in which all individuals were equal, ran counter to prevailing ideas about collective identities defined in guilds and orders. People on all levels of society learned politics by doing it. In the beginning, experience helped. The elites, both noble and bourgeois, had served in government and administration. But the rules of the game under the Old Regime had been very different, with birth and wealth determining power.

After 1789, all men were declared free and equal, in opportunity if not in rights. Men of ability and talent, who had served as middlemen for the privileged elite under the Old Regime, now claimed power as their due. Many of them were lawyers, educated in the rules and regulations of the society of orders. They experienced firsthand the problems of the exercise of power in the Old Regime, and they had their own ideas about reform. But the school of the revolution did not remain the domain of a special class. Women demanded their places but continued to be excluded from the political arena, though the importance of their participation in the revolution was indisputable. Workers talked of seizing their rights, but because of the inherent contradictions of representation and participation, experimenting with democracy led to outcomes that did not look very democratic at all.

The Revolution of the People

The first stage of the French Revolution, lasting from 1789 through the beginning of 1792, was based on liberty—the liberty to compete, to own, and to succeed. The second stage of the French Revolution, which began in 1792, took equality as its rallying cry. It was the revolution of the working people of French cities. The popular movement that spearheaded political action in 1792 was committed to equality of rights in a way not characteristic of the leaders of the revolution of 1789. Urban workers were not benefiting from the revolution, but they had come to believe in their own power as political beings. Organized on the local level into sections, artisans in cities identified themselves as **sans-culottes**—literally, those trousered citizens who did not wear knee breeches (*culottes*)—to distinguish themselves from the privileged elite.

Who constituted the popular movement? The self-designated sans-culottes were the working men and women of Paris. Some were wealthier than others, some were wage earners, but all shared a common identity as consumers in the market-

THE GUILLOTINE AND REVOLUTIONARY JUSTICE

In the sultry summer days of 1792, Parisians found a new way to entertain themselves. They attended executions. French men, women, and children were long accustomed to watching criminals being tortured and put to death in public view. During the Old Regime, spectators could enjoy a variety of methods: drawing and quartering, strangling, or hanging. Decapitation, reputedly a less painful death, was a privilege reserved for nobles sentenced for capital crimes. The French Revolution extended that formerly aristocratic privilege to all criminals condemned to death. What especially attracted people to public squares in the third year of the revolution was the introduction of a novel method of decapitation. In 1792, the new instrument of death, the guillotine, became the center of the spectacle of revolutionary justice.

The guillotine promised to eliminate the suffering of its victims. Axes, swords, and sabers—the traditional tools of decapitation and dismemberment—were messy and undependable, producing slow and bloody ordeals when inept or drunken executioners missed their mark or victims flinched at the fatal moment. The design of the guillotine took all of that into account. On its easel-like wooden structure, victims, lying on their stomachs, were held in place with straps and a pillory. Heavy pulleys guaranteed that the sharp blade would fall efficiently from its great height. A basket was placed at the base of the blade to catch the severed head; another was used to slide the headless body through the base of the scaffolding for removal. In place of unintended torture and gore, the guillotine was devised as a humanitarian instrument to guarantee swift and painless death.

It should have been called the Louisette, after its inventor, Dr. Antoine Louis. In what now seems a dubious honor, the new machine was named instead after its greatest supporter, Dr. Joseph Ignace Guillotin, a delegate to the National Assembly. Both Guillotin and Louis were medical doctors, men of science influenced by Enlightenment ideas and committed to the revolution's elimination of the cruelty of older forms of punishment. In the spirit of scientific experimentation, Louis's invention was tested on sheep, cadavers, and then convicted thieves. In 1792, it was used for the first time against another class of offenders: political prisoners.

Early in the revolution, the Marquis de Condorcet, philosophe and mathematician, had opposed capital punishment with the argument that the state did not have the right to take life. Ironically, Maximilien Robespierre, future architect of the Reign of Terror, was one of the few revolutionaries who agreed with Condorcet. Those who favored justice by execution of the state's enemies prevailed. By the end of 1792, as revolution and civil war swept over France, 83 identical guillotines were constructed and installed in each of the départements of France. For the next two years, the guillotine's great blade was rhythmically raised and lowered daily in public squares all over France. In the name of the revolution, the "axe of the people" dispatched over 50,000 victims.

Although intended as a humanitarian instrument, the guillotine became the

■ Execution of Louis XVI on 21 January 1793.

symbol of all that was arbitrary and repressive about a revolution run amok. Day and night, the Revolutionary Tribunal in Paris delivered the death sentence to the "enemies of the people." Most of those executed were members of what had been the Third Estate: members of the bourgeoisie, workers, and peasants. Only 15 percent of the condemned were nobles and priests. During the Terror, the guillotine could be used to settle old scores. Sans-culottes turned in their neighbors, sometimes over long-standing grievances that owed more to spite than politics. The most fanatical revolutionaries had fantasies that guillotines were about to be erected on every street corner to dispense with hoarders and traitors. Others suggested that guillotines be made portable so that by putting justice on wheels, it could be taken directly to the people.

As usual, Paris set the style. The most famous of the guillotines stood on the Place du Carrousel, deliberately placed in front of the royal palace of the Tuileries. It was eventually moved to the larger Place de la Révolution in order to accommodate the growing numbers of spectators. Famous victims drew especially large crowds. The revolutionary drama took on the trappings of a spectacle as hawkers sold toy guillotines, miniature pikes, and liberty caps as souvenirs, along with the usual food and drink. Troops attended the events, but not to control the crowd. Members of the National Guard in formation, their backs to the people, faced the stage of the scaffold. They, like the citizenry, were there to witness the birth of a new nation and, by their presence, to give legitimacy to the event. The crowd entered into the ritual, cheering the victim's last words and demanding that the executioner hold high the severed head. In the new political culture, death was a festival.

■ This frontispiece from the anti-Robespierre work *Almanach des Prisons* illustrates the results of the Reign of Terror under Robespierre's leadership and the guillotine's blade.

For two centuries, Western societies have debated the legitimacy of the death sentence and have periodically considered the relative merits of the guillotine, the gas chamber, and the electric chair. For the French, the controversy temporarily ceased in 1794, when people were convinced that justice had gotten out of hand and that they had seen enough. The guillotine would return, but for the time being, the government put an end to capital punishment. At the height of its use, between 1792 and 1794, it had played a unique role in forging a new system of justice: the guillotine had been the great leveler. In the ideology of democracy, people were equal—in death as well as in life. The guillotine came to be popularly known as the "scythe of equality." It killed king and commoner alike.

place. They hated the privileged (*les gros*), who appeared to be profiting at the expense of the people. The sans-culottes wanted government power to be decentralized, with neighborhoods ruling themselves through sectional organizations. As the have-nots, they were increasingly intent on pulling down the haves, and they translated the sense of vengeance into a new revolutionary justice. On 10 August 1792, the people of Paris stormed the Tuileries, chanting their demands for "Equality!" and "Nation!" The people tramped across the silk sheets of the king's bed and broke his fine furniture, reveling in the private chambers of the royal family. Love and respect for the king had vanished. What the people of Paris demanded was the right to vote and participate in a popular democracy. Working people were acting independently of other factions, and the bourgeois political leadership became quickly aware of the need to scramble to maintain order. When they invaded the Tuileries Palace on the morning of 10 August, the sans-culottes did so in the name of the people. They saw themselves as patriots whose duty it was to brush the monarchy aside. The people were now a force to be reckoned with and feared.

"Terror Is the Order of the Day"

Political factions characterized revolutionary politics from the start. The terms *Left* and *Right,* which came to represent opposite ends of the political spectrum, originated in a description of where people sat in the Assembly in relation to the podium. Political designations were refined in successive parliamentary bodies. The Convention was the legislative body elected in September 1792 that succeeded the Legislative Assembly and had as its charge determining the best form of government after the collapse of the monarchy. On 21 September 1792, the monarchy was abolished in France; on the following day the Republic, France's first, came into being. Members of the Convention conducted the trial of Louis XVI for treason and pronounced his sentence: execution by the guillotine in January 1793.

The various political factions of the Convention were described in terms borrowed from geography. The Mountain, sitting on the upper benches on the left, was made up of members of the Jacobin Club (named for its meeting place in an abandoned monastery). The **Jacobins** were the most radical element in the National Convention, supporting democratic solutions and speaking in favor of the cause of people in the streets.

Jacobin Ascendancy.

Both **Girondins**, the more moderate revolutionary faction, and Jacobins were from the middle ranks of the bourgeoisie, and both groups were dedicated to the principles of the revolution. Although they controlled the ministries, the Girondins began to lose their hold on the revolution and the war. The renewed European war fragmented the democratic movement, and the Girondins, unable to control violence at home, saw political control slipping away. They became prisoners of the revolution when 80,000 armed Parisians surrounded the National Convention in June 1793.

Girondin power had been eroding in the critical months between August 1792 and June 1793. A new leader was working quietly and effectively behind the scenes to weld a partnership between the popular movement of sans-culottes and the Jacobins. He was Maximilien Robespierre (1758–1794), leader of the Mountain and the Jacobin Club. Robespierre was typical of the new breed of revolutionary politician. Only 31 years old in 1789, he wrote mediocre poems and attended the local provincial academy to discuss the new ideas when he was not practicing law in his hometown of Arras. Elected to the Estates-General, he joined the Jacobin Club and quickly rose to become its leader. He was willing to take controversial stands on issues: unlike most of his fellow members of the Mountain—including his rival, the popular orator Georges-Jacques Danton (1759–1794)—he opposed the war in 1792. Although neither an original thinker nor a compelling orator, Robespierre discovered with the revolution that he was an adroit political tactician. He gained a following and learned how to manipulate it. It was he who engineered the Jacobins' replacement of the Girondins as leaders of the government.

Robespierre and the Reign of Terror.

Robespierre's chance for real power came when he assumed leadership of the Committee of Public Safety in July 1793. Faced with the threat of internal anarchy and external war, the elected body, the National Convention, yielded political control to the 12-man Committee of Public Safety that ruled dictatorially under Robespierre's direction. The Great Committee, as it was known at the time, orchestrated the **Reign of Terror** (1793–1794), a period of systematic state repression that meted out justice in the people's name. Summary trials by specially created revolutionary tribunals were followed by the swift execution of the guilty under the blade of the guillotine.

Influenced by *The Social Contract* (1762) and other writings of Jean-Jacques Rousseau, Robespierre believed that sovereignty resided with the people. For him, individual wills and even individual rights did not matter when weighed against the will of the nation. The king was dead; the people were the new source of political power. Robespierre saw himself in the all-important role of interpreting and shaping the people's will. His own task was to guide the people "to the summit of its destinies." As he explained to his critics, "I am defending not my own cause but the public cause." As head of the Great Committee, Robespierre oversaw a revolutionary machinery dedicated to economic regulation, massive military mobilization, and a punitive system of revolutionary justice characterized by the slogan, "Terror Is the Order of the Day." Militant revolutionary committees and revolutionary tribunals were established throughout France to identify traitors and to mete out the harsh justice that struck hardest against those members of the bourgeoisie perceived as opponents of the government.

The guillotine became the symbol of revolutionary justice, but it was not the only means of execution. (See "A Closer Look: The Guillotine and Revolutionary Justice," pp. 604–605.)

DOCUMENT

Saint-Just on Democracy, Education, and Terror

IMAGE DISCOVERY

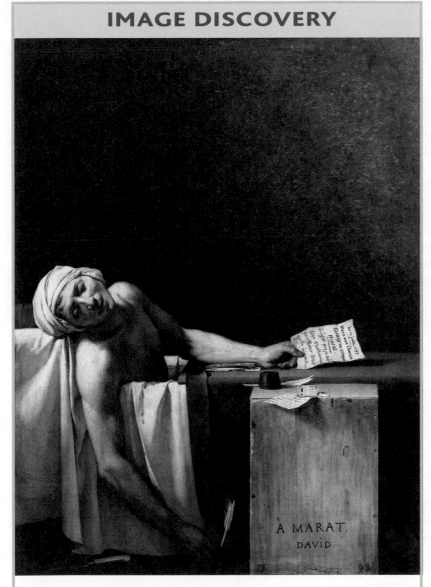

The Death of Marat, 1793, by Jacques-Louis David

The revolutionary Jean-Paul Marat was killed in his medicinal tub (he suffered from a skin disease) by Charlotte Corday, a critic of the Radical politics and mob violence of the Revolution. Marat advocated the use of violence to ensure the success of the revolution. How does the use of lighting and drapery in this canvas convey the political leanings and attitude of the artist toward his subject? The canvas is dedicated to Marat (À Marat). What effect does the artist intend by listing his name—David—under Marat's? Note that the knife used to commit the attack is juxtaposed with the pen in Marat's hand. What is the overall effect of the tableau?

In Lyon, officials of the Reign of Terror had prisoners tied to stakes in open fields and fired on with cannons. In Nantes, a Parisian administrator of the new justice had enemies of the

revolution chained to barges and drowned in the estuary of the Loire. The civil war, which raged most violently in the Vendée in the west of France, consisted often of primitive massacres that sent an estimated quarter of a million people to their deaths. The bureaucratized Reign of Terror was responsible for about 40,000 executions in a nine-month period, resulting in the image of the republicans as "drinkers of blood."

The Cult of the Supreme Being, a civic religion without priests or churches and influenced by Rousseau's ideas about nature, followed de-Christianization. The cathedral of Notre Dame de Paris was turned into the Temple of Reason, and the new religion established its own festivals to undermine the persistence of Catholicism. The cult was one indication of the Reign of Terror's attempt to create a new moral universe of revolutionary values.

Women Excluded. Women remained conspicuously absent from the summit of political power. After 1793, Jacobin revolutionaries, who had been willing to empower the popular movement of workers, turned against women's participation and denounced it. Women's associations were outlawed and the Society of Revolutionary Republican Women was disbanded. Olympe de Gouges, revolutionary author of the Declaration of the Rights of Woman and Citizen (see p. 601), was guillotined. Women were declared unfit for political participation, according to the Jacobins, because of their biological functions of reproduction and child-rearing. Rousseau's ideas about family policy were probably more influential than his political doctrines. His best-selling books, *La Nouvelle Héloïse* (1761) and *Émile* (1762), which combined went into 72 editions before 1789, were moral works that transformed people's ideas about family life. Under his influence, the reading public came to value a separate and private sphere of domestic and conjugal values. Following Rousseau's lead, Robespierre and the Jacobins insisted that the role of women as mothers was incompatible with women's participation in the political realm.

The Thermidorian Reaction. By attacking his critics on both the Left and the Right, Robespierre undermined the support he needed to stay in power. He abandoned the alliance with the popular movement that had been so important in bringing him to power. Robespierre's enemies—and he had many—were able to break the identification between political power and the will of the people that Robespierre had established. As a result, he was branded a traitor by the same process that he had used against many of his own enemies. He saved France from foreign occupation and internal collapse, but he could not save democracy through terror. In the summer of 1794, Robespierre was guillotined. The Reign of Terror ceased with his death in the revolutionary month of Thermidor 1794.

The revolution did not end with the **Thermidorian Reaction,** as the fall of Robespierre came to be known, but his execution initiated a new phase. For some, democracy lost its legitimacy. The popular movement was reviled, and sans-culotte became a term of derision. Jacobins were forced underground. Price controls were abolished, resulting in extreme hardship for most urban residents. Out of desperation, in April 1795 the Jacobins and the sans-culottes renewed their alliance and united to demand "bread and the Constitution of 1793." The politics of bread had never been more accurately captured in slogan. Those who took to the streets in 1795 saw the universal manhood suffrage of the unimplemented 1793 constitution as the way to solve their economic problems. But their demands went unheeded; the popular revolution had failed.

The End of the Revolution

In the four years after Robespierre's fall, a new government by committee, called the Directory, appeared to offer mediocrity, caution, and opportunism in place of the idealism and action of the early years of the revolution. No successor to Robespierre stepped forward to command center stage. There were no heroes like Lafayette or the great Jacobin orator Georges-Jacques Danton to inspire patriotic fervor. Nor were there women like Olympe de Gouges to demand in the public arena equal rights for women. Most people, numbed after years of change, barely noticed that the revolution was over. Ordinary men in parliamentary institutions effectively did the day-to-day job of running the government. They tried to steer a middle path between royalist resurgence and popular insurrection. This nearly forgotten period in the history of the French Revolution was the fulfillment of the liberal hopes of 1789 for a stable constitutional rule.

The Directory, however, continued to be dogged by European war. A mass army of conscripts and volunteers had successfully extended France's power and frontiers. France expelled foreign invaders and annexed territories, including Belgium, while increasing its control in Holland, Switzerland, and Italy. But the expansion of revolutionary France was expensive and increasingly unpopular. Military defeats and the corruption of the Directory undermined government control. The Directory might have succeeded in the slow accretion of a parliamentary tradition, but reinstatement of **conscription** in 1798 met with widespread protest and resistance. No matter what their political leanings, people were weary. They turned to those who promised stability and peace.

In the democratic experiment at the heart of the second stage of the French Revolution, the sovereign will of the peo-

CHRONOLOGY	
The French Revolution	
August 1788	Louis XVI announces meeting of Estates-General to be held May 1789
5 May 1789	Estates-General convenes
17 June 1789	Third Estate declares itself the National Assembly
20 June 1789	Oath of the Tennis Court
14 July 1789	Storming of the Bastille
20 July 1789	Revolution of peasantry begins
26 August 1789	Declaration of the Rights of Man and Citizen
5 October 1789	Parisian women march to Versailles; force Louis XVI to return to Paris
February 1790	Monasteries, convents dissolved
July 1790	Civil Constitution of the Clergy
June 1791	Louis XVI and family attempt to flee Paris; are captured and returned
September 1791	France's first Constitution
April 1792	France declares war on Austria
10 August 1792	Storming of the Tuileries
22 September 1792	Revolutionary calendar implemented
January 1793	Louis XVI executed
July 1793	Robespierre assumes leadership of Committee of Public Safety
1793–1794	Reign of Terror
1794	Robespierre guillotined
1795	Directory rules France
1799	Napoleon overthrows the Directory and seizes power

ple permanently replaced the monarch's claim to divine right to rule. Yet with democracy came tyranny. The severe repression of the terror revealed the pressures that external war and civil unrest created for the new Republic. The Thermidorian Reaction and the elimination of Robespierre as the legitimate interpreter of the people's will ushered in a period of conciliation, opportunism, and a search for stability. Ironically, the savior that France found to answer its needs for peace and a just government was a man of war and a dictator.

THE REIGN OF NAPOLEON, 1799–1815

The great debate that rages to this day about Napoleon revolves around the question of whether he fulfilled the aims of the revolution or perverted them. In his return to a monarchical model, Napoleon resembled the enlightened despots of eighteenth-century Europe. In a modern sense, he was also a dictator, manipulating the French population through a highly centralized administrative apparatus. He locked French society into a program of military expansion that depleted its human and material resources. Yet, in spite of destruction and war, he dedicated his reign to building a French state according to the principles of the Revolution. Napoleon is one of those individuals about whom one can say that if he had not lived, history would have been different. He left his mark on an age and a continent.

Bonaparte Seizes Power

In Paris in 1795 a young, penniless, and unknown military officer moved among the wealthy and the beautiful of Parisian society and longed for fame. Already nicknamed at school "the Little Corporal" on account of his short stature, he was snubbed because of his background and ridiculed for his foreign accent. His story is typical of all stories of thwarted ambition. Yet the outcome of his story is unique: within four years, that young man would become ruler of France. The story of his ascent to power is also a story of the demise of the revolution.

Napoleon's Training and Experience.

Napoleon Bonaparte (1769–1821) was a true child of the eighteenth century. He shared the philosophes' belief in a rational and progressive world. Born in Corsica, which until a few months before his birth was part of the Republic of Genoa, he received his training in French military schools. As a youth, he was arrogant and ambitious. But he could have never aspired to a position of leadership in the army during the Old Regime because he lacked the noble birth necessary for advancement. The highest rank Napoleon could hope to achieve was that of captain or major.

DOCUMENT

The Rise of Napoleon

The revolution changed everything for him. First, it opened up careers previously restricted by birth, including those in the military, to those with talent. Second, the revolution made new posts available when aristocratic generals defected and crossed over to the enemy side, both before and after the execution of the king. Finally, the revolution created great opportunities for military men to test their mettle.

Foreign war and civil war required military leaders devoted to the revolution. Forced to flee Corsica because he had sided with the Jacobins, Napoleon and his troops were given the task of crushing Parisian protesters who rioted against the Directory in 1795. His victories in the Italian campaign in 1796–1797 launched his political career. As he extended French rule into central Italy, he became the embodiment of revolutionary values and energy.

The revolutionary wars had begun as wars to liberate humanity in the name of liberty, equality, and fraternity. Yet concerns for power, territory, and riches soon replaced earlier concerns with defense of the nation and of the revolution. The aggrandizement was nowhere more evident than in the Egyptian campaign of 1798, in which Napoleon Bonaparte headed an expedition whose goal was to enrich France by hastening the collapse of the Turkish Empire, crippling British trade routes, and handicapping Russian interests in the region. With Napoleon's highly publicized campaigns in Egypt and Syria, the war left the European theater and moved to the East, leaving behind its original revolutionary ideals. The Egyptian campaign, which was in reality a disaster, made Napoleon a hero at home.

Napoleon as First Consul.

In 1799, Napoleon Bonaparte readily joined a conspiracy that pulled down the Directory, the government he had earlier preserved, and became the First Consul of a triumvirate of consuls. Napoleon set out to secure his position of power by eliminating his enemies on the Left and weakening those on the Right. He guaranteed the security of property acquired in the revolution, a move that undercut royalists who wanted to return property to its original owners. Through policing forces and special criminal courts, law and order prevailed and civil war subsided. The First Consul promised a balanced budget and appeared to deliver it. Bonaparte spoke of healing the nation's wounds, especially those opened by de-Christianization during the revolution. Realizing the importance of religion in maintaining domestic peace, Napoleon reestablished relations with the pope in 1801 by the Concordat, which recognized Catholicism as the religion of the French and restored the Roman Catholic hierarchy.

Napoleon's popularity as First Consul flowed from his military and political successes and his religious reconciliation. He had come to power in 1799 by appealing for the support of the army. In 1802, Napoleon decided to extend his power by calling for a plebiscite in which he asked the electorate to vote him First Consul for life. Public support was overwhelming. An electoral landslide gave Napoleon greater political power than any of his Bourbon predecessors. Using revolutionary mechanisms, Napoleon laid the foundation for a new dynasty.

Napoleon at War with the European Powers

Napoleon was either at war or preparing for war during his entire reign. He certainly seemed up to the task of defeating the European powers. His military successes before 1799, real and apparent, had been crucial in his bid for political power. By 1802, he had signed favorable treaties with both Austria and Great Britain. He appeared to deliver a lasting peace and to establish France as the dominant power in Europe. But the

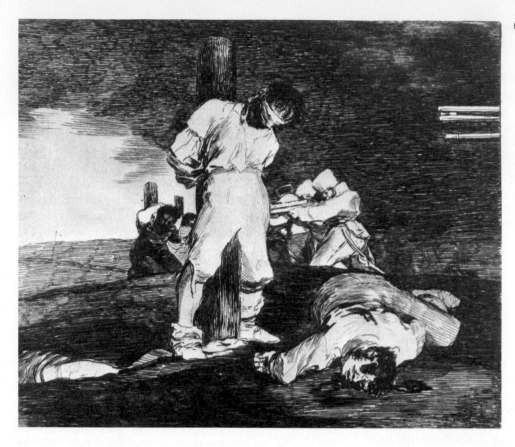

■ This engraving, from the series *Disasters of War* by Francisco Goya, depicts the horrors of war. The series was inspired by Napoleon's invasion and occupation of Spain from 1808 to 1814.

peace was short-lived. In 1803, France embarked on an 11-year period of continuous war. Under Napoleon's command, the French army delivered defeat after defeat to the European powers. Austria fell in 1805, Prussia in 1806, and the Russian armies of Alexander I were defeated at Friedland in 1807. In 1808, Napoleon invaded Spain to drive out British expeditionary forces intent on invading France. The great painter of the Spanish court, Francisco Goya (1746–1828), produced a series of etchings, *The Disasters of War,* that depicted the atrocities accompanying the Napoleonic invasion. Spain became a satellite kingdom of France, though the conflict continued.

Britain was the one exception to the string of Napoleonic victories. Napoleon initially considered sending a French fleet to invade the island nation. Lacking the strength necessary to achieve that, he turned to economic warfare, blockading European ports against British trade. Beginning in 1806, the **Continental System**, as the blockade was known, erected a structure of protection for French manufactures in all continental European markets. The British responded to the tariff walls and boycotts with a naval blockade that succeeded in cutting French commerce off from its Atlantic markets. The Continental System did not prove to be the decisive policy that Napoleon had planned: the British economy was not broken and the French economy did not flourish when faced with restricted resources and the persistence of a black market in smuggled goods.

Still, by 1810 the French leader was master of the Continent. French armies had extended revolutionary reforms and legal codes outside France and brought with them civil equality and religious toleration. They had also drained defeated countries of their resources and had inflicted the horrors of war with armies of occupation, forced billeting, and pillage. Napoleon's empire extended across Europe, with only a diminished Austria, Prussia, and Russia remaining independent. He placed his relatives and friends on the thrones of the new satellite kingdoms of Italy, Naples, Westphalia, Holland, and Spain. It was a fine empire, Napoleon later recalled in the loneliness of exile. Napoleon's empire did not endure, but at its acme, it seemed as though it would never fall.

The First Empire and Domestic Reforms

Napoleon measured domestic prosperity in terms of the stability of his reign. Through the 1802 plebiscite that voted him First Consul for life, he maintained the charade of constitutional rule while he ruled as virtual dictator. In 1804, he abandoned all pretense and had himself proclaimed emperor of the French. Mimicking the rituals of kingship, he staged his own coronation and that of his wife Josephine at the cathedral of Notre Dame de Paris. Breaking the tradition set by Charlemagne, Napoleon took the crown from the hands of Pope Pius VII (1800–1823) and placed it on his own head.

MAP DISCOVERY

Napoleon's Empire

Note the expansion of France under Napoleon's rule. How much of western and central Europe did Napoleon control by 1812? Why did Great Britain remain outside Napoleon's influence? Why were Prussia, Austria, and Denmark and Norway allies of France in 1812?

measures. The metric system was established by 1799. But Napoleon felt the need to go further: France must be first in scientific research and application. To assure French predominance, Napoleon became a patron of science, supporting important work in the areas of physics and chemistry. Building for the future, Napoleon made science a pillar in the new structure of higher education.

The Directory had restored French prosperity through stabilization of the currency, fiscal reform, and support of industry. Napoleon's contribution to the French economy was the much needed reform of the tax system. He authorized the creation of a central banking system. French industries flourished under the protection of the state. The blockade forced the development of new domestic crops such as sugar beets and indigo, which became substitutes for colonial products. Napoleon extended the infrastructure of roads necessary for the expansion of national and European markets.

The New Legal System. Perhaps his greatest achievement was the codification of law, a task begun under the revolution. Many of the new articles of the **Napoleonic Code** were hammered out in Napoleon's presence, as he presided regularly over meetings with legal reformers. Combined with economic reforms, the Napoleonic Code facilitated trade and the development of commerce by regularizing contractual relations and protecting property rights and equality before the law.

The civil laws of the new code carved out a family policy characterized by hierarchy and subordination. Married women were neither independent nor equal to men in ownership of property, custody of children, or access to divorce. Women also lacked political rights. In the Napoleonic Code, women, like children, were subjected to paternal authority. The Napoleonic philosophy of woman's place is well captured in an anecdote told by Madame Germaine de Staël

The Importance of Science and Economic Reforms. Secure in his regime, surrounded by a new nobility that he created based on military achievement and talent and that he rewarded with honors, Napoleon set about implementing sweeping reforms in every area of government. Like many of the men of the revolutionary assemblies who had received scientific educations in their youth, he recognized the importance of science for both industry and war. The revolution had removed an impediment to the development of a national market by creating a uniform system of weights and

THE *CIVIL CODE* OF THE *CODE NAPOLÉON* (1804)

While still First Consul, Bonaparte assembled a group of the country's leading legal specialists to replace the vast agglomeration of feudal, customary, and canon laws, all with their own courts and procedures, with a unified system based on Roman law. The Civil Code, *along with the* Criminal Code, *made up the* Code Napoléon, *and consisted of 2281 articles intended to cover all aspects of civil life from birth to death, all civic aspects relating to family and property, contractual responsibilities, and civil liberties. A unified legal system became the basis for economic development and was arguably Napoleon's greatest achievement as ruler of France. The* Civil Code *replaced the Roman Catholic Church as having authority over marriage, and although divorce was permitted in the* Code, *it was outlawed in 1816 and not permitted again until 1884.*

Focus Questions

What rights do men enjoy in this passage that women do not? What are you able to conclude about the rights of married women who work?

Of the respective rights and duties of parent and children

212. Husband and wife owe each other fidelity, support, and assistance.
213. A husband owes protection to his wife; a wife owes obedience to her husband.
214. A wife is bound to live with her husband and to follow him wherever he deems proper to reside. The husband is bound to receive her, and to supply her with whatever is necessary for the wants of life, according to his means and condition.
215. A wife cannot sue in court without the consent of her husband, even if she is a public tradeswoman or if there is no community or she is separated as to property.
216. The husband's consent is not necessary when the wife is prosecuted criminally or in a police matter.
217. A wife, even when there is no community, or when she is separated as to property, cannot give, convey, mortgage, or acquire property, with or without consideration, without the husband joining in the instrument or giving his written consent.
218. If a husband refuses to allow his wife to sue in court, the Judge may grant the authorization.
219. If a husband refuses to allow his wife to execute an instrument, the wife can cause her husband to be summoned directly before the Tribunal of the First Instance of the common domicile, and such Tribunal shall grant or refuse its consent in the Judges' room after the husband has been heard or has been duly summoned.
220. A wife may, if she is a public tradeswoman, bind herself without the husband's consent with respect to what relates to her trade, and in that case she also binds her husband if there is a community of property between them. She is not considered a public tradeswoman if she merely retails the goods of her husband's business, but only when she has a separate business.
221. When a sentence has been passed upon a husband which carries with it a degrading corporal punishment, even if it has been passed by default, a wife, even of full age, cannot, during the continuance of the punishment, sue in court nor bind herself, unless she has been authorized by the Judge, who may in such cases grant the consent without the husband having been heard or summoned.
222. If a husband has been interdicted or is absent, the Judge may with proper knowledge of the case, authorize the wife to sue in court or to bind herself.
223. Any general authorization, even given by marriage contract, is only valid as to the management of the wife's property.
224. If the husband is a minor, the authorization of the Judge is necessary to the wife, either to sue in court or to bind herself.
225. A nullity based on the want of authorization can only be set up by the wife, the husband, or the heirs.
226. A wife can make a will without her husband's consent.

(1766–1817), a leading intellectual of her day. As the daughter of Jacques Necker, a Swiss financier and adviser to Louis XVI at the time of the revolution, she had been taught Enlightenment ideas from an early age. On finding herself seated next to Napoleon at a dinner party, she asked him what was very likely a self-interested question: Whom did he consider the greatest woman, alive or dead? Napoleon had no name to give her but responded, without pausing: "The one who has had the most children."

Napoleon turned his prodigious energies to every aspect of French life. He encouraged the arts while creating a police force. He had monuments built but did not forget about sewers. He organized French administrative life in a fashion that has endured. In place of the popular democratic movement, he offered his own singular authority. In place of elections, clubs, and free associations, he gave France plebiscites and army service. To be sure, Napoleon believed in constitutions, but he thought they should be "short and obscure." For Napoleon, the great problem of democracy was its unpredictability. His regime solved that problem by eliminating choices.

Decline and Fall

Militarily, Napoleon went too far. The first cracks in the French facade began to show in the Peninsular War (1808–1814) with Spain, in which Spanish guerrilla tactics proved costly for French troops. Napoleon's biggest mistake, the one that shattered the myth of his invincibility, occurred when he decided to invade Russia in June 1812.

The Invasion of Russia and the Battle of Nations.

Having decisively defeated Russian forces in 1807, Napoleon had entered into a peace treaty with Tsar Alexander I that guaranteed Russian allegiance to French policies. Alexander repudiated the Continental System in 1810 and appeared to be preparing for his own war against France. Napoleon seized the initiative, sure that he could defeat Russian forces once again. With an army of 500,000 men, Napoleon moved deep into Russia in the summer

---

CHRONOLOGY

The Reign of Napoleon

1799	Napoleon establishes consulate, becomes First Consul
1801	Napoleon reestablishes relations with pope, restores Roman Catholic hierarchy
1802	Plebiscite declares Napoleon First Consul for life
1804	Napoleon proclaims himself Emperor of the French
1806	Continental System implemented
1808–1814	France engaged in Peninsular War with Spain
June 1812	Napoleon invades Russia
September 1812	French army reaches Moscow; trapped by Russian winter
1813	Napoleon defeated at Battle of Nations at Leipzig
March 1814	Napoleon abdicates and goes into exile on island of Elba
March 1815	Napoleon escapes Elba and attempts to reclaim power
15 June 1815	Napoleon is defeated at Waterloo and exiled to island of Saint Helena

---

of 1812. The tsar's troops fell back in retreat. It was a strange war, one that pulled the French army to Moscow like a bird following bread crumbs. When Napoleon and his men entered Moscow in September, they found a city in flames. The people of Moscow had destroyed their own city to deprive the French troops of winter quarters.

Winter came early in Moscow, Napoleon's men discovered. They had left France basking in the warmth of summer and sure of certain and early victory. They then found themselves facing a severe Russian winter without overcoats, supplies, or food. Russia's strategy has become legendary. The Russians destroyed grain and shelter that might be of use to the French. Napoleon and his starving and frostbitten troops were forced into retreat. The horses of the French cavalry died because they were not properly shod for cold weather. The French army was decimated. Fewer than 100,000 men made it back to France.

Britain, unbowed by the Continental System, remained Napoleon's sworn enemy. Prussia joined Great Britain, Sweden, Russia, and Austria in opposing France anew. In the Battle of Nations at Leipzig in October 1813, France was forced to retreat. Napoleon refused a negotiated peace and fought on until the following March, when the victorious allies marched down the streets of Paris and occupied the French capital. Only then did Napoleon abdicate in favor of his young son, François, the titular king of Rome (1811–1832). Napoleon was exiled to the Mediterranean island of Elba.

The allies refused to accept the young "Napoleon II" and supported instead the Bourbon claimant to the throne, the brother of the guillotined Louis XVI. Naming himself Louis XVIII (skipping "XVII" in deference to his nephew dead at the hands of the Revolution), the new king claimed to rule over a "restored" France.

Napoleon's Final Defeat: Waterloo.

Still it was not quite the end for Napoleon. While the European heads of state sat in Vienna trying to determine the future of Europe and France's place in it, Napoleon returned from his exile on the Mediterranean island of Elba to reclaim leadership of France. On 15 June 1815, Napoleon once again, and for the final time, confronted the European powers in one of the most famous military campaigns in history. With 125,000 loyal French forces, Napoleon seemed within hours of reestablishing the French Empire in Europe.

DOCUMENT

Napoleon's Exile to St. Helena

But he had underestimated his opponents. The defeat of Napoleon's forces at Waterloo was decisive. Napoleon later explained, "Everything failed me just when everything had succeeded!" He had met his Waterloo, and with his defeat a new expression entered the language to describe devastating, permanent, irreversible downfall. Napoleon's return proved brief—it lasted only 100 days. An era had come to an end. Napoleon was exiled to the inhospitable island of Saint Helena in the South Atlantic. For the next six years, Napoleon wrote his memoirs under the watchful eyes of his British jailers. He died a painful death on 5 May 1821 from what today is believed to have been cancer.

■ "The Song of the End." Napoleon is depicted in flight with the whole world chasing him as he stumbles through a graveyard of bones and fallen symbols of power. Behind the globe is the masonic symbol of Providence, a shining eye within a triangle, a symbol also used by the American founding fathers on the Great Seal.

CONCLUSION

The period of revolution and empire from 1789 to 1815 radically changed the face of France. A new, more cohesive elite of bourgeois and nobles emerged, sharing power based on wealth and status. Ownership of land remained a defining characteristic of both old and new elites. A new state bureaucracy, built on the foundations of the old, expanded and centralized state power.

The people as sovereign now legitimated political power. Napoleon at his most imperial never doubted that he owed his existence to the people. In this sense, Napoleon was the king of the revolution—an apparently contradictory fusion of old forms and new ideology. Napoleon channeled democratic forces into enthusiasm for empire. He learned his lessons from the failure of the Bourbon monarchy and the politicians of the revolution. For 16 years, Napoleon successfully reconciled the Old Regime with the new France. Yet he could not resolve the essential problem of democracy: the relationship between the will of the people and the exercise of political power. The picture in 1815 was not dramatically different from the situation in 1789. The revolution might have been over, but changes fueled by the revolutionary tradition were just beginning. The struggle for a workable democratic government continued in France for another century and elsewhere in Europe throughout the twentieth century.

QUESTIONS FOR REVIEW

1. To what extent was the French nobility responsible for the crisis that destroyed the Old Regime?

2. How did commoners, men and women, transform a crisis of government into a revolution?

3. Why did the leaders of the Revolution resort to a "reign of terror," and what effect did that have on the Revolution?

4. What problems in France and beyond contributed to the rise of Napoleon?

5. What did Napoleon accomplish in France, and what brought about his fall?

KEY TERMS

cahiers de doléances, p. 594

conscription, *p. 608*

Continental System, *p. 610*

Estates-General, *p. 593*

Girondins, *p. 606*

Great Fear, *p. 598*

Jacobins, *p. 606*

Napoleonic Code, *p. 611*

National Assembly, *p. 590*

Old Regime, *p. 593*

Reign of Terror, *p. 606*

sans-culottes, *p. 603*

Thermidorian Reaction, *p. 608*

Third Estate, *p. 593*

DISCOVERING WESTERN CIVILIZATION ONLINE

You can obtain more information about the French Revolution and the Napoleonic Era at the Websites listed below. See also the Companion Website that accompanies this text, www.ablongman.com/kishlansky, which contains an online study guide and additional resources.

The French Revolution and the Fall of the Monarchy

Creating French Culture

www.loc.gov/exhibits/bnf/bnf0001.html

Different aspects of French culture as a form of elite power from Charlemagne to Charles de Gaulle are presented by the Library of Congress. Most of the material is from the collections of the Bibliothèque Nationale de France.

Liberty, Equality, Fraternity: Explaining the French Revolution

Chnm.gmu.edu/revolution/

This site contains an extraordinary archive of key images, maps, songs, timelines, and texts from the French Revolution. The site is authored by Professors Lynn Hunt and Jack Censer, leading scholars in the field of French revolutionary history.

Château de Versailles

www.chateauversailles.fr/en/

Devoted to the history and images of Versailles, this site provides brief essays about the people and events significant to court culture during the seventeenth and eighteenth centuries. It also explores the role of Versailles in French culture after the French Revolution.

Experimenting with Democracy, 1789–1792

St. Just

history.hanover.edu/texts/stjust.html

Texts by St. Just, a close colleague of Robespierre and a member of the Committee of Public Safety, which orchestrated the Reign of Terror.

Modern History Sourcebook: Robespierre: The Supreme Being

www.fordham.edu/halsall/mod/robespierre-supreme.html

This site contains Robespierre's words on The Cult of the Supreme Being and links to other sites.

The Reign of Napoleon, 1799–1815

Internet Modern History Sourcebook: French Revolution

www.fordham.edu/halsall/mod/modsbook13.html

This site will direct students to the Modern History Sourcebook section of documents on the French Revolution, Napoleon, and the Napoleonic Wars.

Napoleon

www.napoleon.org/en/home.asp

Sponsored by the Foundation Napoleon for "the furtherance of study and research into the civil and military achievements of the First and Second Empires," this site is aimed at a nonacademic audience providing chronologies, essays, images, videos, and links to other sites on Napoleon.

SUGGESTIONS FOR FURTHER READING

The French Revolution and the Fall of the Monarchy

Keith Michael Baker, *Inventing the French Revolution* (Cambridge: Cambridge University Press, 1992). The author views the French Revolution as a basically political event that can only be understood in the context of the changing political culture of the eighteenth century, with special attention to the use of language and the role of public opinion as a political invention.

Roger Chartier, *The Cultural Origins of the French Revolution*, tr. Lydia G. Cochrane (Durham, NC: Duke University Press, 1991). Argues for the importance of the rise of critical modes of thinking in the public sphere in the eighteenth century and of long-term de-Christianization in shaping the desire for change in French society and politics.

William Doyle, *Origins of the French Revolution* (Oxford: Oxford University Press, 1988). An excellent introduction devoted to the historiography of the Revolution since 1939, followed by an analysis of the breakdown of the Old Regime and the struggle for power.

Lynn Hunt, ed., *The French Revolution and Human Rights*: A *Brief Documentary History* (Bedford: St. Martins, 1996). This edited work contains 38 primary documents on citizenship and civil rights.

Georges Lefebvre, *The Great Fear of 1789* (New York: Pantheon Books, 1973). This classic study analyzes the rural panic that swept through parts of France in the summer of 1789 as a distinct episode in the opening months of the Revolution that had its own internal logic.

Colin Lucas, ed., *Rewriting the French Revolution* (Oxford: Clarendon Press, 1991). Eight scholars present interpretations in the areas of social development, ideas, politics, and religion.

Daniel Roche, *The People of Paris* (Berkeley: University of California Press, 1987). An essay on popular culture in the eighteenth century in which the author surveys the lives of the Parisian popular classes—servants, laborers, and artisans—and examines their housing, furnishings, dress, and leisure activities.

Timothy Tackett, *Becoming a Revolutionary: The Deputies of the French National Assembly and the Emergence of a Revolutionary Culture* (Princeton: Princeton University Press, 1996). This collective biography of the cohort of deputies to the National Assembly demonstrates that their practical experience was distinct from that of the nobility.

Michel Vovelle, *The Fall of the French Monarchy* (Cambridge: Cambridge University Press, 1984). A social history of the origins and early years of the Revolution, beginning with a brief examination of the Old Regime and paying special attention to social and economic changes initiated by the

Revolution, the role of the popular classes, and the creation of revolutionary culture.

Experimenting with Democracy, 1792–1799

Jack Censer and Lynn Hunt, *Liberty, Equality, Fraternity: Exploring the French Revolution* (University Park: Pennsylvania State University Press, 2001). This book is accompanied by a CD-ROM and provides a unique multimedia introduction to the French Revolution.

François Furet, *Interpreting the French Revolution* (Cambridge: Cambridge University Press, 1981). A series of essays challenging many of the assumptions about the causes and outcome of the Revolution and reviewing its historiography.

Dominique Godineau, *The Women of Paris and Their French Revolution* (Berkeley: University of California Press, 1998). A compelling account of the lives of women revolutionaries. Godineau presents women's protests as a mass movement within the Revolution.

Patrice Higonnet, *Goodness Beyond Virtue: Jacobins During the French Revolution* (Cambridge: Harvard University Press, 1998). The author considers the Jacobin politics as a model for modern democrats, not to be reduced to the tragedy of the Terror.

Michael L. Kennedy, *The Jacobin Clubs in the French Revolution, 1793–1795* (New York: Berghahn Books, 2000). The final volume of Kennedy's three-volume history of the Jacobin Club focusing on the period between May 1793 and August 1795.

Sara E. Melzer and Leslie Rabine, eds., *Rebel Daughters: Women and the French Revolution* (New York: Oxford University Press, 1992). Contributors from a variety of disciplines examine the importance of women in the French Revolution, with special attention to the exclusion of women from the new politics.

Albert Soboul, *The Sans-Culottes* (New York: Anchor, 1972). A study of the artisans who composed the core of popular political activism in revolutionary Paris.

The Reign of Napoleon, 1799–1815

David Patrick Geggus, *Haitian Revolutionary Studies* (Bloomington: Indiana University Press, 2002). Using archives from several countries, the author examines little-known aspects of black rebellion from French rule.

Jean Tulard, *Napoleon: The Myth of the Saviour* (London: Weidenfeld and Nicolson, 1984). In this biography of Napoleon, the Napoleonic Empire is presented as a creation of the bourgeoisie, who desired to end the Revolution and consolidate their gains and control over the lower classes.

Isser Woloch, *Napoleon and His Collaborators: The Making of a Dictatorship* (New York: Norton, 2001). Woloch explains the success of Napoleon's regime in terms of the support of his civilian collaborators.

Isser Woloch, *The New Regime: Transformations of the French Civic Order* (New York: Norton, 1994). Woloch's study emphasizes the break of the new regime from the old, placing the institutions created or revamped after 1789 in the context of a new civic order and citizenship.

For a list of additional titles related to this chapter's topics, please see http://www.ablongman.com/kishlansky.

21 INDUSTRIAL EUROPE

PORTRAIT OF AN AGE

THE RAILROAD

THE VISUAL RECORD

The Normandy train has reached Paris. The coast and the capital are once again connected. Passengers in their city finery disembark and are greeted by others who have awaited their scheduled arrival. Workmen stand ready to unload freight, porters to carry luggage. Steam billows forth from the resting engine, which is the object of all human activity. The engine stares as enigmatically as any character in a Renaissance portrait. Yet the train that has arrived in *La Gare Saint-Lazare* by Claude Monet (1840–1926) is as much the central character in this portrait of the industrial age as was any individual in portraits of ages past.

The train's iron bulk dwarfs the people around it. Indeed, iron dominates; tons of it are in view. The rails, the lampposts, the massive frame of the station, no less than the train itself, are all formed from iron—pliable, durable, inexpensive iron—the miracle product of industrialization. The iron station with its glass panels became as central a feature of nineteenth-century cities as stone cathedrals were in the Middle Ages. Railway stations changed the shape of urban settings, just as railway travel changed the lives of millions of people.

There had never been anything like it before. Ancient Romans had hitched four horses to their chariots; nineteenth-century Europeans hitched four horses to their stagecoaches. The technology of overland transportation had hardly changed in 2000 years. Coach journeys were long, uncomfortable, and expensive, and they were governed by the elements and muddy, rutted roads that caused injuries to humans and horses with alarming regularity. First-class passengers rode inside, where they were jostled against one another and breathed the dust that the horses kicked up in front of them. Second-class passengers rode on top, braving the elements and risking life and limb in an accident.

Railway travel was a quantum leap forward. It was faster, cheaper, and safer. Overnight it changed conceptions of time, space, and, above all, speed. People could journey to what once were distant places in a single day. Voyages be-came trips, and the travel holiday was born. Commerce was transformed, as was the way in which it was conducted. Large quantities of goods could be shipped quickly from place to place; orders could instantly be filled. The whole notion of locality changed, as salesmen could board a morning train for what only recently had been an unreachable market. Branch offices could be overseen by regional directors, services and products could be standardized, and the gap between great and small cities and between town and countryside could be narrowed.

Wherever they went, the railroads created links that had never been forged before. In Britain, the railroad schedule led to the creation of official time. Trains that left London were scheduled to arrive at their destinations according to London time, which was now kept at the royal observatory in Greenwich. Trains carried fresh fish inland from the coasts and fresh vegetables from rural farms to city tables. Mail moved farther and more quickly; news spread more evenly. Fashionable ideas from the capital cities of Europe circulated everywhere, as did new knowledge and discoveries. The railroads brought both diversity and uniformity.

They also brought wonderment. The engine seemed to propel itself with unimaginable power and at breathtaking speed. The English actress Fanny Kemble (1809–1893) captured the sensation memorably: "You can't imagine how strange it seemed to be journeying on thus, without any visible cause of progress other than the magical machine, with its flying white breath and rhythmical, unvarying pace. I felt no fairy tale was ever half so wonderful as what I saw." For many, the railroad symbolized the genius of the age in which they were living, an age in which invention, novelty, and progress were everywhere to be seen. It combined the great innovations of steam, coal, and iron that were transforming nearly every aspect of ordinary life. But for others, the railway was just as much a symbol of disquiet, of the passing of a way of life that was easier to understand and to control. "Seated in the old mail-coach we needed no evidence out of ourselves to indicate the velocity," wrote the English author Thomas De

■ Claude Monet, *Arrival of the Normandy Train, Gare Saint-Lazare, 1877*

Quincey (1785–1859) in his obituary for the passing of horse travel. "We heard our speed, we saw it, we felt it. This speed was not the product of blind, insensate agencies, that had no sympathy to give, but was incarnated in the fiery eyeballs of the noblest among brutes."

The fruits of the railways, like the fruits of industrialization, were not all sweet. As the nineteenth century progressed, there could be no doubt that, year by year, one way of life was being replaced by another. More and more laborers were leaving the farms for the factories; more and more products were being made by machines. Everywhere there was change, but it was not always or everywhere for the better. Millions of people poured into cities that mushroomed up without plan or intention. Population growth, factory labor, and ultimately the grinding poverty that they produced overwhelmed traditional means of social control. Families and communities split apart; the expectations of ordinary people were no longer predictable. Life was spinning out of control for individuals,

groups, and even whole societies. It was an engine racing down a track that only occasionally ended as placidly as did the Normandy train at the Gare Saint-Lazare.

LOOKING AHEAD

As this chapter will discuss, industrialization began in Great Britain, spurred by its mineral wealth and entrepreneurial skill. It was the result of changes in agricultural practices that allowed for a larger population to be supported by fewer farmers. It was powered first by coal and its use in the production of iron and then by steam that allowed for powerful engines to mechanize production. The steam engines also allowed for a revolution in transportation as seen in the painting of the Gare Saint-Lazare. Industrialization transformed every aspect of the British economy and soon spread throughout Europe.

THE TRADITIONAL ECONOMY

The curse of Adam and Eve was that they would earn their daily bread by the sweat of their brows. For generation after generation, age after age, economic life was dominated by toil. Man, woman, and child labored to secure their supply of food against the caprice of nature. There was nothing even vaguely romantic about the backbreaking exertion needed to crack open the hard ground, plant seeds in it, and protect the crops from the ravages of insects, birds, and animals long enough to be harvested. Every activity was labor-intensive. Wood for shelter or fuel was chopped with thick, blunt axes. Water was drawn from deep wells by the long, slow turn of a crank or dragged in buckets from the nearest stream. Everything that was consumed was pulled or pushed or lifted. French women carried soil and water up steep terraces in journeys that could take as long as seven hours. "The women seemed from their persons and features to be harder worked than horses," Arthur Young (1741–1820), the English agricultural expert, observed with a combination of admiration and disgust. The capital that was invested in the traditional economy was human capital, and by the middle of the eighteenth century nearly eight out of every ten Europeans still tilled the soil, earning their bread by the sweat of their brow.

Although the traditional economy was dominated by agriculture, an increasing amount of labor was devoted to manufacture. The development of a secure and expanding overseas trade created a worldwide demand for consumer goods. In the countryside, small domestic textile industries grew up. Families would take in wool for spinning and weaving to supplement their income from agriculture. When times were good, they would expend proportionately less effort in manufacturing; when times were bad, they would expend more. Their tasks were set by an entrepreneur who provided raw materials and paid the workers by the piece. Wages paid to rural workers were lower than those paid to urban laborers because they were not subject to guild restrictions and because the wages supplemented farm income. Thus entrepreneurs could profit from lower costs, although they had to bear

the risk that the goods produced in that fashion would be of lesser quality or that markets would dry up in the interval. Although domestic industry increased the supply of manufactured commodities, it demanded even more labor from an already overworked sector of the traditional economy.

Throughout the traditional economy, the limits on progress were set by nature. Good harvests brought prosperity, bad harvests despair. Over the long run, the traditional economy ran in all-too-predictable cycles. Sadly, the adage, "Eat, drink, and be merry, for tomorrow we may die," was good advice. Prosperity was sure to bring misery in its train. The good fortune of one generation was the hard luck of the next, as more people competed for a relatively fixed quantity of food. No amount of sweat and muscle and, as yet, ingenuity could rescue the traditional economy from its pendulum swings of boom and bust.

By the eighteenth century, the process that would ultimately transform the traditional economy was already under way. It began with the **agricultural revolution**, one of the great turning points in human history. Before it occurred, the life of every community and of every citizen was always held hostage to nature. The struggle to secure an adequate food supply was the dominant fact of life to which nearly all productive labor was dedicated. After the agricultural revolution, an inadequate food supply was a political rather than an economic fact of life. Fewer and fewer farmers were required to feed more and more people. In Britain, where nearly 70 percent of the population was engaged in agriculture at the end of the seventeenth century, fewer than 2 percent today work on farms. By the middle of the nineteenth century, the most advanced economies were capable of producing vast surpluses of basic commodities. The agricultural revolution was not an event, and it did not happen suddenly. It would not deserve the label "revolution" at all were it not for its momentous consequences: Europe's escape from the shackles of the traditional economy.

Farming Families

Over most of Europe, agricultural activity in the eighteenth century followed methods of crop rotation that had been in place for more than a thousand years. Fields were divided into strips of land, and each family "owned" a certain number of strips, which they cultivated for their livelihood. Between one-half and one-third of village land lay fallow each year so that its nutrients could be restored. Open-field farming, as the system was called, was communal rather than individual. Decisions about which crops to grow in the productive fields, where animals would be pastured, or how much wood could be cut from the common wastes affected everyone. Moreover, many activities, such as plowing, gleaning, and manuring, could not conveniently observe the distinctions of ownership of separate strips. Nor, given the realities of nature, could individual families be self-sustaining without the services of a village tanner or milkmaid or hog minder drawn from the closely intertwined group of kin and neighbors that consti-

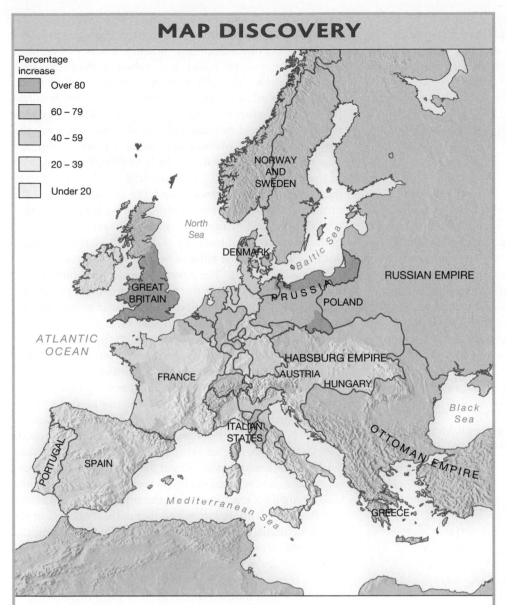

MAP DISCOVERY

Percentage increase

- Over 80
- 60 – 79
- 40 – 59
- 20 – 39
- Under 20

Population Growth in Europe, 1800–1850

Notice which parts of Europe experienced the largest growth in population in the first half of the nineteenth century. Compare the rate of population growth in Spain and Norway and Sweden. Which grew faster? In which parts of Europe did the population increase the most during this period? What impact would you expect such growth to have on the agricultural economy? On the rate of industrialization?

potatoes in the mistaken belief that they caused leprosy. Yet both potatoes and corn became peasant crops and spread rapidly throughout southern Europe, not least because as new commodities they were untaxed. Peasants bartered their surplus, hoarded their profits, and took what few advantages they could out of a system in which the deck was stacked against them.

As the European population entered a new cycle of growth in the second quarter of the eighteenth century, the traditional economy began to increase agricultural productivity in traditional ways. In the east, new lands were colonized and slowly brought under cultivation. Frederick the Great welcomed immigrants to Prussia, where land was plentiful, if not very fertile. In settled communities, less productive land, which had provided fodder for animals at the end of the seventeenth century, now had to provide food for humans. Scrubland was cleared and hillsides terraced. Dry ground was irrigated manually by women and children working in bucket brigades. As always, an increase in population initially meant an increase in productivity. For a time, more able-bodied workers produced more food. In the half century that ended in the 1770s, French peasants increased agricultural production by nearly 60 percent. The intensification of traditional methods rather than innovation accounted for the increase. The number of strips held by each family declined, but each strip was more carefully cultivated.

By the end of the eighteenth century, the European population was reaching the point at which another check on its growth might be expected. Between 1700 and 1800, total European population had increased by nearly 50 percent, and the rate of growth was continuing to accelerate. The vast expansion of rural population placed a grave strain on agricultural production. Decade by decade, more families attempted to eke out an existence from the same amount of land. The gains made by intensive cultivation were now lost to overpopulation. In areas that practiced partible inheritance, farms were subdivided into units too small to

tuted the community. Communal agriculture was effective, but it also limited the number of people that could survive on the produce from a given amount of land.

Agriculture was a profoundly conservative occupation, for the risk of experimentation was nothing less than survival. Lords and peasants both practiced defensive innovation, introducing change only after its practical benefits were easily demonstrable. For example, in the mid-seventeenth century two French provincial parlements banned the cultivation of provide subsistence. Competition for the "morsels" of land, as the French called them, was intense. Older sons bought out younger brothers; better-off families purchased whatever came on the market to prevent their children from slipping into poverty. Even in areas in which primogeniture was the rule, portions for younger sons and daughters ate into the meager inheritance of the eldest son. Over much of Europe, it was becoming increasingly difficult to live by bread alone.

Rural Manufacture

The crisis of overpopulation meant that not only were there more mouths to feed, there were more bodies to clothe. That increased the need for spun and woven cloth, and thus for spinners and weavers. Traditionally, commercial cloth production was the work of urban artisans, but the expansion of the marketplace and the introduction of new fabrics, especially cotton and silk, had eroded the monopoly of most of the clothing guilds. Merchants could sell as much finished product as they could find, and the teeming rural population provided a tempting pool of inexpensive labor for anyone willing to risk the capital to purchase raw materials. Initially, farming families took manufacturing work into their homes to supplement their income. Spinning and weaving were the

■ The European Linen Industry. By the eighteenth century, linen production was dominated by the Low Countries and the north German principalities where skilled labor could still be found for the complicated process of linen weaving.

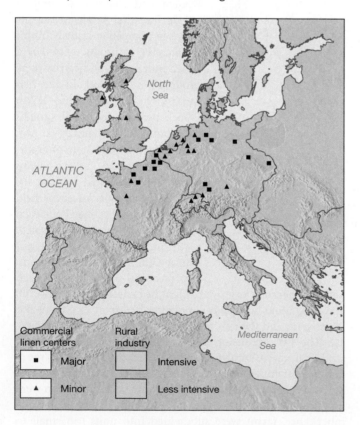

most common occupations, and they were treated as occasional work, reserved for the slow times in the agricultural cycle. This was known as cottage industry. It was side-employment, less important and less valuable than the vital agricultural labor that all members of the family undertook.

But by the middle of the eighteenth century, cottage industry was developing in a new direction. As landholdings grew smaller, even good harvests did not promise subsistence to many families. The oversupply of labor was soon organized into the **putting-out system**, which mobilized the resources of the rural labor force for commercial production of large quantities of manufactured goods. The characteristics of the putting-out system were similar throughout Europe, whether it was undertaken by individual entrepreneurs or lords of the manor, or even sponsored by the state. The process began with the capital of the entrepreneur, which was used to purchase raw materials. The materials were "put out" to the homes of workers where the manufacture, most commonly spinning or weaving, took place. The finished goods were returned to the entrepreneur, who sold them at a profit, with which he bought raw materials to begin the process anew.

The simplicity of the putting-out system was one of its most valuable features. All of its essential elements were already present in rural communities. The small nest egg of a prosperous farmer or small trader was all the money needed to make the first purchase of raw materials. The raw materials could be put out to his kin or closest neighbors and the finished goods then delivered to market along with surplus crops. Not only could a small amount of cash begin the cycle of putting-out, but that capital continued to circulate to keep the process in motion.

The small scale of the initial enterprise can be seen in the fact that many entrepreneurs had themselves begun as workers. In Bohemia, for example, some of the largest putting-out operations were run by serfs who paid their lords fees for the right to engage in trade. At the end of the eighteenth century, there were more than one-quarter million spinners in the Bohemian linen industry alone, most of them organized into small groups around a single entrepreneur, though one monastery employed more than 650 women spinners. Putting-out also required only a low level of skill and common, inexpensive tools. Rural families did their own spinning and rural villages their own weaving. Thus, putting-out demanded little investment, either in plant, equipment, or education. Nor did it inevitably disrupt traditional gender-based tasks in the family economy. In most places spinning was women's work, weaving was done by men, and children helped at whichever task was under way. In fact, certain occupations, such as lacemaking in France, were so gender-based that men would not even act as entrepreneurs. In Austria, lacemaking was considered less honorable than other forms of clothmaking because of its association with women and household-based production. Performed at home, rural manufacture remained a traditional family-oriented occupation.

Gradually, the putting-out system came to dominate the lives of many rural families. From small networks of isolated

■ Linen production is the subject of this 1705 engraving by Franz Philipp Florin. To make linen, it was necessary to soak the stems of the flax plant to soften its tough outer fibers, which were then removed by beating. The more delicate inner fibers were spun into thread, and then were woven into linen cloth on handlooms.

villages, domestic manufacture grew to cover entire regions. Perhaps as many as one-quarter of the inhabitants of the Irish province of Ulster were engaged in manufacturing linen by the end of the eighteenth century. Spinning and weaving became full-time occupations for families that kept no more than a small garden. But without agricultural earnings, piecework rates became starvation wages, and families unable to purchase their subsistence were forced to rely upon loans from the entrepreneurs who set them at work. Long hours in dank cottages performing endlessly repetitive tasks became the lot of millions of rural inhabitants, and their numbers increased annually. While the sons of farmers waited to inherit land before they formed their families, the sons of cottage weavers needed only a loom to begin theirs. They could afford to marry younger and to have more children, for children could contribute to manufacturing from an early age.

Consequently, the expansion of the putting-out system, like the expansion of traditional agriculture, fueled the continued growth of population. Like traditional agriculture, putting-out contained a number of structural inefficiencies. Both entrepreneur and worker were potential victims of unscrupulousness. Embezzlement of raw materials was a problem for the entrepreneur, arbitrary wage cuts for the laborers. Because the tasks were performed at home, the entrepreneur could not supervise the work. Most disputes in domestic manufacturing arose over specifications of quality. Workers would not receive full pay for poorly produced goods that could not be sold for full value. Inexperienced, aged, or infirm workers could easily spoil costly raw materials. One Bohemian nobleman created village spinning rooms on his estates so that young girls could be given four weeks of training before they set up on their own. Finally, the putting-out system was labor- rather than capital-intensive. As long as there were ready hands to employ, there was little incentive to seek better methods or more efficient techniques.

The Agricultural Revolution

The continued growth of Europe's population necessitated an expansion of agricultural output. In most places that was achieved by intensifying traditional practices, bringing more land into production and more labor to work the land. But in the most advanced European economies, first in Holland and then in England, traditional agriculture underwent a long but dynamic transformation, an agricultural revolution. It was a revolution of technique rather than technology. Humans were not replaced by machines nor were new forms of energy substituted for human and animal muscle. Indeed, many of the methods that were to increase crop yields had been known for centuries and practiced during periods of population pressure. But they had never been practiced as systematically as they came to be from the seventeenth century onward, and they were never combined with a commercial attitude toward farming. It was the willingness and ability of owners to invest capital in their land that transformed subsistence farming into commercial agriculture.

Enclosures. As long as farming was practiced in open fields, there was little incentive for individual landowners to invest in improvements to their scattered strips. Although the community as a whole could enclose a small field or plant some fodder crops for the animals, its ability to change

IMAGE DISCOVERY

The Blacksmith's Shop

Joseph Wright of Derby depicts a blacksmith working without many of the technological advances of the eighteenth century. The smith is housed in an abandoned religious building, most likely an old church. What clues in the background would lead one to that conclusion? The image, as a whole, recalls an oft-painted scene from Christianity involving figures gathered around and bending over a source of light. Can you identify it? Why would Joseph Wright have imitated depictions of that foundational Christian event in painting a traditional English blacksmith?

The consolidation of estates along with the enclosure of fields was thus the initial step toward change. It was a long-term process that took many forms. In England, where it was to become most advanced, **enclosure** was already under way in the sixteenth century. Prosperous families had long been consolidating their strips in the open fields, and at some point the lord of the manor and the members of the community agreed to carve up the common fields and make the necessary exchanges to consolidate everyone's lands. Perhaps as much as three-quarters of the arable land in England was enclosed by agreement before 1760. Enclosure by agreement did not mean that the breakup of the open-field community was necessarily a harmonious process. Riots preceding or following agreed enclosures were not uncommon.

Paradoxically, it was the middling rather than the poorest villagers who had the most to lose. The breakup of the commons initially gave the poor more arable land from which to eke out their subsistence, and few of them could afford to sacrifice present gain for future loss. The smallholders were quickly bought out. It was the middle-size holders who were squeezed hardest. Although prosperous in communal farming, those families did not have access to the capital necessary to make agricultural improvements such as converting grass to grain land or purchasing large amounts of fertilizer. They could not compete in producing for the market, and gradually they, too, disappeared from the enclosed village. Their opposition to enclosure by agreement led, in the eighteenth century, to enclosure by act of Parliament. Parliamentary enclosure was legislated by government, a government composed for the most part of large landowners. A commission would view the community's lands and divide them, usually by a prescribed formula. Between 1760 and 1815, more than 1.5 million acres of farmland were enclosed by act of Parliament. During the late eighteenth century, the Prussian and French governments emulated the practice by ordering large tracts of land enclosed.

The enclosure of millions of acres of land was one of the largest expenses of the new commercial agriculture. Hedging or fencing off the land and plowing up the commons required extra labor beyond that necessary for basic agrarian activities. Thus many who sold the small estates that they received on the breakup of the commons remained in villages as agricultural laborers or leaseholders. But they practiced a different form of farming. More and more agricultural activity became market-oriented. Single crops were sown in large enclosed fields and ex-

traditional practice was limited. In farming villages, even the smallest landholder had rights in common lands, which were jealously guarded. Rights in commons meant a place in the community itself. Commercial agriculture was more suited to large rather than small estates and was more successful when the land could be utilized in response to market conditions rather than to the necessities of subsistence.

■ Surveyors measure a field for land enclosure. The enclosure movement eliminated large areas of what had formerly been communal land.

changed at market for the mixture of goods that previously had been grown in the village. Market production turned attention from producing a balance of commodities to increasing the yield of a single one.

Agricultural Innovations.   The first innovation was the widespread cultivation of fodder crops such as clover and turnips. Crops like clover restore nutrients to the soil as they grow, shortening the period in which land has to lie fallow. Moreover, farm animals grazing on clover or feeding on turnips return more manure to the land, further increasing its productivity. Turnip cultivation had begun in Holland and was brought to England in the sixteenth century. But it was not until the late seventeenth century that Viscount Charles "Turnip" Townsend (1675–1738) made turnip cultivation popular. Townsend and other large Norfolk landowners developed a new system of planting known as the four-crop rotation, in which wheat, turnips, barley, and clover succeeded one another. The method kept the land in productive use, and both the turnip and clover crops were used to feed larger herds of animals.

The ability of farmers to increase their livestock was as important as their ability to grow more grain. Not only were horses and oxen more productive than humans—a horse could perform seven times the labor of a man while consuming only five times the food—but the animals also refertilized the land as they worked. Light fertilization of a single acre of arable land required an average of 25,000 pounds of manure. But animals competed with humans for food, especially during the winter months when little grazing was possible. To conserve grain for human consumption, lambs were led to the slaughter and the fatted calf was killed in the autumn. Thus

the development of the technique of meadow floating was a remarkable breakthrough. By flooding low-lying land near streams in the winter, English and Dutch farmers could prevent the ground from freezing during their generally mild winters. When the water was drained, the land beneath it would produce an early grass crop on which the beasts could graze. That meant that more animals could be kept alive during the winter.

The relationship between animal husbandry and grain growing became another feature of commercial agriculture. In many areas farmers could choose between growing grain and pasturing animals. When prices for wool or meat were relatively higher than those for grain, fields could be left in grass for grazing. When grain prices rose, the same fields could be plowed. Consolidated enclosed estates made convertible husbandry possible. The decision to hire field-workers or shepherds could be taken only by large agricultural employers. Whatever the relative price of grain, the open-field village continued to produce grain as its primary crop. Farmers who could convert their production in tune to the market not only could maximize their profits but also could prevent shortages of raw materials for domestic manufacturers or of foodstuffs for urban and rural workers.

Convertible husbandry was but the first step in the development of a true system of regional specialization in agriculture. Different soils and climates favored different use of the land. In southern and eastern England the soil was thin and easily depleted by grain growing. Traditionally, the light soil areas had been used almost exclusively for sheep rearing. On the other hand, the clay soils of central England, though poorly drained and hard to work, were more suited to grain growing. The new agricultural techniques reversed the

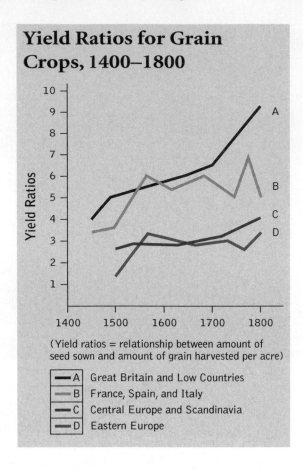

Yield Ratios for Grain Crops, 1400–1800

(Yield ratios = relationship between amount of seed sown and amount of grain harvested per acre)

A	Great Britain and Low Countries
B	France, Spain, and Italy
C	Central Europe and Scandinavia
D	Eastern Europe

own. But as landless laborers, either on farms or in rural manufacturing, they could no longer make that claim and many soon became fodder for the factories, the "dark satanic mills" that came to disfigure the land once tilled in open-field villages. For the destitute, charity was now visited upon them in anonymous parish workhouses or in the good works of the comfortable middle class. In all of those ways the agricultural revolution changed the face of Europe.

THE INDUSTRIAL REVOLUTION IN BRITAIN

Like the changes in agriculture, the changes in manufacturing that began in Britain during the eighteenth century were more revolutionary in consequence than in development. But their consequences were revolutionary indeed. A work force that was predominantly agricultural in 1750 had become predominantly industrial a century later. A population that for centuries had centered on the south and east was now concentrated in the north and west. Liverpool, Manchester, Glasgow, and Birmingham mushroomed into giant cities. While the population of England grew by 100 percent between 1801 and 1851, from about 8.5 million people to more than 17 million, the populations of Liverpool and Manchester grew by more than 1000 percent.

It was the replacement of animal muscle by hydraulic and mineral energy that made the continued population growth possible. Water and coal drove machinery that dramatically increased human productivity. In 1812, one woman could spin as much thread as 200 women had in 1770. What was most revolutionary about the Industrial Revolution was the wave after wave of technological innovation, a constant tinkering and improving of the ways in which things were made, which could have the simultaneous effects of cutting costs and improving quality. It was not just the great breakthrough inventions such as the steam engine, the smelting of iron with coke, and the spinning jenny that were important, but also the hundreds of adjustments in technique that applied new ideas in one industry to another, opened bottlenecks, and solved problems. Ingenuity rather than genius was at the root of the **Industrial Revolution** in Britain.

The Industrial Revolution was a sustained period of economic growth and change brought about by the application of mineral energy and technological innovations to the process of manufacturing. It took place during the century between 1750 and 1850, though different industries moved at different paces and sustained economic growth continued in Britain until World War I. It is difficult to define the timing of the Industrial Revolution with any great precision because, unlike a political event, an economic transformation does not happen all at once. Nor are new systems and inventions ever really new. Coal miners had been using rails and wheeled carriages to move ore since the seventeenth century. In the sixteenth century, "Jack of Newbury" had housed his cloth

pattern. The introduction of fodder crops and increased fertilization rejuvenated thin soils, and southeastern England became the nation's breadbasket. Large enclosed estates provided a surplus of grain throughout the eighteenth century. By the 1760s, England was exporting enough grain to feed more than a half million people. Similarly, the midland clays became the location of great sheep runs and cattle herds. Experiments in herd management, crossbreeding, and fattening all resulted in increased production of wool, milk, meat, leather, soap, and tallow for candles.

There can be no doubt about the benefits of the transformation of agricultural practices that began in Holland and England in the seventeenth century and spread slowly to all corners of the Continent over the next 200 years. Millions more mouths were fed at lower cost than ever before. In 1700, each person engaged in farming in England produced enough food for 1.7 people; in 1800, each produced enough for 2.5 people. Cheaper food allowed more discretionary spending, which fueled the demand for consumer goods, which in turn employed more rural manufacturers. But there also were costs. The transformation of agriculture was also a transformation in a way of life. The open-field village was a community; the enclosed estate was a business. The plight of the rural poor was tragic enough in villages of kin and neighbors, where face-to-face charity might be returned from one generation to the next. With their scrap of land and their common rights, even the poorest villagers laid claim to a place of their workers in a large shed. The one was the precursor of the railroad and the other the precursor of the factory, but each preceded the Industrial Revolution by more than a century. Before 1750, innovations made their way slowly into general use, and after 1850 the pace of growth slowed appreciably. By then, Britain had a manufacturing economy: fewer than one-quarter of its labor force engaged in agriculture and nearly 60 percent were involved in industry, trade, and transport.

Britain First

The Industrial Revolution occurred first in Britain, but even in Britain **industrialization** was a regional rather than a national phenomenon. There were many areas of Britain that remained untouched by innovations in manufacturing methods and agricultural techniques, although no one remained unaffected by the prosperity that industrialization brought. That was the result of both national conditions and historical developments. When industrialization spread to the Continent, it took hold—as it had in Britain—in regions where mineral resources were abundant or where domestic manufacturing was a traditional activity. There was no single model for European industrialization, however often contemporaries looked toward Britain for the key to unlock the power of economic growth. There was as much technological innovation in France, as much capital for investment in Holland. Belgium was rich in coal, while eastern Europe enjoyed an agricultural surplus that sustained an increase in population. The finest cotton in the world was made in India; the best iron was made

in Sweden. Each of those factors was in some way a precondition for industrialization, but none by itself proved sufficient. Only in Britain did those circumstances meld together.

Water and Coal. Among Britain's blessings, water was foremost. Water was its best defense, protecting the island from foreign invasion and making it unnecessary to invest in a costly standing army. Rather, Britain invested heavily in its navy to maintain its commercial preeminence around the globe. The navy protected British interests in times of war and transported British wares in times of peace. Britain's position in the Asian trade made it the leading importer of cottons, ceramics, and teas. Its colonies, especially in North America, not only provided sugar and tobacco but also formed a rich market for British manufacturing.

But the commercial advantages that water brought were not confined to oceanic trade. Britain was favored by an internal water system that tied inland communities together. In the eighteenth century, no place in Britain was more than 70 miles from the sea or more than 30 miles from a navigable river. Water transport was far cheaper than hauling goods overland; a packhorse could carry 250 pounds of goods on its back but could move 100,000 pounds by walking alongside a river and pulling a barge. Small wonder that river transport was one of the principal interests of merchants and traders. Beginning in the 1760s, private concerns began to invest in the construction of canals, first to move coal from inland locations to major arteries and then to connect the great rivers themselves. Over the next 50 years several hundred miles of canals were built by authority of Navigation Acts, which

■ Pictured here is the mouth of the underground tunnel for the Worsley-Manchester Canal, as depicted in Arthur Young's *Six Months' Tour Through the North of England* (1770). Here at Worsley the canal led to a significant coal mine, enabling increased coal production that would improve England's new industrial economy.

allowed for the sale of shares to raise capital. In 1760, the Duke of Bridgewater (1736–1803) lived up to his name by completing the first great canal. It brought coal to Manchester and ultimately to Liverpool. It cost more than £250,000 and took 14 years of labor to build, but it repaid the duke and his investors many times over by bringing an uneconomical coal field into production. Not the least of the beneficiaries were the people of Manchester, where the price of coal was halved.

Coal was the second of Britain's natural blessings on which it improved. Britain's reserves of wood were nearly depleted by the eighteenth century, especially those near centers of population. Coal had been in use as a fuel for several centuries, and the coal trade between London and the northern coal pits had been essential to the growth of the capital. Coal was abundant, much of it almost at surface level along the northeastern coast, and easily transported on water. The location of large coalfields along waterways was a vital condition of its early use. As canals and roadways improved, more inland coal was brought into production for domestic use. Yet it was in industry rather than in the home that coal was put to its greatest use. There again Britain was favored, for large seams of coal were also located near large seams of iron. At first, the coincidence was of little consequence, since iron was smelted by charcoal made from wood and iron foundries were located deep in forests. But ultimately ironmakers learned to use coal for fuel, and then the natural economies of having mineral, fuel, and transport in the same vicinity were given full play.

Economic Infrastructure. The factors that contributed to Britain's early industrialization were not only those of natural advantage. Over the course of years, Britain had developed an infrastructure for economic advancement. The transformation of domestic handicrafts to industrial production depended as much on the abilities of merchants as on those of manufacturers. The markets for domestic manufacturing had largely been overseas, where British merchants built up relationships over generations. Export markets were vital to the success of industrialization as production grew dramatically and most ventures needed a quick turnaround of sales to reinvest the profits in continued growth. The flexibility of English trading houses would be seen in their ability to shift from reexporting Eastern and North American goods to exporting British manufactures. Equally important, increased production meant increased demand for raw materials: Swedish bar iron for casting, Egyptian and American cotton for textiles, and Oriental silk for luxuries. The expansion of shipping mirrored the expansion of the economy, tripling during the eighteenth century to more than one million tons of cargo capacity.

The expansion of shipping, agriculture, and investment in machines, plant, and raw material all required capital. Not only did capital have to exist, but it had to be made productive. Profits in agriculture, especially in the south and east, somehow had to be shifted to investment in industry in the north and west. The wealth of merchants, which flowed into London, had to be redistributed throughout the economy.

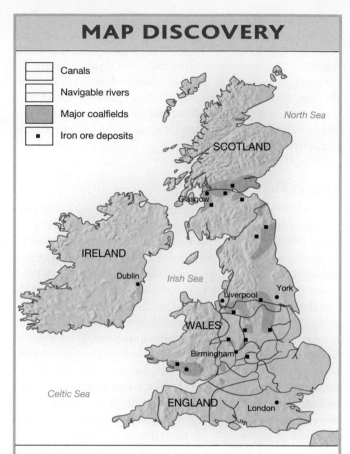

MAP DISCOVERY

Canals
Navigable rivers
Major coalfields
Iron ore deposits

Great Britain: Canals and Natural Resources

Examine the locations of canals, navigable rivers, and coal and iron ore deposits in Great Britain. Which parts of Great Britain did not develop canals? Why? Where are the canals concentrated? What is the relationship between canals and major navigable rivers? What about the relationship between the canals and the coal and iron ore deposits? Where would you expect railroads to be built?

More importantly, short-term investments had to give way to long-term financing. At the end of the seventeenth century, the creation of the Bank of England had begun the process of constructing a reliable banking system. The Bank of England dealt almost entirely with government securities, but it also served as a bill broker. It bought the debts of reputable merchants at a discount in exchange for Bank of England notes; Bank of England notes could then be exchanged between merchants, which increased the liquidity of the English economy, especially in London. It also became the model for provincial banking by the middle of the eighteenth century.

Private family banks also grew in importance in London, handling the accounts of merchants and buying shares in profitable enterprises, of which the canals were a favorite. Regional banks, smaller and less capitalized, began to use the private London banks as correspondents, that is, as extensions of their own banks in the city. That allowed local manufacturers and city merchants to do business with one another. The connections between the regional banks and London facilitated the flow of capital from one section of the nation to the other. In 1700, there were just 12 provincial banks; by 1790, there were nearly 300. Banks remained reluctant to invest for the long term, preferring to discount bills for a few months, but after they developed a relationship with a particular firm, they were usually willing to continue to roll the debt over. Although the banking system was vital to large enterprises, in fact the capital for most industry was raised locally, from kin and neighbors, and grew by plowing back profits into the business. At least at the beginning, manufacturers were willing to take risks and to work for small returns to ensure the survival and growth of their business.

Minerals and Metals

There could have been no Industrial Revolution without coal. It was the black gold of the eighteenth century, the fuel that fed the furnaces and turned the engines of industrial expansion. The coal produced by one miner generated as much energy as 20 horses. Coal was the first capital-intensive industry in Britain, already well developed by the seventeenth century. Owners paid the costs of sinking shafts, building roads, and erecting winding machines. Miners were brought to a pit and paid piecework for their labor. Only the very wealthy could afford to invest in coal mining, and it was by chance that British law vested mineral rights in owners rather than users of the land, as was the case on the Continent. That meant that the largest English coalfields were owned by landed families of means who were able to invest agricultural profits in mining. Britain's traditional elites thus played a crucial role in the industrial transformation of the agrarian economy from which their wealth and social standing had derived.

Early Coal Mining. The technical problems of coal mining grew with demand. As surface seams were exhausted it became necessary to dig deeper shafts, to lower miners farther underground, and to raise the coal greater heights to the surface. Men loosened the coal from the seam; women and children hauled it to the shaft. They also cleared the tons of debris that came loose with the coal. Underground mining was extremely dangerous. In addition to all-too-frequent cave-ins, miners struggled against inadequate ventilation and light. Better ventilation was achieved by the expensive method of sinking second and third shafts into the same seam, allowing for cross breezes. Candles and sparks created by flint wheels addressed the problem of light, though both methods suffered from the disadvantage that most pits contained combustible gases. Even after a fireman walked through the mine exploding gas with a long lighted stick, many miners preferred to work in total darkness, feeling the edges of the seam.

But by far the most difficult mining problem was water. As pits were sunk deeper they reached pools of groundwater, which enlarged as the coal was stripped away from the earth. Dripping water increased the difficulty of hewing, standing water the difficulty of hauling. The pit acted like a riverbed and filled quickly. Water drainage presented the greatest obstacle to deep-shaft mining. Women and children could carry the water out in large skin-lined baskets, which were attached to a winding wheel and pulled up by horses. Primitive pumps, also horse-powered, had been devised for the same purpose. Neither method was efficient or effective when shafts sank deeper. In 1709, Thomas Newcomen (1663–1729) introduced a steam-driven pump that enabled water to be sucked through a pipe directly from the pit bottom to the surface. Although the engine was expensive to build and needed tons of coal to create the steam, it could raise the same amount of water in a day as 2500 humans. Such economies of labor were enormous, and within 20 years of its introduction there were 78 engines draining coal and metal mines in England.

Innovations such as Newcomen's engine helped increase output of coal at just the time that it became needed as an industrial fuel. Between 1700 and 1830, coal production increased tenfold despite the fact that deeper and more difficult seams were being worked. Eventually, the largest demand for coal came from the iron industry. In 1793, just two ironworks consumed as much coal as the entire population of Edinburgh. Like mining coal, making iron was both capital- and labor-intensive, requiring expensive furnaces, water-powered bellows, and mills in which forged iron could be slit into rods or rolled into sheets. Ironmaking depended upon an abundance of wood, for it took the charcoal derived from 10 acres of trees to refine 1 ton of iron ore. After the ore was mined, it was smelted into pig iron, a low-grade, brittle metal. Pig iron was converted to higher-quality bar iron in charcoal-powered forges that burned off some of its impurities. From bar iron came the rods and sheets used in casting household items such as pots and nails or in making finer wrought iron products such as plows and armaments. Because each process in the making of iron was separate, furnaces, forges, and mills were located near their own supplies of wood. The shipping of the bulky ore, pig iron, and bar iron added substantially to its cost, and it was cheaper to import bars from Sweden than to carry them 20 miles overland.

The great innovations in the production of iron came with the development of techniques that allowed for the use of coal rather than wood charcoal in smelting and forging. As early as 1709, Abraham Darby (ca. 1678–1717), a Quaker nail maker, experimented with smelting iron ore with coke, coal from which most of the gas has been burned off. Iron coking greatly reduced the cost of fuel in the first stages of production, but because most ironworks were located in woodlands rather than near coal pits, the method was not widely adopted. Moreover, although coke made from coal was cheaper than charcoal made from wood, coke added its own impurities to the iron ore. Nor could it provide the intense heat needed for smelting without a large bellows. The cost of

■ Britain's ample coal deposits were one of the country's assets as it industrialized. This painting of the pithead of an eighteenth-century coal mine shows the coexistence of the new steam technology with aspects of older forms of production, such as the use of beasts of burden.

the bellows offset the savings from the coke until James Watt (1736–1819) invented a new form of steam engine in 1775.

The Steam Engine. Like most innovations of the Industrial Revolution, James Watt's steam engine was an adaptation of existing technology made possible by the sophistication of techniques in a variety of fields. Although Watt is credited with the invention of the condensing steam engine, one of the seminal creations in human history, the success of his work depended upon the achievements of numerous others. Watt's introduction to the steam engine was accidental. An instrument maker in Glasgow, he was asked to repair a model of a Newcomen engine and immediately realized that it would work more efficiently if there were a separate chamber for the condensation of the steam. Although his idea was sound, Watt spent years attempting to implement it. He was continually frustrated that poor-quality valves and cylinders never fit well enough together to prevent steam from escaping from the engine.

Watt was unable to translate his idea into a practical invention until he became partners with the Birmingham ironmaker and manufacturer Matthew Boulton (1728–1809). At Boulton's works, Watt found craftsmen who could make precision engine valves, and at the foundries of John Wilkinson (1728–1808) he found workers who could bore the cylinders of his engine to exact specifications. Watt's partnership with Boulton and Wilkinson was vital to the success of the steam engine. But Watt himself possessed the qualities necessary to ensure that his ideas were transformed into reality. He persevered through years of unsuccessful experimentation and searched out partners to provide capital and expertise. He saw beyond bare mechanics, realizing the practical utility of his invention long before it was perfected. Watt designed the mechanism to convert the traditional up-and-down motion of the pumping engine into rotary

■ James Watt's rotary beam steam engine. This model was built in 1788 to provide rotary power to the lapping and polishing machines at Matthew Boulton's Soho Engineering Works in Birmingham, England, where Watt and Boulton manufactured steam engines from 1775 to 1810.

motion, which could be used for machines and ultimately for locomotion.

Watt's engine received its first practical application in the iron industry. Wilkinson became one of the largest customers for steam engines, using them for pumping, moving wheels, and ultimately increasing the power of the blast of air in the forge. Increasing the heat provided by coke in the smelting and forging of iron led to the transformation of the industry. In the 1780s, Henry Cort (1740–1800), a naval contractor, experimented with a technique for using coke as fuel in removing the impurities from pig iron. The iron was melted into puddles and stirred with rods. The gaseous carbon that was brought to the surface burned off, leaving a purer and more malleable iron than even charcoal could produce. Because the iron had been purified in a molten state, Cort reasoned that it could be rolled directly into sheets rather than first made into bars. He erected a rolling mill adjacent to his forge and combined two separate processes into one.

Puddling and rolling had an immediate impact upon iron production. There was no longer any need to use charcoal in the stages of forging and rolling. From mineral to workable sheets, iron could be made entirely with coke. Ironworks moved to the coalfields, where the economies of transporting fuel and finished product were great. Moreover, the distinct stages of production were eliminated. Rather than separate smelting, forging, and finishing industries, one consolidated manufacturing process had been created. Forges, furnaces, and rolling machines were brought together and powered by steam engines. Cort's rolling technique alone increased output 15 times. By 1808, output of pig iron had grown from 68,000 to 250,000 tons and of bar iron from 32,000 to 100,000 tons.

Cotton Is King

Traditionally, British commerce had been dominated by the woolen cloth trade, in which techniques of production had not changed for hundreds of years. Running water was used for cleaning and separating fleece; crude wooden wheels spun the thread; simple handlooms wove together the long warp threads and the short weft ones. It took nearly four female spinners to provide the materials for one male weaver, the tasks having long been gender-specific. During the course of the seventeenth century, new fabrics appeared on the domestic market, particularly linen, silk, and cotton. It was cotton that captured the imagination of the eighteenth-century consumer, especially brightly colored, finely spun Indian cotton.

Domestic Industries.   Spinning and weaving were organized as domestic industries. Work was done in the home on small, inexpensive machines to supplement the income from farming. Putters-out were especially frustrated by the difficulty in obtaining yarn for weaving in the autumn, when female laborers were needed for the harvest. Even the widespread development of full-time domestic manufacturers did not satisfy the increased demand for cloth. Limited output and variable quality characterized British textile production throughout the early part of the eighteenth century. The breakthrough came with technological innovation. Beginning in the mid-eighteenth century, a series of new machines dramatically increased output and, for the first time, allowed English textiles to compete with Indian imports.

The first innovation was the flying shuttle, invented by John Kay (1704–1764) in the 1730s. A series of hammers drove the shuttle, which held the weft, through the stretched warp on the loom. The flying shuttle allowed weavers to work alone rather than in pairs, but it was adopted slowly because it increased the demand for spun thread, which was already in

■ In the eighteenth century, a number of British inventors patented new machines that transformed the British textile industry and marked the beginning of the Industrial Revolution. Among the inventions was the spinning jenny, invented by James Hargreaves in 1764, and named for his daughter. The jenny, which permitted the spinning of a number of threads at the same time, made possible the automatic production of cotton thread.

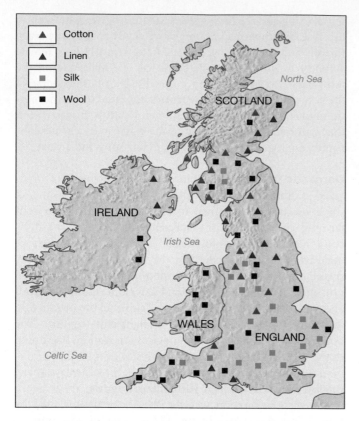

▲	Cotton
▲	Linen
■	Silk
■	Wool

North Sea

SCOTLAND

IRELAND

Irish Sea

WALES

ENGLAND

Celtic Sea

■ Great Britain: Textile Centers. Textiles had been the traditional industrial activity in Britain and almost every region of the country had organized textile production.

short supply. The spinning bottleneck was opened by James Hargreaves (d. 1778), who devised a machine known as the jenny. The jenny was a wooden frame containing a number of spindles around which thread was drawn by means of a hand-turned wheel. The first jennies allowed for the spinning of eight threads at once, and improvements brought the number to more than 100. Jennies replaced spinning wheels by the tens of thousands. The jenny was a crucial breakthrough in redressing the balance between spinning and weaving, though it did not solve all problems. Jenny-spun thread was not strong enough to be used as warp, which continued to be wheel spun. But the jenny could spin cotton in unimaginable quantities.

As is often the case with technological change, one innovation followed another. The problem set by improvements in weaving gave rise to solutions for increasing the output of spinners. The need to provide stronger warp threads posed by the introduction of the jenny was ultimately solved by the development of the water frame. It was created in 1769 by Richard Arkwright (1732–1792), whose name was also to be associated with the founding of the modern factory system. Arkwright's frame consisted of a series of water-driven rollers that stretched the cotton before spinning. The stronger fibers could be spun into threads suitable for warp, and English manufacturers could finally produce an all-cotton fabric. It was not long before another innovator realized that the water frame and the jenny could be combined into a single machine, one that would pro-

duce an even finer cotton yarn than that made in India. The **mule**, so named because it was a cross between a frame and a jenny, was invented by Samuel Crompton (1753–1827), who sold its rights for only £60. It was the decisive innovation in cotton production. By 1811, ten times as many threads were being spun on mules as on water frames and jennies combined.

The original mules were small machines that, like the jennies, could be used for domestic manufactures. But increasingly the mule followed the water frame into purposely built factories, where it became larger and more expensive. The need for large rooms to house the equipment and for a ready source of running water to power it provided an incentive for the creation of factories, but secrecy provided a greater one. The original factories were called "safe-boxes," and whether they were established for the manufacture of silk or cotton, their purpose was to protect trade secrets. Innovators took out patents to prevent their inventions from being copied and fought long lawsuits to prevent their machines from being used. Workers were sworn to secrecy about the techniques they were taught. Imitators practiced industrial espionage as sophisticated as the age would allow: enticing knowledgeable workers; employing spies; copying inventions. Although the factory was designed to protect secrets, its other benefits were quickly realized. Manufacturers could maintain control over the quality of products through strict supervision of the work force. Moreover, workers in shifts could keep the costly machines in continuous use.

Cotton Factories.   Richard Arkwright constructed the first cotton factories in Britain, all of which were designed to house water frames. The first was established in 1769 at Cromford near Nottingham, which was the center of stocking manufacture. The site was chosen for its isolation, since stockings were an article of fashion in which secrecy was most important. The Cromford mill was a four-story building that ultimately employed more than 800 workers. During the next quarter century, Arkwright built more than a dozen other mills, most in partnership with wealthy manufacturers. Arkwright's genius lay in industrial management rather than mechanical innovation. As others switched from frames to mules, Arkwright stubbornly stuck to his own invention. When steam power began to replace water, he failed to make the shift. But his methods of constructing and financing factories were undeniably successful. From a modest beginning as a traveling salesman of wigs, Sir Richard Arkwright died in possession of a fortune worth more than £500,000.

The organization of the cotton industry into factories was one of the pivotal transformations in economic life. Domestic spinning and weaving took place in agricultural villages; factory production took place in mill towns. The location of the factory determined movements of population, and from the first quarter of the eighteenth century onward a great shift toward northeast England was under way. Moreover, the character of the work itself changed. The operation of heavy machinery reversed the traditional gender-based tasks. Mule spinning became men's work, while handloom weaving was taken over by

DOCUMENT

Industrial Society and Factory Conditions

THE WEALTH OF BRITAIN

Cotton was the first of the new industries that led to British economic domination in the nineteenth century. In cotton production, new inventions such as the spinning jenny and the water frame revolutionized manufacture, and the factory system was born. Britain's domination of cotton production impressed contemporaries. In this excerpt, a contemporary tries to explain why Britain took the lead in industrialization.

Focus Questions

How important does the author think geography and natural resources have been to Britain's industrial success? What is the relation between industrialization and forms of government?

In comparing the advantages of England for manufactures with those of other countries, we can by no means overlook the excellent commercial position of the country—intermediate between the north and south of Europe; and its insular situation, which, combined with the command of the seas, secures our territory from invasion or annoyance. The German ocean, the Baltic, and the Mediterranean are the regular highways for our ships; and our western ports command an unobstructed passage to the Atlantic, and to every quarter of the world.

A temperate climate, and a hardy race of men, have also greatly contributed to promote the manufacturing industry of England.

The political and moral advantages of this country, as a seat of manufactures, are not less remarkable than its physical advantages. The arts are the daughters of peace and liberty. In no country have these blessings been enjoyed in so high a degree, or for so long a continuance, as in England. Under the reign of just laws, personal liberty and property have been secure; mercantile enterprise has been allowed to reap its reward; capital has accumulated in safety; the workman has "gone forth to his work and to his labour until the evening"; and, thus protected and favoured, the manufacturing prosperity of the country has struck its roots deep, and spread forth its branches to the ends of the earth.

England has also gained by the calamities of other countries, and the intolerance of other governments. At different periods, the Flemish and French protestants; expelled from their native lands, have taken refuge in England, and have repaid the protection given them by practising and teaching branches of industry, in which the English were then less expert than their neighbours.

From Edward Baines, *The History of the Cotton Manufacture in Great Britain* (1835).

---

women. The mechanization of weaving took longer than that of spinning, both because of difficulties in perfecting a power loom and because of opposition to its introduction by workers known as **Luddites**, who organized machine-breaking riots in the 1810s. The Luddites attempted to maintain the traditional organization of their industry and the independence of their labor. For a time, handloom weavers managed to survive by accepting lower and lower piece rates. But their competition was like that of a horse against an automobile. In 1820, there were more than 250,000 handloom weavers in Britain; by 1850, the number was less than 50,000. Weaving as well as spinning became factory work.

The transformation of cotton manufacture had a profound effect on the overall growth of the British economy. It increased shipping because the raw material had to be imported, first from the Mediterranean and then from America. American cotton—especially after 1794, when American inventor Eli Whitney (1765–1825) patented his cotton gin—fed a nearly insatiable demand. This appetite was met primarily because American cotton plantations used slave labor to plant and harvest their crop. In 1750, Britain imported less than 5 million pounds of raw cotton; a century later the volume had grown to 588 million pounds. And to each pound of raw cotton, British manufacturers added the value of their technology and their labor. By the mid-nineteenth century, nearly a half million people earned their living from cotton, which alone accounted for more than 40 percent of the value of all British exports. Cotton was undeniably the king of manufactured goods.

The Iron Horse

The first stage of the Industrial Revolution in Britain was driven by the production of consumer goods. Pottery, cast-iron tools, clocks, toys, and textiles, especially cottons—all were manufactured in quantities unknown in the early eighteenth century. The products fed a ravenous market at home and abroad. The greatest complaint of industrialists was that they could not get enough raw materials or fuel, nor could they ship their finished products fast enough to keep up with demand. Transportation was becoming a serious stumbling block to continued economic growth. Even with the completion of the canal network that linked the major rivers and improvement in highways and tollways, raw materials and finished goods moved slowly and uncertainly. It was said that it took as long to ship goods from

Manchester to Liverpool on the Duke of Bridgewater's canal as it did to sail from New York to Liverpool on the Atlantic Ocean. Furthermore, once the canals had a monopoly on bulk cargo, transportation costs began to rise.

It was the need to ship increasing amounts of coal to foundries and factories that provided the spur for the development of a new form of transportation. Ever since the seventeenth century, coal had been moved from the seam to the pit on rails, first constructed of wood and later of iron. Broad-wheeled carts hitched to horses were as much dragged as rolled, but that still represented the most efficient form of hauling, and those railways ultimately ran from the seam to the dock. By 1800, there was perhaps as much as 300 miles of iron rail in British mines.

In the same year, Watt's patent on the steam engine expired, and inventors began to apply the engine to a variety of mechanical tasks. Richard Trevithick (1771–1833), whose father managed a tin mine in Cornwall, was the first to experiment with a steam-driven carriage. George Stephenson (1781–1848), who is generally recognized as the father of the modern railroad, made two crucial improvements. In mine railways the wheels of the cart were smooth and the rail was grooved. Stephenson reversed the construction to provide better traction and less wear. Perhaps more importantly, Stephenson made the vital improvement in engine power by increasing the steam pressure in the boiler and exhausting the smoke through a chimney. In 1829, he won a £500 prize with his engine "The Rocket," which pulled a load three times its own weight at a speed of 30 miles per hour and could actually outrun a horse.

The First Railways. In 1830 the first modern railway, the Manchester-to-Liverpool line, was opened. Like the Duke of Bridgewater's canal, it was designed to move coal and bulk goods, but surprisingly its most important function came to be moving people. In its first year, the Manchester–Liverpool line carried more than 400,000 passengers, which generated double the revenue derived from freight. The railway was quicker, more comfortable, and ultimately cheaper than the coach. Investors in the Manchester–Liverpool line, who pocketed a comfortable 9.5 percent when government securities were paying 3.5 percent, learned quickly that links between population centers were as important as those between industrial sites. The London–Birmingham and London–Bristol lines were both designed with passenger traffic in mind.

Railway building was one of the great boom activities of British industrialization. Since it came toward the end of the mechanization of factories, investors and industrialists were psychologically prepared for the benefits of technological innovation. By 1835, Parliament had passed 54 separate acts to establish more than 750 miles of railways. Ten years later, more than 6000 miles had been sanctioned and more than 2500 miles built; by 1852, more than 7500 miles of track were in use. The railways were built on the model of the canals. Private bills passed through Parliament, which allowed a company to raise money through the sale of stock. Most railways were trunk lines, connecting one town to another or joining two longer lines together. They were run by small companies, and few ultimately proved profitable. Only because of the dominant influence of George Stephenson and his son Robert (1803–1859) was there an attempt to establish a standard gauge for tracks and engines. Britain was the only country in which the government did not take a leading role in building the railways. Hundreds of millions of pounds were raised privately, and in the end it is calculated that the railroads cost £40,000 a mile to build, more than three times the cost per mile of railroads on the Continent and in the United States.

From Goods to Passengers. Nevertheless, the investment paid huge dividends. By the 1850s, the original purpose of the railways was being realized as freight revenues finally surpassed passenger revenues. Coal was the dominant cargo shipped by rail, and the speedy, efficient service continued to drive down prices. The iron and steel industries were modernized on the back of demand for rails, engines, and cast-iron seats and fittings. In peak periods—and railway building was a boom-and-bust affair—as much as a quarter of the output of the rolling mills went into domestic railroads, and much more into Continental systems. The railways were also a massive consumer of bricks for beddings, sidings, and especially bridges, tunnels, and stations. Finally, the railways were a leading employer of labor, surpassing the textile mills in peak periods. Hundreds of thousands worked in tasks as varied as engineering and ditch digging, for even in that most ad-

■ Great Britain: Railroads (ca. 1850). All rails led to London as the major lines were built to transport passengers as well as goods.

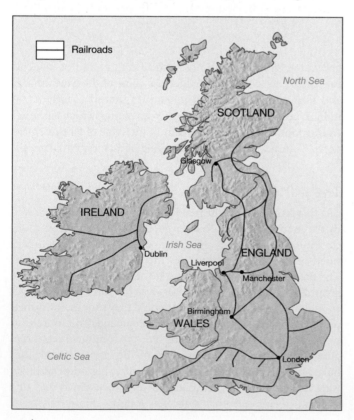

■ Honoré Daumier (1808–1879), *The Third-Class Carriage*. Daumier captured a human condition peculiar to the modern era: "the lonely crowd."

vanced industry, sophisticated mechanized production went hand in hand with traditional drudgery. More than 60,000 workers were permanently engaged in the industry to run trains, mind stations, and repair track. Countless others were employed in manufacturing engines, carriages, boxcars, and the thousands of components that went into making them.

Most of all, the railroads changed the nature of people's lives. Whole new concepts of time, space, and speed emerged to govern daily activities. As Henry Booth, an early railroad official, observed, "Notions which we have received from our ancestors and verified by our own experience are overthrown in a day. What was slow is now quick; what was distant is now near." Coach travel had ordinarily been limited to those with means, not only because it was expensive, but also because it was time-consuming. Ordinary people could not take off the days necessary to complete relatively short round-trip journeys. When passenger rail service began, there was even a debate over whether provision should be made for third-class passengers, a class unknown on the coaches, where the only choices were riding inside for comfort or outside for savings.

Third-class passengers quickly became the staple of railroad service. The cheap excursion was born to provide short holidays or even day trips. The career of Thomas Cook (1808–1892), who became the world's first travel agent, began after he took a short excursion. More than six million people visited London by train to view the Crystal Palace exhibition in 1851, a number equivalent to one-third of the population of England and Wales. The railways did more than link places; they brought people together and helped develop a sense of national identity by speeding up all forms of communication.

Entrepreneurs and Managers

The Industrial Revolution in Britain was not simply invented. Too much credit is given to a few breakthroughs and too little to the ways in which they were improved and dispersed. The Industrial Revolution was an age of gadgets when people believed that new was better than old and that there was always room for improvement. "The age is running mad after innovation," the English moralist Dr. Johnson wrote. "All the business of the world is done in a new way; men are hanged in a new way." Societies for the advancement of knowledge sprang up all over Britain. Journals and magazines promoted new ideas and techniques. Competitions were held for the best invention of the year; prizes were awarded for agricultural achievements. Practical rather than pure science was the hallmark of industrial development.

Yet technological innovation was not the same as industrialization. A vital change in economic activity took place in the organization of industry. Putters-out with their circulating capital and hired laborers could never make the economies necessary to increase output and quality while simultaneously lowering costs. That was the achievement of industrialists, producers who owned workplace, machinery, and raw materials and invested fixed capital by plowing back their profits. Industrial enterprises came in all sizes and shapes. A cotton mill could be started with as little as £300 or as much as £10,000. As late as 1840, fewer than 10 percent of the mills employed more than 500 workers. Most were family concerns with less than 100 employees, and many of them failed. For every story with a happy ending, there was another with a sad one. When Major Edmund Cartwright (1740–1824) erected a cotton mill, he was offered a Watt steam engine built for a distiller who had gone bankrupt. He acquired his machinery at the auction of another bankrupt mill. Cartwright's mill, engine, and machinery ended on the auction block less than three years later. There were more than 30,000 bankruptcies in the eighteenth century, testimony both to the risks of business and to the willingness of entrepreneurs to take them.

To survive against the odds, successful industrialists had to be both entrepreneur and manager. As entrepreneurs, they raised capital, almost always locally from relatives, friends, or members of their church. Quakers were especially active in financing each other's enterprises. The industrial entrepreneur also had to understand the latest methods for building and powering machinery and the most up-to-date techniques for performing the work. One early manufacturer claimed "a practical knowledge of every process from the cotton-bag to the piece of cloth." Finally, entrepreneurs had to know how to market their goods. In those functions, industrial entrepreneurs developed logically from putters-out.

But industrialists also had to be managers. The most difficult task was organization of the workplace. Most gains in productivity were achieved through the specialization of function. The processes of production were divided and subdivided until workers performed a basic task over and over. The education of the work force was the industrial manager's greatest challenge. Workers had to be taught how to use and maintain their machines and disciplined to apply themselves continuously. At least at the beginning, it was difficult to staff the factories. Many employed children as young as seven from workhouses or orphanages, who, though cheap to pay, were difficult to train and discipline. It was the task of the manager to break old habits of intermittent work, indifference to quality, and petty theft of materials. Families were preferred to individuals, for then parents could instruct and supervise their children. There is no reason to believe that industrial managers were more brutal masters than farmers or that children were treated better in workhouses than in mills. Labor was a business asset, what was sometimes called "living machinery," and its control with carrots and sticks was the chief concern of the industrial manager.

Who were the industrialists who transformed the traditional economy? Because British society was relatively open, they came from every conceivable background: dukes and orphans, merchants and salesmen, inventors and improvers. Although some went from rags to riches—such as Richard Arkwright, who was the thirteenth child of a poor barber—it was extremely difficult for a laborer to acquire the capital necessary to set up a business. Wealthy landowners were prominent in capital-intensive aspects of industries—for example, owning ironworks and mines—but few established factories. Most industrialists came from the middle classes, which, while comprising one-third of the British population, provided as much as two-thirds of the first generation of industrialists. That first generation included lawyers, bankers, merchants, and those already engaged in manufacturing, as well as tradesmen, shopkeepers, and self-employed artisans. The career of every industrialist was different, as a look at two—Josiah Wedgwood and Robert Owen—will show.

Josiah Wedgwood. Josiah Wedgwood (1730–1795) was the thirteenth child of a long-established English potting family. He worked in the potteries from childhood, but a deformed leg

■ Jasperware copy of the Portland vase by Josiah Wedgwood. The Portland vase is one of the most famous ancient vases. It was found near Rome in the seventeenth century in a tomb believed to be that of Alexander Severus.

made it difficult for him to turn the wheel. Instead he studied the structure of the business. His head teemed with ideas for improving ceramic manufacturing, but it was not until he was 30 that he could set up on his own and introduce his innovations, which encompassed both technique and organization, the entrepreneurial and managerial sides of his business.

Wedgwood developed new mixtures of clays that took brilliant colors in the kiln and new glazes for both useful and ornamental ware. His technical innovations were all the more remarkable in that he had little education in mineral chemistry and made his discoveries by simple trial and error. But there was nothing of either luck or good fortune in Wedgwood's managerial innovations. He was repelled by the disorder of the traditional pottery, with its waste of materials, uneven quality, and slow output. When he began his first works, he divided the making of pottery into distinct tasks and assigned separate workers to them. One group did nothing but throw the pots on the wheel; another painted designs; a third glazed. To achieve the division of function, Wedgwood had to train his own workers almost from childhood. Traditional potters performed every task from molding to glazing and prized the fact that no two pieces were ever alike. Wedgwood wanted each piece to replicate another, and he stalked the works breaking defective wares on his wooden leg. He invested in schools to help train young artists, in canals to transport his products, and in London shops to sell them. Wedgwood was a marketing genius. He named his famed cream-colored pottery Queen's Ware and made special coffee and tea services for leading aristocratic families. He would then sell replicas by the thousands. In less than 20 years, Wedgwood pottery was prized all over Europe and Wedgwood's potting works were the standard of the industry.

Robert Owen.   Robert Owen (1771–1858) did not have a family business to develop. The son of a small tradesman, he was apprenticed to a clothier at the age of 10. As a teenager he worked as a shop assistant in Manchester, where he audaciously applied for a job as a manager of a cotton mill. At 19, he was supervising 500 workers and learning the cotton trade. Owen was immediately successful, increasing the output of his workers and introducing new materials to the mill. In 1816, he entered a partnership to purchase the New Lanark mill in Scotland. Owen found conditions in Scotland much worse than those in Manchester. More than 500 workhouse children were employed at New Lanark, where drunkenness and theft were endemic. Owen believed that to improve the quality of work one had to improve the quality of the workplace. He replaced old machinery with new, reduced working hours, and instituted a monitoring system to check theft. To enhance life outside the factory, he established a high-quality company-run store, which plowed its profits into a school for village children.

Owen was struck by the irony that in the mills, machines were better cared for than were humans. He thought that with the same attention to detail that had so improved the quality of commodities he could make even greater improvements in the

■ Great Britain: Manufacturing Centers. The growth of manufacturers in the Midlands led to a massive population shift and the development of major urban areas such as Manchester.

quality of life. He prohibited children under 10 from mill work and instituted a 10-hour day for child labor. His local school took infants from one year old, freeing women to work and ensuring each child an education. Owen instituted old-age and disability pensions, funded by mandatory contributions from workers' wages. Taverns were closed and workers were fined for drunkenness and sexual offenses. In the factory and the village, Owen established a principle of communal regulation to improve both the work and the character of his employees. New Lanark became the model of the world of the future, and each year thousands made an industrial pilgrimage to visit it.

The Wages of Progress

Robert Owen ended his life as a social reformer. His efforts to improve the lot of his workers at New Lanark led to experiments to create ideal industrial communities throughout the world. He founded cooperative societies, in which all members shared in the profits of the business, and supported trade unions in which workers could better their lives. His followers planted colonies where goods were held in common and the fruits of labor belonged to the laborers. Owen's agitation for social reform was part of a movement that produced results of lasting consequence. The **Factory Act (1833)** prohibited factory work by children under nine, provided two hours of daily education, and effectively created a 12-hour day in the mills

THE SIN OF WAGES

Robert Owen was both a successful manufacturer and a leading philanthropist. He believed that economic advance had to take place in step with the improvement of the moral and physical well-being of the workers. He organized schools, company shops, and ultimately utopian communities in an effort to improve the lives of industrial laborers. Owen was one of the first social commentators to argue that industrialism threatened the fabric of family and community life.

Focus Questions

What effect does the luxury market have on "the lower orders"? Why are commercial competition and its effects becoming more intense?

The acquisition of wealth, and the desire which it naturally creates for a continued increase, have introduced a fondness for essentially injurious luxuries among a numerous class of individuals who formerly never thought of them, and they have also generated a disposition which strongly impels its possessors to sacrifice the best feelings of human nature to this love of accumulation. To succeed in this career, the industry of the lower orders, from whose labour this wealth is now drawn, has been carried by new competitors striving against those of longer standing, to a point of real oppression, reducing them by successive changes, as the spirit of competition increased and the ease of acquiring wealth diminished, to a state more wretched than can be imagined by those who have not attentively observed the changes as they have gradually occurred. In consequence, they are at present in a situation infinitely more degraded and miserable than they were before the introduction of these manufactories, upon the success of which their bare subsistence now depends. . . .

The inhabitants of every country are trained and formed by its great leading existing circumstances, and the character of the lower orders in Britain is now formed chiefly by circumstances arising from trade, manufactures, and commerce; and the governing principle of trade, manufactures, and commerce is immediate pecuniary gain, to which on the great scale every other is made to give way. All are sedulously trained to buy cheap and to sell dear; and to succeed in this art, the parties must be taught to acquire strong powers of deception; and thus a spirit is generated through every class of traders, destructive of that open, honest sincerity, without which man cannot make others happy, nor enjoy happiness himself.

From Robert Owen, *Observations on the Effect of the Manufacturing System* (1815).

---

until the Ten Hours Act (1847). The Mines Act (1842) prohibited women and children from working underground.

Nor was Owen alone in dedicating time and money to the improvement of workers' lives. The rapid growth of unplanned cities exacerbated the plight of those too poor and overworked to help themselves. Conditions of housing and sanitation were appalling even by nineteenth-century standards. The *Report on the Sanitary Condition of the Laboring Population of Britain* (1842), written by Edwin Chadwick (1800–1890), so shocked Parliament and the nation that it helped to shift the burden of social reform to government. The Public Health Act (1848) established boards of health and the office of medical examiner, while the Vaccination Act (1853) and the Contagious Diseases Act (1864) attempted to control epidemics. (See "A Closer Look: Industry and the Environment," pp. 640–641.)

DOCUMENT

Chadwick, *The Sanitary Condition of the Laboring Population of Britain*

The movement for social reform began almost as soon as industrialization. The Industrial Revolution initiated profound changes in the organization of British society. Cities sprang up from grain fields almost overnight. The lure of steady work and high wages prompted an exodus from rural Britain and spurred an unremitting boom in population. In the first half of the nineteenth century, the population of England doubled from 9 to 18 million, with growth most rapid in the newly urban north and west. In 1750, about 15 percent of the population lived in urban areas; by 1850, about 60 percent did. Industrial workers married younger and produced more children than their agricultural counterparts. For centuries, women had married in their middle twenties, but by 1800, age at first marriage had dropped to 23 for the female population as a whole and to nearly 20 in the industrial areas. That was in part because factory hands did not have to wait until they inherited land or money, and in part because they did not have to serve an apprenticeship. But early marriage and large families were also a bet on the future, a belief that things were better now and would be even better soon, that the new mouths would be fed and the new bodies clothed. It was an investment on the part of ordinary people similar to that made by bankers and entrepreneurs when they risked their capital in new businesses. Was it an investment that paid off?

Expansion of Wealth.   It is difficult to calculate the benefits of the Industrial Revolution or to weigh them against the costs. What is certain is that there was a vast expansion of wealth as well as a vast expansion of people to share it. Agricultural and industrial change made it possible to support comfortably a population more than three times larger than that of the seventeenth century, when it was widely believed that England had reached the limits of expansion. Despite the fact that population doubled between 1801 and 1851, per capita income rose by 75 percent. Had the population remained stable, per capita income would have increased by a staggering 350 percent. At the same time, untold millions of pounds had been sunk into canals, roads, railways, factories, mines, and mills.

But the expansion of wealth is not the same as the improvement in the quality of life, for wealth is not equally distributed. An increase in the level of wealth may mean only that the rich are getting richer more quickly than the poor are getting poorer. Similarly, economic growth over a century involved the lives of several generations, each of which experienced different standards of living. One set of parents may have sacrificed for the future of their children; another may have mortgaged it. Moreover, economic activity is cyclical. Trade depressions, such as those induced by the War of 1812 and the American Civil War, which interrupted cotton supplies, could have disastrous short-term effects. The "Great Hunger" of the 1840s was a time of agrarian crisis and industrial slump. The downturn of 1842 threw 60 percent of the factory workers in the town of Bolton out of work at a time when there was neither unemployment insurance nor a welfare system. Finally, quality of life

cannot be measured simply in economic terms. People with more money to spend may still be worse off than their ancestors, who may have preferred leisure to wealth or independence to the discipline of the clock.

Thus there are no easy answers to the quality-of-life question. In the first stages of industrialization, it seems clear that only the wealthy benefited economically, though much of their increased wealth was reinvested in expansion. Under the impact of population growth, the Napoleonic wars, and regional harvest failure, real wages seem to have fallen from the levels reached in the 1730s. Industrial workers were not substantially better off than agricultural laborers when the high cost of food and rent is considered. But beginning around 1820, there is convincing evidence that the real wages of industrial workers were rising despite the fact that more and more work was semi- and unskilled machine-minding and more of it was being done by women, who were generally paid only two-thirds the wages of men. Although the increase in real wages was still subject to trade cycles, such as the Great Hunger of the 1840s, it continued nearly unabated for the rest of the nineteenth century. Thus, in the second half of the Industrial Revolution, both employers and workers saw a bettering of their economic situation, which was one reason why

---

EXPLOITING THE YOUNG

The condition of child laborers was a concern of English legislators and social reformers from the beginning of industrialization. Most of the attention was given to factory workers, and most legislation attempted to regulate the age at which children could begin work, the number of hours they could be made to work, and the provision of schooling and religious education during their leisure. It was not until the early 1840s that a parliamentary commission was formed to investigate the condition of child labor in the mines. In this extract, the testimony of the child is confirmed by the observations of one of the commissioners.

Focus Questions

How does Mr. Franks's account differ from Ellison Jack's own? Why do you think Ellison offers information about her level of literacy and knowledge of the Bible?

Ellison Jack, 11-years-old girl coal-bearer at Loanhead Colliery, Scotland: I have been working below three years on my father's account; he takes me down at two in the morning, and I come up at one and two next afternoon. I go to bed at six at night to be ready for work next morning: the part of the pit I bear in the seams are much on the edge. I have to bear my burthen up four traps, or ladders, before I get to the main road which leads to the pit bottom. My task is four or five tubs; each tub holds 4G cwt. I fill five tubs in twenty journeys.

I have had the strap when I did not do my bidding. Am very glad when my task is wrought, as it sore fatigues. I can read, and was learning the writing; can do a little; not been

at school for two years; go to kirk occasionally, over to Lasswade: don't know much about the Bible, so long since read.

R. H. Franks, Esq., the sub-commissioner: A brief description of this child's place of work will illustrate her evidence. She has first to descend a nine-ladder pit to the first rest, even to which a shaft is sunk, to draw up the baskets or tubs of coals filled by the bearers; she then takes her creel (a basket formed to the back, not unlike a cockle-shell flattened towards the neck, so as to allow lumps of coal to rest on the back of the neck and shoulders), and pursues her journey to the wall-face, or as it is called here, the room of work. She then lays down her basket, into which the coal is rolled, and it is frequently more than one man can do to lift the burden on her back. The tugs or straps are placed over the forehead, and the body bent in a semicircular form, in order to stiffen the arch.

"Child Labor in the Coal Mines," Testimony to the Parliamentary Investigative Committee (1842).

INDUSTRY AND THE ENVIRONMENT

The Industrial Revolution changed the landscape of Britain. Small villages grew into vast metropolises seemingly overnight. The rates of growth were absolutely staggering: in 1801, there were 75,000 people in Manchester; by 1851, the number had more than quadrupled. The unremitting boom in population did more than strain the resources of local authorities: it broke them apart. It was not that the new industrial cities were unplanned; they were beyond the capacity of planning. Every essential requirement for human survival became scarce and expensive. Shortages of food, water, and basic accommodation were commonplace.

Shantytowns sprang up wherever space would allow, making the flimsily built habitations of construction profiteers seem like palaces. There was loud complaint about those nineteenth-century rip-off artists, but in truth the need for housing was so desperate that people willingly lived anywhere that provided shelter. Houses were built back to back and side by side, with only narrow alleyways to provide sunlight and air. In Edinburgh, one could step through the window of one house into the window of the adjoining one. Whole families occupied single rooms where members slept as others worked, in shifts. In Liverpool, more than 38,000 people were estimated to be living in cellars—windowless underground accommodations that flooded with the rains and the tides.

Most cities lacked both running water and toilet facilities. Districts were provided with either pumps or capped pipes through which private companies ran water for a few hours each day. The water was collected in buckets and brought to the home, where it would stand for the rest of the day and serve indifferently for washing, drinking, and cooking. Outhouse toilets were an extravagant luxury; in one Manchester district, 33 outhouses had to accommodate 7095 people. They were a mixed blessing even in the middle-class districts where they were more plentiful, as there was no system of drainage to flush away the waste. It simply accumulated in cesspools, which were emptied manually about every two years. The thing that most impressed visitors as they approached an industrial city was the smoke; what impressed them most when they arrived was the smell.

The quality of life experienced by most of the urban poor who lived in the squalid conditions has been recorded by a number of contemporary observers. Friedrich Engels was a German socialist who was sent to England to learn the cotton trade. He lived in Manchester for two years and spent much of his time exploring the working-class areas of the city. "In this district I found a man, apparently about sixty years old, living in a cow stable," Engels recounted from one of his walking tours in *The Condition of the Working Class in England in 1844.* "He had constructed a sort of chimney for his square pen, which had neither windows, floor, nor ceiling, had obtained a bedstead and lived there, though the rain dripped through his rotten roof. This man was too old and weak for regular work, and supported himself by removing manure with a hand-cart; the dung-heaps lay next door to his palace!" From his own observations Engels concluded that "in such dwellings only a physically degenerate race, robbed of all humanity, degraded, reduced morally and physically to bestiality, could feel comfortable and at home." And as he was quick to point out, his own observations were no different from those of parliamentary commissioners, medical officers, or civic authorities who had seen the conditions firsthand.

Among the observers, the most influential by far was Sir Edwin Chadwick, who began his government career as a commissioner for the poor law and ended it as the founder of a national system of public health. Chadwick wrote the report of a parliamentary commission, *The Sanitary Condition of the Laboring Population of Britain* (1842), which caused a sensation among the governing classes. Building on the work of physicians, overseers of the poor, and the most technical scholarship available, Chadwick not only painted the same grim picture of urban life as Engels did, he proposed a comprehensive solution to one of its greatest problems, waste management.

A CLOSER LOOK

■ Drawings of workers constructing London's sanitation system.

Chadwick was a civil servant, and he believed that problems were solved by government based on the conclusions of experts. He had heard doctors argue their theories about the causes of disease, some believing in fluxes that resulted from combinations of foul air, water, and refuse; others believing disease was spread by the diseased, in this case Irish immigrants who settled in the poorest parts of English industrial towns. Although medical research had not yet detected the existence of germs, it was widely held that lack of ventilation, stagnant pools of water, and the accumulation of human and animal waste in proximity to people's dwellings all contributed to the increasing incidence of disease. Chadwick fixed upon the last element as crucial. Not even in middle-class districts was there any effective system for the removal of waste. Chamber pots and primitive toilets were emptied into ditches, which were used to drain rain off into local waterways. The few underground sewers that existed were square containers without outlets that were simply emptied once filled. Chadwick's vision was for a sanitation system, one that would carry waste out of the city quickly and deposit it in outlying fields where it could be used as fertilizer.

Chadwick realized that the key to disposing of waste was a constant supply of running water piped through the system. Traditionally, only heavy rainstorms cleared the waste ditches in most cities, and those were too infrequent to be effective. The river had to be the beginning of the sewerage system as well as its end. River water had to be pumped through an underground construction of sewage pits that were built to facilitate the water's flow. Civil engineers had already demonstrated that pits with rounded rather than angular edges were far more effective, and Chadwick advocated the construction of a system of oval-shaped tunnels, built on an incline beneath the city. Water pumped from one part of the river would rush through the tunnels, which would empty into pipes that would carry the waste to nearby farms.

Chadwick's vision took years to implement. He had all of the zeal of a reformer and none of the tact of a politician. He offended nearly everyone with whom he came into contact, because he believed that his program was the only workable one and because he believed that it had to be implemented whatever the price. He was uninterested in who was to pay the enormous costs of laying underground tunnels and building pumping stations and insisted only that the work begin immediately. In the end, he won his point. Sanitation systems became one of the first great public-works projects of the industrial age.

rural workers flocked to the cities and Irish peasants emigrated in the hundreds of thousands to work the lowest paid and least desirable jobs in the factories.

Social Costs. But economic gain had social costs. The first was the decline of the family as a labor unit. In both agricultural and early industrial activity, families labored together. Workers would not move to mill towns without the guarantee of a job for all members of their families, and initially they could drive a hard bargain. The early factories preferred family labor to workhouse conscripts, and it was traditional for children to work beside their parents, cleaning, fetching, or assisting in minding the machines. Children provided an essential part of family income, and youngest children were the agency of care for infirm parents. Paradoxically, it was agitation for improvement in the conditions of child labor that spelled the end of the family work unit. At first, young children were barred from the factories and older ones allowed to work only a partial adult shift. Although reformers intended that schooling and leisure be substituted for work, the separation of children from parents in the workplace ultimately made possible the substitution of teenagers for adults, especially as machines replaced skilled human labor. The individual worker now became the unit of labor, and during economic downturns it was adult males with their higher salaries who were laid off first.

The decline of the family as a labor unit was matched by other changes in living conditions when rural dwellers migrated to cities. Many rural habits were unsuited to both factory work and urban living. The tradition of "Saint Monday," for example,

was one that was deeply rooted in the pattern of agricultural life. Little effort was expended at the beginning of the work week and progressively more at the end. Sunday leisure was followed by Monday recovery, a slow start to renewed labor. The factory demanded constant application six days a week. Strict rules were enforced to keep workers at their stations and their minds on their jobs. More than efficiency was at stake. Early machines were not only crude, they were dangerous, with no safety features to cover moving parts. Maiming accidents were common in the early factories, and they were the fault of both workers and machines. Similarly, industrial workers entered a world of the cash economy. Most agricultural workers were used to being paid in kind and to barter exchange. Money was an unusual luxury that was associated with binges of food, drink, and frivolities, which made adjustment to the wage packet as difficult as adjustment to the clock. Cash had to be set aside for provisions, rent, and clothing. On the farm, the time of a bountiful harvest was the time to buy durable goods; in the factory, "harvest time" was always the same.

Such adjustments were not easy, and during the course of the nineteenth century a way of life passed forever from England. For some, its departure caused profound sorrow; for others, it was a matter of rejoicing. A vertically integrated society in which lord of the manor, village worthies, independent farmers, workers, and servants lived together interdependently was replaced by a society of segregated social classes. By the middle decades of the nineteenth century, a class of capitalists and a class of workers had begun to form and had begun to clash. The middle classes abandoned the city centers, building exclusive suburban

■ *Dudley Street, Seven Dials, London*, by Gustave Doré, depicts life in the London slums of the early nineteenth century.

communities in which to raise their children and insulate their families. Conditions in the cities deteriorated under the pressure of overcrowding, lack of sanitation, and the absence of private investment. The loss of interaction between the different segments of society had profound consequences for the struggle to improve the quality of life for everyone. Leaders of labor saw themselves fighting against profits, greed, and apathy; leaders of capital against drunkenness, sloth, and ignorance. Between the two stereotypes there was little middle ground.

THE INDUSTRIALIZATION OF THE CONTINENT

Industrialization in Europe

Although Britain took the first steps along the road to an industrial economy, it was not long before other European nations followed. There was intense interest in "the British miracle," as it was dubbed by contemporaries. European ministers, entrepreneurs, even heads of state visited British factories and mines in hope of learning the key industrial secrets that would unlock the prosperity of a new age. The **Crystal Palace Exhibition** of manufacturing and industry held in London in 1851 was the occasion for a Continentwide celebration of the benefits of technology and a chance for ambitious Europeans to measure themselves against the mighty British. By then many European nations had begun the transformation of their own economies and had entered a period of sustained growth.

There was no single model for the industrialization of the Continental states. Contemporaries continually made comparisons with Britain, but in truth the process of British industrialization was not well suited to any but the coal-rich regions in Belgium and the Rhineland. Nevertheless, all of Europe benefited from the British experience. No one else had to invent the jenny, the mule, or the steam engine. Although the British government banned the export of technology, none of the pathbreaking inventions remained a secret for long. Britain had demonstrated a way to make cheap, durable goods in factories, and every other state in Europe was able to skip the long stages of discovery and improvement. Thus, while industrialization began later on the Continent, it could progress more quickly.

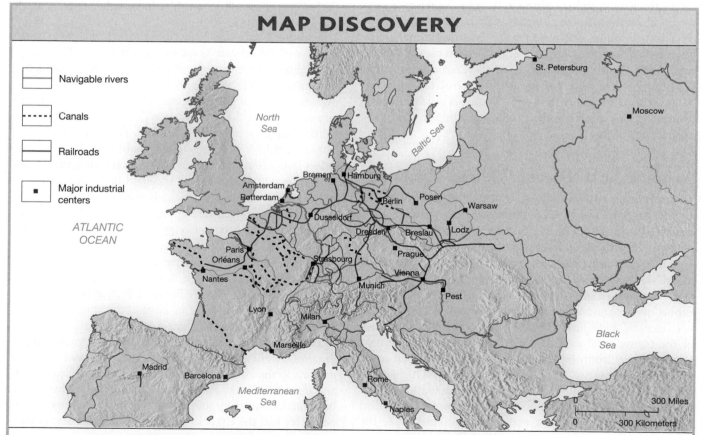

MAP DISCOVERY

Industrial Revolution on the Continent

What were the least industrial parts of Europe outside of Great Britain? In what directions did the major railroads run? How did the progress of industrialization in continental Europe compare with that in Britain? What impact did industrialization have on Spain and Italy?

France and Germany were building a railroad system within years of Britain despite the fact that they had to import most of the technology, raw materials, and engineers.

Britain shaped European industrialization in another way. Its head start made it very difficult for follower nations to compete against British commodities in the world market. Thus European industrialization would be directed first and foremost to home markets, where tariffs and import quotas could protect fledgling industries. Although European states were willing to import vital British products, they placed high duties on British-made consumer goods and encouraged higher-cost domestic production. Britain's competitive advantage demanded that European governments become involved in the industrialization of their countries, financing capital-intensive industries, backing the railroads, and favoring the establishment of factories.

European industrialization was therefore not the thunderclap it was in Britain. In France, it was a slow, accretive development that took advantage of traditional skills and occupations and gradually modernized the marketplace. In Germany, industrialization had to overcome the political divisions of the empire, the economic isolation of the petty states, and the wide dispersion of vital resources. Regions rather than states industrialized in the early nineteenth century, and parts of Austria, Italy, and Spain imported machinery and techniques and modernized their traditional crafts. But most of the states and most of the eastern part of Europe remained tied to a traditional agrarian-based economy that provided neither labor for industrial production nor purchasing power for industrial goods. The areas quickly became sources for raw materials and primary products for their industrial neighbors.

France: Industrialization Without Revolution

The experience of France in the nineteenth century demonstrates that there was no single path to industrialization. Each state blended together its natural resources, historical experiences, and forms of economic organization in unique combinations. While some mixtures resulted in explosive growth, as in Britain, others made for steady development, as in France.

French industrialization was keyed to domestic rather than export markets and to the application of new technology to a vast array of traditional crafts. The French profited, as did all of the Continental states, from British inventions, but they also benefited from the distinct features of their own economy. France possessed a pool of highly skilled and highly productive labor, a manufacturing tradition oriented toward the creation of high-quality goods, and consumers who valued taste and fashion over cost and function. Thus while the British dominated the new mass market for inexpensive cottons and cast-iron goods, a market with high sales but low profit margins, the French were producing luxury items whose very scarcity kept both prices and profits high. Two decisive factors determined the nature of French industrialization: population growth and the French Revolution.

Slow Growth.   From the early eighteenth to the mid-nineteenth centuries, France grew slowly. In 1700, the French population stood at just less than 20 million; in 1850, it was just less than 36 million, a growth rate of 80 percent. In contrast, Germany grew 135 percent, from 15 to 34 million, and England 300 percent, from 5 to 20 million, during the same period. Nevertheless, France remained the most populous nation in western Europe, second on the Continent only to Russia. There is no simple explanation for France's relatively sluggish population growth. The French had been hit particularly hard by subsistence crises in the seventeenth century, and there is reliable evidence that the rural population consciously attempted to limit family size by methods of birth control as well as by delaying marriages. Moreover, France urbanized slowly at a time when city dwellers were marrying younger and producing larger families. As late as the 1860s, a majority of French workers were farmers. Whatever the cause of the moderate population growth, its consequences were clear. France was not pressured by the force of numbers to abandon its traditional agricultural methods, nor did it face a shortage of traditional supplies of energy. Except during crop failures, French agriculture could produce to meet French needs, and there remained more than enough wood for domestic and industrial use.

The Impact of the French Revolution.   The consequences of the French Revolution are less clear. Throughout the eighteenth century, the French economy performed at least as well as the British, and in many areas better. French overseas trade had grown spectacularly until checked by military defeat in the Seven Years' War (1756–1763). French agriculture steadily increased output, while French rural manufactures flourished. A strong guild tradition still dominated urban industries, and although it restricted competition and limited growth, it also helped maintain the standards for the production of high-quality goods that made French commodities highly prized throughout the world. The Revolution disrupted every aspect of economic life. Some of its outcomes were unforeseen and unwelcome. For example, Napoleon's Continental System, which attempted to close European markets to Britain, resulted in a shipping war, which the British won decisively and which eliminated France as a competitor for overseas trade in the mid-nineteenth century. But other outcomes were the result of direct policies, even if their impact could not have been entirely predicted. Urban guilds and corporations were abolished, opening trades to newcomers but destroying the close-knit groups that trained skilled artisans and introduced innovative products. Similarly, the breakup of both feudal and common lands to satisfy the hunger of the peasantry had the effect of maintaining a large rural population for decades.

Despite the efforts of the central government, there had been little change in the techniques used by French farmers over the course of the eighteenth century. French peasants clung tenaciously to traditional rights that gave even the smallest landholder a vital say in community agriculture.

Landlords were predominantly absentees, less interested in the organization of their estates than in the dues and taxes that could be extracted from them. Thus the policies of successive revolutionary governments strengthened the hold of small peasants on the land. With the abolition of many feudal dues and with careful family planning, smallholders could survive and pass a meager inheritance on to their children. Even prosperous farmers could not grow into the large-scale proprietors that had enclosed English fields, for little land came on the market, and many parts of France practiced partible inheritance, which, over time, tended to even out the size of holdings. French agriculture continued to be organized in its centuries-old patterns. While it was able to supply the nation's need for food, it could not release large numbers of workers for purely industrial activity.

Stages of Industrial Progress.

Thus French industrial growth was constrained on the one hand by the relatively small numbers of workers who could engage in manufacturing and on the other by the fact that a large portion of the population remained subsistence producers, cash-poor, and linked only to small rural markets. Throughout the eighteenth century, the French economy continued to be regionally segregated rather than nationally integrated. The size of the state inhibited a highly organized internal trade, and there was little improvement of the infrastructure of transportation. Although some British-style canals were built, canals in Britain were built to move coal rather than staple goods, and France did not have much coal to move. Manufacturing concerns were still predominantly family businesses whose primary markets were regional rather than international. Roads that connected the short distances between producers and consumers were of greater importance to the producers than arterial routes that served the markets of others. Similarly, there was no national capital market until the mid-nineteenth century, and precious few regional ones. French producers were as thrifty and profit-oriented as any others, but they found it more difficult to raise the large amounts of capital necessary to purchase the most expensive new machinery and build the most up-to-date factories. Ironworks, coal mines, and railroads, the three capital-intensive ventures of industrialization, were financed either by government subsidy or by foreign investment.

All those factors determined the slow, steady pace of French industrialization. Recovery after 1815 came in fits and starts. British inventors, manufacturers, and entrepreneurs were enticed to France to demonstrate new machinery and industrial techniques, but in most places the real engine of growth was skilled workers' steady application of traditional methods. By 1820, only 65 French factories were powered by steam engines, and even water-powered machinery was uncommon. Industrial firms remained small and were frequently a combination of putting-out and factory production. It was not until midcentury that sustained industrial growth became evident. This was largely the result of the construction of railroads on a national plan, financed in large part by the central government. Whereas in Britain the railways took advantage of a national market, in France they created one. They also

■ Pierre-Denis Martin's *Waterworks and Aqueduct at Marly* makes clear the transformation of the landscape wrought by the infrastructure of industry in eighteenth-century France.

gave the essential stimulation to the modernization of the iron industry, in which much refining was still done with charcoal rather than coke; of machine making; and of the capital markets. Imported iron and foreign investment were vital ingredients in a process that took several decades to reach fruition.

The disadvantages of being on the trailing edge of economic change were mitigated for a time by conventional practices of protectionism. Except in specialty goods, agricultural produce, and luxury products, French manufactures could not compete with either British or German commodities. Had France maintained its position as a world trader, the comparative disadvantage would have been devastating. But defeat in the wars of commerce had led to a drawing inward of French economic effort. Marseille and Bordeaux, once bustling centers of European trade, became provincial backwaters in the nineteenth century. But the internal market was still strong enough to support industrial growth, and domestic commodities could be protected by prohibitive tariffs, especially against British textiles, iron, and, ironically, coal. Despite the fact that France had to import more than 40 percent of its meager requirements of coal, it still insisted upon slapping high import duties on British supplies. That was in part to protect French mine owners, who had never integrated their operations with iron production and therefore had no interest in keeping fuel costs low. Moreover, the slow pace of French industrialization allowed for the skipping of intermediate stages of development. France had hardly entered the canal age when it began to build its railways. Ultimately, industry moved from hand power to steam power in one long step.

While France achieved industrialization without an industrial revolution, it also achieved economic growth within the context of its traditional values. Agriculture may not have modernized, but the ancient village communities escaped the devastation modernization would bring. The orderly progression of generations of farming families characterized rural France until the shattering experiences of the Franco-Prussian War (1870) and World War I (1914–1918). Nor did France experience the mushroom growth of new cities with all of their problems of poverty, squalor, and homelessness. Slow population growth ameliorated the worst of the social diseases of industrialization while traditional rural manufacturing softened the transformation of a way of life. If France did not reap the windfall profits of the Industrial Revolution, neither did it harvest the bitter crop of social, economic, and spiritual impoverishment that was pulled in its train.

Germany: Industrialization and Union

The process of industrialization in Germany was dominated by the historic divisions of the empire of the German peoples. Before 1815, there were more than 300 separate jurisdictional units within the empire, and after 1815 there were still more than 30. Those included large advanced states such as Prussia, Austria, and Saxony as well as small free cities and the personal enclaves of petty nobles who had guessed right during the Napoleonic wars. Political divisions had more than politi-

cal impact. Each state clung tenaciously to its local laws and customs, which favored its citizens over outsiders. Merchants who lived near the intersection of separate jurisdictions could find themselves liable for several sets of tolls to move their goods and several sets of customs duties for importing and exporting them. The tolls and duties would have to be paid in different currencies at different rates of exchange according to the different regulations of each state. Small wonder that German merchants exhibited an intense localism, preferring to trade with members of their own state and supporting trade barriers against others. Such obstacles had a depressing effect on the economies of all German states but pushed with greatest weight against the manufacturing regions of Saxony, Silesia, and the Rhineland.

Agriculture.   Most of imperial Germany was agricultural land suited to a diversity of uses. The mountainous regions of Bavaria and the Austrian alpine communities practiced animal husbandry; there was a grain belt in Prussia, where the soil was poor but the land plentiful, and one in central Germany in which the soil was fertile and the land densely occupied. The Rhine Valley was one of the richest in all of Europe and was the center of German wine production. The introduction of the potato was the chief innovation of the eighteenth century. While English farmers were turning farms into commercial estates, German peasants were learning how to make do with less land.

Agricultural estates were organized differently in different parts of Germany. In the east, serfdom still prevailed. Peasants were tied to the land and its lord and were responsible for labor service during much of the week. Methods of cultivation were traditional, and neither peasants nor lords had much incentive to adopt new techniques. The vast agricultural domains of the Prussian Junkers, as those landlords were called, were built on the backs of cheap serf labor, and the harvest was destined for the Baltic export trade, where world grain prices rather than local production costs would determine profits. In central Germany, the long process of commuting labor service into rents was nearly completed by the end of the eighteenth century. The peasantry was not yet free, as a series of manorial relationships still tied them to the land, but they were no longer mere serfs. Moreover, western Germany was dominated by free farmers who either owned or leased their lands and who had a purely economic relationship with their landlords. The restriction of peasant mobility in much of Germany posed difficulties for the creation of an industrial work force. As late as 1800, more than 80 percent of the German population was engaged in agriculture, a proportion that would drop slowly over the next half century.

Although Germany was well endowed with natural resources and skilled labor in a number of trades, it had not taken part in the expansion of world trade during the seventeenth century, and the once bustling Hanseatic ports had been far outdistanced by the rise of the Atlantic economies. The principal exported manufacture was linen, which was expertly spun and woven in Saxony and the Prussian province of Silesia. The linen industry was organized traditionally, with a mixture of domestic production managed on the putting-out system and some factory spinning, especially after the introduction of British mechanical innovations. But even the most advanced factories were still being powered by water, and thus they were located in mountainous regions where rapidly running streams could turn the wheels. In the 1840s there were only 22 steam-driven spinning mills in Germany, several of them established by the Prussian government, which imported British machines and technicians to run them. Neither linens nor traditional German metal crafts could compete on the international markets, but they could find a wider market within Germany if only the problems of political division could be resolved.

The Zollverein.

The problems of political division were especially acute for Prussia after the reorganization of European boundaries in 1815 (see Chapter 22). Prussian territory included the coal- and iron-rich Rhineland provinces, but a number of smaller states separated those areas from Prussia's eastern domain. Each small state exacted its own tolls and customs duties whenever Prussian merchants wanted to move goods from one part of Prussia to the other. Such movement became more common in the nineteenth century as German manufacturing began to grow in step with its rising population. Between 1815 and 1865, the population of Germany grew by 60 percent to more than 36 million people. It was an enormous internal market, nearly as large as the population of France, and the Prussians resolved to make it a unified trading zone by creating a series of alliances with smaller states known as the **Zollverein** (1834). The Zollverein was not a free-trade zone, as was the British Empire, but rather a customs union in which member states adopted the liberal Prussian customs regulations. Every state was paid an annual portion of receipts based upon its population, and every state—except Prussia—increased its revenues as a result. The crucial advantage the Prussians received was the ability to move goods and materials from east to west, but Prussia reaped political profits as well. It forced Hanover and Saxony into the Zollverein and kept its powerful rival Austria out. Prussia's economic union soon proved to be the basis for the union of the German states.

The creation of the Zollverein was vital to German industrialization. It permitted the exploitation of natural advantages, such as plentiful supplies of coal and iron, and it provided a basis for the building of railroads. Germany was a follower nation in the process of industrialization. It started late and it self-consciously modeled its success on the British experience. British equipment and engineers were brought to Germany to attempt to plant the seeds of an industrial economy. German manufacturers sent their children to England to learn the latest techniques in industrial management. Friedrich Engels (1820–1895) worked in a Manchester cotton factory, where he observed the appalling conditions of the industrial labor force and wrote *The Condition of the Working Class in England in 1844* (1845). Steam

THE SLAVERY OF LABOR

Although born in Germany, Friedrich Engels witnessed industrialization in England firsthand. His father owned a factory in Manchester of which Engels was put in charge. By day he oversaw industrial production, and by night he wandered the city streets overwhelmed by the suffering of the working classes. His analysis of industrialization developed from his own observations. He became first a socialist and then, with Karl Marx, a founder of the Communist party.

Focus Questions

Why is capital "the all-important weapon in the class war"?
Why does Engels view wage labor as a kind of slavery?

Capital is the all-important weapon in the class war. Power lies in the hands of those who own, directly or indirectly, foodstuffs and the means of production. The poor, having no capital, inevitably bear the consequences of defeat in the struggle. Nobody troubles about the poor as they struggle helplessly in the whirlpool of modern industrial life. The working man may be lucky enough to find employment, if by his labour he can enrich some member of the middle classes. But his wages are so low that they hardly keep body and soul together. If he cannot find work, he can steal, unless he is afraid of the police; or he can go hungry and then the police will see to it that he will die of hunger in such a way as not to disturb the equanimity of the middle classes. . . .

The only difference between the old-fashioned slavery and the new is that while the former was openly acknowledged the latter is disguised. The worker *appears* to be free, because he is not bought and sold outright. He is sold piece-meal by the day, the week, or the year. Moreover he is not sold by one owner to another, but he is forced to sell himself in this fashion. He is not the slave of a single individual, but of the whole capitalist class. As far as the worker is concerned, however, there can be no doubt as to his servile status. It is true that the apparent liberty which the worker enjoys does give him some *real* freedom. Even this genuine freedom has the disadvantage that no one is responsible for providing him with food and shelter. His real masters, the middle-class capitalists, can discard him at any moment and leave him to starve, if they have no further use for his services and no further interest in his survival. . . .

From Friedrich Engels, *The Condition of the Working Class in England in 1844* (1845).

engines were installed in coal mines, if not in factories, and the process of puddling revolutionized ironmaking, though most iron was still smelted with charcoal rather than coke. Although coal was plentiful in Prussia, it was found at the eastern and western extremities of Germany. Even with the lowering of tolls and duties, it was still too expensive to move over rudimentary roads and an uncompleted system of canals.

Thus the railroads were the key to tapping the industrial potential of Germany. There they were a cause rather than a result of industrialization. The agreements hammered out in the creation of the Zollverein made possible the planning necessary to build single lines across the boundaries of numerous states. Initially, German railroads were financed privately, with much foreign investment. But ultimately governments saw the practical advantages of rail transport and took an active part in both planning and financing the system. More than a quarter of the track constructed in Prussia before 1870 was owned directly by the government, and most of the rest had been indirectly financed by the government, which purchased land and guaranteed interest on stock issues.

Germany imported most of its engines directly from Britain and thus adopted standard British gauge for its system. As early as 1850 there were more than 3500 miles of rail in Germany, with important roads linking the manufacturing districts of Saxony and the coal and iron deposits of the Ruhr. Twenty years later, Germany was second only to Britain in the amount of track that had been laid and opened. By then it was no longer simply a follower. German engineers and machinists, trained in Europe's best schools of technology, were turning out engines and rolling stock second to none. And the railroads transported a host of high-quality manufactures, especially durable metal goods that came to carry the most prestigious trademark of the late nineteenth century: "Made in Germany."

The Lands That Time Forgot

Nothing better demonstrates the point that industrialization was a regional rather than a national process than a survey of those states that did not develop industrial economies by the middle of the nineteenth century. The states ranged from the Netherlands, which was still one of the richest areas in Europe, to Spain and Russia, which were the poorest. Also included were Austria-Hungary, the states of the Italian peninsula, and Poland. In all those nations there was some industrial progress. The Bohemian lands of Austria contained a highly developed spinning industry; the Spanish province of Catalonia produced more cotton than did Belgium, and the Basque region was rich in iron and coal. Northern Italy mechanized its textile production, particularly silk spinning, while in the regions around both Moscow and Saint Petersburg, factories were run on serf labor. Nevertheless, the economies of all the states remained nonindustrial and, with the exception of the Netherlands, dominated by subsistence agriculture.

There were many reasons why the states were unable to develop their industrial potential. Some, such as Naples and Poland, were simply underendowed with resources; others,

such as Austria-Hungary and Spain, faced difficulties of transport and communications that could not easily be overcome. Spain's modest resources were located on its northern and eastern edges, while a vast, arid plain dominated the center. To move raw materials and finished products from one end of the country to the other was a daunting task, made more difficult by lack of waterways and the rudimentary condition of Spanish roads. Two-thirds of Austria-Hungary was either mountains or hills, a geographic feature that presented obstacles not even the railroads could easily solve. But there was far more than natural disadvantage behind the failure of those parts of Europe to move in step with the industrializing states. Their social structure, agricultural organization, and commercial policies all hindered the adoption of new methods, machines, and modes of production.

Despite the fact that industrialization created new and largely unmanageable social problems, the follower states were eager for its benefits. All imported the latest products of technology, and the ruling elites in even the most traditional economies lived a material life similar to those in the most advanced. British entrepreneurs and artisans were courted by heads of state and their ministers and were offered riches in exchange for their precious knowledge. British industrialists set up textile factories in Moscow, built spinning machines in Bohemia, and taught Spanish miners how to puddle iron. Railroad pioneer George Stephenson himself surveyed the prospect of creating a passenger rail system in Spain, though he concluded pessimistically, "I have not seen enough people of the right sort to fill a single train." In the later part of the nineteenth century, French, Belgian, and German industrialists served similar roles. There were no traditional economies by choice. Industrialization was seen as a miracle, and the latecomers worshiped avidly at its shrine.

It was work rather than faith that would produce economic salvation. The most common characteristic of the latecomers was a traditional agrarian structure that consumed the lion's share of labor and capital while producing little surplus for any but a small dominant class. In areas as dissimilar as Spain, Italy, and Russia, agriculture was organized in vast estates, which kept the mass of peasants perpetually poor. Sharecropping systems in the west and serfdom in the east differed only in formal organization. Both conditions made it impossible for peasants to accumulate the land necessary to invest in capital improvements or to send their children to towns to engage in industrial occupations. In Hungary, Poland, and Russia, it was illegal for people to change occupations, and serfs who engaged in industrial activity paid their lords for the privilege. Although a number of serfs amassed considerable fortunes in organizing domestic or factory spinning, legal constraints restricted the efforts of potential entrepreneurs.

Similarly, the leaders of traditional economies maintained tariff systems that insulated their own producers from competition. Austrian tariffs were not only artificially high, they were accompanied by import quotas to keep all but the smallest fraction of foreign products from Austrian consumers. The Spanish government prohibited the importation of grain, forcing its eastern provinces to pay huge transport costs for domestic grain despite the fact that cheaper Italian grain was readily available. Such policies sapped much needed capital from industrial investment. There were many reasons for so-called protective tariffs, and it was not only the follower states that imposed them. France and the Zollverein protected domestic industry while Britain was converted to free trade only in the 1840s. But protection was sensible only when it protected rather than isolated. Inefficiently produced goods of inferior quality were the chief results of the protectionist policies of the follower nations. Failure to adopt steam-powered machines made traditionally produced linens and silks so expensive that smuggling occurred on an international scale. Although the goods might find buyers in domestic markets, they could not compete in international trade, and one by one the industries of the follower nations atrophied. Such nations became exporters of raw materials and foodstuffs. The export of Russian linen was replaced by the export of Russian flax. Spain, once the largest exporter of woolen cloth in Europe, exported mainly wines and fruits. Those economies that remained traditionally organized came to be exploited for their resources by those that had industrialized.

The international situation was not all that different from the dual system that came into effect within the nonindustrialized states. In Austria-Hungary, for example, it was Hungary that was kept from industrializing, first by the continuation of serf-based agriculture, then by the high internal tariffs that favored Austrian over Hungarian manufactures. In Italy, the division was between north and south. In Lombardy and Tuscany, machine-based manufacturing took hold alongside mining and metallurgy; in 1860, northern Italy contained 98 percent of the railways and 87 percent of the roads that existed on the entire peninsula. In Naples and Sicily, half-starved peasants eked out a miserable existence on once-rich soil that had become depleted from overuse. It was estimated that of the 400,000 people living in Naples, more than 100,000 were destitute beggars. In Spain, Catalonia modernized while Castile stagnated. Until the loss of its Latin American empire in the first half of the nineteenth century, Spain had a ready market for Catalonian textiles and handicrafts. But since Castile remained the cultural and administrative center of the state, it did little to encourage change, and much government policy was actually counterproductive. The chief problem faced by the dual economies was that neither part could sustain the other. Traditional agriculture could not produce the necessary surplus of either labor or capital to support industry, and industry could not economize sufficiently to make manufactured goods cheap enough for a poor peasantry.

Thus the advantages of being a follower were all missed. Technology could not be borrowed or stages skipped because the ground was not prepared for widespread industrial activity to be cultivated. Even by standing still, followers fell behind. While over the course of the nineteenth century male illiteracy dropped dramatically in the industrialized states—to 30 percent in Britain and France and 10 percent in Prussia—it remained at 75 to 80 percent in Spain and Italy and more than 90 percent in Russia. There was more than irony in the fact that one of the first railroads built on the Continent was built in Austria but was built to be powered by horses rather than engines. The first railways in Italy linked royal palaces to capital cities. Those in Spain radiated from Madrid and bypassed most centers of natural resources. In those states, the railroads

■ A Russian peasant tills a field with a primitive horse-drawn wooden plow. Russian fields produced low yields, partly because of the use of such crude farming methods.

were built to move the military rather than passengers or goods. They were state-financed, occasionally state-owned, and almost always lost money. They were symbols of the industrial age, but in those states they were symbols without substance.

CONCLUSION

The industrialization of Europe in the eighteenth century was an epochal event in human history. The constraints on daily life imposed by nature were loosened for the first time. No longer did population growth in one generation mean famine in the next; no longer was it necessary for the great majority of people to toil in the fields to earn their daily bread. Manufacture replaced agriculture as humanity's primary activity, though the change was longer and slower than the burst of industrialization that took place in the first half of the nineteenth century. For the leaders, Britain especially, industrialization brought international eminence. British achievements were envied, British inventors celebrated, Britain's constitutional and social organization lauded. A comparatively small island nation had become the greatest economic power in Europe. Industrialization had profound consequences for economic life, but its effects ran deeper than that. The search for new markets would result in the conquest of continents; the power of productivity unleashed by coal and iron would result in the first great arms race. Both would reach fruition in World War I, the first industrial war. For better or worse, the industrial era that began in Britain in the middle of the eighteenth century continues today.

QUESTIONS FOR REVIEW

1. Why did early manufacturing develop in the countryside, and what effect did that have on manufacturing practices and social relations?
2. In what ways were the ideas about organization of manufacturers such as Josiah Wedgwood and Robert Owen as significant as new technology in the development of industry in Britain?
3. How did British society address some of the changes in people's lives that were brought about by industrialization?
4. How did industrialization on the Continent differ from industrialization in England?
5. Why did some nations develop little industry at all?

KEY TERMS

agricultural revolution, *p. 620*

Crystal Palace Exhibition, *p. 643*

enclosure, *p. 624*

Factory Act (1833), *p. 637*

industrialization, *p. 627*

Industrial Revolution, *p. 626*

Luddites, *p.633*

mule, *p. 632*

putting-out system, *p. 622*

Zollverein, *p. 647*

DISCOVERING WESTERN CIVILIZATION ONLINE

You can obtain more information about industrial Europe at the Websites listed below. See also the Companion Website that accompanies this text, www.ablongman.com/kishlansky, which contains an online study guide and additional resources.

The Industrial Revolution in Britain

Reminiscences of James Watt

www.history.rochester.edu/steam/hart/
A nineteenth-century account of the life of James Watt and his role as inventor of the steam engine with links to the history of the steam engine.

Women in World History Curriculum: Industrial Revolution

www.womeninworldhistory.com/lesson7.html
Sponsored by Women in World History Curriculum, this site details the plight of working women in industrial England.

Child Labour in the 19th Century

www.spartacus.schoolnet.co.uk/IRchild.main.htm
This site chronicles child labor in Britain, including life in the factory and first-hand experiences.

The Industrialization of the Continent

Modern History Sourcebook: Tables Illustrating the Spread of Industrialization

www.fordham.edu/halsall/mod/indrevtabs1.html
Charts and statistics about industrialization in Europe.

Internet Modern History Sourcebook: Industrial Revolution

www.fordham.edu/halsall/mod/modsbook14.html
An outstanding collection of documents on the Industrial Age with links.

SUGGESTIONS FOR FURTHER READING

General Reading

T. S. Ashton, *The Industrial Revolution* (Oxford: Oxford University Press, 1997). A compelling brief account of the traditional view of industrialization.

Niall Ferguson, *The Cash Nexus: Money and Power in the Modern World, 1700–2000* (New York: Basic Books, 2001). A transnational history of the role of finance in the making of the modern world.

Jordan Goodman and Katrina Honeyman, *Gainful Pursuits: The Making of Industrial Europe, 1600–1914* (London: Edward Arnold, 1988). A brief overview of the entire process of industrialization.

Pat Hudson, *The Industrial Revolution* (London: Oxford University Press, 2007). The latest account of the technological innovation that began the modern era.

The Traditional Economy

Richard Brown, *Society and Economy in Modern Britain, 1700–1850* (London: Routledge, 1991). A comprehensive survey.

J. D. Chambers and G. E. Mingay, *The Agricultural Revolution* (London: Batsford, 1966). The classic survey of the changes in British agriculture.

The Industrial Revolution in Britain

N. F. R. Crafts, *British Economic Growth During the Industrial Revolution* (Oxford: Oxford University Press, 1986). A highly quantitative study by an economic historian arguing the case that economic growth was slow in the early nineteenth century.

François Crouzet, *The First Industrialists* (Cambridge: Cambridge University Press, 1985). An analysis of the social background of the first generation of British entrepreneurs.

Martin Daunton, *Progress and Poverty: An Economic and Social History of Britain, 1700–1850* (Oxford: Oxford University Press, 1995). The best single-volume survey on the Industrial Revolution and its effects on British society.

Phyllis Deane, *The First Industrial Revolution*, 2d ed. (Cambridge: Cambridge University Press, 1979). The best introduction to the technological changes in Britain.

Judith Flanders, *Inside the Victorian Home: A Portrait of Domestic Life in Victorian England* (New York: W. W. Norton, 2005). A detailed depiction of homes and families in nineteenth-century England.

Richard Price, *British Society, 1680–1880: Dynamism, Containment, and Change* (New York: Cambridge University Press, 1999). An argument about the nature of British society in the age of the Industrial Revolution.

John Rule, *The Vital Century: England's Developing Economy, 1714–1815* (London: Longman, 1992). A comprehensive survey of the British economy.

E. P. Thompson, *The Making of the English Working Class* (New York: Random House, 1966). A brilliant and passionate study of the ways laborers responded to the changes brought about by the industrial economy.

The Industrialization of the Continent

W. O. Henderson, *The Rise of German Industrial Power* (Berkeley: University of California Press, 1975). A chronological study of German industrialization that centers on Prussia.

Tom Kemp, *Industrialization in Nineteenth-Century Europe*, 2d ed. (London: Longman, 1985). Survey of the process of industrialization in the major European states.

Sidney Pollard, *Peaceful Conquest* (Oxford: Oxford University Press, 1981). Argues the regional nature of industrialization throughout western Europe.

Roger Price, *The Economic Transformation of France* (London: Croom Helm, 1975). A study of French society before and during the process of industrialization.

Wolfgang Schivelbusch, *The Railway Journey* (Berkeley: University of California Press, 1986). A social history of the impact of railways, drawn from French and German sources.

Clive Trebilcock, *The Industrialization of the Continental Powers, 1780–1914* (London: Longman, 1981). A complex study of Germany, France, and Russia.

For a list of additional titles related to this chapter's topics, please see http://www.ablongman.com/kishlansky.

22 POLITICAL UPHEAVALS AND SOCIAL TRANSFORMATIONS, 1815–1850

POTATO POLITICS

THE PLIGHT OF THE POOR IN EUROPEAN SOCIETIES

Vegetables have histories too. But none has a more interesting history in the West than the humble potato. First introduced to northern Europe from the Andean highlands of South America at the end of the sixteenth century, it rapidly became a staple of peasant diets from Ireland to Russia. The potato's vitamins, minerals, and high carbohydrate content provided a rich source of energy to Europe's rural poor. It was simple to plant, required little or no cultivation, and did well in damp,

THE VISUAL RECORD

cool climates. Best of all, it could be grown successfully on the smallest plots of land. One acre could support a peasant family of four for a year. Potato peelings helped sustain the family cow and pig, further supplementing family income.

In *Potato Planters,* shown here, the French painter Jean-François Millet (1814–1875) provided a view of the peasant labor involved in planting potatoes. Millet, the son of a wealthy peasant family, understood well the importance of the potato crop in the peasant diet. The man and woman in the painting plant their potatoes as a reverent act, bowing as field laborers might in prayer. (Laborers actually do pray in Millet's more sentimental work *The Angelus.*) The primitive nature of the process is striking: the man uses a short hoe to scrape at what seems to be unyielding soil. The peasants seem part of the nature that surrounds them, patient as the beast that waits in the shade, bent and gnarled and lovely as the tree that arches in the background.

The fleshy root not only guaranteed health, it also affected social relations. Traditionally, peasants delayed marrying and starting families because of the unavailability of land. The potato changed that behavior. Now the potato allowed peasants with only a little land to marry and have children earlier. Millet's depiction of the man and woman working together in

the field resonates with the simple fact that potato cultivation aided in the formation of the couple. Millet's couple are parents whose baby sleeps swaddled in a basket and shaded by the tree. In those peasant homes where family members did putting-out work for local entrepreneurs, potato cultivation drew little labor away from the spinning wheel and loom. It permitted prosperous farmers to devote more land to cash crops, since only a small portion of land was required to feed a family. As the sole item of diet, it provided life-sustaining nutrients and a significant amount of the protein so necessary for heavy labor. The Irish adult male ate an average of 12 to 14 pounds of potatoes a day—a figure that may seem preposterous to us today.

Proverbs warned peasants against putting all their eggs in one basket, but no folk wisdom prepared the Irish, many of whom relied on the potato as a single crop, for the potato disaster that struck them. In 1845, a fungus from America destroyed the new potato crop. Although peasants were certainly accustomed to bad harvests and crop failures, they had no precedent for the years of blight that followed. From 1846 to 1850, famine and the diseases resulting from it—scurvy, dysentery, cholera, and typhus fever—killed more than a million people in what became known as the **Great Hunger**. Another million people emigrated, many to the United States. Total dependence on the potato reaped its grim harvest, devastating all levels of Irish society. Within five years, the Irish population was reduced by almost 25 percent.

LOOKING AHEAD

The Irish potato famine has been called the "last great European natural disaster," to distinguish it from the man-made horrors of war and revolution. But it was as much a social and political disas-

■ Jean-François Millet, *Potato Planters* (ca. 1861).

ter as a natural one. As the wealth of European societies expanded in the nineteenth century, so did the number of those who lived on the edge, poised between unemployment and starvation. The Great Hunger in Ireland was the most striking example of the problem that plagued all Western societies in the first half of the nineteenth century: what to do with the poor. In this chapter, we shall see that while the boundaries of European nations were redefined in order to create stability following the Napoleonic Wars, the economic hardships of peasants and workers continued to plague and disrupt European societies internally. The new ideologies of the first half of the nineteenth century grappled with the challenge of reshaping state and society. But social inequities continued to fuel protest and revolution between 1815 and 1850 and pulled down governments across Europe.

GEOGRAPHICAL TOUR
Europe in 1815

Peasants like those depicted by Millet (in this chapter's Visual Record) seldom traveled beyond their own villages. Of course, all of that was different in Napoleon's quest for empire. Napoleon had placed large armies of peasants and workers in motion, crisscrossing the continent, and giving his own troops and Europe a geography lesson. At the heart of that lesson was the fact that no one state had been able to defeat Napoleon and his conscript armies. He had made clear the territorial and political interdependence of the European powers. The lesson was not lost on the leaders of Russia, Austria, Prussia, and France as they sat down to redraw the map of Europe in 1815.

■ **Map A. Europe, 1815.** In a series of treaties following Napoleon's defeat, the European powers redrew the map of Europe to create the most stable territorial arrangement and ensure European security. At the center of Europe stood the German confederation, outlined here in red.

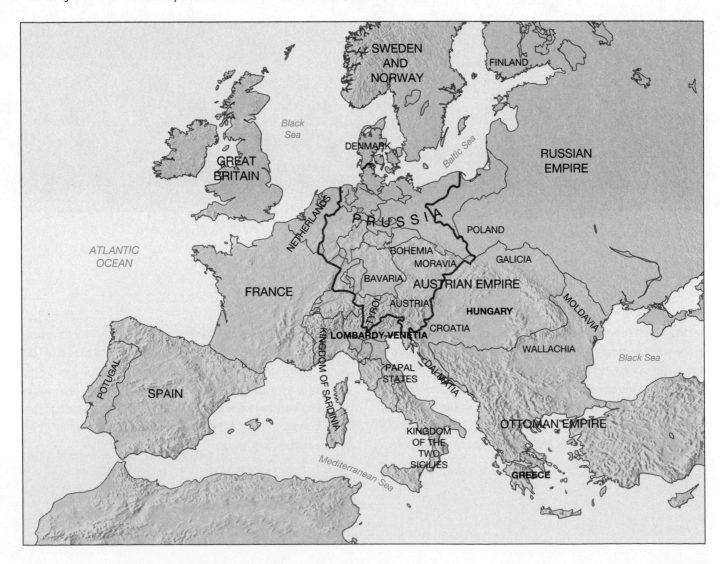

Europe's rulers shared the vision of Europe as a machine that must be kept in running order. Those victorious in defeating Napoleon's Empire looked on the whole of Europe as one entity and conceived of peace in terms of a general European security.

The primary goal of European leaders was to devise the most stable territorial arrangement possible. That goal entailed redrawing the map of Europe (see **Map A**). During the negotiations, traditional claims of the right to rule came head to head with new ideas about stabilization. The equilibrium established in 1815 made possible a century-long European peace. Conflicts erupted, to be sure, but they took on the characteristics of the new system that was constructed at Vienna in 1815.

The Congress of Vienna

In September 1814, representatives of the victorious Allies agreed to convene in the Austrian capital of Vienna for the purposes of mopping up the mess created in Europe by French rule and restoring order to European monarchies.

The central actors of the **Congress of Vienna** were Austrian minister of foreign affairs Prince Klemens von Metternich (1809–1848), British foreign secretary Viscount Castlereagh (1812–1822), French minister of foreign affairs Charles Maurice de Talleyrand (1814–1815), the Russian tsar Alexander I (1801–1825), and the Prussian king Frederick William III (1797–1840). In spite of personal eccentricities, animosities, and occasional outright hostilities among Europe's leaders, all shared a common concern with reestablishing harmony in Europe.

Settling with France.   Because of the concern with establishing harmony at the time of Napoleon's defeat, the peace enforced against France was not a punitive one. After Napoleon's abdication in 1814, the victorious powers of Great Britain, Russia, Prussia, and Austria decided that leniency was the best way to support the restored Bourbon monarchy. After 1793, royalist émigrés referred to the young son of the executed Louis XVI as Louis XVII, although the child died in captivity and never reigned. In 1814, the four powers designated the elder of the two surviving brothers of Louis XVI as the appropriate candidate for the restored monarchy. Because of the circumstances of his restoration, the new king, Louis XVIII (1814–1815; 1815–1824), bore the ignominious image of returning "in the baggage car of the Allies." Every effort was made not to weigh down Louis XVIII with a harsh settlement. The First Peace of Paris, signed by the Allies with France in May 1814, had reestablished the French frontiers at the 1792 boundaries, which included Avignon, Venaissin, parts of Savoy, and German and Flemish territories—none of which had belonged to France in 1789.

Even after the hundred-day return of Napoleon, the "Usurper," the Second Peace of Paris of November 1815 declared French frontiers restricted to the boundaries of 1790 (see **Map B**) and exacted from France an indemnity of 700

■ **Map B. France, 1815.** In determining the borders of France, European heads of state were torn between the need to punish and control France and the importance of reconciliation with France for a stable Europe. The Second Peace of Paris of November 1815 permitted France to return to the borders of 1790 and to resume its role as one of the Great Powers.

million francs. An army of occupation consisting of 150,000 troops was also placed on French soil at French expense but was removed ahead of schedule in 1818. Contrary to the terms of the first treaty, the second treaty also required France to return plundered art treasures to their countries of origin.

New Territorial Arrangements.   The dominant partnership of Austria and Britain at the Congress of Vienna resulted in treaty arrangements that served to restrain the ambitions of Russia and Prussia. No country was to receive territory without giving up something in return, and no one country was to receive enough territory to make it a present or future threat to the peace of Europe. To contain France, some steps taken prior to the Congress were ratified or expanded. In June 1814, the Low Countries had been set up as a unitary state to serve as a buffer against future French expansion on the Continent and a block to the revival of French sea power. The new Kingdom of the Netherlands (see **Map C**), created out of the former Dutch Republic and the Austrian Netherlands, was placed under the rule of William I (1815–1840). The Catholic southern provinces were thus uneasily reunited with the Protestant northern provinces, regions that had been separated since the Peace of Westphalia in 1648. Great Britain gave

■ **Map C. Kingdom of the Netherlands.** As a buffer on France's northernmost border, the new Kingdom of the Netherlands was a forced union of two regions with different languages and religions. The union lasted only until 1831 when the southern provinces revolted to form Belgium.

■ **Map D. Italian Peninsula, 1815.** Austria gained major territorial concessions on the Italian peninsula. The Austrian Empire now included Lombardy and Venetia. Austria was also influential throughout the peninsula in the Papal States, the three small duchies (Tuscany, Parma, Modena), and the Kingdom of the Two Sicilies.

William I of the Netherlands £2 million to fortify his frontier against France.

A reestablished monarchy that united the island kingdom of Sardinia with Piedmont and included Savoy, Nice, and part of Genoa contained France on its southeast border (see **Map D**). To the east, Prussia was given control of the left bank of the Rhine. Switzerland was reestablished as an independent confederation of cantons. Bourbon rule was restored in Spain on France's southwestern border.

Austria's power was firmly established in Italy, either through outright territorial control or influence over independent states (see **Map D**). The Papal States were returned to Pope Pius VII (1800–1823), along with territories that had been Napoleon's Cisalpine Republic and the Kingdom of Italy. Lombardy and the Illyrian provinces on the Dalmatian coast were likewise restored to Austria. The Republic of Venice and the Italian duchies of Tuscany, Parma, and Modena fell under the influence of Habsburg princes.

After the fall of Napoleon, the Allies made no attempt to restore the Holy Roman Empire. Napoleon's Confederation of the Rhine, which organized the majority of German territory under French auspices in 1806, was dissolved. In its place, the lands once divided into 300 petty states in central Europe

were reorganized into 38 states in the German Confederation (see **Map E**). The 38 states, along with Austria as the thirty-ninth, were represented in a new Federal Diet at Frankfurt, dominated by Austria. The German Confederation was intended as a bulwark against France, not to serve any nationalist or parliamentary function.

All of the changes were the result of carefully discussed but fairly uncontroversial negotiations. The question of Poland was another matter indeed. Successive partitions by Russia, Austria, and Prussia in 1772, 1793, and 1795 had completely dismembered the land that had been Poland. Napoleon had reconstituted a small portion of Poland as the Grand Duchy of Warsaw. The Congress faced the dilemma of what to do with the Napoleonic creation and with Polish territory in general. Fierce debate over Poland threatened to shatter congressional harmony (see **Map F**).

Tsar Alexander I of Russia argued for a large Poland that he intended to be fully under his influence, thus extending Russian-controlled territories to the banks of the Oder. He also envisioned extending Russian dominance farther into central and eastern Europe. He based his claim on the significant contribution the Russian army had made to Napoleon's defeat. But such thinking conflicted with the Austrian minis-

■ In this French cartoon satirizing the Congress of Vienna, left to right, Talleyrand is watching and waiting as Castlereagh balks, Metternich leads the "dancing," the king of Saxony clutches his crown in fear, and Genoa jumps up and down on the sidelines.

■ **Map E. German Confederation.** The league of German states created in 1815 replaced the Holy Roman Empire. The 39 states, of which 35 were monarchies and 4 were free cities, existed to ensure the independence of its member states and support in case of external attack. The member states of Austria and Prussia lay partially outside the Confederation.

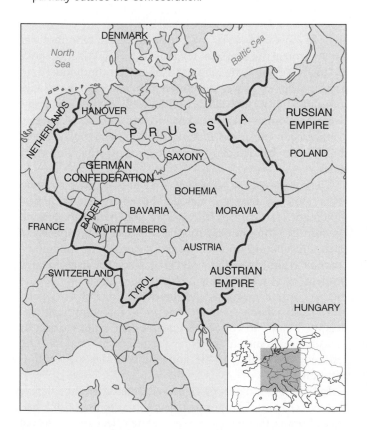

ter Metternich's pursuit of equilibrium. Frederick William III of Prussia contended that if a large Poland were to be created, Prussia would expect compensation by absorbing Saxony (see **Map G**). Both Great Britain and France distrusted Russian and Prussian territorial aims.

In the final arrangement, Prussia retained the Polish territory of Posen and Austria kept the Polish province of Galicia (see **Map F**). Krakow, with its population of 95,000, was declared a free city. Finally, a kingdom of Poland, nominally independent but in fact under the tutelage of Russia, emerged from what remained of the Grand Duchy of Warsaw. It was a solution that benefited no one in particular and disregarded Polish wishes.

In addition to receiving Polish territories, Prussia gained two-fifths of the kingdom of Saxony (see **Map G**). Prussia also received territory on the left bank of the Rhine, the Duchy of Westphalia, and Swedish Pomerania. With the acquisitions, Prussia doubled its population to around 11 million people. The Junkers, the landed class of east Prussia, reversed many of the reforms of the Napoleonic period. The new territories that Prussia gained were rich in waterways and resources but geographically fragmented. The dispersal of holdings that was intended to contain Prussian power in central Europe spurred Prussia to find new ways of uniting its markets. In the endeavor, Prussia constituted a future threat to Austrian power over the German Confederation.

In Scandinavia, the members of the Congress acknowledged Russia's conquest of Finland, and in return Sweden acquired Norway from Denmark. Unlike Austria, Prussia, and Russia, Great Britain made no claim to territories at the Congress. Having achieved its aim of containing France, its

■ **Map F. Poland, 1815.** An independent kingdom in name only, Poland was under the influence of Russia. Prussia carved off Posen, and Austria maintained control of Galicia. Krakow was defined by treaty as an independent republic.

■ **Map G. Saxony.** In 1806, Saxony had sided with France against Prussia and remained allies with the French for the remainder of the Napoleonic Wars. With Napoleon's defeat in 1815, about 40 percent of Saxony became part of Prussia.

greatest rival for dominance on the seas, Britain returned the French colonies it had seized in war. For the time being, the redrawing of the territorial map of Europe had achieved its pragmatic aim of guaranteeing the peace. It was now left to a system of alliances to preserve that peace.

The Alliance System

Only by joining forces had the European powers been able to defeat Napoleon, and a system of alliances continued to be needed even after the battles were over. Two alliance pacts dominated the post-Napoleonic era: the renewed Quadruple Alliance and the Holy Alliance.

The **Quadruple Alliance** (see **Map H**), signed by the victorious powers of Great Britain, Austria, Russia, and Prussia in November 1815, was intended to protect Europe against future French aggression and to preserve the status quo. In 1818, France, having completed its payment of war indemnities, joined the pact, which now became the **Quintuple Alliance**. The five powers promised to meet periodically over the following 20 years to discuss common problems and to ensure the peace.

The **Holy Alliance** (see **Map H**) was the brainchild of Alexander I and was heavily influenced by his mystical and romantic view of international politics. In the pact, the mon-

archs of Prussia, Austria, and Russia agreed to renounce war and to protect the Christian religion. The Holy Alliance spoke of "the bonds of a true and indissoluble brotherhood . . . to protect religion, peace, and justice." Russia was able to give some credibility to the alliance with the sheer size of its army. Career diplomats were aware of its hollowness as a treaty arrangement, but it did indicate the willingness of Europe's three eastern autocracies to intervene in the affairs of other states.

The concept of Europe acting as a whole, through a system of periodic conferences, marked the emergence of a new diplomatic era. Conflict, however, was inherent in the tension between the commitment of parliamentary governments to open consultation and the need for secrecy in diplomacy. Dynastic regimes sought to intervene in smaller states to buoy up despots, as was the case in 1822, when European powers met to consider restoring the Bourbon monarchy in Spain. The British acted as a counterbalance to interventionist tendencies, refused to cooperate, and blocked united action by the Alliance. France took military action on its own in 1823, restored King Ferdinand VII, and abolished the Spanish constitution.

In both the Congress of Vienna and the system of alliances that succeeded it, European nations aimed to establish a balance of power that recognized legitimate rulers and preserved

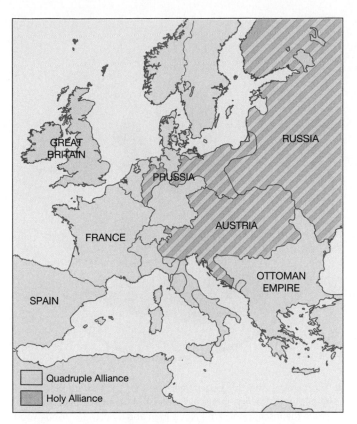

■ **Map H. Quadruple Alliance and Holy Alliance.** The Quadruple Alliance grew out of the need of the Great Powers to create a stable Europe and had as its initial impulse the creation of a buffer against a future French threat. Austria, Great Britain, Prussia, and Russia entered into the agreement as the basis for defining the balance of power in Europe. In the Holy Alliance, Russia, Austria, and Prussia entered an agreement to treat each other according to the precepts of the Christian religion. As a counterweight to the Quadruple Alliance, the Holy Alliance served as a justification for repression against dissent.

CHRONOLOGY

The Alliance System

May 1814	First Peace of Paris
23 September 1814– 9 June 1815	Congress of Vienna
26 September 1815	Formation of the Holy Alliance
20 November 1815	Second Peace of Paris; Formation of the Quadruple Alliance
November 1818	Quadruple Alliance expands to include France in Quintuple Alliance
1823	French restoration of Bourbon Monarchy in Spain

the peace. The upheaval of the French Revolution and the revolutionary and Napoleonic Wars had made clear the interdependence of one nation on another as a guarantee of survival. By maintaining an international equilibrium, Europe's statesmen hoped—erroneously, as it turned out—that by keeping the peace abroad, domestic peace would follow.

THE NEW IDEOLOGIES

After 1815, the world was changing in many ways. As national boundaries were being redefined, the ways in which Europeans regarded their world were also being transformed. Steam-driven mechanical power in production and transportation steadily replaced human and animal power. In deference to what it was replacing, the new mechanical force was measured in units of horsepower. The new technology combined with political changes to challenge old values; new definitions of worth emerged from the increasingly mechanized world of work. The fixed, castelike distinctions of the old aristocratic world were under attack or in disarray. Western intellectuals struggled with the changes as they sought to make sense of the way in which Europeans lived, looked at the world, and defined their place in it.

The political and economic upheavals of the first half of the nineteenth century encouraged a new breed of thinkers to search for ways to explain the transformations of the period. During that period, Europeans witnessed one of the most intellectually fertile periods in the history of the West. The search for understanding during this era gave birth to new ideologies—liberalism, nationalism, romanticism, conservatism, and socialism—that continue to shape the ideas and institutions of the present day.

The New Politics of Preserving Order

European states had been dealing with war for more than two decades. Now they faced the challenge of peace. The French Revolution and Napoleon had not only meant military engagements; they had also brought the force of revolutionary ideas to the political arena, and those ideas did not retire from the field after Waterloo. Nor did treaties restore an old order, in spite of claims to doing so. Governments throughout Europe had to find new ways to deal with the tension between state authority and individual liberty. Conservative and liberal thinkers took very different paths in the pursuit of political stability.

Conservatism. **Conservatism** represented a dynamic adaptation to a social system in transition. In place of individualism, conservatives stressed the corporate nature of European society; in place of reason and progress, conservatives saw organic growth and tradition. Liberty, argued British statesman Edmund Burke (1729–1797) in *Reflections on the Revolution in France* (1790), must emerge out of the gradual development of the old order, and not its destruction. On the Continent, conservatives Louis de Bonald (1754–1840) and Joseph de Maistre (1753–1821) defended the monarchical principle of authority against the onslaught of revolutionary events.

Conservatism took a reactionary turn in the hands of the Austrian statesman Metternich. The Carlsbad decrees of 1819 are a good example of the "Metternich system" of espionage, censorship, and repression in central Europe, which sought to eliminate any constitutional or nationalist sentiments that had arisen during the Napoleonic period. The German Confederation approved decrees against free speech and civil liberties and set up mechanisms to root out "subversive" university students. Students who had taken up arms in the Wars of Liberation (1813–1815) against France had done so in hope of instituting liberal and national reforms. Metternich's system aimed at uprooting those goals. Student fraternities were closed, and police became a regular fixture in the university. Political expression in central Europe was driven underground for at least a decade. Metternich set out to crush any form of democratic government, constitutionalism, and parliamentarianism in central Europe.

Liberalism. The term *liberal* was first used in a narrow political sense to indicate the Spanish party of reform that supported the constitution modeled on the French document of 1791. But the term assumed much broader connotations in the first half of the nineteenth century as its appeal spread among the European middle classes. The two main tenets of belief that underlay **liberalism** were the freedom of the individual and the corruptibility of authority. As a political doctrine, liberalism built on Enlightenment rationalism and embraced the right to vote, civil liberties, legal equality, constitutional government, parliamentary sovereignty, and a free-market economy. Liberals firmly believed that less government was better government and that noninterference would produce a harmonious and well-ordered world. They also believed that human beings were basically good and reasonable and needed freedom to flourish. The sole end of government should be to promote that freedom.

Liberal thinkers tried to make sense of the political conflicts of the revolutionary period and the economic disruptions brought on by industrialization. The Great Revolution at the end of the eighteenth century spawned a vast array of liberal thought in France. Republicans, Bonapartists, and constitutional monarchists cooperated as self-styled "liberals" who shared a desire to preserve the gains of the revolution while ensuring orderly rule. In 1807, British law attempted to eliminate the slave trade with very limited success. William Wilberforce led abolitionists in England who continued to agitate for a parliamentary law that would abolish the slave trade throughout the British Empire. Such a law was finally passed in 1833, and about £20 million was paid in compensation to British plantation owners in the Caribbean. Also influenced by liberal ideas were a variety of political movements in

■ This cameo, made by Josiah Wedgwood for the Society for the Abolition of Slavery, shows a chained and manacled slave and bears the inscription, "Am I Not a Man and a Brother?" Wedgwood sent a batch of the cameos to Benjamin Franklin for distribution among American abolitionists.

the United States, including those demanding the liberation of slaves and the extension of legal and political rights to women. Abolitionists justified their opposition to slavery on humanitarian Christian grounds and on the liberal principles of freedom and equality. American women who were active in antislavery societies extended their liberal crusade against oppression to their own legal and political status.

By the mid-nineteenth century, liberal thinking constituted a dominant strain in British politics. Jeremy Bentham (1748–1832), trained in British law, fashioned himself into a social philosopher. He founded **utilitarianism,** a fundamentally liberal doctrine that argued for "the greatest happiness of the greatest number" in such works as *Introduction to the Principles of Morals and Legislation*. Bentham believed that government could achieve positive ends through limited and "scientific" intervention. Only the pursuit of social harmony justified interference with individual liberty. He found the best testing grounds for his theories in prisons, among convicted criminals. By supporting the reform of penal codes and prison regulations in *Rationale of Punishments and Rewards* (1825), he hoped that rewards and punishments could be meted out to convicts in a measurable "geometry" of pain and pleasure. He was sure that behavior could be improved and that prisoners could be rehabilitated and returned as honest citizens to society. (See "A Closer Look: The Birth of the Prison," pp. 662–663.)

The Scottish philosopher, economist, and historian James Mill (1773–1836) met Jeremy Bentham in 1808 and dedicated the rest of his life to promulgating Bentham's utilitarian philosophy. James Mill's son John Stuart Mill (1806–1873) reacted to his early and intense education in Benthamite ideas by rejecting the tenets of utilitarianism. Forging his own brand of classical liberalism in his treatise *On Liberty* (1859), the younger Mill became the greatest liberal thinker of the age. John Stuart Mill criticized Bentham for ignoring human emotions and for the mass tyranny implicit in his ideas. Mill went beyond existing political analyses by applying economic doctrines to social conditions in *Principles of Political Economy* (1848). With his wife and collaborator Harriet Taylor (d. 1858), he espoused social reform for the poor and championed the equality of women and the necessity of birth control. By 1848, his writings on liberty and equality were questioning the sacredness of private property. In later life, John Stuart Mill came to believe that a more equitable distribution of wealth was both necessary and possible.

DOCUMENT

Mill on Enfranchisement of Women

David Ricardo (1772–1823) was a stockbroker prodigy who by the age of 20 had made his fortune. In *Principles of Political Economy and Taxation* (1817), Ricardo outlined his opposition to government intervention in foreign trade and elaborated his "iron law of wages," which contended that wages would stabilize at the subsistence level. Increased wages would cause the working classes to grow, and the resulting competition in the labor market would drive wages down to the level of subsistence. Other liberals, more concerned with social welfare than Ricardo, argued that state intervention was unavoidable but could be limited.

Romanticism and Change

Unlike liberalism and conservatism, which were fundamentally political ideologies, **romanticism** included a variety of literary and artistic movements throughout Europe that spanned the period from the late eighteenth century to the mid-nineteenth century. One could be a liberal and a romantic just as easily as one could be a conservative and a romantic.

The Romantic World View. Above all, and in spite of variations, romantics shared similar beliefs and a common view of the world. Among the first romantics were the English poets William Wordsworth (1770–1850) and Samuel Taylor Coleridge (1772–1834), whose collaborative *Lyrical Ballads* (1798) exemplified the iconoclastic romantic idea that poetry was the result of "the spontaneous overflow of powerful feelings" rather than a formal and highly disciplined intellectual exercise. Romantics, in general, rebelled against the confinement of classical forms and refused to accept the supremacy of reason over emotions.

The English gardens designed at the end of the eighteenth century provide one of the best visual examples of the new romanticism. The formal gardens that surrounded the castles and manor houses of Europe's wealthy elite throughout the eighteenth century relied on carefully drawn geometric patterns, minutely trimmed hedges and lawns, and symmetrically arranged flowers planted in rows by size and color to achieve the effect of total mastery of nature. The gardens at the great palace of Versailles are a good example of the formal landscaping chosen by France's kings and emulated by the wealthy everywhere in Europe. The romantic or English garden was, by contrast, a rebellious profusion of color in which the landscaper rejected the carefully drawn geometric patterns then in vogue and set out instead, deliberately and somewhat paradoxically, to imitate nature. The romantic aesthetic, whether in landscape gardening or in literature, recognized the beauty of untamed nature and the inspiration produced by the release of human emotions.

Intellectuals, Artists, and Freedom. By rooting artistic vision in spontaneity, romantics endorsed a concept of creativity based on the supremacy of human freedom. The artist was valued in a new way as a genius through whose insight and intuition great art was created. Intuition, as opposed to scientific learning, was endorsed as a valid means of knowing. Building on the work of the eighteenth-century philosopher Immanuel Kant (1724–1804), romanticism embraced subjective knowledge. Inspiration and intuition took the place of reason and science in the romantic pantheon of values.

Germaine de Staël (1766–1817), often hailed as the founder of French romanticism, was an extraordinary woman whose writings influenced French liberal political theory after 1815. Madame de Staël's mother had followed the principles of education spelled out by Jean-Jacques Rousseau in *Emile* (1762), according to which the child was allowed to follow his or her own path of intellectual development. De Staël authored histories, novels, literary criticism, and political tracts that opposed what she judged to be the tyranny of Napoleonic rule. She, like many other romantics, was greatly influenced by the writings of Rousseau, and through him she discovered that "the soul's elevation is born of self-consciousness." The recognition of the subjective meant for de Staël that women's vision was as essential as men's for the flowering of European culture.

"It is within oneself that one must look at what lies outside." Following de Staël's lead, Victor Hugo (1802–1885), one of the great French writers of the nineteenth century, identified another essential ingredient in romanticism. The turning "within oneself" so apparent in Hugo's poetry was profoundly influenced by the political events of the French Revolution and its principles of liberty and equality. His greatest novels, including *Notre-Dame de Paris* (1831) and *Les Misérables* (1862), offer bold panoramic sweeps of the social universe of Paris across the ages. Whether in words or in music or on canvas, romanticism conveyed a new way of understanding the world. The supremacy of the emotions over reason found its way into the works of the great romantic composers of the age. Liberation from the forms that dominated the classical

THE BIRTH OF THE PRISON

There was once a time when modern prisons, what we call penitentiaries, did not exist. Prisons, like modern hospitals and schools, were one of the great achievements of the age of reform in the first half of the nineteenth century. Thanks to the efforts of humanitarians and social reformers, a new rationale for punishment emerged, one claiming that modern prisons were capable of rehabilitating criminals. Reformers argued that the controlled environment of a new prison system would be able to fashion wrongdoers into upstanding citizens through moral instruction, hard work, constant surveillance, and, in some cases, isolation from human contact.

The principles of the new penal arrangement were silence and separation—total or partial, in order to rehabilitate prisoners through supervised activities, including productive work. In French penitentiaries, prisoners were given an occupation and produced goods for the prison system itself—shoes or mattresses, for example—or for sale on the open market. The belief was that through productive labor, prisoners could be taught to be good workers and good citizens. Idle hands were the devil's workshop, so no moment of the prisoner's day was unoccupied or, in theory, unsupervised.

A CLOSER LOOK

Some of the "new" prisons were built in the shells of ancient military garrisons, seminaries, convents, and retreat houses. Before the beginning of the nineteenth century, prisons existed but they served as waystations, holding areas for those who were about to face their "real" punishments, which could be death, mutilation, forced labor in prison ships, or banishment. After 1820, however, incarceration became a punishment in itself throughout western Europe, with the goal to deprive prisoners of liberty and freedom of movement.

A typical prisoner in the new penitentiaries was a man convicted of theft serving a sentence of five to seven years. He entered a prison world where every aspect of his life was prescribed and supervised. The experience of the prison was intended to transform the behavior of the prisoner. Prisoners for the first time were required to wear uniforms. In addition to the regimented routine of work, meals, and sleep, the prisoner now also received moral and religious instruction behind bars.

Although populations in the old prisons of the eighteenth century were mixed with women and men, adults and children confined in the same spaces, by contrast, in the nineteenth century convicted women and children were systematically separated from male prisoners and subject to separate rules of confinement. Religious orders and philanthropic groups supervised women and children in prisons and continued to watch them in their lives after prison. Reformers now spoke of the punishment being made to fit the criminal—not the crime.

The most controversial aspect of the new punishment was solitary confinement. Women were usually exempted from the initial isolation experiments, deemed as too "social" or too weak to support total separation. Young boys on the other hand were targeted for the special experimental punishment of solitary isolation, something French observers such as historian and political philosopher Alexis de Tocqueville greatly admired on his travels in the United States. In one particularly brutal period of experimentation, beginning in 1838 French prison officials confined boys between the ages of six and sixteen to their cells day and night where they were expected to follow a strict regime of silence, discipline, religious instruction, and constant occupation. Most of the children were court custody cases committed by their fathers because of unruly behavior. The results were dire. There was no accurate way to measure recidivism, and, worse, the children's mortality rates increased sharply. Children in solitary confinement may have been protected from the "moral depravity" of other inmates, but they became sick and died more frequently than their counterparts in free society and than other kinds of prisoners. What began as a humanitarian advance was soon denounced as a form of torture for juvenile offenders.

Why did penitentiaries come into being in the first half of the nineteenth century? The new punishment was considered attractive because, in an age confronted with industrial and political transformations and revolutionary upheavals, it seemed to be a way of controlling criminal disruptions and social unrest. The middle classes, whether in London or Paris, grew increasingly fearful about potential threats to their property and well-being. Industrial workers crowded into substandard urban housing could face long periods of unemployment, when it was feared that desperate men and women would commit crimes to feed themselves and their families. The fear of the poor as dangerous influenced many of the prison reforms of the early nineteenth century. Great Britain and France created growing bureaucracies of penal, policing, and judicial institutions to guarantee the safety of honest citizens. At the same time that new prisons opened their doors, policemen started walking their neighborhood beats in European capitals.

Almost from the beginning prisons were deemed a failure. Specialists concluded that prisons did not correct criminals but instead served as schools for crime. Statistics—a new scientific practice in itself—proved them right. Recidivism rates rose dramatically, as penal authorities devised new ways—eventually fingerprinting and photography—to follow the activities of released prisoners. It is very likely that what was increasing in this era was not criminality but the ability of the state to track it.

■ Vincent Van Gogh, *The Prison Courtyard* (1890). The painting is copied after a wood engraving by Gustave Doré representing Newgate—the Exercise Yard in *London, a Pilgrimage* (1872).

The science of the new punishment evolved directly in relation to political and social changes in the first half of the nineteenth century. The three major spurts of prison reform in France, for example, coincided with the revolutionary upheavals of 1789, 1830, and 1848. Social reformers and legislators turned to the prison system as a crucial mechanism in the regulation of civil society. The new prisons were part of the network of institutions created to maintain an orderly working class in the new democratic age.

■ *Liberty Leading the People* (1831) by Eugène Delacroix captures the spirit of the French romantics, who looked upon revolutionary action as a way to achieve union with the spirit of history.

era could be heard in the works of French composer Louis Hector Berlioz (1803–1869), who set Faust's damnation to music; Polish virtuoso Frédéric Chopin (1810–1849), who created lyric compositions for the piano; and Hungarian concert pianist Franz Liszt (1811–1886), who composed symphonic poems and Hungarian rhapsodies.

Artists as different as J. M. W. Turner (1775–1851), the English landscape painter, and Eugène Delacroix (1798–1863), the leader of the French romantic school in painting (see image above), shared a commitment to their iconoclastic art. Turner's intense and increasingly abstract vision of an often turbulent world (see page 665) and Delacroix's epic historical and political masterpieces shared a rebellious experimentation with color and a rejection of classical conventions and forms. Characteristic of a particular strain within romanticism was the political message of Delacroix's art. In the magnificent painting

Liberty Leading the People (1831), for example, Delacroix immortalized the revolutionary events that swept Paris in 1830 in his moving portrayal of valiant revolutionaries of different social classes led into battle by a female Liberty.

In the postrevolutionary years between 1815 and 1850, romanticism claimed to be no more than an aesthetic stance in art, letters, and music, a posture that had no particular political intent. Yet its validation of the individual as opposed to the caste or the estate was the most revolutionary of doctrines, just as its justification of subjective knowledge threatened to erode the authority of classical learning. Artists did not make revolutions, but they supported them. Some stood by on the sidelines; others mounted the barricades; but all romantics, no matter how political or apolitical, helped shape a new way of looking at the world and helped define a new political consciousness.

■ *Ulysses deriding Polyphemus*, as described in Homer's *Odyssey*. J. W. Turner, 1829, National Gallery.

Reshaping State and Society

As another legacy of the French Revolution, the concept of the *nation* as a source of collective identity and political allegiance became a political force after 1815. Just as nationalism put the needs of the people at the heart of its political doctrine, so did socialism focus on the needs of society and especially of the poor.

Nationalism.   In its most basic sense, nationalism between 1815 and 1850 was the political doctrine that glorified the people united against the absolutism of kings and the tyranny of foreign oppressors. The success of the French Revolution and the spread of Napoleonic reforms boosted nationalist doctrines. In Germany, Johann Gottfried von Herder (1744–1803) rooted national identity in German folk culture. The *Fairy Tales* (1812–1814) of the brothers Jacob Ludwig Grimm (1785–1863) and Wilhelm Carl Grimm (1786–1859) had a similar national purpose. The brothers painstakingly captured in print the German oral tradition of peasant folklore. The philosophers Johann Fichte (1762–1814) and Georg Wilhelm Friedrich Hegel (1770–1831) emphasized the importance of the state.

Nationalism gave birth to a search for new symbols, just as the tricolor flag replaced the fleur-de-lis and the image of Marianne replaced the monarch as a result of the Great Revolution in France. There was a new concern with history as nationalists sought to revive a common cultural past.

The nationalist yearning for liberation sometimes meshed with the liberal political program of overthrowing tyrannical rule. Giuseppe Mazzini (1805–1872) represented the new breed of liberal nationalist. A less-than-liberal nationalist was political economist Georg Friedrich List (1789–1846), who formulated a statement of economic nationalism to counter the liberal doctrines of David Ricardo. Arguing that free trade worked only for the wealthy and powerful, List advocated a program of protective tariffs for developing German industries. He perceived British free trade as merely economic imperialism in disguise. List was one of the few nationalists who did not wholeheartedly embrace liberal economic doctrines. Beyond ideology and political practices, nationalism began to capture the imagination of groups who resented foreign domination. Expanding state bureaucracies did little to tame the centrifugal forces of nationalist feeling and probably exacerbated a desire for independence in eastern and central Europe, especially in the Habsburg-ruled lands.

YOUNG ITALY (1832)

Giuseppe Mazzini, an Italian patriot and revolutionary, was the principal theorist of national revolution in Europe in the first half of the nineteenth century. He claimed that his strong commitment to equality and democratic principles stemmed from his readings on the French Revolution of 1789 and his study of the Latin classics. As a young man, he resolved to dress always in black as a sign of mourning for his country, disunited and under foreign oppressors. In 1832 he founded the secret society Young Italy. The goal of the revolutionary group was the unification of Italy under a republican form of government through direct popular action.

Focus Questions

How is Mazzini's message about Italian nationalism reflective of the romantic world view? What is the significance of Mazzini's stress on the role of youth?

We have beheld Italy—Italy, the purpose, the soul, the consolation of our thoughts, the country chosen of God and oppressed by men, twice queen of the world and twice fallen through the infamy of foreigners/ and the guilt of her citizens, yet lovely still though she be dust, unmatched by any other nation whatever fortune has decreed; and Genius returns to seek in this dust the word of eternal life, and the spark that creates the future. . . .

Young Italy: but we chose this term because the one term seems to marshal before the youth of Italy the magnitude of its duties and the solemnity of the mission that circumstances have entrusted to it, so that it will be ready when the hour has struck to arise from its slumber to a new life of action and regeneration. And we chose it because we wanted to show ourselves, writing it, as what we are, to do battle with raised visors, to bear our faith before us, as the knights of medieval times bore their faith on their shields. For while we pity men who do not know the truth, we despise men who, though they know the truth, do not dare to speak it.

Nationalists valued the authenticity of the vernacular and folklore over the language and customs imposed by a foreign ruler. Herder and the brothers Grimm were German examples of the romantic appreciation of the roots of German culture. While French romantics emphasized the glories of their revolutionary heritage, German romantics stressed the importance of history as the source of one's identity. By searching for the self in a historic past, and especially in the Middle Ages, they glorified their collective cultural identity and national origins.

Socialism. Socialists rejected the world as it was. Socialism, like other ideologies of the first half of the nineteenth century, grew out of changes in the structure of daily life and the structure of power. There were as many stripes of socialists as there were liberals, nationalists, and conservatives. Socialists as a group shared a concern with "alienation," though they may not all have used the term.

Henri de Saint-Simon (1760–1825) rejected liberal individualism in favor of social organization and, for this reason, has been called the father of French socialism. To Saint-Simon, the accomplishments and potential of industrial development represented the highest stage in history. In a perfect and just society, productive work would be the basis of all prestige and power. The elite of society would be organized according to the hierarchy of its productive members, with industrial leaders at the top. Work was a social duty. The new industrial society that Saint-Simon foresaw would be both efficient and ethical, based on a religion similar to Christianity.

Like Saint-Simon, the French social theorist Pierre-Joseph Proudhon (1809–1865) recognized the social value of work. But unlike Saint-Simon, Proudhon refused to accept the dominance of industrial society. A self-educated typesetter of peasant origin, Proudhon gained national prominence with his ideas about a just society, free credit, and equitable exchange. In his famous pamphlet *What Is Property?* (1840), Proudhon answered, "Property is theft." That statement was not, however, an argument for the abolition of private ownership. Proudhon reasoned that industrialization had destroyed workers' rights, which included the right to the profits of their own labor. In attacking "property" in the form of profits amassed from the labor of others, Proudhon was arguing for a socialist concept of limited possession—people had the right to own only what they had earned from their own labor. Proudhon, who did not himself participate in political agitation, held a profoundly anarchistic view of society, hated government, and favored instead small self-ruling communities of producers. Proudhon's ideal world would be one of comfort but not great wealth.

At least one socialist believed in luxury. Charles Fourier (1772–1837), an unsuccessful traveling salesman, devoted himself to the study and improvement of society and formulated one of the most trenchant criticisms of industrial capitalism. In numerous writings between 1808 and his death, the eccentric, solitary man put forth his vision of a utopian world organized into units called phalanxes that took into account the social, sexual, and economic needs of their members. With a proper mix of duties, everyone in the phalanx would work only a few hours a day. In Fourier's scheme, work was not naturally abhorrent, but care had to be taken to match temperaments with tasks. Women and men fulfilled themselves and found pleasure and gratification through work. People would be paid according to their contributions in work, capital, and talent. In his vision of a better world, Fourier's phalanxes were always rural and were organized communally, though neither poverty nor property would be eliminated. Education would help alleviate discord, and rich and poor would learn to live together in perfect harmony.

Charles Fourier's work, along with that of Saint-Simon and Proudhon, became part of the tradition of utopian thinking that can be traced back to Thomas More in the sixteenth century. Because he believed in the ability of individuals to shape themselves and their world, Fourier intended his critique of society to be a blueprint for living. Fourier's followers set up communities in his lifetime—40 phalanxes were established in the United States alone—but because of financial problems and petty squabbling, all of them failed.

Women, who were active in demanding their own emancipation, were often joined by men who espoused utopian socialist and liberal views. The issue of increased civil liberties for women, tied as it often was to talk of freeing the slaves, was both a moral and political question for social reformers and utopian thinkers, including Fourier, who put the issue of women's freedom at the center of their plans to redesign society. Saint-Simonians argued for woman's social elevation and searched for a female messiah. Other social reformers joined with conservative thinkers in arguing that women must be kept in their place and that their place was in the home. Proudhon, for example, saw women's only choices as working at home as housewives or working in the streets as prostitutes.

Socialists, along with other ideologues in the decades before the middle of the nineteenth century, were aware of how rapidly their world was changing. Many believed that a revolution that would eliminate poverty and the sufferings of the working class was at hand. Followers of Saint-Simon, Fourier, and Proudhon all hoped that their proposals and ideas would change the world and prevent violent upheaval. Not all social critics were so sanguine.

In January 1848, two young men, one a philosopher living in exile and the other a businessman working for his father, began a collaboration that would last a lifetime with the publication of a short tract entitled ***The Communist Manifesto.*** Karl Marx (1818–1883) and Friedrich Engels (1820–1895) described the dire situation of the European working classes throughout the 1840s. The growing poverty and alienation of the propertyless workers, the authors promised, would bring

THE COMMUNIST MANIFESTO

The Communist Manifesto *is one of the most important documents in world history. Translated into many languages in countless editions, it inspired worker organizations throughout Europe in the second half of the nineteenth century and fired the imagination of Communist leaders in Asia, Latin America, Africa, and Europe well into the twentieth century.*

The pamphlet, which consists of no more than 12,000 words, was written early in 1848 by Karl Marx, founder of modern communism, and his collaborator and friend, Friedrich Engels. Their intention was to urge exploited workers throughout Europe to prepare themselves for the coming revolution by uniting across national boundaries. The Communist Manifesto *is a concise statement of the basic tenets of Marxism. Although mistaken in most of its predictions about the future development of capitalism, it accurately distilled some of the most salient inequities of industrial economies whose remedies, Marx and Engels asserted, could only be found through the revolutionary overthrow of the capitalist system.*

Focus Questions

According to Marx and Engels, how do markets and capitalism promote class struggle? What is the basis of their opposition to private property and their justification of a Communist revolution?

Bourgeois and Proletarians*

The history of all hitherto existing society is the history of class struggles.

Freeman and slave, patrician and plebeian, lord and serf, guild-master and journeyman, in a word, oppressor and oppressed, stood in constant opposition to one another, carried on an uninterrupted, now hidden, now open fight, a fight that each time ended, either in a revolutionary reconstitution of society at large, or in the common ruin of the contending classes. . . .

The modern bourgeois society that has sprouted from the ruins of feudal society has not done away with class antagonisms. It has but established new classes, new conditions of oppression, new forms of struggle in place of the old ones.

Our epoch, the epoch of the bourgeoisie, possesses, however, this distinctive feature: it has simplified the class antagonisms. Society as a whole is more and more splitting up into two great hostile camps, into two great classes directly facing each other: Bourgeoisie and Proletariat. . . .

The bourgeoisie cannot exist without constantly revolutionizing the instruments of production, and thereby the

(continued)

relations of production, and with them the whole relations of society. Conservation of the old modes of production in unaltered form, was, on the contrary, the first condition of existence for all earlier industrial classes. Constant revolutionizing of production, uninterrupted disturbance of all social conditions, everlasting uncertainty and agitation distinguish the bourgeois epoch from all earlier ones. All fixed, fast-frozen relations, with their train of ancient and venerable prejudices and opinions are swept away, all new-formed ones become antiquated before they can ossify. All that is solid melts into air, all that is holy is profaned, and man is at last compelled to face with sober senses, his real conditions of life, and his relations with his kind.

The need of a constantly expanding market for its products chases the bourgeoisie over the whole surface of the globe. It must nestle everywhere, settle everywhere, establish connections everywhere....

The proletariat goes through various stages of development. With its birth begins its struggle with the bourgeoisie. At first the contest is carried on by individual labourers, then by the work-people of a factory, then by the operatives of one trade, in one locality, against the individual bourgeois who directly exploits them. They direct their attacks not against the bourgeois conditions of production, but against the instruments of production themselves; they destroy imported wares that compete with their labour, they smash to pieces machinery, they set factories ablaze, they seek to restore by force the vanished status of the workman of the Middle Ages.

Proletarians and Communists

In what relation do the Communists stand to the proletarians as a whole?

The Communists do not form a separate part opposed to other working-class parties. They have no interests separate and apart from those of the proletariat as a whole....

You are horrified at our [Communists'] intending to do away with private property. But in your existing society, private property is already done away with for nine-tenths of the population; its existence for the few is solely due to its non-existence in the hands of those nine-tenths. You reproach us, therefore, with intending to do away with a form of property the necessary condition for whose existence is the non-existence of any property for the immense majority of society....

In short, the Communists everywhere support every revolutionary movement against the existing social and political order of things.

In all these movements they bring to the front, as the leading question in each, the property question, no matter what its degree of development at the time.

Finally, they labour everywhere for the union and agreement of the democratic parties of all countries.

The Communists disdain to conceal their views and aims. They openly declare that their ends can be attained only by the forcible overthrow of all existing social conditions. Let the ruling classes tremble at a Communistic revolution. The proletarians have nothing to lose but their chains. They have a world to win.

WORKING MEN OF ALL COUNTRIES, UNITE!

*By bourgeoisie is meant the class of modern Capitalists, owners of the means of social production and employers of wage labour. By **proletariat,** the class of modern wage-labourers who, having no means of production of their own, are reduced to selling their labour power in order to live. [*Note by Engels to the English edition of 1888.*]

to industrialized Europe a class war against the capitalists, the owners of the means of production. Exploited workers were to prepare themselves for the moment of revolution by joining with each other across national boundaries: "Workers of the world unite. You have nothing to lose but your chains." In light of subsequent events, the *Manifesto* appears to be a work of great predictive value. But neither Marx nor Engels realized that the hour of revolution was at hand.

Intellectuals and reformers hoped to reshape the world in which they lived with the force of their ideas. Yet the new ideologies were themselves the consequence of the changing role of government and the changing practices of daily life. The technology of industrial production influenced people's values and required a new way of looking at the world. Liberals, nationalists, romantics, conservatives, and socialists addressed the challenges of a changing economy in a political universe buffeted by democratic ideas. The new ideologies did not provide easy answers, but they did serve to incite their followers to take up arms in protests and revolutions throughout Europe.

PROTEST AND REVOLUTION

For European societies that had remained stable, if not stagnant, for centuries, the changes in the first half of the nineteenth century were undoubtedly startling and disruptive. New factories created the arena for exploitation and misery. More people than ever before lived in cities, and national populations faced the prospect of becoming urban. Urban congestion brought crime and disease; patterns of consumption demonstrated beyond dispute that people were not created equal. A new European society that challenged existing political ideas and demanded new political formulations was in the process of emerging.

Causes of Social Instability

The fabric of stability began unraveling throughout Europe in the 1820s. The forces of order reacted to protest with repression everywhere in Europe. Yet armed force proved inadequate to contain the demands for political participation and the increased political awareness of whole segments of the population. Workers, the middle class, and women's political organizations now demanded, through the vote, the right to govern themselves.

Urban Miseries.   In 1800, two of every 100 Europeans lived in a city. By 1850, the number of urban dwellers per hundred had jumped to five and was rising rapidly. In England, the shift was more concentrated than the general European pattern. With one of every two people living in a city, England had become an urban society by mid-century. London was the fastest-growing city in Europe, followed at some distance by Paris and Berlin. The numbers of smaller urban centers were also multiplying.

Massive internal migrations caused most urban growth. People from the same rural areas often lived together in the same urban neighborhoods, and even in the same boarding-houses. Irish emigrants crowded together in the "Little Dublin" section of London. Similarly, districts in other cities were set off by regional accents and native provincial dress. Workers from the same hometowns gravitated to their favorite cafes. The social networks helped make the transition from rural to urban life bearable for the tens of thousands of people who poured into Europe's cities in search of jobs and opportunity. Until mid-century, many migrants returned to their rural homes for the winter when work, especially in the building trades, was scarce in the city. Young migrant women who came to the city to work as servants sent money home to support rural relatives, or worked to save a nest egg—or dowry—with the plan of returning to the village permanently. Before 1850, 20 percent of the workers in London were domestics, and most of them were women.

Despite the support networks that migrants constructed for themselves, the city was not always a hospitable place. Workers were poorly paid, and women workers were more poorly paid than men. When working women were cut free of the support of home and family, uncounted numbers were forced into part-time prostitution to supplement meager in-comes. It is conservatively estimated that in 1850 there were 34,000 prostitutes in Paris and 50,000 in London. The phenomenon of prostitution indicated changing mores about sexuality in the first half of the nineteenth century. The "angel" of middle-class households and the "whore" of the streets were subjects of fascination in fiction and nonfiction. Increased prostitution created a veritable epidemic of venereal diseases, especially syphilis, for which there was no known cure until the twentieth century.

Urban crime also grew astronomically, with thefts accounting for the greatest number of crimes. Social reformers identified poverty and urban crowding as causes of the increase in criminal behavior. In 1829, both Paris and London began to create modern urban police forces to deal with the challenges to law and order. Crime assumed the character of disease in the minds of middle-class reformers. Statisticians and social scientists, themselves a new urban phenomenon, produced massive theses on social hygiene, lower-class immorality, and the unworthiness of the poor. The pathology of the city was widely discussed. Always at the center of the issue was the growing problem of what to do with the poor.

The Role of the State.   State-sponsored work relief expanded after 1830 for the deserving poor: the old, the sick, and children. Able-bodied workers who were idle were regarded as undeserving and dangerous, regardless of the causes of their unemployment. Performance of work became an indicator of moral worth as urban and rural workers succumbed to downturns in the economic cycle. Those unable to work sought relief from the state as a last resort. What has been called a "revolution in government" took place in the 1830s and 1840s as legislative bodies increased regulation of everything from factories and mines to prisons and schools.

Poverty was not just an urban problem, although it was both more conspicuous and more feared in urban areas. Politicians, social reformers, religious thinkers, and revolutionaries all had different solutions that followed one of two general orientations. There were those who argued, as in the

■ The Irish potato famine, one of the worst famines in modern history, afflicted the European poor in the 1840s.

case of the Irish famine, that the government must do nothing to intervene because the problem would correct itself, as Thomas Malthus had predicted 40 years earlier. Malthus had argued that the "positive" means of famine and death would keep population from outgrowing available resources and food supplies. The Irish population, one of the poorest in Europe, had indeed doubled between 1781 and 1841, and for Malthusians the Irish famine was the fulfillment of their vision that famine was the only way to correct overpopulation. Some insisted that poverty was a social necessity; by interfering with it, governments could only make matters worse.

Others contended that poverty was society's problem, and perhaps society's creation, and not a law of nature. Thus it was the social responsibility of the state to take care of its members. The question of how to treat poverty—or the "**social question**" as it came to be known among contemporaries—underlay many of the protests and reforms of the two decades before 1850 and fueled the revolutionary movements of 1848. Parliamentary legislation attempted to improve the situation of the poor, especially the working class, during the 1830s and 1840s. In 1833, British reformers turned their attention to the question of child labor. Against the opposition of those who argued for a free market for labor, Parliament passed the Factory Act of 1833, which prohibited the employment of children under nine years of age and restricted the workweek of children aged nine to thirteen to 48 hours. No child in this age group could work more than nine hours a day. Teenagers between 13 and 18 years could work no more than 69 hours a week. By modern standards, the "reformed" workloads present a shocking picture of the heavy reliance on child labor. The British Parliament commissioned investigations, compiled in the "Blue Books," that reported the abusive treatment of men, women, and children in factories. Similar studies existed for French and Belgian industry.

British legislation marked an initial step in state intervention in the workplace. Additional legislation over the next three decades further restricted children's and women's labor in factories and concerned itself with improving conditions in the workplace. Fundamentally, the "social question" was the question of what the state's role and responsibility were in caring for its citizens.

The Revolutions of 1830

Few Europeans alive in 1830 remembered the age of revolution that spanned the period from 1789 to 1799. Yet the legends were kept alive from one generation to the next. Secret political organizations perpetuated Jacobin republicanism. Mutual aid societies and artisans' associations preserved the rituals of democratic culture. A new generation of radicals seemed to be budding in the student riots in Germany and in the revolutionary waves that swept across southern and central Europe in the early 1820s. In August of 1819, a crowd of 80,000 people gathered outside Manchester, England, in St. Peter's Field to hear speeches for parliamentary reform and universal male suffrage. The cavalry swept down on them in a bloody slaughter that came to be

known as the **"Peterloo" Massacre,** a bitter reference to the Waterloo victory four years before.

Poor harvests in 1829 followed by a harsh winter left people cold, hungry, and bitter. Misery fueled social protest, and political issues of participation and representation commanded new attention. The convergence of social unrest with long-standing political demands touched off apparently simultaneous revolutions all over Europe. Governmental failure to respond to local grievances sparked the revolutions of 1830. Highly diverse groups of workers, students, lawyers, professionals, and peasants rose up spontaneously to demand a voice in the affairs of government.

The French Revolution of 1830. In France, the late 1820s were a period of increasing political friction. Charles X (1824–1830), the former comte d'Artois, had never resigned himself to the constitutional monarchy accepted by his brother and predecessor, Louis XVIII. When Charles assumed the throne in 1824, he dedicated himself to a true restoration of kingship as it had existed before the Revolution. To this end, he realigned the monarchy with the Catholic Church and undertook several unpopular measures, including approval of the death penalty for those found guilty of sacrilege. The king's bourgeois critics, heavily influenced by liberal ideas about political economy and constitutional rights, sought increased political power through their activities in secret organizations and in public elections. The king responded to his critics by relying on his ultraroyalist supporters to run the government. In May 1830, the king dissolved the Chamber of Deputies and ordered new elections. The elections returned a liberal majority unfavorable to the king. Charles X retaliated with what proved to be his last political act, the Four Ordinances, in which he censored the press, changed the electoral law to favor his own candidates, dissolved the newly elected Chamber, and ordered new elections.

Opposition to Charles X might have remained at the level of political wrangling and journalistic protest, if it had not been for the problems plaguing the people of Paris. A severe winter in France had driven up food prices by 75 percent. Most urban dwellers were barely subsisting. The king had erred in hoping that France's recent conquest of Algeria in North Africa would keep the populace quiet. He underestimated the extent of hardship and the political volatility of the population. Throughout the spring of 1830, prices continued to rise and Charles continued to blunder. In a spontaneous uprising in the last days of July 1830, workers took to the streets of Paris. The revolution they initiated spread rapidly to towns and the countryside as people throughout France protested the cost of living, hoarding by grain merchants, tax collection, and wage cuts. In "three glorious days," the restored Bourbon regime was pulled down and Charles X fled to England.

The people fighting in the streets demanded a republic, but they lacked organization and political experience. Liberal bourgeois politicians quickly filled the power vacuum. They presented Charles's cousin Louis-Philippe, formerly the duc d'Orléans, as the savior of France and the new constitutional

■ Barricade in the rue Dauphine, July 1830.

monarch. The July Monarchy, born of a revolution, put an end to the Bourbon Restoration. Louis-Philippe became "king of the French." The charter that he brought with him was, like its predecessor, based on restricted suffrage, with property ownership a requisite for voting. The voting age was lowered from 30 to 25, and the tax requirement was also lowered. The electorate nearly doubled, from 90,000 to 170,000, but nevertheless voting remained restricted to a small fraction of the population.

Unrest in Europe.   Popular disturbances did not always result in revolution. In Britain, rural and town riots erupted over grain prices and distribution, but no revolution followed. German workers broke their machines to protest low wages and loss of control of the workplace, but no prince was displaced. In Switzerland, reformers found strength in the French revolutionary example. Ten Swiss cantons granted liberal constitutions and established universal manhood suffrage, freedom of expression, and legal equality.

In southern Europe, Greece had languished as a subjugated country for centuries. Turkish overlords ruled Greece as part of the Ottoman Empire. The longing for independence smoldered in Greece throughout the 1820s as public pressure to support the Greeks mounted in Europe. Greek insurrections were answered by Turkish retaliations throughout the Ottoman Empire. In 1822, a Turkish fleet captured the island of Chios in the Aegean Sea off the west coast of Turkey and massacred or enslaved the population. The atrocities committed by the Turks against Greeks in Constantinople provoked international reaction in the form of a Philhellenic (literally, "lover of Greece") movement supported by two of Britain's great romantic poets,

Lord Byron (1788–1824) and Percy Bysshe Shelley (1792–1822). Byron sailed to the besieged Greek city of Missolonghi in 1824 to help coordinate the military effort, and there he contracted malaria and died. The sultan of Turkey had been able to call upon his vassal, the pasha of Egypt, to subdue Greece. In response, Great Britain, France, and Russia signed the Treaty of London in 1827, pledging intervention on behalf of Greece. In a joint effort, the three powers defeated the Egyptian fleet. Russia declared war on Turkey the following year, seeking territorial concessions from the Ottoman Empire. Following the Russian victory, Great Britain and France joined Russia in declaring Greek independence.

The concerted action of the three powers in favor of Greek independence was neither an endorsement of liberal ideals nor a support of Greek nationalism. The British, French, and Russians were reasserting their commitment made at the Congress of Vienna to territorial stability. Yet beneath the veneer of their commitment, the Russians intervened, hoping for territorial gains in the Ottoman Empire. The British favored Ottoman stability while distrusting Russian ambitions in the area. The Turks had been unable to maintain stability on their own. Finally, the three powers abandoned their policy of propping up the Ottoman Empire and supported instead the movement for Greek independence. But they did so on their own terms by creating a monarchy in Greece and placing a German-born prince on the new throne.

Belgian, Polish, and Italian Struggles.   The overthrow of the Bourbon monarch in France served as a model for revolution in other parts of Europe. Following the French lead, in the midst of the Greek crisis the Belgian provinces revolted against the Netherlands. The Belgians' desire for their own nation struck at the heart of the Vienna settlement. Provoked by a food crisis similar to that in France, Belgian revolutionaries took to the streets in August 1830. As a symbol of their solidarity with the successful French Revolution, they flew the tricolor in defiance of their Dutch rulers. Belgians protested the deterioration of their economic situation and made demands for their own Catholic religion, their own language, and constitutional rights. Bitter fighting on the barricades in Brussels ensued, and the movement for freedom and independence spread to the countryside.

The Great Powers disagreed on what to do. Russia, Austria, and Prussia were all eager to see the revolution crushed. France, having just established the new regime of the July Monarchy, and Great Britain, fearing the involvement of the central and eastern European powers in an area where Britain had traditionally had interests, were reluctant to intervene. A provisional government in Belgium set about the task of writing a constitution. All five great powers recognized Belgian independence, with the proviso that Belgium was to maintain the status of a neutral state.

Russia, Prussia, and Austria were convinced to accept Belgian independence because they were having their own problems in eastern and southern Europe. Revolution erupted to the east in Warsaw, Poland. Driven by a desire for national independence, Polish army cadets and university students revolted in November 1830, demanding a constitution.

DOCUMENT

The Books of the Polish Nation

Landed aristocrats and gentry helped establish a provisional government but soon split over how radical reforms should be. Polish peasants refused to support either landowning group. Within the year, Russia brought in 180,000 troops to crush the revolution and reassert its rule over Poland.

In February 1831, the Italian states of Modena and Parma rose up to throw off Austrian domination of northern Italy. The revolutionaries were ineffective against Austrian troops. Revolution in the Papal States resulted in French occupation that lasted until 1838 without serious reforms.

Nationalist and republican yearnings were driven underground, kept alive there in the Young Italy movement under the leadership of Giuseppe Mazzini.

Although the revolutions of 1830 are called "the forgotten revolutions" of the nineteenth century, they are important for several reasons. First, they made clear to European states how closely tied together were their fates. The events of 1830 were a test of the Great Powers' commitment to stability and a balance of power in Europe. True to the principles of the Vienna settlements of 1815, European leaders preserved the status quo. Revolutions in Poland and Italy were contained by Russia and Austria without interference from the other powers. Where adaptation was necessary, as in Greece and Belgium, the Great Powers were able to compromise on settlements, though the solutions ran counter to previous policies. Heads of state were willing to use the forces of repression to stamp out protest. Although each revolution followed its own pattern of development, all shared origins in domestic crises unsuccessfully addressed by those in power.

IMAGE DISCOVERY

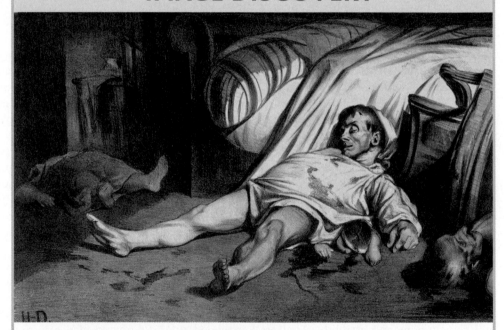

Rue Transnonain by Honoré Daumier

Workers launched an insurrection in Paris in the spring of 1834 against the labor policies of the French government. An officer was killed by sniper fire in the rue Transnonain. Before dawn on the next day, 14 April 1834, troops entered an apartment building on that street and killed many of the occupants by either shooting or bayoneting them. How many bodies do you see in this lithograph? What message about the victims is Daumier, the artist, conveying by the bedroom location of the scene? What story do the dead bodies, including that of the baby, tell? Lithographs were printed in large numbers especially for newspapers and journals. Is this a work of art or propaganda?

The international significance of the revolutions reveals a second important aspect of the events of 1830: the vulnerability of international politics to domestic instability. No state could practice diplomacy in a vacuum. Grain prices and demands for democratic participation had direct impact on the balance of power of European states. The five Great Powers broke down into two ideological camps. On the one hand were the liberal constitutional states of Great Britain and France, on the other stood the autocratic monarchies of Russia, Austria, and Prussia. Yet ideological differences were always less important than the shared desire for internal stability as a prerequisite for international peace.

Finally, the 1830 revolutions exposed a growing awareness of politics at all levels of European society. If policies in 1830 revealed a shared consciousness of events and shared values among ruling elites, the revolutions disclosed a growing awareness among the lower classes of the importance of politics in their daily lives. The cry for "liberty, equality, and fraternity" transcended national borders and the French language. The demands for constitutions, national identity, and civic equality resounded from the Atlantic to the Urals. In a dangerous combination of circumstances, workers and the lower classes throughout Europe were politicized, yet they continued to be excluded from political power.

Reform in Great Britain

The right to vote had been an issue of contention in the revolutions of 1830 in western Europe. Only the Swiss cantons enforced the principle of "one man, one vote." The July Revolution in France had doubled the electorate, but still only a tiny minority of the population (less than 1 percent) enjoyed the vote. Universal male suffrage had been mandated in 1793 during the Great Revolution but not implemented. Those in power believed that the wealthiest property owners were best qualified to govern, in part because they had the greatest stake in politics and society. One also needed to own property to hold office. Because those who served in parliaments received no salary, only the wealthy had the resources and the leisure to represent the electorate. When confronted by his critics, François Guizot (1787–1874), French prime minister and chief spokesman for the July Monarchy, offered this glib advice to an aspiring electorate: "Get rich!"

The Rule of the Landed.   Landowners also ruled Britain. There the dominance of a wealthy elite was strengthened by the geographic redistribution of population resulting from industrialization. Migration to cities had depleted the population of rural areas. Yet the electoral system did not adjust to the changes: large towns had no parliamentary representation, while dwindling county electorates maintained their parliamentary strength. Areas that continued to enjoy representation greater than that justified by their population were dubbed "rotten" or "pocket" boroughs to indicate a corrupt and antiquated electoral system. In general, urban areas were grossly underrepresented and the wealthy few controlled county seats.

Liberal reformers attempted to rectify the electoral inequalities by reassigning parliamentary seats on the basis of density of population, but vested interests balked at attempted reforms and members of Parliament wrangled bitterly. Popular agitation by the lower classes provoked the fear of civil war, which helped break the parliamentary deadlock. The **Great Reform Bill of 1832** proposed a compromise. Although the vast majority of the population still did not have the vote, the new legislation strengthened the industrial and commercial elite in the towns, enfranchised most of the middle class, opened the way to social reforms, and encouraged the formation of political parties.

Years of bad harvests, unemployment, and depression, coupled with growing dissatisfaction with the government's

■ This English cartoon of 1832 is titled "The Clemency of the Russian Monster." It shows Nicholas I in the guise of a bear with menacing teeth and claws addressing the Poles after crushing their rebellion against Russian rule.

'Gentlemen,' says Nicholas I, the bear, to the Polish revolutionaries of 1830, 'I know that you wish to address me; but to spare you from delivering a pack of lies, I desire that you hold your tongues.' The Polish rebellion of 1830–31 was brutally suppressed by the Russians. However, this brutality reinforced Polish national sentiment (the Poles rebelled again in 1863) and engaged the sympathy of the West for the Poles—as this English cartoon shows. (2)

weak efforts to address social problems, put the spur to a new national reform movement in the 1830s. Radical reformers, disillusioned with the 1832 Reform Bill because it strengthened the power of a wealthy capitalist class, argued that democracy was the only answer to the problems plaguing British society.

The Chartist Movement. In 1838, a small group of labor leaders, including representatives of the London Working Men's Association, an organization of craft workers, drew up a document known as the People's Charter. The single most important demand of the charter was that all men must have the vote. In addition, Chartists petitioned for a secret ballot, salaries for parliamentary service, elimination of the requirement that a person must own property in order to run for office, equal electoral districts, and annual elections. The proposal favored direct democracy, guaranteed by frequent elections that would ensure maximum accountability of officials to their constituents.

Chartist appeal was greatest in periods of economic hardship. A violent mood swept through the movement in 1839. The Irish Chartist leader Feargus O'Connor (1794–1855) and the Irish journalist and orator James Bronterre O'Brien (1805–1864) urged an unskilled and poorly organized working class to

MAP DISCOVERY

Unrest of the 1820s and 1830s: Centers of Revolutionary Action

What geographic and political features were common to the centers of popular unrest and revolutionary action in the 1820s and 1830s? How did the French Revolution of 1830 serve as a model for revolutionary action in the Belgian provinces, Poland, and the northern Italian states? How did political actions in Great Britain differ from those of the Continent in this period?

protest inequities through strikes that on occasion became violent. O'Brien thrilled his working-class listeners by haranguing "the big-bellied, little-brained, numbskull aristocracy." **Chartism** blossomed as a communal phenomenon in working-class towns and appeared to involve all members of the family: "Every kitchen is now a political meeting house; the little children are members of the unions and the good mother is the political teacher," one Chartist organizer boasted. Chartist babies were christened with the names of Chartist heroes. When Mrs. King of Manchester, England, attempted to register the birth of her son, James Feargus O'Connor King, her choice of names was challenged. The registrar demanded,

"Is your husband a Chartist?" Mrs. King replied, "I don't know, but his wife is." Women organized Chartist schools and Sunday schools in radical defiance of local church organizations. Many middle-class observers were sure that the moment for class war and revolutionary upheaval had arrived. The government responded with force to the perceived threat of armed rebellion and imprisoned a number of Chartist leaders.

Throughout the 1840s, bad harvests and economic hardships continued to fan the flames of discontent. National petitions signed by millions were submitted to the House of Commons, which stubbornly resisted the idea of universal manhood suffrage. Strikes and attacks on factories spread throughout

England, Scotland, and Wales in 1842. Increased violence served to make the Parliament intransigent and caused the movement to splinter and weaken as moderates formed their own factions. The final moment for Chartism occurred in April 1848 when 25,000 Chartist workers, inspired by revolutionary events on the Continent, assembled in London to march on the House of Commons. They carried with them a newly signed petition demanding the enactment of the terms of the People's Charter. In response, the government deputized nearly 200,000 "special" constables in the streets. The deputized private citizens were London property owners and skilled workers intent on holding back a revolutionary rabble. Tired, cold, and rain-soaked, the Chartist demonstrators disbanded. No social revolution took place in Great Britain, and the dilemma of democratic representation was deferred.

Workers Unite

The word **proletariat** entered European languages before the mid-nineteenth century to describe those workers afloat in the labor pool who owned nothing, not even the tools of their labor, and who were becoming "appendages" to the new machines that dominated production. To workers, machines could mean the elimination of jobs or the de-skilling of tasks; almost always machines meant a drop in wages.

Luddism. Mechanization deprived skilled craft workers of control of the workplace. In Great Britain, France, and Germany, groups of textile workers destroyed machines in protest. Workers demanding a fair wage smashed cotton power looms, knitting machines, and wool-carding machines. Sometimes the machines were a bargaining point for workers who used violence against them as a last resort. Machine-breakers tyrannized parts of Great Britain from 1811 to 1816 in an attempt to frighten masters. The movement was known as Luddism after its mythical leader, Ned Ludd. Workers damaged and destroyed property for more control over the work process, but such destruction met with severe repression. From the 1820s to the 1850s, sporadic but intense outbursts of machine-breaking occurred in continental Europe. Suffering weavers in Silesia and Bohemia resorted to destroying their looms in 1844.

Craft production continued to deteriorate with the rise in industrial competition. Skilled workers, fearing that they would be pulled down into the new proletariat because of mechanization and the increased scale of production, began organizing in new ways after 1830 by forming associations to assert their control over the workplace and to demand a voice in politics.

In Britain, skilled craft workers built on a tradition of citizenship. They resisted the encroachments of factory production, and some channeled their political fervor into the Chartist movement. Skilled workers in France also built on a cultural heritage of shared language and values to create a consciousness of themselves as an exploited class. Uprisings and strikes in France, favoring the destruction of the monarchy and the creation of a democratic republic, increased dra-matically from 1831 to 1834. Many French craft workers grew conscious of themselves as a class and embraced a socialism heavily influenced by their own traditions and contemporary socialist writings. Republican socialism spread throughout France by means of a network of traveling journeymen and tapped into growing economic hardship and political discontent with the July Monarchy. Government repression drove worker organizations underground in the late 1830s, but secret societies proliferated. Increasingly, workers saw the validity of the slogan of the silk workers of Lyon: "Live Working or Die Fighting!"

Women in the Work Force. Women were an important part of the work force in the industrializing societies. Working men were keenly aware of the competition with cheaper female labor in the factories. Women formed a salaried work force in the home, too. In order to turn out products cheaply and in large quantities, some manufacturers turned to subcontractors to perform the simpler tasks in the work process. The new middlemen contracted out work such as cutting and sewing to needy women who were often responsible for caring for family members in their homes. That kind of subcontracting, called "sweated labor" because of the exertion and long hours involved in working in one's own home, was always poorly paid.

Cheap female labor paid by the piece allowed employers to profit by keeping overhead costs low and by driving down the wages of skilled workers. Trade unions opposed women's work, both in the home and in the factories. Women's talents, union leaders explained, were more properly devoted to domestic chores. Unions argued that their members should earn a family wage "sufficient to support a wife and children." Unions consistently excluded women workers from their ranks.

French labor leader Flora Tristan, speaking not only as a worker but also as a wife and mother, had a very different answer for those who wanted to remove women from the workplace and assign them to their "proper place" in the home. She recognized that working women needed to work in order to support themselves and their families. Tristan told audiences in Europe and Latin America that the emancipation of women from their "slave status" was essential if the working class as a whole was to enjoy a better future. She deplored the economic competition between working men and women and denounced the degradation of women in both the home and the workplace. A working woman earned one-third or less of the average working man's wages, and women's working conditions were often deplorable. In the 1840s, British parliamentary commissions heard the horrifying testimony of one young London dressmaker from the country who was forced to work grueling hours—often 20 hours a day—under unhealthy working conditions that had destroyed her health. She concluded that "no men could endure the work enforced from the dressmakers."

Working women's only hope, according to Tristan, lay in education and unionization. She urged working men and

FLORA TRISTAN AND THE RIGHTS OF WORKING WOMEN

Flora Tristan (1803–1844) was a feminist and socialist who in the 1830s was actively involved in efforts to reintroduce divorce and to abolish the death penalty. She made her greatest political efforts for the creation of an international union of workers. The education of women was, Tristan asserted, essential for the success and prosperity of the working class. She toured slums in England and traveled across France on lecture tours to promote workers' unions and the education of women. The excerpt below is taken from her important book, L'Union Ouvriére, 1843. *Tristan's argument for women's education is based not only on the claims of women to basic human rights, but on her assertion that educated women held the key to the betterment of families, the working class, and the whole society.*

Focus Questions

Why is education so important in Tristan's justification of women's rights? Would you describe Tristan as a reformer or a revolutionary?

. . . [I]t is imperative, in order to improve the intellectual, moral, and material condition of the working class, that women of the lower classes be given a rational and solid education, conducive to the development of their good inclinations, so that they may become skillful workers, good mothers, capable of raising and guiding their children, and of tutoring them in their school work, and so that they may act as moralizing agents in the life of the men on whom they exert an influence from the cradle to the grave.

Do you begin to understand, you, men, who cry shame before even looking into the question, why I demand rights for woman? Why I should like her to be placed on a footing of absolute equality with man in society, and that she should be so by virtue of the legal right every human being brings at birth?

I demand rights for women because I am convinced that all the misfortunes in the world result from the neglect and contempt in which woman's natural and inalienable rights have so far been held. I demand rights for woman because it is the only way she will get an education, and because the education of man in general and man of the lower classes in particular depends on the education of woman. I demand rights for woman because it is the only way to obtain her rehabilitation in the Church, the law, and society, and because this preliminary rehabilitation is necessary to achieve the rehabilitation of the workers themselves. All the woes of the working class can be summed up in these two words: poverty and ignorance, ignorance and poverty. Now, I see only one way out of this labyrinth: begin by educating women, because women have the responsibility of educating male and female children. . . .

As soon as the dangerous consequences of the development of the moral and physical faculties of women—dangerous because of women's current slave status—are no longer feared, woman can be taught with great care so as to make the best possible use of her intelligence and work. Then, you, men of the lower classes, will have as mothers skillful workers who earn a decent salary, are educated, well brought up, and quite capable of raising you, of educating you, the workers, as is proper for free men. You will have well brought up and well educated sisters, lovers, wives, friends, with whom daily contacts will be most pleasant for you. Nothing is sweeter or more agreeable to a man's heart than the sensible and gracious conversation of good and well educated women.

women to join together to lay claim to their natural and inalienable rights. In some cases, working women formed their own organizations, like that of the Parisian seamstresses who joined together to demand improved working conditions. On the whole, however, domestic workers in the home remained isolated from other working women, and many women in factories feared the loss of their jobs if they engaged in political activism. The wages of Europe's working women remained low, often below the level of subsistence. In the absence of a man's income, working women and their children were the poorest of the poor in European society in the middle of the nineteenth century.

For some men and women of the working class, the 1840s were a time of mounting unrest, increased organization, and growing protest. Workers used their unity in associations, unions, and mutual aid societies to press for full political participation and government action in times of economic distress.

Revolutions Across Europe, 1848–1850

Europeans had never experienced a year like 1848. Beginning soon after the ringing in of the New Year, revolutionary fervor swept through nearly every European country. By year's end, regimes had been created and destroyed. France, Italy, the German states, Austria, Hungary, and Bohemia were shaken to their foundations. Switzerland, Denmark, and Romania experienced lesser upheavals. Great Britain had survived re-

■ Meeting of Chartists on Kennington Common, 15 April 1848.

formist agitation, and famine-crippled Ireland had endured a failed insurrection. No one was sure what had happened. Each country's conflict was based on a unique mix of issues, but all were connected in their conscious emulation of a revolutionary tradition.

Hindsight reveals warning signs in the two years before the 1848 cataclysm. Beginning in 1846, a severe famine—the last serious food crisis Europe would experience—racked Europe. Lack of grain drove up prices. An increasing percentage of disposable income was spent on food for survival. Lack of spending power severely damaged markets and forced thousands of industrial workers out of their jobs. The famine hurt everyone—the poor, workers, employers, and investors—as recession paralyzed the economy.

The food crisis took place in a heavily charged political atmosphere. Throughout Europe during the 1840s, the middle and lower classes had intensified their agitation for democracy. Chartists in Great Britain argued for a wider electorate. Bourgeois reformers in France campaigned for universal manhood suffrage. Known as the "banquet" campaign because its leaders attempted to raise money by giving speeches at subscribed dinners, the movement for the vote appeared to be developing a mass following by taking its cause directly to the people. In making demands for political participation, those agitating for suffrage necessarily criticized those in power. Freedom of speech and freedom of assembly were demanded as inalienable rights. The food crisis and political activism provided the ingredients for an incendiary situation.

In addition to a burgeoning democratic culture, growing demands for national autonomy based on linguistic and cultural claims spread through central, southern, and eastern Europe. The revolts in Poland in 1846, though failures, encouraged similar movements for national liberation among Italians and Germans. Even in the relatively homogeneous nation of France, concerns with national mission and national glory grew among the regime's critics. National unity was primarily a middle-class ideal. Liberal lawyers, teachers, and businessmen from Dublin to Budapest to Prague agitated for separation from foreign rule. Austria, with an empire formed of numerous ethnic minorities, had the most to lose. Since 1815, Metternich had been ruthless in stamping out nationalist dissent. However, by the 1840s, national claims were assuming a cultural legitimacy that was difficult to dismiss or ignore.

France Leads the Way.   The events in France in the cold February of 1848 ignited the conflagration that swept Europe. Bourgeois reformers had arranged for their largest banquet to date in support of extension of the vote, to take place in Paris on 22 February. City officials became nervous at the prospect of thousands of workers assembling for political purposes and canceled the scheduled banquet. That was the spark that touched off the powder keg. In a spontaneous uprising, Parisians demonstrated against the government's repressive measures. Skilled workers took to the streets, not only in favor of the banned banquet but also with the hope that the government would recognize the importance of labor to the social order. Shots were fired; a demonstrator was killed. The French Revolution of 1848 had begun.

Events moved quickly. The National Guard, a citizen militia of bourgeois Parisians, defected from Louis-Philippe. Many army troops garrisoned in Paris crossed the barricades to join revolutionary workers. The king attempted some reform, but it was too little and too late. Louis-Philippe fled. The Second Republic was proclaimed at the insistence of the revolutionary crowds on the barricades. The Provisional Government, led by the poet Alphonse de Lamartine (1790–1869), included members of both factions of political reformers of the July Monarchy: moderates who sought constitutional reforms and an extension of the suffrage, and radicals who favored universal manhood suffrage and social programs to deal with poverty and work. Only the threat of popular violence held together the uneasy alliance.

The people fighting in the streets had little in common with the bourgeois reformers who assumed power on 24 February. Workers made a social revolution out of a commitment to their "right to work," which would replace the right to property as the organizing principle of the new society. Only one member of the new Provisional Government was a worker, and he was included as a token symbol of the intentions of the new government. He was known as "Albert, the worker," and was not addressed by his surname, Martin. The government acknowledged the demand of the "right to work" and set up two mechanisms to guarantee workers' relief. First, a commission of workers and employers was created to act as a grievance and bargaining board and settle questions of common

concern in the workplace. Headed by the socialist Louis Blanc (1811–1882) and known as the Luxembourg Commission, the worker-employer parliament was an important innovation, but it accomplished little other than deflecting workers' attention away from the problems of the Provisional Government. The second measure was the creation of "national workshops" to deal with the problems of unemployment in Paris. Although the name was taken from Blanc's plan for worker control of production, the national workshops were no more than an inefficient charity program that paid men minimal wages. The national workshops quickly proved disastrous. Workers from all over France poured into Paris with the hope of finding jobs. However, the workshops had a residency requirement that even Parisians had difficulty meeting. As a result, unemployment skyrocketed. Furthermore, the government was going bankrupt trying to support the program. The need to raise taxes upset peasants in the provinces. National pressure mounted to repudiate the programs of the revolution.

French workers were too weak to dominate the revolution. The government dissolved the workshops and recalled General Louis Cavaignac (1802–1857) from service in Algeria to maintain order. In a wave of armed insurrection, Parisian workers rebelled in June. Using provincial troops having no identification with the urban population and employing guerrilla techniques he had mastered in Algeria, Cavaignac put down the uprising. The June fighting was the bloodiest that Paris had ever seen. The Second Republic was placed under the military dictatorship of Cavaignac until December, when presidential elections were scheduled.

Revolutions in Central and Eastern Europe. The overthrow of the July Monarchy at the end of February set off shock waves of protest in central and eastern Europe. Long-suppressed desires for civil liberties and constitutional reforms erupted in widespread popular disturbances through-

■ Club-wielding police break up a radical demonstration in Berlin, the capital of Prussia, in 1848. In March, King Frederick William of Prussia acceded to the demands of liberal reformers. But in November, after uprisings against conservative regimes elsewhere in Europe had been put down, the monarch allowed the Prussian army to regain control of Berlin.

MAP DISCOVERY

Revolutions of 1848

The Revolutions of 1848

In less than a generation, a second major wave of revolutions swept across Europe from west to east in 1848. What were the centers of revolutionary action in 1848 and what was their relationship to the seats of political power? How do you explain the timing of the eastern trajectory of successive revolutions? How did the map of Europe change as a result of these revolutions?

out Prussia and the German states. Fearing a war with France and unable to count on Austria or Russia for support, the princes who ruled Baden, Württemberg, Hesse-Darmstadt, Bavaria, Saxony, and Hanover followed the advice of moderate liberals and acceded quickly to revolutionary demands. In Prussia, Kaiser Friedrich Wilhelm IV (1840–1861) preferred to use military force to respond to popular demonstrations. Only in mid-March 1848 did the Prussian king yield to the force of the revolutionary crowds building barricades in Berlin by ordering his troops to leave the city and by promising to create a national Prussian assembly. The king was now a prisoner of the revolution.

Meanwhile, the collapse of absolute monarchy in Prussia gave further impetus to a constitutional movement among the liberal leaders of the German states. The governments of all the German states were invited to elect delegates to a national parliament in Frankfurt. The Frankfurt Assembly, which was convened in May 1848, had as its dual charge the framing of a constitution and the unification of Germany. It was composed for the most part of members of the middle class, with civil servants, lawyers, and intellectuals predominating. In spite of the principle of universal manhood suffrage, no members of the working class served among the 800 men elected. To most of the delegates, who had been trained in universities and shared a social and cultural identity, nationalism and constitutionalism were inextricably related.

As straightforward as the desire for a German nation appeared to be, it was complicated by two important facts. First, there were non-German minorities living in German states. What was to be done with the Poles, Czechs, Slovenes, Italians, and Dutch in a newly constituted and autonomous German nation? Second, there were Germans living outside the German states under Habsburg rule in Austria, in Danish Schleswig and Holstein, in Posen (Poznan), in Russian Poland, and in European Russia. How were they to be included within the linguistically and ethnically constituted German nation? No matter how small the circle was drawn, it included non-Germans; no matter how wide, it excluded Germans. After much wrangling over a "small" Germany that excluded Austrian Germans and a "large" Germany that included them, the Frankfurt Assembly opted for the small-Germany solution in March 1849. The crown of the new nation was offered to the unpredictable Friedrich Wilhelm IV of Prussia, head of the largest and most powerful of the German states. Unhappy with his capitulation to the revolutionary crowd in March 1848, the Prussian king refused to accept a "crown from the gutter." He had his own plans to rule over a middle-European bloc, but not at the behest of a liberal parliament. The attempt to create a German nation crumbled with his unwillingness to lead.

Revolution in Austrian-dominated central Europe was concentrated in three places: Vienna, where German-speaking students, workers, and middle-class liberals were agitating for constitutional reform and political participation; Budapest, where the Magyars, the dominant ethnic group in Hungary, led a movement for national autonomy; and Prague, where Czechs were attempting self-rule. By April 1848, Metternich had fallen from power and the Viennese revolutionaries had set up a constituent assembly. In Budapest, the initial steps of the patriot Lajos Kossuth (1802–1894) toward establishing a separate Hungarian state seemed equally solid as the Magyars defeated Habsburg troops. Habsburg armies were more successful in Prague, where they crushed the revolution in June 1848. In December 1848, Emperor Ferdinand I (1835–1848), whose authority had been weakened irreparably by the overthrow of Metternich, abdicated in favor of his 18-year-old nephew, Franz Josef I (1848–1916).

DOCUMENT

Metternich on
Revolutions of
1848

Italian Nationalism. The Habsburg Empire was also under siege on the Italian Peninsula, where the Kingdom of the Two Sicilies, Tuscany, and Piedmont declared new constitutions in March 1848. Championed by Charles Albert of Piedmont, Venice and Lombardy rose up against Austria. Italian middle-class intellectuals and professionals championed the idea of national unification and the expulsion of the hated Austrian overlords. Nationalist sentiments had percolated underground in the Young Italy movement, founded in 1831 by Giuseppe Mazzini. A tireless and idealistic patriot,

CHRONOLOGY

Protest and Revolution

August 1819	Peterloo Massacre
1824	Charles X assumes French throne
1827	Treaty of London to support liberation of Greece
July 1830	Revolution in Paris; creation of July Monarchy under Louis-Philippe
August 1830	Revolution in Belgium
November 1830	Revolution in Poland
1831–1838	Revolutions in Italian states
1831–1834	Labor protests in France
1832	Britain's Great Reform Bill
1838	Drawing up of the first People's Charter in Britain
1846	Beginning of food crisis in Europe; revolts in Poland
1846–1848	Europewide movements for national liberation
February 1848	Revolution in France; overthrow of the July Monarchy; proclamation of the French Second Republic and creation of Provisional Government
March 1848	Uprisings in some German states; granting of a constitution in Prussia
March 1848– June 1849	Revolutions in Italy
April 1848	Revolutions in Vienna, Budapest, Prague
May 1848	Frankfurt Assembly
June 1848	Second revolution in Paris, severely repressed by army troops under General Cavaignac
December 1848	Presidential elections in France; Louis Napoleon wins

Mazzini favored a democratic revolution. In spite of his reputation as a liberal, Pope Pius IX (1846–1878) lost control of Rome and was forced to flee the city. Mazzini became head of the Republic of Rome, created in February 1849.

The French government decided to intervene to protect the pope's interests and sent in troops to defeat the republicans. One of Mazzini's disciples, Giuseppe Garibaldi (1807–1882), returned from exile in South America to undertake the defense of Rome. Garibaldi was a capable soldier who had learned the tactics of guerrilla warfare by joining independence struggles in Brazil and Argentina. Although his legion of poorly armed patriots and soldiers of fortune, known from their attire as the Red Shirts, waged a valiant effort to defend the city from April to June 1849, they were no match for the highly trained French army. French troops restored Pius IX as ruler of the Papal States.

Meanwhile, from August 1848 to the following spring, the Habsburg armies fought and finally defeated each of the revolutions. Austrian success can be explained in part because the various Italian groups of Piedmontese, Tuscans, Venetians, Romans, and Neapolitans continued to identify with their local concerns and lacked coordination and central organization. Both Mazzini and Pius IX had failed to provide the focal point of leadership necessary for a successful national movement. By the fall of 1849, Austria had solved the problems in its own capital and with Italy and Hungary by military repression.

Europe in 1850. In 1850, Austrians threatened the Prussians with war if they did not give up their plans for a unified Germany. In November of that year, Prussian ministers signed an agreement with their Austrian counterparts in the Moravian city of Olmütz. The convention became known as "the humiliation of Olmütz" because Prussia was forced to accept Austrian dominance or go to war. In every case, military force and diplomatic measures prevailed to defeat the national and liberal movements within the German states and the Austrian Empire.

By 1850, a veneer of calm had spread over central Europe. In Prussia, the peasantry were emancipated from feudal dues, and a constitution, albeit conservative and based on a three-class system, was established. Yet beneath the surface, there was the deeper reality of Austrian decline and Prussian challenge. The great Habsburg Empire needed to call on outside help from Russia to defeat its enemies within. The imperial giant was again on its feet, but for how long? In international relations, Austria's dominance in the German Confederation had diminished, while Prussia assumed greater political and economic power.

The 1848 revolutions spelled the end to the concert of Europe as it had been defined in the peace settlement of 1815. The European powers were incapable of united action to defend established territorial interests.

The revolutions of 1848 failed in part because of the irreconcilable split between moderate liberals and radical democrats. The participation of the masses had frightened members of the middle classes, who were committed to moderate reforms that did not threaten property. In France, working-class revolutionaries had attempted to replace property with labor as the highest social value. Property triumphed. In the face of more extreme solutions, members of the middle class were willing to accept the increased authority of existing rule as a bulwark against anarchy. In December 1848, Prince Louis Napoleon, nephew of the former emperor, was elected president of the

Second Republic by a wide margin. The first truly modern French politician, Louis Napoleon managed to appeal to everyone—workers, bourgeois, royalists, and peasants—by making promises that he did not keep. Severe repression forced radical protest into hiding. The new Bonaparte bided his time, apparently as an ineffectual ruler, until the moment in 1851 when he seized absolute power.

Similar patterns emerged elsewhere in Europe. In Germany, the bourgeoisie accepted the dominance of the old feudal aristocracy as a guarantee of law and order. Repressive government, businessmen were sure, would restore a strong economy. The attempts in 1848 to create new nations based on ethnic identities were in shambles by 1850.

Nearly everywhere throughout Europe, constitutions had been systematically withdrawn with the recovery of the forces of reaction. With the French and Swiss exceptions, the bid for the extension of the franchise failed. The propertied classes remained in control of political institutions. Radicals willing to use violence to press electoral reforms were arrested, killed, or exiled. The leadership of the revolutionary movements had been decapitated, and there seemed no effective opposition to the rise and consolidation of state power. The 1848 revolutions have been called a turning point at which modern history failed to turn. Contemporaries wondered how so much action could have produced so few lasting results.

CONCLUSION

The perception that nothing had changed was wrong. The revolutions of 1848 and subsequent events galvanized whole societies to political action. Conservatives and radicals alike turned toward a new realism in politics. Everywhere governments were forced to adapt to new social realities. No longer could the state ignore economic upheavals and social dislocations if it wanted to survive. Revolutionaries also learned the lesson of repression. The state wielded powerful forces of violence against which nationalists, socialists, republicans, and liberals had all been proved helpless. Organizing, campaigning, and lobbying were newly learned political skills, as was outreach across class lines—from bourgeoisie to peasantry—around common political causes. In these ways, 1848 was a turning point in the formation of a modern political culture.

QUESTIONS FOR REVIEW

1. What problems did European peacemakers confront at the Congress of Vienna, and how did they attempt to resolve the problems?
2. How did industrialization change European families?
3. In what ways were liberalism and nationalism compatible with each other; how were they in conflict?
4. What are the connections between various ideologies—for instance, liberalism, romanticism, or socialism—and the revolutions of 1830 and 1848?

KEY TERMS

Chartism, *p. 674*

The Communist Manifesto, p. 667

Congress of Vienna, *p. 655*

conservatism, *p. 659*

Great Hunger, *p. 652*

Great Reform Bill of 1832, *p. 673*

Holy Alliance, *p. 658*

liberalism, *p. 660*

"Peterloo" Massacre, *p. 670*

proletariat, *p. 675*

Quadruple Alliance, *p. 658*

Quintuple Alliance, *p. 658*

romanticism, *p. 661*

"social question," *p. 670*

utilitarianism, *p. 660*

DISCOVERING WESTERN CIVILIZATION ONLINE

You can obtain more information about political upheavals and social transformations between 1815 and 1850 at the Websites listed below. See also the Companion Website that accompanies this text, www.ablongman.com/kishlansky, which contains an online study guide and additional resources.

Geographical Tour: Europe in 1815

Internet Modern History Sourcebook: Conservative Order

www.fordham.edu/halsall/mod/modsbook16.html

The site provides documents, discussions, and bibliographies on the Congress of Vienna and charts the development of conservative thought.

The New Ideologies

McMaster University Archive for the History of Economic Thought

socserv.mcmaster.ca/econ/ugcm/3ll3

A site for texts in modern economic theory.

Internet Modern History Sourcebook: Liberalism

www.fordham.edu/halsall/mod/modsbook18.html

A collection of links to primary documents and bibliographies on liberalism.

Internet Modern History Sourcebook: Nationalism

www.fordham.edu/halsall/mod/modsbook17.html

The Nationalism Project

www.nationalismproject.org/

These sites provide links to primary documents and bibliographies of nationalism.

Internet Modern History Sourcebook: Romanticism

www.fordham.edu/halsall/mod/modsbook15.html

This site provides links to primary texts on romantic philosophy and literature.

Voice of the Shuttle

vos.ucsb.edu/index.asp

This comprehensive database for humanities research provides links to general resources, criticism, and primary texts. Type "Romantics" into the search function for resources on romantic philosophy and literature.

Marxist Internet Archive: Marxist Writers

www.marxists.org/archive/index.htm

The site provides translated texts of Marx and Engels as well as other prominent Social Democrats and Communists.

Protest and Revolution

Child Labour in the 19th Century

www.spartacus.schoolnet.co.uk/IRchild.htm

A collection of biographies of reformers and promoters of child labor laws, electronic texts of major child labor legislation, and excerpts from primary sources concerning child labor in nineteenth-century Britain.

The Emancipation of Women: 1750–1920

www.spartacus.schoolnet.co.uk/women.htm

The site contains links to biographies of major figures, essays on the major organizations and societies, and electronic texts of the women's movement in Britain.

Internet Modern History Sourcebook: 1848

www.fordham.edu/halsall/mod/modsbook19.html

The site provides documents, discussions, bibliographies and other links on the revolutions of 1848.

SUGGESTIONS FOR FURTHER READING

Geographical Tour: Europe in 1815

Tim Chapman, *The Congress of Vienna: Origins, Processes, and Results* (New York: Routledge, 1998). A brief, comprehensive survey of how the European powers victorious against Napoleon redrew Europe's frontiers. It follows the impact of the Settlement to its demise in the twentieth century.

Robert Gildea, *Barricades and Borders, Europe 1800–1914* (Oxford: Oxford University Press, 1996). A synthetic overview of economic, demographic, political, and international trends in European society.

Robin Okey, *The Habsburg Monarchy: From Enlightenment to Eclipse* (New York: St. Martin's Press, 2001). An informative survey of Austrian rule from the mid-eighteenth century to the end of World War I, which contains an annotated bibliography and materials drawn from historiographic material in Magyar, Serbo-Croat, Czech, and other eastern European language sources.

The New Ideologies

Jonathan Beecher, *Charles Fourier: The Visionary and His World* (Berkeley: University of California Press, 1986). An intellectual biography that traces the development of Fourier's theoretical perspective and roots it firmly in the social context of nineteenth-century France.

Gareth Stedman Jones, *Languages of Class: Studies in English Working Class History, 1832–1982* (Cambridge: Cambridge University Press, 1983). A series of essays, on topics such as working-class culture and Chartism, that examine the development of class consciousness.

William H. Sewell, Jr., *Work and Revolution in France: The Language of Labor from the Old Regime to 1848* (Cambridge: Cambridge University Press, 1980). Traces nineteenth-century working-class socialism to the corporate culture of Old Regime guilds through traditional values, norms, language, and artisan organizations.

Denis Mack Smith, *Mazzini* (New Haven, CT: Yale University Press, 1994). Mazzini is presented as an important force in legitimizing Italian nationalism by associating it with republicanism and the interests of humanity.

Edward P. Thompson, *The Making of the English Working Class* (New York: Pantheon Books, 1963). A classic in social history that spans the late eighteenth to mid-nineteenth centuries in examining the social, political, and cultural contexts in which workers created their own identity and put forward their own demands.

Protest and Revolution

Maurice Agulhon, *The Republican Experiment, 1848–1852* (Cambridge: Cambridge University Press, 1983). Traces the Revolution of 1848 from its roots to its ultimate failure in 1852 through an analysis of the republican ideologies of workers, peasants, and the bourgeoisie.

Clive Church, *Europe in 1830: Revolution and Political Change* (London: Allen & Unwin, 1983). Considers the origins of the 1830 revolutions within a wider European crisis through a comparative analysis of European regions.

Dieter Dowe, H. G. Haupt, D. Langewiesche, J. Sperber, and D. Higgins, eds., *Europe in 1848: Revolution and Reform* (New York: Berghahn Books, 2001). A collection by leading nineteenth-century European historians.

R. J. W. Evans and Hartmut Pogge von Strandmann, eds., *The Revolutions in Europe, 1848–1849: From Reform to Reaction* (Oxford: Oxford University Press, 2000). A focused collection of articles on the mid-nineteenth-century collapse of authority across Europe.

Alan J. Kidd, *State, Society, and the Poor in Nineteenth-Century England* (New York: St. Martin's Press, 1999). This volume is part of the *Social History in Perspective* series; it provides an overview of poverty in industrializing England, the role of the poor laws, public welfare, and charitable organizations in the nineteenth century.

Catherine J. Kudlick, *Cholera in Post-Revolutionary Paris: A Cultural History* (Berkeley: University of California Press, 1996). Examines the cultural values of ruling elites and demonstrates the role disease played in shaping political life and class identity in nineteenth-century France.

Patricia O'Brien, *The Promise of Punishment: Prisons in Nineteenth-Century France* (Princeton: Princeton University Press, 1982). An overview of the creation of the penitentiary system in nineteenth-century France and the rise of the new science of punishment, criminology, and the eventual appearance of alternatives to the penitentiary system.

Cormac O'Grada and A. Eriksson, *Ireland's Great Famine: Interdisciplinary Essays* (Dublin: University College Dublin Press, 2006). These authors have done extensive work in the Famine Archives of Ireland.

Redcliffe N. Salaman, *The History and Social Influence of the Potato,* revised impression edited by J. G. Hawkes (Cambridge: Cambridge University Press, 1985). The classic study of the potato. A major portion of the work is devoted to the potato famine.

Jonathan Sperber, *Revolutionary Europe, 1780–1850* (New York: Longman, 2000). Considers the revolutions of 1848 within the context of economic and social changes rooted in Old Regime politics and society and from the perspective of the twenty-first century.

For a list of additional titles related to this chapter's topics, please see http://www.ablongman.com/kishlansky.

STATE BUILDING AND SOCIAL CHANGE IN EUROPE, 1850–1871

THE CRYSTAL PALACE EXHIBITION OF 1851

SYMBOL OF A NEW AGE

On 1 May 1851, Queen Victoria inaugurated the first world's fair in history. The "Great Exhibition of Works of Industry of All Nations" was an extraordinary international display of science and technology combined with industry and commerce. Nations sought to highlight their achievements with submissions that included everything from looms to reapers to envelope folders. Labor-saving devices for the kitchen stood alongside steel-making displays.

THE VISUAL RECORD Perhaps the greatest display of all was the very building in which the Exhibition of 1851 was housed—the Crystal Palace, so named because its walls and roof were made of clear glass, held in place by iron girders. The building was a third of a mile long with 800,000 square feet of floor space. Designed by Joseph Paxton, a gardener and landscaper, the Crystal Palace resembled a giant greenhouse dedicated to the fruits of industrial civilization. Trees and statuary stood within the giant pavilion, which housed exhibits off a central avenue and in upstairs galleries. Twelve thousand fountains surrounded the Palace in open park space. In the five and a half months in which the Exhibition was open, it welcomed over six million visitors. The Crystal Palace was hailed as an unprecedented marvel of engineering and excess, all the more impressive because it was a temporary structure, taken down from its site in London's Hyde Park in 1852.

In hosting such an exhibition, Great Britain made clear to the world its role as industrial leader. It also showcased its new empire with exhibits from India, Australia, and New Zealand. Products from all regions of the world were represented. Following two difficult decades of political and social upheaval in Europe, the Exhibition gave viewers the sense that a corner had been turned and that technology promised a rosy future.

Spectators were dazzled by what they saw. On a self-congratulatory note a British magazine of the time reported: "Seventeen thousand exhibitors, who like the visitors were of almost every nation and kindred under heaven, entrusted the most valuable evidences of their wealth, their skill, their industry, and their enterprise to the guardianship of some fifty policemen, armed with no better weapon than a wooden baton. Day after day and night after night passed on, and no added force was requisite for the safety of the almost countless wealth deposited within these fragile walls. In no other country of the world could such an exhibition of the industrial arts have taken place." Yet the French won more medals for design and style than any other country.

Some subsequent commentators consider the Crystal Palace Exhibition a defining event in the history of the nineteenth century. Not everyone agreed. Karl Marx denounced the Crystal Palace Exhibition as the worst kind of capitalist fetishism. But it was Prince Albert, Victoria's consort, who captured the essence of the Crystal Palace when he characterized the 1851 event as "a new starting point from which all nations would be able to direct their further exertions."

LOOKING AHEAD

In this chapter we will examine the period between 1850 and 1871, when unification of territories was an important part of the process of building a nation in both Germany and Italy. Successful statesmen were diplomats who used alliances to further national interests. They were also realists willing to use force to further national interests. The existing nation-states of France, Great Britain, and Russia, with little in common save their commitment to progress, pursued different paths to state reform and consolidation of national power.

The changing values and force of new ideas so evident in the symbolic power of the Crystal Palace also characterized the changing world of politics, home and family. Just as realism was a dominant force in politics, realism in arts and sciences became a means of promoting material progress. With the convergence of these changes in a variety of realms, Europeans witnessed the birth of the modern age in the third quarter of the nineteenth century.

■ The main entrance to the central exhibit hall of the Crystal Palace, built in Hyde Park, London, 1851.

BUILDING NATIONS: THE POLITICS OF UNIFICATION

The revolutions of 1848 had occurred in a period of experimentation from below. Radicals enlisting popular support had tried and failed to reshape European states for their own nationalist, liberal, and socialist ends. Governments in Paris, Vienna, Berlin, and a number of lesser states had been swept away as revolutions created a power vacuum but no durable solutions. To fill that vacuum, a new breed of politician emerged in the 1850s and 1860s, men who understood the importance of the centralized nation-state and saw the need of reforms from above. They shared a new realism about means and ends and about using foreign policy successes to further domestic programs.

The Crimean War

After 1815 Russia, as the greatest military power in Europe, honored its commitment to preserving the status quo by acting as police officer for the continent. Russia supported Austria against Hungary and Prussia in 1849 and 1850. But Russia sought greater power to the south, in the Balkans. The Bosporus, the narrow strait connecting the Black Sea with the Sea of Marmara, and the strait of the Dardanelles, which connects the Sea of Marmara with the Aegean Sea, were controlled by the Ottoman Empire. Russia hoped to benefit from Ottoman weakness caused by internal conflicts and gain control of the straits, which were the only outlet for the Russian fleet to the warm waters of the Mediterranean, Russia's southern outlet to the world.

The Eastern Question. Each of the Great Powers—including Russia, Great Britain, Austria, Prussia, and France—hoped to benefit territorially from the collapse of Ottoman control. In 1853, Great Power rivalry over the "**Eastern question,**" as the anticipated disintegration of the Ottoman Empire was termed, created an international situation that led to war.

In 1853, the Russian government demanded that the Turkish government recognize Russia's right to protect Greek Orthodox believers in the Ottoman Empire. The Russian action was a response to measures taken by the French government during the previous year, when France had gained from the Turkish government rights for Roman Catholic religious orders in certain sanctuaries in the Holy Land. In making its claims as protector, Russia demanded that the rights granted Roman Catholic orders also be rescinded. The Turkish government refused Russian demands and the Russians, feeling that their prestige had been damaged, ordered troops to enter the Danubian Principalities held by the Turks.

In October 1853, the Turkish government, counting on support from Great Britain and France, declared war on Russia. Russia easily prevailed over its weaker neighbor to the south. In a four-hour battle, a Russian squadron destroyed the Turkish fleet off the coast of Sinope. Tsar Nicholas I (1825–1855) drew up the terms of a settlement with the Ottoman Empire and submitted them to Great Britain and France for review.

The two western European powers, fearing Russian aggrandizement at Turkish expense, responded by declaring war on Russia on 28 March 1854, a date that marked a new phase in the Crimean War. Both Great Britain and France, like Russia, had ambitions in the Balkans and the eastern Mediterranean. Great Britain feared Russian expansion as a threat to its trade and holdings in India and had a vested interest in an independent but weak Turkey presiding over the straits. The French hoped that by entering into a partnership with the British to defeat the Russians, they would be able to lay claim to greater power and status in European international politics. The Italian kingdom of Piedmont-Sardinia joined the war on the side of the western European powers in January 1855, hoping to make its name militarily and win recognition for its aim to unite Italy into a single nation. Although Great Britain, France, and the Italian state of Piedmont-Sardinia did not have explicit economic interests, they were motivated by ambition, prestige, and rivalry in the Balkans.

British and French troops landed in the Crimea, the Russian peninsula extending into the Black Sea, in September 1854, with the intention of capturing Sevastopol, Russia's heavily fortified chief naval base on the Black Sea. In March 1855, Nicholas I died and was succeeded by his son Alexander II (1855–1881), who wanted to bring the war to a speedy end. His attempts to negotiate a peace in the spring of 1855 repeatedly failed. In battle, the Russians continued to resist as the allies laid siege to the fortress at Sevastopol, which fell only after 322 days of battle, on 11 September 1855. The defeated Russians abandoned Sevastopol, blew up their forts, and sank their own ships. Facing the threat of Austrian entry into the war, Russia agreed to preliminary peace terms.

In the **Peace of Paris of 1856**, Russia relinquished its claim as protector of Christians in Turkey. The British gained the neutralization of the Black Sea. The mouth of the Danube was returned to Turkish control, and an international commission was created to oversee safe navigation on the Danube. The

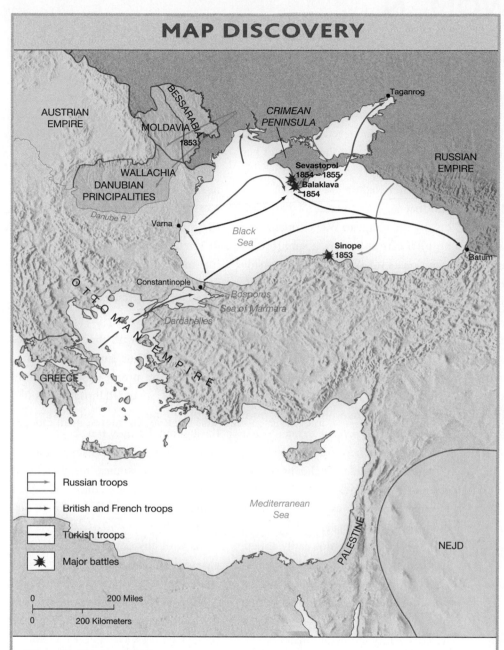

MAP DISCOVERY

AUSTRIAN
EMPIRE

BESSARABIA

MOLDAVIA
1853

CRIMEAN
PENINSULA

Taganrog

WALLACHIA
DANUBIAN
PRINCIPALITIES

Danube R.

RUSSIAN
EMPIRE

Sevastopol
1854 – 1855
Balaklava
1854

Varna

*Black
Sea*

Sinope
1853

Batum

Constantinople

Bosporus
Sea of Marmara

Dardanelles

O T T O M A N   E M P I R E

GREECE

*Mediterranean
Sea*

→ Russian troops

→ British and French troops

→ Turkish troops

✴ Major battles

PALESTINE

NEJD

0   200 Miles
0   200 Kilometers

The Crimean War

The Crimean War, which was Russia's war against the Ottoman Empire, Great Britain, France, and Sardinia, ended Russia's influence over southeastern Europe. What was the strategic importance of control of the Dardanelles Straits for Russia? Why did Russia fear Turkish control of its access to the Mediterranean Sea? Russia controlled a naval base at Sevastopol and resisted French, British, Turkish, and Sardinian attacks for over 11 months during the Crimean War. In excluding Russian influence from southern Europe, why was defeat in the Crimean War such a catastrophe for Russia? Finally, why did a dispute among Christians in the Holy Land result in a war in the Crimea?

The Human Costs of the War. The Crimean War had the highest number of casualties of any European war between 1815 and 1914. Three-quarters of a million soldiers—Russian, French, British, and Turkish—died. Because no sanitary practices were observed in caring for the wounded, four out of five succumbed to disease, especially typhus and cholera. The English nurse Florence Nightingale (1820–1910) brought medical reforms to the theater of war, introduced sanitation, and organized barracks hospitals, all of which saved the lives of countless British soldiers. (See "A Closer Look: A Working Woman," pp. 688–689.) Russians suffered disproportionately, claiming two-thirds of all dead and wounded; 450,000 Russian soldiers died. Of those who died in battle, many died needlessly, under poorly prepared leaders. A typical example occurred during the battle of Balaklava when 600 troops of the British Light Brigade were ordered into battle by incompetent and confused commanders. British soldiers charged down a narrow valley flanked by Russian guns on the heights on both sides and into the teeth of yet another battery at the head of the valley. The battlefield became known as the Valley of Death and was commemorated in Alfred Tennyson's poem, "The Charge of the Light Brigade." When the dust of the fighting had settled, the battlefield lay strewn with the bodies of nearly two-thirds of the soldiers of the Light Brigade. Their horses, slain too, lay beside them.

It was a war no one really won, a war over obscure disagreements in a faraway peninsula in the Black Sea. Nevertheless, it had dramatic and enduring conse-

Danubian Principalities were placed under joint guarantee of the powers, and Russia gave up a small portion of Bessarabia. In 1861, the Principalities were united in the independent nation of Romania.

quences. Russia ceased playing an active role in European affairs and turned toward expansion in central Asia. Its withdrawal opened up the possibility for a move by Prussia in central Europe. The rules of the game had changed. The

A WORKING WOMAN

Women have always worked, but how society has valued women's work has changed over time. After 1850, women were expected to retire from the workplace upon marrying. Woman's proper role was that of wife and mother in the home, caring for her husband and family, watching over her children. Young women worked before they married to help their parents and to save for dowries. There is no doubt that many women continued to work for wages because they had to; they were too poor to live by society's norms. But mid-nineteenth-century European culture reinforced the idea that a woman's place was in the separate domestic sphere of private pleasures and unpaid labor. To be a "public" man was a valued trait. The same adjective applied to a woman meant that she was a harlot.

A CLOSER LOOK

Yet it is this culture that immortalized Florence Nightingale, a woman who valued what she called "my work" above home and family. She was a single woman in an age when more and more women were making the choice to remain unmarried; but it was also an age in which "spinster" was a term of derision and a sign of failure. Miss Nightingale, as she was known, received the British Empire's Order of Merit for her achievements. Queen Victoria, the most maternal and domestic of queens, hailed her as "an example to our sex." Nightingale was widely regarded as the greatest woman of her age, among the most eminent of Victorians. A highly visible and outspoken reformer, Nightingale deviated from woman's unpaid role as nurturer in the private sphere. How could she be an example to the women of her time?

Florence Nightingale was hailed as a national heroine because of her work during the Crimean War in organizing hospital care at Scutari, a suburb outside Constantinople on the Asiatic side of the Bosporus. In the Crimea, she entered her own field of battle, attacking the mismanagement, corruption, and lack of organization characteristic of medical treatment for British soldiers. She campaigned for better sanitation, hygiene, ventilation, and diet, and in 1855 the death rate plummeted from 42 percent to 2 percent thanks to her efforts. The London *Times* declared, "There is not one of England's proudest and purest daughters who at the moment stands on as high a pinnacle as Florence Nightingale."

It was a pinnacle not easily scaled. Blocked by her family and publicly maligned, Nightingale struggled against prevailing norms to carve out her occupation. She was the daughter of a wealthy gentry family, and from her father she received a man's classical education. Women of her milieu were expected to be educated only in domestic arts. The fashion of the day emphasized woman's confinement to the home: crinolines, corsets, and trains restricted movement and suggested gentility. That was the life of Nightingale's older sister, a life that "the Angel of the Crimea" fiercely resisted. Nightingale railed at the inequity of married life: "A man gains everything by marriage: he gains a 'helpmate,' but a woman does not." Her memoirs are filled with what she called her "complaints" against the plight of women.

Nightingale was not a typical working woman. She struck out on her career as a rebel. Because of her wealth, she did not need to work, yet she felt driven to be useful. Her choice of nursing much alarmed her family, who considered the occupation to be on a level with domestic service. For them, nursing was worse, in fact, because nurses worked with the naked bodies of the sick. Thus nurses were either shameless or promiscuous, or both. Nightingale shattered those taboos. She visited nursing establishments throughout Europe, traveling alone—another feat unheard of for women in her day—and studied their methods and techniques. She conceived of her own mission to serve God through caring for others.

As with any exceptional individual, character and capabilities must figure in an explanation of achievements. Nightingale was a woman of drive and discipline who refused to accept the limited choices available to Victorian women. She possessed, in her sovereign's words, "a wonderful, clear and comprehensive head." Yet her unique talents are not enough to explain her success. In many ways, Nightingale was not a rebel, but rather an embodiment of the changing values of her age. In 1860, she established a school to train nurses, just as similar institutions were being created to train young women as teachers. Those occupations were extensions of women's roles from the arena of the home into society. In keeping with their domestic roles, women remained nurturers in the classroom and at the sickbed.

Florence Nightingale spent a good part of the last 45 years of her life in a sickbed suffering from what she called "nervous fever." During that period she wrote incessantly and continued to lobby for her programs, benefiting, one of her biographers claimed, from the freedom to think and write provided by her illness. It may well be true that her invalidism protected her from the claims on her time made by her family and by society. It may also be true that she, like many of her middle-class female contemporaries, experienced debilitation or suffered from hypochondria in direct proportion to the limitations they experienced.

New occupations labeled "women's work" were essential to the expansion of industrial society. A healthy and literate population guaranteed a strong citizenry, a strong army, and a strong work force. As helpmates, women entered a new work sector identified by the adjective *service*. Women were accepted as clerical workers, performing the "housekeeping" of business firms and bureaucracies.

After midcentury, gender differences, socially defined virtues for men and women, became more set. Individualism, competition, and militarism were the values of the world of men. Familial support, nurturance, and healing were female virtues. Those were the separate and unequal worlds created by the factory and the battlefield. The virtues of the private sphere were extended into the public world with the creation of new forms of poorly paid female labor. In that sense, Florence Nightingale was not a rebel. The "Lady with the Lamp," whom fever-ridden soldiers called their mother, was another working woman.

■ Florence Nightingale, known as the Lady with the Lamp, is depicted in this contemporary drawing helping soldiers injured in the Crimean War.

concert of Europe so carefully crafted by European statesmen in 1815 came to an end with the Crimean War. With the Peace of Paris of 1856, the hope that goals could be achieved by peaceful means also died. Piedmont-Sardinia, an empty-handed victor, realized that only the force of the cannon could achieve the unification of Italy.

Unifying Italy

Italy had not been a single political entity since the end of the Roman Empire in the West in the fifth century. The movement to reunite Italy culturally and politically was known as the **Risorgimento** (literally, "resurgence") and had its roots in the eighteenth century. Hopes for unification encouraged by reorganization during the Napoleonic era had been repeatedly crushed throughout the first half of the nineteenth century. Revolutionary movements had failed to cast out foreign domination by Austria in 1848.

Cavour's Political Realism. Both Giuseppe Mazzini's Young Italy movement and Giuseppe Garibaldi's Red Shirts had as their goal in 1848 a united republican Italy achieved through direct popular action. But both movements had failed. Mazzini had been a moralist; and Garibaldi was a fighter. But Camillo Benso di Cavour (1810–1861) was an opportunistic politician and a realist. He knew that only as a unified nation could Italy lay claim to status as a great power

in Europe. And he saw that a united Italy could be achieved only through the manipulation of diplomacy and military victory. He understood that international events could be made to serve national ends.

As premier for Piedmont-Sardinia from 1852 to 1859 and again in 1860–1861, Cavour was well placed to launch his campaign for Italian unity. The kingdom of Piedmont-Sardinia had made itself a focal point for unification efforts. Its king, Carlo-Alberto (1831–1849), had stood alone among Italian rulers in opposing Austrian domination of the Italian peninsula in 1848 and 1849. Severely defeated by the Austrians, he was forced to abdicate. He was succeeded by his son Victor Emmanuel II (1849–1861), who had the good sense to appoint Cavour as his first minister. From the start, Cavour undertook liberal administrative reforms that included tax reform, stabilization of the currency, improvement of the railway system, the creation of a transatlantic steamship system, and the support of private enterprise. With these programs, Cavour created for Piedmont-Sardinia the dynamic image of progressive change. He involved Piedmont-Sardinia in the Crimean War, thereby securing its status among the European powers.

Most important, however, was Cavour's alliance with France against Austria in 1858. Cavour shrewdly secured the French pledge of support, including military aid if necessary, against Austria in the Treaty of Plombières, signed by Napoleon III in 1858. The treaty was quickly followed by an arranged provocation against the Habsburg monarchy. Austria

■ Soldiers battle during the Crimean War, ca. 1855. This was the first war to be documented by photographers.

■ The Unification of Italy. By 1860, the majority of the Italian "boot" was under the rule of Piedmont-Sardinia. By 1870, the unification was complete.

the Italian mainland to expel Francis II from Naples. Garibaldi next turned his attention to the liberation of the Holy City, where a French garrison protected the pope. After his defeat in Rome in 1849, Garibaldi had never lost sight of his mission to free all of Italy from foreign rule, even in the 1850s when he had lived on New York's Staten Island as a candlemaker and had become a naturalized citizen of the United States.

As Garibaldi's popularity as a national hero grew, Cavour became alarmed by his competing effort to unite Italy and took secret steps to block the advance of the Red Shirts and their leader. To seize the initiative, Cavour directed the Piedmontese army into the Papal States. After defeating the pope's troops, Cavour's men crossed into the Neapolitan state and scored important victories against forces loyal to the king of Naples. Cavour proceeded to annex southern Italy for Victor Emmanuel II, using plebiscites to seal the procedure.

A King for a United Italy. At this point, in 1860, Garibaldi yielded his own conquered territories to the Piedmontese ruler, making possible the declaration of a united Italy under Victor Emmanuel II, who reigned as king of Italy from 1861 to 1878.

The new king of Italy was now poised to acquire Venetia, still under Austrian rule, and Rome, still ruled by Pope Pius IX, and he devoted much of his foreign policy in the 1860s to those ends.

■ In this British cartoon of 1860, Garibaldi surrenders his power to Victor Emmanuel II, king of Piedmont-Sardinia (soon to be king of a united Italy). The caption reads "Right Leg in the Boot at Last."

declared war in 1859 and was easily defeated by French forces in the battles of Magenta and Solferino. The peace, signed in November 1859 at Zürich, joined Lombardy to Piedmont-Sardinia. Cavour wielded the electoral weapon of the plebiscite—a method of direct voting that gives to electors the choice of voting for or against an important public question—to unite Tuscany, Parma, and Modena under Piedmont's king.

Cavour's approach was not without its costs. His partnership with a stronger power meant sometimes following France's lead. French bullying provoked fits of rage and forced Cavour to resign from office temporarily in 1859 over a war ended too early by Napoleon III. The need to solicit French support meant enriching France with territorial gain in the form of Nice and Savoy. However, Piedmont-Sardinia gained more than it gave up. In the summer of 1859, revolutionary assemblies in Tuscany, Modena, Parma, and the Romagna, wanting to eject their Austrian rulers, voted in favor of union with the Piedmontese. By April 1860, those four areas of central Italy were under Victor Emmanuel II's rule. Piedmont-Sardinia had doubled in size to become the dominant power on the Italian peninsula.

Southern Italians took their lead from events in central Italy and in the spring of 1860 initiated disturbances against the rule of King Francis II (1859–1861) of Naples. Uprisings in Sicily inspired Giuseppe Garibaldi to return from his self-imposed exile to organize his own army of Red Shirts, known as the Thousand, with whom he liberated Sicily and crossed to

In 1866, when Austria lost a war with Prussia, Italy struck a deal with the victor and gained control of Venetia. When Prussia prevailed against France in 1870, Victor Emmanuel II took over Rome. The boot of Italy, from top to toe, was now a single nation. The pope remained in the Vatican, opposed to an Italy united under King Victor Emmanuel II. The new national government sought to impose centralization with a heavy hand and had little interest in preserving regional differences and regional cultures. Cavour's liberal constitutional principles, combined with moderately conservative stands on social issues, produced alienation, especially in southern Italy, among both the peasantry and the nobility.

Cavour did not live to see the united Italy that he had worked so hard to fashion. He had succeeded where poets and revolutionaries had failed in preparing the ground for unification because he understood that the world had changed dramatically in the first half of the nineteenth century. He appreciated the relationship between national and international events and was able to manipulate it for his own ends. Both Cavour and his counterpart in Germany, Otto von Bismarck, considered themselves realists who shared a recognition of diplomacy as an instrument of domestic policy.

Unifying Germany

Seldom in modern history does an individual emerge as a chess master, overseeing international politics and domestic affairs as if the world were a great board game with movable pieces. Otto von Bismarck was such an individual. He was aware that he was playing a game of high risks and high

IMAGE DISCOVERY

The Proclamation of Kaiser Wilhelm I by Anton von Werner

In this painting, the German painter Anton von Werner portrays the declaration of the German Empire in the Hall of Mirrors at Versailles on 18 January 1871. Why was such a momentous event in German history taking place on French soil? Otto von Bismarck stands in the center in a white military jacket. Why is he not the one making the proclamation, although the painting has him at its center? Why is such a political event accomplished with such military pomp and circumstance?

The Unification
of Germany

stakes. His vision was limited to the pragmatic pursuit of preserving the power of his beloved Prussia. For him the empire was not an end in itself but a means of guaranteeing Prussian strength. In an age of realistic politicians, Bismarck emerged as the supreme practitioner of **Realpolitik,** the ruthless pursuit by any means, including illegal and violent ones, to advance the interests of his country.

Bismarck was a Junker, an aristocratic estate owner from east of the Elbe River, who entered politics in 1847. As a member of the United Diet of Prussia, he made his reputation as a reactionary when he rose to speak in favor of hunting privileges for the nobility: "I am a Junker and I want to enjoy the advantages of it." In the 1850s, he became aware of Prussia's future in the center of Europe: he saw that the old elites must be allied with the national movement in order to survive. The problem was that nationalism was the property of the liberals, who had been defeated in 1848. Bismarck appropriated it. Liberals and Junkers shared an interest in unification, but for different political ends. As a politician, Bismarck learned how to exploit their common ground.

Prussia's Seven Weeks' War with Austria. In 1850, Prussia had been forced to accept Austrian dominance in central Europe or go to war. Throughout the following decade, however, Prussia systematically undermined Austrian power by wielding the trade agreements of the Zollverein as a tool to exclude Austria from German economic affairs. In 1862, at the moment of a crisis provoked by the new king, Wilhelm I, over military reorganization, Bismarck became minister-president of the Prussian cabinet as well as foreign minister. He overrode the parliamentary body, the Diet, by reorganizing the Prussian army without a formally approved budget. In 1864, he constructed an alliance between Austria and Prussia for the purpose of invading Schleswig, a predominantly German-speaking territory controlled by the king of Denmark. Within five days of the invasion, Denmark yielded the duchies of Schleswig and Holstein, to be ruled jointly by Austria and Prussia.

Ascertaining that he had a free hand in central Europe, Bismarck skillfully provoked a crisis between Austria and Prussia over management of the

MAP DISCOVERY

The Unification of Germany

In this map, regard the diversity in size and type of political entities that were combined to form the new state of Germany. What annexation did the War of 1866 make possible? How did the peace settlement with France affect the creation of the German state? Why was the North German Confederation so important in determining the formation of the new German Empire?

territories. Counting on the neutrality of France and Great Britain, the support of Piedmont-Sardinia, and good relations with Russia, Bismarck led his country into war with Austria in June 1866. In this Seven Weeks' War, Austrian forces proved to be no match for the better-equipped and better-trained Prussian army. Bismarck dictated the terms of the peace, which demonstrated that he had no desire to cripple Austria, only to exclude it from a united Germany in which Prussia would be the dominant force. Austria's exclusion from Germany forced the Austrian government to deal with its own internal problems of imperial organization. In 1867, in response to pressures from the subject nationalities, the Habsburg Empire transformed itself into a **dual monarchy** of two independent and equal states under one ruler, who would be both the emperor of Austria and the king of Hungary. In spite of the reorganization, the problem of nationalities persisted, and ethnic groups began to agitate for total independence from imperial rule.

The Franco-Prussian War.

Bismarck's biggest obstacle to German unification was laid to rest with Austria's defeat. The south German states, however, continued to resist the idea of Prussian dominance, but growing numbers of people in Baden, Württemberg, Bavaria, and the southern parts of Hesse-Darmstadt recognized the necessity of uniting under Prussian leadership.

Many French observers were troubled by the Prussian victory over Austria and were apprehensive over what a united Germany might portend for the future of French dominance in Europe. Napoleon III attempted unsuccessfully to contain Prussian ambitions through diplomatic maneuverings. Instead, France found itself stranded without important European allies. In the spring of 1870, Bismarck decided to seize the initiative and provoke a crisis with France.

Bismarck recognized that war with France could be the dramatic event needed to forge cooperation and unity among all German states. The issue of succession to the Spanish throne gave him the opportunity he sought. Bismarck skillfully created the impression that the French ambassador had insulted the Prussian king, then leaked news of the incident to the press in both countries. Enraged and inflamed French and Prussian publics both demanded war.

As a direct result of this contrived misunderstanding, France declared war on Prussia in July 1870. As Bismarck hoped, the southern German princes immediately sided with the Prussian king. For years before hostilities broke out, the Prussians had been preparing for war. They had been sending Prussian army officers disguised as landscape painters into France to study the terrain of battle. French troops carried maps of Germany but were ignorant of the geography of their own country, where the battles were waged. Sent into battle against the Germans, French troops roamed around in search of their commanders and each other.

The Germans had learned new deployment strategies from studying the use of railroads in the American Civil War of 1861–1865. Unlike the Germans, the French had not coordinated deployment with the new technology of the railroad. Although French troops had the latest equipment, they were sent into battle without instructions on how to use it. Finally, the Prussian-led German army was superior, outnumbering French troops 450,000 to 260,000. All those factors combined to spell disaster for the French. Within a matter of weeks, it was obvious that France had lost the Franco-Prussian War, and its eastern territories of Alsace and Lorraine. The path was now clear for the **Proclamation of the German Empire** in January 1871.

Prussian Dominance of United Germany.

The newly established Second Reich, successor to the Holy Roman Empire, united the German states into a single nation. After years of foreign wars and endless wrangling among the heads of the 38 German states, Bismarck obtained what he wanted: a German Empire under the leadership of the Prussian king. The Proclamation of the German Empire was signed on 18 January 1871 in a ceremony in the French palace of Versailles. Bismarck, always the pragmatist, understood clearly that Europe was not the same place that it had been a decade or two earlier. "Anyone who speaks of Europe is wrong—it is nothing but a set of national expressions." That understanding was the key to his success. In unifying Germany, Bismarck built on the constitution of the North German Confederation formed in 1867, which guaranteed Prussian dominance. Bismarck used the bureaucracy as a mainstay of the emperor. The new **Reichstag**—the national legislative assembly—was to be elected by means of universal male suffrage, a concession to the liberals. Yet the constitution was not a liberal one, since the Reichstag was not sovereign and the chancellor was accountable only to the emperor. Policy was made outside the domain of electoral politics. The federal structure of the constitution, especially with regard to taxation, also kept the central parliament weak. Most liberals supported the constitution, but a minority persisted in a tradition of radical dissent. Critics believed that true constitutional government had been sacrificed to the demands of empire. As one liberal remarked, "Unity without freedom is a unity of slaves." Bismarck spoke in confidence of his aim "to destroy parliamentarianism by parliamentarianism." According to that formula, Bismarck hoped that a weak Reichstag would undermine parliamentary institutions better than any dictatorial ruler.

The United States: Civil War and Reunification

In the 1860s, another crisis in state–building was resolved across the Atlantic. The United States cemented political unity through the use of force in its Civil War (1861–1865). The president of the United States, Abraham Lincoln (1809–1865), mobilized the superior resources of the industrial Northern states against the heavily agrarian, slave-owning South. The United States worked to achieve national unity and territorial integrity in another sense through ongoing expansion westward by eliminating and subduing Native American peoples.

With the emancipation of the slaves, republican democracy appeared to triumph in the United States. Newly created European nation-states followed a different path: plebiscites were manipulated by those in power in Italy, and a neo-absolutism emerged in Germany. Yet the Civil War in the United States and the successful bids for unification in Italy and Germany shared remarkable similarities. In all three countries, wars eventually resulted in a single national market and a single financial system without internal barriers. Unified national economies, particularly in Germany and the United States, paved the way for significant economic growth and the expansion of industrial power.

Nationalism and Force

It is commonplace in the Western historical tradition to speak of nations as if they were individuals possessing emotions, making choices, taking actions, having ideas. "Russia turned inward"; "Germany chose its enemies as well as its friends"; "France vowed revenge"; "Great Britain took pride in its achievements." On one level, to attribute volition, feeling, and insight to an abstract entity such as a nation is nonsense. But on another level, the personification of nation-states was one of the great achievements of statesmen throughout Europe between 1850 and 1870. The language and symbols they put in place created the nation itself, a new political reality whose forms contained a modern political consciousness. The nation-state became an all-knowing being whose rights had to be protected, whose destiny had to be assured.

The nation was above all a creation that minimized or denied real differences in dialect and language, regional loyalties, local traditions, and village identities. The crises in state building in Italy and Germany had been resolved finally by violence. No power was acknowledged to exist above the nation-state. No power could sanction the nation's actions but itself. Force was an acceptable alternative to diplomacy. War was a political act and a political instrument, a continuation of political relations. Violence and nationalism were inextricably linked in the unification of both Italy and Germany in the third quarter of the nineteenth century.

National unification had escaped the grasp of liberals and radicals between 1848 and 1850 with the failure of revolutionary and reform movements. In the 1850s and 1860s, those committed to national transformations worked from within the existing system. The new realists subordinated liberal nationalism to the needs of conservative state building. Military force validated what intellectuals and revolutionaries had not been able to legitimate through ideological claims.

REFORMING EUROPEAN SOCIETY

After the revolutions of 1848, government repression silenced radical movements throughout Europe. But repression could not maintain social harmony and promote growth and prosperity. In the third quarter of the nineteenth century, Europe's leaders recognized that reforms were needed to build dynamic and competitive states. Three different models for social and political reform developed in France, Great Britain, and Russia after 1850. All three sets of reforms took place in unified nation-states. The three societies had little in common with each other ideologically, but all reflected a commitment to progress and an awareness of the state's role and responsibility in achieving it.

The Second Empire in France, 1852–1870

One model was that of France, where the French emperor worked through a highly centralized administrative structure and with a valued elite of specialists to achieve social and economic transformations. The French model was a technocratic one that emphasized the importance of specialized knowledge to achieve material progress. Reform in France relied on both autocratic direction and liberal participation.

Napoleon III.   Napoleon III ruled France from the middle of the century until 1870. His apprenticeship for political leadership had been an unusual one. Louis Napoleon (1808–1873) was a nephew of the emperor Napoleon I. The child Louis, born at the peak of French glory, was old enough to remember the devastation of his uncle's defeat in 1815. He dedicated his exiled youth to preparing for his family's restoration as rulers of France. With the death of Napoleon's son, the duc de Reichstadt, in 1832, Louis was aware that the mantle of future power and the family destiny fell to him.

In comparing Louis Napoleon with his uncle, Napoleon I, Karl Marx observed that history happens the first time as tragedy and the second time as farce. There was much that passed as farcical before Louis Napoleon established France's Second Empire in 1852, as one attempt after another to seize power failed. Yet those who viewed Louis Napoleon as a figure of derision were misled: by 1848 he understood the importance of shaping public opinion to suit his own ends. He wielded the Napoleonic legend to play on the dissatisfaction of millions. He understood that to succeed in an electoral system, he had to promise something to everyone. He spoke of prosperity, order, and the end of poverty, slogans that sent different and incompatible messages to a bourgeoisie who wanted social peace, workers who wanted jobs and social justice, and peasants who wanted land and freedom from taxes. As the dark-horse candidate, he swept the field and in December 1848 became France's first president elected by universal manhood suffrage. The politicians were sure that he could be managed, so insignificant did he seem. They and the rest of France were literally caught sleeping before dawn on 2 December 1851 when the nephew of the great Napoleon seized power in a coup d'état and became dictator of France. Exactly one year later, he proclaimed himself Emperor Napoleon III and set about the tasks of establishing his dynasty and reclaiming French imperial glory.

Napoleon III's regime has been condemned for its decadence and its spectacle. On the surface, the world of the

Second Empire glittered like a fancy-dress ball, with men in sparkling uniforms and women in full-skirted, low-necked gowns waltzing to gay tunes. Courtesans in open carriages, parading through the newly landscaped Bois de Boulogne, became as famous as cabinet members. But to judge the empire on superficial criteria alone would be a mistake. The Second Empire achieved significant successes in a variety of areas. Napoleon III supported economic expansion and industrial development. During his reign, the French economy prospered and flourished. The discovery of gold in California and Australia fueled a demand for French products in international markets and initiated a period of sustained economic growth that lasted beyond Napoleon III's reign into the 1880s. A new private banking system, founded in 1852 by financiers and key political figures, enabled the pooling of investors' resources, small and large, to finance industrial expansion. Stable authoritarian government encouraged increased investment in state public works programs.

Napoleon III surrounded himself with advisers who saw in prosperity the answer to all social problems. Between 1852 and 1860, the government supported a massive program of railroad construction. Jobs multiplied and investment increased. Agriculture expanded as railroad lines opened new markets. The rich became richer, but the extreme poverty of the first half of the nineteenth century was diminishing. Brutal misery in city and countryside did not disappear, but on the whole, the standard of living increased as wages rose faster than prices.

Rebuilding Paris.   The best single example of the energy and commitment of the imperial regime was the rebuilding of the French capital. As Sir Edwin Chadwick (1800–1890), Britain's leading public health reformer, put it, Napoleon III found Paris stinking and left it sweet. Before midcentury, Paris was one of the most unsanitary, crime-ridden, and politically volatile capitals in Europe. Within 15 years it had been transformed into a city of lights, wide boulevards and avenues, monumental vistas, parks, and gardens. Napoleon III was the architect of the idea for a new Paris, something his uncle never had the time or resources to accomplish. But the real credit for carrying through the municipal improvements should be attributed to Baron Georges Haussmann (1809–1891).

As Prefect of the Seine from 1853 to 1870, Baron Haussmann typified the technocrat in power. He was called "the Attila of the Straight Line" for the ruthless manner in which his protractor cut through city neighborhoods, destroying all that lay in his pencil's path. Poor districts were turned into rubble to make way for the elegant apartment buildings of the Parisian bourgeoisie. The new housing was too expensive for workers, who were pushed out of Paris into the suburbs. The boundaries of the city expanded. As workers from all over France migrated to the capital in search of jobs, the population nearly doubled, increasing by just under one million in the 1850s and 1860s. A poor and volatile population encircled the city of monuments and museums. Paris as the radical capital of France was being physically dismantled and a new, more conservative political entity rose in its place

■ Inauguration of the Boulevard du Prince-Eugène during the rebuilding of Paris. The renovations were carried out under the direction of Baron Georges Haussmann, who was called "the Attila of the Straight Line" for the ruthless manner in which his pencil cut through city neighborhoods on the map.

as the middle classes took over the heart of the city. The process was very different from the development of other urban areas such as London, where the middle class fled to the suburbs, leaving behind the problems of urban life.

Much has been made of the policing benefits of rebuilding the city of Paris. Wider streets facilitated the movement of troops, which could more easily crush revolutionary disturbances. While the control aspect of urban reconstruction was not lost on Haussmann and Napoleon III, it was not the primary purpose of the vast public works project that lasted for the whole regime. Napoleon wanted Paris to be the center of Western culture and the envy of the world. Its wide, straight avenues served as the model for other French cities. The new Paris became an international model copied in Mexico City, Brussels, Madrid, Rome, Stockholm, and Barcelona between 1870 and 1900. American city planners of the City Beautiful movement were also influenced by the **"Haussmannization"** of Paris. In spite of financial scandals that plagued the reconstruction near the end of the regime, few disputed that Napoleon III had transformed Paris into one of the world's most beautiful cities.

The Foreign Policy of the Second Empire.   Just as a new Paris would make France the center of culture, Napoleon III intended his blueprint for foreign policy to restore France to its pre-1815 status as the greatest European power. By involving France in both the Crimean War and the war for Italian unification, Napoleon III returned France to adventurous foreign policies. The emperor had undertaken both wars with the hope of further increasing French economic and diplomatic prominence on the Continent. Napoleon III supported Piedmont-Sardinia not out of any sense of altruism, in spite of his claim that he was "doing something for Italy." The accession of Nice and Savoy increased French territory—and reversed the settlements of 1815.

The Italian campaign complicated relations with Great Britain, which feared a resurgent French militarism. French construction of the Suez Canal between the Red Sea and the Mediterranean also created tensions with Great Britain, protective of its own dominance in the Mediterranean and the Near East. Nevertheless, the free-trade agreement between the British and the French in 1860—the Chevalier-Cobden Treaty—was a landmark in overseas policy and a commitment to liberal economic policies.

The Second Empire's involvement in Mexico was a fiasco. The Mexican government had been chronically unable to pay its foreign debts, and France was Mexico's largest creditor. Napoleon III hoped that by intervening in Mexican affairs he could strengthen ties with Great Britain and Spain, to whom the Mexicans also owed money. The emperor planned to turn Mexico into a satellite empire that would be economically profitable to France. The United States, occupied with civil war, did not interfere in 1861 when Napoleon III sent a military expedition to "pacify" the Mexican countryside. With the backing of Mexican conservatives who opposed Mexican president Benito Juárez (1806–1872), Napoleon III supported the Austrian archduke Maximilian (1832–1867) as emperor of Mexico. After he

was crowned in 1863, the new Mexican emperor struggled to rule in an enlightened manner, but he was stymied from the beginning by his ineptitude and lack of popular support. Following the recall of the 34,000 French troops that, at considerable expense, were keeping Maximilian's troubled regime in place, Maximilian was captured and executed by a firing squad in the summer of 1867. The Mexican disaster damaged the prestige of Napoleon III's regime in the international arena. Intensely aware of public criticism, the emperor undertook the reorganization of the army and a series of liberal reforms, including increasing parliamentary participation in affairs of state, and granting to trade unions the right of assembly.

The Prussian victory over Austria in the Seven Weeks' War had dramatically changed the situation on the Continent. Pundits in Paris were fond of saying that the Austrian loss really marked the defeat of France. France's position within Europe was threatened, and Napoleon III knew it. In 1870, the humiliatingly rapid defeat of French imperial forces in the Franco-Prussian War brought to an end the experiment in liberal empire.

In 1870, France remained a mixture of old and new. Although industrial production had doubled between 1852 and 1870, France was still an agricultural nation. Foreign trade expanded by 300 percent, growing faster than that of any other nation in Europe. Six times as many miles of railroad track crisscrossed France at the time Napoleon III went into exile as when he came into power. Napoleon III did not create the economic boom from which all of Europe benefited between 1850 and 1880, but he did build on it, using the state to stimulate and enhance prosperity. His policies favored

■ Edouard Manet, *The Execution of the Emperor Maximilian* (1868). The United States pressured France to withdraw support for the Mexican imperial venture, which led to disaster for Maximilian and the reinstatement of Benito Juárez as president of Mexico.

business and initiated a financial revolution of enduring benefits. However, the technocratic model of rule by specialists was not applied to the army in forcing it to modernize. Nor had foreign policy benefited from the careful calculations employed in domestic administration. The empire had become the victim of its own myth of invincibility.

Victorian Political Reforms

Great Britain provided another model of reform, which was fostered through liberal parliamentary democracy. In government by "amateurs," with local rather than a highly centralized administration, British legislation alternated between a philosophy of freedom and one of protection. But reforms were always hammered out by parliamentary means with the support of a gradually expanding electorate.

Parliamentary Reforms. Contemporaries were aware of two facts of life about Great Britain in 1850: first, that Britain had an enormously productive capitalist economy of sustained growth, and second, that Britain enjoyed apparent social harmony without revolution and without civil war. As revolutions ravaged continental Europe in 1848, the British took pride in a parliamentary system that valued a tradition of freedom. British statesmen were not reluctant to point out to the rest of the world that Great Britain had achieved industrial growth without rending the social fabric.

The political rhetoric of stability and calm was undoubtedly exaggerated. Great Britain at midcentury had its share of serious social problems. British slums rivaled any in Europe. Poverty, disease, and famine ravaged the kingdom. Many feared that British social protests of the 1840s would result in upheavals similar to those in continental Europe. Yet Great Britain avoided a revolution. One explanation for Britain's relative calm lay in the shared political tradition that emphasized liberty as the birthright of English citizens. Building on an established political culture, the British Parliament was able to adapt to the demands of an industrializing society. Adaptation was gradual, but as slow as it seemed, a compromise was achieved among competing social interests. The great compromise of Victorian society was the reconciliation of industrialists' commitment to unimpeded growth with workers' need for the protection of the state. The British political system was democratized slowly after 1832.

The Reform Bill of that year gave increased political power to the industrial and manufacturing bourgeoisie, who joined a landed aristocracy and merchant class. Yet, the property qualification meant that only 20 percent of the population was able to vote. The next step toward democracy was not taken for another 35 years. In 1867, under conservative leadership, a second Reform Bill was introduced. Approval of the bill doubled the electorate, giving the vote to a new urban population of shopkeepers, clerks, and workers. In 1884, farm laborers were enfranchised. Women, however, remained disfranchised; they were not granted the vote until after World War I. Through parliamentary cooperation between Liberals and Conservatives, the male franchise was slowly implemented without a revolution.

■ William Gladstone rides in an omnibus in this painting titled *One of the People* by Alfred Morgan. This mode of transport was thought of as a social leveler because all classes of people could afford the fares.

Gladstone and Disraeli. The lives and careers of two men, William Ewart Gladstone (1809–1898) and Benjamin Disraeli (1804–1881), exemplify the particular path the British government followed in maintaining social peace. Rivals and political opponents, both men served as prime ministers and both left their mark on the age. From different political perspectives, they contributed to British reform in the second half of the nineteenth century.

William Gladstone was an example of a British statesman with no counterpart elsewhere in Europe: he was a classical liberal who believed in free enterprise and was opposed to state intervention. Good government, according to Gladstone, should remove obstacles to talent, competition, and individual initiative but should interfere as little as possible in economy and society. Surprisingly, the leader of the Liberal party began his long parliamentary career at the other end of the political spectrum, as a Tory. The son of a successful merchant and slave trader, Gladstone enjoyed the benefits of wealth and attended Eton and Oxford, where he studied classics and mathematics. Discouraged by his father from a career in the Church of England, Gladstone used his connections to launch a parliamentary career in 1832. He gradually left behind his conservative opposition to parliamentary reform and his support of protective tariffs. In 1846, as a member of the government, Gladstone broke with Tory principles and voted in favor of free trade. The best government, he affirmed in true liberal fashion, was the one that governed least.

Those who knew Gladstone in the early years were struck not by his brilliance but by his capacity for hard work and assiduous application to the task at hand. He chopped wood for relaxation. In his spare time he wrote a three-volume study on Homer and the Homeric age. He practiced an overt morality, targeting prostitutes in the hope of convincing them to change their lives. Gladstone was not blind to social problems, but he considered private philanthropy the best way to correct them.

Many of the significant advances of the British liberal state were achieved during Gladstone's first term as prime minister (1868–1874). Taking advantage of British prosperity, Gladstone abolished tariffs, cut defense expenditures, lowered taxes, and sponsored sound budgets. He furthered the liberal agenda by disestablishing the Anglican Church in Ireland in 1869. The Church had been the source of great resentment to the vast majority of Irish Catholics, who had been forced to pay taxes to support the Protestant state church.

Gladstone reformed the army, in disrepute after its poor performance in the Crimea, so that commissions no longer could be purchased. Training and merit would have to justify all future advancements. Similarly, Gladstone reformed the civil service system by separating it from political influence and seniority. A merit system and examinations were intended to ensure the most efficient and effective government administration. The secret ballot was introduced to prevent coercion in voting. Finally, the Liberals stressed the importance of education for an informed electorate and passed an education act that aimed to make elementary schooling available to everyone.

■ This *Punch* cartoon, "Rival Actors," depicts William Gladstone (left) as popular character William Tell exiting the stage, while Benjamin Disraeli (right), as farcical character Jeremy Diddler, sulks in the wings.

The reforms added up to a liberal philosophy of government. Liberal government was, above all, an attack on privilege. It sought to remove restraints on individual freedom and to foster opportunity and talent. Liberal government sought to protect democracy through education. Voting men must be educated men. As one Liberal put it, "We must educate our masters." Liberals governed in the interests of the bourgeoisie and with the belief that what was good for capitalism was good for society. Tariffs, therefore, were kept low or eliminated to promote British commerce. Gladstone believed that all political questions were moral questions and that fairness and justice could solve political problems. In spite of his moral claims, his programs made him enemies among special interests, including farmers and the Church of England, because his policies undermined their security and privileges.

During those years, another political philosophy also left its mark on British government. It was conservatism. Under the flamboyant leadership of Benjamin Disraeli, the Conservative party supported state intervention and regulation on behalf of the weak and disadvantaged. Disraeli sponsored the Factory Act of 1875, which set a maximum of 56 hours for the factory work week. The Public Health Act established a sanitary code. The Artisans Dwelling Act defined minimum housing standards. Probably the most important conservative legislation was the Trade Union Act, which permitted picketing and other peaceful labor tactics.

Disraeli's personal background and training were very different from Gladstone's and made him unique in British parliamentary politics. He was known primarily as a novelist, social critic, and failed financier before he entered the political arena in 1837. His father was a Jewish merchant descended from a family of Spanish refugees in Venice. The senior Disraeli became a British subject in 1801, three years before Benjamin's birth. In embracing English culture, the senior Disraeli had his children baptized in the Anglican Church.

The split between Disraeli and Gladstone was clearly apparent in 1846 when they, both Tories, disagreed over the issue of free trade versus tariffs. Disraeli moved on to champion protection and throughout the early 1860s consistently opposed Gladstone's financial system. Unlike the Liberals, Disraeli insisted on the importance of traditional institutions including the monarchy, the House of Lords, and the Church of England. Queen Victoria named him the First Earl of Beaconsfield for his strong foreign policy and social reforms. "Dizzy's" real cleverness and contribution to British politics were in an area that few contemporaries appreciated at the time. Disraeli's work in organizing a national party machinery facilitated the adaptation of the parliamentary system to mass politics. His methods of campaigning and building a mass base of support were used by successful politicians regardless of political persuasion.

The terms liberal and conservative hold none of the meaning today that they did for men and women in the nineteenth century. Classical liberalism has little in common with its twenty-first-century counterpart, which favors an active interventionist state. Disraeli is a far more likely candidate for the twenty-first-century liberal label than is Britain's leading nineteenth-century liberal statesman, Gladstone. Disraeli placed value in the ability of the state to correct and protect. Because of his interventionist philosophy, he may be compared with the Continental statesmen Bismarck and Napoleon III.

In spite of Liberal hopes, Great Britain never had a purely laissez-faire economy. As the intersecting careers of Gladstone and Disraeli demonstrate, the British model combined free enterprise with intervention and regulation. The clear issues and the clear choices of the two great parties—Liberal and Conservative—dominated parliamentary life after midcentury. In polarizing parliamentary politics, the parties also invigorated it.

Reforming Russia

Russia offered a third model for reform in the nineteenth century. Like Britain, Russia had avoided revolution at midcentury. Like Britain, it hoped to preserve social peace. Yet the Russian model for reform stands in dramatic contrast to Britain's. Russia was an unreformed autocracy, a form of government in which the tsar held absolute power. Without a parliament, a constitution, or civil liberties for its subjects, the Russian ruler governed

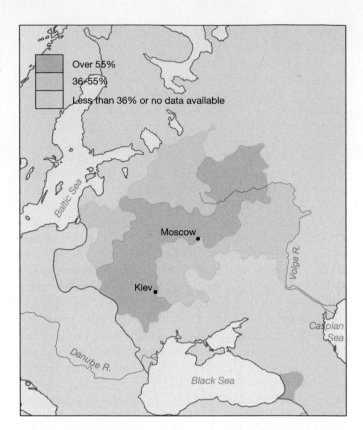

Over 55%

36–55%

Less than 36% or no data available

■ **Russian Serfs.** Serfdom was created in the sixteenth century as a system of virtual enslavement of Russian peasants. Its greatest density was in areas with a strong presence of landed gentry.

through a bureaucracy and a police force. Russia was a semifeudal agrarian economy with a class of privileged aristocrats supported by serf labor on their estates.

A Serf-Holding Nation. For decades—since the reign of Alexander I (1801–1825)—the tsars and their advisers realized that they were out of step with developments in western Europe. An awareness was growing that serfdom was uncivilized and morally wrong. The remnants of feudalism had been swept away in France in the Great Revolution at the end of the eighteenth century. Prussia had abolished hereditary serfdom beginning in 1806. Among the European powers, only Russia remained a serf-holding nation. Russian serfs were tied to the land and owed dues and labor services in return for the lands they held. Peasant protests mounted, attracting public attention to the plight of the serfs. A Russian aristocrat, Baron N. Wrangel (1847–1920), recounted in his memoirs a story from his childhood in the 1850s, when he was about ten years old, that exemplifies the growing social awareness of the problem:

One day we were sitting quietly on the terrace listening to the reading aloud of *Uncle Tom's Cabin,* a recently translated book that was then in fashion. My sisters could not get over the horrors of slavery and wept at the sad fate of poor Uncle Tom. "I cannot conceive," said one of them, "how such atrocities can be tolerated. Slavery is horrible." "But," said Bunny, in her shrill little voice, "we have slaves too."

In spite of growing moral concern, there were many reasons to resist the abolition of serfdom. Granting freedom to all serfs was a vastly complicated affair. How were serf-holders to be compensated for the loss of labor power? What was to be the freed serf's relationship to the land? Personal freedom would be worthless without a land allotment. Yet landowners opposed loss of land as strongly as loss of their work force. A landless work force would be a serious social threat, if western European experience could be taken as an example.

Alexander II and the Emancipation of the Serfs.

Hesitation about abolition evaporated with the Russian defeat in the Crimean War. The new tsar, Alexander II (1855–1881), viewed Russia's inability to repel an invasion force on its own soil as proof of its backwardness. Russia had no railroads and was forced to transport military supplies by carts to the Crimea. It took Moscow three months to provision troops, whereas the enemy could do so in three weeks. Alexander II believed in taking matters into his own hands. Russia must be reformed. Abolition of serfdom would permit a well-trained reserve army to exist without fear of rebellion. Liberating the serfs would also create a system of free labor so necessary for industrial development. Alexander interpreted rumblings within his own country as the harbinger of future upheavals similar to those that had rocked France and the Austrian Empire. He explained to the Muscovite nobility, "It is better to abolish serfdom from above than to wait until the serfs begin to liberate themselves from below."

In March 1861, the tsar signed the emancipation edict that liberated the serfs. Serfdom was eliminated in Poland three years later. Alexander II, who came to be known as the "Tsar-Liberator," compromised between landlord and serf by allotting land to freed peasants, while requiring from the former serfs redemption payments that were spread out over a period of 49 years. The peasant paid the state in installments; the state reimbursed the landowner in lump sums. To guarantee repayment, the land was not granted directly to individual peasants but to the village commune (*mir*), which was responsible for collecting redemption payments.

Emancipation of the serfs, Alexander's greatest achievement, was a reform of unprecedented scale. It affected 52 million peasants, more than 20 million of them enserfed to private landowners. By comparison, Abraham Lincoln's Emancipation Proclamation less than two years later freed four million American slaves. However, beneath the surface of the Russian liberation, peasants soon realized that the repayment schedule increased their burdens and responsibilities.

THE RUSSIAN EMANCIPATION PROCLAMATION, 1861

Aleksandr Vasilievich Nikitenko, a former serf who had managed through luck and talent to gain an education and a place in the Russian bureaucracy, recorded the joy and excitement he and others felt when Alexander II freed Russia's serfs. Many hoped, and some feared, that the change would revolutionize Russian agriculture and society.

Focus Questions

How do you explain the joy of this state bureaucrat in learning of the emancipation of the serfs? Why was the manor serf who is quoted here indignant about the ongoing obligations of the manor serfs?

5 March. A great day: the emancipation manifesto! I received a copy around noon. I cannot express my joy at reading this precious act which scarcely has its equal in the thousand-year history of the Russian people. I read it aloud to my wife, my children and a friend of ours in my study, under Alexander II's portrait, as we gazed at it with deep reverence and gratitude. I tried to explain to my ten-year-old son as simply as possible the essence of the manifesto and bid him to keep inscribed in his heart forever the date of March 5 and the name of Alexander II, the Liberator.

I couldn't stay at home. I had to wander about the streets and mingle, so to say, with my regenerated fellow citizens. Announcements from the governor-general were posted at all crossways, and knots of people were gathered around them. One would read while the others listened. I encountered happy, but calm faces everywhere. Here and there people were reading the proclamation aloud, and, as I walked, I continually caught phrases like "decree on liberty," "freedom." One fellow who was reading the announcement and reached the place where it said that manor serfs were obligated to their masters for another two years, exclaimed indignantly "The hell with this paper! Two years? I'll do nothing of the sort." The others remained silent. I ran into my friend, Galakhov. "Christ has risen!" I said to him. "He has indeed!" he answered, and we expressed our great joy to each other.

Then I went to see Rebinder. He ordered champagne and we drank a toast to Alexander II.

From Aleksandr Nikitenko, *The Diary of a Russian Censor* (1861).

The peasants resented being forced to pay for land they considered rightfully theirs. An old peasant saying reflected that belief: "We are yours"—they acknowledged to the landlords—"but the land is ours." It was not an accident that the mir arrangement prevented mobility; Alexander had no intention of creating a floating proletariat similar to that of western Europe. He wanted his people closely tied to the land, but freed from the servility of feudal obligations.

Russian Serfs

The abolition of serfdom did not solve the problem of Russian backwardness. Farming methods and farming implements remained primitive. Russian agriculture did not become more productive. Nor did emancipation result in a contented and loyal peasantry. Frustrations festered. A large proportion of peasants received too little land to make their redemption payments. Many peasants in the south received smaller plots of land than they had farmed under serfdom. The commune replaced the landowner in a system of peasant bondage. Redemption payments were finally abolished in 1907, but not before exacerbating social tensions in the countryside.

The Great Reforms.   The real winner in the abolition of serfdom was not the landowners, and certainly not the peasantry, but the state. A bureaucratic hierarchy and a financial infrastructure were expanded. Other reforms in the system of credit and banking contributed significantly to rapid economic growth. With the help of foreign—especially French—investment, railway construction increased dramatically, from 660 miles of track in 1855 to 14,000 by 1880. Thanks in large part to the new transportation network, Russia became a world grain supplier during the period, with exports increasing threefold. But development was uneven and remained uncoordinated. The coexistence of the old alongside the new, combined with the speed of change, created friction and promised future unrest.

Alexander II, a man conservative by temperament but aware that Russia must move forward, did not stop there. In 1864, he introduced *zemstvos*, local elected assemblies on the provincial and county levels, to govern local affairs. The three classes of landowners, townspeople, and peasants elected representatives who were responsible for implementing educational, health, and other social welfare reforms. Similar statutes governing towns were passed in 1870. In the spirit of modernization, the state also undertook judicial reforms. New provincial courts were opened in 1866. Corporal punishment was to be eliminated. Separate courts for peasants still endured, however, preserving the impression that peasants were a lower class of citizens subject to different jurisdiction.

With the military triumph of Prussia over France in 1870–1871, the tsar found the excuse he had been looking for in the 1860s to push through fundamental military reforms. Alexander II had admired the Prussian military model since his childhood. In 1874 he used that model to require that all young men upon reaching the age of 20 be eligible for conscription "in defense of the fatherland." Fifteen years of service were specified, but only six were served in active duty.

That was a significant reduction from the 25 years of active service that peasant and lower-class conscripts had formerly served. Although length of service was reduced according to educational level, the military reforms were, on the whole, democratizing because they eliminated an important privilege of the wealthy.

In spite of the vast array of "Great Reforms"—emancipating the serfs, creating local parliamentary bodies, reorganizing the judiciary, and modernizing the army—Russia was not sufficiently liberalized or democratized to satisfy the critics of autocracy. Between 1860 and 1870, a young generation of intelligentsia, radical intellectuals who benefited from the democratization of education and were influenced by the rhetoric of revolution in the West, assumed a critical stance in protest against the existing order. Although not itself a class, many members of the intelligentsia shared a similar background as the student sons and daughters of petty officials or priests. Young women, who often sought the education in Switzerland that was denied to them at home, were especially active in supporting ideas of emancipation.

The Populist Movement.   In 1873, the imperial government considered the Western liberal and socialist ideas of the intelligentsia so threatening that it ordered Russian students studying in Switzerland to return home. Many returning students combined forces with radical intellectuals in Russia and decided to "go to the people." About 2500 educated young men and women traveled from village to village to educate, to help, and, in some cases, to attempt to radicalize the peasants. The populist crusaders sought to learn from what they considered to be the source of all morality and justice, the Russian peasantry. They paid dearly for what proved to be a fruitless commitment to populism in the mass trials and repression of the late 1870s.

Some of the tsarist regime's critics fled into exile to reemerge as revolutionaries in western Europe, where they continued to oppose the tsarist regime and helped shape the tradition of revolution and dissent in Western countries. Other educated men and women who remained in Russia chose violence as the only effective weapon against absolute rule. Terrorists who called themselves "Will of the People" decided to assassinate the tsar; in the "emperor hunt" that followed, numerous attempts were made on the tsar's life. Miraculously, Alexander II escaped even the bombing of his own living quarters in the Winter Palace. The tsarist state responded with stricter controls, but repression only fanned the flames of discontent.

In response to attempts on his life and the assassination of public officials, which were intended to cripple the central regime, Alexander II put the brakes on reform in the second half of his reign. The Great Reforms could not be undone, however, and they had set in motion sweeping economic and social changes. The state encouraged capitalist growth and witnessed the rise of a professional middle class and the formation of an embryonic factory proletariat. Serfdom was dead for-

Growth of Russia to 1914

■ Russian peasants at a village meeting. With the abolition of serfdom in 1861, village leaders gained considerable power.

ever. Yet reforms had increased expectations for an equally dramatic political transformation that failed to materialize. In the end, the "Will of the People" movement succeeded in its mission. A terrorist bomb killed Alexander II, the "Tsar-Liberator," in St. Petersburg in 1881.

The Politics of Leadership

Modern politics emerged in Europe only after 1850. Until that time, traditional political categories had prevailed. When faced with revolutionary upheavals, regimes aimed for stability and permanence. Only after 1850 did a new breed of political leader appear who understood the world of politics and directed it to their own ends. Three statesmen typified the new approach to the public world of power: Camillo di Cavour, Otto von Bismarck, and Louis Napoleon.

The Demise of Royal Authority.   In Old Regime Europe, power flowed downward from the monarch, who was perched atop a hierarchically organized social system often depicted as a pyramid. The source of royal power was both timeless and historic. As God's appointed agents, the sovereigns of Europe reinforced their right to rule with the continuity of their dynasties. Men of great political acumen ministered to their royal masters and were legitimated by royal power. In the years between 1789 and 1850, that system was challenged as kings were displaced—sometimes restored to power, sometimes executed.

Divine authority was an archaic idea to the growing numbers of those who spoke of democratic principles and rallied to banners that represented new concepts of liberty and equality.

In the first half of the nineteenth century, men and women had learned that those in power could be questioned. The good of the people was the primary justification for government. Power now flowed upward from the citizenry to their appointed and elected representatives. The new power brokers were those who could control and direct the flow, not merely be carried along or swept away by it. The new political men were realists in the same tradition as Machiavelli and reflected the new political culture of the nineteenth century.

Political realists such as Cavour, Bismarck, and Louis Napoleon understood the importance of public opinion. Public opinion had been a central fact of political life from the eighteenth century, but as revolutionary events in France demonstrated, public opinion proved unreliable building material for a stable government. The new political leaders appreciated public opinion for what it was—an unreliable guide for policy making, often a dangerous beast that had to be controlled and tamed. But above all, it was a tool for the shaping of consensus, the molding of support. The new political realists also understood the power of the press. Cavour achieved first prominence and then power by founding his own newspaper, *Il Risorgimento*. Louis Napoleon ran Europe's first modern political campaign, manipulating the printed word to shape his image and tailor his message to different audiences.

Bismarck used public opinion and fashioned an image of German power that served his political ends.

DOCUMENT

A Letter from Bismarck

The Supremacy of the Nation-State. The new political men also shared, to varying degrees, a disregard for traditional morality in decision making. As Bismarck succinctly put it at the end of his long career in public life, "Politics ruins the character." The new political men forged their own standards by which they judged the correctness of decisions and policies.

The nation-state was the supreme justification for all actions. Cavour, Bismarck, and Louis Napoleon saw struggle as the central fact of life. Nation-states were inherently competitive, with conflicting objectives. Realpolitik meant that statesmen had to think in terms of military capability, technological dominance, and the acceptable use of force. Without a traditional morality of right and wrong, the leaders recognized that there could be no arbiter outside the interests of the nation-state. From exile in England following his military defeat and his abdication, Napoleon III placed the welfare of France above his failed ambitions. At the former emperor's funeral, his son led a cheer, not for the empire but for France.

Modern European statesmen did not, however, share a common ideological outlook. Cavour leaned toward liberal ideas, while Bismarck was unquestionably conservative and Louis Napoleon held a blend of liberal and conservative views. Yet the leaders willingly enacted similar policies and sponsored similar legislation, not from any shared political commitment, but because of their desire to strengthen and promote their nations. In order to maintain power, they adapted to circumstance; they did not insist on principle. As Bismarck explained it, he always had more than one arrow in his quiver.

The new political men were risk takers. They acted without the safety net of tradition or political legitimacy. Bismarck saw himself on a tightrope, but one he felt prepared to walk. Just as Jeremy Bentham, earlier in the century, had figured the relationship between actions and outcomes in terms of profits and losses, the new statesmen were calculators; they weighed levels of risk appropriate for the ends they sought to achieve. Realpolitik was less the invention of a particular statesman and more a characteristic of the new age of gamesmanship in statecraft.

CHANGING VALUES AND THE FORCE OF NEW IDEAS

Like the political world, the material world was changing rapidly after 1850. The world of ideas that explained the place of women and men in the new universe was rapidly changing as well. The railroad journey became the metaphor for the new age. The locomotive hurtling forward signified the strength, power, and progress of materialism. Yet the passenger was strangely dislocated, the landscape between one point and another a blur seen through a carriage window. New points of reference had to be found; new roots had to be put down. In the period between 1850 and 1870, a materialist system of values emerged as behaviors changed. That was as true for the private world of the home as it was for the public world of high politics.

In any age, changes in material life find their way into literature, philosophy, science, and art. Changes in the environment affect the way people look at the world. In turn, intellectuals can have a profound effect on values and behavior. Truly great thinkers not only reflect their times, they also shape them. The third quarter of the nineteenth century was especially rich in both the creativity and critical stance that shaped modern consciousness. Amid the tumult of new ideas in the period after 1850, two titans stand out. Not artists, but scientists—one of biology, the other of society—they sought regularity and predictability in the world they observed and measured. The ideas of Charles Darwin and Karl Marx both reflected and changed the world in which they lived. People alive during the third quarter of the nineteenth century called themselves "modern." They were, indeed, "modern," since in their values and view of the world they were closer to their twentieth-century progeny than they were to their eighteenth-century grandparents.

The Politics of Homemaking

At the Great Exhibition of 1851 in London, the achievements of modern industry were proudly displayed for all the world to see. Engineering marvels and mechanistic wonders dwarfed the thousands of visitors who came to the Crystal Palace to view civilization at its most advanced. In the midst of the machinery of the factory, household items took their place. Modern kitchens with coal-burning stoves were showcased, and the artifacts of the ideal home were carefully displayed. Predictably, mechanical looms, symbols of the new age, were exhibited; but inkstands, artificial flowers, thermostats, and cooking utensils were also enshrined. Visitors did not find strange the juxtaposition of the public world of production with the private world of the home in an exhibition celebrating British superiority.

The world of the home, not immune to changes in society and the economy, was invested with new power and meaning in mid-nineteenth-century Europe. Home was glorified as the locus of shelter and comfort where the harsh outside world could be forgotten. In 1870, an article in a popular Victorian magazine explained that the home functioned as a haven: "Home is emphatically man's place of rest, where his wife is his friend who knows his mind, where he may be himself without fear of offending, and relax the strain that must be kept out of doors: where he may feel himself safe, understood, and at ease."

Throughout Europe, the home served another function, as a symbol of status and achievement. Objects of a proper sort indicated wealth, upward mobility, and taste. In the belief that the more objects that could be displayed the better, the middle-class home of the third quarter of the nineteenth century was usually overdecorated. Drapes hung over doors and windows, pictures and prints covered the walls, and overstuffed furniture filled the rooms. All were intended to convey gentility and comfort.

Woman's Place.   Industrialization had separated the workplace from the home. Protective legislation before midcentury attempted to ease women out of the work force. Middle-class women were expected to assume primary responsibility for the domestic goals of escape and status. Just as the workplace was man's world, the private world of the home was woman's domain. After 1850, magazines, handbooks, and guidebooks that instructed women on how to fulfill their domestic duties proliferated. The most famous of the instruction manuals in Britain was *Mrs. Beeton's Book of Household Management* (1861). The title is instructive. The business concept of management could now be applied to the home. Mrs. Beeton told

■ The cover of the 1890 edition of *Mrs. Beeton's Everyday Cookery and Housekeeping Book.* Preparing an elaborate table like that shown in the cover illustration was one of women's principal domestic duties, according to Mrs. Beeton.

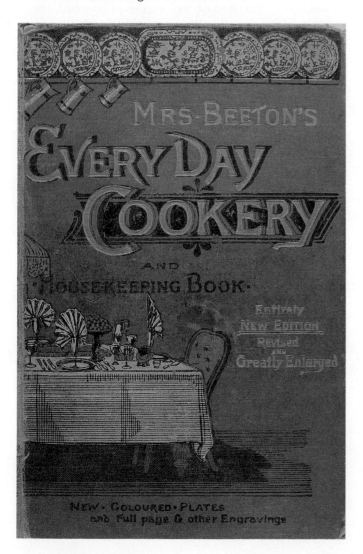

her readers, "The functions of the mistress of the house resemble those of the general of an army or the manager of a great business concern." "Home economics" was invented during this period. As the marketplace had its own rules and regulations that could be studied in the "dismal science" of economics, so too, women were told, the domestic sphere could benefit from the application of rational principles of organization.

Women were targeted by popular literature about how to get a man and keep him. Manuals cautioned women not to be too clever, since women with opinions were not popular with men. Mrs. Beeton's advice centered on food as the way to a man's heart. A wife's duty, she explained, was above all to provide her husband with a hot meal, prepared well and served punctually. Meals became elaborate occasions of several courses requiring hours of work. Women's magazines bombarded a growing readership with menus and recipes for the careful housewife. Status was communicated not by expensive foods, but by extravagant preparation. Meal planning was an art, women learned, one whose practice required and assumed the assistance of household servants. Before that time, women had produced in the home products they could now buy in the marketplace. Purchases of bread, beer, soap, and candles saved housewives hours of labor every week. But with rising expectations about the quality of life in the home, women had more rather than less to do each day. Handbooks prescribed rules on etiquette and proper manners. The rituals of domestic life, from letter writing to afternoon visits and serving tea, were minutely detailed for middle-class audiences. The woman of the house was instructed in the care and education of her children; in health, cleanliness, and nutrition; and in the management of resources. Thrift, industry, and orderliness, the virtues of the business world, had their own particular meaning in the domestic sphere.

To the Victorian mind, gentility and morality were inextricably interwoven. A woman who failed in her duty to maintain a clean and comfortable home threatened the safety of her family. An 1867 English tract warned:

> The man who goes home on a Saturday only to find his house in disorder, with every article of furniture out of its place, the floor unwashed or sloppy from uncompleted washing, his wife slovenly, his children untidy, his dinner not yet ready, or spoilt in the cooking, is much more likely "to go on a spree" than the man who finds his house in order, the furniture glistening from the recent polishing, the burnished steel fire-irons looking doubly resplendent from the bright glow of the cheerful fire, his well-cooked dinner laid on a snowy cloth, and his wife and children tidy and cheerful.

Working-Class Wives and Mothers.   The "ideal" was very far from the experiences of most families throughout Europe after the middle of the century. The "science" of homemaking presupposed a cushion of affluence out of reach to the men, women, and children who made up the vast majority of the population. Working-class wives and mothers often had to earn wages if their families were to survive. One

MISTRESS OF THE HOUSE

Mrs. Beeton's Book of Household Management was first published in 1861 and in less than a year sold 60,000 copies. Isabella Beeton was 23 years old when the book first appeared and she died at the age of 28 before she saw its vast success as one of the most published and reissued guidebooks of all time. The book is filled with practical advice on a wide variety of subjects ranging from wet-nursing to care of a sick child, etiquette, fashion, and cooking. Mrs. Beeton also provided a strong rationale for the importance of the domestic sphere in the modern world. The sections below are from Chapter 1: The Mistress.

Focus Questions

What is Mrs. Beeton's purpose in using military and business comparisons to describe the housewife's role? What is Mrs. Beeton's view of servants and of the mistress's responsibility as their manager? Why is an orderly household so important to the author?

As with the commander of an army, or the leader of any enterprise, so it is with the mistress of a house. Her spirit will be seen through the whole establishment; and just in proportion as she performs her duties intelligently and thoroughly, so will her domestics follow her path. Of all those acquirements, which more particularly belong to the feminine character, there are none which take a higher rank, in our estimation, than such as enter into a knowledge of household duties, for on these are perpetually dependent the happiness, comfort, and well-being of a family. . . .

Early rising is one of the most essential qualities which enter into good Household Management, as it is not only the parent of health, but of innumerable other advantages. Indeed, when a mistress is an early riser, it is almost certain that her house will be orderly and well-managed. On the contrary, if she remain in bed till a late hour, then the domestics, who, as we have before observed, invariably partake somewhat of their mistress's character, will surely become sluggards. To self-indulgence all are more or less disposed, and it is not to be expected that servants are freer from fault than the heads of houses. The great Lord Chatham thus gave his advice in reference to this subject— "I would have inscribed on the curtains of your bed, and the walls of your chamber, 'If you do not rise early, you can make progress in nothing.'"

From Mrs. Isabella Beeton, *The Book of Household Management* (1861).

Englishwoman, Lucy Luck (1848–1922), began her working career in a silk mill at the age of eight. By law allowed to work only half a day, the child Lucy returned to her foster home at the end of her shift to labor late into the night plaiting straw for baskets. In her reminiscences, she looked back over her life: "I have been at work for forty-seven years, and have never missed one season, although I have a large family of seven surviving children." Lucy, who married at the age of 18, learned that on her own she could not survive without a man's income or without resorting to the "bad life" of crime and prostitution. In the marriage, the couple could not survive without Lucy's wages.

Like Lucy Luck, many women held jobs outside the home or did piecework to supplement meager family incomes. In 1866, women constituted a significant percentage of the French labor force, including 45 percent of all textile workers. At the height of the rhetoric about the virtues of domesticity, as many as two married English women in five worked in the mills in industrial areas such as Lancashire. Working women often chose the "sweated labor" that they could perform in their home because it allowed them to care for their children while being paid by the piece. Home workers labored in the needle trades, shoemaking, and furniture making in their cramped living quarters under miserable conditions; and they worked for a third or less of what men earned.

Troubles at Home.   The "haven" of the home was not insulated from the perils of the outside world. Nor was every home a happy one. Venereal diseases rose dramatically in Western nations, belying the image of the devoted couple. By the end of the nineteenth century, 14 to 17 percent of all deaths in France were attributable to sexually transmitted diseases. The diseases were blind to class distinctions. Illegitimacy rates rose in the first half of the nineteenth century and remained high after 1850 among the working classes, defying middle-class standards of propriety. Illegitimate births were highest in urban areas, where household life assumed its own distinctive pattern among working-class families, with couples often choosing free union instead of legal marriage.

Because virtue was defined in terms of woman's roles as wife and mother, working women were regarded as immoral. Social evils were, according to that reasoning, easily attributed to the "unnatural" phenomenon of women leaving the home to work in a man's world. Women continued to work and, in some cases, to organize to demand their rights. Women like Lucy Luck did not and could not accept the prescription that good mothers should not work, since their wages fed their children. The politics of homemaking defined women as mothers and hence legitimated the poor treatment and poor pay of women as workers. Yet the labor of women outside as well as inside the home remained the norm.

Nor did all middle-class women accept approved social roles. Increasing numbers of middle-class women in western Europe protested their circumscribed sphere. Critics argued that designating the home as woman's proper domain stifled individual development. Earlier in the century, Jane Austen, one of Britain's greatest novelists, had to keep a piece of muslin work on her writing table in the family drawing room to cover her papers lest visitors detect evidence of literary activity. In the next generation, Florence Nightingale refused to accept the embroidery and knitting to which she was relegated at home. That period in Western society witnessed both the creation of the cult of domesticity and the stirrings of feminism among middle-class women, whose demand for equal treatment for women was to become more important after 1870. Patterns of behavior changed within the family, and they were not fixed immutably in social practice. Woman's place and woman's role proved to be much-disputed questions in the new politics of homemaking.

Realism in the Arts

Realism in the arts and literature was a rejection of romantic idealism and subjectivity. The realist response to the disillusionment with the political failures of the post-1848 era characterized a wide array of artistic and literary endeavors. Realists depicted the challenges of urban and industrial growth by confronting the alienation of modern life.

The Social World of the Artist.   The term **realism** was first used in 1850 to describe the paintings of Gustave Courbet (1819–1877). In *The Artist's Studio* (1855), Courbet portrayed himself surrounded by the intellectuals and political figures of his day. He may have been painting a landscape, but contemporary political life crowded in; a starving Irish peasant and her child crouch beneath his easel. Of his unrelenting canvases, none more fittingly portrays the harsh realism of bourgeois life than the funeral ceremony depicted in *Burial at Ornans* (1849–1850) or better depicts the brutality of workers' lives than *The Stone Breakers* (1849) (see below).

Other artists shared Courbet's desire to reject the conventions prevailing in the art world in favor of portraying reality in its natural and social dimensions. Jean-Francois Millet's paintings of peasants and workers (see p. 653) sought for a truth deeper than a surface beauty. Images of ordinary people, the working classes, and the poor populated realist art. Realist artists often strove to make a social commentary such as that of Honoré Daumier's *Washerwoman,* which shows a woman of the lower classes, clearly weary, climbing up a flight of stairs with a small child in tow. Daumier captures scenes from the daily life of the poor that would not have been considered a fit subject for art a generation before.

Realist Novels.   After midcentury, idealization in romantic literature yielded to novels depicting the objective and unforgiving social world. Through serialization in journals and newspapers, fiction reached out to mass audiences, who obtained their "facts" about modern life through stories that often cynically portrayed the monotony and boredom of daily existence. In *Hard Times* (1854), set in the imaginary city of Coketown, Charles Dickens (1812–1870) created an allegory that exposed the sterility and soullessness of industrial society through "fact, fact, fact everywhere in the material aspect of the town; fact, fact, fact everywhere in the immaterial."

■ Gustave Courbet (1819–1877), *The Stone Breakers* (1849). Courbet realistically portrays menial labor with the two laborers' faces obscured.

Gustave Flaubert (1821–1880), the great French realist novelist, critiqued the Western intellectual tradition in his unfinished *Dictionary of Accepted Ideas* (1881). In the novel *Bouvard et Pécuchet* (1881), Flaubert satirized modern man's applications of Enlightenment ideas about the environment and progress by showing that they were foolish and often at odds with common sense. The main characters of the novel know everything there is to know about theories and applied sciences, but they know nothing about life. His best-known work, *Madame Bovary* (1856), recounts the story of a young country doctor's wife whose desire to escape from the boredom of her provincial existence leads her into adultery and eventually results in her destruction. Flaubert was put on trial for obscenity and violating public morality with his tale of the unrepentant Emma Bovary. The beautifully crafted novel is marked by an ironic detachment from the hypocrisy of bourgeois life. Mary Ann Evans (1819–1880), writing under the pseudonym George Eliot, was also concerned with moral choices and responsibilities in her novels, including *Middlemarch* (1871–1872), a tale of idealism disappointed by the petty realities of provincial English life.

The problem of morality in the realist novel is nowhere more apparent than in the works of the Russian writer Fyodor Dostoyevsky (1821–1881). Dostoyevsky's protagonists wrestle with a universe where God no longer exists and where they must shape their own morality. The impoverished student Raskolnikov in *Crime and Punishment* (1866) justifies his brutal murder of an old woman that occurs in the opening pages of the novel. Realist art and literature addressed an educated elite public but did not flinch before the unrelenting poverty and harshness of contemporary life. The morality of the realist vision lay not in condemning the evils of modern life and seeking their political solutions, as an earlier generation of romantics did, but in depicting social evils for what they were, failures of a smug and progressive middle class.

The New World of Photography.   It is perhaps difficult for us to imagine a world before the accurate visual images that modern photography and the media revolution of the twentieth century made an integral part of our daily lives. Yet it was not until 1839 that Western men and women saw the first modern photographs.

Nineteenth-century photography was the result of wedding art and science. Although various techniques that made it possible to capture images and landscapes on paper existed in the early decades of the nineteenth century, Louis Daguerre (1789–1851) can be credited as a pioneer in the photographic process with the invention of the daguerreotype in 1839. Daguerre was both a French scene painter and a physicist, and he brought both his sensibilities and scientific training to the process of capturing images on silver-coated copper plates treated with iodine vapor. The images were often clouded and not able to be reproduced, as from a negative. Successive discoveries of new techniques allowed for the creation and reproduction of lasting images in still photography.

■ Calotype of the Adamson family, ca. 1844, by pioneer photographers Robert Adamson (shown at far right) and David Octavius Hill of Scotland. The new technology of photography enabled middle-class families to have their portraits taken, a luxury once only available to those wealthy enough to commission artists.

The fascination with photography in the nineteenth century can be observed in its use for portraits by growing numbers of ordinary people, just as in an earlier time the wealthy and powerful sat for oil portraits. With the achievement of greater portability and precision, the camera, still a cumbersome object, was used for country landscapes, urban landmarks, and recording the horrors and glory of battle. Within a generation, cameras altered the way people understood the world around them and how they recorded human life. An increasing emphasis on the real world, reflected in literature, art, and discoveries in science was fueled by the altered worldview and the new consciousness that photography made possible.

Charles Darwin and the New Science

Science had a special appeal for a generation of Europeans disillusioned with the political failures of idealism in the revolutions of 1848. It was not an age of great scientific discovery,

■ Charles Darwin as a young man. Darwin was only 22 years old in 1831 when he signed on for a five-year cruise as the official naturalist aboard the *Beagle*. By this age he had already tried and rejected careers in medicine and the ministry.

but rather one of synthesis of previous findings and their technological applications. Science was, above all, to be useful in promoting material progress.

DOCUMENT

On Darwin

Charles Darwin (1809–1882), the preeminent scientist of the age, was a great synthesizer. Darwin began his scientific career as a naturalist with a background in geology. As a young man, he sailed around the world on the *Beagle* (1831–1836). He collected specimens and fossils as the ship's naturalist, with his greatest finds in South America, especially the Galápagos Islands. He spent the next 20 years of his life taking notes of his observations of the natural world. In chronically poor health, Darwin produced 500 pages of what he called "one long argument." *On the Origin of Species by Means of Natural Selection* (1859) was a book that changed the world.

Darwin's argument was a simple one: life forms originated in and perpetuated themselves through struggle. The outcome of the struggle was determined by **natural selection,** or what came to be known as "survival of the fittest." Better-adapted individuals survived, while others died out. Competition between species and within species produced a dynamic model of organic evolution. Darwin did not use the word evolution in the original edition, but a positivist belief in an evolutionary process permeated the 1859 text.

Evolutionary theory was not new, nor was materialism a new concept in organic biology. In the 1850s, others were coming forward with similar ideas about natural selection, including most notably A. R. Wallace (1823–1913), who stressed geographic factors in biological evolution. Darwin's work was a product of discoveries in a variety of fields—philosophy, history, and science. He derived his idea of struggle from Malthus's *Essay on Population* and borrowed across disciplines to construct a theory of "the preservation of favored races in the struggle for life" (part of the book's subtitle). The publication of *On the Origin of Species* made Darwin immediately famous. Scientific theory was the stuff of front-page headlines. Like Samuel Smiles, a businessman who published the best-seller *Self-Help* in 1860, Darwin spoke of struggle and discipline, though in nature, not in the marketplace. In the world of biology, Darwin's ideas embodied a new realist belief in progress based on struggle. Force explained the past and would guarantee the future as the fittest survived. Those were ideas that a general public applied to a whole range of human endeavors and to theories of social organization.

Karl Marx and the Science of Society

"Just as Darwin discovered the law of development of organic nature, Marx discovered the law of development of human history." So spoke Friedrich Engels (1820–1895), longtime friend of and collaborator with Karl Marx (1818–1883), over Marx's grave. Marx would have been pleased with Engels's eulogy: he called himself the Darwin of sociology. Marx footnoted as corroborating evidence Darwin's "epoch-making work on the origin of species" in his own masterwork, *Das Kapital*, the first volume of which appeared in 1867. As the theorist of the socialism that he called "scientific," Marx viewed himself as an evolutionist who demonstrated that history is the dialectical struggle of classes.

The son of a Prussian lawyer who had converted from Judaism to Christianity, Marx had rejected the study of the law and belief in a deity. In exile because of his political writings, Marx was the most brilliant of the German young Hegelians, intellectuals heavily influenced by the ideas of Georg Friedrich Hegel (1770–1831), which held sway over the German intellectual world of the 1830s and 1840s. By the mid-1840s, Marx was in rebellion against Hegel's idealism and was developing his own materially grounded view of society.

The philosophy that evolved in the years of collaboration with Engels was built on a materialist view of society. Human beings were defined not by their souls but by their labor. Labor was a struggle to transform nature by producing commodities useful for survival. Their ability to transform nature by work differentiated men and women from animals. Building on that fundamental concept of labor, Marx and

ON THE ORIGIN OF SPECIES, 1859

For the 20 years prior to the publication of On the Origin of Species, *Charles Darwin gathered data in support of his theory of evolution. He was not alone in advancing a theory of natural selection, but he was unique in basing his conclusions on carefully compiled data.* On the Origin of Species *was based on his scientific observations resulting from a five-year cruise aboard the* Beagle, *which took him to the Galápagos Islands off the coast of Ecuador.*

Focus Questions

How did Charles Darwin construct his case and deploy his thesis for the evolution of the human species without using the word "evolution"? What words did he use? What did he mean by the term "species," and how did he see species as interrelated?

I have now recapitulated the chief facts and considerations which have thoroughly convinced me that species have changed, and are still slowly changing by the preservation and accumulation of successive slight favorable variations. Why, it may be asked, have all the most eminent living naturalists and geologists rejected this view of the mutability of species? It cannot be asserted that organic beings in a state of nature are subject to no variation; it cannot be proved that the amount of variation in the course of long ages is a limited quantity; no clear distinction has been, or can be, drawn between species and well-marked varieties. It cannot be maintained that species when intercrossed are invariably sterile, and varieties invariably fertile; and that

sterility is a special endowment and sign of creation. The belief that species were immutable productions was almost unavoidable as long as the history of the world was thought to be of short duration; and now that we have acquired some idea of the lapse of time, we are too apt to assume, without proof, that the geological record is so perfect that it would have afforded us plain evidence of the mutation of species, if they had undergone mutation.

But the chief cause of our natural unwillingness to admit that one species have given birth to other and distinct species, is that we are always slow in admitting any great change of which we do not see the intermediate steps. The difficulty is the same as that felt by so many geologists, when Lyell [Sir Charles Lyell (1797–1875), English geologist] first insisted that long lines of inland cliffs had been formed, and great valleys excavated, by the slow action of the coast-waves. The mind cannot possibly grasp the full meaning of the term of a hundred million years; it cannot add up and perceive the full effects of many slight variations, accumulated during an almost infinite number of generations.

Engels saw society as divided into two camps: those who own property and those who do not. Nineteenth-century capitalist society was divided into two classes: the bourgeoisie, those who owned the means of production as their private property, and the proletariat, the propertyless working class.

The Class Struggle.   This materialist perspective on society was the engine driving Marx's theory of history. For Marx, every social system based on a division into classes carries within it the seeds of its own destruction. Marx and Engels used a biological metaphor to explain the destruction: the growth of a plant from a seed is a dialectical process in which the germ is destroyed by its opposite, the plant. The mature plant produces seed while continuing its form. For Marx and Engels, the different stages of history are determined by different forms of the ownership of production. In a feudal-agrarian society, the aristocracy controlled and exploited the unfree labor of serfs. In a world of commerce and manufacturing, the capitalist bourgeoisie are the new aristocracy exploiting free labor for wages.

Marx was more than an observer: he was a critic of capitalism. His labor theory of value was the wedge he drove into the self-congratulatory rhetoric of the capitalist age. Labor is the source of all value, he argued, and yet the bourgeois employer

denies workers the profit of their work by refusing to pay them a decent wage. Instead, the employer pockets the profits. Workers are separated, or alienated, from the product of their labor. But more profoundly, Marx believed that in a capitalist system all workers are alienated from the creation that makes them human; they are alienated from their labor.

Marx predicted that capitalism would produce more and more goods but would continue to pay workers the lowest wages possible. By driving out smaller producers, the bourgeoisie would increase the size of the proletariat. Yet Marx was optimistic. As workers were slowly pauperized, they would become conscious of their exploitation and would revolt.

Marx's Legacy.   The force of Karl Marx's ideas mobilized thousands of contemporaries aware of the injustices of capitalism. Few thinkers in the history of the West have left a more lasting legacy than Marx. The legacy has survived the fact that much of Marx's analysis rested on incorrect predictions about the increasing misery of workers and the inflexibility of the capitalist system. Marx was a synthesizer who combined economics, philosophy, politics, and history in a wide-ranging critique of industrial society.

Marxism spread across Europe as workers responded to its message. Marx did not cause the increase in the organization

Although I am fully convinced of the truth of the views given in this volume under the form of an abstract, I by no means expect to convince experienced naturalists whose minds are stocked with a multitude of facts all viewed, during a long course of years, from a point of view directly opposite to mine. It is so easy to hide our ignorance under such expressions as the "plan of creation," "unity of design," etc., and to think that we give an explanation when we only restate a fact. Any one whose disposition leads him to attach more weight to unexplained difficulties than to the explanation of a certain number of facts will certainly reject my theory.

A few naturalists, endowed with much flexibility of mind, and who have already begun to doubt on the immutability of species, may be influenced by this volume; but I look with confidence to the future, to young and rising naturalists, who will be able to view both sides of the question with impartiality. Whoever is led to believe that species are mutable will do good service by conscientiously expressing his conviction; for only thus can the load of prejudice by which this subject is overwhelmed be removed. . . .

It may be asked how far I extend the doctrine of the modification of species. The question is difficult to answer, because the more distinct the forms are which we may consider, by so much the arguments fall away in force. But some arguments of the greatest weight extend very far. All the members of whole classes can be connected together by chains of affinities, and all can be classified on the same principle, in groups subordinate to groups. Fossil remains sometimes tend to fill up very wide intervals between existing orders. Organs in a rudimentary condition plainly show that an early progenitor had the organ in a fully developed state; and this in some instances necessarily implies an enormous amount of modification in the descendants. Throughout whole classes various structures are formed on the same pattern, and at an embryonic age the species closely resemble each other. Therefore I cannot doubt that the theory of descent with modification embraces all the members of the same class. I believe that animals have descended from at most only four or five progenitors, and plants from an equal or lesser number.

Analogy would lead me one step further, namely, to the belief that all animals and plants have descended from some one prototype. But analogy may be a deceitful guide. Nevertheless all living things have much in common, in the chemical composition, their germinal vesicles, their cellular structure, and their laws of growth and reproduction. We see this even in so trifling a circumstance as that the same poison often similarly affects plants and animals; or that the poison secreted by the gall-fly produces monstrous growths on the wild rose or oak-tree. Therefore I should infer from analogy that probably all the organic beings which have ever lived on this earth have descended from some one primordial form, into which life was first breathed.

From Charles Darwin, *On the Origin of Species* (London, 1859), pp. 480–490.

---

of workers that took place in the 1860s, but his theories did give shape and focus to a growing critique of labor relations in the second half of the nineteenth century. Political parties throughout Europe coalesced around Marxist beliefs and programs. Marxists were beginning to be heard in associations of workers, and in 1864 they helped found the International Working Men's Association in London, an organization of French, German, and Italian workers dedicated to "the end of all class rule." The promise of a common association of workers transcending national boundaries became a compelling idea to those who envisioned the end of capitalism. The importance of the international exchange of ideas and information cannot be underestimated as a means of promoting labor organization in western Europe. In 1871, Marx and his followers turned to Paris for proof that the revolution was at hand.

A New Revolution?

Soundly defeated on 2 September 1870, Napoleon III and his fighting force of 100,000 men became Prussia's prisoners of war. With the emperor's defeat, the Second Empire collapsed. But even with the capture of Napoleon III, the French capital city of Paris refused to capitulate. The dedication of Parisians to the ongoing war with the Prussians was evident from the first. The regime's liberal critics in Paris seized the initiative to proclaim France a republic. If a corrupt and decadent empire could not save the nation, then France's Third Republic could.

The Siege of Paris.   In mid-September 1870, two German armies surrounded Paris and began a siege that lasted for more than four months. Only carrier pigeons and balloon-transported passengers linked Paris with the rest of France. In the beginning, Parisian heroism, unchallenged by battle, seemed festive and unreal. Bismarck's troops were intent on bringing the city to its knees not by fighting but by cutting off its vital supply lines. By November, food and fuel were dwindling and Parisians were facing starvation. Undaunted, they began to eat dogs, cats, and rats. By December, famine threatened to become a reality. Most people had no vegetables and no meat. Rationing was ineffective, and a black market prevailed in which the wealthy could buy whatever was available. Horses disappeared from the streets and the zoo was emptied as antelope, camel, donkey, mule, and elephant became desirable table fare. The Bois de Boulogne, the city's largest park, was leveled for timber to build barricades and for fuel. But the wood was too green and would not burn. The bitter cold of one of the century's most severe winters heightened the horror. Yet the population was committed to fighting on. Men

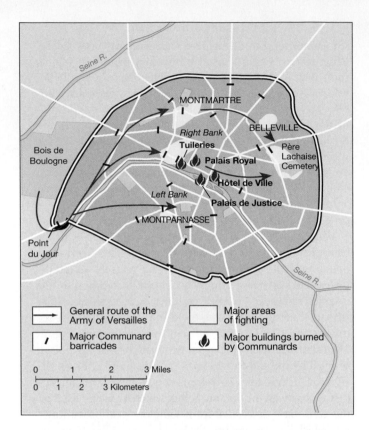

■ The Paris Commune. French troops, under the direction of the French government sitting in Versailles, penetrated the fortifications ringing the city of Paris, and within one "Bloody Week," crushed the Parisian Communards.

and women became part of the city's citizen militia, the National Guard, and trained for combat against the Germans. "Siege fever" swept the city. In spite of dire conditions, there were moments of euphoria. Collective delusions, perhaps intensified by empty stomachs, convinced Parisians that they were invincible against the enemy. Citizens joined clubs to discuss politics and preparedness, and probably to keep warm. Patents on inventions to defeat the Germans proliferated. Most of them were useless and silly, like the musical machine gun that was intended to lure its victims within firing range. The enemy at their gates absorbed the total attention of the urban population. There was no life other than the war.

Apparently with the goal of terrorizing the population, the Germans began a steady bombardment of the city at the beginning of January 1871. The shells fell for three weeks, but Parisian resistance prevailed. However, the rest of France wanted an end to the war. The Germans agreed to an armistice at the end of January 1871 in order that French national elections could be held to elect representatives to the new government. In the elections, French citizens outside Paris repudiated the war and returned an overwhelmingly conservative majority to seek peace.

Thus the siege came to an end. Yet it left deep wounds that still festered. Parisians believed they had been betrayed by the rest of France. Through four months as a besieged city, they had sacrificed, suffered, and died. Parisians believed that they were defenders of the true republic, the true patriots. Among Parisians, disparities of wealth were more obvious than ever before. Some wealthy citizens had abandoned the city during the siege. The wealthy who did stay ate and kept warm. Poor women who stood in food lines from before dawn every day to provision their families knew that there was food—but not for them.

The Paris Commune.   The war was over, but Paris was not at peace. The new national government, safely installed outside Paris at Versailles, attempted to reestablish normal life. The volatility of the city motivated the government's attempt in March 1871 to disarm the Parisian citizenry by using army troops. In the hilly neighborhood of northern Paris, men, women, and children poured into the streets to protect their

CHRONOLOGY	
State Building and Social Change	
1853–1856	Crimean War
1859	Austria declares war on Kingdom of Sardinia; France joins forces with Italians
1860	Piedmont-Sardinia annexes duchies in central Italy; France gains Nice and Savoy
3 March 1861	Emancipation of Russian serfs
14 March 1861	Kingdom of Italy proclaimed with Victor Emmanuel II as king
1861–1865	American Civil War
1863	Maximilian crowned emperor of Mexico
1863	Prussians and Austrians at war with Denmark
1866	Seven Weeks' War between Austria and Prussia; Italy acquires Venetia
1867	Emperor Maximilian executed
July 1870	Franco-Prussian War begins
2 September 1870	French Second Empire capitulates with Prussian victory at Sedan
20 September 1870	Italy annexes Rome
18 January 1871	German Empire proclaimed
March–May 1871	Paris Commune

cannons and to defend their right to bear arms. In the fighting that followed, the Versailles troops were driven from the city. Paris was in a state of siege once again.

The spontaneity of the March uprising was soon succeeded by organization. Citizens rallied to the idea of the city's self-government and established the **Paris Commune**, as other French cities followed the capital's lead. Karl Marx hailed the event as the beginning of the revolution that would overthrow the capitalist system and saw in it the beginning of the dictatorship of the proletariat. But what occurred between March and May 1871 was not a proletarian revolution. Rather, it was a continuation of the state of siege that had held Paris through the fall and early winter months. Parisians were still at war. It was not war against a foreign enemy, nor was it a class war. It was a civil war against the rest of France.

The social experiment of self-defense in the Commune lasted for 72 days. Armed women formed their own fighting units, the city council regulated labor relations, and neighborhoods ruled themselves. In May 1871, government troops reentered the city and brutally crushed the Paris Commune. In one "Bloody Week," 25,000 Parisians were massacred and 40,000 others were arrested and tried. Of the 10,000 rebels convicted, 5000 were sent to a penal colony in the southwestern Pacific Ocean. Such reprisals inflamed radicals and workers all over Europe. The myth of the Commune became a rallying cry for revolutionary movements throughout the world and inspired the future leaders of the Russian revolutionary state.

The Commune was important at the time, but not as a revolution. It offered two lessons to men and women at the end of the third quarter of the nineteenth century. First, it demonstrated the power of patriotism. Competing images of the nation were at stake, one Parisian and the other French, but no one could deny the power of national identity to inspire a whole city to suffer and to sacrifice. Second, the Commune made clear the power of the state. No revolutionary movement could succeed without controlling the massive forces of repression at the state's command. The Commune had tried to recapture a local, federal view of the world but failed to take sufficient account of the power of the state that it opposed. In writing of the episode two decades later, Friedrich Engels wondered if revolution would ever again be possible in the West.

CONCLUSION

Western societies had crossed the threshold into the modern age in the third quarter of the nineteenth century. Strong states from Great Britain to Russia were committed to creating and preserving the conditions of industrial expansion. The machine age, railroads, and metallurgy were spreading industrial development much more widely through western and central Europe than had been possible before 1850. Italians and Prussians, in attempting to join the ranks of nation-states, realized that the road to a strong nation could only be achieved with industrial development and social reforms.

State building in Western societies went hand in hand with growth in the social responsibilities of government. The national powers that would dominate world politics and economy in the twentieth century all underwent modernizing transitions in the 1860s. The powers included the United States, France, Great Britain, and Germany. The Austrian Empire, too, undertook programs to modernize its government and economy, and the Russian Empire established social reforms of unparalleled dimensions. New nations came into existence in this period through the limited use of armed force. With the establishment of the German Empire, Otto von Bismarck, the most realistic of politicians, was intent on preserving the peace in Europe by balancing the power of the great European states. Europeans prided themselves on being both modern and realistic in the third quarter of the nineteenth century. Peace was possible if it was armed and vigilant. Reform, not revolution, many were sure, was the key to the future progress of European societies.

QUESTIONS FOR REVIEW

1. How did the process of creating nation-states in Germany and Italy differ?
2. What social and political circumstances explain the different reforms undertaken in France, Britain, and Russia?
3. How did industrialization change women's lives, and how did such changes depend on a woman's social class?
4. What were the connections between Darwin's ideas about nature and Marx's ideas about society?
5. What forces inspired the creation of the Paris Commune, and what did its fate suggest about the possibility of revolution in the late nineteenth century?

KEY TERMS

dual monarchy, *p. 694*

"Eastern question", *p. 686*

"Haussmannization," *p. 696*

natural selection, *p. 709*

Paris Commune, *p. 713*

Peace of Paris of 1856, *p. 686*

Proclamation of the German Empire, *p. 694*

realism, *p. 707*

Realpolitik, *p. 693*

Reichstag, *p. 694*

Risorgimento, *p. 690*

zemstvos, p. 702

DISCOVERING WESTERN CIVILIZATION ONLINE

You can obtain more information about state building and social change in Europe between 1850 and 1871 at the Websites listed below. See also the Companion Website that accompanies this text, www.ablongman.com/kishlansky, which contains an online study guide and additional resources.

Building Nations: The Politics of Unification

The Crimean War (1853–1856)
www.hillsdale.edu/oldacademics/history/war/19Crim.htm
Electronic texts of officers' and soldiers' accounts of the battles of the Crimean War.

Internet Modern History Sourcebook: 19th Century Italy
www.fordham.edu/halsall/mod/modsbook23.html
This site focuses on documents relating to the unification of Italy and the Risorgimento.

Modern History Sourcebook: Documents of German Unification, 1848–1871
www.fordham.edu/halsall/mod/germanunification.html
This site provides translations of major primary documents concerning the unification of Germany.

Reforming European Society

The Victorian Web
www.victorianweb.org
A comprehensive collection of links to Victorian England.

Age of Liberalism: 1848–1914
campus.northpark.edu/history/WebChron/WestEurope/LiberalAge.html
A collection of links to chronologies for the "Age of Liberalism," 1848–1914.

Internet Modern History Sourcebook: Russian Revolution
www.fordham.edu/halsall/mod/modsbook39.html
This site, a repository for links to the Russian Revolution, provides links to documents on nineteenth-century tsarist Russia.

Changing Values and the Force of New Ideas

Florence Nightingale
www.kings.edu/womens_history/florence.html
Annotated bibliography of literature on Florence Nightingale.

The Eighteenth Brumaire of Louis Napoleon
csf.colorado.edu/psn/marx/Archive/1852-18brum/
The electronic text of Karl Marx's *Eighteenth Brumaire of Napoleon*.

1851 Project: The Great Exhibition
www.nal.vam.ac.uk/projects/1851.html
This site draws upon the collection of the National Library of Art in London to chronicle the Great Exhibition of 1851.

The Darwin Page
web.clas.ufl.edu/users/rhatch/pages/02-TeachingResources/readingwriting/darwin/05-DARWIN-PAGE.html
Web page of Professor Robert Hatch of the University of Florida, which provides links to bibliographies, texts, and other resources on Charles Darwin.

Paris Commune Archive
dwardmac.pitzer.edu/Anarchist_Archives/pariscommune/Pariscommunearchive.html
A Pitzer College political studies site providing summaries of the major players and events of the Paris Commune as well as an extensive bibliography.

Internet Women's History Sourcebook
www.fordham.edu/halsall/women/womensbook.html
This section of the Modern History Sourcebook focuses on women's history from antiquity to the present. The subchapter on modern European women's history provides links to texts on the structure of working women's lives as well as texts on feminism and the suffrage movement.

SUGGESTIONS FOR FURTHER READING

Building Nations: The Politics of Unification

David Blackbourn, *The Long Nineteenth Century: A History of Germany, 1780–1918* (New York: Oxford University Press, 1998). This book examines the emergence of Germany from the late eighteenth century through the First World War in terms of politics, economics, and culture.

John A. Davis, ed., *Italy in the Nineteenth Century, 1796–1900* (New York: Oxford University Press, 2000). The essays of nine specialists provide an historical analysis of Italian society, politics, and culture.

Peter H. Hoffenberg, *An Empire on Display: English, Indian, and Australian Exhibitions from the Crystal Palace to the Great War* (Berkeley: University of California Press, 2001). The author examines over 30 colonial exhibitions from three different continents.

Dieter Langewiesche, *Liberalism in Germany* (Princeton, NJ: Princeton University Press, 2000). This study traces the roots of German liberalism to the late eighteenth century and emphasizes the role of individual German states, with a special chapter on the local influences on the formation of the nation-state between 1815 and 1860.

Lucy Riall, *The Italian Risorgimento: State, Society, and National Unification* (New York: Routledge, 1999). Riall examines the historiography of Italian unification and presents the turbulent period of "resurgence" as a turning point in Italian history.

Denis Mack Smith, *Cavour* (London: Weidenfeld and Nicolson, 1985). Smith contrasts Cavour and his policies with those of Garibaldi and Mazzini and considers the challenge of regionalism to the unification process.

Reforming European Society

Jane Burbank and David Ransel, eds., *Imperial Russia: New Histories for the Empire* (Bloomington: Indiana University Press, 1998). A collection of essays using new methodologies for understanding Russian history in the eighteenth and nineteenth centuries.

Judith Flanders, *Inside the Victorian Home: A Portrait of Domestic Life in Victorian England* (New York: W.W. Norton & Co., 2004). This examination of the daily lives of ordinary people reconstructs the drudgery of Victorian domesticity and "the different mental world" of that era.

Catherine Hall, Keith McClelland, and Jane Rendall, *Defining the Victorian Nation: Class, Race, Gender and the British Reform Act of 1867* (Cambridge: Cambridge University Press, 2000). This co-authored study presents a cultural, social, and gender history of the extension of the vote in 1867, accompanied by strong bibliographic aids.

Sudhir Hazareesingh, *From Subject to Citizen: The Second Empire and the Emergence of Modern French Democracy* (Princeton, NJ: Princeton University Press, 1998). In showing the relationship between the local and the national, the author provides a reevaluation of the emergence of republican citizenship in the Second Empire.

Margaret Homans, *Royal Representations: Queen Victoria and British Culture, 1837–1876* (Chicago: University of Chicago Press, 1998). Victoria is examined as a monarch, a symbol, and a wife and mother and as a key to British culture.

Alain Plessis, *The Rise and Fall of the Second Empire, 1852–1871,* tr. Jonathan Mandelbaum (Cambridge: Cambridge University Press, 1985). Discusses the Second Empire as an important transitional period in French history, when the conflict was between traditional and modern values in political, economic, and social transformations.

Changing Values and the Force of New Ideas

Jenni Calder, *The Victorian Home* (London: B. T. Batsford, 1977). A cultural and social history of Victorian domestic life in which the author describes both bourgeois and working-class domestic environments.

Katharine Anne Lerman, *Bismarck* (Longman, 2004). A new introduction to the life of the man who unified Germany.

Bonnie G. Smith, *Ladies of the Leisure Class: The Bourgeoises of Northern France in the Nineteenth Century* (Princeton, NJ: Princeton University Press, 1981). Explores the impact of industrialization on the lives of bourgeois women in northern France and demonstrates how the cult of domesticity emerged in a particular community.

Robert Tombs, *The Paris Commune, 1871* (London: Longman, 1999). A synthetic overview of the events of the Commune and their impact on the course of French and European history.

Martha Vicinus, *Independent Women: Work and Community for Single Women, 1850–1920* (Chicago: University of Chicago Press, 1985). Chronicles the choices that Victorian women made to live outside the norms of marriage and domesticity in various women's communities, including sisterhoods, nursing communities, colleges, boarding schools, and settlement houses.

For a list of additional titles related to this chapter's topics, please see http://www.ablongman.com/kishlansky.

SPEEDING TO THE FUTURE

MASS SOCIETY AND THE REJECTION OF TRADITION

"We want to demolish museums and libraries." These are not the words of an anarchist or a terrorist but of a poet. The Italian writer Emilio Marinetti (1876–1944) endeavored—symbolically, at least, through the power of his pen—to destroy the citadels of Western culture at the beginning of the twentieth century. Marinetti was not alone in wanting to pull down all that preserved art and learning in the West. Joined by other artists and writers who called themselves **futurists,** Marinetti represented a desire to break free of the past. By shocking complacent bourgeois society with their art, futurists hoped to fashion a new and dynamic civilization. Although they were a small group with limited influence, their concerns were shared by a growing number of intellectuals who judged European culture to be in the throes of a serious moral and cultural crisis. Futurist ideas also reflected the growing preoccupation with the future common among European men and women who spurned the value of tradition.

THE VISUAL RECORD

The futurist painter Umberto Boccioni (1882–1916) captured an aspect of the dynamic intensity of the changing world in his *Riot in the Galleria* (1910) shown here. The setting is a galleria, the equivalent of a modern shopping mall, in front of a respectable *caffé* (an Italian coffee shop), frequented by well-dressed men and women, clearly members of the middle class. It shows a modern urban scene, a public space in every way characteristic of the new age of enjoyment and consumption.

The painting tells a story. In a flurry of light and shadow, a rush of figures moves toward the middle ground of the canvas. At the center of the movement are two women engaged in a brawl that seems to pull the figures of shoppers and strollers toward it. The fact that the brawlers are female is intended to underscore the irrationality of the incident. Yet the brawl itself is not compelling our attention. Rather it is the movement of the crowd, like moths to a flame, that Boccioni intended viewers to

see. It is a painting about movement. The objects in motion are little more than vibrations in space, faceless and indistinguishable as individuals. The crowd does not walk or run; it appears instead to be in flight. In his studies for the canvas, Boccioni reduced movement to a series of lines both swirling and directed.

The riot Boccioni depicts is an irrational event. It is no ordinary rabble: it is a well-dressed mob, as the blurred but sumptuously flowered hats and the occasional yellow straw boaters make clear. Movement is taking place without forethought, fueled by the attraction of violence and the possibility of participating in it. There are those on the periphery who have not joined the frenzy, but it appears likely that they will be swept up in the action as the energy of the brawl sucks everything to its center, like the vortex of a tornado. European society seemed to many contemporaries to be moving into an abyss, a world of tumultuous change but without values.

In the violence of the riot we are shown beauty of movement that surpasses that of an orderly waltz. Boccioni uses the warm glow of the electric lights, symbol of the modern age, to illuminate a "new reality." Golden tones, warm oranges and rosy hues, shadowed in delicate purples, create a mosaic whose beauty in the play of color is strangely at odds with the theme of the two brawling figures who activate the crowd. There is no meaning beyond the movement.

Riot in the Galleria reflects the preoccupation with change in the early twentieth century. Life was moving so fast that by 1900 European society seemed to have outrun its own heritage. Technology was transforming Europe with a breakneck speed unmatched in human history. Science undermined the way people thought about themselves by challenging moral and religious values as hollow and meaningless. The natural sciences threw into doubt the existence of a creator. New forms of communication and transportation—the telephone, the wireless telegraph, the bicycle, the automobile, the airplane—were obliterating traditional understandings of time and space. The cinema and the X ray altered visual perception and redefined the ways people saw the world around them. It was a period of intense excitement and vitality in the history of the West, one that traditional values did not always explain.

Like the political revolutionaries of an earlier age, futurist artists sought the liberation of the human spirit from a world that could no longer be understood or controlled. Liberation could only be achieved through immersion in mass society and rapid change. Boccioni's goal was a revolutionary one: "Let's turn everything upside down. . . . Let's split open our figures and place the environment inside them."

Boccioni has been recognized as one of the great artists of the twentieth century. In his sculpture and painting, he aimed to capture the vitality and excitement of the new age. The individual was no longer at the center of the new culture. Change, technology, and, above all, violence were exalted. As the First Futurist Manifesto urged, "Let us leave Wisdom behind. . . . Let us throw ourselves to be devoured by the Unknown." With the figures in his canvas swept up into an irrational mass, Boccioni emphasizes the rush and unpredictability of daily life. Boccioni met his own death in 1916 as a soldier in the war that he welcomed as a purifying event.

■ Umberto Boccioni, *Riot in the Galleria* (1910).

LOOKING AHEAD

As Europe passed from the nineteenth to the twentieth century, the new, grand scale of industrial production and political life was matched by the emergence of mass society. This chapter will discuss how the need for regulation and control in mass democracy challenged the liberal, nineteenth-century emphasis on individual rights and parliamentary rule in Great Britain, Germany, France, and Austria. Mass democracy drew new social groups, workers and peasants, into the political arena, but it also continued to exclude others, including women, ethnic minorities, and Jews, whose pursuit of inclusion further challenged parliamentary forms.

The sciences and the new scientific study of society known as the social sciences contributed to attempts to understand how the physical world functioned, its predictability, and its improvement through technological and applied advances in knowledge. And a new artistic vision influenced by breakthroughs in science, technology, new knowledge about other cultures, and the study of the unconscious greatly enriched the way Europeans and the broader global community viewed the world. A new consciousness shaped ideas about family life, gender roles, and patterns of consumption as Europeans entered the twentieth century.

EUROPEAN ECONOMY AND THE POLITICS OF MASS SOCIETY

Between 1871 and 1914, the scale of European life was radically altered. Industrial society had promoted largeness as the norm, and growing numbers of people worked under the same roof. Large-scale heavy industries fueled by new energy sources dominated the economic landscape. Great Britain, the leader of the first phase of the Industrial Revolution of the eighteenth century, slipped in prominence as an industrial power at the end of the nineteenth century, as Germany and the United States devised successful competitive strategies of investment, protection, and control.

Regulating Boom and Bust

The organization of factory production throughout Europe and the proximity of productive centers to distribution networks meant ever greater concentration of populations in urban areas. Like factories, cities were getting bigger at a rapid rate and were proliferating in numbers. Berlin, capital of the new German nation, mushroomed in size in the last quarter of the nineteenth century. In the less industrialized parts of eastern Europe, cities also underwent record growth. Warsaw, St. Petersburg, and Moscow all expanded by at least 400,000 inhabitants each. Budapest, the city created by uniting the towns of Buda and Pest in 1872, tripled in size between 1867 and 1914 and was typical of the booming growth of provincial cities throughout Europe. With every passing year proportionately fewer people remained on the land. Those who did stay in the agricultural sector were linked to cities and tied into national cultures by new transportation and communications networks.

The Need for Regulation.   Between 1873 and 1895, an epidemic of slumps battered the economies of European nations.

■ This bustling Berlin street scene in 1909 in a fashionable quarter of the city is typical of European urban life at the beginning of the twentieth century.

The slumps, characterized by falling prices, downturns in productivity, and declining profits, have been called the "Great Depression" of the nineteenth century. In reality, the economic downturn of the period was not a great depression like the one that followed the crash of 1929, but instead was a period of economic uncertainty and fluctuation. It did not strike European nations simultaneously, nor did it affect all countries with the same degree of severity. But the so-called Great Depression of the late nineteenth century and the boom period of intense economic expansion from 1895 to 1914 did teach industrialists, financiers, and politicians one important lesson: alternative booms and busts in the business cycle were dangerous and had to be regulated.

Too much of a good thing brought on the steady deflation of the last quarter of the nineteenth century. In the world economy, there was an overproduction of agricultural products—a sharp contrast to the famines that had ravaged Europe only 50 years earlier. Overproduction resulted from two new factors in the world economy: technological advances in crop cultivation and the low cost of shipping and transport, which

had opened up European markets to cheap agricultural goods from the United States, Canada, and Argentina. The absolute numbers of those employed in agriculture remained more or less constant, but world output soared. Cheap foreign grains, especially wheat, flooded European markets and drastically drove down agricultural prices. The drop in prices affected purchasing power in other sectors and resulted in long-term deflation and unemployment.

Financiers, politicians, and businessmen dedicated themselves to eliminating the boom-and-bust phenomenon, which they considered dangerous. The application of science and technology to industrial production required huge amounts of capital. The two new sources of power after 1880, petroleum and electricity, could only be developed with heavy capital investment. Large mechanized steel plants were costly and out of reach for small family firms of the scale that had industrialized textiles so successfully earlier in the century. Heavy machinery, smelting furnaces, buildings, and transport were all beyond the abilities of the small entrepreneur. To raise the capital necessary for the new heavy industry at the end of the nineteenth century, firms had to look outside themselves to the stock market, banks, or the state to find adequate capital resources. Because investment in heavy industry meant tying up capital for extended periods of time, banks insisted on safeguards against falling prices. The solution they demanded was the elimination of uncertainty through the regulation of markets.

Cartels.   Regulation was achieved through the establishment of **cartels**, combinations of firms in a given industry united to fix prices and to establish production quotas. Not as extreme as the monopolies that appeared in the United States

in the same period and for the same purpose, cartels were agreements among big firms intent on controlling markets and guaranteeing profits. Trusts were another form of collaboration that resulted in the elimination of unprofitable businesses. Firms joined together horizontally within the same industry—for example, all steel producers agreed to fix prices and set quotas. Or they combined vertically by controlling all levels of the production process, from raw materials to the finished product, and all other ancillary products necessary to or resulting from the production process. That type of cartel was exemplified by a single firm that controlled the entire production process and the marketing of a single product, from raw materials and fuel through sales and distribution.

Firms in Great Britain, falling behind in heavy industry, failed to form cartels and for the most part remained in private hands. But heavy industry in Germany, France, and Austria, to varying degrees, sought regulation of markets through cartels. International cartels appeared that regulated markets and prices across national borders within Europe. Firms producing steel, chemicals, coke, and pig iron all minimized the effects of competition through the regulation of prices and output.

Banks, which had been the initial impetus behind the transformation to a regulated economy, in turn formed consortia to meet the need for greater amounts of capital. A consortium—paralleling a cartel—was a partnership among banks, often international in character, in which interest rates and the movement of capital were regulated by mutual agreement. The state, too, played an important role in directing the economy. In capital-poor Russia, the state used indirect taxes on the peasantry to finance industrialization and railway construction at the end of the nineteenth century. Russia industrialized with the sweat of its peasants. Russia also needed to

■ A cartoon from a pamphlet published in Britain by the Tariff Reform League in 1903. The tree represents Britain's free trade policy. The other nations of the world are harvesting the benefits of the British policy.

import capital, primarily from France after 1887. The state had to guarantee foreign loans and regulate the economy to pay interest on foreign capital investment. Foreign investors were not willing to leave the export of capital to chance or the vagaries of the business cycle. The state must intervene.

Throughout Europe, nation-states protected domestic industries by erecting tariff barriers that made foreign goods noncompetitive in domestic markets. Only Great Britain among the major powers stood by a policy of free trade. Europe was split into two tiers, the haves and the have-nots—those countries with a solid industrial core and those that had remained unindustrialized. The division had a geographic character, with the north and west of Europe more heavily developed and capitalized and the southern and eastern parts of Europe remaining heavily agricultural. For both the haves and the have-nots, tariff policies were an attractive form of regulation by the state to protect established industries and to nurture those industries struggling for existence.

Economic regulation was not a twentieth-century creation, as critics of the welfare state contend. Intervention and control began in the late nineteenth century, very much under the impetus of bankers, financiers, and industrialists. Capitalists looked on state intervention not as an intrusion but as a welcome corrective to the ups and downs of the business cycle. Regulation did not emerge from any philosophical or ideological assumption about government but came about as a result of the very real need for capital to enable heavy industry to expand and the equally compelling need to protect profits in order to encourage financiers to invest.

Challenging Liberal England

Great Britain experienced the transformation in political organization and social structure before other European nations. But after 1870, changes in politics influenced by the scale of the new industrial society spread to every European country. Mass democracy was on the rise and was pushing aside the liberal emphasis on individual rights valued by parliamentary governments everywhere.

Great Britain had avoided revolution and social upheaval. It prided itself on the progress achieved by a strong parliamentary tradition. One writer caught the self-congratulatory spirit of the age in an 1885 book on popular government: "We Englishmen pass on the Continent as masters of the art of government." Parliamentary government was based on a homogeneous ruling elite. Aristocrats, businessmen, and financial leaders shared a common educational background in England's elitist educational system of the "public schools," which were really exclusive, private ones, and the universities of Oxford or Cambridge. Schooling produced a common outlook and common attitudes toward parliamentary rule, whether in Conservative or Liberal circles, and guaranteed a certain stability in policies and legislation.

Trade Unions.   In the 1880s, issues of unemployment, housing, public health, and education challenged the attitudes of Britain's ruling elite and fostered the advent of an independent working-class politics. Between 1867 and 1885, extension of the suffrage increased the electorate fourfold. Protected by the markets of its empire, the British economy did not experience the roller-coaster effect of recurrent booms and busts after 1873. Nor did Britain experience severe economic crisis between 1890 and 1914, a period of growing labor unrest. But after 1900, wages stagnated while prices continued to rise. Traditional parliamentary politics had little to offer those workers whose standard of living suffered a real decline. The quality of urban housing deteriorated, as exemplified by the severe overcrowding of London's East End.

Workers responded to their distress by supporting militant trade unions. Trade unions, drawing on a long tradition of working-class associations, were all that stood between workers and the economic dislocation caused by unemployment, sickness, or old age. In addition, new unions of unskilled and semiskilled workers flourished, beginning in the 1880s and 1890s. A Scottish miner, James Keir Hardie (1856–1915), attracted national attention as the spokesman for a new political movement, the Labour party, whose goal was to represent workers in Parliament. In 1892, Hardie was the first independent working man to sit in the House of Commons. Hardie and his party convinced trade unions that it was in their best interests to support Labour candidates instead of Liberals in parliamentary elections after 1900. Unions, as extraparliamentary groups, worked successfully toward achieving a parliamentary voice. By 1906, the new Labour party had 29 seats in Parliament.

Parliamentary Reforms.   Yet Parliament seemed to be failing the poor. So argued a group of intellectuals concerned with social welfare who called themselves **Fabians.** They named themselves after the Roman dictator Fabius, who was noted for his delaying tactics, which enabled him to avoid decisive battle with Hannibal in the Punic Wars. Fabius believed in cutting off the supplies of his enemies and engaging in skirmishes. Following his lead, the Fabians were socialists, not in a Marxist sense of ultimate revolutionary confrontation, but in a gradualist sense of a reformist commitment to social justice. Led by Beatrice Webb (1858–1943) and Sidney Webb (1859–1947), and including in their number playwright and critic George Bernard Shaw (1856–1950), theosophist Annie Besant (1847–1943), and novelist H. G. Wells (1866–1946), the Fabians proved to be successful propagandists who were able to keep issues of social reform in the public eye. They advocated collective ownership of factories and workshops and state direction of production through gradual reform. At the turn of the century, the Fabian Society threw its support and the power of its tracts on social issues behind Labour party candidates. Intellectuals now joined with trade unionists in demanding public housing, better public sanitation, municipal reforms, and improved pay and benefits for working people.

The existence of the new Labour party pressured Conservatives and Liberals to develop more enlightened social policies and programs. After 1906, under threat of losing votes to the Labour party, the Liberal party heeded the pressures for reform. The "new" Liberals supported legislation to strengthen the right of unions to picket peacefully. Led by David Lloyd George (1863–1945), who was chancellor of the exchequer, Liberals sponsored the National Insurance Act of 1911. Modeled after Bismarck's social welfare policies (see p. 722), the act provided compulsory payments to workers for sickness and unemployment benefits. In order to gain approval to pay for the new legislation, Lloyd George recognized that Parliament itself had to be renovated. The Parliament Bill of 1911 reduced the House of Lords, dominated by Conservatives resistant to proposed welfare reforms, from its status as equal partner with the House of Commons. Commons could and now did raise taxes without the consent of the House of Lords to pay for new programs that benefited workers and the poor.

Extraparliamentary Protest.   Social legislation did not silence unions and worker organizations. To the contrary, protest increased in the period up to the beginning of World War I in 1914. There was little doubt about the ability of militant trade unions to mobilize workers. In 1910, three of every ten manual workers belonged to a union, and that figure doubled to 60 percent of the work force between 1910 and 1914. In those years, waves of strikes broke over England. Unions threatened to paralyze the economy. Coal miners, seamen, railroad workers, and dockers protested against stagnant wages and rising prices.

The high incidence of strikes was a consequence of growing distrust of Parliament and distrust, too, of a regulatory state bureaucracy responsible for the social welfare reforms. Workers felt manipulated by a system unresponsive to their needs. Labour's voice grew more strident. The Trade Unions Act of 1913 granted unions legal rights to settle their grievances with management directly. In the summer of 1914, a railway worker boasted, "We are big and powerful enough to fight our own battle without the aid of Parliament or any other agency. There could be no affection between the robber and the robbed." Only the outbreak of war in 1914 ended the possibility of a general strike by miners, railwaymen, and transport workers.

The question of Irish Home Rule also plagued Parliament. In Ulster in northern Ireland, army officers of Protestant Irish background threatened to mutiny. In addition, women agitating for the vote shattered parliamentary complacence. The most advanced industrial nation in the world, with its tradition of peaceful parliamentary rule, had entered the age of mass politics.

Political Struggles in Germany

During his reign as chancellor of the German Empire (1871–1890), Otto von Bismarck formed shrewd alliances that hampered the development of effective parliamentary government. He repeatedly and successfully blocked the emergence of fully democratic participation. In Germany, all males had the right to vote, but the German parliament, the Reichstag, enjoyed only restricted powers in comparison to the British Parliament. Bismarck's objective remained always the successful unification of Germany, and he promoted cooperation with democratic institutions and parties only as long as that goal was enhanced.

Bismarck and the German Parliament.   Throughout the 1870s, the German chancellor collaborated with the German liberal parties in constructing the legal codes, the monetary and banking system, the judicial apparatus, and the railroad network that pulled the new Germany together. Bismarck backed German liberals in their antipapal campaign, in which the Catholic Church was declared the enemy of the German state. He suspected the identification of Catholics with Rome, which the liberals depicted as an authority in competition with the nation-state. The anti-Church campaign, launched in 1872, was dubbed the *Kulturkampf*, the "struggle for civilization," because its supporters contended that it was a battle waged in the interests of humanity.

The legislation of the *Kulturkampf* expelled Jesuits from Germany, removed priests from state service, attacked religious education, and instituted civil marriage. Bishops and priests who followed the instructions of Pope Pius IX (1846–1878) not to obey the new laws were arrested and expelled from Germany. Many Germans grew concerned over the social costs of such widespread religious repression, and the Catholic Center party increased its parliamentary representation by rallying Catholics as a voting bloc in the face of state repression. With the succession of a new pontiff, Leo XIII (1878–1903), Bismarck took advantage of the opportunity to negotiate a settlement with the Catholic Church, cutting his losses and bringing the *Kulturkampf* to a halt. Bismarck had grown wary of the demands of the National Liberal party for an increasing share of political power.

The Social Democratic Party.   Bismarck's repressive policies also targeted the Social Democratic party. The Social Democrats were committed to a Marxist critique of capitalism and to international cooperation with other socialist parties. Seeing them as a threat to stability in Germany and in Europe as a whole, he set out to smash them. In 1878, using the opportunity for repression presented by two attempts on the emperor's life, Bismarck outlawed the fledgling Socialist Party. The Anti-Socialist Law forbade meetings among Socialists, fundraising, and distribution of printed matter. The law relied on expanded police powers and was a fundamental attack on civil liberties and freedom of choice within a democratic electoral system. Nevertheless, individual Social Democratic candidates stood for election in the period and quickly learned how to work with middle-class parties in order to achieve electoral successes. By 1890, Social Democrats had captured 20 percent of the electorate and controlled 35 Reichstag seats, in spite of Bismarck's anti-Socialist legislation.

Throughout the 1880s, as his ability to manage Reichstag majorities declined and as Socialist strength steadily mounted, Bismarck grew disenchanted with universal manhood suffrage. Beginning in 1888, the chancellor found himself at odds with the new emperor, Wilhelm II (1888–1918), over his foreign and domestic policies. The young emperor dismissed Bismarck in March 1890 and abandoned the chancellor's anti-Socialist legislation. The Social Democratic party became the largest Marxist party in the world and, by 1914, the largest single party in Germany.

The socialism of the German Social Democrats was modified in the 1890s. Although it had never been violent or insurrectionary, social democracy moved away from a belief in a future revolution and toward a democratic **revisionism** that favored gradual reform through parliamentary participation. Those who continued to maintain a more orthodox Marxist position, such as August Bebel (1840–1913) and Karl Kautsky (1854–1938), believed capitalism would destroy itself, as Karl Marx had predicted, without any violent action by German Social Democrats. Bebel confided to Friedrich Engels in 1885 that he went to bed every night with the confidence that "the last hour of bourgeois society strikes soon."

Revisionism was both practical and democratic. Its leading advocate, Eduard Bernstein (1850–1932), introduced aspects of Fabian state socialism into the German movement. The grassroots transformation favored evolutionary rather than revolutionary political action. Workers were the primary force behind the shift away from the catastrophe theory of Bebel and Kautsky. Their standard of living had been improving in Germany, and the prospect of the imminent collapse of capitalism seemed slight to workers intent on achieving further gains. Union membership grew dramatically among unskilled workers after 1895. Working-class organizations, tolerated earlier by Social Democrats for their future potential, now became centers of power and pressed for practical benefits for their members.

During the period when the Social Democratic movement had been outlawed, Bismarck had employed carrot-and-stick methods to woo the working class away from the Marxists. The stick with which Bismarck beat back the political opposition had been the Anti-Socialist Law. The carrot that he and then Wilhelm II used to win mass support was social welfare legislation, including accident insurance, sick benefits, and old age and disability benefits introduced by the state. But such legislation did not undermine the popularity of socialism, nor did it attract workers away from Marxist political programs, as the mounting electoral returns demonstrated. Social democracy built its rank-and-file union membership by employing sophisticated organizational techniques in order to expand its mass base of support.

The success and popularity of the Social Democratic party cemented a stronger alliance on the Right among Conservatives. Realizing that they could not beat the Left, right-wing groups decided to copy it. Unable to defeat social democracy by force or by state-sponsored welfare policies,

Bismarck's successors set out to organize mass support. Agrarian and industrial interests united strongly behind state policies. An aggressive foreign policy was judged as the surest way to win over the masses. Leagues were formed to exploit nationalism and patriotism among the electorate over issues of naval and military expansion and colonial development.

In the end, the Reichstag failed to defy the absolute authority of Emperor Wilhelm II, who was served after 1890 by a string of ineffectual chancellors. Despite its constitutional forms, Germany was ruled by a state authoritarianism in which the bureaucracy, the military, and various interest groups exercised influence over the emperor. A high-risk foreign policy that had mass appeal was one way to circumvent a parliamentary system incapable of decision making. Constitutional solutions had been short-circuited in favor of authoritarian rule.

Political Scandals and Mass Politics in France

The Third Republic in France had an aura of accidental origins and precarious existence. Founded in 1870 with the defeat of Napoleon III's empire by the Germans, the Third Republic claimed legitimacy by placing itself squarely within the revolutionary democratic tradition. Yet its early days were marked by bloody social conflict, and its existence was plagued by ongoing struggles among contenders on the Right and Left who sought to control it.

Creating Citizens.   In spite of surface indications of political conflict, the Third Republic successfully worked toward the creation of a national community based on a common identity for its citizens. Compulsory schooling, one of the great institutional transformations of French government in 1885, socialized French children by implanting in them common values, patriotism, and identification with the nation-state. Old ways, local dialects, superstitious practices, and peasant insularity dropped away or were modified under the persistent pressure of a centralized curriculum of reading, writing, arithmetic, and civics. Compulsory service in the army for the generation of young men of draft age served the same end of communicating national values to a predominantly peasant population.

Technology also accelerated the process of shaping a national citizenry as railroad lines tied people together and the infrastructure of roads made distances shrink. People could now travel back and forth between village and city, town and countryside, with ease and frequency. Common expectations for a better life and upward mobility moved through rural populations that for most of the nineteenth century had not looked beyond the horizon of the village. Young working women were particularly influential in transferring values from urban to rural areas as they moved from villages to towns in search of domestic and industrial jobs and then returned to their villages with new outlooks and new goals for their families.

Information was controlled at the center—Paris—and distributed on a national scale. Villagers in southern France read Parisian newspapers over their morning bowls of coffee and learned—with a previously unimaginable immediacy—about French foreign exploits and parliamentary wrangles. A truly national mass culture emerged in the period between 1880 and 1914. Common symbols such as the bust of Marianne appeared in every city hall in France, and a common vocabulary of patriotism spread across the land. French people were not necessarily more political, but they were political in a new way that enabled them to identify their own local interests with national issues.

The Boulanger Affair.   A political crisis, known as the Boulanger Affair, temporarily threatened the stability of the Republic and served as a good indication of the extent of the transformation in French political life at the end of the nineteenth century. As minister of war, General Georges Boulanger (1837–1891) became a hero to French soldiers when he undertook needed reforms of army life. He won over businessmen by leading troops against strikers. Above all, he cultivated the image of a patriot ready to defend France's honor at any cost. But Boulanger was a shallow man whose success and national popularity were created by a carefully orchestrated publicity campaign that made him the most popular man in France by 1886.

Boulanger's potential in the political arena attracted the attention of right-wing backers, including monarchists who hoped eventually to restore kingship to France. Supported by big-money interests who favored a strengthened executive and a weaker parliamentary system, Boulanger undertook a nationwide political campaign, hoping to appeal to those unhappy with the Third Republic and promising vague constitutional reforms. General Boulanger's 1889 campaign managers successfully manipulated images that were recognizable to a rural electorate. Religious lithographs carried likenesses of the modern "messiah," the blond-bearded general, in place of Jesus.

By 1889, Boulanger was able to amass enough national support to frighten the defenders of parliamentary institutions. The charismatic general ultimately failed in his bid for power and fled the country because of allegations of treason. But he left in his wake an embryonic mass movement on the Right that operated outside the channels of parliamentary institutions.

The Dreyfus Affair.   A very different type of crisis began to take shape in 1894 with the controversy surrounding the trial of Captain Alfred Dreyfus (1859–1935) that came to be known simply as "the Affair." Dreyfus was an Alsatian Jewish army officer accused of selling military secrets to the Germans. His trial for treason served as a lightning rod for xenophobia—the hatred of foreigners, especially Germans—and **anti-Semitism,** the hatred of Jews. Dreyfus was stripped of his commission and honors and sentenced to solitary confinement for life on Devil's Island, a convict colony off French Guiana in South America.

Illegal activities and outright falsifications by Dreyfus's superiors in order to secure a conviction came to light in the mass press. The nation was soon divided. Those who supported Dreyfus's innocence, the pro-Dreyfusards, were for the most part on the left of the political spectrum and spoke of

■ This caricature portrays Captain Alfred Dreyfus as a dragon for the alleged leaking of military secrets.

the Republic's duty to uphold justice and freedom. The anti-Dreyfusards were associated with the traditional institutions of the Catholic Church and the army and considered themselves to be defending the honor of France. Among those who upheld the conviction were right-wing groups, monarchists, and virulent anti-Semites.

Dreyfus was eventually exonerated and granted a full pardon in 1905. On the personal level, the Affair represented the ability of an individual to seek redress against injustice. On the national level, the Affair represented an important transformation in the nature of French political life. Existing parliamentary institutions had been found wanting and unable to cope with the mass politics stirred up by Dreyfus's conviction. New groups entered public life after 1894, coalescing around the question of the guilt or innocence of an individual man. The newspaper press vied with parliament and the courts as a forum for investigation and decision making. Intellectuals, too, organized. Leagues on the left and on the right took shape; unions, cooperatives, and professional societies all raised their voices. The organizations manipulated propaganda around issues of national defense and republican justice.

The crises provoked by Boulanger's attempt at power and the Dreyfus Affair demonstrated the major role of the press

"J' ACCUSE"

The central role of the press during the Dreyfus Affair is nowhere more apparent than in the impact of the novelist Émile Zola's front-page letter to the president of the Third Republic published in Georges Clemenceau's newspaper L'Aurore, on 13 January 1898. "J'Accuse" was an impassioned appeal to the French nation for justice in which Zola pointed to those truly guilty of betraying France in a cascade of ringing accusations. This letter, which was ultimately instrumental in freeing Captain Dreyfus, resulted in Zola's own prosecution and exile for libel.

Focus Questions

What institutions of the French Third Republic was Zola attacking in "J'Accuse"? Why were Zola's words considered so libelous?

I accuse Lieutenant-Colonel du Paty de Clam of having been the diabolical artisan of the judicial error, without knowing it, I am willing to believe, and then of having defended his nefarious work for three years throughout the most grotesque and culpable machinations.

I accuse General Mercier of having become an accomplice, out of mental weakness at the least, in one of the greatest iniquities of the century. . . .

I accuse the three handwriting experts, Mssrs. Belhomme, Varinard, and Couard, of having composed deceitful and fraudulent reports, unless a medical examination declares them to be stricken with an impairment of vision or judgment.

I accuse the offices of War of having conducted in the press, particularly in *L'Éclair* and in *L'Echo de Paris*, an abominable campaign designed to mislead public opinion and to conceal their wrongdoing.

Finally, I accuse the first Court Martial of having violated the law in convicting a defendant on the basis of a document kept secret, and I accuse the second Court Martial of having covered up that illegality on command by committing in turn the juridical crime of knowingly acquitting a guilty man.

In bringing these accusations, I am not without realizing that I expose myself in the process to Articles 30 and 31 of the press law of July 29, 1881, which punishes offenses of slander. And it is quite willingly that I so expose myself.

As for those whom I accuse, I do not know them, I have never seen them, I have neither rancor nor hatred for them. They are for me no more than entities, spirits of social malfeasance. And the act that I hereby accomplish is but a revolutionary means of hastening the explosion of truth and justice.

I have but one passion, one for seeing the light, in the name of humanity which has so suffered and which is entitled to happiness. My fiery protest is but the cry of my soul. Let me be brought then before a criminal court and let the investigation be conducted in the light of day!

I am waiting.

---

and the importance of public opinion in exerting pressure on the system of government. The press emerged as a mythmaker in shaping and channeling public opinion. Émile Zola (1840–1902), the great French novelist, spearheaded the pro-Dreyfusard movement with his damning article "I Accuse!" in which he pointed to the military and the judiciary as the "spirits of social evil" for persecuting an innocent man. The article appeared in a leading French newspaper and was influential in securing Dreyfus's eventual exoneration and the discovery of the real culprit, one of Dreyfus's colleagues in the General Staff. The Third Republic had never been in danger of collapsing, but it was transformed. The locus of power in parliament was challenged by pressure groups outside it.

Defeating Liberalism in Austria

In the 1870s, the liberal values of the bourgeoisie dominated the Austro-Hungarian Empire. The Habsburg monarchy had adjusted to constitutional government, which was introduced throughout Austria in 1860. Faith in parliamentary government based on a restricted suffrage had established a tenuous

foothold. After the setbacks of 1848 and the troublesome decade of the 1860s, when Prussia had trounced Austria and Bismarck had routed the hope of an Austrian-dominated German Empire, the Austrian bourgeoisie counted on a peaceful future with a centralized multinational state dedicated to order and progress.

Vienna and the Bourgeoisie.   There is no better symbol of middle-class political and cultural aspirations in the period than the monumental rebuilding of the city of Vienna that took place after 1860. The belt of public and private buildings on the Ringstrasse, or "Ring Street," girding the old central city and separating it from its suburbs was dramatic testimony to bourgeois self-confidence. Grandiose buildings, likened to "cakes on platters," glorified constitutional government, economic vitality, the fine arts, and educational values. Monumental architecture was intended to legitimize bourgeois claims to power and to link Austrian institutions with the great cultural heritage of the West. The buildings were blatant copies of past architectural styles— massive Gothic for the city hall, Renaissance for the university, and early baroque for the theater. Yet the rebuilding was more than a self-confident statement of Austria's inheritance of a rich cultural tradition. Vienna's ruling class was fortifying itself behind the edifices of Western politics and culture against the onslaught of the new age.

In reality, the Austrian bourgeoisie was weaker than its French or British counterparts. The Austrian ruling class was heavily dependent on the Habsburg emperor and identified itself with the values of the aristocracy. Rapid economic growth had strengthened bourgeois status between 1840 and 1870, but it had also unleashed new social forces that existing institutions were unable to control. Liberal values of constitutional monarchy, centralization, restricted suffrage, and multinational government came up against new and threatening forces of anti-Semitism, socialism, nationalism, and mass politics.

The New Right.   By 1900, liberal politicians were being eliminated as a directing force in national politics. The new politicians who replaced them rejected the liberal-rational values of progress and order and moved into a realm colored by charisma, fantasy, and demagoguery. A new Right wielded mass political strategies that embraced the irrational and the violent.

The new groups laying claim to political power and displacing a weak Austrian bourgeoisie were peasants, workers, urban artisans and shopkeepers, and the colonized Slavic peoples of the empire. Bourgeois politics and laissez-faire economics had offered little or nothing to those varied groups, who were claiming the right of participation. Mass parties were formed based on radical pan-Germanic feeling; anticapitalism, which appealed to peasants and artisans; hatred of the Jews, shared by students and artisans; and nationalist aspirations that attracted the lower middle classes.

In 1895, Karl Lueger (1844–1910) used anti-Semitism in his successful campaign for the office of mayor of Vienna. Lueger's election was the first serious sign of the collapse of Austrian liberalism. Jews were identified with capitalists, and the irrational hatred directed at them unified different groups and helped to sweep Lueger into office.

Austrian poet and playwright Hugo von Hofmannsthal (1874–1929) understood the rejection of bourgeois politics in the age of expanded suffrage: "Politics is magic. He who knows how to summon the forces from the deep, him will they follow." The creation of a scapegoat by means of anti-Semitism and racism became the means of uniting the masses against a common foe and in favor of a common nationalist program. In Austria, antiliberal politics grew stronger in the years before 1914. The great buildings on the Ringstrasse that had attempted to connect Austrian political life with the glories of the European past were mocked as relics of a dead age. Centrifugal forces of pan-Germanism and nationalism were pulling the parliamentary system apart. An urban and capitalist middle class that ruled Austria by virtue of a limited suffrage based on property had lost ground to new groups that were essentially anticapitalist and antiliberal in their outlook and for whom parliamentary deliberations held no promise. The rejection of liberalism was a "revolt against the fathers." A new style of leader had emerged in Vienna at the end of the

century, charismatic in style and violent in appeal. The "politics of fantasy" based on a new electorate was fast becoming the nightmare of parliamentary disintegration.

The political experiences of Great Britain, Germany, France, and Austria between 1871 and 1914 make clear the common challenges confronting Western parliamentary systems in a changing era of democratic politics. In spite of variations, each nation experienced its own challenge to liberal parliamentary institutions, and each shaped its own variety of responses to a new international phenomenon—the rise of the masses as a political force.

OUTSIDERS IN MASS POLITICS

By the end of the nineteenth century, a faceless, nameless electorate became the basis of new political strategies and a new political rhetoric. A concept of class identification of workers was devalued in favor of interest-group politics in which lobbies formed around single issues to pressure European governments. But the apparently all-inclusive concept of mass society continued to exclude women, ethnic minorities, and Jews. Outsiders in mass politics had little in common with one another except for the common experience of repression by the state. But they did not remain quietly on the periphery. Women and ethnic minorities learned to incorporate strategies and techniques of politics and organization that permitted them to challenge the existing political system. Others, including anarchists, rejected both the organizational techniques of mass society and the values of the nation-state. Outsiders, then, were both those intent on being integrated into mass politics and those who sought its destruction.

Feminists and Politics

Women's drive for emancipation had been a recurrent motif of European political culture throughout the nineteenth century. In the areas of civil liberties, legal equality with men, and economic autonomy, only the most limited reforms had been enacted. The glorification of domesticity, important throughout the nineteenth century, assigned women to a separate sphere and was a recognition of women's unique contribution to society in the home. But it was also a means of keeping women "in their place."

Women's Rights.   European women were paid at most one-third to one-half of what men earned for the same work. In Great Britain, women did not enjoy equal divorce rights until the twentieth century. In France, married women had no control over their own incomes: all their earnings were considered their husbands' private property. From the Atlantic to the Urals, women were excluded from economic and educational opportunities. Serfs had been liberated. Working-class men had gained the right to vote. But the new electoral politics that emerged in the last quarter of the nineteenth century explicitly excluded women.

Growing numbers of women, primarily from the middle classes, began calling themselves "feminist," a term coined in France in the 1830s. The new feminists throughout western Europe differed from earlier generations in their willingness to organize mass movements and to appropriate the techniques of interest-group politics. The first international congress of women's rights, held in Paris in 1878, initiated an era of international cooperation and exchange among women's organizations. Women's groups now positioned themselves for sustained political action.

Feminism as a historic term is worth pondering. Like liberalism, which had pulled down kings and destroyed privilege, feminism aimed at eliminating social inequalities. Like socialism, feminism was a set of principles for action whose purpose was to build a better world. At its base, feminism recognized the equality of the sexes, without denying difference. As John Stuart Mill in Great Britain and Ernest Legouvé (1807–1903), a French dramatist and leading proponent of women's rights, had demonstrated, one need not be female to be a feminist. It was the belief that men and women were equal and should enjoy equal rights that identified the feminist. Most feminists, however, were women, and the leadership of the movement for equal rights was in women's hands. The converse—that most women were feminists—was not true. Contemporary critics often dismissed feminism on the grounds that it represented no more than a tiny minority of women. The same minority status characterized the trade union movement—which in France, for example, had a smaller membership at the end of the nineteenth century than did feminist organizations.

European feminist organizations did not share a common agenda but instead grouped themselves around a series of related concerns for legal, educational, economic, and political emancipation. Rather than speaking of a single feminism, it is more appropriate to speak of different feminisms. The General German Women's Association agitated for educational opportunities and democratic participation for women. In France, women working for the vote were a minority of the women's organizations. Many French feminists defended a "maternal politics," by which they sought protection for women's responsibilities in the home. Other feminists were involved in abortion reform, birth control issues, and repeal of state control of prostitution. The French League for the Rights of Women stood steadfastly against the vote as an end in itself and worked instead for legal and economic reforms. On the whole, however, feminist organizations were divided into two camps. In the first were those who agitated for the vote; the second included those who thought that the vote was beside the point and that the central issues were economic, social, and legal reforms of women's status. Constituting the left wing of the second group were socialist women who were dedicated to needs of women of the working class.

Movements for the Vote. The lessons of the new electoral politics were not lost on feminists seeking women's emancipation through the vote. The feminist leaders Hubertine Auclert (1848–1914) in France and Emmeline Pankhurst (1858–1928) in Great Britain recognized the need for a mass base of support. If women's organizations were to survive as competing interest groups, they needed to form political alliances, control their own newspapers and magazines, and keep their cause before the public eye. Just as cartels, trade unions, and political parties had learned the game of influence and leverage so important for survival in the modern political milieu, so too did feminists rely on organization to achieve their ends. There was a growing willingness by a variety of women's organizations to hold mass demonstrations and rallies and to use violent tactics.

■ A strike meeting of women workers at Millwall, England, 1914. Women speaking in public, especially on economic and political matters, was a highly unusual phenomenon.

No movement operated more effectively in that regard than the British suffrage movement. In 1903, the Women's Social and Political Union (WSPU) was formed by a group of eminently respectable middle-class and aristocratic British women. At the center of the movement was Emmeline Pankhurst, an attractive middle-aged woman with a frail appearance but a will of iron and a gift for oratory. Emmeline Pankhurst and her two daughters—Christabel (1880–1958), a lawyer by training, and Sylvia (1882–1960), an artist—succeeded in keeping women's suffrage before the British public and brought the plight of British women to international attention. During the following seven years, the WSPU made considerable progress, attracting a growing number of followers and successfully aligning itself with parliamentary supporters.

Women's demands for political power were the basis of an unheralded revolution in Western culture. In Great Britain, the decade before the Great War of 1914 was a period of profound political education for women seeking the vote. An unprecedented 250,000 women gathered in Hyde Park in 1908 to hear more about female suffrage. Laughed at by men, ridiculed in the press, taunted in public demonstrations, women activists refused to be quiet and to "know their place." If respectable women would never demonstrate for their rights, then the suffragists were willing to cease being respectable. Because they spoke out for voting rights, feminists were demeaned, humiliated, and accused of not being *real* women by their detractors. One of the best examples of the rebellion of women against the limitations of their social roles took place on 18 November 1910, a day that came to be known among feminists as Black Friday. On that day, suffragists marched on Parliament, which had failed to support the vote for women. In a confrontation that lasted six hours, unarmed women battled with police to hold their ground. Rather than returning home as they were ordered, the women relentlessly pushed forward, meeting the blows and the wrath of London's bobbies. Many women were injured and many arrested.

The year 1910 marked the beginning of an era of increased militancy among women, who were derisively called **suffragettes** in the press in order to distinguish them from the nonmilitant suffragists. A basic element in the new militancy was the willingness to use violence to achieve political emancipation. As Emmeline Pankhurst explained it, "The argument of the broken window pane is the most valuable argument in modern politics." Militant women set mailboxes on fire or poured glue and jam over their contents, threw bombs into country houses, and slashed paintings in the National Gallery. All over London the tinkling of thousands of shattered windowpanes ushered in a new age of women's political action.

Mrs. Pankhurst was not naive about what her followers were doing: "There is something which governments care for more than human life and that is the security of property, and so it is through property that we shall strike the enemy." Suffragettes set fires in public buildings, churches, and hotels. As frustration grew, some assaulted members of the cabinet. One suffragette, Emily Wilding Davison (1872–1913), probably intent on suicide as an act of protest, was trampled to death when she threw herself under the king's horse on Derby Day at Epsom Downs in 1913. Mrs. Pankhurst and others advocated violence against personal property to highlight the violence done to women by denying them their rights. The tactics seemed to accomplish little before the war, although they certainly kept the issue of female suffrage in the public eye until the outbreak of war in 1914. It was not until 1918 that British women were granted limited suffrage, and not until 1928 that women gained voting rights equal to those of men.

Women suffered for their militancy, for civil disobedience evoked harsh repressive measures from the British government. Previous benevolence toward middle-class female prisoners arrested for attacks on property gave way to a new harshness that included the force-feeding of convicted suffragettes. Using tubes, hoses, and metal jaw clamps, prison guards and doctors poured gruel down the throats of imprisoned women who, as a form of protest, refused to eat. Such repressive measures only increased the solidarity within the women's movement and won the suffragettes international sympathy and support. Stymied, the government passed the

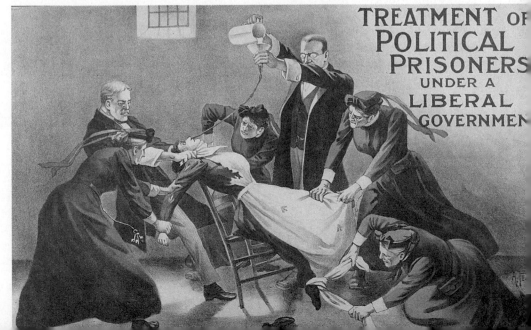

■ This British suffragette poster, published by the Women's Social and Political Union, graphically depicts the extreme methods used to force-feed women prisoners. A prison guard pulls back the prisoner's head, others hold down her arms and legs, and another ties her foot to the chair. A doctor holds a hose through which he forces gruel into the woman's nose.

TREATMENT OF POLITICAL PRISONERS UNDER A LIBERAL GOVERNMEN

Cat and Mouse Act in 1913. Imprisoned women who refused to eat were released, then reincarcerated once they had resumed eating and regained their strength. The "cat-and-mouse" pattern of release and reimprisonment could double or extend indefinitely a three-year sentence served in three-day segments. Many of the more dramatic tactics of the suffragettes, including getting arrested, were not available to working-class activists, who could not put aside their family responsibilities to serve jail sentences.

European women did not easily gain the right to vote. In France and Germany, moderate and left-wing politicians opposed extension of the vote to women because they feared that women would strengthen conservative candidates. Many politicians felt that women were not "ready" for the vote and that they should receive it only as a reward—an unusual concept in democratic societies. Queen Victoria condemned women's agitation for the vote as a "mad, wicked folly." Only after war and revolution was the vote extended to women in the West—in Germany in 1918, in the United States in 1920, and in France at the end of World War II.

Women and Social Reform. Not all activist women saw the right to vote as the solution to women's oppression. Those who agitated for social reforms for poor and working-class women parted ways with the militant suffragettes. Sylvia Pankhurst, for example, left her mother and sister to their political battles in order to work for social reform in London's poverty-stricken East End. Differing from those who focused on woman's right to vote as a primary goal, women socialists were concerned with working-class women's "double oppression" in the home and in the workplace. The largest women's socialist movement existed in Germany, with 175,000 members by 1914. With its own newspaper, it operated independently of the men's socialist movement. German socialist

women were opposed to suffrage on the grounds that giving middle-class women the vote did not address social issues.

Socialist women's lot was not an easy one, since union members often denied women's right to work and saw women's employment as a threat to men in the workplace. In Germany, socialist men opposed women industrial workers. Unions supported the concept of separate spheres for men and women and based their demands for a family wage on the need to maintain a separate private domain of the home. Socialist men argued that women's work often resulted in the neglect of children and could lead to the physical degeneration of the family. Working women, socialist men argued, undermined existing wage scales and aided the exploitation of workers by their willingness to work for lower wages. Class oppression, countered German socialist leader and theorist Clara Zetkin (1857–1933), was the basis of women's oppression. For militants like Zetkin, socialism offered the only means to eliminate sexual inequalities.

DOCUMENT

Working Conditions of Women in Factories

The women's movements of the period from 1871 to 1914 differed socially and culturally from nation to nation. Yet in one sense the women's movements constituted an international phenomenon. The rise in the level of women's political consciousness occurred in the most advanced Western coun-

IMAGE DISCOVERY

A Suffragette's Protest on Derby Day

In this photograph, the suffragette Emily Davison has just been trampled by the king of England's horse at the Derby. The date is 4 June 1913. She died four days later of a fractured skull. What do you imagine Davison hoped to achieve, and what is the significance of her stepping onto the track at this event? Do you consider Emily Davison a deranged person? An anarchist? (See the discussion of anarchism on p. 732.) Or perhaps she is a terrorist? Consider her motives and other means of protest at her disposal as you contemplate this photo.

CONSTANCE LYTTON

Civil disobedience by British women demanding the right to vote often led to their arrest. In protest, incarcerated suffragettes went on hunger strikes to publicize their cause. The British government responded with a brutal policy of force-feeding of prisoners. Constance Lytton, a British aristocrat and suffragette, recounts here the agony of being forcibly fed in prison. Her own health was seriously weakened by the experience.

Focus Questions

How did Constance Lytton express civil disobedience? Why was the government intent on force-feeding women incarcerated in this way, a practice not common with other prisoners?

[The prison's senior medical officer] urged me to take food voluntarily. I told him that was absolutely out of the question, that when our legislators ceased to resist enfranchising women then I should cease to resist taking food in prison.... I offered no resistance to being placed in position, but lay down voluntarily on the plank bed. Two of the wardresses took hold of my arms, one held my head and one my feet. One wardress helped to pour the food. The doctor leant on my knees as he stooped over my chest to get at my mouth. I shut my mouth and clenched my teeth.... The doctor offered me the choice of a wooden or steel gag; he explained elaborately, as he did on most subsequent occasions, that the steel gag would hurt and the wooden one not, and he urged me not to force him to use the steel gag. But I did not speak nor open my mouth, so that after playing about for a moment or two with the wooden one he finally had recourse to the steel. He seemed annoyed at my resistance and he broke into a temper as he plied my teeth with the steel implement.... The pain of it was intense and at last I must have given way for he got the gag between my teeth, when he proceeded to turn it much more than necessary until my jaws were fastened wide apart, far more than they could go naturally. Then he put down my throat a tube which seemed to me much too wide and was something like four feet in length. The irritation of the tube was excessive. I choked the moment it touched my throat until it had got down. Then the food was poured in quickly; it made me sick a few seconds after it was down and the action of the sickness made my body and legs double up, but the wardresses instantly pressed back my head and the doctor leant on my knees. The horror of it was more than I can describe. I was sick over the doctor and wardresses, and it seemed a long time before they took the tube out. As the doctor left he gave me a slap on the cheek, not violently, but, as it were, to express his contemptuous disapproval, and he seemed to take for granted that my distress was assumed.... I had been sick over my hair, which, though short, hung on either side of my face, all over the wall near my bed, and my clothes seemed saturated with it, but the wardresses told me they could not get me a change that night as it was too late, the office was shut. I lay quite motionless, it seemed paradise to be without the suffocating tube, without the liquid food going in and out of my body and without the gag between my teeth. Before long I heard the sounds of the forced feeding in the next cell to mine. It was almost more than I could bear, it was Elsie Howey, I was sure. When the ghastly process was over and all quiet, I tapped on the wall and called out at the top of my voice, which wasn't much just then, "No surrender," and there came the answer past any doubt in Elsie's voice. "No surrender."

From Constance Lytton, *Prisons and Prisoners* (1914).

tries almost simultaneously and had a predominantly middle-class character. Working-class women, most notably in Germany, united feminism with socialism in search of a better life. In spite of concerted efforts, women remained outside societies that excluded them from political participation, access to education, and social and economic equality.

The Jewish Question and Zionism

Two million eastern European Jews migrated westward between 1868 and 1914 in search of peace and refuge. Seventy thousand settled in Germany. Others continued westward, stopping in the United States. Another kind of Jewish migration took place in the nineteenth century—the movement of Jews from rural to urban areas within nations. In eastern Europe, Jewish migrations coincided with downturns in the economic cycle, and Jews became scapegoats for the high rates of unemployment and high prices that seemed to follow in their wake. Most migrants were peddlers, artisans, or small shopkeepers who were seen as threatening to small businesses. Differing in language, culture, and dress, they were viewed as alien in every way.

Anti-Semitism.   The term anti-Semitism, meaning hostility to Jews, was first used in 1879 to give a pseudoscientific legitimacy to bigotry and hatred. Persecution was a harsh reality for Jews in eastern Europe at the end of the nineteenth century. In Russia, Jews could not own property and were restricted to living in certain territories. Organized massacres, or **pogroms,** in Kiev, Odessa, and Warsaw followed the assassination of Tsar

MAP DISCOVERY

Legend:
- The Pale: area where Russian Jews were allowed to live
- Other areas of large Jewish population
- Cities with large Jewish population
- General routes of Jewish exodus

Jewish Migration

Persecution and expulsions drove two million Jews out of Russia and eastern Europe between 1868 and 1914. Some settled in central Europe, others traveled to Palestine and the Americas. According to this map, what features do the areas of large Jewish population have in common? What are the major general routes of Jewish exodus? Based on the chapter discussion, why did Jews migrate into and out of The Pale in western Russia? What were the major stopover points in the Jewish migrations to the south and west?

In western Europe, Jews considered themselves "assimilated" into their national cultures, identifying with their nationality as much as with their religion. Austrian and German Jews were granted full civil rights in 1867 on the principle that citizens of all religions enjoyed full equality. In France, Jews had been legally emancipated since the end of the eighteenth century. But western and central European politics of the 1890s had a strong dose of anti-Semitism. Demagogues such as Georg von Schönerer (1842–1921) of Austria were capable of whipping up a frenzy of riots and violence against Jews. They did not distinguish between assimilated and immigrant Jewish populations in their irrational denunciations.

Western and central European anti-Semitism assumed a new level of virulence at the end of the nineteenth century. Fear of an economic depression united aristocrat and worker alike in blaming a Jewish conspiracy. German anti-Semitism proliferated in the 1880s. "It is like a horrible epidemic," the scholar Theodor Mommsen (1817–1903) observed.

Fear of the Jews was connected with hatred of capitalism. In France and Germany, Jews controlled powerful banking and commercial firms that became the targets of blame in hard times. Upwardly mobile sons of Jewish immigrants entered the professions of banking, trading, and journalism. They were also growing in numbers as teachers and academics. In the 1880s, more than half of Vienna's physicians (61 percent in 1881) and lawyers (58 percent of barristers in 1888) were Jewish. Their professional success only heightened tensions and condemnations of Jews as an "alien race." Anti-Semitism served as a violent means of mobilizing mass support, especially among those groups who felt threatened by capitalist concentration and large-scale industrialization. For anti-Semitic Europeans, Jews embodied the democratic,

Alexander II in 1881 and recurred after the failed Russian revolution of 1905. Russian authorities blamed the Jews, seen as perennial outsiders, for the assassination and revolution and the social instability that followed them. Pogroms resulted in the death and displacement of tens of thousands of Russian and eastern European Jews.

■ Maurycy Minkowski, *After the Pogrom* (ca. 1910). Minkowski's works depict Jewish life in Poland before the Russian Revolution. In this painting he has expertly captured the weariness, hopelessness, and fear of the refugees who have interrupted their flight to rest. The sense of isolation and dislocation evoked in the painting may derive from the deaf and mute artist's personal perception of profound separation and detachment.

liberal, and cosmopolitan tendencies of the culture that they were consciously rejecting in their new political affiliations.

Zionism.   A Jewish leadership emerged in central and western Europe that treated anti-Semitism as a problem that could be solved by political means. For their generation at the end of the nineteenth century, the assimilation of their fathers and mothers was not the answer. Jews needed their own nation, it was argued, since they were a people without a nation. **Zionism** was the solution to what Jewish intellectuals called "the Jewish problem." Zion, the ancient homeland of Biblical times, would provide a national territory, and a choice, to persecuted Jews. Zionism became a Jewish nationalist movement dedicated to the establishment of a Jewish state. Although Zionism did not develop mass support in western Europe among assimilated Jews, its program for national identity and social reforms appealed to a large following of eastern European Jews in Galicia (Poland), Russia, and the eastern lands of the Habsburg Empire—those directly subjected to the extremes of persecution.

Theodor Herzl (1860–1904), an Austrian Jew born in Budapest, was the founder of Zionism in its political form. As a student in Vienna he had encountered discrimination, but his commitment to Zionism developed as a result of his years as a journalist in Paris. Observing the anti-Semitic attacks in republican France provoked by the scandals surrounding the misappropriation of funds by leading French politicians and businessmen during the construction of the Panama Canal and the divisive conflict over the Dreyfus Affair in the 1890s, Herzl came to appreciate how deeply imbedded anti-Semitism was in European society. He despaired of the ability of corrupt parliamentary governments to solve the problem of anti-Semitism. In *The Jewish State* (1896), Herzl concluded that Jews must have a state of their own. Under his direction, Zionism developed a worldwide organization and its own newspaper with the aim of establishing a Jewish homeland in Palestine.

Jews began emigrating to Palestine. With the financial backing of Jewish donors, including the French banker Baron de Rothschild, nearly 90,000 Jews had established settlements there by 1914. Calculated to tap a common Jewish identification with an ancient heritage, the choice of Palestine as a homeland was controversial from the beginning. The problems arising from the choice have persisted into the twenty-first century.

The promised land of the Old Testament, Zion is a holy place in Judaism. The Austrian psychoanalyst Sigmund Freud (1856–1939), who described himself as "a Jew from Moravia," was sympathetic to the Zionist cause but critical of the idea of Palestine as a Jewish state. He considered the idea unworkable and one bound to arouse Christian and Islamic opposition. Freud feared that Palestine would arouse the suspicions of the Arab world and challenge "the feelings of the local natives." He would have preferred a "new, historically unencumbered soil."

Some Jewish critics of Zionism believed that a separate Jewish state would prove that Jews were not good citizens of their respective nation-states and would exacerbate hostilities toward Jews as outsiders. Yet Zionism had much in common with the European liberal tradition because it sought in the creation of a nation-state for Jews the solution to social injustice. Zion, the Jewish nation in the Middle East, was a liberal utopia for the Jewish people. Zionism learned from other mass movements of the period the importance of a broad base of support. By the time of the First Zionist Congress, held in Basel, Switzerland, in 1897, it had become a truly international movement. Herzl was also well aware of the necessity for a charismatic leader and cast himself in the role of messiah for his people.

Zionism did not achieve its goals before World War I, and the Jewish state of Israel was not recognized by the world community until 1948. Before World War I, anti-Semitism and antifeminism were strongly linked in nationalist political programs, which insisted that the place for Jews was on the periphery and the place for women was in the home. Through the Zionist movement, Jews victimized by nationalism planned for their own nation-state as a solution.

Workers and Minorities on the Margins

Changes in the scale of political life paralleled the rise of heavy industry and the increasing urbanization of European populations. New industrial and financial leaders assumed positions of power among Europe's ruling elite. A new style of politics brought new political actors into the public arena at the beginning of the twentieth century. Extraparliamentary groups grew in influence and power and came to exert pressure on the political process. The politics of mass society made clear the contradictions inherent in democracy. Propaganda, the ability to control information, became the avenue to success.

Anarchism.   There was no single anarchist doctrine, but the varieties of **anarchism** all shared a hope in a future free from constraints. Mikhail Bakunin (1814–1876), a member of the Russian nobility, absorbed the works and the message of the French social critic Pierre-Joseph Proudhon. Bakunin became Europe's leading anarchist spokesman. Unlike Proudhon, Bakunin was a man of revolutionary action who espoused the use of violence to achieve individual liberation. He believed that all existing institutions had to be swept away before ownership of production could be collectivized. Bakunin broke with Marx, whom he considered a "scientific bourgeois socialist" out of touch with the mass of workers.

In 1892, the Parisian trial of a bomb-throwing anarchist named Ravachol attracted great public attention. He and other French anarchists had captured the popular imagination with their threats to destroy bourgeois society by bombing private residences, public buildings, and restaurants. Ravachol's terrorist deeds represented the extreme rejection of participation in electoral politics. The public was frightened—but also fascinated. Ravachol opposed the state and the capitalist economy as the dual enemy that could only be destroyed through individual acts of random physical violence. For his crimes he was condemned to death and publicly executed.

The best-known anarchists of the late nineteenth century were those, like Ravachol, who engaged in terrorist assassinations and bombings. Although not all anarchists were terrorists intent on destruction, all shared a desire for a revolutionary restructuring of society. Most anarchists were loners. They dreamed of the collapse of the capitalist system with its exploitation and inequality and of the emergence of a society based on personal freedom, autonomy, and justice. Anarchists spurned the Marxist willingness to organize and participate in parliamentary politics. They disdained the tyranny of new organizations and bureaucracies that worked for gradual reforms at the expense of principles of justice.

Bakunin's successor in international anarchist doctrine was also a Russian of aristocratic lineage—Prince Petr Kropotkin (1842–1921). Kropotkin joined together communism and anarchism, arguing that goods should be communally distributed, "from each according to his ability, to each according to his needs." On the basis of his own empirical observations, Kropotkin argued that competition and dominance were not laws of nature and instead stressed human interdependence.

It is difficult to measure the extent of Bakunin's or Kropotkin's influence, since whatever followers they might have inspired were not overtly or formally organized. Anarchism's greatest appeal was in the less industrialized countries of southern Europe: Spain, Italy, and southern France. In those countries, grassroots anarchism germinated in working-class communities. In the second half of the nineteenth century, Russia too had developed a strong populist tradition similar to anarchism in its opposition to state tyranny. But anarchism was primarily a western European phenomenon.

Anarchism had special appeal to workers in skilled trades staggering under the blows of industrial capitalism. Calling themselves **anarcho-syndicalists**, artisans—especially in France—were able to combine local trade union organization with anarchist principles. Unlike union movements in the industrialized countries of Great Britain and Germany, French trade unions remained small, weak, and local. The contrast between the Labour party in Great Britain and the German Social Democrats on the one hand and the French anarcho-syndicalists on the other highlighted the split between advanced industrial countries and less-developed areas of Europe, where an artisan class was attempting to preserve autonomy and control.

The General Strike.   The journalist and social thinker Georges Sorel (1847–1922) captured the philosophy of anarcho-syndicalism in his book *Reflections on Violence* (1908). Sorel described the "myth," or shared belief, in the **general strike,** a kind of final judgment day when justice would prevail. Unlike the trade unions of other western European states, anarcho-syndicalist unions were militantly opposed to issues of improved wages and better working conditions. They believed that in order to be ready for the collapse of bourgeois society, anarcho-syndicalists must not collaborate with the existing system by accepting benefits and improvements from it. Instead, workers were to hold themselves ready by employing a technique of "direct action" to maintain worker solidarity. "Direct action" was a symbolic gesture that did not advance the revolution but did help workers remain aware of their exploitation. A typical example of "direct action" was the agreement among the militantly revolutionary barbers' union to nick their customers periodically with the razor while shaving them. Acts such as this were meaningless in themselves—

except perhaps to those who experienced them—but were intended to raise the level of commitment to a common cause.

The problems of disaffected groups in general intensified before 1914. Anarchists and anarcho-syndicalist workers deplored the centralization and organization of mass society. Yet anarchism posed no serious threat to social stability because of the effectiveness of policing in most European states. As Friedrich Engels observed at the turn of the century, random violence directed against politics and the economy was no match for the repressive forces at the command of the nation-state. The politics of mass society excluded diverse groups—including women, Jews, and ethnic minorities—from participation. Yet the techniques, values, and organization of the world of politics remained available to all those groups. It was the outbreak of war in 1914 that silenced, temporarily at least, the challenge of the outsiders.

SHAPING THE NEW CONSCIOUSNESS

Both science and art contributed to the new world view that emerged in western society in the late nineteenth century. Not only was the European imagination opened up to new influences from the culture and aesthetics of other lands, but Europeans developed a critique of traditional values and rationalist thought from within through new developments in philosophy and science.

The Authority of Science

The discoveries of science had ramifications that extended beyond the laboratory, the hospital, and the classroom. What may seem commonplace at the beginning of the twenty-first century was nothing less than spectacular at the end of the nineteenth. Imagine a world that discovered how to eliminate the difference between night and day. Imagine further a civilization that could obliterate distance or shrink it. Imagine a people who could see for the first time into solid mass, into their own bodies, and send images through space. Those are the imaginings of fable and fantasy that can be traced back to prehistory. But what had always been the stuff of magic became reality between 1880 and 1914. The people of the West used science and technology to reshape the world and their understanding of it.

Discoveries in the Physical Sciences.   Scientific discoveries in the last quarter of the century pushed out the frontiers of knowledge. In physics, James Clerk Maxwell (1831–1879) discovered the relationship between electricity and magnetism. Maxwell showed mathematically that an oscillating electric charge produces an electromagnetic field and that such a field radiates outward from its source at a constant speed—the speed of light. His theories led to the discovery of the electromagnetic spectrum, comprising radiation of different wavelengths, including X rays, visible light, and radio waves. The discovery had

■ Marie Curie was born Manya Sklodowska in Warsaw, Poland. She shared the Nobel Prize in physics in 1903 and was awarded the Nobel Prize in chemistry in 1911. She is one of two women interred in the French Pantheon, commemorated as a hero of France.

important practical applications for the development of the electrical industry and led to the invention of radio and television. Within a generation, the names of Edison, Westinghouse, Marconi, Siemens, and Bell entered the public realm.

Discoveries in the physical sciences succeeded one another with great rapidity. The periodic table of chemical elements was formulated in 1869. Radioactivity was discovered in 1896. Two years later, Marie Curie (1867–1934) and her husband Pierre (1859–1906) discovered the elements radium and polonium. At the end of the century, Ernest Rutherford (1871–1937) identified alpha and beta rays in radioactive atoms. Building on the new discoveries, Max Planck (1858–1947), Albert Einstein (1879–1955), and Niels Bohr (1885–1962) dismantled the classical physics of absolute and determined principles and left in its place modern physics based on relativity and uncertainty. In 1900, Planck propounded a theory that renounced the emphasis in classical physics on energy as a wave phenomenon in favor of a new "quantum theory" of energy as emitted and absorbed in minute, discrete amounts.

In 1905, Albert Einstein formulated his special theory of relativity, in which he established the relationship of mass and energy in the famous equation $E = mc^2$. In 1916, he published his general theory of relativity, a mathematical formulation that created a new conception of space and time. Einstein disproved the Newtonian view of gravitation as a force and instead saw it as a curved field in the time-space continuum created by the presence of mass. No one foresaw that the application of Einstein's theory—that a particle of matter could be converted into a great quantity of energy—would unleash the greatest destructive power in history. Einstein, a pacifist, lived to see atomic and hydrogen bombs developed.

Achievements in Biology.   Although there were no more dramatic discoveries than those in the physical sciences, the biological sciences also witnessed great breakthroughs. Research biologists dedicated themselves to the study of disease-causing microbes and to the chemical bases of physiology. French chemist Louis Pasteur (1822–1895) studied microorganisms to find methods of preventing the spread of diseases in humans, animals, and plants. He developed methods of inoculation to provide protection against anthrax in sheep, cholera in chickens, and rabies in animals and humans.

The pace of breakthroughs in biological knowledge and medical treatment was staggering. The malaria parasite was isolated in 1880. The control of diseases such as yellow fever contributed to improvement in the quality of life. Knowledge burst the bounds of disciplines, and new fields developed to accommodate new concerns. Research in human genetics, a field that was only beginning to be understood, was begun in the first decade of the twentieth century. The studies of Austrian botanist Gregor Mendel (1822–1884) in the crossbreeding of peas in the 1860s led to the Mendelian laws of inheritance.

Applied Knowledge.   Biological discoveries resulted in new state policies. Public health benefited from new methods of prevention and detection of diseases caused by germs. A professor at the University of Berlin, Rudolf Virchow (1821–1902), discovered the relationship between microbes, sewage, and disease that led to the development of modern sewer systems and pure water for urban populations. Biochemistry, bacteriology, and physiology promoted a belief in social progress through state programs. After 1900, health programs to educate the general public spread throughout Europe.

Discoveries that changed the face of the twentieth century proliferated in a variety of fields. It was a time of many firsts. Airplane flights and deep-sea expeditions based on technological applications of new discoveries pushed out boundaries of exploration above the land and below the sea. In 1909, the same year that work began in human genetics, American explorer Robert E. Peary (1856–1920) reached the North Pole. In that year, too, plastic was first manufactured, under the trade name Bakelite. In the period, Irish-born British astronomer Agnes Mary Clerke (1842–1907) did pioneering work in the new field of astrophysics. Ernest Rutherford proposed a new spatial reality in his theory of the nuclear structure of the atom,

which stated that the atom could be divided and that it consisted of a nucleus surrounded by electrons revolving in orbits.

The values of an age are often revealed in the accomplishments it chooses to honor. In 1896, Swedish industrialist Alfred Nobel (1833–1896), who had invented dynamite and amassed a fortune through the manufacture of explosives, established the Nobel Prizes. To be drawn from a bequest of $9.2 million, the prizes were to recognize achievement internationally in five areas: physics, physiology or medicine, chemistry, literature, and peace. Literary figures, peacemakers, poets, and philosophers had long been recognized as shapers of Western culture. At the end of the nineteenth century, scientists assumed pride of place in their company.

Establishing the Social Sciences

Innovations in the social sciences paralleled the drama of discovery in the biological and physical sciences. The "scientific" study of society purported to apply the same methods of observation and experimentation to human interactions. After 1870, the fields of sociology, economics, history, psychology, anthropology, and archaeology took shape at the core of new social scientific endeavors. They, like the "hard" sciences, had benefits to offer Western women and men that improved the quality of life. But just as scientific advances could be applied to destructive ends, so too did the social sciences promote inequities and prejudices in the Western world.

Economics.   The social scientific study of economics came to the aid of businessmen. Influenced by the quantum theory of physics, economists posited a new view of the economy that revised the classical models of Adam Smith and David Ricardo. The neoclassical economic theory of Alfred Marshall (1842–1924) and others recognized the centrality of individual choice in the marketplace, while dealing with the problem of overproduction: how could businesses know they have produced enough to maximize profits? Economists concerned with how individuals responded to prices devised a theory of marginal utility, by which producers could calculate costs and project profits in a reliable fashion based on a pattern of consumer response to price changes.

Psychology and Studying Human Behavior.   "Scientific" psychology developed in a variety of directions. Wilhelm Wundt (1832–1920) established the first laboratory devoted to psychological research in Leipzig in 1879. From his experiments he concluded that thought is grounded in physical reality. The Russian physiologist Ivan Pavlov (1849–1936) had already received the Nobel Prize for physiology and medicine for his study of the dog's digestive system when he began his famous series of experiments demonstrating the conditioned reflex in dogs. With his theory of personality development and the creation of psychoanalysis, the science of the unconscious, Sigmund Freud (1859–1939) greatly influenced the direction of psychology. Freudian probing of the unconscious was a model greatly at odds with the behavioral perspective of conditioned responses based on Pavlov's work, yet both influenced psychological studies into the twentieth century.

The new social science of criminology claimed scientific veracity after 1880. In 1885, Sir Francis Galton (1822–1911), a cousin of Charles Darwin, proved the individuality of fingerprints through scientific study and thereby initiated an important method of identifying criminals. Criminologists joined psychiatrists as expert witnesses in criminal trials for the first time at the end of the nineteenth century. Galton also propagated pseudoscientific ideas about **eugenics,** the improvement of the human race through selective breeding. Anthropological studies of primitive cultures influenced eugenic assumptions about inferiority and superiority based on racial differences.

The new specialties of forensic medicine and criminal anthropology came into being at the end of the century. *The Criminal Man* (1876), written by Italian criminologist Cesare Lombroso (1836–1909), claimed to be a scientific study of the physical attributes of convicted criminals. Through observation and statistical compilation, Lombroso discovered "born criminals," individuals whose physical characteristics proved their deviance. Criminals, he claimed, could be identified by their looks. With statistics, Lombroso demonstrated, for example, that left-handed, redheaded people with low foreheads were naturally disposed to a life of crime. Even during his lifetime, Lombroso's ideas were widely disputed, and subsequently they were discredited, but their temporary legitimacy was a good indication of how scientific claims justified prejudicial assumptions. Opposing Lombroso's ideas, the French school of criminology stressed the social determinants of crime, seeing poverty and malnutrition as explanations for the different physical appearance of criminals.

The psychology of crowd behavior originated in the work of the French physician Gustave Le Bon (1841–1931). In *Psychology of Crowds* (1895), Le Bon argued that the masses were instinctively irrational. Through his "science" he arrived at the political judgment that democracy was a despicable and dangerous form of government. Émile Durkheim (1858–1917) is regarded as the founder of modern sociology. In his famous study of suicide as a social phenomenon, Durkheim pitted sociological theory against psychology and argued that deviance was the result not of psychic disturbances but of environmental factors and hereditary forces.

Heredity became a general explanation for behavior of all sorts. The novels of Émile Zola presented a popular view of biological determinism. Zola's protagonists were doomed by self-destructive characteristics they inherited from their parents. Everything from poverty, drunkenness, and crime to a declining birthrate could be attributed to biologically determined causes. For some theorists, the reasoning teetered on the edge of racism and ideas about "better blood." Intelligence was now measured "scientifically" for the first time with intelligence quotient (IQ) tests developed at the Sorbonne by the psychologist Alfred Binet (1857–1911) in the 1890s. The tests did not acknowledge the importance of cultural factors in the development of intelligence, and they scientifically legitimated a belief in natural elites. Not least of all, science was also invoked in support of a particular system of gender relations, one that itself was undergoing assault and upheaval between 1871 and 1914 (See "Biology and Woman's Destiny" below.)

Science changed the way people thought and the way they lived. It improved the quality of life by defeating diseases, improving nutrition, and lengthening life span. But scientific knowledge was not without its costs. Scientific discoveries led to new forces of destruction. Scientific ideas challenged moral and religious beliefs. Science was invoked to justify racial and sexual discrimination. Traditional values and religious beliefs also did combat with the new god of science, with philosophers proclaiming that God was dead. Not least of all, science and the progress it promised came under attack by those like Friedrich Nietzsche (1844–1900), the German philosopher who questioned rational values as well as the emphasis on religion in Western thought.

The "New Woman" and the New Consciousness

As women continued to be excluded from national political participation, the right to vote was gradually being extended to all men in western Europe, regardless of property or social rank. New pseudoscientific ideas colluded with political prejudices to justify denying women equal rights. The natural sciences had a formative impact on prevailing views of gender relations and female sexuality and were employed to prove the inferiority of women in the species.

Biology and Woman's Destiny.   In *The Descent of Man* (1871), Charles Darwin, the giant of evolutionary theory, concluded that the mental power of man was higher than that of woman. The female's need for male protection, the father of evolution reasoned, had increased her dependence over time while at the same time increasing the competition of natural selection among men. The result, Darwin argued, was inequality between the sexes. Darwin went on to reject women's emancipation as out of step with biological realities. What Darwin presented was a vicious circle in which women's dependence had made them inferior and their inferiority kept them dependent. The attitudes toward gender and race marked the advent of biological "proofs" to justify social policies. Those of Darwin's disciples who applied biological principles to society came to be known as **social Darwinists,** specialists who claimed that "survival of the fittest" was a concept that could be applied to all social interactions between races and the sexes.

Darwin was not the only man of science who had ideas about a woman's proper place. Others made a dubious case for brain size as an index of superiority. The French physiologist Paul Broca (1824–1880), a contemporary of Darwin, countered in 1873 that the skull capacity of the two sexes was very similar and that a case for inferiority could not be based on measurement. But Broca was atypical. Most scientific opinion argued in favor of female frailty and outright inferiority. Social Darwinists adapted evolutionary biology to the debate over inequality between the sexes. They complemented their race theories with

"ANGEL" OR WOMAN?

Victorian domestic ideals viewed woman as an "Angel in the House" (the title of a poem by Coventry Patmore) who created a paradise of love and nurturance for her husband and children. By the end of the nineteenth century, many women recognized that the description, however rosy, kept women in the home and out of public life. Here Maria Desraismes, a French feminist and republican, rebuts republican and historian Jules Michelet for his popular books that romanticized women and marriage. Desraismes advocated legal rights for women.

Focus Questions

How did the formulation of woman as angel limit the rights of women at the end of the nineteenth century? What is the concept of freedom grounded on in this passage?

Of all woman's enemies, I tell you that the worst are those who insist that woman is an angel. To say that woman is an angel is to impose on her, in a sentimental and admiring fashion, all duties, and to reserve for oneself all rights; it is to imply that her specialty is self-effacement, resignation, and sacrifice; it is to suggest to her that woman's greatest glory, her greatest happiness, is to immolate herself for those she loves; it is to let her understand that she will be *generously* furnished with every opportunity for exercising her aptitudes. It is to say that she will respond to absolutism by submission, to brutality by meekness, to indifference by tenderness, to inconstancy by fidelity, to egotism by devotion.

In the face of this long enumeration, I decline the honor of being an angel. No one has the right to force me to be both dupe and victim. Self-sacrifice is not a habit, a custom; it is an *extra!* It is not on the program of one's duties. No power has the right to impose it on me. Of all acts, sacrifice is the freest, and it is precisely because it is free that it is so admirable.

From Maria Desraismes, "La Femme et le droit" public address published in *Eve dans l'humanité* (1891).

---

evolutionary theories of sexual division: "What was decided among the prehistoric Protozoa cannot be annulled by an Act of Parliament" was one argument against women's right to vote. In general, the natural sciences worked to reinforce the idea of women as reproducers whose proper role was nurturing and whose proper domain was the home. The social sciences, in particular sociology, echoed the findings by asserting that the male-dominated household was a proof of social progress.

The "scientific" arguments justified the exclusion of women from educational opportunities and from professions such as medicine and law. Biology became destiny as women's attempts at equal education came up against closed doors. Stalwarts broke the prohibitions, but women who gained higher education in those decades were the exception that proved the rule. The women who were able to get an education were blocked from using it. There was a generalized fear in Western societies that women who attempted to exceed their "natural" abilities would damage their reproductive functions and neglect their nurturing roles. The specter of sickly children and women with nervous disorders was invoked as grounds for opposing demands for coeducation. Women's education was assigned to churches and was intended to meet the needs of the family. The creation of the first separate women's colleges in the late 1860s marked the beginning of the pioneering era of higher education for women.

The New Woman. In the age of scientific justification of female inferiority, the "new woman" emerged. All over Europe the feminist movement had demanded social, economic, and political progress for women. But the "new woman" phenom-enon exceeded the bounds of the feminist movement and can be described as a general cultural phenomenon. The search for independence was overwhelmingly a middle-class phenomenon that had a psychological as well as a political significance in the years between 1880 and 1914. Victorian stereotypes of the angel at the hearth were crumbling. The "new woman" was a woman characterized by intelligence, strength, and sexual desire—in every way man's equal. The Norwegian playwright Henrik Ibsen (1828–1906) created a fictional embodiment of the phenomenon in Nora, the hero of *A Doll's House* (1879), who was typical of the restive spirit for independence among wives and mothers confined to suffocating households and relegated to the status of children. Contemporary opinion condemned Nora as immoral for abandoning her home, her husband, and her children.

The "new woman's" pursuit of independence included control over her own body. The term *birth control* was first used by an American, Margaret Sanger (1879–1966), although the reality itself was not new. Women had always known of and employed contraceptive and abortive techniques to limit family size. What was different in the period before 1914 was the militant public discussion of ways to prevent conception and an awareness of the death and debilitation that resulted from primitive methods. The development of a process of vulcanizing rubber in the mid-nineteenth century had made condoms available to a mass market, but they were seldom employed. A growing number of women, among whom were medical doctors, decided to take information to the public. Annie Besant, advocating birth control in Great Britain, was charged with corrupting youth by distributing books that dealt with contraception. Aletta Jacobs (1849–1929), the first woman to practice medicine in Holland, opened a contraceptive clinic in 1882. Leagues for distributing contraceptive information were formed elsewhere in Europe. Birth-control advocates aimed to preserve women's health and to give them some control over their reproductive lives.

Discussions of contraception brought into the public arena the premise that women, like men, were sexual beings. That was reinforced by the frank discussions of sexuality in the works of Sigmund Freud. The first English translation of Freud's *The Interpretation of Dreams* appeared in 1913 with a warning note from the publisher that its sale should be limited to doctors, lawyers, and clerics. Richard von Krafft-Ebing (1840–1902) and Havelock Ellis (1859–1939) also contributed to the public discussion of sex in their works on sexuality and sexual deviance. By 1900, sexuality and reproduction were openly connected to discussions of women's rights.

Scientific discoveries had worked to change the world. At the same time, those intent on preserving traditional values invoked scientific authority. But as the uncertainty over gender roles at the beginning of the twentieth century makes clear, science was a way of thinking as well as a body of doctrine. Traditional ideas might be scientifically justified, but they would not go unchallenged.

Art and the New Age

In the last quarter of the nineteenth century, the world of art in western Europe and the United States was characterized by new discoveries, new subjects, and new modes of expression.

At least a half dozen major and distinct art movements caught the imagination of artists and the general public. Beginning in the 1860s, impressionist painters led the way in rebelling against the conventions of the formal painting of the academic salons. Choosing unlikely subjects such as railway stations and haystacks in the works of Claude Monet (1840–1926), impressionists made a revolution in capturing on canvas the nature of light and atmosphere. Post-impressionists in the 1880s and 1890s built on the insights of their impressionist colleagues but went in new and less predictable directions, as exemplified in the work of Paul Cezanne (1839–1906), Vincent Van Gogh (1853–1890), and Henri Rousseau (1844–1910). Pointillism, well exemplified in the work of Georges Seurat (1859–1891), also followed the discoveries of the impressionists by using tiny dots to convey light and a spectrum of color.

Symbolism in painting brought a new concern with the unconscious and dream imagery to the canvas and influenced important movements in the twentieth century. The Norwegian painter Edvard Munch (1863–1944), for example, brought an eerie sense of disquiet to works such as *The Scream*. In France, Odilon Redon (1840–1916) used color and light to convey mysticism through recurrent symbols. Color took on dramatic power as well for the fauvists, who used it to convey primitive emotions, such as in the works of Paul Gauguin (1848–1903), also labeled post-impressionist, and in the bold compositions of Henri Matisse (1869–1954). In Italy, the particular movement of futurism flourished in this same period. As discussed in "The Visual Record" (pp. 716–717), futurist Umberto Boccioni embraced the new age in his art and broke free of the more sedate art that had characterized

■ Claude Monet, *Arrival of the Normandy Train, Gare Saint-Lazare,* 1877. French impressionist painter Claude Monet frequently painted a subject repeatedly under varying light conditions or during different seasons to emphasize light and atmosphere, hallmarks of impressionism. This painting of a bustling Paris train station is one of seven paintings of the station by Monet.

AFRICAN ART AND EUROPEAN ARTISTS

The limited definition of civilization held by the Western world for more than a millennium began to broaden in the late nineteenth century. Anthropologists studying non-Western cultures argued that the social structure, habits, beliefs, and products of communities elsewhere in the world formerly dismissed as primitive or exotic were, in their own way, as complex and evolved as those based on European tradition. In the late nineteenth century, the world view of Europeans was expanded by two characteristic European institutions: world fairs and public museums. European countries and the United States hosted international exhibitions such as the London Great Exhibition of 1851 and the Chicago Columbian Exposition of 1893 that introduced art and cultural artifacts from all over the world to a mass public audience. Curiosity led to awareness and gave way to growing appreciation and understanding of the cultures of different continents. For example, European exposure to the art forms and costumes of the Far East changed European style and painting in the second half of the nineteenth century. The discovery of Japanese painting, wood-block prints, and calligraphy provided an important influence on the new direction of European impressionists and postimpressionists. Japanese design was incorporated into the work of such leading Western artists as Edgar Degas and James Whistler.

THE WEST AND THE WIDER WORLD

No less important was the artistic influence of Africa, portrayed as the "dark continent" and the "white man's burden" by colonizing forces (see Chapter 25), on leading lights of the European art world. Pablo Picasso encountered African carvings for the first time as a young man in the ethnographic collections of the Trocadéro Museum in Paris. The Spanish artist was so fascinated by the directness and strength of the African aesthetic that he was inspired to abandon all traces of traditional form in his work and seek a new means of expression. In one of his best known works from the early twentieth century, *Les Desmoiselles d'Avignon* (1907, France, Figure 1), Picasso used the formula of African masks to cover the faces of the two women on the right of the canvas. Mask-like features were incorporated into the faces of the three women to the left. The denial of natural appearance in these women is coupled with the denial of a similar Western art convention, the illusion of three-dimensional space. Picasso fragments the planes of the background and the planes of some of the bodies, breaking them into the jagged slabs that would become the hallmark of Cubism. Picasso knew little about the cultural significance of the African masks he so admired and collected; he saw them as emblems of primitivism, appropriate for the spirit of danger and mystery he

■ Figure 1. Pablo Picasso, *Les Demoiselles d'Avignon* (1907). Museum of Modern Art, New York/Art Resource, NY. © 2007 Estate of Pablo Picasso/Artists Rights Society (ARS), New York.

wanted to convey in a portrait of Avignon prostitutes. He saw in African art the point of departure and the source of inspiration for a new and radical art in the West.

The dynamic of cultural exchange in the arts flowed in both directions. While leading European artists such as Picasso were forging new art forms by appropriating an African art aesthetic identified as primitive, African artists were borrowing and incorporating Western-inspired forms into their art. See this staff finial from the Kongo (ca. 16th–19th century, Figure 2) of an ivory figure representing a Kongo man, indicated by his broken teeth and beardless chin, with blue eyes and dressed in Western clothing. Wooden staffs topped with ivory carvings symbolized power and status to Kongo peoples. This particular figure, reddened by pigment and use, embodies the further status conferred by Western hat, high-collared jacket, and earring

■ Figure 2. Staff finial of the Kongo peoples (ca. 16th–19th century).

typical of the earliest Westerners to trade in Africa. The man's garb positions him in a new wider world, associating Westernization with power and progress.

The Mami Wata cult of west Africa demonstrates another kind of cultural intersection. Images of this foreign water spirit seen here in a mask of the Guro peoples from the Ivory Coast in the mid-twentieth century (Figure 3) record the layering of ideas and aesthetics from abroad. Her posture and her attribute of the coiling snake have been traced back to a German color lithograph of an East Indian snake charmer, circulated throughout the Ivory Coast in the late nineteenth century. Here the Mami Wata figure is superimposed on the top of a beautiful and colorful tribal mask, demonstrating the graceful coexistence of cultures and influences. The combination of the Mami Wata icon with the traditional African mask, similar to those collected by Picasso, is intended to connote a particular spiritual force of imported ideas and influences. The cult of Mami Wata has endured through the twentieth century, and her image is associated with more than a dozen cultures from Senegal to Tanzania. Dressed according to modern Western standards, Mami Wata's form has continued to change with the times. Her iconography is a dynamic one that continues to develop.

Beyond form and content, one of the major differences that should be noted in considering the dynamic between the West and the wider world of African art is the presence of the individual artist in the Western aesthetic. We know *Les Desmoiselles d'Avignon* as the work of the great artist Pablo Picasso, but in the African examples

■ Figure 3. Mask with carving of Mami Wata, foreign water spirit (mid-20th century, Ivory Coast).

considered here, no artist's name was recorded. We know the art by the region and the community in which it was produced. The African emphasis on the role of the community in the production of art is quite different from the Western glorification of the individual artist and his or her creative act.

QUESTIONS FOR DISCUSSION

What African art form influenced Picasso, and how did his use of it lead to changes in Western art? What symbols did African artists in the same period import from the West and from other cultures? What qualities did Picasso attempt to convey by using African art forms? And what qualities did African artists recognize in appropriating Western symbols?

the Western tradition. Other movements that were contemporaneous with impressionism and post-impressionism included the British pre-Raphaelites and the arts and crafts movement.

All the widely varied art of this period also had certain features in common. The artists reflected the values and mores of a changing society in their work, both in their choice of subject matter and their choice of perspective. They were also influenced by breakthroughs in science and technology that allowed the understanding of how light worked through the new realism of the photographic medium and new discoveries in physics and the science of the material world. New knowledge about non-Western cultures and Europeans' widening view of the world also influenced artistic subjects and styles. (See "The West and the Wider World: African Art and European Artists," pp. 738–739.) The new art movements of the late nineteenth century also indicated a dramatic shift in the class base of art out of the salons of the elite and the aristocracy and into the venues of middle class life—the home, the public spheres of the café, the theater, and the railway station.

The New Consumption

The great Russian novelist Lev Tolstoy (1828–1910) was an astute observer of the world in which he lived. In 1877, he condemned the materialism that characterized European society: "Money is a new form of slavery, and distinguishable from the old simply by the fact that it is impersonal—that there is no human relation between master and slave." Although he was speaking as a moral philosopher, Tolstoy had put his finger on something that economists were just beginning to understand—the extension of a money economy. Tolstoy was aware of how peasants freed from the land became entangled in a web of financial obligations that constituted a new form of serfdom.

Disposable Income. At the end of the nineteenth century, the role of money changed in ways affecting all of Western society. Workers were beginning to share in the benefits of industrial prosperity. The prosperity differed dramatically by geographic region and occupation. But the expansion in the ranks of a salaried working class augured a shift in patterns of behavior. Lagging behind the industrial revolutions but no less important was a revolution in consumption patterns among European populations. The new consumer age is best illustrated by the creation of the big department stores of the last quarter of the nineteenth century. The Bon Marché Department Store in Paris occupied more than 52,000 square feet and contained a vast selection of goods. Everything from initialed toilet paper to household furniture was now located under a single roof. The department store was intended to satisfy every need. Advertising and the art of display became industries in themselves, the goal of which was to encourage people to buy things they did not need. The promise of the good life, epitomized in the department store and preached by advertising, now seemed accessible to everyone.

Leisure as Consumption. Leisure time also became a consumer item in the late nineteenth century. In 1899, the American economist Thorstein Veblen (1857–1929) published a pathbreaking work that was little appreciated at the time. *The Theory of the Leisure Class* argued that leisure was a form of "conspicuous consumption," a term Veblen coined. More than a theory, his work constituted a critique of the values of Western culture. Women and the family were, for Veblen, the primary vehicles for conspicuous consumption. Elegant dress, for example, conveyed status and served as a sign of leisure just as it had done in aristocratic society. Expensive clothing was designed to show that the wearer had no need to earn wages. For this purpose, women were actually "mutilated," in Veblen's term, by the corset that constricted their vitality and rendered them unfit for work. Women immobilized by their clothes and shoes became the ultimate symbols of social status.

The middle and upper classes controlled sufficient disposable income to allow them to spend time in such leisure pur-

■ Ad for toys for the Bon Marché Department Store in Paris, 1911. Such advertisements lured consumers (and their children) to the big department stores with vast selections of goods on display.

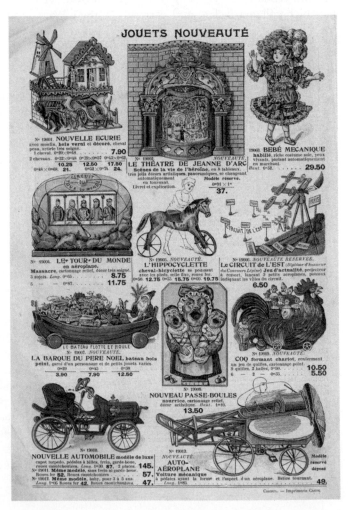

throughout Europe and to the United States. Spectator sports grew in importance, with audiences of more than 100,000 people at British soccer matches at the beginning of the twentieth century. Victorians saw the necessity of recreation and endorsed the renewing, relaxing, and entertaining aspects of organized play.

Scouting also originated at the end of the nineteenth century as another form of organized leisure. Uniformed boys were taught "manly" virtues of self-reliance and teamwork. Team spirit was tied to patriotism. Scouting organizations for girls emphasized domestic virtues and household tasks. Amateur athletics and track-and-field events grew in popularity, especially after the establishment of an international Olympics competition, modeled on the ancient Greek games. The first modern Olympiad was held in Athens in 1896, and—except for upheavals caused by war—the Olympic Games continue to be held at four-year intervals.

Cycling became a popular competitive sport on the Continent with the establishment of the Tour de France at the beginning of the twentieth century. Some saw in the new pastime of bicycling a threat to the social order. Women, attracted by the exercise and mobility afforded by the new means of transportation, altered their costumes in favor of freedom of movement. They discarded their corsets and bustles and shortened their skirts. As women gained greater mobility, some observers saw in the "new woman" on the bicycle seat the decline of true womanhood and Western values.

■ A poster for the World Exhibition held in Paris in 1889 features the star attraction of the show—the Eiffel Tower. Most of the other exhibition buildings were subsequently demolished.

suits as flocking to seaside resorts in Great Britain and on the Continent. However, resort vacations remained out of the financial reach of most working-class people. Instead, in pursuit of leisure-time activities, working-class men congregated in cafes and pubs. Starting in the 1880s, vaudeville and music halls rose in popularity, their low admission price attracting ever larger crowds. There were at least 30 striptease shows in Paris in the 1890s. Such activities fostered fear among the middle classes that working-class leisure was degenerate. The newly invented cinema also exercised a growing appeal for European men and women of all ages and classes.

Not least important in the new leisure was the rise of organized sports. The strict organization of work life in mature industrial societies may have made sports an attractive way of organizing leisure. Men—there were few organized sports for women—worked by the clock and now played by the clock as well. Sports also promoted national and regional identification. Beginning in the 1860s, men began playing the games they had learned as boys in English public schools. Rugby, football (soccer), and cricket soon developed national followings. Golf originated in Scotland in the period and spread

CONCLUSION

The engineering marvel of the Eiffel Tower, built in 1889 for the World Exposition held in Paris, became a symbol not only of the French capital but of the values of the new age. New artifacts of European culture proliferated. Photography, motorcars, bicycles, motion picture cameras, and X rays all created sensations when they appeared. London's Inner Circle underground railway was completed in 1884, and other lines soon followed, forming a vast urban subterranean network. In 1898, the miracle of underground transportation became a reality in Paris with the opening of the Métro, or subway. Yet some observers saw in the new age upheaval and disruption of traditional liberal values, the collapse of the family, and the disruptions of women and workers who did not know their place.

The Eiffel Tower was criticized more than it was praised. It was a building, yet it was not. Its inside and its outside were confused. The admirers of classic architecture lamented the girdered monument whose main function was to demonstrate structural innovation for its own sake. Critics lamented that science disrupted people's understanding of the world and their place in it in the same way. The Eiffel Tower—like the values of the new age (speed, progress, technological innovation, and mass consumption), critics warned—was hollow and would not endure.

QUESTIONS FOR REVIEW

1. Why did European economies run through cycles of boom and bust in the late nineteenth century, and how did European governments attempt to regulate the economy?
2. What challenges did liberal ideals and institutions confront in England, Germany, France, and Austria?
3. What social forces brought women and others into the new mass politics of the late nineteenth century?
4. What new ideas were being generated in psychology and the social sciences at the turn of the century, and what impact did they have on the way Europeans thought about gender relations?

KEY TERMS

anarchism, *p. 732*	general strike, *p. 732*
anarcho-syndicalists, *p. 732*	*Kulturkampf, p. 721*
anti-Semitism, *p. 723*	pogroms, *p. 729*
cartels, *p. 719*	revisionism, *p. 722*
eugenics, *p. 735*	social Darwinists, *p. 735*
Fabians, *p. 720*	suffragettes, *p. 727*
futurists, *p. 716*	Zionism, *p. 731*

DISCOVERING WESTERN CIVILIZATION ONLINE

You can obtain more information about the crisis of European culture between 1871 and 1914 at the Websites listed below. See also the Companion Website that accompanies this text, www.ablongman.com/kishlansky, which contains an online study guide and additional resources.

European Economy and the Politics of Mass Society

Encyclopaedia of British History: Socialism
www.spartacus.schoolnet.co.uk/socialism.htm
This is a fairly comprehensive site on the English labor movement, including texts, biographies of major figures, and other links.

Project Social Insurance in Germany
www.erziehung.uni-giessen.de/studis/Robert/inhver_e.html
A brief overview of the development of social welfare legislation in Germany in the latter half of the nineteenth century.

Habsburg Source Texts Archive
www2.h-net.msu.edu/~habsweb/sourcetexts
Sponsored by the H-Net Discussion list HABSBURG, this site provides electronic texts relating to the creation of the Dual Monarchy.

Outsiders in Mass Politics

The Emancipation of Women: 1750–1920
www.spartacus.schoolnet.co.uk/women.htm
This site contains links to biographies of major figures, essays on the major organizations and societies, and electronic texts of the women's movement in Britain.

The Genesis Project
www.genesis.ac.uk
This mapping project on women's history research sources is provided by the Women's Library of London and the Research Support Libraries Programme.

Shaping the New Consciousness

Sigmund Freud: Conflict & Culture
www.loc.gov/exhibits/freud
A Library of Congress virtual exhibit on the life and times of Sigmund Freud.

Sigmund Freud and the Freud Archives
users.rcn.com/brill/freudarc.html
An exhaustive collection of links to archives, electronic texts, bibliographies, and other resources on Freud and the history of psychoanalysis.

Internet History of Science Sourcebook
www.fordham.edu/halsall/science/sciencesbook.html
A comprehensive collection of links to primary source materials, Websites, and bibliographies on major scientists, discoveries, and theories in the nineteenth century.

Art History Resources: 19th-Century Art & 20th-Century Art
witcombe.sbc.edu/ARTHLinks5.html
witcombe.sbc.edu/ARTH20thcentury.html
The first Web page contains numerous links on the artists, styles, and schools of art in the nineteenth century, including impressionism, post-impressionism, and symbolism. The second page includes links to resources on art and artists of the twentieth century.

SUGGESTIONS FOR FURTHER READING

European Economy and the Politics of Mass Society

Edward Arnold, ed., *The Development of the Radical Right in France: From Boulanger to Le Pen* (New York: St. Martin's Press, 2000). Part I examines Boulangism, Socialism, anti-Semitism, right-wing working-class politics, and roots of right-wing radicalism.

Sudhir Hazareesingh, *Political Traditions in Modern France* (New York: Oxford University Press, 1994). In examining the particularities of French political life, the author focuses on the relationship between political movements and ideologies since 1789.

Martin P. Johnson, *The Dreyfus Affair* (New York: St. Martin's Press, 1999). A concise and comprehensive overview of the Affair as a defining event in French history.

Beian Porter, *When Nationalism Began to Hate: Imagining Modern Politics in Nineteenth-Century Poland* (New York: Oxford University Press, 2001). In examining Polish nationalism, the author offers a broader understanding of modern European politics.

Kevin Repp, *Reformers, Critics, and the Paths of German Modernity, 1890–1914* (Cambridge, MA: Harvard University Press, 2000). The author looks at the reformers, intellectuals, and activists who shaped the modernist movement in Germany.

Outsiders in Mass Politics

Karen Offen, *European Feminisms, 1750-1950: A Political History* (Stanford: Stanford University Press, 2000). A leading historian of French feminism, Offen provides a comprehensive account of the varieties of European feminism over 250 years.

June Purvis and Sandra Stanley Holton, eds., *Votes for Women* (New York: Routledge, 2000). The editors have brought together a collection of essays that reappraise the history of British suffragism by examining the activities of various women's groups and individuals from the nineteenth century to the interwar period.

Richard Stites, *The Women's Liberation Movement in Russia: Feminism, Nihilism, and Bolshevism, 1860–1930* (Princeton, NJ: Princeton University Press, 1978). Situates the Russian women's movement within the contexts of both nineteenth-century European feminism and twentieth-century communist ideology and traces its development from the early feminists through the rise of the Bolsheviks to power. Includes a discussion of the Russian Revolution's impact on the status of women.

Sophia A. van Wingerden, *The Women's Suffrage Movement in Britain, 1866–1928* (New York: St. Martin's Press, 1999). A chronological overview of the history of the British suffrage movement.

Shaping the New Consciousness

Geoffrey Crossick and Serge Jaumain, eds., *Cathedrals of Consumption: The European Department Store, 1850–1939* (Aldershot, England: Ashgate Publishing, 1999). A collection of articles about the creation of department stores in different European countries from the perspectives of culture, consumption, gender, and urban life.

Stephen Kern, *The Culture of Time and Space, 1880–1918* (Cambridge, MA: Harvard University Press, 1983). Describes how late-nineteenth-century technological advances created new modes of thinking about and experiencing time and space.

Robert A. Nye, *Crime, Madness, and Politics in Modern France: The Medical Concept of National Decline* (Princeton, NJ: Princeton University Press, 1984). Nye shows how the medical concept of deviance was linked to a general cultural crisis in fin-de-siécle France.

Theodore M. Porter, *The Rise of Statistical Thinking, 1820–1900* (Princeton, NJ: Princeton University Press, 1986). This work traces the origins of modern statistical innovation of the early 1900s and shows the interdependence of the natural and social sciences.

William M. Reddy, *Money and Liberty in Modern Europe: A Critique of Historical Understanding* (Cambridge: Cambridge University Press, 1987). This essay on the role of money in modern Europe contends that its widespread use in exchange influenced social structure. Arguing that monetary exchange intensified existing social inequities, Reddy examines the expansion of commerce in France, Germany, and England.

Vanessa Schwartz, *Spectacular Realities: Early Mass Culture in Fin-de-Siécle Paris* (Berkeley: University of California Press, 1998). This work examines the formation and emergence of mass urban culture in late nineteenth-century Paris.

John Tosh, *A Man's Place: Masculinity and the Middle-Class Home in Victorian England* (New Haven, CT: Yale University Press, 1999). This work examines the roles of men in the private world of the domestic sphere and argues that Victorian masculinity was constructed not only in terms of work and male associations but also in terms of the home.

For a list of additional titles related to this chapter's topics, please see http://www.ablongman.com/kishlansky.

25 EUROPE AND THE WORLD, 1870–1914

THE POLITICS OF MAPMAKING
THE FIRST STANDARDIZED MAP OF THE WORLD

People drew maps before they knew how to write. Yet in 1885 only one-ninth of the land surface of the earth had been surveyed. In the ten-year period before 1900, European and American surveyors and cartographers fanned out around the globe to every continent including Antarctica. The result was that for the first time comprehensive and accurate world maps could be drawn.

THE VISUAL RECORD The great leap forward in knowledge of the earth's terrain did not produce a standardized map of the world. Representatives of different countries argued over the units for measurement, and even the symbols and colors that should be used on official maps. Mapmakers from Europe and the United States began to gather regularly at their own international conventions with the goal of devising a uniform map of the world that would satisfy everyone. They failed repeatedly.

The French, for example, argued that the meter should be the standard measurement for the world map. The British countered with yards and miles, unscientifically developed units of measurement to which they had been committed for centuries. Those scientists who acknowledged the logic of using the meter could not agree on which prototype meter should be taken as standard. Should the meter be measured according to the common method of the movement of a pendulum? If so, gravitation varying from one place to another on the earth's surface would result in different meter lengths. Most agreed that the meter should be measured in reference to the arc of the meridian. But where should the prime meridian, the place on the map that indicates zero longitude, be located since it was not a fixed phenomenon?

The debate over the prime meridian is a perfect example of the politics of mapmaking. Unlike the equator, which is midway between the North and South Poles, zero longitude can be drawn anywhere. Paris, Philadelphia, and Beijing were just three of the competing sites designated as zero longitude in the nineteenth century.

Uniformity, the cartographers insisted, would have advantages for everyone. Not least of all, a standardized map would make standardized timekeeping easier. Standard times could be calculated according to zones of longitude. Germany had five different time zones in 1891. In France, every city had its own time taken from solar readings. The United States had more than 200 time zones from one coast to the other. In modern industrial societies with railroad timetables and legal contracts, time had to be controlled and it had to be exact. In other words, time had to be standardized. Specialists suggested that the Royal Observatory in Greenwich, England, was the best place to locate the prime meridian in order to calculate a standard time system. The French balked, insisting on Paris as the only candidate for the designation. In the end, there was a compromise. The metric system, created during the French Revolution, prevailed as the standard of measurement, and the prime meridian passed through the Royal Greenwich Observatory, where standard time was calculated for most of the globe. Standard time zones and uniform maps were possible for the first time only at the end of the nineteenth century, and the key to standardization, its touchstone, was determined by geopolitical dominance. Great Britain, the most powerful imperial power, became the starting point for measuring time and space.

The accompanying map provides a dramatic example of the conquest of territories by the British Empire in 1886. The importance of territorial expansion is underlined by the presence of the inset in the upper right, which shows the extent of British territories a century earlier. The map is Great Britain's report card of success between 1785 and 1886. Britannia, sitting astride the "world" in the bottom center, is held up by

■ Map of the world highlighting the reaches of the British Empire in 1886.

Human Labor and attended by women of color with fans. Prospectors, explorers, men of the military, and a British schoolboy all witness Britannia's triumph. In the right panel, native women are erotically presented amid garlands and tropical flora, mirroring the people from colder climes on the opposing panel. British presence provides the only color on the world's continents, which are, it appears, ready to be suffused by the rosy glow of British rule.

In 1891, a young Viennese geographer named Albrecht Penck proposed an international map of the world. His idea was to produce a map using standard symbols and colors and omitting political boundaries. Penck's proposal came up against the harsh realities of mapmaking. In the age of imperialism, being able to indicate the extent of territorial control of nations on maps became a supreme value. The imperialist nation-states of Europe at the end of the nineteenth century sought to tout their territorial successes, not always with the greatest attention to accuracy. As technology made more accurate mapmaking possible, national pride resisted standardization. Penck's global vision remained subordinate to the limits of national boundaries and to the politics of mapmaking.

LOOKING AHEAD

This chapter begins by considering the territorial arrangements and conflicts within Europe between 1870 and 1914 that created a new kind of foreign policy based on mutual interests and national vulnerabilities. The chapter then turns to European rivalries in the global arena and the territorial and market expansion into Africa and Asia that characterized the new imperialism. Finally, the chapter considers how imperial encounters changed both the colonized and the colonizer and produced interdependent markets and a new world economy.

THE EUROPEAN BALANCE OF POWER, 1870–1914

Between 1870 and 1914, European states were locked in a competition within Europe for territorial dominance and control. Rising nationalist movements in southern Europe and the Ottoman Empire contributed to a mood of increasing confrontation among Europe's great powers. The European balance of power so carefully crafted by Germany's Otto von Bismarck began to disintegrate with his departure from office in 1890. By 1914, a Europe divided into two camps was no longer the sure guarantee of peace that it had been a generation earlier.

Upsetting the European Balance of Power

The map of Europe had been redrawn in the two decades after 1850. By 1871, Europe consisted of five great powers, known as the Big Five—Britain, France, Germany, Austria-Hungary, and Russia—and a handful of lesser states. The proclamation of a German Empire in 1871 and the emergence of Italy with Rome as its capital in 1870 unified numerous disparate states. Although not always corresponding to linguistic and cultural differences among Europe's peoples, national boundaries appeared fixed, with no country aspiring to territorial expansion at the expense of its neighbors. But the creation of the two new national units of Germany and Italy had legitimized nationalist aspirations and the militarism necessary to enforce them.

The Three Emperors' League. Under the chancellorship of Otto von Bismarck, Germany led the way in forging a new alliance system based on the realistic assessment of power politics within Europe. In 1873, Bismarck joined together the three most conservative powers of the Big Five—Germany, Austria-Hungary, and Russia—into the Three Emperors' League. Consultation over mutual interests and friendly neutrality were the cornerstones of the alliance. Identifying enemies and choosing friends in the new configuration of power came in large part to depend on geographic weaknesses. The Three Emperors' League was one example of the geographic imperatives driving diplomacy. Bismarck was determined to banish the specter of a two-front war by isolating France on the Continent.

Each of the Great Powers had a vulnerability, a geographic Achilles' heel. Germany's vulnerability lay in its North Sea ports. German shipping along its only coast could easily be bottlenecked by a powerful naval force. Such an event, the Germans knew, could destroy their rapidly growing international trade. What was worse, powerful land forces could "encircle" Germany. As Britain's century-old factories slowly became obsolete under peeling coats of paint, Germany enjoyed the advantages of a latecomer to industrialization—forced to start from scratch by investing in the most advanced machinery and technology. The German Reich was willing to support industrial expansion, scientific and technological training, and social programs for its workers. Yet as Germany surged forward to seize its share of world markets, it was acutely aware that it was hemmed in on the Continent. Germany could not extend its frontiers the way Russia had to the east. German gains in the Franco-Prussian War in Alsace and Lorraine could not be repeated without risking greater enmity. German leaders saw the threat of encirclement as a second geographic weakness. Bismarck's awareness of those geographic facts of life prompted his engineering of the Three Emperors' League in 1873, two years after the founding of the German Empire.

Austria-Hungary was Europe's second largest nation in land and the third largest in population. The same factors that had made it a great European power—its size and its diversity—now threatened to destroy it. The ramshackle empire of Europe, it had no geographical unity. Its vulnerability came from within, from the centrifugal forces of linguistic and cultural diversity. Weakened by nationalities clamoring for independence and self-rule and by an unresponsive political system, Austria-Hungary remained backward agriculturally and unable to respond to the Western industrial challenge. It seemed most likely to collapse from social and political pressures.

Russia's vulnerability was reflected in its preoccupation with maintaining free access to the Mediterranean Sea. Russia, clearly Europe's greatest landed power, was vulnerable because it could be landlocked by frozen or blockaded ports. The ice that crippled its naval and commercial vessels in the Baltic Sea drove Russia east through Asia to secure another ice-blocked port on the Sea of Japan at Vladivostok in 1860 and to seek ice-free Chinese ports. Russia was equally obsessed with protecting its warm-water ports on the Black Sea. Whoever controlled the strait of the Bosporus controlled Russia's grain export trade, on which its economic prosperity depended.

The Ottoman Empire. Another great decaying conglomeration was the Ottoman Empire, bridging Europe and Asia. Politically feeble and on the verge of bankruptcy, the Ottoman

Empire, with Turkey at its core, was composed of a vast array of ethnically, linguistically, and culturally diverse peoples. In the hundred years before 1914, increasing social unrest and nationalist bids for independence had plagued the Ottoman Empire. As was the case with the Habsburgs in Austria-Hungary, the Ottomans maintained power with increasing difficulty over the myriad ethnic groups struggling to be free. The Ottoman Empire, called "the sick man of Europe" by contemporaries, found two kinds of relations sitting at its bedside: those who would do anything to ensure its survival, no matter how weak, and those who longed for and sought to hasten its demise. Fortunately for the Ottoman Empire, rivalries among its enemies helped to preserve it.

The Ottomans had already seen parts of their holdings lopped off in the nineteenth century. Britain, ever conscious of its interests in India, had acquired Cyprus, Egypt, Aden, and Sudan from the Ottomans. Germany insinuated itself into Turkish internal affairs and financed the **Baghdad Railway** in the attempt to link the Mediterranean to the Persian Gulf. Russia acquired territories on the banks of the Caspian Sea and had plans to take Constantinople. But it was the volatile Balkan Peninsula that threatened to upset the European power balance. The Balkans appeared to be a territory that begged for dismemberment. Internally, the Slavs sought independence from their Habsburg and Turkish oppressors. External pressures were equally great, with each of the major powers following its own political agenda.

The Instability of the Alliance System

The system of alliances formed between and among European states was guided by two political realities: the tension between France and Germany, and Russia's fear of becoming landlocked.

Franco-German Tensions. A major destabilizing factor in the European balance of power was the tension between France and Germany. France had lost its dominance on the Continent in 1870–1871, when it was easily defeated by Prussia at the head of a nascent German Empire. With its back to the Atlantic, France faced the smaller states of Belgium, Luxembourg, Switzerland, and Italy and the industrially and militarily powerful Germany. It had suffered the humiliation of losing territory to Germany—Alsace and Lorraine in 1871. France felt trapped and isolated geographically and in need of powerful friends as a counterweight to German power.

Russian Aspirations and the Congress of Berlin. Ostensibly, Russia had the most to gain from the extension of its frontiers and the creation of pro-Russian satellites. It saw that by championing Pan-Slavic nationalist groups in southeastern Europe, it could greatly strengthen its own position at the expense of the two great declining empires, Ottoman Turkey and Austria-Hungary. Russia hoped to draw the Slavs into its orbit by fostering the creation of independent states in the Balkans. A Serbian revolt began in two Ottoman provinces,

Bosnia and Herzegovina, in 1874. International opinion pressured Turkey to initiate reforms. Serbia declared war on Turkey on 30 June 1876; Montenegro did the same the next day. Britain, supporting the Ottoman Empire because of its trading interests in the Mediterranean, found itself in a delicate position of perhaps condemning an ally when it received news of Turkish atrocities against Christians in Bulgaria. Prime Minister Disraeli insisted that Britain was bound to defend Constantinople because of British interests in the Suez Canal and India. While Britain stood on the sidelines, Russia, with Romania as an ally, declared war against the Ottoman Empire. The war was quickly over, with Russia capturing all of Armenia, forcing the Ottoman sultan, Abdul Hamid II (1842–1918), to sue for peace on 31 January 1878.

Great Britain did not share Germany's and Russia's fears of strangulation by blockade. And although the question of Irish home rule was a nationalities problem for Britain, it paled in comparison with Austria-Hungary's internal challenge. As an island kingdom, however, Great Britain relied on imports for its survival. The first of the European nations to become an urban and industrial power, Britain was forced to do so at the expense of its agricultural sector. It could not feed its own people without importing foodstuffs. Britain's geographic vulnerability was its dependence on access to its empire and the maintenance of open sea-lanes. Britain saw its greatest menace coming from the rise of other sea powers—notably Germany.

Bismarck, a seemingly disinterested party acting as an "honest broker," hosted the peace conference that met at Berlin. The British succeeded in blocking Russia's intentions for a Bulgarian satellite and keeping the Russians from taking Constantinople. Russia abandoned its support of Serbian nationalism, and Austria-Hungary occupied Bosnia and Herzegovina. The peace concluded at the 1878 Congress of Berlin disregarded Serbian claims, thereby promising continuing conflict over the nationalities question.

The Berlin Congress also marked the emergence of a new estrangement among the Great Powers. Russia believed itself betrayed by Bismarck and abandoned in its alliance with Germany. Bismarck in turn cemented a Dual Alliance between Austria-Hungary and Germany in 1879 that survived until the collapse of the two imperial regimes in 1918. The Three Emperors' League was renewed in 1881, now with stipulations regarding the division of the spoils in case of a war against Turkey.

The Alliance System Revamped. In 1882, Italy was asked to join the Dual Alliance with Germany and Austria-Hungary, thus converting it into the **Triple Alliance,** which prevailed until the Great War of 1914. Germany, under Bismarck's tutelage, signed treaties with Italy, Russia, and Austria-Hungary and established friendly terms with Great Britain. A new Balkan crisis in 1885, however, shattered the illusion of stable relations.

Hostilities erupted between Bulgaria and Serbia. Russia threatened to occupy Bulgaria, but Austria stepped in to prevent Russian domination of the Balkans, thus threatening the alliance of the Three Emperors' League. Russia was further

BABYLON DISCOVERED

While European nations were engaged in laying claim to other lands for economic development and imperial conquest, a different kind of exploration was occurring at the end of the nineteenth century. The relatively new social science of arachaeology uncovered lost civilizations. Heinrich Schliemann (1882–1890) discovered Troy. Schliemann, a German businessman, captured the imagination of Europeans when he used his own fortune to open up what he believed to be the ruins of the sites mentioned in Homeric verse. Sir Arthur Evans (1851-

1941) began excavations in Crete in 1900 and over the next eight years unearthed the remains of Minoan culture. Both men used scientific procedures to reconstruct ancient cultures.

After 1870, other archaeologists employing increasingly scientific techniques worked on "digs" in Italy, Greece, and Turkey, deepening western knowledge of ancient civilizations. Archaeologists also broadened their vision to include new areas. For centuries adventurers and explorers had been traveling back and forth to the lands around the Persian Gulf. In the

geographic area that came to be known as the "Middle East," new archaeological discoveries were being made now about the world's earliest civilizations.

Beginning in 1899, German archaeologist Robert Koldewey (1855–1925) began an 18-year-long endeavor to find the city of ancient Babylon, a land of biblical and legendary fame. He worked in the region between the Tigris and Euphrates rivers, the site of ancient Mesopotamia, which is included in present-day Iraq. (See pp. 11-19 of this book for a discussion of Mesopotamian civilization.) And

■ Ishtar Gate of the inner city of Babylon, dedicated to the Assyrian goddess, discovered by Koldewey.

THE WEST AND THE WIDER WORLD

■ Ziggurat of Manduk, a pyramidal-shaped temple with a flat roof, was one of the largest of such structures in ancient Mesopotamia.

here Koldewey made phenomenal discoveries. Through careful excavation and the invention of new techniques that allowed him to identify mudbrick architecture, he uncovered much of ancient Babylon including the Temple of Marduk, a ziggurat-shaped building of ascending terraces capped by an astronomical observatory. He unearthed the elaborate and ceremonial Ishtar gate, as well as the elaborate fortification walls that surrounded the city. Some believe that Koldewey also discovered the fabulous Hanging Gardens of Babylon, long revered as one of the Seven Wonders of the World. He did uncover a terraced

structure that might have housed roof gardens; and he located a nearby engineered well. Whatever use was made of such a structure, it is clear that a sophisticated ancient society laid out irrigation canals to harness and direct water supplies for city dwellers.

Mesopotamia has been recognized as the cradle of civilization. Here historians joined archaeologists at the end of the nineteenth century in reconstructing this civilization that made many contributions to knowledge including the invention of the concept of zero, writing, the seed plow, irrigation, sanitation, wind-harnessed power, and the wheel.

In the same period that Koldewey was meticulously excavating mounds that held archaeological treasures, German bankers were negotiating with the Ottoman Empire on behalf of Germany to build a railroad from Berlin to Baghdad, begun in 1888 but not completed before World War I. The trade and sea advantages of the Persian Gulf and the recognition of the significance of plentiful oil resources in the region attracted international attention and competition among the Great Powers, something that still dominates international politics.

angered by German unwillingness to support its interests against Austrian actions in the Balkans. Germany maintained relations with Russia in a new Reinsurance Treaty drawn up in 1887, which stipulated that each power would maintain neutrality should the other find itself at war. Bismarck now walked a fine line, balancing alliances and selectively disclosing the terms of secret treaties to nonsignatory countries with the goal of preserving the peace. His successor described him as the only man who could keep five glass balls in the air at the same time.

After Bismarck's resignation in 1890, Germany allowed the arrangement with Russia to lapse. Russia, in turn, allied itself in 1894 with France. Also allied with Great Britain, France had broken out of the isolation that Bismarck had intended for it two decades earlier. The **Triple Entente** came into existence following the Anglo-Russian understanding of 1907. Now it was the Triple Entente of Great Britain, France, and Russia against the Triple Alliance of Germany, Austria-Hungary, and Italy.

There was still every confidence that the two camps could balance each other and preserve the peace. But in 1908–1909, the unresolved Balkan problem threatened to topple Europe's precarious peace. Against Russia's objections, Austria-Hungary annexed Bosnia and Herzegovina, the provinces it had occupied since 1878. Russia supported Serbia's discontent over Austrian acquisition of the predominantly Slavic territories that Serbia believed should be united with its own lands. Unwilling to risk a European war at this point, Russia was ultimately forced to back down under German pressure. Germany had to contend with its own fear of geographic vulnerability with hostile neighbors, France and Russia, on its western and eastern frontiers.

A third Balkan crisis erupted in 1912 when Italy and Turkey fought over the possession of Tripoli in North Africa. The Balkan states took advantage of the opportunity to increase their holdings at Turkey's expense. The action quickly involved Great

■ The Baghdad Railway was launched by Germany and the Ottoman Empire in extending the Orient Express to link Constantinople with Baghdad.

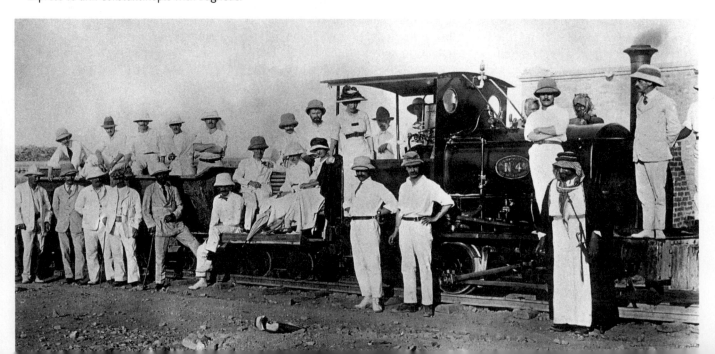

Power interests once again. A second war broke out in 1913 over Serbian interests in Bulgaria. Russia backed Serbia against Austro-Hungarian support of Bulgaria. The Russians and Austrians prepared for war while the British and Germans urged peaceful resolution. Although hostilities ceased, Serbian resentment toward Austria-Hungary over its frustrated nationalism was greater than ever. Britain, in its backing of Russia, and Germany, in its support of Austria-Hungary, were enmeshed in alliances that could involve them in a military confrontation.

THE NEW IMPERIALISM

Europeans in the last third of the nineteenth century did not invent the idea of empire: ancient civilizations had valued territorial conquest. Even before 1870 in Europe, the influence of Great Britain stretched far beyond the limits of its island holdings to India and South Africa. Russia held Siberia and central Asia, and France ruled Algeria and Indochina. Older empires—Spain, for example—had survived from the sixteenth century but as hollow shells. What, then, was new about the **new imperialism** practiced by England, France, and Germany after 1870?

In part, the new imperialism was the acquisition of territories on an intense and unprecedented scale. Industrialization created the tools of transportation, communication, and domination that permitted the rapid pace of global empire building. Above all, what distinguished the new imperialism was the domination by the industrial powers over the nonindustrial world. The United States also participated in the new imperialism, less by territorial acquisition and more by developing an "invisible" empire of trade and influence in the Pacific. The forms of imperialism may have varied from nation to nation, but the basically unequal relationship between an industrial power and an undeveloped territory did not.

Only nation-states commanded the technology and resources necessary for the new scale of imperialist expansion. Rivalry among a few European nation-states—notably Great Britain, France, and Germany—was a common denominator that set the standards by which the nations and other European nation-states gained control of the globe by 1900. Why did the Europeans create vast empires? Were empires built for economic gain, military protection, or national glory? Questions about motives may obscure common features of the new imperialism. Industrial powers sought to take over nonindustrial regions, not in isolated areas but all over the globe. In the attempt they necessarily competed with one another, successfully adapting the resources of industrialism to the needs of conquest.

The Technology of Empire

For Europeans at the end of the nineteenth century, the world had definitely become a smaller place. Steam, iron, and electricity—the great forces of Western industrialization—were responsible for seemingly shrinking the globe. Technology not only allowed Europeans to accomplish tasks and to mass produce goods efficiently, but it also altered the previous conception of time and space.

Steam, which powered factories, proved equally efficient as an energy source in transportation. Great iron steamships fueled by coal replaced the smaller, slower, wind-powered wooden sailing vessels that had ruled the seas for centuries. Steam-powered vessels transported large cargoes of people and goods more quickly and more reliably than the sailing ships. Iron ships were superior to wood in their durability, lightness, water-tightness, cargo space, speed, and fuel economy. For most of the nineteenth century, British trading ships and the British navy dominated the seas, but after 1880 other nations, especially Germany, challenged England by building versatile and efficient iron steamers. In a society in which time was money, steamships were important because, for the first time, ocean-going vessels could meet schedules as precisely and as predictably as railroads could. Just as the imperial Romans had used their network of roads to link far-flung territories to the capital, Europeans used sea-lanes to join their colonies to the home country.

Until 1850, Europeans had ventured no farther on the African continent than its coastal areas. The installation of coal-burning boilers on smaller boats permitted navigation of previously uncharted and unnavigable rivers. Steam power made exploration and migration possible and greatly contributed to knowledge of terrain, natural wealth, and resources. Smaller steam-powered vessels also increased European inland trade with China, Burma, and India.

Engineering Empire. While technology improved European mobility on water, it also literally moved the land. Harbors were deepened to accommodate the new iron- and then steel-hulled ships. One of the greatest engineering feats of the century was the construction of a hundred-mile-long canal across the Isthmus of Suez in Egypt. The Suez Canal, completed in 1869, joined the Mediterranean and Red Seas and created a new, safer trade route to the East. No longer did trading vessels have to make the long voyage around Africa's Cape of Good Hope. The Suez Canal was built by the French under the supervision of Ferdinand de Lesseps (1805–1894), a diplomat with no technical or financial background who was able to promote construction because of concessions he received from Said Pasha, the viceroy of Egypt. The canal could accommodate ships of all sizes. Great Britain purchased a controlling interest in the Suez Canal in 1875 to benefit its trade with India.

De Lesseps later oversaw the initial construction of the Panama Canal in the Western Hemisphere. The combination of French mismanagement, bankruptcy, and the high incidence of disease among work crews enabled the United States to acquire rights to the Panama project and complete the canal by 1914. Fifty-one miles long, the Panama Canal connected the world's two largest bodies of water, the Atlantic and Pacific Oceans, across the Isthmus of Panama by a waterway containing a series of locks. The passage from the Atlantic Ocean to the Pacific Ocean took less than eight hours—much less time than it took using the various overland routes or voyaging

■ The transatlantic telegraph cable was the first intercontinental communications link of the electric age. This illustration shows the *Great Eastern*, the largest ship afloat, which finally succeeded in laying the cable in 1866.

around the tip of South America. Both the Suez and Panama canals were built in pursuit of speed. Shorter distances meant quicker travel, which in turn meant higher profits.

Europeans carried the technologies of destruction as well as survival with them into less-developed areas of the world. New types of firearms produced in the second half of the nineteenth century included breech-loading rifles, repeating rifles, and machine guns. The new weapons gave the advantages of both accurate aim and rapid fire. The spears of African warriors and the primitive weaponry of Chinese rebels were no match for sophisticated European arms, which permitted their bearers to lie down while firing and to remain undetected at distances of up to a half mile.

Technology also altered time by increasing the speed with which Westerners communicated with other parts of the world. In 1830, for example, it took about two years for a person sending a letter from Great Britain to India to receive a reply. In 1850, steam-powered mail boats shortened the time required for the same round-trip correspondence to about two or three months. But the real revolution in communication came through electricity. Thousands of miles of copper telegraph wire laced countries together; insulated underwater cables linked continents to each other. By the late nineteenth century, a vast telegraph network connected Europe to every area of the world. In 1870, a telegram from London to Bombay arrived in a matter of hours, instead of months, and a response could be received back in London on the same day. Faster communications extended power and control throughout empires. Europeans could communicate immediately with their distant colonies, dispatching troops, orders, and supplies. The communication network eliminated the problem of overextension that had plagued Roman

imperial organization in the third century. For the first time, continents discovered by Europeans five centuries earlier were brought into daily contact with the West.

Medical Advances. Advances in medicine helped foster European imperialism in the nineteenth century by permitting European men and women to penetrate disease-ridden swamps and jungles. After 1850, European explorers, traders, missionaries, and adventurers carried **quinine** pills. Quinine, the bitter-tasting derivative of cinchona tree bark, was discovered to be an effective treatment for malaria. The treatment had its first important test during the French invasion of Algeria in 1830, and it allowed the French to stay healthy enough to conquer that North African country between 1830 and 1847. David Livingstone (1813–1873) and Henry M. Stanley (1841–1904) were just two of the many explorers who crossed vast terrains and explored the waterways of Africa, after malaria—the number one killer of European travelers—had been controlled.

The new technology did not cause the new imperialism. The Western powers used technological advances as a tool for establishing their control of the world. Viewed as a tool, however, the new technology does explain how vast areas of land and millions of people were conquered so rapidly.

Motives for Empire

If technology was not the cause but only a tool, what explains the new imperialism of the late nineteenth century? Were wealthy financiers, searching for high-yielding opportunities for investments, the driving force? Was profit the main motive?

Were politicians and heads of state in the game for the prestige and glory that territorial expansion could bring them at home?

There are no easy or simple explanations for the new imperialism. Individuals made their fortunes overseas, and heavy industries such as the Krupp firm in Germany prospered with the expansion of state-protected colonies. Yet many colonies were economically worthless. Tunisia and Morocco, acquired for their strategic and political importance, constituted an economic loss for the French, who poured more funds into their administration than they were able to extract. Each imperial power held one or more colonies whose costs outweighed the return. Yet that does not mean that some Europeans were simply irrational in their pursuit of empire and glory.

Economics.   The test for economic motivation cannot simply be reduced to a balance sheet of debits and credits because, in the end, an account of state revenues and state expenditures provides only a static picture of the business of empire. Even losses cannot be counted as proof against the profit motive in expansion. In modern capitalism, profits, especially great profits, are often predicated on risks. Portugal and Italy, as smaller nations with limited resources, failed as players in the game in which the great industrial powers called the shots. Prestige through the acquisition of empire was one way of keeping alive in the game.

Imperialism was influenced by business interests, market considerations, and the pursuit of individual and national fortunes. Not by accident did the great industrial powers control the scramble and dictate the terms of expansion. Nor was it merely fortuitous that Great Britain, the nation that provided the model for European expansion, dedicated itself to the establishment of a profitable worldwide network of trade and investment. Above all, the search for investment opportunities—whether railroads in China or diamond mines in South Africa—lured Europeans into a world system that challenged capitalist ingenuity and imagination. Acquiring territory was only one means of protecting investments. But there were other benefits associated with the acquisition of territory that cannot be reduced to economic terms, and those too must be considered.

Geopolitics.   Geopolitics, or the politics of geography, is based on the recognition that certain areas of the world are valuable for political reasons. The term was first used at the end of the nineteenth century by statesmen who recognized the strategic value of land. Some territory was considered important because of its proximity to acquired colonies or to territory targeted for takeover. France, for example, occupied thousands of square miles of the Sahara Desert to protect its interests in Algeria.

IMAGE DISCOVERY

A German View of How the British Treated Africans

This political cartoon offers a German view of British imperialism. An African man is trapped and helpless in a giant press, being force-fed and producing wealth as symbolized by the coins falling to the right. What groups in British society are symbolized by the three standing figures to the left, right, and center of the cartoon? If you were to draw a cartoon of German imperialism, how would it differ from the one here?

LEOPOLD II OF BELGIUM, SPEECH TO AN INTERNATIONAL CONFERENCE OF GEOGRAPHERS, 12 SEPTEMBER 1876

Leopold II reigned as king of the Belgians from 1865 until his death in 1909. Although the ruler of a small European country, he had vast territorial aspirations in Africa. As the personal ruler of the Congo Free State, Leopold amassed an immense fortune until abuses of African workers forced him to hand over his authority over what is now the Democratic Republic of the Congo to the Belgian government. In addressing geographers, Leopold evinced some of the self-serving goals that made him the architect of the scramble for territory.

Focus Questions

How does King Leopold's speech rely on the concept of the "White Man's burden" to justify occupation of territory? What are Leopold's motives for occupying Africa?

The matter which brings us together today is one most deserving the attention of the friends of humanity. For bringing civilization to the only part of the earth which it has not yet reached and lightening the darkness in which whole peoples are plunged, is, I venture to say, a crusade worthy of this century of progress, and I am glad to find how favourable public opinion is to the accomplishment of this task. We are swimming with the tide. Many of those who have closely studied Africa have come to realize that it would be in the interest of the object they are all seeking to achieve for them to meet and consult together with a view to regulating the course to be taken, combining their efforts and drawing on all available resources in a way which would avoid duplication of effort.... Among the matters which remain to be discussed, the following may be mentioned:

1. Deciding exactly where to acquire bases for the task in hand . . . on the Zanzibar coast and near the mouth of the Congo, either by means of conventions with chiefs or by purchasing or renting sites from individuals.
2. Deciding on the routes to be successively opened up into the interior, and on the medical, scientific and peacekeeping stations which are to be set up with a view to abolishing slavery, and bringing about good relations between the chiefs by providing them with fair-minded, impartial persons to settle their disputes, and so forth.
3. Setting up—once the task to be done has been clearly defined—a central, international committee with national committees, each to carry out this task in the aspects of it which concern them, to explain the object to the public of all countries, and to appeal to the feeling of charity to which no worthy cause has ever appealed in vain.

These are some of the points which seem worthy of your attention. . . . My wish is to serve the great cause for which you have already done so much, in whatever manner you may suggest to me. It is with this object that I put myself at your disposal, and I extend a cordial welcome to you.

Other territory was important because of its proximity to sea routes. Egypt had significance for Great Britain not because of its inherent economic potential but because it permitted the British to protect access to lucrative markets in India through the Suez Canal. Beginning in 1875, the British purchased shares in the canal. By 1879, Egypt was under the informal dual rule of France and Great Britain. The British used the deterioration of internal Egyptian politics to justify their occupation of the country in 1882. Protected access to India also accounted for Great Britain's maintenance of Mediterranean outposts, its acquisition of territory on the east coast of Africa, and its occupation of territory in southern Asia.

A third geopolitical motive for annexation was the necessity of fueling bases throughout the world. Faster and more reliable than wind-powered vessels, coal-powered ships were nonetheless dependent on guaranteed fueling bases in friendly ports of call. Islands in the South Pacific and the Indian Ocean were acquired primarily to serve as coaling stations for the great steamers carrying manufactured goods to colonial ports and returning with foodstuffs and raw materi-

als. Ports along the southern rim of Asia served the same purpose. The need for protection of colonies, fueling ports, and sea-lanes led to the creation of naval bases such as those on the Red Sea at Djibouti by the French, along the South China Sea at Singapore by the British, and in the Pacific Ocean at Honolulu by the Americans.

In turn, the acquisition of territories justified the increase in naval budgets and the size of fleets. Britain still had the world's largest navy, but by the beginning of the twentieth century, the United States and Germany had entered the competition for dominance of sea-lanes. Japan joined the contest by expanding its navy as a vehicle for its own claims to empire in the Pacific.

The politics of geography was land- as well as sea-based. As navies grew to protect sea-lanes, armies expanded to police new lands. Between 1890 and 1914, military expenditures of Western governments grew phenomenally, with war machines doubling in size. In both its impact on domestic budgets and its protection of markets and trading routes, geopolitics had a strong economic component. Governments became consumers of heavy industry; their predictable participation in markets for armaments and military supplies helped control fluctuations in the business cycle and reduce unemployment at home. A side effect of the growing importance of geopolitics was the increased influence of military and naval leaders in foreign and domestic policy making.

Nationalism.   Many European statesmen in the last quarter of the nineteenth century gave stirring speeches about the importance of empire as a means of enhancing national prestige. National prestige was not an absolute value but one weighed relatively. Possessing an empire may have meant "keeping up with the Joneses," as it did for smaller countries such as Italy. Imperial status was important to a country such as Portugal, which was willing to go bankrupt to maintain its territories. But prestige without economic power was the form of imperialism without its substance. Nation-states could, through the acquisition of overseas territories, gain bargaining chips to be played at the international conference table. In that way, smaller nations hoped to be taken seriously in the system of alliances that preserved "the balance of power" in Europe.

Western newspapers deliberately fostered the desire for the advancement of national interests. Newspapers competed for readers, and their circulation often depended on the passions they aroused. Filled with tales calculated to titillate and entertain, and with advertisements promising miracle cures, newspapers wrested foreign policy from the realm of the specialist and transformed politics into another form of entertainment. The drama and vocabulary of sporting events, whose mass appeal as a leisure activity also dates from the era, were now applied to imperialist politics. Whether it was a rugby match or a territorial conquest, readers backed the "home" team, disdained the opposition, and competed for the thrill of victory. It marked quite a change for urban dwellers whose grandparents worked the land and did not look beyond the horizon of their home villages. Newspapers forged a national consciousness whereby individuals learned to identify with collective causes they often did not fully comprehend. Some observed what was happening with a critical eye, identifying a deep-seated need in modern men and women for excitement in their lives.

Information conveyed in newspapers shaped opinion, and opinion, in turn, could influence policy. Leaders had to reckon with the new creation of "public opinion." In a typical instance, French newspaper editors promoted feverish public outcry for conquest of the Congo by pointing out the need to revenge British advances in Egypt. "Colonial fever" in France was so high in the summer of 1882 that French policy makers were pressured to pursue claims in the Congo Basin without adequate assessment or reflection. As a result, the French government evicted Belgians and Portuguese from the northern

■ Great Britain originally opposed construction of the Suez Canal but soon recognized its crucial role in the route to India. In this cartoon, *The Lion's Share,* British Prime Minister Disraeli purchases a controlling interest in the Suez Canal Company from the khedive of Egypt. The British lion in the foreground guards the key to India, the symbol of the canal.

THE LION'S SHARE.

"GARE À QUI LA TOUCHE!"

Congo territory and enforced questionable treaty claims rather than risk public censure for appearing weak and irresolute.

Public opinion was certainly influential, but it also could be manipulated. In Germany, the government often promoted colonial hysteria through the press in order to advance its own political ends. Chancellor Otto von Bismarck used his power over the press to support imperialism and to influence electoral outcomes in 1884. His successors were deft at promoting the "bread and circuses" atmosphere that surrounded colonial expansion in order to direct attention away from social problems at home and to maintain domestic stability.

The printed word was also manipulated in Britain, critics asserted, by business interests during the Boer War (1899–1902) to keep public enthusiasm for the war effort high. J. A. Hobson (1858–1940), a journalist and theorist of imperialism, denounced the "abuse of the press" in his hard-hitting *Psychology of Jingoism* (1901), which appeared while the war was still being waged. Hobson recognized **jingoism** as the appropriate term for the "inverted patriotism whereby the love of one's own nation is transformed into hatred of another nation, and into the fierce craving to destroy the individual members of that other nation."

Jingoism was not a new phenomenon in 1900, nor was it confined to Britain. Throughout Europe a mass public appeared increasingly willing to support conflict to defend national honor. Xenophobia (hatred of foreigners) melded with nationalism, both nurtured by the mass press, to put new pressures on the determination of foreign policy. Government elites, who formerly had operated behind closed doors far removed from public scrutiny, were now accountable in new ways to faceless masses.

Every nation in Europe had its jingoes, those willing to risk war for national glory. Significantly, the term *jingo* was coined in 1878 during a British showdown with the Russians over Turkey. The sentiment that "the Russians shall not have Constantinople" was so strong that the acceptability of war was set to music:

> *We don't want to fight,*
> *But, by Jingo, if we do,*
> *We've got the men,*
> *We've got the ships,*
> *We've got the money too.*

This was the most popular music-hall song in Britain that year, and long after the crisis had faded the tune and its lyrics lingered.

To varying degrees, all of the factors—economics, geopolitics, and nationalism—motivated the actions of the three great imperialist powers—Britain, France, and Germany—and their less-powerful European neighbors. The same reasons account for the global aspirations of non-European nations such as the United States and Japan. Each of the powers was aware of what the others were doing and tailored its actions accordingly. Imperialism followed a variety of patterns but always had a built-in component of emulation and acceleration. It was both a cause and a proof of a world system of states in which the actions of one nation affected the others.

THE SEARCH FOR TERRITORY AND MARKETS

Most western Europeans who read about the distant regions that their armies and statesmen were bringing under their national flags tended to regard the new territories as no more than entries on a great tally sheet or as colors on a map. The daily press recorded the numbers of square miles gained and the captive populations taken, and for readers that was often the end of the story. Few Europeans looked on imperialism as a relationship of power between two parties and, like all relationships, one influenced by both partners. Fewer still understood or appreciated the distinctive qualities of the conquered peoples.

The areas European imperialism affected varied widely in their political organization. Throughout Africa, states were generally small or even nonexistent, and Europeans considered their governmental institutions too ineffectual to produce the economic changes and growth of trade Europe wanted. Military takeover and direct rule by European officials seemed the only feasible way to establish empire there. In Asia, on the other hand, societies such as China and India were territorially large and possessed efficient institutions of government dominated by established political hierarchies. Although they were more difficult to conquer, their leaders were also more likely to cooperate with the imperial powers because their own interests were often similar to those of the Westerners. For those reasons, European empire builders pursued a variety of models: formal military empires (as in Africa), informal empires (as in China), or formal but indirect rule over hierarchical societies (as in India). The United States provided yet another model, one that relied on hegemonic influence as well as outright control.

The Scramble for Africa: Diplomacy and Conflict

From about 1875 to 1912 European powers engaged in the pursuit of territorial control and conquest of Africa. The conflict and competing claims that resulted are known as the **scramble for Africa**.

Africa is a large and complex continent, and the reasons of Europeans for pursuing control over specific pieces of African territory were similarly complex. The explanations for the acquisition of a particular colony, therefore, depend largely on the historical context of that particular case. In certain areas, such as the West African desert zones of the Sudan and the Sahara, ambitious French military men sought to advance their careers by carving out grand colonies.

The existence of valuable minerals motivated the scramble for the area now called Zimbabwe, the Zambian-Zairian copper belt, and other areas. Along the West African coast,

JOSEPH CHAMBERLAIN'S SPEECH TO THE BIRMINGHAM RELIEF ASSOCIATION

Joseph Chamberlain (1836–1914) was an English businessman and statesman and, from 1873 to 1876, the mayor of one of Great Britain's leading industrial cities, Birmingham. He was a national advocate for an expansionist colonial policy as the means of keeping his country strong. On 22 January 1894, with no regard for African people, he spoke before a community group to convince them that British imperialism helped the working class.

Focus Questions

What are the motives evoked by Chamberlain to justify colonial expansion? How does he appeal to the patriotism of the English working classes?

Believe me, if in any one of the places [in Africa] to which I have referred any change took place which deprived us of that control and influence of which I have been speaking, the first to suffer would be the working-men of this country. Then, indeed, we should see a distress which would not be temporary, but which would be chronic, and we should find that England was entirely unable to support the enormous population which is now maintained by the aid of her foreign trade. If the working-men of this country understand, as I believe they do—I am one of those who have had good reason through my life to rely upon their intelligence and shrewdness—if they understand their own interests, they will never lend any countenance to the doctrines of those politicians who never lose an opportunity of pouring contempt and abuse upon the brave Englishmen, who, even at this moment, in all parts of the world are carving out new dominions for Britain, and are opening up fresh markets for British commerce, and laying out fresh fields for British labour. [Applause.] If the Little Englanders[i] had their way, not only would they refrain from taking the legitimate opportunities which offer for extending the empire and for securing for us new markets, but I doubt whether they would even take the pains which are necessary to preserve the great heritage which has come down to us from our ancestors. [Applause.]

When you are told that the British pioneers of civilisation in Africa are filibusters,[ii] and when you are asked to call them back, and to leave this great continent to the barbarism and superstition in which it has been steeped for centuries, or to hand over to foreign countries the duty which you are unwilling to undertake, I ask you to consider what would have happened if 100 or 150 years ago your ancestors had taken similar views of their responsibility? Where would be the empire on which now your livelihood depends? We should have been the United Kingdom of Great Britain and Ireland; but those vast dependencies, those hundreds of millions with whom we keep up a mutually beneficial relationship and commerce would have been the subjects of other nations, who would not have been slow to profit by our neglect of our opportunities and obligations. [Applause.]

From Joseph Chamberlain, M.P., *Foreign and Colonial Speeches* (1897).

[i] Britain's anti-imperialists.

[ii] A person engaged in a private military action against a foreign government.

chronic disputes between traders working in a souring economy seemed to demand European annexation. Some colonies, such as those in what are now Uganda and Malawi, were created to please missionaries already working there. Britain took Egypt and France took Djibouti for strategic reasons. And in Mozambique, Tanzania, Namibia, and Botswana, some Europeans seized areas to keep other Europeans from doing the same. In seeking territorial control, Europeans were willing to use force. Only Ethiopia escaped the European grasp.

Colonization in Africa

The Drive for Markets and Profits. An important factor influencing imperialist expansion was the economic downturn in Europe that lasted from 1873 until 1896. The downturn, coupled with Germany's rapid rise to economic power during the second phase of the Industrial Revolution in the 1870s and 1880s, was deeply unsettling to many Europeans. Protectionist policies springing from new economic anxieties eroded the earlier European faith in free trade. Many Europeans favored acquiring African territory just in case it should turn out to be economically useful. Even Britain, long the major champion of free trade, became ever more protectionist and imperialistic as the century neared its end.

Historians generally agree that the person who provided the catalyst for the scramble was Leopold II, king of Belgium (1835–1909). Sheer greed motivated Leopold. In early 1876, he had read a report about the Congo Basin that claimed it was "mostly a magnificent and healthy country of unspeakable richness" that promised "to repay any enterprising capitalist." Leopold, an ambitious and frustrated king ruling over a small country, went to work at once to acquire the Congo Basin, an area one-third the size of the United States. Cloaking

IN THE RUBBER COILS.

■ A contemporary cartoon characterized King Leopold of the Belgians as a monstrous snake crushing the life out of the black population of the Congo Free State. The territory was under the personal rule of the Belgian king from 1885 to 1908.

himself in the mantle of philanthropy and asserting that all he desired was to stamp out the remnants of the East African slave trade, in late 1876 Leopold organized the International African Association. Leopold II's association soon established trading stations on the region's rivers and coerced much valuable ivory from the people. Belgian settlers, missionaries, and traders set out to create a common language among disparate tribes, and imposed Swahili on Congolese natives.

Leopold skillfully lobbied in Europe for formal recognition of his association's right to rule the Congo Basin. The action provoked objections from France and Portugal, and, after much diplomatic wrangling, an international conference was finally held in Berlin in late 1884 to decide who should rule the Congo. The Berlin Conference was important, not only because it yielded the Congo Basin to Leopold as the Congo Free State, but also because it laid down the ground rules for all other colonial acquisitions in Africa. For international recogni-

tion of a claim, "effective occupation" would be required. That meant that no longer would planting a flag in an area be considered adequate for establishing sovereignty; instead, a real presence calculated to produce "economic development" would be needed. If Leopold's actions began the scramble by panicking the European states, the Berlin Conference organized it. However, it is clear in retrospect that the scramble would have occurred even without Leopold II's greedy intervention.

European Agreements and African Massacres. In their disputes over apportioning Africa, the Europeans were remarkably pacific with each other. Although Britain threatened Portugal with war in 1890 in a conflict over the area around Lake Malawi, and although it appeared for a while that Britain and France were headed toward armed conflict in 1898 at Fashoda in a dispute over the Nile headwaters, peaceful diplomatic settlements that satisfied the imperial powers were always worked out. Deals where states traded territory were common, and peace was maintained. Africa was not worth a war to Europeans. Yet in every instance of expansion in Africa, Europeans were ready to shoot Africans. With Hiram Maxim's invention in 1884 of a machine gun that could fire 11 bullets per second, and with the sale of modern weapons to Africans banned by the Brussels Convention of 1890, the military advantage passed overwhelmingly to the imperialists. As the British poet Hillaire Belloc tellingly observed,

> Whatever happens, we have got
> The Maxim gun, and they have not.

The conquest of "them" became more like hunting than warfare. In 1893, for example, in Zimbabwe, 50 Europeans, using only six machine guns, killed 3000 Ndebele people in less than two hours. In 1897, in northern Nigeria, a force of 32 Europeans and 500 African mercenaries defeated the 31,000-man army of the emir of Sokoto. The nature of such warfare is well summed up in a report by Winston Churchill about the battle at Omdurman, in the Sudan, in 1898:

> The [British] infantry fired steadily and stolidly, without hurry or excitement, for the enemy were far away and the officers careful. Besides the soldiers were interested in the work and took great pains. . . . And all the time out on the plain on the other side bullets were shearing through flesh, smashing and splintering bone: blood spouted from terrible wounds; valiant men were struggling on through a hell of whistling metal, exploding shells, and spurting dust—suffering, despairing, and dying.

After five hours of fighting, the number killed were 20 Britons, 20 Egyptian allies, and more than 11,000 Sudanese. Technology had made bravery and courage obsolete for the majority of Africans.

Ethiopia as an Exception. One exception to the general rule of easy conquest was Ethiopia. The history of the country illustrates the overriding importance of guns in understanding the essential dynamic of the scramble. In the middle of the nineteenth century, the emperor of Ethiopia possessed little more than a grand title. The empire had broken down into its ethnic and regional components, each of which was fueled by its own "big men," local rulers with little regard for the emperor. Yet the dream of a united empire was alive and pursued by the emperors of the time, Amharic-speaking "big men" with their political base on the fertile plateau that constituted the heartland of the country. In their campaigns to rebuild the empire, they relied increasingly on modern weapons imported from Europe. Their work went forward with some success.

By the early 1870s, however, the emperor realized that his accomplishments in recreating the Ethiopian Empire were endangered by the resistance of the people whom he was then trying to force into his empire and, more ominously, by interference from the outside world, especially Egypt to the north and the Sudan to the west. An expansionary Egypt actually invaded Ethiopian territory, and it was only the Egyptian government's bankruptcy in 1876 that gave the emperor breathing room. The opening of the Suez Canal in 1869 had made the Red Sea and its surroundings attractive not only to Egypt but also to European countries eager to ensure their trade routes to Asia. By the end of the 1870s, when the scramble for Africa was getting seriously under way, Britain, France, and Italy were all contemplating acquiring land in the region. Soon thereafter, Britain occupied Egypt (1882), France took Djibouti (1884), and Italy seized Eritrea (1885).

The Ethiopian emperor, Menelik II (1889–1913), realized that he could exploit rival European interests in the area by playing off one European power against the others to obtain the weapons he needed for expanding his empire's boundaries. Thus he gave certain concessions to France in return for French weapons. Italy, upset by the growing French influence in Ethiopia, offered weapons as well, and Menelik accepted them. Russia and Britain joined in. More and more modern weapons flowed into Ethiopia during the 1870s and 1880s and into the early 1890s, and Menelik steadily strengthened his military position, both to stop internal unrest and to block encroachment from without. Because each European power feared its rivals' influence in Ethiopia, each sold arms to Menelik, and Ethiopia remained largely unaffected by the scramble going on around it.

In the early 1890s, Menelik's stratagems began to unravel. In 1889 he had signed the Treaty of Wichale with Italy, granting it certain concessions in return for more arms shipments. Italy then claimed that Ethiopia had become an Italian protectorate and moved against Menelik when he objected. By 1896, Italy was ready for a major assault on the Ethiopian army. The Italians were heady with confident racism, believing that their forces could defeat the "primitive" Ethiopians with ease. However, General Oreste Baratieri (1841–1901), the commander of the 18,000-man Italian army in Eritrea, was wisely cautious. He understood that modern weapons functioned the same, whether they were fired by Africans or by Italians. Baratieri knew that Menelik's army of some 100,000 troops had very long supply lines, and his strategy was to wait until Menelik could no longer supply his troops with food. Then, he assumed, the soldiers would simply disappear and the Italians would walk in. But the prime minister of Italy, Francesco Crispi (1819–1901), wanted a quick, glorious victory to enhance his political reputation. Crispi ordered Baratieri to send his army of 18,000 men into battle at once. Hopelessly outnumbered, the Italians lost more than 8000 at the decisive battle of Adowa on 1 March 1896. With its army destroyed and its artillery lost to the Ethiopians, Italy had no choice but to sue for peace.

Italy's acceptance of Ethiopia as a sovereign state with greatly expanded imperial boundaries was soon ratified by France and Britain. As a consequence of its victory at Adowa—and attesting to the crucial importance of modern weaponry for survival in late-nineteenth-century Africa—Ethiopia was the only African country aside from the United States' quasi-colony of Liberia not to be occupied in the scramble for Africa. After 1896, Menelik, with his access to modern weapons assured by his country's international recognition, continued his campaign to extend his control forcefully over the Ethiopian Empire's subordinate peoples.

Gold, Empire Building, and the Boer War

Europeans fought white African settlers as well as black Africans during the scramble, as they seized their lands and resources. In South Africa, for example, the British engaged in

■ This cartoon shows Cecil Rhodes astride the continent of Africa like a colossus, fulfilling his dream of a British Africa from the Cape to Cairo.

THE RHODES COLOSSUS
STRIDING FROM CAPE TOWN TO CAIRO.

MAP DISCOVERY

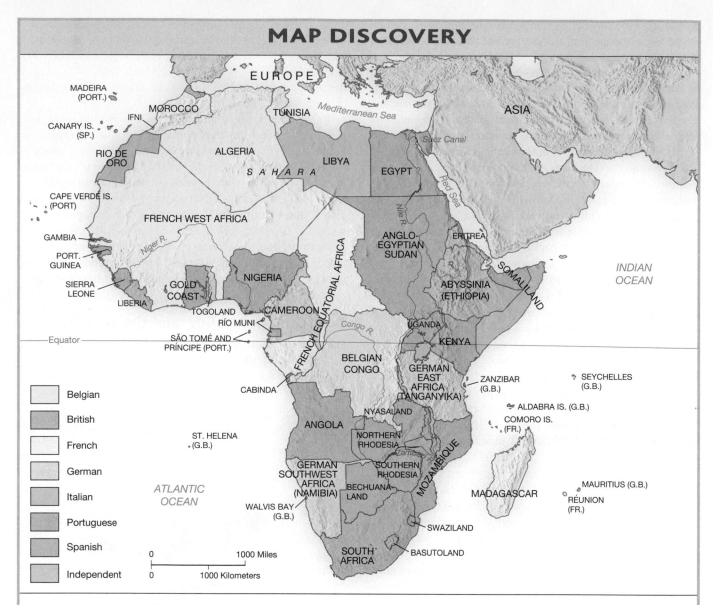

Africa, 1914

By 1914, the map of Africa emerged as a colorful patchwork indicating competing European interests. Do you perceive any patterns in the way the seven European nations laid claim to territory? What were the geopolitical imperatives that motivated the British to seek a swathe of territory from north to south? What are the only two states in 1914 not under the control or oversight of European powers? Based on the chapter discussion, how do you explain why they were exceptions?

a long war over access to the world's largest supply of gold with a group of "Afrikaners"—white settlers who had emigrated, mostly from the Netherlands, and settled in South Africa during the eighteenth and early nineteenth centuries.

Afrikaner Rule. After the Great Trek (1837–1844), in which a large number of Afrikaners had withdrawn from the British-controlled Colony of the Cape of Good Hope (or Cape Colony), the British had grudgingly recognized the independence of the

Orange Free State and the Transvaal—the Afrikaner republics in the interior—in a series of formal agreements. The British complacently believed that the Afrikaners, economically weak and geographically isolated, could never challenge British preeminence in the region. Two events of the mid-1880s shattered British complacency. First, in 1884, Germany—Britain's greatest rival—inserted itself into the region by annexing Namibia as a colony as part of its imperial adventures. The British, aware that the Germans and the Afrikaners were as sympathetic to one another as both were hostile to them, worried about the German threat to their regional hegemony and economic prospects.

Britain's War in South Africa.

British fear of the Germans redoubled in 1886 when, in the Witwatersrand area of the Transvaal Republic, huge deposits of gold were discovered. A group of rich British diamond-mine owners moved in quickly to develop the gold mines in the Witwatersrand area, for the gold lay deep in the ground and could be mined only with a large capital investment, which the Afrikaners lacked. The best known of the British investors was Cecil Rhodes (1853–1902), a politician and financier intent upon expanding his wealth through an expansion of British power.

After a failed attempt prompted by Rhodes and backed by the British government to overthrow Afrikaner rule, war had become inevitable, and in October it broke out. The British confidently expected to win the war by Christmas, but the Afrikaners did not cooperate. Inept British commanders opposed by skillful Afrikaner guerrilla-warfare leaders guaranteed that the so-called Boer War would drag on and on.

The British eventually sent 350,000 troops to South Africa, but the forces could not decisively defeat the 65,000 Afrikaner fighting men. Casualties were high, not merely from the fighting, but because typhus epidemics broke out in the concentration camps in which the British interred Afrikaner women and children as they pursued their scorched-earth policies. By the war's end in April 1902, 25,000 Afrikaners, 22,000 British imperial troops, and 12,000 Africans had died. Britain had also been widely criticized for having treated white Afrikaners as if they were black Africans.

In April 1902, the British accepted the conditional surrender of the Afrikaners. The British annexed the Afrikaners to the empire and had the opportunity of making the gold industry efficient. However, they had to promise the Afrikaners that no decisions regarding the political role of the black African majority in a future South Africa would be made before returning political power to the Afrikaners. That crucial concession ensured that segregation would remain the model for race relations in South Africa throughout the twentieth century.

When World War I broke out in 1914, the scramble for Africa was over and the map of the continent was colored in imperial inks. France had secured the largest chunk of the continent—some four million square miles—but it was mostly desert and tropical forest. Britain had the second-largest empire, but it was richer in minerals and agricultural potential than France's. Germany was the proud possessor of two West African colonies, Togo and Cameroon, as well as Namibia and Tanganyika. Belgium had inherited Leopold II's Congo in 1908. Portugal had finally consolidated its feeble hold on Angola, Mozambique, and Portuguese Guinea. Italy and Spain held unimportant bits of coastal territory. Only Ethiopia and Liberia were politically independent. With the conquest of Africa, the colonial powers had to face the issue of how their new colonies could be made to pay off; Africans had to face the issue of how they might regain their political independence.

Imperialism in Asia

During the first half of the nineteenth century, strong Asian powers had grown stronger. China increased its control over Inner Asian territories; Vietnam and Siam, predecessor to modern Thailand, enhanced their powers in southeast Asia. By the end of the nineteenth century, Asian political dynasties had suffered reversals. China had been permanently weakened in Inner Asia; Vietnam had fallen under French colonial rule; Siam had lost half its territories. India had long constituted an important part of the British Empire. By contrast, Japan became an aggressive power, itself an imperialist presence.

India.   The British Parliament proclaimed that on New Year's Day, 1877, Queen Victoria (1837–1901) would add the title of Empress of India to her many honors. India, the great jewel in the imperial crown, was a land Victoria had never seen. The queen's new title, not universally popular in Britain and unnoticed by most famine-stricken Indian peasants, in fact changed nothing about the way the British ruled India. Yet it was more than merely a symbolic assertion of dominance over a country long controlled by the British.

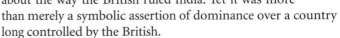

DOCUMENT

Arrival of British in Punjab

India was the starting point of all British expansion, and it stood at the center of British foreign policy. To protect its sea routes to India and to secure its Indian markets, Britain acquired territories and carved out concessions all over the world. Devised by Prime Minister Benjamin Disraeli to flatter an aging monarch, the new title of empress was really a calculated warning to Russia—present on India's northern frontier in Afghanistan—and to France, busily pursuing its own interests in Egypt.

Formal British rule in India began in 1861 with the appointment of a viceroy, assisted by legislative and executive councils. Both of the bodies included some Indian representatives. British rule encountered the four main divisions of the highly stratified Hindu society. At the top were Brahmans—the learned and priestly class—followed by warriors and rulers, then by farmers and merchants, and finally by peasants and laborers. On the outside of Hindu society were the "untouchables"—a fifth division relegated to performing society's most menial tasks. Rather than disrupt the divisive caste system, the British found it to their advantage to maintain the status quo.

Britain's relationship with India originated in the seventeenth century, when the British East India Company—a joint-stock venture free of government control—began limited trading in Indian markets. The need for regulation and protection firmly established British rule by the end of the eighteenth century. Conquest of the Punjab in 1849 brought the last independent areas of India under British control. Throughout this period, Britain invested considerable overseas capital in India, and in turn India absorbed one-fifth of the total of British exports. The market for Indian cotton, for centuries exported to markets in Asia and Europe, collapsed under British tariffs, and India became a ready market for cheap Lancashire cotton. The British also exploited India's agricultural products, salt, and opium.

China.

At the end of the eighteenth century, the British were trading English wool and Indian cotton for Chinese tea and textiles. But Britain's thirst for Chinese tea grew, while Chinese demand for English and Indian textiles slackened. Britain discovered that Indian opium could be used to balance the trade deficit created by tea. British merchants and local Chinese officials, especially in the entry port of Canton, began to expand their profitable involvement in a contraband trade in opium. The British East India Company held a monopoly over opium cultivation in Bengal. Opium exports to China mounted phenomenally: from 200 chests in 1729 to 40,000 chests in 1838. By the 1830s, opium was probably Britain's most important crop in world markets. The British prospered as opium was pumped into China at rates faster than tea was flowing out. Chinese buyers began paying for the drug with silver.

Concerned about the sharp rise in opium addiction, the accompanying social problems, and the massive exporting of silver, the Chinese government reacted. As Chinese officials saw it, they were exchanging their precious metal for British poison. Addicts were threatened with the death penalty. In 1839, the Chinese government destroyed British opium in the port of Canton, touching off the so-called Opium War (1839–1842). British expeditionary forces blockaded Chinese ports, besieged Canton, and occupied Shanghai. In protecting the rights of British merchants engaged in illegal trading, Great Britain became the first Western nation to use force to impose its economic interests on China. The Treaty of Nanking (1842) initiated a series of unequal treaties between Europeans and the Chinese and set the pattern for exacting large indemnities.

Between 1842 and 1895, China fought five wars with foreigners and lost all of them. Defeat was expensive, as China had to pay costs to the winners. Before the end of the century, Britain, France, Germany, and Japan had managed to establish major territorial advantages in their "**spheres of influence,**" sometimes through negotiation and sometimes through force. By 1912, more than 50 major Chinese ports had been handed over to foreign control as "treaty ports." British spheres included Shanghai, the lower Yangzi, and Hong Kong. France maintained special interests in South China. Germany controlled the Shandong peninsula. Japan laid claim to the northeast.

Treaty Ports and Boxer Rebellion

Spheres of influence grew in importance at the beginning of the twentieth century, when foreign investors poured capital into railway lines, which needed treaty protection from competing companies. Railways necessarily furthered foreign encroachment and opened up new territories to the claims of foreigners. As one Chinese official explained it, the railroads were like scissors that threatened to cut China into many pieces. As a result, China lost control of its trade and was totally unable to protect its infant industries. Foreigners estab-

lished no formal empires in China, but the treaty ports certainly were evidence of both informal rule and indisputable foreign dominance.

Treaty ports were centers of foreign residence and trade, where rules of **extraterritoriality** applied. That meant that foreigners were exempt from Chinese law enforcement and that, though present on Chinese territory, they could be judged only by officials of their own countries. Extraterritoriality, a privilege not just for diplomats but one shared by every foreign national, implied both a distrust of Chinese legal procedures and a cultural arrogance about the superiority of Western institutions. The arrangements stirred Chinese resentment and contributed considerably to growing antiforeign sentiment.

To preserve extraterritoriality and maintain informal empires, the European powers appointed civilian representatives known as consuls. Often merchants themselves—in the beginning unpaid in their posts—and consuls acted as the chieftains of resident merchant communities, judges in all civil and criminal cases, and spokesmen for the commercial interests of the home country. They clearly embodied the commercial intentions of Western governments. Initially they stood outside the diplomatic corps; later they were consigned to its lower ranks. Consuls acted as brokers for commerce and interpreted the international commercial law being forged. Consulates spread beyond China as Western nations used consuls to protect their own interests elsewhere. In Africa, consuls represented the trading concerns of European governments and were instrumental in the transition to formal rule.

The rise of Western influence in China coincided with and benefited from Chinese domestic problems, including dynastic decline, famine, and successive rebellions. The European powers were willing to prop up the crumbling structure for their own ends, but the Boxer Rebellion of 1900 made clear to the Western powers their limited ability to control social unrest in China. The Boxers—peasants so named by Westerners because of the martial rites practiced by their secret society, the Harmonious Fists—rose up against the foreign and Christian exploitation in north China. At the beginning of the summer of 1900, the Boxers—with the concealed encouragement of the Chinese government—killed Europeans and seized the foreign legations in Beijing. An international expeditionary force of 16,000 well-armed Japanese, Russian, British, American, German, French, Austrian, and Italian troops entered Beijing in August to defend the treaty interests of their respective countries. Led by a German general, the international force followed Kaiser Wilhelm II's urging to remember the Huns: "Show no mercy! Take no prisoners!" Systematic plunder and slaughter followed. Beijing was sacked.

Abandoning earlier discussions of partitioning China, the international powers accepted the need for a central Chinese government—even one that had betrayed their interests—that would police a populace plagued by demographic pressures, famine, discrimination against minorities, excessive

■ The claims of the Boxer troops to invulnerability were believed by millions of Chinese. In this Chinese print, the Boxer forces use cannons, bayonets, dynamite, and sabers to drive the Western "barbarians" from the Middle Kingdom.

taxation, exorbitant land rents, and social and economic dislocations created by foreign trade. During the previous year (1899), the United States had asserted its claims in China in the Open Door policy. The policy, formulated by U.S. Secretary of State John Hay, was as much concerned with preserving Chinese sovereignty as it was with establishing equal economic opportunity for foreign competition in Chinese markets. Europeans and Americans wanted to send bankers to China, not gunboats. A stable central government facilitated their aims. By operating within delineated spheres of influence and using established elites to further their own programs, Westerners protected their financial interests without incurring the costs and responsibilities of direct rule.

European Powers in Southeast Asia

Southeast Asia and Japan. European nations pursued imperialist endeavors elsewhere in Asia, acquiring territories on China's frontiers and taking over states that had formerly paid tribute to the Chinese Empire. The British acquired Hong Kong in 1842, Burma in 1886, and Kowloon in 1898. The Russians took over the Maritime Provinces in 1858.

With the Dutch already well established in Java, France, Great Britain, and the United States each established a center of power in southeast Asia and sought a balance of strength there to complement their global efforts to keep any one of them from getting ahead of the others. The French creation of Indochina was administratively the most complex. Composed of five territories administered separately, only Cochinchina (south Vietnam) was a formal colony; the other four regions were protectorates—Annam (central Vietnam), Tonkin (northern Vietnam), Cambodia, and Laos. French power remained strongest in south Vietnam and weakest in the center where, as in the north, local government was under a combined French and Vietnamese rule. The French approach to colonial rule combined hierarchical administration, economic exploitation, and cultural elitism. They introduced plantation agriculture for coffee and tea; together with rubber, the plantations were concentrated in the southern region of Indochina. Some light industry developed in the north at Hanoi. Because of its economic growth, Hanoi became the capital of the Indo-Chinese Union in 1902.

The French established their dominion in Laos at the expense of Siam (Thailand). The French provoked a crisis over Laos with the Thai, who hoped for British backing in the dispute. The British, however, saw French control over Laos as a reasonable part of the regional balance of European power. Laos, Cambodia, and central Vietnam all stagnated under French colonial rule. While the Mekong Delta in the south continued to export raw materials and crops, political power became more concentrated in the north in Hanoi.

■ This 1904 cartoon of the United States' imperial expansion shows an American eagle stretching its wings from Panama to the Philippines.

Thailand was the only country in southeast Asia to escape direct control by the Western powers. Yet it was forced to yield half the territory it once controlled, and to accept the treaty port system with its tariffs and extraterritoriality. Through government reforms, the Thai attempted to meet the demands of facing foreign powers without forsaking their traditional institutions of Buddhist monarchy and monkhood.

In the Philippines, Spanish suppression of nationalist sentiments led to increasingly bitter feelings in the 1870s and 1880s. Separate groups of educated and poor people who opposed Spanish rule were unified by the Spanish execution of elite leader José Rizal (1861–1896). His martyrdom inspired broadly based resistance. The United States took control of the Philippines from the Spanish during the Spanish-American War over Cuba. Facing continued Filipino resistance, the United States opposed Filipino nationalism with its new colonial rule. American colonialism collaborated with a conservative landowning Filipino oligarchy that controlled huge sugar plantations. The plantations impeded the development of a more balanced agriculture that could feed the country's population. American colonial rule, like colonial regimes elsewhere in the region, fostered an acute Philippine economic dependency on the colonial power.

The Sino-Japanese War of 1894–1895 revealed Japan's intentions to compete as an imperialist power in Asia. The modernized and Westernized Japanese army easily defeated the ill-equipped and poorly led Chinese forces. As a result, Japan gained the island of Taiwan. Pressing its ambitions on the continent, Japan locked horns with Russia over claims to the Liaotung peninsula, Korea, and South Manchuria. Following its victory in the Russo-Japanese War of 1904–1905, Japan expanded into all of those areas, annexing Korea outright in 1910. The war sent a strong message to the West about the ease with which the small Asian nation had defeated the Russian giant and contributed to the heightening of anti-imperialist sentiments in China.

The Imperialism of the United States

The United States provided another variation on imperial expansion. Its westward drive across the North American continent, beginning at the end of the eighteenth century, established the United States as an imperial power in the Western Hemisphere. By 1848, the relatively young American nation stretched over 3000 miles from one ocean to the other. It had met the opposition and resistance of the Native Americans with armed force, decimated them, and "concentrated" the survivors in assigned territories, and later on reservations.

At the end of the nineteenth century, the United States, possessing both the people and the resources for rapid industrial development, turned to the Caribbean and the Pacific islands in pursuit of markets and investment opportunities. By acquiring stepping stones of islands across the Pacific Ocean in the Hawaiian Islands and Samoa, it secured fueling bases and access to lucrative east Asian ports. And by intervening repeatedly in Central America and building the Panama

Canal, the United States had established its hegemony in the Caribbean by 1914. Growing in economic power and hegemonic influence, both Japan and the United States had joined the club of imperial powers and were making serious claims against European expansion.

RESULTS OF A EUROPEAN-DOMINATED WORLD

Europeans fashioned the world in their own image, but in doing so, Western values and Western institutions underwent profound and unintended transformations. Family values were articulated in an imperialist context, and race emerged as a key

cultural factor. The discovery of new lands, new cultures, and new peoples altered the ways in which European women and men regarded themselves and viewed their place in the world. With the rise of new contenders for power—the United States and Japan—and growing criticism about the morality of capitalism, the Western world was not as predictable in 1914 as it had appeared to be in 1870.

A World Economy

Imperialism produced an interdependent world economy, with Europe at its center. Industrial and commercial capitalism linked together the world's continents in a communications and transportation network unimaginable in earlier ages. As a

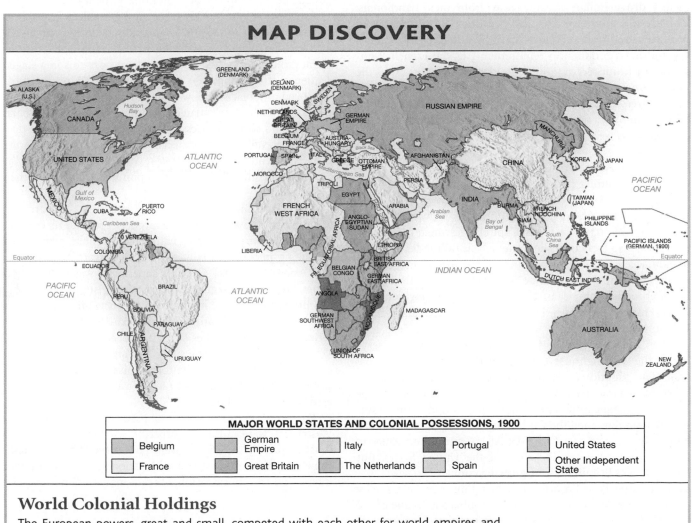

MAP DISCOVERY

MAJOR WORLD STATES AND COLONIAL POSSESSIONS, 1900

Belgium	German Empire	Italy	Portugal	United States
France	Great Britain	The Netherlands	Spain	Other Independent State

World Colonial Holdings

The European powers, great and small, competed with each other for world empires and world influence between 1870 and 1914. In terms of territory occupied, which nation held the largest global empire? What is the meaning of the expression "the sun never sets on the British Empire"? Based on what you have read in the chapter, how do you explain the fact that the Netherlands held colonies in southeast Asia and Latin America, but had no holdings in Africa? How did the United States become an imperial power in this period? How do you explain the locations of U.S. colonial acquisitions?

result, foreign trade increased from 3 percent of world output in 1800 to 33 percent by 1913. The greatest growth in trade occurred in the period from 1870 to 1914 as raw materials, manufactured products, capital, and men and women were transported across seas and continents by those seeking profits.

Meeting Western Needs.   Most trading in the age of imperialism still took place among European nations and North America. But entrepreneurs in search of new markets and new resources saw in Africa and Asia opportunities for protected exploitation. In nonindustrialized areas of the world new markets were shaped to meet the needs of Western producers and consumers. European landlords and managers trained Kenyan farmers to put aside their traditional agricultural methods and grow more "useful" crops such as coffee, tea, and sugar. The availability of cheaper British textiles of inferior quality drove Indian weavers away from their handlooms. Chinese silk producers changed centuries-old techniques to produce silk thread and cloth that was suited to the machinery and mass-production requirements of the French. Non-European producers undoubtedly derived benefits from the new international trading partnership, but those benefits were often scarce. Trade permitted specialization, but at the choice of the colonizer, not the colonized. World production and consumption were being shaped to suit the needs of the West.

Investment Abroad.   Capital in search of profits flowed out of the wealthier areas of Europe into the nonindustrialized regions of Russia, the Balkans, and the Ottoman Empire, where capital-intensive expenditures (on railways, for instance) promised high returns. Capital investment in overseas territories also increased phenomenally as railroads were built to gain access to primary products. Great Britain maintained its overwhelming dominance in overseas investment, with loans abroad greater than those of its five major competitors—France, Germany, Holland, the United States, and Belgium—combined.

The City of London had become the world's banker, serving as the clearinghouse for foreign investment on a global scale. The adoption of gold as the standard for exchange for most European currencies by 1874 further facilitated the operation of a single interdependent trading and investment system. Britain remained the world's biggest trading nation, with half of its exports going to Asia, Africa, and South America and the other half to Europe and the United States. But Germany was Britain's fastest-growing competitor, with twice as many exports to Europe and expanding overseas trade by 1914. The United States had recently joined the league of the world's great trading nations and was running a strong third in shares of total trade.

Foreign investments often took the form of loans to governments or to enterprises guaranteed by governments. Investors might be willing to take risks, but they also expected protection, no less so than merchants and industrialists trading in overseas territories. Together, trade and investment interests exerted considerable pressure on European states for control through acquisition and concessions. The vast amounts of money involved help explain the expectations of state involvement and the reasons why international competition, rivalry, and instability threatened to lead to conflict and war.

Race and Culture

After 1870 pseudoscientific racist ideas spread that Europeans were a superior race and that Africans were inferior. The writings of Charles Darwin were critical in gaining broad popular acceptance for the concept of a racial hierarchy governed by natural laws and operating within an evolutionist dynamic. That was not merely because Darwin's *On the Origin of Species* (1859) and *The Descent of Man* (1871) explicitly suggested the applicability of evolutionary theory to humanity. His suggestion was quickly taken up by intellectuals such as Herbert Spencer (1820–1903) and subsequently popularized as social Darwinism. According to the notion, the various racial groups not only occupied distinct positions in a staged sequence of "development" over time, with whites the most advanced and blacks the least so, but also were engaged in a natural conflict or struggle with one another. Social Darwinism's strongest message was that the fittest were destined to prevail, an idea especially welcome to racists of the later nineteenth century because it could be used to justify as "natural" the imperial expansion upon which they were then embarked.

The West's ability to kill and conquer as well as to cure was, as one Victorian social observer argued, proof of its cultural superiority. Every colonizing nation had its spokesmen for the "civilizing mission" to educate and to convert African and Asian "heathens." Cultural superiority was only a short step from arguments for racial superiority. Prompted by the U.S. involvement in the Philippines, the British poet Rudyard Kipling (1865–1936) characterized the responsibilities of the advanced West as "the White Man's burden." The smug and arrogant attitude of his poem about the white man's mission revealed a deep-seated and unacknowledged racism toward peoples considered "half-devil and half-child."

Rudyard Kipling, "The White Man's Burden"

Race and culture were collapsed into each other. If Westerners were culturally superior, as they claimed, they must be racially superior as well. The "survival of the fittest" came to justify conquest and subjugation as "laws" of human interaction and, by extension, of relations among nations.

Women and Imperialism

Ideas about racial and cultural superiority were not confined to books by pseudoscientists and to discussions among policy makers. Public discussions about marriage, reproduction, motherhood, and child-rearing reflected new concerns about furthering "the imperial race"—the racial identity of white

■ A British family in India poses with their domestic staff in front of their bungalow. An 1878 handbook on upper-class life in India recommended 27 servants per family. Note the dimensions of the "bungalow."

Westerners. Women throughout Western societies were encouraged by reformers, politicians, and doctors to have more children and instructed to take better care of them. "Children are the most valuable of imperial assets," one British doctor instructed his readers. Healthy young men were needed in the colonies, they were told, to defend Western values. State officials paid new attention to infant mortality at the end of the nineteenth century, set up health programs for children, and provided young women with training in home management, nutrition, and child care. The programs were no coincidence in an age of imperialism. Their rhetoric was explicitly imperialist and often racist in urging women to preserve the quality of the white race.

In the poem "White Man's Burden," Kipling advised, "Send forth the best ye breed." All over Europe, newly formed associations and clubs stressed the need for careful mate selection. In Britain, Francis Galton (1822–1911) founded eugenics, the study of genetics for the purpose of improving inherited characteristics of the race. Imperialism, the propagandists proclaimed, depended on mothers—women who would nurture healthy workers, strong soldiers and sailors, and intelligent and capable leaders. High infant mortality and poor health in children were attributed directly to maternal failings and not to environmental factors or poverty. Kaiser Wilhelm

II stressed that German women's attention to the "three Ks"— *Kinder, Küche, Kirche* (children, kitchen, church)—would guarantee a race of Germans who would rule the world. British generals and French statesmen publicly applied similar sentiments to their own countries and stressed that the future depended on the devotion of women to their family obligations.

Some European women participated directly in the colonizing experience. As missionaries and nurses, they supported the civilizing mission. As wives of officials and managers, they were expected to embody the gentility and values of Western culture. Most men who traded and served overseas did so unaccompanied by women. But when women were present in any numbers, as they were in India before 1914, they were expected to preserve the exclusivity of Western communities and to maintain class and status differentiations as a proof of cultural superiority.

Ecology and Imperialism

Ecology—the relationship and adjustment of human groups to their environment—was affected by imperial expansion, which dislocated the societies that it touched. Early explorers had disrupted little as they arrived, observed, and then moved

KARL PEARSON AND THE DEFENSE OF EUGENICS

The following is an excerpt from a lecture titled "National Life from the Standpoint of Science," given by a British professor of mathematics, Karl Pearson (1857–1936), in 1900. Pearson held the first chair in eugenics at the University of London, where he applied statistical methods to the study of heredity and evolution. The term eugenics *was introduced by Francis Galton, of whom Pearson was a follower. Pearson was heavily influenced by the pseudoscientific assumptions of social Darwinism and combined prejudices about race and nationalism to justify British imperialism as a proof of "survival of the fittest."*

Focus Questions

What does Pearson mean by "the scientific view of the nation"? And how "scientific" are the views he employs to arrive at that view?

The ... great function of science in national life ... is to show us what national life means, and how the nation is a vast organism subject as much to the great forces of evolution as any other gregarious type of life. There is a struggle of race against race and of nation against nation. In the early days of that struggle it was a blind, unconscious struggle of barbaric tribes. At the present day, in the case of the civilized white man, it has become more and more the conscious, carefully directed attempt of the nation to fit itself to a continuously changing environment. The nation has to foresee how and where the struggle will be carried on; the maintenance of national position is becoming more and more a conscious preparation for changing conditions, an insight into the needs of coming environments. ...

If a nation is to maintain its position in this struggle, it must be fully provided with trained brains in every department of national activity, from the government to the factory, and have, if possible, *a reserve of brain and physique* to fall back upon in times of national crisis. ...

You will see that my view—and I think it may be called the scientific view of a nation—is that of an organized whole, kept up to a high pitch of internal efficiency by insuring that its numbers are substantially recruited from the better stocks, and kept up to a high pitch of external efficiency by contest, chiefly by way of war with inferior races, and with equal races by the struggle for trade-routes and

for the sources of raw material and of food supply. This is the natural history view of mankind, and I do not think you can in its main features subvert it. ...

Is it not a fact that the daily bread of our millions of workers depends on their having somebody to work for? That if we give up the contest for trade-routes and for free markets and for waste lands, we indirectly give up our food supply? Is it not a fact that our strength depends on these and upon our colonies, and that our colonies have been won by the ejection of inferior races, and are maintained against equal races only by respect for the present power of our empire? ...

We find that the law of the survival of the fitter is true of mankind, but that the struggle is that of the gregarious animal. A community not knit together by strong social instincts, by sympathy between man and man, and class and class, cannot face the external contest, the competition with other nations, by peace or by war, for the raw material of production and for its food supply. This struggle of tribe with tribe, and nation with nation, may have its mournful side; but we see as a result of it the gradual progress of mankind to higher intellectual and physical efficiency. It is idle to condemn it; we can only see that it exists and recognize what we have gained by it—civilization and social sympathy. But while the statesman has to watch this external struggle, ... he must be very cautious that the nation is not silently rotting at its core. He must insure that the fertility of the inferior stocks is checked, and that of the superior stocks encouraged; he must regard with suspicion anything that tempts the physically and mentally fitter men and women to remain childless.

From Karl Pearson, *National Life from the Standpoint of Science* (1905).

---

on. The missionaries, merchants, soldiers, and businessmen who came later required that those with whom they came into contact must change their thought and behavior. In some cases, dislocation resulted in material improvements, better medical care, and the introduction of modern technology. For the most part, however, the initial ecological impact of the imperialist was negative. Western men and women carried diseases to people who did not share the Westerners' immunity. Traditional village life was destroyed in rural India, and African tribal societies disintegrated under the European onslaught.

Education of native populations had as its primary goal the improvement of administration and productivity in the colonies. When foreigners ruled indirectly through existing indigenous hierarchies, they often created corrupt and tyrannical bureaucracies that exploited natives. The indirect rule of the British in India was based on a pragmatic desire to keep British costs low.

When Asian and African laborers started producing for the Western market, they became dependent on its fluctuations. Victimized for centuries by the vagaries of weather, they now had to contend with the instability and cutthroat competition of cash crops in world markets. Individuals migrated from place to place in the countryside and from the countryside to newly formed cities. The fabric of tribal life unraveled. Such migrations necessarily affected family life, with individuals marrying later because they lacked the resources to set up households. The situation paralleled similar disruptions in English society at the beginning of the Industrial Revolution. Women as well as men migrated to find jobs. Many women, cut free of their tribes (as was the case in Nairobi), turned to prostitution—literally for pennies—as a means of survival.

In an extreme example of the colonizers' disdain for the colonized, some European countries used their overseas territories as dumping grounds for hardened and incorrigible convicted criminals. Imitating the earlier example of the British in Australia, the French developed Guiana and New Caledonia as prison colonies in the hope that they could solve their social problems at home by exporting prisoners.

CONCLUSION

From the very beginning of the competition for territories and concessions, no European state could act in Africa or Asia without affecting the interests and actions of its rivals in Europe. The scramble for Africa made clear how interlocking the system of European states had become after 1870. The development of spheres of influence in China underlined the value of world markets and international trade for the survival and expansion of Western nations.

A "balance of power" among states guaranteed national security and independence until the end of the nineteenth century. But between 1870 and 1914, industrialization, technology, and accompanying capital formation created vast economic disparities. Conflict and disequilibrium challenged European stability and balance. Ultimately, it was the politics of geography on the European continent, not confrontations in distant colonies, that polarized the European states into two camps. Despite the unresolved conflicts behind all of the crises, European statesmen prided themselves on their ability to settle disputes through reason and negotiation. Yet it was the problems at home in Europe and not abroad in the colonies that were to exacerbate geopolitical vulnerabilities and detonate a conflict far worse than the world had ever seen.

QUESTIONS FOR REVIEW

1. What geopolitical factors made the European balance of power so unstable around the turn of the century?
2. What social, political, and economic forces encouraged the nations of Europe to create overseas empires in the late nineteenth century?
3. How and why did European imperialism differ in Africa and Asia?
4. How did imperial expansion around the globe transform the lives of Europeans at home?

KEY TERMS

Baghdad Railway, *p. 747*

extraterritoriality, *p. 762*

geopolitics, *p. 753*

jingoism, *p. 756*

new imperialism, *p. 751*

quinine, *p. 752*

scramble for Africa, *p. 756*

spheres of influence, *p. 762*

Triple Alliance, *p. 747*

Triple Entente, *p. 750*

DISCOVERING WESTERN CIVILIZATION ONLINE

You can obtain more information about Europe and the world between 1870 and 1914 at the Websites listed below. See also the Companion Website that accompanies this text, www.ablongman.com/kishlansky, which contains an online study guide and additional resources.

The European Balance of Power, 1870–1914

Internet Modern History Sourcebook: World War I

www.fordham.edu/halsall/mod/modsbook38.html

This site is part of a larger site on World War I primary and secondary sources, but it contains a section on the developments among the great powers from the 1870s to 1914.

The New Imperialism

Internet Modern History Sourcebook: Imperialism

www.fordham.edu/halsall/mod/modsbook34.html

A comprehensive site of links arranged by continent to primary source materials and bibliographies on imperialism.

Colonialism and Postcolonialism: Selected Biographies

landow.stg.brown.edu/post/misc/bibl.html

Another site of links to bibliographies on colonialism and post-colonialism.

European Imperialism

www.winsor.edu/library/euroimpe.htm

This site is sponsored by the Winsor School and contains an extensive list of links by region on European imperialism.

The European Search for Territory and Markets

Francophone Africa: Bibliographies

www.hum.port.ac.uk/slas/francophone/bibliographies.htm

A collection of bibliographies on the partition of Africa and the impact of colonization in Africa.

South African War Virtual Library

www.bowlerhat.com.au/sawvl/

A virtual library of essays, photos, and further links on the Boer War.

China: A Traveling Exhibit, 1903–1904

www.chinaexhibit.org

A virtual museum exhibit of photographs taken in 1903 of the Chinese countryside after the Boxer Rebellion.

SUGGESTIONS FOR FURTHER READING

The European Balance of Power, 1870–1914

Norman Rich, *Great Power Diplomacy, 1814–1914* (New York: McGraw-Hill Higher Education, 1992). This work surveys diplomatic activities from the end of the Napoleonic Wars to the eve of World War I.

Alan Sked, *The Decline and Fall of the Habsburg Empire, 1815–1918* (London: Longman, 1989). An overview of the Habsburg Empire's history from Metternich to World War I. The author interprets the various historiographical debates over the collapse of Habsburg rule. Rather than treating the late empire as a case of inevitable decline, the book examines the monarchy as a viable institution within a multinational state.

The New Imperialism

Antoinette Burton, ed., *After the Imperial Turn: Thinking With and Through the Nation* (Durham, NC: Duke University Press, 2003). This collection provides a critical cultural analysis of nationalism and imperialism by showing the inadequacies of the nation as an analytic category.

David Cannadine, *Ornamentalism: How the British Saw Their Empire* (New York: Oxford University Press, 2001). The author approaches the history of the British Empire as interconnected with the history of the British nation and considers this "entire interactive system" in terms of a social construction and social perceptions.

Alice L. Conklin and Ian Christopher Fletcher, eds., *European Imperialism, 1830–1930: Climax and Contradiction* (Boston: Houghton Mifflin, 1999). A selection of essays on conflicting views of imperialism.

Richard Drayton, *Nature's Government: Science, Imperial Britain, and the 'Improvement' of the World* (New Haven, CT: Yale University Press, 2000). A fascinating examination of the role scientists, and especially botanists, played as partners with bureaucratic government in British imperial expansion.

Daniel R. Headrick, *The Tentacles of Progress: Technology Transfer in the Age of Imperialism, 1850–1940* (New York: Oxford University Press, 1988). Argues that the transfer of technology to Africa and Asia by the Western imperial powers produced colonial underdevelopment.

Robert H. MacDonald, *The Language of Empire: Myths and Metaphors of Popular Imperialism, 1880–1918* (Manchester, England: Manchester University Press, 1994). In studying the new metaphors of imperialism, the author examines the role of mythmakers, such as Rudyard Kipling, and popular fiction in shaping imperial perceptions and experiences. The author argues that the very shaping of language about non-European lands and peoples helped determine the form empire took in Great Britain.

The Search for Territory and Markets

Peter Cain and Tony Hopkins, *British Imperialism, 1688–2000* (New York: Longman, 2001). This volume stresses the role of finance and commercial services and the central role of the city of London in shaping British imperialism.

William D. Bowman, Frank M. Chiteji, J. Megan Greene, *Imperialism in the Modern World: Sources and Interpretations* Englewood Cliffs, NJ: Prentice Hall, 2006). A collection of primary and secondary texts with visual materials on nineteenth and twentieth century imperialism.

Eric Hobsbawm, *The Age of Empire, 1875–1914* (New York: Pantheon, 1987). A wide-ranging interpretive history of the late nineteenth century that spans economic, social, political, and cultural developments.

Thomas Pakenham, *The Scramble for Africa* (New York: Random House, 1991). A narrative history of how Europeans subdivided Africa among themselves.

Results of a European-Dominated World

Tony Ballantyne, *Orientalism and Race: Aryanism in the British Empire* (New York: Palgrave, 2002). Ballantyne traces how the idea of an Aryan race became an important feature of British imperial culture in the nineteenth century.

Alfred W. Crosby, *Ecological Imperialism: The Biological Expansion of Europe, 900–1900* (Cambridge: Cambridge University Press, 2004). Approaching imperialism from a biological rather than an economic or military perspective, the author shows the ecological impact of European expansion.

Johannes Fabian, *Language and Colonial Power: The Appropriation of Swahili in the Former Belgian Congo* (Cambridge: Cambridge University Press, 1986). Demonstrates how colonial power was exercised in the Belgian Congo through the study of the growth of Swahili as a lingua franca. The author pays particular attention to the uses of Swahili in industrial and other work situations.

Leila Tarazi Fawaz and C. A. Bayly, eds., *Modernity and Culture: From the Mediterranean to the Indian Ocean* (New York: Columbia University Press, 2002). This collection of essays demonstrates how cities in this vast region were increasingly cosmopolitan loci for a new kind of modernity that responded to political, economic, social, and cultural change.

Anne McClintock, *Imperial Leather: Race, Gender, and Sexuality in the Colonial Contest* (New York: Routledge, 1995). By using novels, diaries, advertisements, and other sources, the author demonstrates the relationship between images of domestic life and an ideology of imperial domination and focuses on the role of women in the colonial experience.

For a list of additional titles related to this chapter's topics, please see http://www.ablongman.com/kishlansky.

SELLING THE GREAT WAR
MOBILIZING THE HOME FRONT

THE VISUAL RECORD

Advertising is a powerful influence in modern life. Some believe that it makes people buy goods they do not need. Others insist that advertising is an efficient way of conveying information, on the basis of which people make choices. The leaders of Western nations discovered the power of advertising during the years of World War I, from 1914 to 1918. Advertising did not create the conflict that came to be known as the Great War. Nor did it produce the enthusiasm that excited millions of Europeans when war was declared in 1914. But when death counts mounted, prices skyrocketed, food supplies dwindled, and the frenzy and fervor for the war flagged, governments came to rely more heavily on the art of persuasion. Survival and victory required the support and coordination of the whole society. For the first time in history, war had to advertise.

By the early decades of the twentieth century, businessmen had learned that it was not enough to develop efficient technologies and to mass-produce everything from hair oil to corsets—they had to sell their goods to the public. People would not buy goods they did not know about and whose merits they did not understand. Modern advertising pioneered sales techniques that convinced people to buy. Now political leaders came to realize that the advertising techniques of the marketplace could be useful. Governments took up the "science" of selling—not products but the idea of war. It was not enough to have a well-trained and well-equipped army to ensure victory. Citizens had to be persuaded to join, to fight, to work, to save, and to believe in the national war effort. Warring nations learned how to organize enthusiasm and how to mobilize the masses in support of what proved to be a long and bloody conflict.

The poster on the facing shows a dramatic appeal to German women to support war work. A stern soldier whose visage and bearing communicate strength and singleness of purpose is backed up by an equally determined young woman. She is in the act of handing him a grenade as she stands with him, her arm on his shoulder, facing the unseen enemy. Grenades hang from his belt and from his left hand, giving the sense that he is able to enter battle properly armed, thanks to the dedicated woman's ef-

forts. The poster is a good representation of the centrality of women's work to the waging of a new kind of war in the twentieth century. The battlefront had to be backed up by a *home front*—the term used for the first time in the Great War—of working men, women, and even children. The poster communicates the dignity and worth that lay in the concerted partnership of soldiers and civilians to defeat the enemy.

Early war posters stressed justice and national glory. Later, as weariness with the war spread, the need for personal sacrifice became the dominant theme. The poster on this page shows a sad female figure rising from a sea of suffering and

■ "Take Up the Sword of Justice" by Sir Bernard Partridge, England, 1915.

Deutsche Frauen arbeitet im Heimat-heer!

Kriegsamtstelle Magdeburg

■ World War I poster by George Kirchbach, Germany, 1914–1918.

death. The woman, both goddesslike and vulnerable, symbolizes Great Britain. She is making a strong visual plea for action, seeking soldiers for her cause. The appeal for volunteers for the armed forces was unique to Great Britain, where conscription was not established until 1916. Yet the image is typical of every nation's reliance on a noble female symbol to emphasize the justice of its cause. The dark suffering and death in the waters lapping at her robes are reflected in her eyes. She evinces a fierce determination as she exhorts, "Take up the sword of justice." In February 1915, Germany declared the waters around the British Isles to be a war zone. All British shipping was subject to attack, as were neutral merchant vessels, which were attacked without warning. In May 1915, the *Lusitania* was sunk, taking with it more than 1000 lives, including those of 128 Americans. The poster frames an illuminated horizon where a ship that is probably the *Lusitania* is sinking. The poster is a clear call to arms against the perfidy of an enemy who has killed innocent civilians. The female figure's determined jaw, clenched fist, and outstretched arms communicate the nobility of the cause and the certainty of success.

Civilians had to be mobilized for two reasons. First, it became evident early in the fighting that the costs of the war in terms of human lives were high. Soldiers at the front had to be constantly replaced by civilian reserves. Second, the costs of the war in terms of food, equipment, and productive materials were so high that civilian populations had to be willing to endure great hardships and to sacrifice their own well-being to produce supplies for soldiers at the front. Advertising was used by nations at war to coordinate civilian and military contributions to a common cause. Selling the Great War required selectively communicating information and inspiring belief and a commitment to total victory, no matter how high the cost.

LOOKING AHEAD

The European governments proudly "selling" war to their citizens in 1914 expected quick victories and a war of short duration. Instead, as this chapter will show, what they experienced was a prolonged global war, costly in human life and material destruction, stretching out over four devastating years. In adjusting to the unexpected, military technology and timetables called the tune in a defensive war fought from the trenches with sophisticated weapons capable of maiming and killing in new ways. In the case of Russia, the war signaled political and social collapse and a revolution of unprecedented scale. The intervention of the United States and German defeat preceded a peace that reshaped Europe as a whole in fundamental ways.

THE WAR EUROPE EXPECTED

In 1914, Europe stood confidently at the center of the world. Covering only seven percent of the earth's surface, it dominated the world's trade and was actively exporting both European goods and European culture all over the globe. Proud of the progress and prosperity of urban industrial society, Europeans had harnessed nature to transform their environment. They extended their influence beyond their continent, sure that their achievements marked the pinnacle of civilization.

Westerners took stability and harmony for granted as preconditions for progress. Yet they also recognized the utility of war. In recent times, local confrontations between European states in Africa had been successfully contained in bids for increased territory. While warfare was accepted as an instrument of policy, no one expected or wanted a general war. Statesmen decided there were rules to the game of war that could be employed in the interests of statecraft. Science and technology also served the goals of limited war. Modern weapons, statesmen and generals were sure, would prevent a long war. Superiority in armed force became a priority for European states seeking to protect the peace.

The beginning of the modern arms race resulted in "armed peace" as a defense against war. Leaders nevertheless expected and planned for a war, short and limited, in which the fittest and most advanced nation would win. Planners believed that their rivals could not triumph. War was acceptable because it would be quick and decisive. Previous confrontations among European states had been limited in duration and destruction, as in the case of Prussia and France in 1870, or confined to peripheries, as squabbles among the Great Powers in Africa

■ European Alliances on the Eve of World War I. Alliance systems divided Europe into two great blocs with few countries remaining neutral.

indicated. The alliance system was expected to defend the peace by defining the conditions of war.

As international tensions mounted, the hot summer days of 1914 were a time of hope and glory. The hope was that war, when it came, would be "over by Christmas." The glory was the promise of ultimate victory in the "crusade for civilization" that each nation's leaders held out to their people. Declarations of war were greeted with songs, flowers, wild enthusiasm, and dancing in the streets. Crowds welcomed the battles to come with the delirium of cheering a favorite team in a sports match. Some embraced war as a test of greatness, a purification of a society that had become lazy and complacent. When war did come in 1914, it was a choice, not an accident. Yet it was a choice that Europeans did not understand, one whose limits they could not control. Their unquestioned pride in reason and progress, which ironically had led them to the war, did not survive the four years of barbaric slaughter that followed.

Separating Friends from Foes

At the end of the nineteenth century, the world appeared to be coming together in a vast international network linked by commerce and finance. A system of alliances based on shared interests also connected states to one another. After 1905, the intricate defensive alliances between and among the European states maintained the balance of power between two blocs of nations and helped prevent one bloc from dominating the other. Yet by creating blocs, alliances identified foes as well as friends. On the eve of the war, France, Great Britain, and Russia stood together in the Triple Entente. Since 1882, Germany, Austria-Hungary, and Italy had joined forces in the Triple Alliance. Other states allied with one or the other of the blocs in pacts of mutual interest and protection. Throughout the world, whether in North Africa, the Balkans, or Asia, the power of some states was intended to balance the power of others. Yet the balance of power did not exist simply to preserve the peace. It existed to preserve a system of independent national societies—nation-states—in a precarious equilibrium. Gains in one area by one bloc had to be offset by compromises in another to maintain the balance. Nations recognized limited conflict as a legitimate means of preserving equilibrium.

The alliance system of blocs reflected the growing impact of public opinion on international relations. Statesmen had the ability to manipulate the newspaper images of allies as good and rivals as evil. But controlling public opinion served to lock policy makers into permanent partnerships and "blank checks" of support for their allies. Western leaders understood that swings in public opinion in periods of crisis could hobble their efforts in the national interest. Permanent military alliances with clearly identified "friends," therefore, took the place of more fluid arrangements.

Although alliances that guaranteed military support did not cause war, they did permit weak nations to act irresponsibly, with the certainty that they would be defended by their

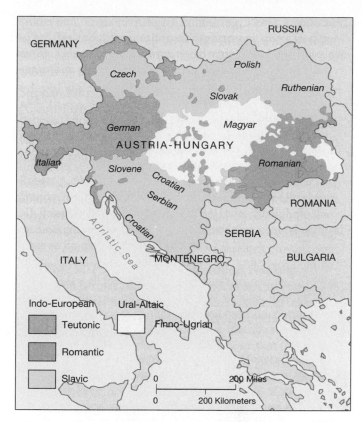

■ Linguistic Groups in Austria-Hungary. The significant linguistic and cultural diversity of Habsburg lands made Austria-Hungary difficult to govern. Although Germany counted on Austria-Hungary as a key ally in promoting a balance of power, its internal challenges made it a weak partner.

more powerful partners. France and Germany were publicly committed to their weaker allies Russia and Austria-Hungary, respectively, in supporting imperialist ambitions in the Balkans from which they themselves derived little direct benefit. Because of treaty commitments, no country expected to face war alone. The interlocking system of defensive alliances was structured to match strength against strength—France against Germany, for example—thereby making a prolonged war more likely than would be the case if a weak nation confronted a strong enemy.

Military Timetables

As Europe soon discovered, military timetables restricted the choices of leaders at times of conflict. The crisis of the summer of 1914 revealed the extent to which politicians and statesmen had come to rely on military expertise and strategic considerations in making decisions. Germany's military preparations are a good example of how war strategy exacerbated crises and prevented peaceful solutions.

The Schlieffen Plan.   Alfred von Schlieffen (1833–1913), the Prussian general and chief of the German General Staff

(1891–1905) who developed the war plan, understood little about politics but spent his life studying the strategic challenges of warfare. His war plan was designed to make Germany the greatest power on the Continent. The **Schlieffen Plan,** which he set before his fellow officers in 1905, was a bold and daring one: in the likely event of war with Russia, Germany would launch a devastating offensive against France. Schlieffen reasoned that France was a strong military presence that would come to the aid of its ally, Russia. Russia, lacking a modern transportation system, would not be able to mobilize as rapidly as France.

Russia also had the inestimable advantage of the ability to retreat into its vast interior. If Germany were pulled into a war with Russia, its western frontier would be vulnerable to France, Russia's powerful ally. The Schlieffen Plan recognized that France must first be defeated in the west before Germany

could turn its forces to the task of defeating Russia. The Schlieffen Plan thus committed Germany to a war with France, regardless of particular circumstances. Furthermore, the plan, with its strategy of invading the neutral countries of Belgium, Holland, and Luxembourg in order to defeat France in six weeks, ignored the rights of the neutral countries.

Russia's Mobilization Plan and the French Plan XVII. Germany was not alone in being driven by military timetables when conflicts arose. Russian military strategists planned full mobilization if war broke out with Austria-Hungary, which was menacing the interests of Russia's ally Serbia. Russia foresaw the likelihood that Germany would come to the aid of Austria-Hungary. Russia knew, too, that because of its primitive railway network it would be unable to mobilize troops rapidly. In order to compensate for that

IMAGE DISCOVERY

A Cartoon Conveys the Politics of a Deadly Tug of War

By 1914 political cartoons with mass distribution in the daily press sought to convey complex political realities with humorous images. Here, Italy assumes the part of the referee in a deadly tug of war that culminated in World War I. Why is Italy, rather than another country, the umpire? Note the players on each side and their dress. Are any of the major participants in the war missing from the "game"? What might the cartoon imply as to the balance of power in this conflict?

MAP DISCOVERY

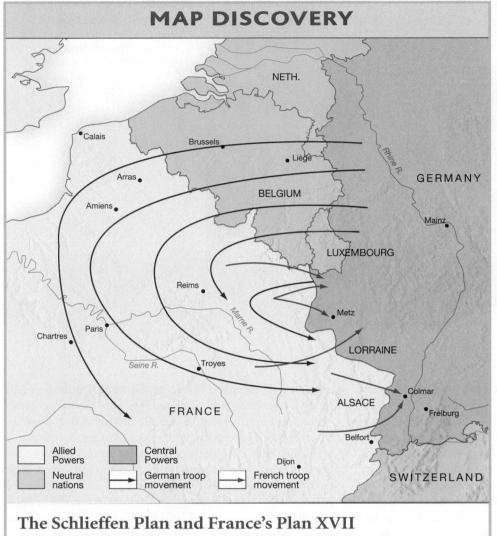

The Schlieffen Plan and France's Plan XVII

The Schlieffen Plan was a German plan of attack devised in the event of a war against Russia. Why was the plan based on the principle that the road to St. Petersburg (to the east) ran through Paris (to the west)? What countries on this map were neutral countries? Why was Germany willing to violate their neutrality in order to move troops across their territory? The French meanwhile were devising their own war plan, called Plan XVII. Where did they plan to concentrate their offensive? Why was it not successful?

German drive through Belgium called for in the Schlieffen Plan.

Military leaders throughout Europe argued that if their plans were to succeed, speed was essential. Delays to consider peaceful solutions would cripple military responses. Diplomacy bowed to military strategy. When orders to mobilize went out, armies would be set on the march. Like a row of dominoes falling with the initial push, the two alliance systems would be at war.

Assassination at Sarajevo

A teenager with a handgun started the First World War. On 28 June 1914, in Sarajevo, the sleepy capital of the Austro-Hungarian province of Bosnia, Gavrilo Princip (1895–1918), a 19-year-old Bosnian Serb, repeatedly pulled the trigger of his Browning revolver, killing the designated heir of the Habsburg throne, Archduke Franz Ferdinand, and his wife, Sophie. Princip belonged to the Young Bosnian Society, a group of students, workers, some peasants, Croats, Muslims, and intellectuals who wanted to free Slavic populations from Habsburg control. Princip was part of a growing movement of South Slavs struggling for national liberation who believed they were being held in colonial servitude by Austria-Hungary.

DOCUMENT

Borijove Jevtic on the Assassination of Archduke Franz Ferdinand

weakness, Russian leaders planned to mobilize *before* war was declared. German military leaders had no choice in the event of full Russian mobilization but to mobilize their own troops immediately and to urge the declaration of war. There was no chance of containing the conflict once a general mobilization on both sides was underway. Mobilization would mean war.

Like the Schlieffen Plan, the French Plan XVII called for the concentration of troops in a single area, with the intention of decisively defeating the enemy. The French command, not well informed about German strengths and strategies, designated Alsace and Lorraine for the immediate offensive against Germany in the event of war. Plan XVII left Paris exposed to the

Struggle over control of the Balkans had been a long-standing issue that had involved all the major European powers for decades. As Austria-Hungary's ally since 1879, Germany was willing to support Vienna's showdown in the Balkans as a way of stopping Russian advances in the area. The alliance with Germany gave Austria-Hungary a sense of security and confidence to pursue its Balkan aims. Germany had its own plans for domination of the Continent and feared that a weakened Austria-Hungary would undermine its own position in central Europe. Independent Balkan states to the south and east were also a threat to Germany's plans. German leaders hoped that an Austro-Serbian war would remain

■ Austrian Archduke Franz Ferdinand and his wife, Sophie, leave the Senate House in Sarajevo on 28 June 1914. Five minutes later, Serbian terrorist Gavrilo Princip assassinated the couple.

localized and would strengthen their ally, Austria-Hungary. While Austria-Hungary had Germany's support, Serbia was backed by a sympathetic Russia that favored nationalist movements in the Balkans. Russia, in turn, had been encouraged by France, its ally by military pact since 1894, to take a firm stand in its struggle with Austria-Hungary for dominance among Balkan nationalities.

The interim of five weeks between the assassination of Archduke Ferdinand and the outbreak of the war was a period of intense diplomatic activity. The assassination gave Austria-Hungary the excuse it needed to bring a troublesome Serbia into line. Austria-Hungary held Serbia responsible for the shootings. Leaders in Vienna had no evidence at the time to justify their allegations of a Serbian conspiracy, but they saw in the event the perfect pretext for military action. On 23 July 1914, Austria-Hungary issued an ultimatum to the small Balkan nation and secretly decided to declare war regardless of Serbia's response. The demands were so severe that, if met, they would have stripped Serbia of its independence. Austria's aim was to destroy Serbia. In spite of a conciliatory, though not capitulatory, reply from Serbia to the ultimatum, Austria-Hungary declared war on the Balkan nation on 28 July 1914. Russia mobilized two days after the Austro-Hungarian declaration of war against Serbia. Germany mobilized in response to the Russian action and declared war on Russia on 1 August, and on France on 3 August. France had begun mobilizing on 30 July, when its ally, Russia, entered the war.

Britain's dependence on its alliance with France as a means of protecting British sea routes in the Mediterranean meant that Great Britain could not remain neutral once France declared war. On 4 August, after Germany had violated Belgian neutrality in its march to France, Great Britain honored its treaty obligations and declared war on Germany. Great Britain entered the war because it judged that a powerful Germany could use ports on the English Channel to invade the British Isles. Italy alone of the major powers remained for the moment outside the conflict. Although allied with Germany and Austria-Hungary, its own aspirations in the Balkans kept it from fighting for the Austrian cause in 1914.

Self-interest, fear, and ambition motivated the Great Powers in different ways in the pursuit of war. The international diplomatic system that had worked so well to prevent war in the preceding decades now enmeshed European states in interlocking alliances and created a chain reaction. The Austro-Serbian war of July 1914 became a Europe-wide war within a month.

A NEW KIND OF WARFARE

Early in the war, the best-laid plans of political and military leaders collapsed. In the first place, Europe experienced a war that was not quickly and decisively won, but spread throughout Europe and became global. Switzerland, Spain, the Netherlands, and all of Scandinavia remained neutral, but every other European nation was pulled into the war. In August 1914, Japan cast its lot with the **Allies,** as the Entente came to be known, and in November the Ottoman Empire joined the **Central Powers** of Germany and Austria-Hungary. In the following year, Italy joined the war—not on the side of its long-term treaty partners, Germany and Austria-Hungary, but on the side of the Allies, with the expectation of benefiting in the Balkans from Austrian defeat. Bulgaria joined Germany and Austria-Hungary in 1915, seeking territory at Serbia's expense. By the time the United States entered the war in 1917, the war had become a world war.

The second surprise for the European powers was that they did not get a war of movement, nor did they get one of short duration. Within weeks, that pattern had given way to what promised to be a long and costly war of attrition. The war started as German strategists had planned, with German victory in battle after battle. The end seemed near. But in the space of less than a month, the war changed in ways that no one had predicted. Technology was the key to understanding the change and explaining the surprises.

Technology and the Trenches

In the history of nineteenth-century European warfare, armies had relied on mobile cavalry and infantry units, whose greatest asset was speed. Rapid advance had been decisive in the Prussian victory over the French in 1870, which had resulted in the formation of the German Empire.

Digging In. Soldiers of the twentieth century were also trained for a war of movement, high maneuverability, and maximum territorial conquest. But after the first six weeks of battle, soldiers were ordered to do something unimaginable to strategists of European warfare: they were ordered to dig ditches and fight from fixed positions. Soldiers on both sides shoveled out trenches four feet deep, piled up sandbags, mounted their machine guns, and began to fight an unplanned defensive war.

The front lines of Europe's armies in the west wallowed in the 400 miles of trenches that ran from the English Channel to the Swiss frontier. The British and French on one side and the Germans on the other fought each other with machine guns and mortars, backed up by heavy artillery to the rear. Strategists on both sides believed they could break through enemy lines. As a result, the monotony of trench warfare was punctuated periodically by infantry offensives in which immense concentrations of artillery caused great bloodshed. Ten million men were killed in the bizarre and deadly combination of old and new warfare. The glamour of battle that had attracted many young men disappeared quickly in the daily reality of living in mud with rats and constantly facing death.

DOCUMENT

Wilfred Owen, "Dulce et Decorum Est"

New Weapons. The invention of new weaponry and heavy equipment had transformed war into an enterprise of increasing complexity. Military and naval staffs expanded to meet the

■ A typical World War I trench. Millions of soldiers lived amid mud, disease, and vermin, awaiting death from enemy shells. After the French army mutiny in 1916, the troops wrung the concession from their commanders that they would not have to charge German machine guns while armed only with rifles.

ALL QUIET ON THE WESTERN FRONT

Eyewitness accounts described the horrors of the new trench warfare. But no one captured the war better than the German novelist Erich Maria Remarque (1898–1970), who drew on his own wartime experiences in All Quiet on the Western Front. *Published in 1928 and subsequently translated into 25 languages, this powerful portrayal of the transformation of a schoolboy into a soldier indicts the inhumanity of war and pleads for peace. Stressing the camaraderie of fighting men and sympathy for the plight of the enemy soldier, Remarque also underscored the alienation of a whole generation—the lost generation of young men who could not go home again after the war.*

Focus Questions

In the final paragraph, the narrator tells us his age. Would you have guessed his age from the opening three paragraphs? How does the narrator's description of his generation transcend enemy lines?

Attack, counter-attack, charge, repulse—these are words, but what things they signify! We have lost a good many men, mostly recruits. Reinforcements have again been sent up to our sector. They are one of the new regiments, composed almost entirely of young fellows just called up. They have had hardly any training, and are sent into the field with only a theoretical knowledge. They do know what a hand-grenade is, it is true, but they have very little idea of cover, and what is most important of all, have no eye for it. A fold in the ground has to be quite eighteen inches high before they can see it.

Although we need reinforcement, the recruits give us almost more trouble than they are worth. They are helpless in this grim fighting area; they fall like flies. Modern trench-warfare demands knowledge and experience; a man must have a feeling for the contours of the ground, an ear for the sound and character of the shells, must be able to decide beforehand where they will drop, how they will burst, and how to shelter from them.

The young recruits of course know none of these things. They get killed simply because they hardly can tell shrapnel from high-explosive, they are mown down because they are listening anxiously to the roar of the big coal-boxes falling in the rear, and miss the light, piping whistle of the low spreading daisy-cutters. They flock together like sheep instead of scattering, and even the wounded are shot down like hares by the airmen.

Their pale turnip faces, their pitiful clenched hands, the fine courage of these poor devils, the desperate charges and attacks made by the poor brave wretches, who are so terrified that they dare not cry out loudly, but with battered chests, with torn bellies, arms and legs only whimper softly for their mothers and cease as soon as one looks at them.

Their sharp, downy, dead faces have the awful expressionlessness of dead children. . . .

I am young, I am twenty years old; yet I know nothing of life but despair, death, fear, and fatuous superficiality cast over an abyss of sorrow. I see how peoples are set against one another, and in silence, unknowingly, foolishly, obediently, innocently slay one another. I see that the keenest brains of the world invent weapons and words to make it yet more refined and enduring. And all men of my age, here and over there, throughout the whole world see these things; all my generation is experiencing these things with me. What would our fathers do if we suddenly stood up and came before them and proffered our account? What do they expect of us if a time ever comes when the war is over? Through the years our business has been killing;—it was our first calling in life. Our knowledge of life is limited to death. What will happen afterwards? And what shall come out of us?

From Erich Maria Remarque, *All Quiet on the Western Front.*

new needs of warfare, but old ways persisted. Outmoded cavalry units survived despite more efficient mechanization. In their bright blue coats and red trousers, French and Belgian infantrymen made easy targets. The railroad made the mobilization, organization, and deployment of mass armies possible. Specialists were needed to control the new war machines that heavy industry had created.

The shovel and the machine gun had transformed war. The Maxim machine gun had been used by the British in Africa. Strategists regarded the carnage that resulted as a stunning achievement but failed to ask how a weapon of such phenom-

enal destructive power would work against an enemy armed with machine guns instead of spears. Military strategists drew all the wrong conclusions. They continued to plan an offensive strategy when the weaponry developed for massive destruction had pushed them into fighting a defensive war from the trenches. Both sides resorted to concentration of artillery, increased use of poison gas, and unrestricted submarine warfare in desperate attempts to break the deadlock caused by meeting armed force with force.

The necessity of total victory drove the Central Powers and the Allies to grisly new inventions. Chlorine gas was first used

■ The British invented the tank, which made its combat debut in 1916. The new weapon terrified the German troops when it was first used on the western front. The British had developed it in heavy secrecy under the pretext of constructing water tanks; hence the name.

in warfare by the Germans in 1915. Mustard gas, which was named for its distinctive smell and which caused severe blistering, was introduced two years later. The Germans were the first to use flame throwers, especially effective against mechanized vehicles with vulnerable fuel tanks. Barbed wire, invented in the American Midwest to contain farm animals, became an essential aspect of trench warfare, as it marked off the no-man's-land between combatants and prevented surprise attacks.

Late in the war, the need to break the deadlock of trench warfare ushered in the airplane and the tank. Neither was decisive in altering the course of the war, although the airplane was useful for reconnaissance and for limited bombing and the tank promised the means of breaking through defensive lines.

New weapons sometimes produced their antidotes. For example, the invention of deadly gas was followed soon after by gas masks. Each side was capable of matching the other's ability to devise new armaments. Deadlocks caused by technological parity forced both sides to resort to desperate concentrations of men and weaponry that resulted not in decisive battles but in ever-escalating casualty rates. By improving their efficiency at killing, the European powers were not finding a way to end the war.

The German Offensive

German forces seized the offensive in the west and invaded neutral Belgium at the beginning of August 1914. The Belgians resisted stubbornly but unsuccessfully. Belgian forts were systematically captured, and the capital of Brussels fell under the German advance on 20 August. After the fall of Belgium, German military might swept into northern France with the intention of defeating the French in six weeks.

Germany on Two Fronts.   In the years preceding the war, the German General Staff, unwilling to concentrate all of its troops in the west, had modified the Schlieffen Plan by committing divisions to its eastern frontier. The absence of the full German fighting force in the west did not appreciably slow the German advance through Belgium. Yet the Germans had underestimated both the cost of holding back the French in Alsace-Lorraine and the difficulty of maneuvering German forces and transporting supplies in an offensive war. Eventually, unexpected Russian advances in the east also siphoned off troops from the west. German forces in the west were so weakened by the offensive that they were unable to swing west of Paris, as planned, and instead chose to enter the French capital from the northeast by crossing the Marne River. The shift exposed the German First Army on its western flank and opened up a gap on its eastern flank.

First Battle of the Marne.   Despite an initial pattern of retreat and a lack of coordination of forces, Allied French and British troops were ready to take advantage of the vulnerabilities in the German advance. In a series of battles between 6 and 10 September 1914 that came to be known as the First Battle of the Marne, the Allies counterattacked and advanced into the gap. The German army was forced to drop back. In the following months, each army tried to outflank the other in what has been called "the race to the sea." By late fall, it was clear that the battles from the Marne north to the border town of Ypres in northwest Belgium near the English Channel

"DULCE ET DECORUM EST"

Some of the best and most moving poetry of modern times was produced in the trenches of World War I. Wilfred Owen (1893–1918), a company commander for the British Army, died in battle one week before the war ended. His poems stand as a strong testimonial to the horrors of battle and the camaraderie of the trenches.

Focus Questions

In this poem, Owen uses his schoolboy Latin to quote the patriotic sentiment that "It is sweet and fitting to die for one's country." What leads him to conclude that this noble thought is "the old Lie"? Notice how he contrasts images of "old beggars under sacks" who are "coughing like hags" to youthful images, a reference to boys, "innocent tongues," and "children ardent for some desperate glory." What effect does his use of words like "ecstasy" and "dreams" have in conveying the horrors of war? This is a poem full of sounds; consider how those sounds are orchestrated to emphasize the poem's theme.

Bent double, like old beggars under sacks,
Knock-kneed, coughing like hags, we cursed through sludge,
Till on the haunting flares we turned our backs
And towards our distant rest began to trudge.
Men marched asleep. Many had lost their boots
But limped on, blood-shod. All went lame; all blind;
Drunk with fatigue; deaf even to the hoots
Of tired, outstripped Five-Nines that dropped behind.

Gas! Gas! Quick, boys!—An ecstasy of fumbling,
Fitting the clumsy helmets just in time;
But someone still was yelling out and stumbling
And flound'ring like a man in fire or lime. . .
Dim, through the misty panes and thick green light,
As under a green sea, I saw him drowning.
In all my dreams, before my helpless sight,
He plunges at me, guttering, choking, drowning.

If in some smothering dreams you too could pace
Behind the wagon that we flung him in,
And watch the white eyes writhing in his face,
His hanging face, like a devil's sick of sin;
If you could hear, at every jolt, the blood
Come gargling from the froth-corrupted lungs,
Obscene as cancer, bitter as the cud
Of vile, incurable sores on innocent tongues,—
My friend, you would not tell with such high zest
To children ardent for some desperate glory,
The old Lie: Dulce et decorum est
Pro patria mori.

From Wilfred Owen, *Poems*, 1920.

had ended an open war of movement on the western front. Soldiers now dug in along a line of battle that changed little in the long three and a half years until March 1918.

The Allies gained a strategic victory in the First Battle of the Marne by resisting the German advance in the fighting that quickly became known as the "miracle of the Marne." The legend was further enhanced by true stories of French troops being rushed from Paris to the front in taxicabs. Yet the real significance of the Marne lay in the severe miscalculations of military leaders and statesmen on both sides who had expected a different kind of war. They did not understand the new technology that made a short war unlikely. Nor did they understand the demands that the new kind of warfare would make on civilian populations. Those Parisian taxi drivers foreshadowed how European civilians would be called upon again and again to support the war in the next four years. The Schlieffen Plan was dead. But it was no more a failure than any of the other military timetables of the Great Powers.

"I don't know what is to be done—this isn't war." So spoke Lord Horatio Kitchener (1850–1916), one of the most decorated British generals of his time. He was not alone in his bafflement over the stalemate of trench warfare at the end of 1914. By that time, Germany's greatest fear, a simultaneous war on two fronts, had become a grim reality. The Central Powers were under a state of siege, cut off from the world by the great battlefront in the west and by the Allied blockade at sea. The rules of the game had changed, and the European powers settled in for a long war.

War on the Eastern Front

War on Germany's eastern front was a mobile war, fought over vast distances. The Russian army was the largest in the world. Yet it was crippled from the outbreak of the war by inadequate supplies and poor leadership. At the end of August 1914, the smaller German army, supported by divisions drawn from the west, delivered a devastating defeat to the Russians in the one great battle on the eastern front. At Tannenberg, the entire Russian Second Army was destroyed, and about 100,000 Russian soldiers were taken prisoner.

The German general Paul von Hindenburg (1847–1934), a veteran of the Franco-Prussian war of 1870, had been recalled from retirement to direct the campaign against the Russians because of his intimate knowledge of the area. Assisted by Quartermaster General Erich Ludendorff (1865–1937),

Hindenburg followed the stunning victory of Tannenberg two weeks later with another devastating blow to Russian forces at the Masurian Lakes.

The Russians were holding up their end of the bargain in the Allied war effort, but at great cost. They kept the Germans busy and forced them to divert troops to the eastern front, weakening the German effort to knock France out of the war.

In the south, the tsar's troops defeated the Austro-Hungarian army at Lemberg in Galicia in September. The Russian victory gave Serbia a temporary reprieve. But by mid-1915, Germany had thrown the Russians back and was keeping Austria-Hungary propped up in the war. By fall, Russia had lost most of Galicia, the Polish lands of the Russian Empire, Lithuania, and parts of Latvia and Byelorussia to the advancing enemy.

MAP DISCOVERY

World War I

The Central Powers were in the unenviable position of fighting wars on two major fronts. The inset shows the stabilized western front of trench warfare in northern France and Belgium. Why did warfare focus in the west on this area, and why did it bog down for such a long period along this front? How did warfare along the eastern front differ, and why did the eastern front cover a much greater expanse? Note the major battles in western and eastern Europe and the Ottoman Empire. Why was none of these battles decisive in ending the war? Were the British naval blockade and the German submarine war zone effective? Finally, note the reduced Russian territory as a result of the Treaty of Brest-Litovsk. Why was Russia willing to agree to such a loss of land to Germany before the war ended?

The losses amounted to 15 percent of its territory and 20 percent of its population. The Russian army staggered, with more than one million soldiers taken as prisoners of war and at least as many killed or wounded.

The Russian army, as one of its own officers described it, was being bled to death. Russian soldiers were poorly led into battle, or not led at all because of the shortage of officers. Munitions shortages meant that soldiers often went into battle without rifles, armed only with the hope of scavenging arms from their fallen comrades. Despite the difficulties, the Russians, under the direction of General Aleksei Brusilov (1853–1926), commander of the Russian armies in the southern part of the eastern front, remarkably managed to throw back the Austro-Hungarian forces in 1916 and almost eliminated Austria as a military power. Russia's near-destruction of the Austrian army tremendously benefited Russia's allies. In order to protect its partner, Germany was forced to withdraw 8 divisions from Italy—alleviating the Allied situation in the Tyrol—and 12 divisions from the western front, providing relief for the French at Verdun and the British at the Somme. In addition, Russia sent troops to the aid of a new member of the Allied camp, Romania, an act that probably further weakened Brusilov's efforts. In response to Brusilov's challenge, the Germans established control over the Austrian army, assigning military command of the coalition to General Ludendorff. But that was the last great campaign on the eastern front and Russia's last show of strength in the Great War.

War on the Western Front

Along hundreds of miles of trenches, the French and British tried repeatedly to expel the Germans from Belgium. Long periods of inactivity were punctuated by orgies of heavy bloodletting. The German phrase "All quiet on the western front," used in military communiqués to describe those periods of silence between massive shellings and infantry attacks, reported only the uneasy calm before the next violent storm.

Verdun.   Military leaders on both sides cherished the dream of a decisive offensive, the breakthrough that would win the war. In 1916, the Allies planned a joint strike at the Somme, a river in northern France flowing west into the English Channel, but the Germans struck first at Verdun, a small fortress city in northeast France. By concentrating great numbers of troops, the Germans outnumbered the French five to two. As General Erich von Falkenhayn (1861–1922), chief of the General Staff of the German army from 1914 to 1916, explained it, the German purpose in attacking Verdun was "to bleed the French white by virtue of our superiority in guns."

On the first day of battle, one million shells were fired. The battlefield was a living hell as soldiers stumbled across corpse after corpse. Against the German onslaught, French troops were instructed to hold out, though they lacked adequate artillery and reinforcements. General Joseph Joffre (1852–1931), commander in chief of the French army, was unwilling to divert reinforcements to Verdun.

The German troops advanced easily through the first lines of defense. But the French held their position for ten long, horrifying months of continuous mass slaughter from February to December 1916. General Henri Philippe Pétain (1856–1951), a local commander who had been planning an early retirement before the war, bolstered morale by constantly rotating his troops to the point that most of the French army—259 of 330 infantry battalions—saw action at Verdun. Nearly starving and poorly armed, the French stood alone in the bloodiest offensive of the war. Attack strategy backfired on the Germans as their own death tolls mounted.

Pétain and his flamboyant general Robert Georges Nivelle (1856–1924) were both hailed as heroes for fulfilling the instruction to their troops: "They shall not pass." Falkenhayn fared less well and was dismissed from his post. Yet no real winners emerged from the scorched earth of Verdun, where observers could see the nearest thing to a desert created in Europe. Verdun was a disaster. The French suffered more than half a million total casualties. German casualties were almost as high. A few square miles of territory had changed hands back and forth. In the end, no military advantage was gained, and almost 700,000 lives had been lost. Legends of the brilliant leadership of Pétain and Nivelle, who both went on to greater positions of authority, and the failed command of Falkenhayn, who retired in disgrace, obscured the real lesson of the battle: an offensive war under those conditions was impossible.

The Somme.   Still, new offensives were devised. The British went ahead with their planned offensive on the Somme in July 1916. For an advance of seven miles, 400,000 British and 200,000 French soldiers were killed or wounded. The American writer F. Scott Fitzgerald (1896–1940), who had served as an army officer in World War I, wrote of the battle of the Somme in his novel *Tender Is the Night* (1934). One of his characters describes a visit to the Somme Valley after the war: "See that little stream. We could walk to it in two minutes. It took the British a whole month to walk to it—a whole empire walking very slowly, dying in front and pushing forward behind. And another empire walked very slowly backward a few inches a day, leaving the dead like a million bloody rugs." German losses brought the total casualties of the offensive to one million men.

Despite his experience at Verdun, the French general Robert Nivelle planned his own offensive in the Champagne region in spring 1917, sure that he could succeed where others had failed in "breaking the crust." The Nivelle offensive resulted in 40,000 deaths, and Nivelle was dismissed. The French army was falling apart, with mutiny and insubordination everywhere.

The British believed they could succeed where the French had failed. Under General Douglas Haig (1861–1928), the commander in chief of British expeditionary forces on the

■ British machine gunners wearing gas masks at the battle of the Somme in 1916.

Continent, the British launched an attack in Flanders throughout the summer and fall of 1917. Known as the *Passchendaele offensive* for the village and ridge in whose "porridge of mud" much of the fighting took place, the campaign resulted in the slaughter of almost 400,000 British soldiers for insignificant territorial gain. The Allies and the Germans finally recognized that "going over the top" in offensives was not working and could not work. The war must be won by other means.

War on the Periphery

Recognizing the stalemate in the west, the Allies attempted to open up other fronts where the Central Powers might be vulnerable. In the spring of 1915, the Allies were successful in convincing Italy to enter the war on their side by promising that it would receive, at the time of the peace, the South Tyrol, the southern part of Dalmatia, and key Dalmatian islands, which would ensure Italy's dominance over the Adriatic Sea. By thus capitalizing on Italian antagonism toward Austria-Hungary over control of that territory, the Allies gained 875,000 Italian soldiers for their cause. Although the Italian troops were in no way decisive in the fighting that followed, Great Britain, France, and Russia saw the need to build up

Allied support in southern Europe in order to reinforce Serbian attempts to keep Austrian troops beyond its borders. The Allies also hoped that by pulling Germans into the southern front, some relief might be provided for British and French soldiers on the western front.

Germany, in turn, was well aware of the need to expand its alliances beyond Austria-Hungary if it was to compete successfully against superior Allied forces. Trapped as they were to the east and west, the Central Powers established control over a broad corridor stretching from the North Sea through central Europe and down through the Ottoman Empire to the Suez Canal that was so vital to British interests.

In the Balkans, where the war had begun, the Serbs were consistently bested by the Austrians. By late 1915, the Serbs had been knocked out of the war in spite of Allied attempts to assist them. Serbia paid a heavy price in the Great War: it lost one-sixth of its population through war, famine, and disease. The promise of booty persuaded Bulgaria to join Germany and Austria-Hungary. Over the next year and a half, the Allies responded by convincing Romania and then Greece to join them.

War in the Ottoman Empire. The theater of war continued to expand. Although the Ottoman Empire had joined the

■ Paul Nash, *We Are Making a New World* (1918), depicts the destructiveness of war. Nash was one of many artists who used their work to communicate their moral outrage against the war.

DOCUMENT

Turkish Officer Describes Armenian Massacres

war in late 1914 on the side of the Central Powers, its own internal difficulties attenuated its fighting ability. As a multinational empire consisting of Turks, Arabs, Armenians, Greeks, Kurds, and other ethnic minorities, it was plagued by Turkish misrule and Arab nationalism. Hence the Ottoman Empire was the weakest link in the chain of German alliances. Yet it held a crucial position. The Turks could block shipping of vital supplies to Russia through the Mediterranean and Black Seas. Coming to the aid of their Russian ally, a combined British and French fleet attacked Turkish forces at the straits of the Dardanelles in April 1915. In the face of political and military opposition, First Lord of the Admiralty Winston Churchill (1874–1965) supported the idea of opening a new front by sea. Poorly planned and mismanaged, the expedition was a disaster. When the naval effort in the German-mined strait

failed, the British foolishly decided to land troops on the Gallipoli Peninsula, which extended from the southern coast of European Turkey. There British soldiers were trapped on the rocky terrain, unable to advance against the Turks and unable to fall back. Gallipoli was the first large-scale attempt at amphibious warfare. The Australian and New Zealand forces (ANZACs) showed great bravery in some of the most brutal fighting of the war.

Britain sought to protect its interests in the Suez Canal. Turkish troops menaced the canal effectively enough to terrify the British into maintaining an elaborate system of defense in the area and concentrating large troop reinforcements in Egypt. War with the Ottoman Empire also extended battle into the oil fields of Mesopotamia and Persia. The attempt at a new front was initially a fiasco for the British and Russian forces that threatened Baghdad. The

Allies proceeded not only without plans, but also without maps. They literally did not know where they were going. Eventually, British forces recovered and took Baghdad in 1917, while Australian and New Zealand troops captured Jerusalem. The tentacles of war spread out, following the path of Western economic and imperial interests throughout the world.

War at Sea.   Most surprising of all was the indecisive nature of the war at sea. The great battleships of the British and German navies avoided confrontation on the high seas. The only major naval battle of the Great War, the Battle of Jutland in the North Sea, took place in early 1916. Each side inflicted damage on the other but, through careful maneuvering, avoided a decisive outcome to the battle. Probably the enormous cost of replacing battleships deterred both the British and the Germans from risking their fleets in engagements on the high seas. With the demands for munitions and equipment on the two great land fronts of the war, neither side could afford to lose a traditional war at sea. Instead, the British used their seapower as a policing force to blockade German trade and strangle the German economy.

The German navy, much weaker than the British, relied on a new weapon, the submarine, which threatened to become decisive in the war at sea. Submarines were initially used in the first months of the war for reconnaissance. Their potential for inflicting heavy losses on commercial shipping became apparent in 1915. Undergoing technological improvements throughout the war, U-boats (*Unterseebooten*), as

German submarines were called, torpedoed six million tons of Allied shipping in 1917. With cruising ranges as far as 3600 miles, German submarines attacked Allied and neutral shipping as far away as off the shore of the United States and the Arctic supply line to Russia. German insistence on unrestricted use outraged neutral powers, which considered the Germans in violation of international law. The Germans rejected the requirements of warning an enemy ship and boarding it for investigation as too dangerous for submarines, which were no match for battleships above water. The Allies invented depth charges and mines capable of blowing German submarines out of the water. Those weapons, combined with the use of the convoy system in the Atlantic Ocean and the Mediterranean Sea, produced a successful blockade and an antisubmarine campaign that put an end to the German advantage.

ADJUSTING TO THE UNEXPECTED: TOTAL WAR

The war that Europe experienced differed from all previous experiences and expectations of armed conflict. Technological advances, equally matched on both sides, introduced a war of attrition, defensive and prolonged. Nineteenth-century wars that lasted six to eight weeks, were confined to one locale, and were determined by a handful of battles marked by low casualties had nothing in common with the long, dirty,

■ Crew on the deck of a German World War I submarine at sea.

lice-infested reality of trench warfare. Warring European nations faced enemies to the west, to the east, and on the periphery, with no end to the slaughter in sight.

The period from 1914 to 1918 marked the first time in history that the productive activities of entire populations were directed toward a single goal: military victory. The Great War became a war of peoples, not just of armies. Wars throughout history have involved noncombatants caught in the crossfire or standing in the wrong place at the wrong time. But the unexpected war of attrition required civilian populations to adjust to a situation in which what went on at the battlefront transformed life on the home front. For this reason, the Great War became known as history's first **total war.**

Adjusting to the unexpected war of 1914, governments intervened to centralize and control every aspect of economic life. Technology and industrial capacity made possible a war of unimaginable destruction. The scale of production and distribution of war-related materials required for victory was

unprecedented. To persuade civilians to suffer at home for the sake of the war, leaders pictured the enemy as evil villains who had to be defeated at any cost. The sacrifice required for a total war made total victory necessary. And total victory required an economy totally geared to fighting the war.

Mobilizing the Home Front

While soldiers were fighting on the eastern and western fronts, businessmen and politicians at home were creating bureaucracies to control wages and prices, distribute supplies, establish production quotas, and mobilize human and material resources. Just as governments had conscripted the active male population for military service, the Allies and the Central Powers now mobilized civilians of all ages and both sexes to work for the war.

WAR AT HOME

The total character of World War I meant that it changed life for noncombatants as much as it did for those at the front. Women had to fend for themselves, organizing relief societies, working the fields, and manufacturing weapons and war goods. They often took jobs men had held before. In London, taxi driving had been a male monopoly before the war. Articles from 16 March 1917 in the Manchester Guardian *show what could happen when both women and men shared jobs. Conflicts could break out when men felt threatened by women's new positions.*

Focus Questions

Why does this newspaper coverage consider that a strike by taxi-men "could be no more than a vain and selfish protest" against competition from women drivers? Is the question here women's competence or something else?

Women Taxi-Cab Drivers

The taxi-cab drivers of London threaten to try to bring about a strike, which will include motor-'bus drivers and conductors, if the London County Council does not abandon its intention to license women to drive taxi-cabs. To be successful a strike must in the ultimate event be in defense of a principle that commands a measure of public assent. The only principle for which the men stand in this strike is that even where women are fitted to do men's work they should be debarred from it. It is a principle never tenable in justice, and utterly discredited in the popular mind by the war. If the employment of women as motor-drivers meant a decrease in the general level of skill in the trade, a worsening of conditions, or a lowering of wages a real principle would be involved. Stress of war might make the setting aside of it temporarily necessary, but the point would be at least arguable. In this matter such considera-

tions do not arise. Hundreds of women have taken the place of men as motor-drivers for the army and the Red Cross at home and abroad, thousands more are employed in driving commercial motors. They have proved, if proof were needed, that this work is well within their compass. The woman who can take a man's place fully in the harder sort of tasks involved in work on the railways or in agriculture is an exception, and the employment of women for such work is a war-time necessity that may not to any great extent survive when peace comes. But the woman motor-driver has come to stay, and a strike of taxi-men could be no more than a vain and selfish protest against her arrival.

"Down Cabs" Again

The London taxi-drivers are again threatening trouble—this time because the Home Office refuses to give way on the question of licensing women drivers. Sir George Cave told a deputation of the Licensed Vehicle Workers the other day that there is no intention at present of licensing women as tram and 'bus drivers, but that competent women will certainly be licensed for taxi-driving. The men are holding indignation meetings on Sunday, and threaten to bring all the cab, 'bus, and tram drivers of London out on strike—about 20,000 workers, inclusive of garage men.

Women's Roles.   Women played an essential role in the mobilization of the home front. They had never been isolated from the experiences and hardships of war, but they now found new ways to support the war effort. In cities, women went to work in munitions factories and war-related industries that had previously employed only men. Women filled service jobs, from fire fighting to trolley-car conducting—jobs that were essential to the smooth running of industrial society and that had been left vacant by men. On farms, women literally took up the plow after both men and horses had been requisitioned for the war effort.

By 1918, 650,000 French women were working in war-related industries and in clerical positions in the army, and they had counterparts throughout Europe. In Germany, two out of every five munitions workers were women. Women became more prominent in the work force as a whole, as the case of Great Britain makes clear: there the number of women workers jumped from 250,000 at the beginning of the war to five million by the war's end. Women also served in the auxiliary units of the armed services, in the clerical and medical corps, in order to free men for fighting at the front. In eastern European nations, women entered combat as soldiers. Although most women were displaced from their wartime jobs with the return of men after the armistice, they were as important to the war effort as the men fighting at the front.

Government Controls.   In the first months of the war, the private sector had been left to its own devices, with nearly disastrous results. Shortages, especially of shells, and bottlenecks in production threatened military efforts. Governments were forced to establish controls and to set up state monopolies in order to guarantee the supplies necessary to wage war. In Germany, industrialists Walther Rathenau (1867–1922) and Alfred Hugenberg (1865–1951) worked with the government. By the spring of 1915, they had eliminated the German problem of munitions scarcity. France was in trouble six weeks after the outbreak of the war: it had used up half of its accumulated munitions supplies in the First Battle of the Marne. German occupation of France's northern industrial basin further crippled munitions production. Through government intervention, France improvised and relocated its war industries. The British government became involved in production, too, by establishing in 1915 the first Ministry of Munitions under the direction of David Lloyd George (1863–1945). Distinct from the Ministry of War, the Ministry of Munitions was to coordinate military needs with the armaments industry.

In a war that leaders soon realized would be a long one, food supplies assumed paramount importance. Germany, dependent on food imports to feed its people and isolated from the world market by the Allied blockade, introduced rationing five months after the outbreak of the war. Other continental nations followed suit. Government agents set quotas for agricultural producers. Armies were fed and supplied at the expense of domestic populations. Great Britain, which enjoyed a more reliable food supply by virtue of its sea power, did not impose food rationing until 1917.

■ Women played a key role in the munitions industry during the war. In this ca. 1914 photograph of a British munitions factory, workers handle artillery shells.

Three factors put food supplies at risk. First, the need for large numbers of soldiers at the front pulled farmers and peasants off the land. The resultant drop in the agricultural work force meant that land was taken out of production and what remained was less efficiently cultivated, so that productivity declined. A second factor was fear of requisitioning and the general uncertainties of war that caused agricultural producers to hoard supplies. What little was available was traded on black markets. Finally, because all European countries depended to some extent on imports of food and fertilizers, enemies successfully targeted trade routes for attack.

Silencing Dissent

The strains of total war were becoming apparent. Two years of sacrificing, scrimping, and, in some areas, starving began to take their toll among soldiers and civilians on both sides.

With the lack of decisive victories, war weariness was spreading. Work stoppages and strikes, which had virtually ceased with the outbreak of war in 1914, began to climb rapidly in 1916. Between 1915 and 1916 in France, the number of strikes by dissatisfied workers increased by 400 percent. Underpaid and tired workers went on strike, staged demonstrations, and protested exploitation. Labor militancy also intensified in the British Isles and Germany. Women, breadwinners for their families, were often in the forefront of the protests throughout Europe. Social peace between unions and governments was no longer held together by patriotic enthusiasm for war.

Politicians, too, began to rethink their suspension of opposition to government policies as the war dragged on.

Dissidents among European socialist parties regained their prewar commitment to peace. Most socialists had enthusiastically supported the declarations of war in 1914. By 1916, the united front that political opponents had presented against the enemy was crumbling under growing demands for peace.

In a total war, unrest at home guaranteed defeat. Governments knew that all opposition to war policies had to be eliminated. In a dramatic extension of the police powers of the state, whether among the Allies or the Central Powers, criticism of the government became treason. Censorship was enforced and propaganda became more virulent. Those who spoke for peace were no better than the enemy. The governments of every warring nation resorted to harsh measures. Parliamentary bodies were stripped of power, civil liberties were suspended, democratic procedures were ignored. The civilian governments of Premier Georges Clemenceau (1841–1929) in France and Prime Minister Lloyd George in Great Britain resorted to rule by emergency police power to repress criticism. Under Generals von Hindenburg and Ludendorff in Germany, military rule became the order of the day. Nowhere was "government as usual" possible in total war.

Every warring nation sought to promote dissension from within the societies of its enemies. Germany provided some aid for the Easter Rebellion in Ireland in 1916 in the hope that the Irish demand for independence that predated the war would deflect British attention and undermine fighting strength and morale. Germany also supported separatist movements among minority nationalities in the Russian Empire and was responsible for returning the avowed revolutionary V. I. Lenin under escort to Russia in April 1917. The British engaged in similar tactics. The British foreign secretary Arthur Balfour (1848–1930) worked with Zionist leaders in 1917 in drawing up the **Balfour Declaration**, which promised to "look with favor" on the creation of a Jewish homeland in Palestine. The British thereby encouraged Zionist hopes among central European Jews, with the intent of creating difficulties for German and Austrian rulers. Similarly, the British encouraged Arabs to rebel against Turks with the same promise of Palestine. Undermining the loyalties of colonized peoples and minorities would be at minimum a nuisance to the enemy. Beyond that, it could erode war efforts from within.

THE RUSSIAN REVOLUTION AND ALLIED VICTORY

For the Allies, 1917 began with a series of crises. Under the hammering of one costly offensive after another, French morale had collapsed and military discipline was deteriorating. A combined German-Austrian force had eliminated the Allied states of Serbia and Romania. The Italians experienced a military debacle at Caporetto and were effectively out of the war. The peril at sea had increased with the opening of unrestricted U-boat warfare against Allied and neutral ships.

Two events proved decisive in 1917 in determining the course of the war: the collapse of the Russian army and the entry of the United States into the war. Russia, in the throes of domestic revolution, ceased to be an effective opponent, and Germany was able to concentrate more of its resources in the west, fight a one-front war, and utilize the foodstuffs and raw materials of its newly acquired Russian territories to buoy its home front.

The war had gone from a stalemate to a state of crisis for both sides. Every belligerent state was experiencing war weariness that undermined civilian and military morale. Both Austria-Hungary and the Ottoman Empire teetered on the verge of collapse, with internal difficulties increasing as the war dragged on. Germany suffered from labor and supply shortages and economic hardship resulting from the blockade and an economy totally dedicated to waging war. It was at this point of crisis and defeatism that the entry of the United States into the war on the side of the Allies proved decisive.

Revolution in Russia

In order to understand Russia's withdrawal from the war, it is important to understand that Russia's ruler, Tsar Nicholas II (1894–1917), presided over an empire in the process of modernization with widening social divisions in 1914. Nicholas believed that a short, successful war would strengthen his monarchy against the domestic forces of change. Little did Nicholas know, when he committed Russia to the path of war instead of revolution, that he had guaranteed a future of war *and* revolution. He was delivering his nation up to humiliating defeat in global war and a devastating civil war. His own days were numbered, with his fate to be determined at the hands of a Marxist dictatorship.

The Last Tsar. In 1914, Russia was considered backward by the standards of Western industrial society. Russia still recalled a recent feudal past. The serfs had been freed in the 1860s, but the nature of the emancipation exacerbated tensions in the countryside and peasant hunger for land. Russia's limited, rapid industrialization in the 1880s and 1890s was an attempt to catch up with Great Britain, France, and Germany as a world industrial power. But the speed of such change brought with it severe dislocation and worker protests, especially in the industrial city of Moscow and the capital, St. Petersburg.

Unrest among factory workers revived on the eve of the Great War, a period of rapid economic growth and renewed trade union activity. Between January and July 1914, Russia experienced 3500 strikes. The tsar certainly weighed the workers' actions in his decision to view war as a possible diversion from domestic problems.

Russia was least prepared for war of the belligerents. Undoubtedly it had more soldiers than other countries, but it lacked arms and equipment. Problems of provisioning such a huge fighting force placed great strains on the domestic economy and on the work force. Under government coercion to

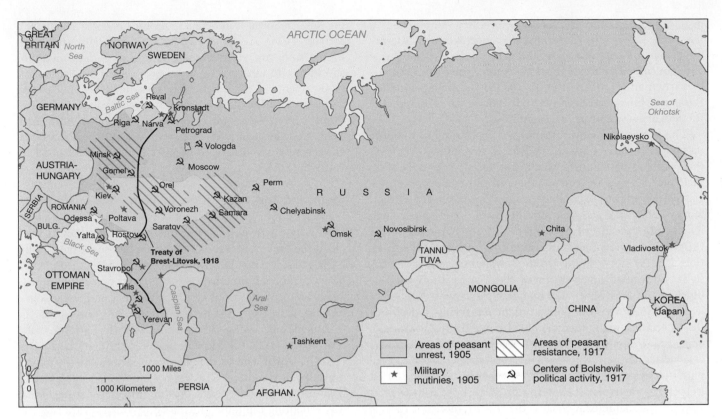

■ Revolution and Civil War in Russia, 1914–1920. Revolutionary and civil unrest was greatest in
those areas of Russia with the greatest concentrations of peasants. Kulaks, the more prosperous
peasants, were severely repressed for resisting the requisitioning of food after 1918.

meet the needs of war, industrial output doubled between 1914 and 1917, while agricultural production plummeted. The tsar, who unwisely insisted on commanding his own troops, left the government in the hands of his wife, the Tsarina Alexandra, a German princess by birth, and her eccentric peasant adviser, Rasputin. Scandal, sexual innuendo, and charges of treason surrounded the royal court. The incompetence of a series of unpopular ministers further eroded confidence in the regime. (See "A Closer Look: The Women Who Started the Russian Revolution," pp. 794–795.)

In the end, the war sharpened long-standing divisions within Russian society. Led by exhausted and starving working women, poorly paid and underfed workers toppled the regime in the bitter winter of March 1917. The event was the beginning of a violent process of revolution and civil war. The tsar abdicated, and all public symbols of the tsardom were destroyed. The banner bearing the Romanov two-headed eagle was torn down, and in its place the red flag of revolution flew over the Winter Palace.

Dual Power.   With the tsar's abdication, two centers of authority replaced autocracy. One was the Provisional Government, appointed by the Duma and made up of progressive liberals led by Prince Georgi Lvov (1861–1925), prime minister of the new government, who also served as

minister of the interior. Aleksandr Kerenski (1881–1970), the only socialist in the Provisional Government, served as minister of justice. The members of the new government hoped to establish constitutional and democratic rule. The other center of authority was the **soviets**—committees or councils elected by workers and soldiers and supported by radical lawyers, journalists, and intellectuals in favor of socialist self-rule. The Petrograd Soviet was the most prominent among the councils. The duality of power was matched by duality in policies and objectives, which guaranteed a short-lived and unstable regime.

Peasants, who made up 80 percent of the Russian population, accepted the revolution and demanded land and peace. Without waiting for government directives, peasants began seizing the land. Peasants tried to alleviate some of their suffering by hoarding what little they had. The food crisis of winter persisted throughout the spring and summer as breadlines lengthened and prices rose. Workers in cities gained better working conditions and higher wages. But wage increases were invariably followed by higher prices that robbed workers of their gains. Real wages declined.

In addition to the problems of land and bread, the war itself presented the new government with other insurmountable difficulties. Hundreds of thousands of Russian soldiers at the front deserted the war, having heard news from home of peasant land grabs and rumors of a new offensive planned for July. The Provisional Government, concerned with Russia's territorial integrity and its position in the international system, continued to honor the tsar's commitments to the Allies by participating in the war. By spring 1917, six to eight million Russian soldiers had been killed, wounded, or captured. The Russian army was incapable of fighting.

The Provisional Government tried everything to convince its people to carry on with the war. In the summer of 1917, the Women's Battalion of Death, composed exclusively of female recruits, was enlisted into the army. Its real purpose, officials admitted, was to "shame the men" into fighting. The all-female unit, like its male counterparts, experienced high losses: 80 percent of the force suffered casualties. The Provisional Government was caught in an impossible situation: it could not withdraw from the war, but neither could it fight. Continued involvement in the lost cause of the war blocked any consideration of social reforms.

While the Provisional Government was trying to deal with the calamities, many members of the intelligentsia—Russia's educated class, who had been exiled by the tsar for their political beliefs—now rushed back from western Europe to take part in the great revolutionary experiment. Theorists of all stripes put their cases before the people. Those who were in favor of gradual reform debated the relative merits of various government policies with those who favored violent revolution. The months between February 1917 and July 1917 were a period of great intellectual ferment. The Marxists, or Social Democrats, had the greatest impact on the direction of the revolution.

The Social Democrats believed that there were objective laws of historical development that could be discovered. Russia's future could be understood only in terms of the present situation in western Europe. Like Marxists in the West, the Russian Social Democrats split over how best to achieve a socialist state. The more moderate Mensheviks (the term means "minority") wanted to work through parliamentary institutions and were willing to cooperate with the Provisional Government. A smaller faction—despite its name—calling themselves **Bolsheviks** (meaning "majority") dedicated themselves to preparation for revolutionary upheaval. After April 1917, the Bolsheviks refused to work with the Provisional Government and organized themselves to take control of the Petrograd Soviet.

Lenin and the Opposition to War.   The leader of the Bolsheviks was Vladimir Ilyich Ulyanov (1870–1924), best known by his revolutionary name, Lenin. Forty-seven years old at the time of the revolution, Lenin had spent most of his life in exile or in prison. More a pragmatist than a theoretician, he argued for a disciplined party of professional revolutionaries, a vanguard that would lead the peasants and workers in a socialist revolution against capitalism. In contrast to the Mensheviks, he argued that the time was ripe for a successful revolution and that it could be achieved through the soviets.

In his **April Theses,** Lenin promised the Russian people peace, land, and bread. The war must be ended immediately, he argued, because it represented an imperialist struggle that was benefiting capitalists. Russia's duty was to withdraw and wait for a world revolution. His years in exile in the West and news of mutinies and worker protests convinced him that revolution was imminent. His revolutionary policies on land were little more than endorsements of the seizures already taking place all over Russia. Even his promises of bread had little substance. But on the whole, the April Theses constituted a clear critique of the policies of the Provisional Government.

Dissatisfaction with the Provisional Government increased as the war dragged hopelessly on and bread lines lengthened.

■ As late as August 1917, the Provisional Government of Aleksandr Kerenski was determined to carry on the war, but the war-weary troops began to quit. In this scene from Galicia, demoralized Russian soldiers throw down their arms and flee after hearing that German cavalry has broken through the lines.

In the midst of the calamities, a massive popular demonstration erupted in July 1917 against the Provisional Government and in favor of the soviets, which excluded the upper classes from voting. The Provisional Government responded with repressive force reminiscent of the tsardom. The July Days were proof of the growing influence of the Bolsheviks among the Russian people. Although the Bolshevik leadership had withdrawn support for the demonstrations at the last moment, Bolshevik rank-and-file party members strongly endorsed the protest. Indisputably, Bolshevik influence was growing in the soviets despite repression and the persecution of its leaders. Lenin himself was forced to flee to Finland.

As a result of the July Days, Kerenski, who had been heading the Ministry of Justice, was named prime minister and continued the Provisional Government's moderate policies. In order to protect the government from a coup on the right, Kerenski permitted the arming of the Red Guards, the workers' militia units of the Petrograd Soviet. The traditional chasm between the upper and lower classes was widening as the policies of the Provisional Government conflicted with the demands of the soviets.

The October Revolution.   The second revolution came in November (October according to the Russian calendar). It was not a spontaneous street demonstration by thousands of working women that triggered the second revolution, but rather the seizure of the Russian capital by the Red Guards of the Petrograd Soviet. The revolution was carefully planned and orchestrated by Lenin and his vanguard of Bolsheviks, who now possessed majorities in the soviets in Moscow and Petrograd and in other industrial centers. Returning surreptitiously from Finland, Lenin moved through the streets of Petrograd disguised in a curly wig and head bandages, watching the Red Guards seize centers of communication and public buildings. The military action was directed by Lev Bronstein, better known by his revolutionary name, Leon Trotsky (1879–1940). The Bolshevik chairman of the Petrograd Soviet, Trotsky used the Red Guards to seize political control and arrest the members of the Provisional Government. Kerenski escaped and fled the city.

The takeover was achieved with almost no bloodshed and was immediately endorsed by the All-Russian Congress of Soviets, which consisted of representatives of local soviets from throughout the nation who were in session amid the takeover of the capital. A Bolshevik regime under Lenin now ruled Russia. Tsar Nicholas II and the royal family were executed by the Bolshevik revolutionaries in July 1918.

The Treaty of Brest-Litovsk.   Lenin immediately set to work to end the Great War for Russia. After months of negotiation, Russia signed a separate peace with the Germans in March 1918 in the **Treaty of Brest-Litovsk.** By every measure, the treaty was a bitter humiliation for the new Soviet regime. The territorial losses sustained were phenomenal. In a vast amputation, Russia was reduced to the size of its Muscovite

CHRONOLOGY
The Russian Revolution

January–July 1914	Protests and strikes
30 July 1914	Russia enters World War I
March 1917	First Russian Revolution; Abdication of Tsar Nicholas II; Creation of Provisional Government
April 1917	Bolsheviks take control of Petrograd
July 1917	Massive demonstration against Provisional Government; Lenin is forced to flee Russia
November 1917	Bolsheviks and Red Guards seize political control in what comes to be known as the October Revolution
March 1918	Russia withdraws from World War I and signs Treaty of Brest-Litovsk
July 1918	Tsar Nicholas II and family are executed

period: it recognized the independence of the Ukraine, Georgia, and Finland; it relinquished its Polish territories, the Baltic States, and part of Byelorussia to Germany and Austria-Hungary; it handed over other territories on the Black Sea to Turkey. Lenin believed that he had no choice: he needed to buy time in order to consolidate the revolution at home, and he hoped for a socialist revolution in Germany that would soften the results of the treaty.

The Treaty of Brest-Litovsk was judged a betrayal, not only outside Russia among the Allied powers, but also inside Russia among some army officers who had sacrificed much for the tsar's war. To those military men, the Bolsheviks were no more than German agents who held the country in their sway.

To deal with the anarchy caused by the fratricidal struggle, Lenin had to strengthen the government's dictatorial elements at the expense of its democratic ones. The new Soviet state used state police to suppress all opposition. The dictatorship of the proletariat yielded to the dictatorship of the repressive forces.

In the course of the civil war, Lenin was no more successful than Kerenski and the Provisional Government had been in solving the problems of food supplies. Human costs of the civil war were high, with more than 800,000 soldiers dead on both sides and two million civilian deaths from dysentery and diseases caused by poor nutrition. Industrial production ceased, and people fled towns to return to the countryside.

THE WOMEN WHO STARTED THE RUSSIAN REVOLUTION

Women in Russia, like their counterparts throughout Europe in 1914, took over new jobs in the workplace as men marched off to war. Four of every ten Russian workers were women, up from three of ten on the eve of the war. The situation was more dramatic in Petrograd, Russia's capital and principal industrial center, where by 1917 women constituted 55 percent of the labor force. Russian working women faced greater hardships than their sisters in the West. Most women workers in Petrograd held unskilled, poorly paid jobs in the textile industries and worked grueling 12- and 13-hour days. They left work only to stand for hours in long bread lines and then returned home to care for their elderly relatives and often sick children. Infant mortality was alarmingly high, with as many as half of all children dying before the age of three. Factory owners reported that nothing could be done. "The worker mother drudges and knows only need, only worry and grief," one commentator observed. "Her life passes in gloom, without light."

A CLOSER LOOK

Russia was suffering badly in the war, with more than two million soldiers killed by the beginning of 1917. News of disasters at the front reached mothers, wives, and sisters at home in spite of the government's efforts to hide the defeats. In the less than three years since the war had begun, prices had increased 400 percent and transport lines for food and coal had broken down. Bread was the main staple of meager diets. Supplies of flour and grain were not reaching towns and cities. People were starving and freezing to death. Young children were now working 11½ hour days in the factories. The situation was dire, and working women knew that something must be done if their families were to survive.

The working women of Petrograd correctly understood that the intolerable state of affairs had come about because the government was unable to control distribution and to ration limited supplies. Carrying a double burden of supporting those at home unable to work and of producing in the factory the armaments essential for the war effort, women workers began demanding that labor organizations take action to alleviate the situation. In the winter of 1916–1917, labor leaders advised exhausted and starving workers to be cautious and patient: workers must wait to strike until the time was ripe. Women workers did not agree. On 8 March 1917 (23 February by the Russian calendar), more than 7000 women went on strike in acknowledgment of International Women's Day, an event initiated in the United States in 1909 to recognize the rights of working women. The striking women were angry, frustrated, hungry, and tired of watching their families starve while their husbands, brothers, and sons were away at the battlefront. One week earlier, the city had been placed on severe rationing because Petrograd was down to its last few days' supply of flour. Although the principal concern of the striking women was bread, their protest was more than just a food riot. Women left their posts in the textile mills to demand an end to the war and an end to the reign of Tsar Nicholas II. They were responding not to revolutionary propaganda but to the politics of hunger. Singing songs of protest, they marched through the streets to take their cause to the better-paid and more radical male metalworkers. Women appealed to working men to join the strike. By the end of the day, 100,000 workers had left their jobs to join demonstrations against the government.

The women did not stop there. They took justice into their own hands and looted bakeries and grocery shops in search of food. In the street demonstrations of the next several days, women and men marched by the thousands, attracting growing support from workers throughout the city and the suburbs. Forty demonstrators were killed when government troops fired into a crowd. Still the women were not deterred. Bolshevik leader Leon Trotsky recalled women's bravery in going up to detachments of soldiers: "More boldly than men, they take hold of the rifles and beseech, almost command: 'Put down your bayonets—join us!'" Stories abound of how poor working women persuaded officers and soldiers of the Cossacks—the tsar's privileged fighting force—to lay down

■ Women workers on strike march through Petrograd, Russia, in 1917.

their arms. It was rumored that soldiers abandoned the tsar because they would not fire on the crowds of women. A participant in one confrontation reported that women workers stood without flinching as a detachment of Cossacks bore down upon them. Someone in the crowd shouted out that the women were the wives and sisters of soldiers at the front. The Cossacks lowered their rifles and turned their horses around. Troops like those, tired of the war, mutinied all over Petrograd. Within four days of the first action taken by women textile operatives, the government had lost the support of Petrograd workers, women and men, and its soldiers, who had joined the demonstrators. The tsar was forced to abdicate. From that point on, the Romanov monarchy and the Russian war effort were doomed.

In those first days of protest, the women of Petrograd took action into their own hands, pouring into the streets to call for bread, peace, and the end of tsardom. They rejected autocracy and war in defense of their communities and their families. The Russian Revolution had begun.

The United States Enters the Great War

The Allies longed for the entry of the United States into the war. Although the United States was a neutral country, from the beginning of the war it had been an important supplier to the Allies. U.S. trade with the Allies had jumped from $825 million in 1914 to $3.2 billion in 1916. American bankers also made loans and extended credit to the Allies to the amount of $2.2 billion. The United States had made a sizable investment in the Allied war effort, and its economy was prospering.

Beginning with the sinking of the *Lusitania* in 1915, German policy on the high seas had incensed the American public. Increased U-boat activity in 1916 led U.S. President Woodrow Wilson (1856–1924) to issue a severe warning to the Germans to cease submarine warfare. The Germans, however, were driven to desperate measures. The great advantage of submarines was in sneak attacks—a procedure against international rules, which required warning. Germany initiated a new phase of unrestricted submarine warfare on 1 February 1917, when the German ambassador informed the U.S. government that U-boats would sink on sight all ships, including passenger ships—even those neutral and unarmed.

The United States Declares War.   German machinations in Mexico were also revealed on 25 February 1917, with the interception of a telegram from Arthur Zimmermann (1864–1940), the German foreign minister. The telegram, known as the **"Zimmerman Note,"** communicated Germany's willingness to support Mexico's recovery of "lost territory" in New Mexico, Arizona, and Texas in return for Mexican support of Germany in the event of U.S. entry into the war. U.S. citizens were outraged. On 2 April 1917, Wilson, who had won the presidential election of 1916 on the promise of peace, asked the U.S. Congress for a declaration of war against Germany.

The entry of the United States was the turning point in the war, tipping the scales dramatically in favor of the Allies. The United States contributed its naval power to the large Allied convoys formed to protect shipping against German attacks. In a total war, control and shipment of resources had become crucial issues, and it was in those areas that the U.S. entry gave the Allies indisputable superiority. The United States was also able to send "over there" tens of thousands of conscripts fighting with the American Expeditionary Forces under the leadership of General John "Black Jack" Pershing (1860–1948). They reinforced British and French troops and gave a vital boost to morale.

However, for such a rich nation, the help that the United States was able to give at first was very little. The U.S. government was new to the business of coordinating a war effort, but it displayed great ingenuity in creating a wartime bureaucracy that increased a small military establishment of 210,000 soldiers to 9.5 million young men registered before the beginning of summer 1917. By July 1918, the Americans were sending a phenomenal 300,000 soldiers a month to Europe. By the end of the war, 2 million Americans had traveled to Europe to fight in the war.

The U.S. entry is significant not just because it provided reinforcements, fresh troops, and fresh supplies to the beleaguered Allies. From a broader perspective, it marked a shift in the nature of international politics: Europe was no longer able to handle its own affairs and settle its own differences without outside help.

U.S. troops, though numerous, were not well trained, and they relied on France and Great Britain for their arms and equipment. But the Germans correctly understood that they could not hold out indefinitely against the superior Allied force. Austria-Hungary was effectively out of the war. Germany had no replacements for its fallen soldiers, but it was able to transfer troops from Russia, Romania, and Macedonia to the west. It realized that its only chance of victory lay in swift action. The German high command decided on a bold measure: one great, final offensive that would knock the combined forces of Great Britain, France, and the United States out of the war once and for all by striking at a weak point and smashing through enemy lines. The great surprise was that it almost worked.

German Defeat.   Known as the **Ludendorff offensive,** after the general who devised it, the final German push began in March 1918, almost a year after U.S. entry into the war.

CHRONOLOGY

Fighting the Great War

1905	Development of the Schlieffen Plan
28 June 1914	Assassination of Archduke Franz Ferdinand and his wife, Sophie
28 July 1914	Austria-Hungary declares war on Serbia
30 July– 4 August 1914	Russia, France, Britain, and Germany declare war in accordance with system of alliances
August 1914	Germany invades Belgium
6–10 September 1914	First Battle of the Marne
1915	Germany introduces chlorine gas
April 1915–January 1916	Gallipoli Campaign
May 1915	Sinking of the *Lusitania*
February–December 1916	Battle at Verdun
1917	First use of mustard gas
2 April 1917	United States enters war
March 1918	Russia withdraws; Ludendorff offensive
11 November 1918	Armistice

■ British soldiers, blinded by gas in Germany's final offensive in the spring of 1918, lead each other toward a medical aid station.

Secretly amassing tired troops from the eastern front pulled back after the Russian withdrawal, the Germans counted on the element of surprise to enable them to break through a weak sector in the west. On the first day of spring, Ludendorff struck. The larger German force gained initial success against weakened British and French forces. Yet in spite of breaches in its defense, the Allied line held. Allied Supreme Commander General Ferdinand Foch (1851–1929) coordinated the war effort that withstood German offensives throughout the spring and early summer of 1918.

The final drive began in mid-July. More than one million German soldiers had already been killed, wounded, or captured in the months between March and July. German prisoners of war gave the French details of Ludendorff's plan. The Germans, now exposed and vulnerable, were placed on the defensive. On the other side, tanks, plentiful munitions, and U.S. reinforcements fueled an Allied offensive that advanced steadily throughout the summer of 1918. The German army retreated, destroying property and equipment as it went. With weak political leadership and indecision in Berlin, the Germans held on until early November, when their efforts

collapsed. On 11 November 1918, an armistice signed by representatives of the German and Allied forces took effect.

Thus came to an end a war of slightly more than four years in duration that had consumed the soldiers, material, and productive resources of the European nations on both sides. Nothing matched the destructiveness of the Great War. Of the 70 million who were mobilized, about one in eight were killed. Battlefields of scorched earth and mud-filled ditches, silent at last, scarred once-fertile countrysides as grim memorials to history's first total war. Home fronts, too, served as battlefields, with those who demanded peace silenced as traitors. The war to end all wars was over; the task of settling the peace now loomed.

SETTLING THE PEACE

In the aftermath of war, the task of the victors was to define the terms of a settlement that would guarantee peace and stabilize Europe. Russia was the ghost at the conference table, excluded from the negotiations because of its withdrawal from the Allied

The representatives of the victorious Allies at Versailles: (left to right) David Lloyd George of Great Britain, Vittorio Orlando of Italy, Georges Clemenceau of France, and Woodrow Wilson of the United States.

camp in 1917 and its separate peace with Germany in March 1918. The Bolsheviks were dealing with problems of their own following the revolution, including a great civil war that lasted through 1920. Much of what happened in the peace settlements reflected the unspoken concern with the challenge of revolution that the new Soviet Russia represented. A variety of goals marked the peace talks: the idealistic desire to create a better world, the patriotic pursuit of self-defense, a commitment to the self-determination of nations, and the desire to fix blame for the outbreak of the war. In the end, the peace treaties satisfied none of those goals. Meanwhile, Russia's new leaders carefully watched events in the West, looking for opportunities that might permit them to extend their revolution to central Europe.

From January to June 1919, an assembly of nations convened in Paris to draw up the new European peace. Although the primary task of settling the peace fell to the Council of Four—Premier Georges Clemenceau of France, Prime Minister David Lloyd George of Great Britain, Prime Minister Vittorio Emanuele Orlando of Italy, and President Woodrow Wilson of the United States—small states, newly formed states, and non-European states, Japan in particular, joined in the task of forging the peace. The states of Germany, Austria-Hungary, and Soviet Russia were excluded from the negotiating tables where the future of Europe was to be determined.

Wilson's Fourteen Points

President Wilson, who captured international attention with his liberal views on the peace, was the central figure of the conference. He was firmly committed to the task of shaping a better world: before the end of the war he had proclaimed the **Fourteen Points** as a guideline to the future peace and as an appeal to the people of Europe to support his policies. Believing that secret diplomacy and the alliance system were responsible for the events leading up to the declaration of war in 1914, he put forward as a basic principle "open covenants of peace, openly arrived at." Other points included the reduction of armaments, freedom of commerce and trade, self-determination of peoples, and a general association of nations to guarantee the peace that became the League of Nations. The Fourteen Points were, above all, an idealistic statement of the principles for a good and lasting peace. Point 14, which stipulated "mutual guarantees of independence and territorial integrity" through the establishment of the League of Nations, was endorsed by the peace conference. The League, which the United States refused to join despite Wilson's advocacy, was intended to arbitrate all future disputes among states and to keep the peace.

Georges Clemenceau of France represented a different approach to the challenge of the peace, one motivated primarily by a concern for his nation's security. France had suffered the greatest losses of the war in both human lives and property destroyed. In order to prevent a resurgent Germany, Clemenceau supported a variety of measures to cripple it as a military force on the Continent. Germany was disarmed. The territory west of the Rhine River was demilitarized, with occupation by Allied troops to last for a period of 15 years. With Russia unavailable as a partner to contain Germany, France supported the creation of a series of states in eastern Europe carved out of former Russian, Austrian, and German territory.

Wilson supported the new states out of a concern for the self-determination of peoples. Clemenceau's main concern was self-defense.

Much time and energy were devoted to redrawing the map of Europe. New states were created out of the lands of three failed empires. To allow self-determination, Finland, Latvia, Estonia, Lithuania, Poland, Czechoslovakia, Austria, Hungary, and Yugoslavia were all granted status as nation-states. However, the rights of ethnic and cultural minorities were violated in some cases because of the impossibility of redrawing the map of Europe strictly according to the principle of self-determination. In spite of good intentions, every new nation had its own national minority, a situation that held the promise of future trouble.

Treaties and Territories

The peace conference produced separate treaties with each of the defeated nations: Austria, Hungary, Turkey, Bulgaria, and Germany. The Austria settlement acknowledged the fundamental disintegration of the Austrian Empire, recognizing an independent Czechoslovakian republic and preparing the way for a fusing of Croatia, Dalmatia, Bosnia and Herzegovina with the Kingdom of Serbia, into the nation of Yugoslavia. Hungary and Poland also emerged as independent nations thanks to territorial losses by Germany and Austria-Hungary. Bulgaria lost territory on the Aegean Sea to Greece, and Yugoslavia assumed control of Bulgarian holdings in Macedonia. Romania gained Hungarian and Bulgarian territory.

In the Middle East, a separate treaty acknowledged Great Britain's mandate in Palestine, Mesopotamia, and Transjordan; and France's mandate in Syria. Hejaz emerged as an independent state. Many aspects of the post-war settlement affecting Turkey and the Middle East were renegotiated in the early 1920s, but British and French gains were preserved, and Hejaz remained as an independent state.

In November 1917 the British issued the Balfour Declaration, to affirm their support for a national home for the Jewish people (see p. 790). This declaration, however, was considered as a violation of promises made to the Arabs during the war that they would be given control of Palestine in return for supporting the Allied war effort. Although Arab rulers were given control of British mandates, and Prince Faisal assumed the title of king of Iraq, Arab resentment festered as increased numbers of European Jews moved into Palestine and Arab hopes for the creation of an Arab kingdom were dashed.

Amid these other treaty negotiations, the treaty signed with Germany on 28 June 1919, known as the **Treaty of Versailles,** dealt exclusively with defeated Germany.

The principle of punitive reparations was included in the German settlement. Germany learned it had to make a down

■ Europe After World War I. The need for security on the continent led France to support a buffer zone of new nations between Russia and Germany, carved out of the former Austrian Empire. German territory along the French border was demilitarized out of the same concern for protection.

THE TREATY OF VERSAILLES

*Of the various treaties negotiating the peace at the end of World War I, the Treaty of Versailles, signed in 1919, was the most important. This treaty dealt with Germany as a defeated nation and was signed in the great Versailles palace outside of Paris in the same location where in 1871 Germany as victor signed a treaty with its defeated enemy, France, at the close of the short Franco-Prussian War (see pp. 694). In the 1919 treaty, the Allies, represented by President Woodrow Wilson of the United States, Prime Minister David Lloyd George of Great Britain, Prime Minister Georges Clemenceau of France, and Prime Minister Vittorio Orlando of Italy, imposed sole blame for the war on Germany and its expansionist aims. According to the treaty, the war was Germany's fault, and Germany must pay reparations for all the destruction of Allied property by its military. Germany lost territories and suffered a greatly reduced military capability. Especially burdensome was article 231 of the treaty, which came to be known as the **War Guilt Clause,** which spelled out Germany's responsibility and the basis for the need to make restitution.*

Focus Questions

In article 42, for whose benefit were the left and right banks of the Rhine demilitarized? How many different forms of reparation can you identify in the articles cited here? For whose benefit was the German navy scaled back? Examine carefully article 231—the War Guilt Clause. What is your judgment of its validity in light of what you know about the causes of the war?

Part III. Political Clauses for Europe

Article 42. Germany is forbidden to maintain or construct any fortifications either on the left bank of the Rhine or on the right bank to the west of a line drawn 50 kilometers to the east of the Rhine. . . .

Article 45. As compensation for the destruction of the coal-mines in the north of France and as part payment towards the total reparation due from Germany for the damage resulting from the war, Germany cedes to France in full and absolute possession, with exclusive rights of exploitation, unencumbered and free from all debts and charges of any kind, the coal-mines situated in the Saar Basin. . . .

The High Contracting Parties, recognizing the moral obligation to redress the wrong done by Germany in 1871 both to the rights of France and to the wishes of the population of Alsace and Lorraine, which were separated from their country in spite of the solemn protest of their representatives at the Assembly of Bordeaux.[1]

Agree upon the following Articles:

Article 51. The territories which were ceded to Germany in accordance with the Preliminaries of Peace signed at Versailles on February 26, 1871, and the Treaty of Frankfurt of May 10, 1871, are restored to French sovereignty as from the date of the Armistice of November 11, 1918.

The provisions of the Treaties establishing the delimitation of the frontiers before 1871 shall be restored. . . .

Article 87. Germany, in conformity with the action already taken by the Allied and Associated Powers, recognizes the complete independence of Poland. . . .

[1] The recovery of Alsace and Lorraine had been a major goal of the French ever since the two provinces had been lost after the Franco-Prussian War (1870–1871).

Article 89. Poland undertakes to accord freedom of transit to persons, goods, vessels, carriages, wagons, and mails in transit between East Prussia and the rest of Germany over Polish territory, including territorial waters, and to treat them at least as favorably as the persons, goods, vessels, carriages, wagons, and mails respectively of Polish or of any other more favored nationality, origin, importation, starting-point, or ownership as regards facilities, restrictions and all other matters.[2] . . .

Part IV. German Rights and Interests Outside Germany

Article 119. Germany renounces in favor of the Principal Allied and Associated Powers all her rights and titles over her overseas possessions. (This renunciation includes Germany's concessions in China.) . . .

Part V. Military, Naval, and Air Claims

Article 159. The German military forces shall be demobilized and reduced as prescribed hereinafter.

Article 160. (1) By a date which must not be later than March 31, 1920, the German Army must not comprise more than seven divisions of infantry and three divisions of cavalry.

After that date the total number of effectives in the Army of the States constituting Germany must not exceed one hundred thousand men, including officers and establishments of depots. The Army shall be devoted exclusively to the maintenance of order within the territory and to the control of the frontiers.

The total effective strength of officers, including the personnel of staffs, whatever their composition, must not exceed four thousand. . . .

(3) The German General Staff and all similar organizations shall be dissolved and may not be reconstituted in any form. . . .

Article 180. All fortified works, fortresses, and field works situated in German territory to the west of a line drawn fifty kilometers to the east of the Rhine shall be disarmed and dismantled. . . .

[2] The establishment of an independent Poland separated the German province of East Prussia from the rest of the nation.

Article 181. After the expiration of a period of two months from the coming into force of the present Treaty the German naval forces in commission must not exceed: 6 battleships of the *Deutschland* or *Lothringen* type, 6 light cruisers, 12 destroyers, 12 torpedo boats, or an equal number of ships constructed to replace them as provided in Article 190.

No submarines are to be included.

All other warships, except where there is provision to the contrary in the present Treaty, must be placed in reserve or devoted to commercial purposes. . . .

Article 198. The armed forces of Germany must not include any military or naval air forces. . . .

Part VIII. Reparation

Article 231. The Allied and Associated Governments affirm and Germany accepts the responsibility of Germany and her allies for causing all the loss and damage to which the Allied and Associated Governments and their nationals have been subjected as a consequence of the war imposed upon them by the aggression of Germany and her allies.

Article 232. The Allied and Associated Governments recognize that the resources of Germany are not adequate, after taking into account permanent diminutions of such resources which will result from other provisions of the present Treaty, to make complete reparation for all such loss and damage.

The Allied and Associated Governments, however, require, and Germany undertakes, that she will make compensation for all damage done to the civilian population of the Allied and Associated Powers and to their property during the period of the belligerency of each as an Allied or Associated Power against Germany by such aggression by land, by sea and from the air, and in general all damages as defined in Annex I hereto. . . .

Article 233. The amount of the above damage for which compensation is to be made by Germany shall be determined by an Inter-Allied Commission, to be called the *Reparation Commission* and constituted in the form and with the powers set forth hereunder and in Annexes II to VII inclusive hereto.

This Commission shall consider the claims and give to the German Government a just opportunity to be heard.

The findings of the Commission as to the amount of damage defined as above shall be concluded and notified to the German Government on or before May 1, 1921, as representing the extent of that Government's obligations.[3]

[3] The total demand on Germany was placed at $32 billion.

---

payment of $5 billion against a future bill of $32 billion; had to hand over a significant proportion of their merchant ships, including all vessels of more than 1600 tons; had to lose all German colonies; and had to deliver coal to neighboring countries. In addition, Germany lost the territory gained from Russia in 1918; returned Alsace and Lorraine to France; ceded territory to Belgium and eventually to Lithuania; and gave up parts of Prussia with large Polish populations. Furthermore, Germany lost control of the Saar, a coal-producing region, to France for fifteen years; and the German Baltic port of Danzig was declared an international "free city." By stripping Germany of key resources, territory, and population, its ability to pay reparations was also weakened. These harsh clauses dictated by the determination of German war guilt, more than any other aspect of the peace settlement, came to haunt the Allies in the succeeding decades.

In the end, no nation obtained what it wanted from the peace settlement. The defeated nations believed that they had been badly abused. The victorious nations were aware of the compromises they had reluctantly accepted. Cooperation among nations was essential if the treaty was to work successfully. It had taken the combined resources, not only of France and the British Empire but also of Russia with its vast population and the United States with its great industrial and financial might, to defeat the power of Germany and the militarily ineffective Austro-Hungarian Empire. A new and stable balance of power depended on the participation of Russia, the United States, and the British Empire. But Russia was excluded from and hostile to the peace settlement, the United States was uncommitted to it, and the British Empire declined to guarantee it. All three Great Powers backed off from their European responsibilities at the end of the war. By 1920, all aspects of the treaty, but especially the reparations clause, had been questioned and criticized by the very governments that had written and accepted them. The search for a lasting peace had just begun.

CONCLUSION

By every measure, the Great War was disastrously expensive. Some European nations suffered more than others, but all endured significant losses of life, property, and productive capacity. The cost in human lives was enormous. In western Europe, 8.5 million were dead; total casualties amounted to 37.5 million. France lost 20 percent of its men between the ages of 20 and 44, Germany lost 15 percent, and Great Britain 10 percent. The war also resulted in huge losses in productive capacity. National economies buckled under the weight of foreign debts, and governments resorted to a variety of methods to bail themselves out, including taxes, loans, and currency inflation. The people of Europe continued to pay for the war long after the fighting had ended.

■ A German cartoon by Lindloff depicts German reaction to the terms of the Treaty of Versailles and to the Allies' brand of justice. Greed, revenge, and other devils gloat over the settlement.

The big winner in the war was the United States, now a creditor nation owed billions of dollars in loans from the Allies and operating in new markets established during the war. The shift was not a temporary move but a structural change. The United States now took its place as a great power in the international system. The world that had existed before 1914 was gone, and what was to replace it was still very much in flux. To the east, Russia was engaged in the vast experiment of building a new society. In the west, the absence of war was not peace.

QUESTIONS FOR REVIEW

1. Why did so many in Europe look forward to war by the summer of 1914, and what had they done to bring it about?
2. How and why did the Great War differ so much from the expectations of both the generals and the majority of Europeans?
3. What is total war, and what made World War I the first such war in history?

4. How was peace achieved, and what were the terms of that peace?
5. In what ways did the Great War contribute to revolution in Russia?

KEY TERMS

Allies, *p. 778*

April Theses, *p. 792*

Balfour Declaration, *p. 792*

Bolsheviks, *p. 792*

Central Powers, *p. 778*

Fourteen Points, *p. 798*

Ludendorff offensive, *p. 796*

Schlieffen Plan, *p. 776*

soviets, *p. 791*

total war, *p. 788*

Treaty of Brest-Litovsk, *p. 793*

Treaty of Versailles, *p. 799*

War Guilt Clause, *p. 800*

Zimmerman Note, *p. 796*

DISCOVERING WESTERN CIVILIZATION ONLINE

You can obtain more information about war and revolution between 1914 and 1920 at the Websites listed below. See also the Companion Website that accompanies this text, www.ablongman.com/kishlansky, which contains an online study guide and additional resources.

The War Europe Expected

Photos and Posters of the Great War
www.geocities.com/SoHo/Gallery/8054
These are sites of posters, photos, and art of World War I.

A New Kind of Warfare

Military History: World War I (1914–1918)
wps.cfc.dnd.ca/links/milhist/wwi.html
Sponsored by Canadian Forces College, this site provides an extensive set of links about World War I with emphasis on military history.

Adjusting to the Unexpected: Total War

World War I: Trenches on the Web
www.worldwar1.com/
This site on World War I is sponsored by the History Channel.

The Great War (1914–1918)
www.pitt.edu/~pugachev/greatwar/ww1.html
A comprehensive site containing primary text, summaries, and photos of the major events in World War I.

The War Poems & Manuscripts of Wilfred Owen
www.hcu.ox.ac.uk/jtap/warpoems.htm
This site contains 57 of Wilfred Owens's war poems.

The Russian Revolution and Allied Victory

Russian Revolution Resources

www.historyguide.org/europe/rusrev_links.html
This site provides electronic texts in English of Lenin and Trotsky and several other links to sites on the Russian Revolution.

Settling the Peace

The Versailles Treaty

history.acusd.edu/gen/text/versaillestreaty/vercontents.html
This site is devoted to the Versailles Treaty, including the text of all articles of the treaty.

SUGGESTIONS FOR FURTHER READING

The War Europe Expected

Keith Robbins, *The First World War* (Oxford: Oxford University Press, 1984). The author explores the major cultural, political, military, and social developments between 1914 and 1918, including the course of the land war and modes of warfare.

Jeffrey Verhey, *The Spirit of 1914: Militarism, Myth, and Mobilization in Germany* (Cambridge: Cambridge University Press, 2000). The author captures the fervor and patriotism that surrounded the August experiences and the declaration of war and chronicles the survival of the memory of the "spirit of 1914" in the postwar period.

A New Kind of Warfare

Roger Chickering, *Imperial Germany and the Great War, 1914–1918* (Cambridge: Cambridge University Press, 1998). The author offers a synthetic treatment of the history of the war and its impact on German society.

Frans Coetzee and Marilyn Shevin-Coetzee, eds., *Authority, Identity and the Social History of the Great War* (Providence: Berghahn Books, 1995). Recognizing that 1914 marks the beginning of the twentieth century, contributors examine the variety of national responses involved in waging total war and stress the interrelatedness of the home fronts and the battlefronts in affecting individual lives and identities.

Mark Cornwall, *The Undermining of Austria-Hungary: The Battle for Hearts and Minds* (New York: St. Martin's Press, 2000). This study presents extensive research on how propaganda was used by and against Austria-Hungary as a weapon of war.

Paul Fussell, *The Great War and Modern Memory* (New York: Oxford University Press, 2000). This twenty-fifth anniversary edition is a cultural history of World War I that treats the patterns and tendencies in war literature within the framework of a literary tradition.

James Joll and Gordon Martel, *The Origins of the First World War* (New York: Longman, 2007). This up-to-date edition of a classic work deals with the complexity of the causes of the war and the ongoing historiographical debate.

John Keegan, *The First World War* (New York: Vintage, 2000). Keegan offers the definitive military history of the war based on diaries, letters, and reports, and in so doing illuminates the origins and progress of the war and the experience of the combatants.

Hew Strachan, ed., *The Oxford Illustrated History of the First World War* (Oxford: Oxford University Press, 1998). This extensively illustrated volume contains 23 chapters on key themes in the history of the Great War covering military issues, the home front, and the role of propaganda.

Adjusting to the Unexpected: Total War

Roger Chickering and Stig Förster, eds., *Great War, Total War: Combat and Mobilization on the Western Front, 1914–1918* (Cambridge: Cambridge University Press, 2000). In a collection of specialist essays, the authors consider the nineteenth-century origins of total industrialized warfare in search of a consensus on what constitutes total war.

Belinda J. Davis, *Home Fires Burning: Food, Politics, and Everyday Life in World War I Berlin* (Chapel Hill: University of North Carolina Press, 2000). This thorough study examines the actions of women, especially poorer women, in Berlin during the war and the impact they had on politics and policy.

Patrick Fridenson, ed., *The French Home Front, 1914–1918* (Providence: Berg Publishers, 1992). The collection of articles demonstrates that unity on the home front concealed deep divisions, which led to open resistance and a redefined political universe at the end of the war.

Susan R. Grayzel, *Women and the First World War* (New York: Longman, 2002). A cultural history of women's roles in World War I on the European home fronts and in Asia, Africa, Australia, and New Zealand.

Aviel Roshwald and Richard Stites, eds., *European Culture in the Great War: The Arts, Entertainment, and Propaganda, 1914–1918* (Cambridge: Cambridge University Press, 1999). This volume encompasses Europe to include western and eastern Europe and the South Slavic lands and examines the relationship between culture and politics during the war.

Jay Winter, Geoffrey Parker, and Mary Habeck, eds., *The Great War and the Twentieth Century* (New Haven, CT: Yale University Press, 2000). This volume of essays by leading scholars contributes to a comparative history of total war in the twentieth century.

The Russian Revolution and Allied Victory

Jane Burbank, *Intelligentsia and Revolution: Russian Views of Bolshevism, 1917–1922* (New York: Oxford University Press,

1982). The author examines Russian intellectuals from the beginnings of revolution to the consolidation of Bolshevik power.

Sheila Fitzpatrick, *The Russian Revolution, 1917–1932* (Oxford: Oxford University Press, 1982). An analysis of the October Revolution of 1917 from the perspective of Stalinist society. The February and October revolutions of 1917, the civil war, and the economic policies of the 1920s are treated as various aspects of a single revolutionary movement.

Jane McDermid and Anna Hillyar, *Midwives of the Revolution: Female Bolsheviks and Women Workers in 1917* (Athens, OH: Ohio University Press, 1999). This work provides a good overview of the importance of women's actions in the Russian Revolution.

Settling the Peace

Manfred E. Boemeke, Gerald D. Feldman, Elisabeth Glaser, eds., *The Treaty of Versailles: A Reassessment After 75 Years* (Cambridge: Cambridge University Press, 1998). The volume is a synthetic reappraisal of the peace treaty, divergent peace aims, and postwar context in which it was developed.

David Stevenson, *The First World War and International Politics* (Oxford: Oxford University Press, 1988). A study of the global ramifications of World War I, this work traces the development of war aims on both sides, the reasons peace negotiations failed, and why compromise proved elusive.

For a list of additional titles related to this chapter's topics, please see http://www.ablongman.com/kishlansky.

THE EUROPEAN SEARCH FOR STABILITY, 1920–1939

THE HARD LESSONS OF INFLATION

For many who survived the horrors of the Great War, worse disruptions were in store. Inflation, like combat, wreaked havoc with people's lives. During the war, prices had doubled in Great Britain, the United States, Germany, Canada, and Japan. Prices had tripled in France and Sweden; in Italy, they had quadrupled. But all of that was nothing compared to what happened after the war in Germany, Austria, Hungary, Poland, and Russia. Inflation was so great, with prices increasing astronomically—by tens of thousands of times as much—

THE VISUAL RECORD

that a new term had to be created for the runaway inflation: *hyperinflation*. As prices reached staggering heights, currencies collapsed. In Germany in 1918, one prewar gold mark was worth two paper marks; by 1923, it took one billion paper marks to match a single gold mark in value. The currency was worthless. German people's hopes and futures disappeared into the abyss of the nine zeroes it took to write a numerical billion.

In war it is important to identify the enemy. So too in hyperinflation did people seek out the adversary. The German expressionist artist George Grosz (1893–1959) was renowned for portraying the decadence and corruption of bourgeois society in the 1920s. In the painting shown on the facing page entitled *The Pillars of Society*, Grosz caricatured postwar Germany as composed of corrupt judges, greedy businessmen, mercenary militarists, and hypocritical pacifists.

Many believed that the postwar republican government of Germany was to blame because it had accepted a harsh peace treaty and made reparations payments. Socialists and Communists were singled out for special disdain. Jewish politicians, bankers, and financiers became scapegoats for Germany's economic problems. Confidence in the state evaporated. The German people learned that the economy was neither stable nor self-correcting. They learned in the harshest way possible that the economy responded to political choices and international events. Social groups accused one another. Small businessmen blamed big capitalists. Civil servants saw unionized workers as the problem. Retailers blamed wholesalers.

■ German children with stacks of inflated currency, virtually worthless in 1923.

Men and women who spend money on food, clothing, and shelter do not have to be schooled in basic facts about money; they learn on a daily basis how the prices of coffee, orange juice, or gasoline fluctuate in relation to factors far beyond their control. But no amount of sophistication in the marketplace could have prepared people for the harsh realities of the German economy in the 1920s.

Inflation began in Germany during the war. It was caused by the government's decision to print money rather than levying taxes to pay off war debts. After the war, inflation continued because big business in need of new capital and organized labor in search of jobs benefited from it. The inflation was further aggravated by depreciation of the currencies in central and eastern European countries. Depreciation was prompted by the hollow hope that by making currencies worth less, exports would be more attractive and would earn the foreign exchange so necessary for prosperity. The Allied demands for reparations payments further undermined confidence in the German mark. The result was that double-digit inflation turned into hyperinflation in the spring of 1922. When the French army occupied the Ruhr and the German government printed money to subsidize the miners and trainmen who were conducting passive resistance, inflation became astronomical.

More and more paper money came into circulation without any corresponding increase in the amount of goods and services. Almost 2000 printing presses ran around the clock. As the value of money plummeted, prices soared. A handful of apples cost cartloads of paper currency—hundreds of billions of marks—at the height of the inflation in the summer of 1923. People were paid twice a day so that they could rush to stores during their breaks and spend their earnings before their money became worth even less.

Working people were malnourished, the unemployed starved. Only one in three German workers was fully employed by the end of 1923. Death rates rose as sicknesses related to poor diets spread. Few people could afford hospital care or doctors' fees. The middle classes suffered most from hyperinflation. Their savings were wiped out, their investments destroyed, their property stripped from them. Widows and the aged living on pensions were reduced to poverty, and civil servants and teachers became paupers overnight, as previously comfortable salaries dwindled. Hyperinflation gave new meaning to the old saying that the money wasn't worth the paper it was printed on, a saying that is seen in action on the facing page in the photograph of German children playing with a huge pile of worthless bills. With soaring prices, people lost security and stability just as surely as if they had been in a military upheaval.

■ George Grosz, *The Pillars of Society*. bpk, Berlin/Art Resource, NY/© Estate of George Grosz/Licensed by VAGA, New York, NY

LOOKING AHEAD

In this chapter, we shall begin with a geographical tour of Europe that allows us to consider how economic and security issues fueled national and territorial tensions. The Germans blamed the French for their reparations demands and their invading troops for the plight of Germany. Hyperinflation had extremely negative repercussions for democracy, as extremists on both the left and right blamed their liberal political leaders. When the Great Depression that began in 1929 hit European economies, the fear of new inflation prevented governments from using deficit spending to bring back prosperity. The Soviet Union, isolated from international politics and international markets, pursued its own separate path of forced economic development at great human and social costs. In Italy and Germany, fascist dictatorships promised solutions to all economic problems. People, having grown cynical and defiant through suffering, sought security in extraordinary and extra-democratic solutions.

GEOGRAPHICAL TOUR
Europe After 1918

The armistice that ended World War I in 1918 did not stop the process of social upheaval and transformations challenging attempts to restore order throughout Europe (see **Map A**). In 1918, parts of war-torn Europe faced the possibility of revolution. Russia, where revolution had destroyed tsardom, expectantly watched revolutionary developments in countries from the British Isles to eastern Europe. The Bolshevik leaders of Russia's revolution counted on the capitalist system to destroy itself. That did not happen. By 1921, revolutions had been brutally crushed in Berlin, Munich, and Budapest. The Soviets, meanwhile, had won the civil war against the Whites and survived the intervention of the British, French, Japanese, and Americans. But the new Russian regime was diplomatically isolated and in a state of almost total economic collapse.

In 1917–1918, the United States had played a significant and central role in the waging of war and in the pursuit of peace. Under U.S. President Woodrow Wilson, who urged his country to guarantee European security and guide Europe's future, the United States seemed promising as an active and positive force in international politics. By 1921, however, the United States had retreated to a position, not of isolation, but of selective in-

volvement. With one giant, Russia, devastated and isolated, and the other, the United States, reluctant, Europeans faced an uncertain future.

New Nation-States, New Problems

Before World War I, east-central Europe was a region divided among four great empires—the Ottoman, the Habsburg, the Russian, and the German. Under the pressure of defeat, those empires collapsed into a dozen sovereign states (see **Map B**). The victorious Allies hoped that independent states newly created from fragments of empire would buffer Europe from the spread of communism westward and the expansion of German power eastward.

New independent states emerged at the center of Europe because of national movements and local leadership. Finland achieved independence from Russia in 1917. Estonia, Latvia, and Lithuania, also formerly under Russian rule, comprised the now independent Baltic states (see **Map B**). After more than a century of dismemberment among three empires, Poland successfully laid claim to being a single nation once again. Czechoslovakia was carved out of former Habsburg lands. Austria and Hungary shriveled to small, independent states. Yugoslavia was pieced together from a patchwork of territories. Romania swelled, fed on a diet of settlement concessions. The new nations assured the victorious powers, especially France, that the new political geography of east-central Europe would guarantee the peace.

The Instability of Self-Determination.   World War I victor nations, hoping that the new states would stabilize European affairs, erred in three important ways in their calculations. Many of the new states were internally unstable precisely because of the principle of national self-determination, the idea that nationalities had the right to rule themselves. Honoring the rights of nationalities was simple in the abstract, but application of the principle proved complicated and at times impossible. Religious, linguistic, and ethnic diversity abounded in the newly formed nations, and recognizing nationality often meant ignoring the rights of minorities. In Czechoslovakia, the Czechs dominated the Slovaks and the Germans even though the Czechs were fewer in number. Ethnic unrest plagued all of eastern Europe. Minority tensions weakened and destabilized the fragile governments.

The struggle for economic prosperity further destabilized the new governments. East-central Europe was primarily agricultural, and the existence of the great empires had created guaranteed markets. The war disrupted the economy and generated social unrest. The peace settlements only compounded the economic problems of the region. When the Habsburg Empire disintegrated, the Danube River basin ceased to be a cohesive economic unit. New governments were saddled with borders that made little economic sense.

Creating cohesive economic units proved an insurmountable task for newly formed governments and administrations

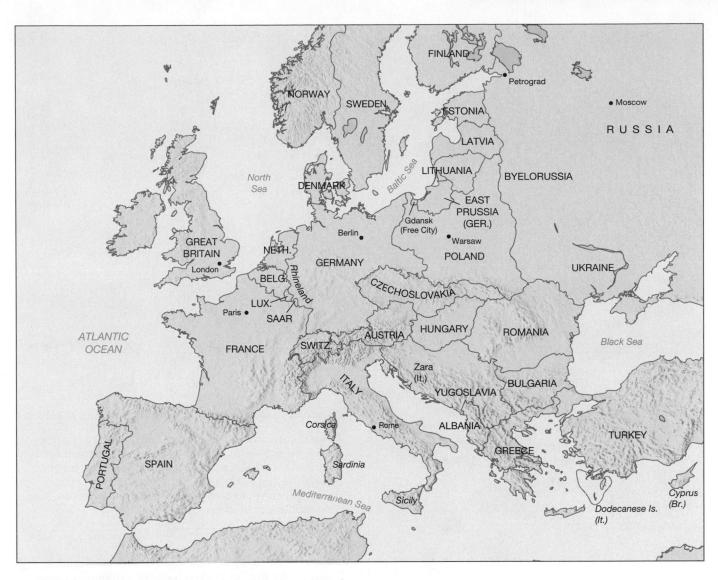

■ **Map A. Europe After World War I.** The peace settlement dismantled the four great empires in Europe—the Ottoman, Habsburg, Russian, and German—and created new sovereign states.

that lacked both resources and experience. Low productivity, unemployment, and overpopulation characterized most of east-central Europe. Attempts to industrialize and to develop new markets confronted many obstacles. Much of the land was farmed on a subsistence basis. What agricultural surplus was created was difficult to sell abroad. East-central Europeans—including Poles, Czechs, Yugoslavs, and Romanians, all tied to France through military and political commitments—were excluded from western European markets and were isolated economically from their treaty allies. Economic ties with Germany endured in ways that perpetuated economic dependence and threatened future survival.

Border Disputes.   Common borders produced tensions over territories. The peace settlements made no one happy.

Poland quarreled with Lithuania; Czechoslovakia vied with Poland over territorial claims. War broke out between Poland and Russia for six months in 1920 over the creation of an independent Ukrainian state. The Bolsheviks counterattacked and tried to turn the conflict into a revolutionary war in order to spread communism to central Europe. The Poles turned the Russians back. The Treaty of Riga, signed in March 1921, gave Poland much but not all of the territory it claimed.

Hungary, having lost the most territory in World War I, held the distinction of having the greatest number of territorial grievances against its neighbors—Czechoslovakia, Romania, and Yugoslavia. Yugoslavia made claims against Austria. Bulgaria sought territories controlled by Greece and Romania. Ethnicity, strategic considerations, and economic

■ **Map B. East-Central Europe.** A dozen sovereign states were created in east-central Europe in the hope that they would serve as an independent buffer between Russia and Germany and guarantee peace.

needs motivated claims for territory. Disputes festered, fed by the intense nationalism that prevented the cooperation necessary for survival.

Germany, the Soviet Union, and Italy further complicated the situation with their own territorial claims against their east-central European neighbors. The new German government refused to accept the loss of the "corridor" controlled by Poland that severed East Prussia from the rest of Germany. Nor was Germany resigned to the loss of part of Silesia to Poland (see **Map C**). Russia refused to forget its losses to Romania, Poland, Finland, and the Baltic states. Italy, too weak to act on its own, nevertheless dreamed of expansion into Yugoslavia, Austria, and Albania. The redefined borders of eastern and central Europe produced animosity and the seeds of ongoing conflict. The new states of

■ **Map C. Germany.** France hoped to hem Germany in, according to the terms of the peace settlement. France regained from Germany the territories of Alsace and Lorraine that France had lost in the Franco-Prussian War in 1870. In the 1920s, the French began building massive fortifications, known as the Maginot Line, along the frontier with Germany.

eastern Europe stood as a picket fence between Germany and Russia, a fence that held little promise of guaranteeing the peace or of making good neighbors.

German Recovery

Germany, the most populous nation in western Europe with 60 million people, emerged apparently strong from defeat. In 1919, the German people endorsed a new liberal and democratic government, the **Weimar Republic,** so named for the city in which its constitution had been written. The constitution of the new government was unusually progressive, with voting rights for women and extensive civil liberties for German citizens. Because World War I had not been fought in Germany, German transportation networks and industrial plants had escaped serious damage. Its industry was fed by raw materials and energy resources unsurpassed anywhere in Europe outside Russia.

Territorial Advantages and Goals. In east-central Europe, Germany had actually benefited from the dismantling of the Habsburg Empire and the removal of Poland and the Baltic states from Russian control. Replacing its formerly large neighbor to the east were weak states potentially susceptible to Germany's influence. Because the governments of east-central Europe feared communism, they were not likely to ally themselves with the Soviet state. The existence of the small buffer states left open the possibility of German collaboration with Russia, since the two large nations might be able to negotiate their interests in the area.

On its western frontier, Germany's prospects were not so bright. Alsace and Lorraine had been returned to France (see **Map C**). From German territory, a demilitarized zone had been created in the Rhineland. The Saar district was under the protection of League of Nations commissioners, and the Saar coal mines were transferred to French ownership until 1935, when a plebiscite returned the region to Germany. Humiliated and betrayed by the geographic consequences of its defeat, Germany looked to recover its status.

Germany's primary foreign policy goal was revision of the treaty settlements of World War I. German politicians and military leaders perceived disarmament, loss of territory, and payment of reparations as serious obstacles in restoring Germany's position as a great power. German statesmen sought liberation of the Rhineland from foreign military occupation, return of the Saar basin, and recovery of the Corridor and Upper Silesia from Poland.

German leaders set economic recovery as the basis of their new foreign policy. In 1922, Germany signed the **Treaty of Rapallo** with Russia, a peacetime partnership that shocked the Western powers. Economics motivated the new Russo-German alliance: German industry needed markets, and the Russians needed loans to reconstruct their economy. Both states wanted to break out of the isolation imposed on them by the victors of World War I. However, Germany quickly learned that markets in Russia were limited and that hopes for recovery depended on financial cooperation with western Europe and the United States. At the end of 1923, Gustav Stresemann (1878–1929) assumed direction of the German Foreign Ministry and began to implement a conciliatory policy toward France and Britain. By displaying peaceful intentions, he hoped to secure American capital for German industry and to win the support of the West for the revision of the peace settlement.

The Locarno Treaties.   Stresemann joined his French and British counterparts, Aristide Briand (1862–1932) and Austen Chamberlain (1863–1937), in fashioning a series of treaties at Locarno, Switzerland, in 1925. In a spirit of cooperation, Germany, France, and Belgium promised never again to go to war against each other and to respect the demilitarized zone that separated them. Britain and Italy "guaranteed" the borders of all three countries and ensured the integrity of the demilitarized zone. The treaties initiated an atmosphere of goodwill, a "**spirit of Locarno**," that heralded a new age of security and nonaggression.

However, Germany did not renounce its ambitions in eastern Europe. Stresemann expected Germany to recover the territory lost to Poland. He also knew that Germany must rearm

and expand to the east. From the early 1920s until 1933, Germany secretly rearmed. Undercover, Germany rebuilt its army and trained its soldiers and airmen on Russian territory. In violation of Versailles treaty agreements, Germany planned to be once again a great power with the same rights as other European countries.

France's Search for Security

Having learned the harsh lessons of 1870–1871 and 1914–1918, France understood well the threat posed by a united, industrialized, and well-armed Germany. During the years immediately following World War I, France deeply distrusted Germany. France had a smaller population of 40 million people and lower industrial production than Germany. France had been devastated by the war, and Germany had not. But France did have certain advantages in 1921. It had the best-equipped army in the world. Germany was disarmed. The Rhineland was demilitarized and occupied. But France knew that without the support of Great Britain and the United States, it could not enforce the Treaty of Versailles and keep Germany militarily weak.

The Americans and the British refused to conclude a long-term peacetime alliance with the French. In search of allies on the Continent, therefore, France committed itself to an alliance in the east with Poland and the Little Entente nations of Czechoslovakia, Romania, and Yugoslavia. Treaties with the four states of east-central Europe gave France some security in the event of an attack. But the treaties were also liabilities because France would have to fight to defend east-central Europe.

To keep Germany militarily and economically weak, the French attempted to enforce the Treaty of Versailles fully in 1921–1923. They were willing to do so alone if necessary. In 1923, the French army invaded the Ruhr district of Germany and occupied it with the intention of collecting reparations payments. But the Ruhr invasion served only to isolate France further from its wartime allies. France depended on loans from American banks to balance its budget, and the Americans disapproved of the French use of military might to enforce the treaty.

In 1924–1925, France decided to cooperate with the United States and Great Britain rather than to continue a policy of enforcing the treaty alone and attempting to keep Germany weak. France withdrew its army from the Ruhr and some troops from the Rhineland. It agreed to lower German reparations payments. In addition, by signing the Locarno treaties, France cooperated with the Anglo-American policy that rejected the use of military force against Germany and promoted German economic recovery.

French anxiety about security continued, however. Nothing indicated the nature of that anxiety more clearly than the construction, beginning in the late 1920s, of the **Maginot Line**, a system of defensive fortifications between Germany and France (see **Map C**).

Throughout the 1920s, French political leaders tried to engage Great Britain in guaranteeing the security of France and

Europe. The British agreed to defend France and Belgium against possible German aggression. They stopped short, however, of promising to defend Poland and Czechoslovakia. After settling the matter at Locarno, Britain largely reverted to its prewar pattern of withdrawing from continental Europe and concentrating its attention on the demands of its global empire.

The United States in Europe

The Treaty of Versailles marked the demise of European autonomy. American intervention had boosted French and British morale during the crucial months of 1917. In providing financial help, ships, troops, and supplies, the United States had rescued the Allied powers. After the war, a balance of power in Europe could not be maintained without outside help. Germany had been defeated, but if it recovered, France and Britain alone probably would not be able to contain it. Security and peace now depended on the presence of the United States to guarantee a stable balance of power in Europe and to defend Western hegemony in the world.

The United States was unwilling to assume a new role as political leader of Europe and mediator of European conflict. It refused to sign a joint peace, arranging instead a separate peace with Germany. It also refused to join the **League of Nations.** Following the war, the League had been devised as an international body of nations committed, according to article 10 of its covenant, to "respect and preserve as against external aggression the territorial integrity and existing political independence" of others. Germany was excluded from membership until 1926, and the Union of Soviet Socialist Republics (USSR) was denied entry until 1934. Otherwise, the League of Nations claimed a global membership. But the absence of U.S. support and the lack of any machinery to enforce its decisions undermined the possibility of the League's long-term effectiveness. Hopes that the international body could serve as a peacekeeper collapsed in 1931 with the League's failure to deal with the crisis of Japanese aggression against Manchuria.

The United States persisted in avoiding political and military obligations in Europe, with the idea of protecting its own freedom and autonomy. Instead, it sought to promote German economic recovery and reasoned that a peaceful and stable Europe would be reestablished without a real balance of power in Europe and without a commitment from the United States.

Many feared that territorial settlements of the peace held the promise of another war. Even efforts at comprehensive international cooperation such as the League of Nations did not overcome the problem of competitive nations, nor did the **Kellogg-Briand Pact,** signed by 23 nations in 1928. Named for U.S. Secretary of State Frank B. Kellogg (1856–1937) and French foreign minister Aristide Briand, who devised the plan, the pact renounced war. In the atmosphere of the 1920s, a time of hope and caution, the agreement carried all the weight of an empty gesture.

CRISIS AND COLLAPSE IN A WORLD ECONOMY

In 1918, the belligerent nations—winners and losers alike—had big bills on their hands. Although nations at war had borrowed from their own populations through the sale of war bonds, private citizens could not provide all the money needed to finance four years of war.

International Loans and Trade Barriers

France borrowed from Great Britain. Both Great Britain and France took loans from the United States. When all else failed, belligerent nations could and did print money not backed by productive wealth. Because more money had claims on the same amount of national wealth, the money in circulation was worth less. When the people who had purchased war bonds were then paid off with depreciated currency, they lost real wealth. Inflation had the same effect as taxation. The people had less wealth and the government had less debt.

The United States, for the first time in history the leading creditor nation in the world, had no intention of wiping the slate clean by forgiving war debts. Nor did it intend to accept repayment in less valuable postwar currencies: loans were tied to gold. Britain, France, and Belgium counted on reparations from Germany to pay their war debts and to rebuild their economies. Reparations were calculated on the basis of the damages Germany had inflicted on the Allies. The postwar Reparations Commission determined that Germany owed the victors 132 billion gold marks ($32 billion), to be paid in annual installments of 2 billion gold marks ($500 million), plus 26 percent of the value of German exports.

For the German people and for German leaders, reparations were an unacceptable punitive levy that mortgaged the prosperity of future generations. Germany, too, wanted to recover from the years of privation of the war. Substantial reparations payments would have transferred real wealth from Germany to the Allies. Transferring wealth would have cut into any increase in the German standard of living in the 1920s, and it would have diminished the investment needed to make the German economy grow. Instead, the German government printed huge amounts of currency. The mark collapsed and world currencies were endangered.

With financial disaster looming, the British and Americans decided to intervene. A plan had to be devised that would permit Germany to prosper while funneling payments to France, which was so dependent on reparations for its own recovery and for its war debt payments to the United States. In 1924, the American banker Charles G. Dawes (1865–1951), along with a group of international financial experts appointed by the Allied governments, devised a solution to the reparations problem. The **Dawes Plan** aimed to end inflation and restore economic prosperity in Germany by giving Germany a more modest and realistic schedule of payments and by extending a loan from American banks to get payments started.

■ "Married Again." This 1928 cartoon shows the wicked world once again pledging eternal fidelity to peace with the signing of the Kellogg-Briand Pact. The cynical attitude of the artist was vindicated by subsequent events.

MARRIED AGAIN

IRELAND, *THE COLUMBUS DISPATCH*

As important as reparations and war debts are in understanding the Western world in the 1920s, they cannot be considered in isolation. Debtor nations, whether Allies paying back loans to the United States or defeated nations paying reparations to the victors, needed to be able to sell their goods in world markets. They saw trade as the principal way to accumulate enough national income to pay back what they owed and to prosper domestically without burying their citizens under a mountain of new taxes.

The United States recognized that a stable Europe would give it a market for its own agricultural and industrial products and provide a guarantee for recovery of its loans and investments. Yet the proverbial monkey wrench in a smoothly functioning international economy was the trade policy of the United States. Republican political leaders in the United States insisted on high tariffs to protect domestic goods against imports. But high tariffs prevented Europeans from selling in the United States and earning the dollars they needed to repay war debts.

While blocking imports, the United States planned to expand its own exports to world markets, especially to Europe. The problem for American exporters, however, was the insta-

bility of European currencies in the first half of the 1920s. All over Europe, governments allowed inflation to rise with the expectation that depreciating currencies would make their goods cheaper in world markets and hence more salable.

Depreciating European currencies on the one hand meant an appreciating dollar on the other. For the "grand design" of U.S. trade expansion, a strong dollar was no virtue. More and more German marks, British pounds, and French francs had to be spent to purchase American goods. The result was that fewer American exports were sold in European markets. Because two-thirds of Germany's long-term credits came from the United States, Germany's fate was directly linked to the fortunes of American financial centers. Conversely, the soundness of American banks depended on a solvent Germany, which now absorbed 18 percent of U.S. capital exports.

Despite the scaled-down schedule of the Dawes Plan, reparations remained a bitter pill for German leaders and the German public to swallow. In 1929, American bankers devised another plan under the leadership of the American businessman Owen D. Young (1874–1962), chairman of the board of General Electric. Although the **Young Plan** initially transferred $100

PASSING THE BUCK.

■ A British cartoonist's view of the reparations problem following World War I.

crash set off the **Great Depression** in an international economic system already plagued with structural problems. It also marked the beginning of a long period of worldwide economic stagnation and depression.

Dependence on the American Economy. A confluence of factors made Europe and the rest of the world vulnerable to reversals in the American economy. Heavy borrowing and reliance on American investment throughout the 1920s contributed to the inherent instability of European economies. Even Great Britain, itself a creditor, relied on short-term loans; "borrowing short and lending long" proved to be disastrous when loans were recalled. Excessive lending and leniency were fatal mistakes of creditor nations, especially the United States. When, in the summer of 1929, American investors turned off the tap of the flow of capital to search for higher profits at home, a precarious situation began to get worse.

■ This poster for the October 1931 British General Election reflects the National Government's concern over mass unemployment and industrial stagnation. The coalition National Government swamped the opposition Labour Party, taking 556 Parliament seats to Labour's 51.

million to Germany, Germans saw the twentieth century stretching before them as year after year of nothing but humiliating reparations payments. To make matters worse, after 1928 American private loans shriveled in Germany as American investors sought the higher yields of a booming stock market at home.

Europe as a whole made rapid progress in manufacturing production during the second half of the decade, and by 1929 it had surpassed its prewar (1913) per capita income. Yet structural weaknesses were present, although they went almost unnoticed. The false security of a new gold standard masked the instability and interdependence of currencies. Low prices prevailed in the agricultural sector, keeping the incomes of a significant segment of the population depressed. But the low rate of long-term capital investment was obscured in the flurry of short-term loans, whose disappearance in 1928 spelled the beginning of the end for European recovery. The protectionist trade policy of the United States conflicted with its insistence on repayment of war debts. Germany's resentment over reparations was in no way alleviated by the Dawes and Young repayment plans. The irresponsibility of American speculation in the stock market pricked the bubble of prosperity. None of those factors operated in isolation to cause the collapse that began in 1929. Taken together, however, they caused a depression of previously unimagined severity in the international economic system.

The Great Depression

In the history of the Western world, the year 1929 has assumed mythic proportions. During one week in October of that year, the stock market in the United States collapsed. That

Smokeless Chimneys and— **ANXIOUS MOTHERS!**

THE REMEDY

VOTE FOR THE **NATIONAL GOVERNMENT**

Oral Account of the Great Depression

A depression is a severe economic downturn marked by sharp declines in income and production as buying and selling slow down to a crawl. Depressions were not new in the business cycles of modern economies, but what happened in October 1929 was more serious in its extent and duration than any depression before or since. The bottom was not reached until three years after the Great Depression began. In 1932, one in four American workers was without a job. One in three banks had closed its doors. People lost their homes, unable to pay their mortgages; farmers lost their land, unable to earn enough to survive. The great prosperity of the 1920s had vanished overnight.

The plight of the United States rippled through world markets. Americans stopped buying foreign goods. The Smoot-Hawley Tariff Act, passed by the U.S. Congress in 1930, created an impenetrable tariff fortress against agricultural and

THE DEPRESSION FOR WOMEN

Winifred Holtby (1898–1935) was a British novelist, journalist, and social reformer who covered European political events throughout the interwar period. In this selection from her writings she chronicles the differential impact that war and economic depression had on women's lives. Expectations about woman's proper role, whether of housewife and mother or serving her country in the workplace, were profoundly political and hotly contested.

Focus Questions

What are the resentments Holtby describes as being caused by the gender division of labor? Why does Holtby place the word "natural" in quotes when speaking of "house-keeping and child-bearing"?

The effect of the slump upon women's economic position is most obvious, not only in the problems of unemployment among both industrial and professional women, but still more in the bitterness surrounding the question of married women's paid employment, "pin money" office girls, unorganized casual female factory labour, and claims to alimony, maintenance, and separation allowances. These are the dilemmas of scarcity. It is here that the shoe pinches when national purchasing power has failed to distribute adequately the products of industry.

During the War, women entered almost every branch of industry and most of the professions. . . . In transport, engineering, chemicals, textiles, tailoring and woodwork, women took the places which, ever since the sorting-out process which followed the first disorganized scramble of the Industrial Revolution, had been reserved to men. They took and they enjoyed them.

Then the men returned, and on demobilization demanded again the jobs which they had left. The position was not simple.

Some of the men had received promises that their work should be kept for them; but of these, some did not return. Some women surrendered their shovels, lathes, and hoes without a grievance. Their work had been "for the duration of the war" and they had no desire to retain it.

But others thought differently. Women, they told themselves, had been excluded from the more highly-skilled and better-paid industrial posts for two or more generations. They had been told that certain processes were beyond their power. It was a lie. During the war they had proved it to be so, by their own skill and efficiency. Why surrender without a word opportunities closed to them by fraud and falsehood? They had as much right to wheel, loom, or cash-register as any man. Why then pretend that they were intruders in a world which was as much their own as their brothers'? . . .

After 1928, jobs became not duties which war-time propaganda taught girls that it was patriotic to perform, but privileges to be reserved for potential bread-winners and fathers of families. Women were commanded to go back to the home.

The bitterness began which has lasted ever since—the women keeping jobs and the men resenting it—the men regaining the jobs and the women resenting it. . . .

In Italy, Germany, and Ireland a new dream of natural instinctive racial unity was arising, which designed for women a return to their "natural" functions of house-keeping and child-bearing; while in the English-speaking countries a new anti-rational philosophy combined with economic fatalism, militated against the ebullient hopes which an earlier generation had pinned to education, effort, and individual enterprise.

All generalizations are false. In every civilized country are little groups of older women with memories of suffrage struggles, and young women who grew up into the post-war optimism, and whose ideas remain unchanged by the fashions of the hour. It is they who still organize protests against reaction; who in national and international societies defend the political, civil, and economic equality of men and women; who invade new territories of achievement; who look towards a time when there shall be no wrangling over rights and wrongs, man's place and woman's place, but an equal and cooperative partnership, the individual going unfettered to the work for which he is best suited, responsibilities and obligations shared alike.

From Winifred Holtby, *Women in a Changing Civilization* (1934).

manufactured imports and hampered foreign producers. The major trading nations of the world, including Great Britain, enacted similar protectionist measures. American investment abroad dried up as the lifelines of American capital to Europe were cut.

European nations tried to staunch the outward flow of capital and gold by restricting the transfer of capital abroad. Large amounts of foreign-owned gold ($6.6 billion from 1931 to 1938) nevertheless were deposited in American banks. In 1931, President Herbert Hoover (1874–1964) supported a moratorium on the payment of reparations and war debts. The moratorium, combined with the pooling of gold in the United States, led to a run on the British pound sterling in 1931 and the collapse of Great Britain as one of the world's great financial centers.

Political Repercussions.   The gold standard disappeared from the international economy, never to return. So, too, did reparations payments and war debts when the major nations of Europe met without the United States at a special conference held in Lausanne, Switzerland, in 1932. Something else died at the end of the 1920s: confidence in a self-adjusting economy, an "invisible hand" by which the business cycle would be righted. During 1932–1933, the Great Depression, showing no signs of disappearing, reached its nadir and became a global phenomenon. Economic hardship transformed political realities. The Labour cabinet in Great Britain was forced to resign, and a new national government composed of Conservative, Liberal, and Labour leaders was formed to deal with the world economic emergency. Republican government was torn by bitter divisions in France. In the United States, the Republican party, which had been in power since 1920, was defeated in 1932. Franklin D. Roosevelt (1882–1945), a Democrat, was elected president in a landslide victory with a mandate to transform the American economy. German democratic institutions were pulled down in favor of fascist dictatorship.

In the decade following the Great War, peace settlements did not promote a stable international community. Instead, self-determination of peoples created new grounds for national rivalries in eastern Europe, and the lack of any effective means of guaranteeing the peace only exacerbated prewar animosities. The economic interdependence of nation-states through an international system of reparations payments and loans increased the vulnerability of governments to external pressures. With the collapse of the international finance system in 1929, political stability and international cooperation seemed more elusive than ever.

THE SOVIET UNION'S SEPARATE PATH

In the 1920s, the Soviet state was also faced with solving its economic problems. Lenin's successor, Joseph Stalin (1879–1953), obliged the Soviet people to achieve in a single generation and in isolation what it had taken the West a century and a half to accomplish.

The Soviet Regime at the End of the Civil War

Echoing Karl Marx, the Bolshevik leader Lenin declared that the revolution and the civil war had been won in the name of "the dictatorship of the proletariat." The hammer and sickle on the Soviet flag represented the united rule of workers and peasants and were symbolic reminders of the commitment to rule from below. But at the end of the civil war in 1921, the Bolsheviks, not the people, were in charge.

DOCUMENT

Lenin Calls for Electrification of All Russia

The industrial sector, small as it was, was in total disarray by 1921. Famine and epidemics in 1921–1922 killed and weakened more people than the Great War and the civil war combined. The countryside had been plundered to feed the Red and White armies. The combination of empty promises and a declining standard of living left workers and peasants frustrated and discontented. Urban strikes and rural uprisings defied short-term solutions. The proletarian revolutionary heroes of 1917 were rejecting the new Soviet regime. The Bolshevik party now faced

■ As members of the Politburo, Leon Trotsky (left), Nikolai Bukharin (center), and Joseph Stalin (right) each tried to direct Soviet economic policy. Only the politically shrewd Stalin would emerge victorious.

the task of restoring a country exhausted by war and revolution, its resources depleted, its economy destroyed.

At the head of the Soviet state was Lenin, the first among equals in the seven-man Politburo. The Central Committee of the Communist party decided "fundamental questions of policy, international and domestic," but in reality the Politburo, the inner circle of the Central Committee, held the reins of power.

Among seven members of the Politburo, three in particular attempted to leave their mark on the direction of Soviet policy: Leon Trotsky, Nikolai Bukharin (1888–1938), and Joseph Stalin. The great drama of Soviet leadership in the 1920s revolved around how the most brilliant (Trotsky) and the most popular (Bukharin) failed at the hands of the most shrewdly political (Stalin).

The two extremes in the debate over the direction of economic development were, on the one hand, a planned economy totally directed from above and, on the other hand, an economy controlled from below. In 1920–1921, Leon Trotsky, at that time the people's commissar of war, favored a planned economy based on the militarization of labor. Trade unions opposed such a proposal and argued for a share of control over production. Lenin, however, favored a proletarian democracy and supported unions organized independently of state control.

The controversy was resolved in the short run at the Tenth Party Congress in 1921, when Lenin chose to steer a middle course between trade union autonomy and militarization by preserving the unions and at the same time insisting on the state's responsibility for economic development. His primary goal was to stabilize Bolshevik rule in its progress toward socialism. He recognized that nothing could be achieved without the peasants. As a result, Lenin found himself embracing a new economic policy that he termed a "temporary retreat" from Communist goals.

The New Economic Policy, 1921–1928

In 1921, Lenin ended the forced requisitioning of peasant produce that had been in effect during the civil war. In its place, peasants were to pay a tax in kind, that is, a fixed portion of their yield, to the state. Peasants, in turn, were permitted to reinstate private trade on their own terms. Party leaders accepted the dramatic shift in economic policy because it held the promise of prosperity so necessary for political stability. The actions of Lenin to return the benefits of productivity to the economy, combined with those of the peasants to reestablish markets, created the **New Economic Policy (NEP)** that emerged in the spring and summer of 1921.

Bukharin's Role.   It remained for Nikolai Bukharin to give shape and substance to the economic policy that permitted Russian producers to engage in some capitalist practices. As one of the founding fathers of the Soviet state and the youngest of the top Bolshevik leaders, Bukharin took his place on the Central Committee of the Communist party and on the Politburo as well.

Bukharin set about solving Russia's single greatest problem: how could Russia, crippled by poverty, find enough capital to industrialize? Insisting on the need for long-term economic planning, Bukharin counted on a prosperous and contented peasantry as the mainstay of his policy. Bukharin was also strongly interested in attracting foreign investment to Soviet endeavors as a way of ensuring future productivity.

Bukharin appreciated the importance of landholding to Russian peasants and defended a system of individual farms and private accumulation. Agriculture would operate through a market system, and the peasants would have the right to control their own surpluses. Rural prosperity would generate profits that could be used for gradual industrial development. Bukharin's policy stood in stark contrast to Stalin's later plan to feed industry by starving the agricultural sector.

Collective and large-scale farming had to be deferred indefinitely in order to reconcile the peasantry to the state—a policy profoundly at odds with the programs of the Communist state to pull down the capitalist system and establish socialism. In 1924, the tax in kind was replaced with a tax in cash. With that shift, the state now procured grain through commercial agencies and cooperative organizations instead of directly from the peasants. The move toward Western capitalist models seemed more pronounced than ever to critics of the NEP.

Beginning in 1922, Lenin suffered a series of strokes, which virtually removed him from power by March 1923. When he died on 21 January 1924, the Communist leadership split over the ambiguities of the NEP. The backward nature of agriculture did not permit the kind of productivity that the NEP policy makers had anticipated. Cities demanded more food as their populations swelled with the influx of unskilled workers

from rural areas. In 1927, peasants held back their grain. The Soviet Union was then experiencing a series of foreign policy setbacks in the West and in China, and Bolshevik leaders spoke of an active anti-Soviet conspiracy by the capitalist powers, led by Great Britain. The Soviet state lowered the price of grain, thereby squeezing the peasantry. The war scare, combined with the drop in food prices, soon led to an economic crisis.

Stalin Takes Charge. By 1928, the NEP was in trouble. Stalin, general secretary of the Communist party of the Soviet Union, saw his chance. Under his supervision, the state intervened to prevent peasants from disposing of their own grain surpluses. The peasants responded to requisitioning by hoarding their produce and violently rioting. Bukharin and the NEP were in danger. Stalin exploited the internal crisis and external dangers to eliminate his political rivals. Trotsky had been expelled from the Communist party in November 1927 on charges that he had engaged in antiparty activities. Banished from Russia in 1929, he eventually found refuge in Mexico, where he was assassinated in 1940 at Stalin's command.

THE RESULTS OF THE FIRST FIVE-YEAR PLAN

Under Joseph Stalin the Soviet Union embarked on rapid industrialization that transformed the peasant-based economy into a leading iron and steel producer. The Five-Year Plan achieved in four years what the Western industrialized nations took 150 years to accomplish. The Soviet leader did not tally the cost in human lives or the impact on the quality of life that such brutal economic transformation entailed.

Focus Questions
How is capitalism depicted as the enemy in this document? How are the impacts of the First Five-Year Plan similar for industry and agriculture? What elements of style and tone in the document indicate the propagandistic intent of Stalin, the author?

The fundamental task of the five-year plan was to transfer our country, with its backward, and in part medieval, technique, to the lines of new, modern technique.

The fundamental task of the Five-Year Plan was to convert the USSR from an agrarian and weak country, dependent upon the caprices of the capitalist countries, into an industrial and powerful country, fully self-reliant and independent of the caprices of world capitalism.

The fundamental task of the Five-Year Plan was, in converting the USSR into an industrial country, fully to eliminate the capitalist elements, to widen the front of socialist forms of economy, and to create the economic base for the abolition of classes in the USSR, for the construction of socialist society....

The fundamental task of the Five-Year Plan was to transfer small and scattered agriculture to the lines of large-scale collective farming, so as to ensure the economic base for so-

cialism in the rural districts and thus to eliminate the possibility of the restoration of capitalism in the USSR.

Finally, the task of the Five-Year Plan was to create in the country all the necessary technical and economic prerequisites for increasing to the utmost the defensive capacity of the country, to enable it to organize determined resistance to any and every attempt at military intervention from outside, to any and every attempt at military attack from without....

What are the results of the Five-Year Plan in four years in the sphere of *industry?*

Have we achieved victory in this sphere?

Yes, we have....

We did not have an iron and steel industry, the foundation for the industrialization of the country. Now we have this industry.

We did not have a tractor industry. Now we have one.

We did not have an automobile industry. Now we have one.

We did not have a machine-tool industry. Now we have one.

We did not have a big and up-to-date chemical industry. Now we have one.

We did not have a real and big industry for the production of modern agricultural machinery. Now we have one.

Bukharin's popularity in the party also threatened Stalin's aspirations. Bukharin was dropped from the Politburo in 1929. Tolerated throughout the early 1930s, he was arrested in 1937, and tried and executed for alleged treasonous activities the following year. The fate that befell Trotsky and Bukharin was typical of what happened to those who stood in the way of Stalin's pursuit of dictatorial control. Stalin was, in a colleague's words, "a gray blur." Beneath his apparently colorless personality, however, was a dangerous man of great political acumen, a ruthless behind-the-scenes politician who controlled the machinery of the party for his own ends and was not averse to employing violence in order to achieve them.

Stalin's Rise to Power

Joseph Stalin was born Iosif Vissarionovich Dzhugashvili in 1879. His self-chosen revolutionary name, Stalin, means "steel" in Russian and is as good an indication as any of his opinion of his own personality and will. Stalin, the man who ruled the Soviet Union as a dictator from 1928 until his death

in 1953, was not a Russian. He was from Georgia, an area between the Black and Caspian seas, and spoke Russian with an accent. Georgia, with its land occupied and its people subjugated by invading armies for centuries, was annexed to the expanding Russian Empire in 1801.

As the youngest of four and the only surviving child of Vissarion and Ekaterina Dzhugashvili, Stalin endured a childhood of brutal misery. Stalin's father was a poor and often unemployed shoemaker who intended that his son be apprenticed in the same trade. Under his mother's protection, young Iosif received an education and entered a seminary against his father's wishes. Iosif's schooling, extraordinary for someone of his poverty-stricken background, gave him the opportunity to learn about revolutionary socialist politics. At the turn of the century, Georgia had a strong Marxist revolutionary movement that opposed Russian exploitation. Iosif dropped out of the seminary in 1899 to engage in underground Marxist activities, and he soon became a follower of Lenin.

Stalin's association with Lenin kept him close to the center of power after the October Revolution of 1917. First as people's

---

We did not have an aircraft industry. Now we have one.

In output of electric power we were last on the list. Now we rank among the first.

In output of oil products and coal we were last on the list. Now we rank among the first.

We had only one coal and metallurgical base—in the Ukraine—which we barely managed to keep going. We have not only succeeded in improving this base, but have created a new coal and metallurgical base—in the East—which is the pride of our country.

We had only one center of the textile industry—in the North of our country. As a result of our efforts we will have in the very near future two new centers of the textile industry—in Central Asia and Western Siberia.

And we have not only created these new great industries, but have created them on a scale and in dimensions that eclipse the scale and dimensions of European industry.

And as a result of all this the capitalist elements have been completely and irrevocably eliminated from industry, and socialist industry has become the sole form of industry in the USSR.

And as a result of all this our country has been converted from an agrarian into an industrial country; for the proportion of industrial output, as compared with agricultural output, has risen from 48 percent of the total in the beginning of the Five-Year Plan period (1928) to 70 percent at the end of the fourth year of the Five-Year Plan period (1932)....

The object of the Five-Year Plan in the sphere of agriculture was to unite the scattered and small individual peasant farms, which lacked the opportunity of utilizing tractors and modern agricultural machinery, into large collective farms, equipped with all the modern implements

of highly developed agriculture, and to cover unoccupied land with model state farms....

The party has succeeded, in a matter of three years, in organizing more than 200,000 collective farms and about 5000 state farms specializing mainly in grain growing and livestock raising, and at the same time it has succeeded, in the course of four years, in enlarging the crop area by 21,000,000 hectares.

The party has succeeded in getting more than 60 percent of the peasant farms, which account for more than 70 percent of the land cultivated by peasants, to unite into collective farms, which means that we have *fulfilled* the Five-Year Plan *threefold*.

The party has succeeded in creating the possibility of obtaining, not 500,000,000 to 600,000,000 poods[1] of marketable grain, which was the amount purchased in the period when individual peasant farming predominated, but 1,200,000,000 to 1,400,000,000 poods of grain annually.

The party has succeeded in routing the kulaks as a class, although they have not yet been dealt the final blow; the laboring peasants have been emancipated from kulak bondage and exploitation, and a firm economic basis for the Soviet government, the basis of collective farming, has been established in the countryside.

The party has succeeded in converting the USSR from a land of small peasant farming into a land where agriculture is run on the largest scale in the world.

Such, in general terms, are the results of the Five-Year Plan in four years in the sphere of agriculture.

From Joseph Stalin, *Selected Writings* (1942).

[1]Pood—a unit of weight equivalent to 36.1 pounds.

commissar for nationalities (1920–1923) and then as general secretary of the Central Committee of the Communist party (1922–1953), Stalin showed natural talent as a political strategist. His familiarity with non-Russian nationalities was a great asset in his dealings with the ethnic diversity and unrest in the vast Soviet state. Unlike party leaders who had lived in exile in western Europe before the revolution, Stalin had little knowledge of the West.

After Lenin's death in 1924, Stalin shrewdly bolstered his own reputation by orchestrating cult worship of Lenin. In 1929, Stalin used the occasion of his fiftieth birthday to fashion for himself a reputation as the living hero of the Soviet state. Icons, statues, busts, and images of all sorts of both Lenin and Stalin appeared everywhere in public buildings, schoolrooms, and homes. He systematically began eliminating his rivals so that he alone stood unchallenged as Lenin's true successor.

The First Five-Year Plan

The cult of Stalin coincided with the First Five-Year Plan (1929–1932), which launched Stalin's program of rapid industrialization. Between 1929 and 1937, the period covered by the first two five-year plans (truncated because of their proclaimed success), Stalin laid the foundation for an urban industrial society in the Soviet Union. By brutally squeezing profits out of the agricultural sector, Stalin managed to increase heavy industrial production between 300 and 600 percent.

Stalin committed the Soviet Union to rapid industrialization as the only way to preserve socialism. The failure of revolutionary movements in western Europe meant that the Soviet Union must preserve "**socialism in one country**," the slogan of the political philosophy that justified Stalin's economic plans. Stalin made steel the idol of the new age. The Soviet state needed heavy machinery to build the future. An industrial labor force was created virtually overnight as peasant men and women were placed at workbenches and before the vast furnaces of modern metallurgical plants. The number of women in the industrial work force tripled in the decade after 1929. The reliability of official indices varied, but there is little doubt that heavy industrial production soared between 1929 and 1932. The Russian people were constantly reminded that no sacrifice could be too great in producing steel and iron.

By the end of 1929, the increasingly repressive measures instituted by the state against the peasants had led both to **collectivization** and to the deportation of *kulaks,* the derisive term for wealthy peasants that literally means "the tight-fisted ones." Stalin achieved forced collectivization by confiscating land and establishing collective farms run by the state. By 1938, private land had been virtually eliminated. The state set prices, controlled distribution, and selected crops with the intention of ensuring a steady food supply and freeing a rural labor force for heavy industry. Collectivization meant misery for the 25 million peasant families who suffered under it. At

DOCUMENT

Stalin Demands
Rapid
Industrialization

■ This 1931 Soviet political poster exhorts workers "Join our kolkhoz [collective farm]." A year later, the process of collectivization of Soviet agriculture was nearly complete.

least 5 million peasants died between 1929 and 1932. Collectivization ripped apart the fabric of village life, destroyed families, and sent homeless peasants into exile. Peasants who resisted collectivization retaliated by destroying their own crops and livestock. Rapid industrial development shattered the lives of millions of people.

The Comintern, Economic Development, and the Purges

In addition to promoting its internal economic development, the Soviet Union had to worry about survival in a world political system composed entirely of capitalist countries. By 1924, all the major countries of the world—with the exception of the United States—had established diplomatic relations with the Soviet Union. In 1928, the USSR cooperated in the preparation of a world disarmament conference to be held in Geneva and joined western European powers in a commitment to peace.

The United States and the Soviet Union exchanged ambassadors for the first time in 1933.

The Comintern.   In addition to diplomatic relations, the Soviet state in 1919 encouraged various national Communist parties to form an association for the purpose of promoting and coordinating the coming world revolution. The Communist International, or Comintern, was based in Moscow and by 1920 included representatives from 37 countries. As it became clear that a world revolution was not imminent, the Comintern concerned itself with the ideological purity of its member parties. Under Lenin's direction, the Soviet Communist party determined policy for all the member parties.

Bukharin and Stalin shared a view of the Comintern that prevailed from 1924 to 1929: since the collapse of capitalism was not imminent, the Comintern should work to promote the unity of working classes everywhere and should cooperate with existing worker organizations. In 1929, however, Stalin argued that advanced capitalist societies were teetering on the brink of new wars and revolutions. As a result, the Comintern must seek to sever the ties between foreign Communist parties and social democratic parties in order to prepare for the revolutionary struggle. Stalin purged the Comintern of dissenters, and he decreed a policy of noncooperation in Europe from 1929 to 1933. As a result, socialism in Europe was badly split between Communists and democratic socialists.

The Second Five-Year Plan, announced in 1933, succeeded in reducing the Soviet Union's dependence on foreign imports, especially in the areas of heavy industry, machinery, and metal works. The basic physical plant for armaments production was in place by 1937, and resources continued to be shifted away from consumer goods to heavy industrial development. The industrial development and the collectivization of agriculture brought growing urbanization. By 1939, one in three Soviet people lived in cities, compared to one in six in 1926. In his commitment to increased production, Stalin introduced into the workplace incentives and differential wage scales at odds with the principles and programs of the original Bolshevik revolution. Stricter discipline was enforced; absenteeism was punished with severe fines or loss of employment. Workers who exceeded their quotas were rewarded and honored.

The Great Purge.   Amid the rapid industrialization, Stalin inaugurated the **Great Purge,** which actually was a series of purges lasting from 1934 to 1938. Those whom Stalin believed to be his opponents—real and imagined, past, present, and future—were labeled *class enemies*. The most prominent of them, including leaders of the Bolshevik revolution who had worked with Stalin during the 1920s, appeared in widely publicized *show trials*. They were intimidated and tortured into making false confessions of crimes against the regime, humiliated by brutal prosecutors, and condemned to death or imprisonment. Stalin wiped out the Bolshevik old guard, Communist party members whose first loyalty was to the international Communist movement rather than to Stalin himself, and all potential opposition within the Communist party.

Probably 300,000 people were put to death, among them engineers, managers, technical specialists, and officers of the army and navy. In addition, seven million people were placed in labor camps. Stalin now had unquestioned control of the Communist party and the country.

The purges dealt a severe blow to the command of the army and resulted in a shortage of qualified industrial personnel, slowing industrial growth. The Great Purge coerced the Soviet people into making great sacrifices in the drive for industrialization. It prevented any possible dissension or opposition within the USSR at a time when the "foreign threat" posed by Nazi Germany was becoming increasingly serious.

The human suffering associated with the dislocation and heavy workloads of rapid, coerced industrialization cannot be

■ Soviet women were mobilized into the labor force. Here four women are shown in a factory in the 1930s.

measured. Planned growth brought with it a top-heavy and often inefficient bureaucracy, and that bureaucracy ensured that the Soviet Union was the most highly centralized of the European states. The growing threat of foreign war meant an even greater diversion of resources from consumer goods to war industries beginning with the Third Five-Year Plan in 1938.

Women and the Family in the New Soviet State

The building of the new Soviet state exacted particularly high costs from women. Soviet women had been active in the revolution from the beginning. Lenin and the Bolshevik leaders were committed to the liberation of women, who, like workers, were considered to be oppressed under capitalism. Lenin denounced housework as "barbarously unproductive, petty, nerve-wracking, stultifying, and crushing drudgery." In its early days, the Soviet state pledged to protect the rights of mothers without narrowing women's opportunities or restricting women's role to the family.

After the October Revolution of 1917, the Bolsheviks passed a new law establishing equality for women within marriage. In 1920, abortion was legalized. New legislation established the right to divorce and removed the stigma from illegitimacy. Communes, calling themselves "laboratories of revolution," experimented with sexual equality. Russian women were enfranchised in 1917, gaining the right to vote before women in the industrialized countries of western Europe. The Russian revolution went further than any revolution in history toward the legal liberation of women within such a short span of time.

Those advances, as utopian as they appeared to admirers in western European countries, did not deal with the problems faced by the majority of Russian women. Bolshevik legislation did little to address the special economic hardships of peasant and factory women. Although paid maternity leaves and nursing breaks were required by law, those guarantees became a source of discrimination against women workers, who were the last hired and first fired by employers trying to limit expenses. Divorce legislation was hardly a blessing for women with children, since men incurred no financial responsibility toward their offspring in terminating a marriage. Even as legislation was being passed in the early days of the new Soviet state, women were losing ground in the struggle for equal rights and independent economic survival.

THE LAW ON THE ABOLITION OF LEGAL ABORTION, 1936

In his drive to industrialize the Soviet Union as rapidly as possible, Stalin recognized the economic importance of women's roles both as workers and as mothers. At the height of the Second Five-Year Plan, many women's rights were revoked, including the right to an abortion. The "New Woman" of the revolutionary period gave way to the post-1936 woman, depicted by the state as the perfect mother who matched her husband's productivity in the workplace, ran the household, and raised a large family.

Focus Questions

In this excerpt, can you identify why Stalin considers abortion a threat to the Soviet state? Why does a working woman fulfill her duties as a citizen through motherhood?

When we speak of strengthening the Soviet family, we are speaking precisely of the struggle against the survivals of a bourgeois attitude towards marriage, women and children. So-called "free love" and all disorderly sex life are bourgeois through and through, and have nothing to do with either socialist principles or the ethics and standards of conduct of the Soviet citizen. Socialist doctrine shows this, and it is proved by life itself.

The elite of our country, the best of the Soviet youth, are as a rule also excellent family men who dearly love their children. And vice versa: the man who does not take marriage seriously, and abandons his children to the whims of fate, is usually also a bad worker and a poor member of society.

Fatherhood and motherhood have long been virtues in this country. This can be seen at the first glance, without searching enquiry. Go through the parks and streets of Moscow or of any other town in the Soviet Union on a holiday, and you will see not a few young men walking with pink-cheeked, well-fed babies in their arms. . . .

The toilers of our land have paid with their blood for the right to a life of joy, and a life of joy implies the right to have one's own family and healthy, happy children. Millions of workers beyond the frontiers of our land are still deprived of this joy, for there unemployment, hunger and helpless poverty are rampant. Old maids and elderly bachelors, a rare thing in our country, are frequent in the West, and that is no accident.

We alone have all the conditions under which a working woman can fulfill her duties as a citizen and as a mother responsible for the birth and early upbringing of her children.

A woman without children merits our pity, for she does not know the full joy of life. Our Soviet women, full-blooded citizens of the freest country in the world, have been given the bliss of motherhood. We must safeguard our family and raise and rear healthy Soviet heroes!

CHRONOLOGY

CHRONOLOGY

The Soviet Union's Separate Path

November 1917	Bolsheviks and Red Guard seize power
1919	Creation of the Communist International (Comintern)
1920	Legalization of abortion and divorce
1921	End of the civil war
1921	Introduction of the New Economic Policy
3 April 1922	Stalin becomes secretary general of the Communist party
21 January 1924	Lenin dies
1924–1929	Comintern policy of "Unity of the Working Classes"
1927	Dissatisfied peasants hoard grain
November 1927	Trotsky expelled from Communist party
1928	Stalin introduces grain requisitioning
November 1929	Bukharin expelled from Politburo
1929	Introduction of First Five-Year Plan and the collectivization of agriculture
1929–1933	Comintern policy of noncooperation with Social Democratic parties
1933–1937	Second Five-Year Plan
1934–1938	Great Purge
1936	Abortion declared illegal
1938	Third Five-Year Plan

By the early 1930s, reforms affecting women were in trouble in large part because of a plummeting birthrate. The decline created special worries for Soviet planners, who forecast doom if the trend was not reversed. In 1936, a woman's right to choose to end a first pregnancy was revoked. In the following decade, all abortions were made illegal. Homosexuality was declared a criminal offense. The family was glorified as the mainstay of the communist order, and the independence of women was challenged as a threat to Soviet productivity. While motherhood was idealized, the Stalinist drive to industrialize could not dispense with full-time women workers.

Women's double burden in the home and workplace became heavier during Stalin's reign. Most Russian women held full-time jobs in the factories or on the farms. They also worked what they called a "second shift" in running a household and taking care of children. In the industrialized nations of western Europe, the growth of a consumer economy lightened to some extent women's labor in the home. In the Soviet Union, procuring the simplest necessities was woman's work that required waiting in long lines for hours. Lack of indoor plumbing meant that women spent time hauling water for their families at the end of a working day. In such ways, rapid industrialization exacted its special price from Soviet women.

In the 1920s and 1930s, the Soviet search for stability and prosperity took the Soviet Union down a path very different from that of the states of western Europe. Rejecting an accommodation with a market economy, Stalin committed the Soviet people to planned rapid industrialization that was accomplished through mass repression and great human suffering. Insulated from world markets and the devastation of the Great Depression, the Soviet Union relied on a massive state bureaucratic system to achieve "socialism in one country" and to make the Soviet state into an industrial giant.

THE RISE OF FASCIST DICTATORSHIP IN ITALY

Throughout western Europe, parliamentary institutions, representative government, and electoral politics offered no ready solutions to the problems of economic collapse and the political upheaval on the left and the right. **Fascism** promised what liberal democratic societies failed to deliver—a way out of the economic and political morass. Fascism, which emerged first in Italy out of the political and social upheaval following World War I, is a totalitarian political system that glorifies the state and totally subordinates the individual to the state's needs. Italy was the first fascist state, followed in the 1930s by Germany and Spain. In all three cases, fascist rule meant dictatorship by a strong, charismatic leader. It promised to those subjected to its rule an escape from parliamentary chaos, party wranglings, and the threat of communism. Fascism promised more: by identifying ready enemies—scapegoats for failed economic and national ambitions—fascism promised that it held the answer for those who sought protection and security.

Fascism sounded very like socialism. In the Soviet Union, Bolshevik leaders reassured their people that socialism was the only way of dealing with the weaknesses and inequities of the world capitalist system laid bare in the world war. In their initial condemnations of the capitalist economy and liberal political institutions and values, fascists employed revolutionary language similar to that of the Left while manipulating in radically new ways the political symbols of the Right—the nation, the flag, and the army. However, fascism rejected the socialist tenet of the collective or government ownership of production and property. It was violently opposed to socialist egalitarianism. Instead, fascism promised to steer a course between the uncertainties and exploitation of a liberal capitalist system and the revolutionary upheaval and expropriation of a socialist system. Fascism was ultranationalist, and the use of force was central to its appeal.

The word *fascism* is derived from the Latin *fasces,* the name for the bundle of rods with ax head carried by the magistrates of the Roman Empire. Fascism was rooted in the mass political movements of the late nineteenth century, which glorified the nation, emphasized antiliberal values, and pursued a politics of violence. The electoral successes of the German variant—National Socialism, or **Nazism**—were just beginning in the late 1920s. In the same period, fascist movements were making their appearance in England, Hungary, Spain, and France. But none was more successful and none demanded more attention than the fascist experiment in Italy, which inspired observers throughout Europe to emulate it.

Mussolini's Italy

Italy was a poor nation. Although Italy was one of the victorious Allies in World War I, Italians believed that their country had been betrayed by the peace settlement of 1919 by being denied the territory and status it deserved. A recently created electoral system based on universal manhood suffrage had produced parliamentary chaos and ministerial instability. The lack of coherent political programs only heightened the general disapproval with government that accompanied the peace negotiations. People were beginning to doubt the parliamentary regime's hold on the future. It was under those circumstances that the Fascist party, led by Benito Mussolini (1883–1945), entered politics in 1920 by attacking the large Socialist and Popular (Catholic) parties.

The Rise of Mussolini.   Mussolini had begun his prewar political career as a Socialist. The young Mussolini was arrested numerous times for Socialist political activities and placed under state surveillance. An ardent nationalist, he volunteered for combat in World War I and was promoted to the rank of corporal. Injured in early 1917 by an exploding shell detonated during firing practice, he returned to Milan to continue his work as editor of *Il Populo d'Italia* ("The People of Italy"), the newspaper he founded in 1914 to promote Italian participation in the war.

Mussolini yearned to be the leader of a revolution in Italy comparable to that directed by Lenin in Russia. Although his doctrinal allegiance to socialism was beginning to flag, Mussolini, like Lenin, recognized the power of the printed word to stir political passions. Emphasizing nationalist goals and vague measures of socioeconomic transformation, Mussolini identified a new enemy for Italy—bolshevism. He organized his followers into the Fascist party, a political movement that, by utilizing strict party discipline, quickly developed its own national network.

Many Fascists were former Socialists and war veterans like Mussolini who were disillusioned with postwar government.

■ Gerardo Dottori, *Portrait of the Duce* (1933). Dottori was one of a group of Italian Futurist artists whose works reflected their fascination with aircraft, flight, and extraterrestrial fantasy. In 1929, they published a manifesto in which they launched the idea of an art linked to the most exciting aspect of contemporary life. During the 1930s the artists sought to align themselves with Mussolini's Fascist regime.

They dreamed of Italy as a great world power, as it had been in the days of ancient Rome. Their enemies were not only Communists with their international outlook but also the big businesses, which they believed drained Italy's resources and kept its people poor and powerless. Panicky members of the lower middle classes sought security against the economic uncertainties of inflation and were willing to endorse violence to achieve it. Unions were to be feared because they used strikes to further their demands for higher salaries and better working conditions for their members while other social groups languished. Near civil war erupted as Italian Communists and Fascists clashed violently in street battles in the early 1920s. The Fascists entered the national political arena and succeeded on the local level in overthrowing city governments. In spite of its visibility on the national political scene, however, the Fascist party was still very much a minority party when Mussolini refused to serve as a junior minister in the new government in 1922.

The March on Rome.   His refusal to serve as representative of a minority party reflected Mussolini's belief that the

Fascists had to be in charge. On 28 October 1922, the Fascists undertook their famous **March on Rome**, which followed similar Fascist takeovers in Milan and Bologna. Mussolini's followers occupied the capital. The event marked the beginning of the end of parliamentary government and the emergence of Fascist dictatorship and institutionalized violence. Rising unemployment and severe inflation contributed to the politically deteriorating situation that helped bring Mussolini to power.

Destruction and violence, not the ballot box, became fascism's most successful tools for securing political power. *Squadristi*—armed bands of Fascist thugs—attacked their political enemies (both Catholic and Socialist), destroyed private property, dismantled the printing presses of adversary groups, and generally terrorized both rural and urban populations. By the end of 1922, Fascists could claim a following of 300,000 members endorsing the new politics of intimidation.

The Fascists achieved their first parliamentary majority by using violent tactics of intimidation to secure votes. One outspoken Socialist critic of Fascist violence, Giacomo Matteotti (1885–1924), was murdered by Mussolini's subordinates. The deed threatened the survival of Mussolini's government as 150 Socialist, Liberal, and Popular party deputies resigned in protest. Mussolini chose that moment to consolidate his position by arresting and silencing his enemies to preserve order. Within two years, Fascists were firmly in control, monopolizing politics, suppressing a free press, creating a secret police force, and transforming social and economic policies. Mussolini destroyed political parties and made Italy into a one-party dictatorship.

Dealing with Big Business and the Church.   In 1925, the Fascist party entered into an agreement with Italian industrialists that gave industry a position of privilege protected by the state in return for its support. Mussolini presented the partnership as the end to class conflict, but in fact it ensured the dominance of capital and the control of labor and professional groups.

A corrupt bureaucracy filled with Mussolini's cronies and run on bribes orchestrated the new relationship between big business and the state. In spite of official claims, Fascist Italy had not done well in riding out the Great Depression. A large rural sector masked the problems of high unemployment by absorbing an urban work force without jobs. Corporatism, a system of economic self-rule by interest groups promoted on paper by Mussolini, was a sham that had little to do with the dominance of the Italian economy by big business. By lending money to Italian businesses on the verge of bankruptcy, the government acquired a controlling interest in key industries, including steel, shipping, heavy machinery, and electricity.

Mussolini, himself an atheist, recognized the importance of the Catholic Church in securing his regime. In 1870, when Italy had been unified, the pope had been deprived of his territories in Rome. That event, which became known as the "Roman Question," proved to be the source of ongoing problems for Italian governments. In February 1929, Mussolini settled matters with Pope Pius XI in the Lateran Treaty and the accompanying Concordat, which granted to the pope sovereignty over the territory around St. Peter's Basilica and the Vatican. The treaty also protected the role of the Catholic Church in education and guaranteed that Italian marriage laws would conform to Catholic dogma.

By 1929, *Il Duce* (the leader), as Mussolini preferred to be called, was at the height of his popularity and power. Apparent political harmony had been achieved by ruthlessly crushing fascism's opponents. The agreement with the pope, which restored harmony with the Church, was matched by a new sense of order and accomplishment in Italian society and the economy.

Mussolini's Plans for Empire

As fascism failed to initiate effective social programs, Mussolini's popularity plummeted. In the hope of boosting his sagging image, *Il Duce* committed Italy to a foreign policy of imperial conquest.

Italy had conquered Ottoman-controlled Libya in North Africa in 1911. Now, in the 1930s, Mussolini targeted Ethiopia for his expansionist aims and ordered Italian troops to invade the east African kingdom in October 1935. Using poison gas and aerial bombing, the Italian army defeated the native troops of Ethiopian Emperor Haile Selassie (1892–1975). European democracies, under the pressure of public opinion, cried out against the wanton and unwarranted attack, but Mussolini succeeded in proclaiming Ethiopia an Italian territory.

The invasion of Ethiopia exposed the ineffectiveness of the League of Nations to stop such flagrant violations of its covenant. Great Britain and France took no action other than to express their disapproval of Italy's conquest. Yet a rift opened between the two western European nations and Italy. Mussolini had distanced himself from the Nazi state in the first years of the German regime's existence, and he was critical of Hitler's plans for rearmament. Now, in light of disapproval from Britain and France, Mussolini turned to Germany for support. In October 1936, Italy aligned itself with Germany in what Mussolini called the Rome-Berlin Axis. The alliance was little more than a pledge of friendship. However, less than three years later, in May 1939, Germany and Italy agreed to offer support in any offensive or defensive war. The agreement, known as the Pact of Steel, in fact bound Italy militarily to Germany.

Mussolini pursued other imperialist goals within Europe. The small Balkan nation of Albania entered into a series of agreements with Mussolini beginning in the mid-1920s that made it dependent financially and militarily on Italian aid. By 1933, Albanian independence had been undermined by its "friendship" with its stronger neighbor. In order not to be outdone by Hitler, who was at the time dismantling Czechoslovakia, Mussolini invaded and annexed Albania in April 1939, ending the fiction that Albania was an Italian protectorate.

■ Ethiopian chieftain and armed forces wait to encounter Mussolini's invading troops, 1935.

HITLER AND THE THIRD REICH

Repeated economic, political, and diplomatic crises of the 1920s buffeted Germany's internal stability. Most Germans considered reparations to be an unfair burden, so onerous that payment should be evaded and resisted in every way possible. The German government did not promote inflation in order to avoid paying reparations, but rather to avoid a postwar recession, revive industrial production, and maintain high employment. But the moderate inflation that stimulated the economy spun out of control into destructive hyperinflation.

The fiscal problems of the Weimar Republic obscure the fact that, in the period after World War I, Germany experienced real economic growth. German industry advanced, productivity was high, and German workers flexed their union muscles to secure better wages. Weimar committed itself to large expenditures for social welfare programs, including unemployment insurance. By 1930, social welfare was responsible for 40 percent of all public expenditures, compared to 19 percent before the war. All those changes, apparently fostering the well-being of the German people, aggravated the fears of German big businessmen, who resented the trade unions and the perceived trend toward socialism. The lower middle classes also felt cheated and economically threatened by inflation. They were a politically volatile group, susceptible to the antidemocratic appeals of some of Weimar's critics.

Growing numbers of Germans expressed disgust with parliamentary democracy. The Great Depression dealt a staggering blow to the Weimar Republic in 1929 as American loans were withdrawn and German unemployment skyrocketed. By 1930, the antagonisms among the parties were so great that the parliament was no longer effective in ruling Germany. As

chancellor from 1930 to 1932, Centrist leader Heinrich Brüning (1885–1970) attempted to break the impasse by overriding the Weimar constitution. The move opened the door to enemies of the republic, and Brüning was forced to resign.

Hitler's Rise to Power

Adolf Hitler (1889–1945) knew how to exploit the Weimar Republic's weaknesses for his own political ends. He denounced reparations. He made a special appeal to Germans who saw their savings disappearing, first in inflation and then in the Great Depression. He promised a way out of economic hardship and the reassertion of Germany's claim to status as a world power.

Hitler was born an Austrian, outside the German fatherland he came to rule. The son of a customs agent who worked on the Austrian side of the border with Germany, he came from a middle-class family with social pretensions. Aimlessness and failure marked Hitler's early life. Denied admission to architecture school, he took odd jobs to survive. Hitler welcomed the outbreak of war in 1914, which put an end to his self-described sleepwalking. He volunteered immediately for service in the German army. Wounded and gassed at the front, he was twice awarded the Iron Cross for bravery in action.

Hitler later described what he had learned from war in terms of the solidarity of struggle against a common enemy and the purity of heroism. The army provided him with a sense of security and direction. What he learned from the peace that followed was an equally powerful lesson that determined his commitment to a career in politics. Hitler profoundly believed in the stab-in-the-back legend: Germany had not lost the war, he insisted, it had been defeated from within—or stabbed in the back by Communists, Socialists, liberals, and Jews. The Weimar Republic signed the humiliating Treaty of Versailles and continued to betray the German people by taxing wages to pay reparations. Hitler's highly distorted and false view of the origins of the republic and its policies was the basis for his demand that the "Weimar System" must be abolished and replaced by a Nazi regime.

The Beer Hall Putsch of 1923.

For his failed attempt to seize control of the Munich municipal government in 1923, in an event that became known as the Beer Hall Putsch because of the locale in which Hitler attempted to initiate the "national revolution," he served nine months of a five-year sentence in prison. There he began writing the first volume of his autobiography, *Mein Kampf* ("My Struggle"). In that turgid work, he condemned the decadence of Western society and singled out for special contempt Jews, Bolsheviks, and middle-class liberals. From his failed attempt to seize power, Hitler learned the important lesson that he could succeed against the German republic only from within, by coming to power legally. By 1928, he had a small party of about 100,000 Nazis. Modifying his anticapitalist message, Hitler appealed to the discontented small farmers and tailored his nationalist sentiments to a frightened middle class. has to gain the support of the Germans

Hitler as Chancellor.

Adolf Hitler became chancellor of Germany in January 1933 by legal, constitutional, and democratic means. The Nazi party was supported by farmers, small businessmen, civil servants, and young people. In the elections of 1930 and 1932, the voters made the Nazi party the largest party in the country—although not the majority one. President Paul von Hindenburg (1925–1934) invited Hitler to form a government. Hitler claimed that Germany was on the verge of a Communist revolution and persuaded Hindenburg and the Reichstag to consent to a series of emergency laws, which the Nazis used to establish themselves firmly in power. Legislation outlawed freedom of the press and public meetings and approved of the use of violence against Hitler's political enemies, particularly the Socialists and the Communists. Within two months after Hitler came to office, Germany was a police state and Hitler was a "legal" dictator who could issue his own laws without having to gain the consent of either the Reichstag or the president. After carrying out the "legal revolution" that incapacitated representative institutions and ended civil liberties, the Nazis worked to consolidate their position and their power. They abolished all other political parties, established single-party rule, dissolved trade unions, and put their own people into state governments and the bureaucracy.

Many observers at the time considered the new Nazi state to be a monolithic structure, ruled and coordinated from the center. That was not, however, an accurate observation. Hitler actually issued few directives. Policy was set by an often chaotic jockeying for power among rival Nazi factions. Hitler's political alliance with traditional conservative and nationalist politicians, industrialists, and military men helped give the state created by Adolf Hitler a claim to legitimacy based on continuity with the past. Hitler called that state the **Third Reich.** (The first Reich was the Holy Roman Empire; the second Reich was the German Empire created by Bismarck in 1871.)

The first of the paramilitary groups so important in orchestrating violence to eliminate Hitler's enemies was the SA (Sturmabteilung), or the storm troopers, under Ernst Röhm (1887–1934). Röhm helped Hitler achieve electoral victories by beating up political opponents on the streets and using other thuglike tactics. SA followers, also known as Brownshirts, adopted a military appearance for their terrorist operations. By the beginning of 1934, there were 2.5 million members of the SA, vastly outnumbering the regular army of 100,000 soldiers.

Heinrich Himmler (1900–1945) headed an elite force of the Nazi party within the SA called the SS (Schutzstaffel, or protection squad), a group whose members wore black uniforms and menacing skull-and-crossbones insignia on their caps. Himmler seized control of political policing and emerged as Röhm's chief rival. In 1934, with the assistance of the army, Hitler and the SS purged the SA and executed Röhm, thereby making the SS Hitler's exclusive elite corps, entrusted with carrying out his extreme programs and responsible later for the greatest atrocities of World War II.

Nazi Goals

Hitler identified three organizing goals for the Nazi state: *Lebensraum* (living space), rearmament, and economic recovery. The goals were the basis of the new foreign policy Hitler forged for Germany, and they served to fuse that foreign policy with the domestic politics of the Third Reich. These goals served the ultimate purpose of securing totalitarian power for the German state. All three were based on Hitler's version of social Darwinism—that the German race was the fittest and would survive and prosper at the expense of others.

Living Space.

Key to Hitler's worldview was the concept of *Lebensraum*, living space, in which he considered the right and the duty of the German master race to be the world's greatest empire, one that would endure for a thousand years. Hitler first stated his ideals about living space in *Mein Kampf*, where he argued that superior nations had the right to expand into the territories of inferior states. Living space meant for him German domination of central and eastern Europe at the expense of Slavic peoples. The Aryan master race would dominate inferior peoples. Colonies were unacceptable because they weakened rather than strengthened national security; Germany must annex territories within continental Europe. Hitler's primary target was what he called "Russia and her vassal border states."

Rearmament.

Hitler continued the secret rearmament of Germany begun by his Weimar predecessors in violation of

■ Adolf Hitler salutes a huge crowd of Hitler Youth at a rally. The mass meetings were used by the Nazi mythmakers to enhance Hitler's image as the savior of Germany.

the restrictions of the Treaty of Versailles. He withdrew Germany from the League of Nations and from the World Disarmament Conference, signaling a new direction for German foreign policy. In 1935, he publicly renounced the Treaty of Versailles and announced that Germany was rearming. The following year he openly defied the French and moved German troops into the Rhineland, the demilitarized security zone that separated the armed forces of the two countries. Hitler also reversed the cooperative relationship his nation had established with the Soviet Union in the 1920s. In 1933, the German state was illicitly spending 1 billion Reichsmarks on arms. By 1939, annual expenditures to prepare Germany for war had climbed to 30 billion.

Hitler knew that preparation for war meant more than amassing weapons; it also required full economic recovery. One of Germany's great weaknesses in World War I had been its dependence on imports of raw materials and foodstuffs. To avoid a repetition of that problem, Hitler instituted a program of autarky, or economic self-sufficiency, by which Germany aimed to produce everything that it consumed. He encouraged the efforts of German industry to develop synthetics for petroleum, rubber, metals, and fats.

NATIONAL INCOME OF THE POWERS IN 1937 AND PERCENTAGE SPENT ON DEFENSE

	National Income (billions of dollars)	Percentage Spent on Defense
United States	68	1.5
British Empire	22	5.7
France	10	9.1
Germany	17	23.5
Italy	6	14.5
USSR	19	26.4
Japan	4	28.2

Economic Recovery. The state pumped money into the private economy, creating new jobs and achieving full employment after 1936, an accomplishment unmatched by any other European nation. Recovery was built on armaments as well as consumer products. The Nazi state's concentration of economic power in the hands of a few strengthened big businesses. The victims of corporate consolidation were the small firms that could no longer compete with government-sponsored corporations such as the chemical giant I. G. Farben.

In 1936, Hitler introduced his Four-Year Plan, dedicated to the goals of full-scale rearmament and economic self-sufficiency. Before the third year of the Four-Year Plan, however, Hitler was aware of the failure to develop synthetic products sufficient to meet Germany's needs. But if Germany could not create substitutes, it could control territories that provided fuel, metals, and foodstuffs. Germany had been importing raw materials from southeastern Europe and wielding increasing economic influence over the Balkan countries. Hitler now realized that economic self-sufficiency could be directly linked to the main goal of the Nazi state: *Lebensraum*.

Thus Hitler was committed to territorial expansion from the time he came to power. He rearmed Germany for that purpose. When economists and generals cautioned him, he refused to listen. Instead, he informed them of his commitment to *Lebensraum* and of his intention to use aggressive war to acquire it. He removed his critics from their positions of power and replaced them with Nazis loyal to him.

Propaganda, Racism, and Culture

To reinforce his personal power and to sell his program for the "total state," Hitler created a Ministry of Propaganda under Joseph Goebbels (1897–1945), a former journalist and Nazi party district leader in Berlin. Goebbels was a master of manipulating emotions in mass demonstrations held to whip up enthusiasm for Nazi policies. Flying the flag and wearing the swastika signified identification with the Nazi state. With his magnetic appeal, Hitler inspired and manipulated the devotion of hundreds of thousands of those who heard him speak. Leni Riefenstahl, a young filmmaker working for Hitler, made a documentary of a National Socialist party rally at Nüremberg. In scenes of swooning women and cheering men, her film, called *Triumph of the Will,* recorded the dramatic force of Hitler's rhetoric and his ability to move the German people. Hitler's public charisma masked a profoundly troubled and incomplete individual capable of irrational rage and sick hatred of his fellow human beings. His warped views of the world were responsible for the greatest outrages ever committed in the name of legitimate power. Yet millions, including admirers in western Europe and the United States, succumbed to his appeal.

Targeting the Young and Women. Family life, too, was carefully regulated through the propaganda machinery. Loyalty only to the state meant less loyalty to the family. In 1939, 82 percent of all German boys and girls between the

■ The *Frauen Warte* was the Nazi Party's official magazine for women. In this cover from an August 1938 issue, a happy family is presented as the best foundation of the German people.

ages of 10 and 18 were members of Nazi-controlled organizations. Special youth organizations, including the Hitler Youth, indoctrinated boys with nationalistic and military values. Organizations for girls were intended to mold them into worthy wives and mothers. Woman's natural function, Hitler argued, was to serve in the home. Education for women beyond the care of home and family was a waste. Adult women had their own organizations to serve the Nazi state. The German Women's Bureau under Gertrud Scholtz-Klink instructed women in their "proper" female duties. In an effort to promote large families, the state paid allowances to couples for getting married, subsidized families according to their size, and gave tax breaks to large families. Abortion and birth control were outlawed, and women who sought such measures risked severe penalties and imprisonment.

By 1937, the need for women workers conflicted with the goals of Nazi propaganda. With the outbreak of war in 1939, women were urged to work, especially in jobs such as munitions manufacture formerly held by men. For working women with

ADOLF HITLER ON "RACIAL PURITY"

The purity of German blood was a recurrent theme in Hitler's speeches and writings from the beginning of his political career. In attacking both liberalism and socialism, Hitler offered racial superiority as the essence of the National Socialist "revolution." This speech, delivered in Berlin on 30 January 1937, lays out his attack on the concept of individual rights and humanity in favor of the folk *community.*

Focus Questions

In this diatribe, how does race function to promote the "folk" and to undermine the individual's rights? Is Hitler's goal here to create "a better understanding" among nations?

The most important plank in the National Socialist program is to abolish the liberal idea of the individual and the Marxist idea of humanity and to substitute for them the folk community rooted in the soil and held together by the bond of common blood. This sounds simple, but it involves a principle which has great consequences.

For the first time and in the first country our people are being taught to understand that, of all the tasks we have to face, the most noble and the most sacred for all mankind is the concept that each racial species must preserve the purity of blood which God has given to it.

The greatest revolution won by National Socialism is that it has pierced the veil which hid from us the knowledge that all human errors may be attributed to the conditions of the time and hence can be remedied, but there is one error that cannot be set right once it has been made by men—that is, the failure to understand the importance of keeping the blood and the race free from intermingling, and in this way to alter God's gift. It is not for human beings to discuss why

Providence created different races. Rather it is important to understand the fact that it will punish those who pay no attention to its work of creation. . . .

I hereby prophesy that, just as knowledge that the earth moves around the sun led to a revolutionary change in the world picture, so will the blood-and-race doctrine of the National Socialist movement bring about a revolutionary change in our knowledge. . . . It will also change the course of history in the future.

This will not lead to difficulties between nations. On the contrary, it will lead to a better understanding between them. But at the same time it will prevent the Jews, under the mask of world citizenship, from thrusting themselves among all nations as an element of domestic chaos. . . .

The National Socialist movement limits its domestic activities to those individuals who belong to one people. It refuses to permit those of a foreign race to have any influence whatever on our political, intellectual, or cultural life. We refuse to give any members of a foreign race a dominant position in our national economic system.

In our folk community, which is based on ties of blood, in the results which National Socialism has obtained by training the public in the idea of this folk-community, lies the deepest reason for the great success of our Revolution.

---

families, the double burden was a heavy one, as women were required to work long shifts—60-hour workweeks were not unusual—for low wages. Many women resisted entering the work force if they had other income or could live on the cash payments they received as the wives of soldiers. At the beginning of 1943, the German people were ordered to make sacrifices for a new era of "total war." Female labor became compulsory, and women were drafted into working for the war. *a lot of parallels to Mussolini*

Enemies of the State.   Propaganda condemned everything foreign, including Mickey Mouse, who was declared an enemy of the state in the 1930s. Purging foreign influences meant purging political opponents, especially members of the Communist party, who were rounded up and sent to concentration camps in Germany. Communism was identified as an international Jewish conspiracy to destroy the German *Volk,* or people. Nazi literature also identified "asocials," those who were considered deviant in any way, including homosexuals, who were likewise to be expelled. Euthanasia was used against the mentally ill and the mentally disabled in the 1930s.

Concentration camps were expanded to contain enemies of the state. Later, when concentration camps became sites of extermination and forced labor, gypsies, homosexuals, criminals, and religious offenders had to wear insignia of different colors to indicate the reason for their persecution. The people who received the greatest attention for exclusion from Nazi Germany, and then from Europe, were the Jews.

Scapegoating Jews.   The first measures against German Jews—their exclusion from public employment and higher education—began almost immediately in 1933. In 1935, the Nuremberg Laws were enacted to identify Jews, to deprive them of their citizenship, and to forbid marriage and extramarital sexual relations between Jews and non-Jews. On the night of 9 November 1938, synagogues were set afire and books and valuables owned by Jews were confiscated throughout Germany. Jews were beaten, about 91 were killed, and 20,000 to 30,000 were imprisoned in concentration camps. The night came to be called *Kristallnacht,* meaning "night of broken glass," which referred to the Jewish shop windows smashed under orders from Goebbels. The government claimed that *Kristallnacht* was an outpouring of the German people's will. An atmosphere of state-sanctioned hate prevailed.

Racism was nothing new in European culture, nor was its particular variant, anti-Semitism—hatred of Jews—the creation of the Third Reich. The link the Nazis cultivated between racism and politics was built on cultural precedents. In the 1890s, in France and Austria and elsewhere in Europe, anti-Semitism was espoused by political and professional groups that formed themselves around issues of militant nationalism, authoritarianism, and mass politics. Hitler was a racist and an anti-Semite, and he placed theories of race at the core of his fascist ideology. "Experts" decided that sterilization was the surest way to protect "German blood." In 1933, one of the early laws of Hitler's new Reich decreed compulsory sterilization of "undesirables" in order to "eliminate inferior genes." The Nazi state decided who the undesirables were and forced the sterilization of 400,000 men and women.

The Third Reich was a government that delivered on its promises to end unemployment, to improve productivity, to break through the logjam of parliamentary obstacles, and to return Germany to the international arena as a contender for power. Hitler's Nazi state ruled by violence, coercion, and intimidation. With a propaganda machine that glorified the leader and vilified groups singled out as scapegoats for Germany's problems, Hitler undermined democratic institutions and civil liberties in his pursuit of German power.

DEMOCRACIES IN CRISIS

Democracies in the 1930s turned in on themselves in order to survive. In contrast to the Fascist mobilization of society and the Soviet restructuring of the economy, European democracies took small, tentative steps to respond to the challenges of the Great Depression. Democratic leaders lacked creative vision or even clear policy. Both democratic France and Great Britain were less successful than Nazi Germany in responding to the challenges of the Great Depression. France paid a high price for parliamentary stalemate and was still severely depressed on the eve of war in 1938–1939. Great Britain maintained a stagnant economy and stable politics under Conservative leadership. Internal dissension ripped Spain apart. Its civil war assumed broader dimensions as the Soviet Union, Italy, and Germany struggled over Spain's future while Europe's democratic nations stood by and accepted defeat.

The Failure of the Left in France

France's Third Republic, like most European parliamentary democracies in the 1930s, was characterized by a multiparty system. Genuine political differences often separated one party from another. The tendency toward parliamentary stalemate was aggravated by the Great Depression and by the increasingly extremist politics on both the left and the right in response to developments in the Soviet Union and Germany.

■ This photograph of striking workers at the Argenteuil car factories in Lorraine captures the spirit of optimism that swept France in 1936.

Mussolini does similar things but is unsuccessful

The belief of the French people in a private enterprise economy was shaken by the Great Depression, but no new unifying belief replaced it. Some believed that state planning was the answer; others were sure that state intervention had caused the problem. Distrusting both the New Deal model of the United States and the Nazi response to depression politics, the Third Republic followed a haphazard, wait-and-see policy of insulating the economy, discouraging competition, and protecting favored interests in both industry and agriculture. Stimulating the economy by deficit spending was considered anathema. Devaluation of the franc, which might have helped French exports, was regarded by policy makers as an unpatriotic act. France stood fast as a bastion of liberal belief in the self-adjusting mechanism of the market, and it suffered greatly for it. Party politics worked to reinforce the defensive rather than the offensive response to the challenges of depression and a sluggish economy.

In 1936, an electoral mandate for change swept the Left into power. The new premier, Léon Blum (1872–1950), was a Socialist. Lacking the votes to rule with an exclusively Socialist government, Blum formed a coalition of Left and Center parties intent on economic reforms known as the **Popular Front.** Before Blum's government could take power, a wave of strikes swept France. Although reluctant to intervene in the economy, the Popular Front nevertheless was pushed into some action. It promised wage increases, paid vacations, and collective bargaining to the great public jubilation of workers. The reduced workweek of 40 hours caused a drop in productivity, as did the short-lived one-month vacation policy. The government did nothing to prevent the outflow of investment capital from France. Higher wages failed to generate increased consumer demand because employers raised prices to cover their higher operating costs.

German rearmament, now publicly known, forced France into rearmament, which it could ill afford. Blum's government failed in 1937, with France still bogged down in a sluggish and depressed economy. The last peacetime government of the

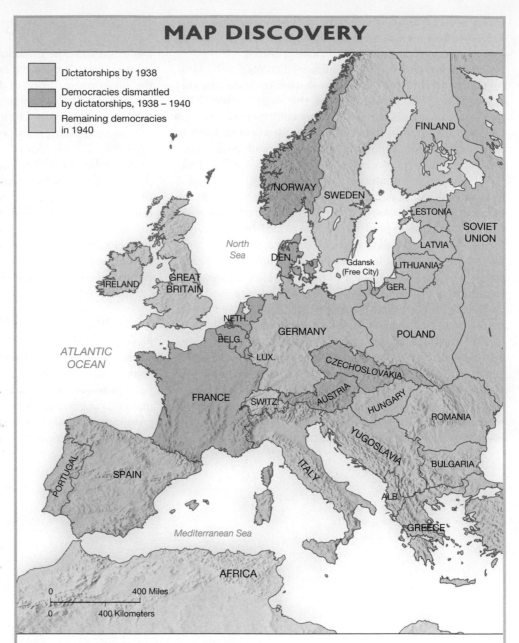

MAP DISCOVERY

Dictatorships by 1938

Democracies dismantled by dictatorships, 1938 – 1940

Remaining democracies in 1940

Europe: Types of Government

Note the prevalence of dictatorships throughout Europe in 1940. How many democracies were dismantled by dictatorships between 1938 and 1940? What were the similarities and differences among these dictatorships? By 1940, most European nations were ruled by dictatorships. What five countries were the exceptions? What generalizations, if any, might you make about those five democracies?

1930s represented a conservative swing back to laissez-faire policies that put the needs of business above those of workers and brought a measure of revival to the French economy.

The radical Right drew strength from the Left's failures. Right-wing leagues and organizations multiplied, appealing to a frightened middle class. The failure of the Socialists, in turn, drove many sympathizers further to the left to join the Communist party. A divided France could not stand up to the foreign policy challenges of the 1930s posed by Hitler's provocations.

Muddling Through in Great Britain

Great Britain was hard hit by the Great Depression of the 1930s; only Germany and the United States experienced comparable economic devastation. It took a coalition of moderate groups from the three parties—Liberal, Conservative, and Labour—to address the issues of high unemployment, a growing government deficit, a banking crisis, and the flight of capital. The National Government (1931–1935) was a centrist, nonpartisan coalition whose members included Ramsay MacDonald, retained as prime minister, and Stanley Baldwin (1867–1947), a Conservative with a background in iron and steel manufacturing.

Slow Recovery. In response to the endemic crisis, the National Government took Britain off the international gold standard and devalued the pound. In order to protect domestic production, tariffs were established. The British economy showed signs of slow recovery, probably due less to the gov-

ernment measures than to a gradual improvement in the business cycle. The government had survived the crisis without resorting to the kinds of creative alternatives devised in the Scandinavian countries, where, for example, consumer and producer cooperatives provided widespread economic relief. Moderates and classical liberals in Great Britain persisted in defending the nonintervention of the government in the economy, despite new economic theories such as that of John Maynard Keynes (1883–1946), who urged government spending to stimulate consumer demand as the best way to shorten the duration of the Great Depression.

The British Union of Fascists.   In 1932, Sir Oswald Mosley (1896–1980) founded the British Union of Fascists (BUF), consisting of goon squads and bodyguards. The BUF was opposed to free trade liberalism and communism alike. Mosley developed a corporate model for economic and political life in which interest groups rather than an electorate would be represented in a new kind of parliament. He favored, above all, national solutions by relying on imperial development; he rejected the world of international finance as corrupt.

The BUF shared similarities with European Fascist organizations. BUF squads beat up their political opponents and began attacking Jews, especially the eastern European émigrés living in London. The British fascists struck a responsive chord among the poorest working-class people of London's East End; at its peak the group claimed a membership of 20,000. Public alarm over increasingly inflammatory and anti-Semitic rhetoric converged with parliamentary denunciation. Popular support for the group was already beginning to

■ A British Union of Fascists unit salutes founder Sir Oswald Mosley in London, October 1936.

THE SCREAMS FROM GUERNICA

Rarely does a piece of art scream out. The mural *Guernica* is different. *Listen* to the painting shown here. It is a painting whose images convey sounds: the shrieks of terror, fear, suffering, and death. There is a chaos of noise here that seems at odds with the drab grays, black, and white, the monochromatic colorlessness of the artist's palette. But no, the lack of color only heightens the noise and allows us to focus on the sound, the screams that come from the open mouths of human and beast on the canvas. Death and brutality reverberate throughout the painting. The open mouths of the dead baby's mother, the bull standing behind her, the small bird to the right of the bull, and the wounded horse at the center of the canvas emit fear like projectiles—beak and tongues thrusting forth in pointed daggers.

The artist Pablo Picasso (1881–1973) painted the great mural in May and June 1937 for the Spanish Pavilion of the International Exhibition to be held in Paris. He called it *Guernica* in commemoration of the bombing of the small Basque town in Spain by German planes at the end of April 1937. The destruction of Guernica was an event that shocked the world and devastated the Spanish artist, then living in France. Working in collaboration with the insurgent forces of Francisco Franco (1892–1975), German planes dropped bomb after bomb on the ancient city, destroying it in three and a half hours. Their purpose was to cut off the retreat of loyalist government troops and to terrorize civilians through saturation bombing. Picasso demonstrates here vividly that noncombatants, represented by the women and child, were no longer just hapless bystanders but were, in fact, the very targets of indiscriminate killing.

Guernica is a huge canvas, measuring more than 11 feet high and 25 feet wide. It dwarfs spectators who stand before it, enveloping them in a modern-day apocalypse of contorted bodies. We do not look at war directly in the mural but at the terror it creates in this vision of needless slaughter. Picasso deliberately used the traditional religious symbols of the Madonna and Child and the Pietà as models for his terrifying image of maternity. The lips of the baby, who hangs like a rag doll in the arms of its despairing mother on the far left of the canvas, are sealed in the silence of death. The mother finds her counterpoint in the figure of the limping woman in the right foreground, who drags behind her a wounded arm and a swollen knee. Above her a woman, gaping in disbelief and clutching her breasts in anguish, raises a lamp over the scene. On the far right, a fourth woman, trapped in the flames of a burning building, appears to be exploding upward in terrified petition. On the ground under the horse lies a dead man with his head and arm severed from his body, clutching a broken sword and flower whose petals wait to be picked in his right hand. The presentation of his head as a piece of statuary fallen from its pedestal reinforces the bloodless horror of his death. His left palm is crisscrossed with the lines of fate, or perhaps marked with the toil of heavy labor. Suspended over the scene like a huge eye is a naked light bulb, a modern image illuminating the timelessness of the theme of the horror of war.

In one of his rare moments of self-interpretation, Picasso explained to a public eager to grasp the mural's symbolism that the horse whose side is opened by a terrible gash is "the people," victimized by incomprehensible cruelty. The bull is an enigmatic figure

■ Pablo Picasso, *Guernica,* 1937. Museo Reina Sofia, Madrid. © 2000 Estate of Pablo Picasso/Artists Rights Society (ARS), New York.

symbolizing, Picasso said, darkness and brutality. The horned beast appears as a powerful and vulnerable witness to the scene of needless destruction.

Guernica has been hailed as the most significant painting of the twentieth century. His greatness as an artist, Picasso claimed, derived from his ability to understand his time. In the stripped-down, almost cartoonlike figures of *Guernica,* Picasso presents a picture of European society that is brutal and horrible. It is a condemnation of the modern technological war that targets civilian populations; there on the horrifying canvas are portrayed the consequences of totalitarianism and the failure of democracy that characterized the European search for stability between 1920 and 1939. Subsequent events made Germany's actions in the Spanish Civil War seem like a dress rehearsal for atrocities against the population centers of Warsaw, Rotterdam, and London and made this canvas seem a prophecy of horrors to come. Some years later, during World War II, a Nazi official challenged Picasso with a photograph of the great mural: "So it was you who did this." The artist answered, "No, you did."

- The Spanish Civil War. The Civil War in Spain lasted from 1936 to 1939, with the Nationalists controlling only the south and west until they defeated the Republicans in their strongholds in the north and east.

erode when the BUF was outlawed in 1936. By that time, anti-Hitler feeling was spreading in Great Britain.

The Spanish Republic as Battleground

In 1931, Spain became a democratic republic after centuries of Bourbon monarchy and almost a decade of military dictatorship. In 1936, the voters of Spain elected a Popular Front government. The Popular Front in Spain was more radical than its French counterpart. The property of aristocratic landlords was seized; revolutionary workers went on strike; the Catholic Church and its clergy were attacked.

The social revolution initiated three years of civil war. On one side were the Republicans, the Popular Front defenders of the Spanish Republic and of social revolution in Spain. On the other side were the Nationalists, those who sought to overthrow the republic—aristocratic landowners, supporters of the monarchy and the Catholic Church, and much of the Spanish army.

The Spanish Civil War began in July 1936 with a revolt against the republic from within the Spanish army. It was led by General Francisco Franco (1892–1975), a tough, shrewd, and stubborn man, a conservative nationalist allied with the Falange, the Fascist party in Spain. The conflict soon became a bloody military stalemate, with the Nationalists led by

Franco controlling the more rural and conservative south and west of Spain and the Republicans holding out in the cities of the north and east—Madrid, Valencia, and Barcelona.

Almost from the beginning, the Spanish Civil War was an international event. Mussolini sent ground troops, "volunteers," to fight alongside Franco's forces. Hitler dispatched technical specialists, tanks, and the Condor Legion, an aviation unit, to support the Nationalists. The Germans regarded Spain as a testing ground for new equipment and new methods of warfare, including aerial bombardment. (See "A Closer Look: The Screams from Guernica," pp. 834–835.) The Soviet Union intervened on the side of the Republic, sending armaments, supplies, and technical and political advisers. Because the people of Britain and France were deeply divided in their attitudes toward the war in Spain, the British government stayed neutral, and the government of France was unable to

aid its fellow Popular Front government in Spain. Although Americans volunteered to fight with the Republicans, the American government did not prevent the Texas Oil Company from selling 1.9 million tons of oil to Franco's insurgents, nor did it block the Ford Motor Company, General Motors, and Studebaker from supplying them with trucks.

The Spanish government pleaded, "Men and women of all lands! Come to our aid!" In response, 2800 American volunteers—among them college students, professors, intellectuals, and trade unionists—joined the loyalist army and European volunteers in defense of the Spanish Republic. Britons and antifascist émigrés from Italy and Germany also joined the International Brigades, which were vital in helping the city of Madrid hold out against the Nationalist generals. The Russians withdrew from the war in 1938, disillusioned by the failure of the French, British, and Americans to come to the aid of the Republicans. Madrid fell to the Nationalists in March 1939. The government established by Franco sent one million of its enemies to prison or concentration camps.

IMAGE DISCOVERY

General Franco's Parade of Power

This Republican poster, intended to depict General Francisco Franco, dates from late 1936 or early 1937. Why is the leader of the Spanish Nationalists depicted as a skeleton in a Nazi uniform? Look at the three figures carrying the Generalisimo's train. What groups do they represent, and what about their depiction makes them seem ludicrous?

CONCLUSION

The fragile postwar stability of the 1920s crumbled under the pressures of economic depression, ongoing national antagonisms, and insecurity in the international arena. Europe after 1932 was plagued by the consequences of economic collapse, Fascist success, and the growing threat of armed conflict. Parliamentary institutions were fighting and losing a tug-of-war with authoritarian movements. A Fascist regime was in place in Italy. Political and electoral defeats eroded democratic and liberal principles in Germany's Weimar Republic. Dictatorships triumphed in Spain and in much of eastern and central Europe. Liberal parliamentary governments were failing to solve the economic and social problems of the postwar years. In the democratic nations of France, Great Britain, and, during the brief period from 1931 to 1936, Spain, parliamentary institutions appeared to be persevering. But even there, polarization and increasing intransigence on both the left and the right threatened the future of democratic politics. The exclusion of the Soviet Union from Western internationalism in the 1920s both reflected and exacerbated the crisis.

QUESTIONS FOR REVIEW

1. What problems for European stability were created or left unresolved by the armistice ending World War I?
2. What did Stalin's victory over Trotsky mean for economic development in the Soviet Union?
3. What is fascism, and why was it so alluring to Italians, Germans, and other Europeans?
4. How were rearmament, anti-Semitism, and autarky all part of Hitler's vision of *Lebensraum?*
5. Why did Europe's remaining democracies prove to be so frail during the 1930s?

KEY TERMS

collectivization, *p. 820*

Dawes Plan, *p. 812*

fascism, *p. 823*

Great Depression, *p. 814*

Great Purge, *p. 821*

Kellogg-Briand Pact, *p. 812*

Kristallnacht, p. 830

League of Nations, *p. 812*

Lebensraum, p. 827

Maginot Line, *p. 811*

March on Rome, *p. 825*

Nazism, *p. 824*

New Economic Policy (NEP), *p. 817*

Popular Front, *p. 832*

"socialism in one country," *p. 820*

"spirit of Locarno," *p. 811*

Third Reich, *p. 827*

Treaty of Rapallo, *p. 811*

Weimar Republic, *p. 810*

Young Plan, *p. 813*

DISCOVERING WESTERN CIVILIZATION ONLINE

You can obtain more information about the European search for stability between 1920 and 1939 at the Websites listed below. See also the Companion Website that accompanies this text, www.ablongman.com/kishlansky, which contains an online study guide and additional resources.

Geographical Tour: Europe After 1918

League of Nations Statistical and Disarmament Documents
www.library.nwu.edu/govpub/collections/league/index.html
This is the home page of a project to digitize documents published by the League of Nations.

Internet Modern History Sourcebook: Age of Anxiety
www.fordham.edu/halsall/mod/modsbook40.html
A collection of links to electronic texts and materials on the interwar period, focusing on the cultural crisis in European and American societies as a result of World War I.

Internet Modern History Sourcebook: The Depression
www.fordham.edu/halsall/mod/modsbook41.html
Comprehensive collection of primary sources and links to materials on the Great Depression in Europe and the United States.

The Soviet Union's Separate Path

NEP: A Bibliography of Soviet and Western Literature
www.lib.duke.edu/ias/slavic/nep.htm
This site contains an exhaustive bibliography on Soviet history during the period of the New Economic Policy.

Revelations from the Russian Archives
www.loc.gov/exhibits/archives
A virtual exhibit by the Library of Congress on material from the secret archives of the Central Committee of the Communist Party of the USSR.

The Rise of Fascist Dictatorship in Italy

Internet Modern History Sourcebook: Fascism in Europe
www.fordham.edu/halsall/mod/modsbook42.html
This site refers to fascism in general, but it focuses on a speech of Mussolini and Spanish Civil War materials.

Hitler and the Third Reich

The National Socialist Era, 1933–1945
www2.h-net.msu.edu/~german/gtext/nazi/index.html
Sponsored by the H-German list, this is a small collection of electronic texts relating to the rise of the Nazis, the creation of the Third Reich, and World War II.

Internet Modern History Sourcebook: Nazism
www.fordham.edu/halsall/mod/modsbook43.html
A collection of primary documents and links on the Weimar Republic and the rise of Nazism.

Third Reich Stamps
www.geocities.com/WallStreet/Exchange/5456/third.html
A Web site of stamps issued during the Third Reich with brief descriptions depicting the cultural values propagated by the Nazis.

Democracies in Crisis

Spanish Civil War Archive
dwardmac.pitzer.edu/anarchist_archives/spancivwar/Spanishcivilwar.html
This site was created by a political studies professor at Pitzer College (see link for Paris Commune in Chapter 23) and contains essays, bibliography, and photographs.

SUGGESTIONS FOR FURTHER READING

Geographical Tour: Europe After 1918

Manfred E. Boemeke, Gerald Feldman, and Elisabeth Glaser, eds., *The Treaty of Versailles: A Reassessment After 75 Years* (Cambridge: Cambridge University Press, 1998). This collection of essays constitutes a reappraisal of the divergent peace aims of the United States, France, Germany, and Great Britain and a new understanding of the period of temporary stability created by the treaty after the war.

Igor Lukes, *Czechoslovakia Between Stalin and Hitler: The Diplomacy of Edvard Beneš in the 1930s* (New York: Oxford University Press, 1996). By examining the Czech statesman Edvard Beneš role this book provides an important perspective on the Munich crisis of 1938 and of Czechoslovakia's fate in the battle between East and West.

Crisis and Collapse in a World Economy

Gerald Feldman, *The Great Disorder: Politics, Economy, and Society in the German Inflation, 1914–1924* (New York: Oxford University Press, 1993). Feldman's monumental study of the German inflation provides a detailed historical account of the economic conditions and monetary policy in Germany during and after the war.

Harold James, *The End of Globalization: Lessons from the Great Depression* (Cambridge: Harvard University Press, 2002). The author examines the impact of protectionism on the worldwide depression of the 1930s.

The Soviet Union's Separate Path

Stephen F. Cohen, *Bukharin and the Bolshevik Revolution: A Political Biography, 1888–1938* (Oxford: Oxford University Press, 1980). This milestone work is a general history of the period, as well as a political and intellectual biography of Bukharin, "the last Bolshevik," who supported an evolutionary road to modernization and socialism and whose policies were an alternative to Stalinism.

Sheila Fitzpatrick, *Everyday Stalinism—Ordinary Life in Extraordinary Times: Soviet Russia in the 1930s* (New York: Oxford University Press, 1999). The author explores the rituals, family life, and institutions of the Stalinist era, what the author calls the "distinctive Stalinist habitat" of Russian urban life in the 1930s.

Robert Service, *Stalin: A Biography* (New York: Belknap Press, 2006). A carefully researched biography based on recently released material from the Soviet archives.

Chris Ward, ed., *The Stalinist Dictatorship* (New York: Oxford University Press, 1998). A collection of leading Soviet scholars examine Stalin's character, his role within the Soviet Union, and how Stalinism was a lived experience.

The Rise of Fascist Dictatorship in Italy

MacGregor Knox, *Dictatorship, Foreign Policy, and War in Fascist Italy and Nazi Germany* (London: Cambridge University Press, 2000). Expanding on his earlier work on Mussolini's foreign policy, the author offers a comparative perspective of Italy's and Germany's moves from unification to militant dictatorships, the similar forces that shaped their creation, and the differences in expansionist zeal, military traditions, and fighting power.

Zeev Sternhell with Mario Sznajder and Maia Asheri, *The Birth of Fascist Ideology: From Cultural Rebellion to Political Revolution* (Princeton, NJ: Princeton University Press, 1994). Approaches fascism as an ideology rather than a social movement and argues that it was already fully formed before World War I.

Hitler and the Third Reich

Ian Kershaw, *Hitler, 1889–1936: Hubris* (New York: W.W. Norton & Company, 1998); and *Hitler, 1936–1945: Nemesis* (New York: W.W. Norton & Company, 2000). The definitive two-volume biography provides a history of Germany society through Hitler's extraordinary political domination.

Dieter Langewiesche, *Liberalism in Germany*, trans. Christiane Banerji (Princeton, NJ: Princeton University Press, 2000). This translated work traces the history of German liberalism from the early nineteenth century to post-1945 politics in West Germany as it was embodied in political movements, organizations, and values.

Bernd Widdig, *Culture and Inflation in Weimar Germany* (Berkeley: University of California Press, 2001). Through literary and filmic sources, the author provides a cultural analysis of a defining economic event in Germany history.

Democracies in Crisis

Ivan T. Berend, *Decades of Crisis: Central and Eastern Europe Before World War II* (Berkeley: University of California Press, 1998). The author offers a comprehensive overview of central and eastern Europe in the first half of the twentieth century and argues that the region "embarked on a historical detour" in rejecting the parliamentary system and turning to nationalist authoritarian regimes.

John Hiden and Patrick Salmon, *The Baltic Nations and Europe: Estonia, Latvia, and Lithuania in the Twentieth Century* (London and New York: Longman, 1991). Surveys the development of the Baltic states in the twentieth century, discussing Baltic independence, the period between the wars, and the states' incorporation into the Soviet Union, as well as renewed efforts toward independence in the Gorbachev era.

Julian Jackson, *The Popular Front in France: Defending Democracy, 1934–1938* (Cambridge: Cambridge University Press, 1988). An in-depth study of Léon Blum's government, with a special emphasis on cultural transformation and the legacy of the Popular Front.

Michael Jackson, *Fallen Sparrows: The International Brigades in the Spanish Civil War* (Philadelphia: American Philosophical Society, 1994). A careful description of the members and activities of the International Brigades, which were organized under the direction of the Comintern to save the Spanish Republic.

Stanley G. Payne, *Fascism in Spain, 1923–1977* (Madison: The University of Wisconsin Press, 1999). The author presents a comprehensive history of Spanish fascism from its origins to the death of Franco.

Michael Richards, *A Time of Silence: Civil War and the Culture of Repression in Franco's Spain, 1936–1945* (Cambridge: Cambridge University Press, 1998). This work examines Spanish society during and after the Spanish Civil War in relation to Franco's policy of "moral and economic reconstruction" based on self-sufficiency.

For a list of additional titles related to this chapter's topics, please see http://www.ablongman.com/kishlansky.

28 GLOBAL CONFLAGRATION: WORLD WAR II, 1939–1945

PRECURSOR OF WAR

THE ANNEXATION OF AUSTRIA

Adolf Hitler's entry into Vienna, capital city of his native country of Austria, was planned as a media event. The accompanying photograph displays a triumphant Hitler leading what appears to be a parade on 14 March 1938. Standing in his open Mercedes in order to be visible to thousands of cheering Austrians and protected by thirteen police cars, Hitler was no less the conqueror. The motorcade of limousines moved slowly along the Ringstrasse, Vienna's most important street of monumental public buildings, greeted by wildly cheering crowds. The Nazi swastika fluttered on flagpoles and draped facades. The viewer is left to wonder how the flags and banners could have been manufactured and positioned over the course of a weekend to greet the Fuhrer's unannounced and "friendly visit." The independent nation of Austria had, overnight and with virtually no bloodshed, become part of the German Reich.

THE VISUAL RECORD

On the first page of *Mein Kampf*, Hitler had promised, "Germany-Austria must return to the great German mother-country, and not because of any economic considerations. . . . One blood demands one Reich." By 1938 Hitler had consolidated power at home by removing the non-Nazi conservatives from positions of power in Germany. Now he alone determined foreign policy. As a cornerstone of that policy, Hitler aimed to unite all German people in one nation by extending German control over territories that included those not ethnically German, but that could provide "living space" and economic self-sufficiency for the German race. (See "Nazi Goals" on page 827 in Chapter 27.) Becoming increasingly impatient, Hitler feared that Germany could fail to achieve its destiny as a world power by waiting too long to act. He became more aggressive and willing to use military force as he set out to re-move, one by one, the obstacles to German domination of central Europe—Austria, Czechoslovakia, and Poland.

The annexation of Austria was the first step in Hitler's plans for conquest. Using the threat of invasion, Hitler intimidated the Austrian government into legalizing the Nazi party, which thereby brought pro-Nazis into the Austrian cabinet and German troops into the country. Many Austrians wanted to be joined to Germany; others had no desire to be led by Nazis. A rigged plebiscite in April 1938, organized by Goebbels's Propaganda Ministry, delivered a 99.75 percent vote of approval in Austria for annexation by Germany. With the union of Austria and Germany, the Third Reich claimed a population of 80 million people as it prepared itself for a war to the east. What appeared to be a parade of pomp and circumstance in March 1938 was really the precursor of a terrible conflagration that would last for six years and claim 50 million lives around the globe.

LOOKING AHEAD

This chapter considers the events leading to the outbreak of the war in 1939 and how collaboration and resistance developed across Europe as the German army advanced. Virulent racism played a central role in directing the war against Jews, Slavs, and others identified as inferior by Nazi racial policies. The power of Soviet patriotism and bravery and the entry of the United States into the war ensured Allied victory. Allied cooperation gave way, however, even as the peace was being forged under the direction of the two superpowers. The dropping of the atom bomb on Japan hastened the war's end, but it would taint the ensuing peace.

■ A triumphant Hitler enters Austria in 1938.

AGGRESSION AND CONQUEST

The years between 1933 and 1939 marked a bleak period in international affairs when the British, the French, and the Americans were unwilling or unable to recognize the dire threat to world peace posed by Hitler and his Nazi state. The leaders of those countries did not comprehend Hitler's single-minded goal to extend German living space eastward as far as western Russia. They failed to understand the seriousness of the Nazi process of consolidation at home. They took no action against Hitler's initial acts of aggression. The war that began in Europe in 1939 eventually became a global conflict that pitted Germany, Italy, and Japan—the **Axis Powers**—against the British Empire, the Soviet Union, and the United States—the Grand Alliance.

Even before war broke out in Europe, there was armed conflict in Asia. The rapidly expanding Japanese economy depended on Manchuria for raw materials and on China for markets. Chinese boycotts against Japanese goods and threats to Japanese economic interests in Manchuria led to a Japanese military occupation of Manchuria and the establishment of a Japanese puppet state there in 1931–1932. When the powers of the League of Nations, led by Great Britain, refused to recognize that state, Japan withdrew from the League. Fearing that the Chinese government was becoming strong enough to exclude Japanese trade from China, Japanese troops and naval units began an undeclared war in China in 1937. Many important Chinese cities—Peking, Shanghai, Nanking, Canton, and Hankow—fell to Japanese forces. Relentless aerial bombardment of Chinese cities and atrocities committed by Japanese troops against Chinese civilians outraged Europeans and Americans. The governments of the Soviet Union, Great Britain, and the United States, seeking to protect their own ideological, economic, and security interests in China, gave economic, diplomatic, and moral support to the Chinese government of Chiang Kai-shek. Thus the stage was set for major military conflicts in Asia and in Europe.

Hitler's Foreign Policy and Appeasement

For Hitler a war against the Soviet Union for living space was inevitable. It would come, he told some of his close associates, in the years 1943–1945. However, he wanted to avoid fighting anew the war that had led to Germany's defeat in 1914–1918. World War I was a war fought on two fronts—in the east and in the west. It was a war in which Germany had to face many enemies at the same time, and a war that lasted until German soldiers, civilians, and resources were exhausted. In the next war, Hitler wanted above all to avoid fighting Great Britain while battling Russia for living space. He convinced himself that the British would remain neutral if Germany agreed not to attack the British Empire. Would they not appreciate his willingness to abolish forever the menace of communism? Were they not Aryans too?

The Campaign Against Czechoslovakia.   Encouraged by his success in the annexation of Austria in March 1938, Hitler provoked a crisis in Czechoslovakia in the summer of the same year. He demanded "freedom" for the German-speaking people of the Sudetenland area of Czechoslovakia. His main objective, however, was not to protect the Germans of Czechoslovakia but to smash the Czech state, the major obstacle in central Europe to the launching of an attack on living space farther east.

Western statesmen did not understand Hitler's commitment to destroying Czechoslovakia or his willingness to fight a limited war against the Czechs to do so. Hitler did everything possible to isolate Czechoslovakia from its neighbors and its treaty partners. France, an ally of Czechoslovakia, appeared distinctly unwilling to defend it against Germany's menace. Britain, seeking to avoid a war that the government did not think was necessary and for which the British were not prepared, sent Prime Minister Neville Chamberlain (1869–1940) to reason with Hitler. Believing that transferring the Sudetenland, the German-speaking area of Czechoslovakia, to Germany was the only solution—and one that would redress some of the wrongs done to Germany after World War I—Chamberlain convinced France and Czechoslovakia to yield to Hitler's demands.

Appeasement at Munich.   Chamberlain's actions were the result of British self-interest. British leaders agreed that their country could not afford another war like the Great War of 1914–1918. Defense expenditures had been dramatically reduced to devote national resources to improving domestic social services, protecting world trade, and fortifying Britain's global interests. Britain understood well its weakened position in its dominions. In the British hierarchy of priorities, defense of the British Empire ranked first, above defense of Europe; Britain's commitment to western Europe ranked above the defense of eastern and central Europe.

Hitler's response to being granted everything he requested was to renege and issue new demands. One final meeting was held at Munich to avert war. On 29 September 1938, one day before German troops were scheduled to invade Czechoslovakia, Mussolini and the French prime minister, Édouard Daladier (1884–1970), joined Hitler and Chamberlain at Munich to discuss a peaceful resolution to the crisis.

At Munich, Chamberlain and Daladier again yielded to Hitler's demands. The Sudetenland was ceded to Germany, and German troops quickly moved to occupy the area. The policy of the British and French was dubbed **appeasement** to indicate the willingness to concede to demands in order to preserve peace. Appeasement became a dirty word in twentieth-century European history, taken to mean weakness and cowardice. Yet Chamberlain was neither weak nor cowardly. His great mistake in negotiating with Hitler was in assuming that Hitler was a reasonable man, who like all reasonable persons wanted to avoid another war.

Chamberlain thought his mediation at Munich had won for Europe a lasting peace—"peace for our time," he reported. The people of Europe received Chamberlain's assessment with a sense of relief and shame—relief over what had been avoided, shame at having deserted Czechoslovakia. In fact, the policy of appeasement further destabilized Europe and accelerated Hitler's plans for European domination. Within months, Hitler cast aside the Munich agreement by annihilating Czechoslovakia. German troops occupied the western, Czech part of the state, including the capital of Prague. The Slovak eastern part became independent and a German satellite. At the same time, Lithuania was pressured into surrendering Memel to Germany, and Hitler demanded that Germany control Gdansk and the Polish Corridor. No longer could Hitler be ignored or appeased. No longer could his goals be misunderstood.

Hitler's War, 1939–1941

In the tense months that followed the Munich meeting and the occupation of Prague, Hitler readied himself for war in western Europe. To strengthen his position, in May 1939 he formed a military alliance, the **Pact of Steel**, with Mussolini's Italy. Then Hitler and Stalin, previously self-declared enemies, shocked the West by joining their two nations in a pact of mutual neutrality, the Non-Aggression Pact of 1939. Opportunism lay behind Hitler's willingness to ally with the Communist state that he had denounced throughout the 1930s. A German alliance with the Soviet Union would, Hitler believed, force the British and the French to back down and to remain neutral while Germany conquered Poland—the last obstacle to a drive for expansion eastward—in a short, limited war. Stalin recognized the failure of the western European powers to stand up to Hitler. There was little possibility, he thought, of an alliance against Germany with the virulently anti-Communist Neville Chamberlain. The best Stalin could hope for was that the Germans and the Western powers would fight it out while the Soviet Union waited to enter the war at the most opportune moment. As an added bonus, Germany promised not to interfere if the Soviet Union an-

■ A German motorized detachment rides through a bomb-shattered town during the Nazi invasion of Poland in 1939. The invasion saw the first use of the *blitzkrieg*—lightning war—in which air power and rapid tank movement combined for swift victory.

nexed eastern Poland, Bessarabia, and the Baltic republics of Latvia and Estonia.

Finally recognizing Hitler's intent, the British and the French also signed a pact in the spring of 1939 promising assistance to Poland in the event of aggression. Tensions mounted throughout the summer as Europeans awaited the inevitable German aggression. On 1 September 1939, Germany attacked Poland. By the end of the month, in spite of valiant resistance, the vastly outnumbered Poles surrendered. Although the German army needed no assistance, the Russians invaded Poland ten days before its collapse, and Germany and Russia divided the spoils. Not trusting his alliance with Hitler, Stalin almost immediately took measures to defend Russia against a possible German attack. The Soviet Union assumed military control in the Baltic states and demanded of Finland territory and military bases from which the city of Leningrad could be defended. When Finland refused, Russia invaded. In the snows of the "Winter War" of 1939–1940, the Finns initially fought the Russian army to a standstill, much to the encouragement of the democratic West. The Finns, however, were eventually defeated in March 1940.

War in Europe.   Hitler's war, the war for German domination of Europe, had begun. But it had not begun the way he intended. Great Britain and France, true to their alliance with Poland and contrary to Hitler's expectations, declared war on Germany on 3 September 1939, even though they were unable to give any help to Poland. In the six months after the fall of Poland, no military action took place between Germany and the Allies as Hitler postponed offensives in northern and western Europe because of poor weather conditions. That strange interlude, which became known as **"the phony war,"** was a period of suspended reality in which France and Great Britain waited for Hitler to make his next move. Civilian morale in France deteriorated among a population that still remembered the death and destruction that France had endured in the Great War. An attitude of defeatism germinated and grew before the first French soldier fell in battle.

With the arrival of spring, Germany attacked Denmark and Norway in April 1940. Then, on 10 May 1940, Hitler's armies invaded the Netherlands, Belgium, and Luxembourg. By the third week of May, German mechanized forces were racing through northern France toward the English Channel, cutting off the British and Belgian troops and 120,000 French forces from the rest of the French army. With the rapid defeat of Belgium, the forces were crowded against the Channel and had to be evacuated from the beaches of Dunkirk. France, with a large and well-equipped army, nevertheless relied on Allied support and was in a desperate situation without it.

In France, the German army fought a new kind of war called a *blitzkrieg*, or "lightning war," so named because of its speed. The British and the French had expected the German army to behave much as it had in World War I, concentrating its striking forces in a swing through coastal Belgium and Holland in order to capture Paris. French strategists believed that France was safe because of hilly and forested terrain they thought was impassable. They also counted on the protection of the fortress wall known as the Maginot Line that France had built in the period between the wars. The Maginot Line stretched for hundreds of miles but was useless against mobile tank divisions, which outflanked it. With stunning speed, Germany drove its tanks—panzers—through the French defenses at Sedan in eastern France.

The Fall of France.   The French could have pinched off the advance of the overextended panzers, but the French army, suffering from severe morale problems, collapsed and was in retreat. On 17 June 1940, only weeks after German soldiers had stepped on French soil, Marshal Henri-Philippe Pétain, the great hero of the Battle of Verdun in World War I, petitioned the Germans for an armistice. Three-fifths of France, including the entire Atlantic seaboard, was occupied by the German army and placed under direct German rule. In the territory that remained unoccupied, Pétain created a collaborationist government that resided at Vichy—a spa city in central France—and worked in partnership with the Germans for the rest of the war. Charles de Gaulle (1890–1970), a brigadier general opposed to the armistice, fled to London, where he set up a Free French government in exile.

The Battle of Britain.   French capitulation in June 1940 followed Italian entry into the war on the side of Germany in the same month. The British were now alone in a war against the two Axis Powers as Germany made plans for an invasion of the British Isles from across the English Channel. To prepare the way, the German air force, under Reich marshal Hermann Göring (1893–1946), launched a series of air attacks against England—the Battle of Britain. The German air force first attacked British aircraft, airfields, and munitions centers and then shifted targets to major population centers such as London and industrial cities such as Coventry.

■ The Division of France, 1940–1944. The collaborationist Vichy regime governed the southern portion of France, while the Germans occupied the north and west and reannexed the provinces of Alsace and Lorraine.

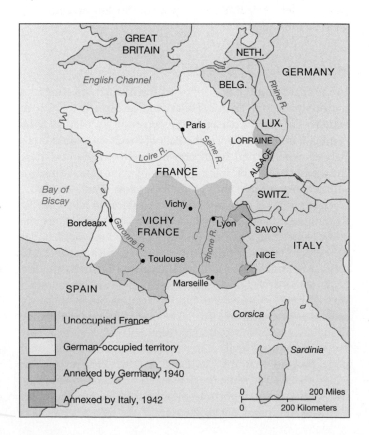

Between 7 September and 2 November 1940, the German air force bombed the city of London every night, inflicting serious damage on the city and killing 15,000 people.

The British resisted the attacks under the leadership of Winston Churchill, who had succeeded Chamberlain as prime minister in 1940. Churchill was a master public speaker who, in a series of radio broadcasts, inspired the people of Britain with the historic greatness of the task confronting them—holding out against Nazism until the forces of the overseas British Empire and the United States could be marshaled to liberate Europe. The British Royal Air Force inflicted serious losses on German aircraft, while British industry was able to maintain steady production of planes, bombs, and armaments. Civilians endured the nightly destruction and air raids in what Churchill termed Britain's "finest hour." Recognizing his lack of success in establishing air superiority over the Channel or in breaking the will of the British people, Hitler abandoned the Battle of Britain and canceled the invasion.

The Balkans at War. It was not in Great Britain but in the Balkans that Hitler was able to engage the British enemy and inflict serious losses. The British had a presence in the Greek Peloponnese, where their air units were deployed to support the valiant resistance of the Greeks against Italian aggression. In his original plans for a limited war, Hitler hoped to establish control over the Balkans by peaceful diplomatic means. But Mussolini's disastrous attempt to achieve military glory by conquering Greece impelled Hitler to make his own plans to attack Greece in Operation Marita. Using Bulgaria as the base of operations, Germany invaded Yugoslavia, whose government had been weakened by a recent military coup. The capital of Belgrade fell in April 1941. Internal ethnic enmity between the Croats and the Serbs led to the mutiny of Croatian soldiers and to the formation of an autonomous Croatian government favorably disposed to the Germans in Zagreb.

German troops then crossed the Yugoslav border into Greece. Moving quickly down the Greek mainland, German soldiers captured the capital of Athens on 27 April 1941. German forces then turned their attention to the Greek island of Crete, where fleeing British soldiers sought refuge. In the first mass paratroops attack in history, Crete was rapidly subdued, forcing the British to evacuate to Egypt. The British were routed and experienced humiliating defeat by the German blitzkrieg.

The Balkans were important to Hitler for a number of reasons. Half of Germany's wheat and livestock came from the countries of southeastern Europe. Romanian and Hungarian oil fields supplied Germany's only non-Russian oil. Greece and Yugoslavia were important suppliers of metal ores, including aluminum, tin, lead, and copper, so vital for industry and the war effort.

The necessity of protecting resources, especially the oil fields in Romania, also gave the area geopolitical importance for Germany. In launching an attack against the Soviet Union, Hitler was well aware of the strategic significance of control-

■ The London Underground was pressed into service as a bomb shelter during the persistent Nazi attacks on London in the Battle of Britain.

ling the straits linking the Mediterranean and Black seas. The British lifeline to its empire could also be cut by control of the eastern Mediterranean.

Collaboration and Resistance

No one nation has ever controlled the Balkans, and Hitler understood that he must rule not by occupation but by collaboration. Some Balkan collaborators joined puppet governments out of an ideological commitment to fascism. They were hostile to communism and believed that Hitler's Nazism was far preferable to Stalin's communism. They saw in the German victory the chance to put their beliefs into practice.

Motives for Collaboration. Some governments collaborated with the Germans out of national self-interest. Just as the

MAP DISCOVERY

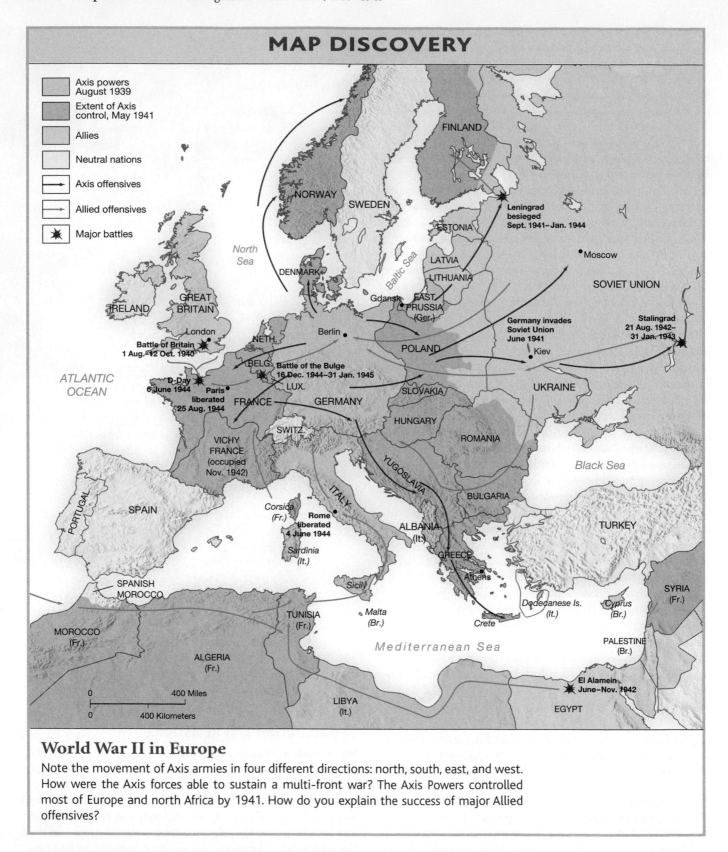

World War II in Europe

Note the movement of Axis armies in four different directions: north, south, east, and west. How were the Axis forces able to sustain a multi-front war? The Axis Powers controlled most of Europe and north Africa by 1941. How do you explain the success of major Allied offensives?

government of Hungary allied with Germany in the hope of winning back territory lost at the end of World War I, Romania allied with Russia. The government of Slovakia was loyal to the Third Reich because Hitler had given it independence from the Czechs. A German puppet state was set up in the Yugoslav province of Croatia. Other collaborators were pragmatists who believed that by taking political office they could negotiate with the German conquerors and soften the effects of the Nazi conquest on their people. Hitler had little affection for local ideological fascists and sometimes smashed their movements. He preferred to work with local generals and administrators. Pragmatic collaborators often could not or would not negotiate with the German authorities. The help they gave in rounding up opponents of Nazi Germany—resistance fighters and Jews—resulted in their punishment after the war.

Forms of Resistance.   Resistance against German occupation and collaborationist regimes took many forms. Resisters wrote subversive tracts, distributed them, gathered intelligence information for the Allies, sheltered Jews or other enemies of the Nazis, committed acts of sabotage or assassination or other violent acts, and carried on guerrilla warfare against the German army. Resisters ran the risk of endangering themselves and their families, who, if discovered, would be tortured and killed. Resistance movements developed after the German attack on the Soviet Union in 1941, when the Communist parties of occupied Europe formed the core of the violent resistance against the Nazi regime. Resistance grew when the Germans began to draft young European men for work on German farms and in German factories. Many preferred to go underground rather than to Germany.

One of the great resistance fighters of the Second World War was Josip Broz (1892–1980), alias Tito. He was a Croatian Communist and a Yugoslav nationalist. Instead of waiting to be liberated by the Allies, his partisans fought against Italian and German troops. Ten or more German divisions that might otherwise have fought elsewhere were tied up combating Tito's forces. He gained the admiration and the support of Churchill, Roosevelt, and Stalin. After liberation, Tito's organization won 90 percent of the vote in the Yugoslav elections, and he became the leader of the country in the postwar era. Resistance entailed enormous risks and required secrecy, moral courage, and great bravery. On the whole, however, the actions of resistance fighters seldom affected military timetables and did little to change the course of the war and Hitler's domination of Europe.

By the middle of 1941, Hitler controlled a vast continental empire that stretched from the Baltic to the Black Sea and from the Atlantic Ocean to the Russian border. Either the German army occupied territories and controlled satellites, or Hitler relied on collaborationist governments for support. Having destroyed the democracies of western Europe, with the exception of Great Britain, Hitler's armies absorbed territory and marched across nations at rapid speed with technical and strategic superiority. Military conquest was not the only horror that the seemingly invincible Hitler inflicted on European peoples.

RACISM AND DESTRUCTION

War, as the saying goes, is hell. But the horrors perpetrated in World War II exceeded anything ever experienced in Western civilization. Claims of racial superiority were invoked to justify inhuman atrocities. The Germans and Japanese used spurious arguments of racial superiority to fuel their war efforts in both the European and Asian theaters of battle. But the Germans and the Japanese were not alone in using racist propaganda. The United States employed racial stereotypes to depict the inferiority of the enemy, and the government interned Japanese-Americans living on the West Coast in camps and seized their property.

German racist ideology, based on the concept of "the master race," was used to identify those human beings worthy of living; those not worthy were designated "subhuman." Hitler promised the German people a purified Reich of Aryans free of the Jews and the racially and mentally inferior. Slavic peoples—Poles and Russians—were designated as subhumans who could be displaced in the search for "living space" for German citizens and German destiny. With the war in eastern Europe, anti-Semitism changed from a policy of persecution and expropriation in the 1930s into a program of systematic extermination beginning in 1941.

Enforcing Nazi Racial Policies

Social policies erected on horrifying biomedical theories discriminated against a variety of social groups in the Third Reich. Beginning in 1933, police harassment of those identified as gypsies began in earnest. In 1936, the Nazi bureaucracy expanded to include the Reich Central Office Against the Gypsy Nuisance, where files on gypsies were assiduously maintained. They were subject to all racialist legislation and could be sterilized because of their "inferiority" without any formal hearing process. In September 1939, even as the war was beginning, high-ranking Nazis planned the removal of 30,000 gypsies to Poland. More than 200,000 German, Russian, Polish, and Balkan gypsies were killed in the course of the war by internment in camps and by systematic extermination.

Mixed-race children were also singled out for special opprobrium under Nazi racial policies. A generational cohort of children born of white German mothers and black fathers was a consequence of the presence in the Rhineland of French colonial troops from Senegal, Morocco, and Malaga as part of the French occupation forces during the 1920s and 1930s. The press during both the Weimar Republic and the Nazi regime attacked the children of those unions, probably numbering no more than 500 to 800 individuals, as "Rhineland bastards." In 1937, the Nazis decided to sterilize them without any legal proceedings.

Those suffering from hereditary illnesses were labeled as a biological threat to the racial purity of the German people. Illegitimate medical tests were devised by state doctors to establish who was feeble-minded and genetically defective. Since the society of the Third Reich was treated as one huge laboratory for the production of the racially fit and the "destruction of worthless life," categories were constructed according to subjective criteria that claimed scientific validation. Medical officials examined children, and those judged to be deformed were separated from their families and transferred to special pediatric clinics where they were either starved to death or injected with lethal drugs. In the summer of 1939, euthanasia programs for adults were organized, and 65,000 to 70,000 Germans were identified

Schreibers rassenkundliche Anschauungstafel: Deutsche Rassenköpfe

Bearbeitet von Dr Alfred Eydt

Nordisch   Westisch

Fälisch   Dinarisch

Ostbaltisch   Ostisch

■ The Nazis attempted to cloak their self-serving racial theories in scientific respectability. A Nazi "race-identification table" displays what were asserted to be the typical heads of different German "races"—a classification that has no basis in anthropology.

for death. Asylums were asked to rank patients according to their race, state of health, and ability to work. The rankings were used to determine candidates for death. In Poland, mental patients were simply shot; in other places they were starved to death. The uncooperative, the sick, and the disabled were purged as racially undesirable.

The umbrella covering hereditary illnesses was broad but not broader than the category covering the "asocial." In that designation, asocial behavior itself came to be interpreted as a hereditary trait. Criminals, beggars, vagrants, and the homeless could be compulsorily sterilized. Alcoholics, prostitutes, and people with sexually transmitted diseases could be labeled asocial and treated accordingly. Those forms of behavior were considered to be hereditary and determined by blood.

Homosexuals were likewise treated as "community aliens" by Nazi social policies. The persecution of homosexual men intensified after 1934, when any form of "same-sex immorality" became subject to legal persecution. "Gazing and lustful intention" were left to the definition of the police and the courts. Criminal sentences could involve a term in a concentration camp. But because homosexuality was judged to be a sickness rather than an immutable biological trait, gays did not become the primary object of Nazi extermination policies that began to be enforced against the "biologically inferior." Instead, Nazi treatment of homosexuality might involve castration or indefinite incarceration in a concentration camp.

Gay men in Nazi concentration camps during the war were singled out with the badge of a pink triangle. Although it is not clear how many gay men were actually killed by the Nazis, estimates run as high as 200,000. Gay men rather than lesbians were singled out by officials of the Third Reich because their behavior was considered a greater threat to the perpetuation of the German race.

The Destruction of Europe's Jews

Although anti-Semitism was an integral part of Hitler's view of the world, he did not think the peoples of Germany and Europe were ready for harsh measures against the Jews. When they came to power in 1933, the Nazis did not have a blueprint for the destruction of Europe's Jews; the anti-Semitic policies of the Third Reich evolved incrementally in the 1930s and 1940s.

After 1938, German civil servants expropriated Jewish property as rightfully belonging to the state. When the war began, Jews were rounded up and herded into urban ghettos in Germany and in the large cities of Poland. For a time, the German foreign ministry considered the possibility of deporting the more than three million Jews under German control to Madagascar, an island off the southeast coast of Africa. Until 1941, Nazi policies against the Jews were often uncoordinated and unfocused.

The "Final Solution."   Confinement in urban ghettos was the beginning of a policy of concentration that ended in annihilation. After having identified Jews, seized their property, and then confined them to ghettos, German authorities began to implement a step-by-step plan for extermination. There appears to have been no single order from Hitler that decreed what became known to German officials as the "**Final Solution**"—the total extermination of European Jews. But Hitler's recorded remarks make it clear that he knew and approved of what was being done to the Jews. A spirit of shared purpose permeated the entire administrative system, from the civil service through the judiciary. Administrative agencies competed to interpret the Führer's will. SS guards in the camps and police in the streets embraced Hitler's "mission" of destruction. Those involved in carrying out the plan for extermination understood what was meant by the Final Solution and what their responsibilities were for enforcing it. To ensure that the whole process operated smoothly, a planning conference for the Final Solution was conducted by Reinhard Heydrich (1904–1942), leader of the Sicherheitsdienst (SD),

or Security Service of the SS, for the benefit of state and party officials at Wannsee, a Berlin suburb, in January 1942.

Mass racial extermination began with the German conquest of Poland, where both Jews and non-Jews were systematically killed. It continued when Hitler's army invaded the Soviet Union in 1941. That campaign, known as Operation Barbarossa, set off the mass execution of eastern Europeans declared to be enemies of the Reich. The tactics of the campaign pointed the way to the Final Solution. To the Nazi leadership, Slavs were subhuman. Russian Jews were, by extension, the lowest of the low, even more despised than German Jews. Nazi propaganda had equated Jews with Communists, and Hitler had used the expression *Judeocommunist* to describe what he considered to be the most dangerous criminal and enemy of the Third Reich, the enemy who must be annihilated at any cost.

The executions were the work of the SS, the elite military arm of the Nazi party. Special mobile murder squads of the SD under Heydrich were organized behind the German lines in Poland and Russia. Members of the army were aware of what the SS squads were doing and participated in some of

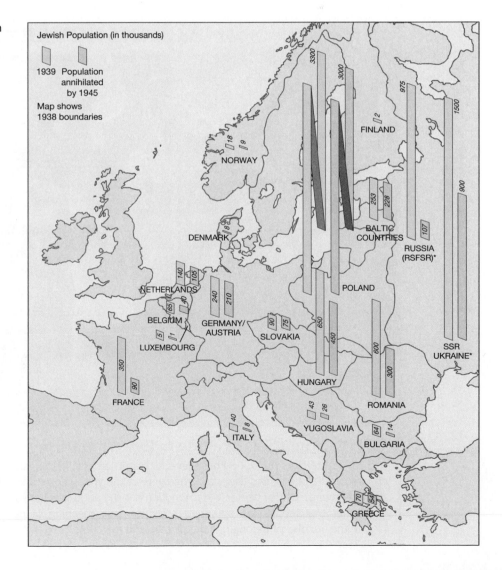

■ The Holocaust. The greatest loss of Jewish life in the Holocaust took place in Poland and the Soviet Union.

the extermination measures. In the spring of 1941, Hitler ordered a massive propaganda campaign to be conducted among the armed forces. The army was indoctrinated to believe that the invasion of the Soviet Union was more than a military campaign: it was a "holy war," a crusade that Germany was waging for civilization. SS chief Heinrich Himmler set about to enforce the Führer's threats with concrete extermination policies. Fearful that the SS would be outstripped by the regular army in the Führer's favor, Himmler exhorted his men to commit the worst atrocities.

Firing squads shot Russian victims en masse, then piled their bodies on top of each other in open graves. Reviewing the procedures for mass killings, Himmler—ever competitive with other Nazi agencies—suggested a more efficient means of extermination that would require less manpower and would enhance the prestige of the SS. As a result, extermination by gas was introduced, using vans whose exhaust fumes were piped into the enclosed cargo areas that served as portable gas chambers. In Poland, Himmler replaced the vans with permanent buildings housing gas chambers using Zyklon B, a gas developed by the chemical firm I. G. Farben for the purpose.

The Third Reich began erecting its vast network of death in 1941. The first extermination camp was created in Chelmno, Poland, where 150,000 people were killed between 1941 and 1944. The camps practiced systematic extermination for the savage destruction of those groups deemed racially inferior, sexually deviant, or politically dangerous. The term **holocaust** has been used to describe the mass slaughter of European Jews, most of which took place in the five major killing centers in what is now Polish territory—Chelmno, Belzec, Sobibor, Treblinka, and Auschwitz. *Holocaust,* drawn from the Greek term for "burnt sacrifice," came to be used more generally after World War II to describe genocide and nuclear annihilation.

Many victims died before ever reaching the camps, transported for days in sealed railroad cars without food, water, or sanitation facilities. Others died within months as forced laborers for the Reich. People of all ages were starved, beaten, and systematically humiliated. Guards taunted their victims ver-

IMAGE DISCOVERY

"Resettlement" as Prelude to Extermination

Armed Nazi soldiers round up Polish Jews for "resettlement" in the east. Notice the children in the photo, and especially the figure of the young boy standing apart in the foreground, right of center. What emotion has the photographer captured? Is it likely that the people photographed knew the true meaning of resettlement? Notice the bundles of belongings the women and men hold.

bally, degraded them physically, and tortured them with false hope. Promised clean clothes and nourishment, camp internees were herded into "showers" that dispensed gas rather than water. Descriptions of life in the camps reveal a systematized brutality and inhumanity on the part of the German, Ukrainian, and Polish guards toward their victims. In all, 11 million people died by the extermination process—6 million Jews and almost as many non-Jews, including children, the aged, homosexuals, Slavic slave laborers, Soviet prisoners of war, Communists, members of the Polish and Soviet leadership, various resistance elements, gypsies, and Jehovah's Witnesses.

The words ARBEIT MACHT FREI ("Work Makes You Free") were emblazoned over the main gate at Auschwitz, the largest of the concentration camps. It was at Auschwitz that the greatest number of persons died in a single place, including more than one million Jews. The healthy and the young were kept barely alive to work. Hard labor, starvation, and disease—especially typhus, tuberculosis, and other diseases that spread rapidly because of the lack of sanitation—claimed many victims.

On entering the camps, the sick and the aged were automatically designated for extermination because of their uselessness as a labor force. Many children were put to work, but some were designated for extermination. Many mothers chose to accompany their children to their deaths to comfort them in their final moments. Pregnant women were considered useless in the

DOCUMENT

Memoirs from Commandant of Auschwitz

forced labor camps and were sent immediately to the "showers." The number of German Jewish women who died in the camps was 50 percent higher than the number of German Jewish men. Starvation diets meant that women stopped menstruating. Because the Nazis worried that women of childbearing age would continue to reproduce, women who showed signs of menstruation were killed immediately. Women who were discovered to have given birth undetected in the camp were killed, as were their infants. It soon became clear that even those allowed to live were only intended to serve the short-term needs of the Nazis.

Resisting Destruction. The impossibility of any effective resistance was based on two essential characteristics of the process of extermination. First, the entire German state and its bureaucratic apparatus were involved in the policies, laws, and decrees of the 1930s that singled out victims, while most Germans stood silently by. There was no possibility of appeal and no place to hide. Those who understood early what was happening and who had enough money to buy their way out emigrated to safer places, including Palestine and the United States. But most countries blocked the entry of German and eastern European refugees with immigration quotas. Neither Britain nor the United States was willing to deal with the mass influx of European Jews. Jews in the occupied countries and the Axis nations had virtually no chance to escape. They were trapped in a society where all forces of law and administration worked against them.

A second reason for the impossibility of effective resistance was the step-by-step nature of the process of extermination, which meant that few understood the final outcome until it

was too late. Initially, in the 1930s, many German Jews believed that things could get no worse and obeyed the German state as good citizens. Even the policy of removing groups from the ghetto militated against resistance because the hope was that sending 1000 Jews to "resettlement" would allow 10,000 Jews remaining behind to be saved. The German authorities deliberately controlled information to cultivate misunderstanding of what was happening.

Isolated instances of resistance in the camps—rioting at Treblinka, for example—only highlight how impossible rebellion was for physically debilitated people in the heavily guarded centers. In the Warsaw ghetto, a resistance movement was organized with a few firearms and some grenades and homemade Molotov cocktails in April 1943. Starvation, overcrowding, and epidemics made Warsaw, the largest of the ghettos, into an extermination camp. As news reached the ghetto that "resettlement" was the death warrant of tens of thousands of Polish Jews, armed rebellion erupted. It did not succeed in blocking the completion of the Final Solution against the Warsaw ghetto the following year, when the SS

■ Felix Nussbaum, *Self-Portrait with a Jewish Identity Card* (1943). Nussbaum left Germany when the Nazis came to power in 1933. During the Holocaust he went underground, moving from place to place in constant fear of discovery. He painted this work, which captures his deep anxiety, while he was in hiding. Nussbaum and his wife were arrested in 1944, and both perished at Auschwitz. Kulturgeschichtliches Museum, Osnäbruck, © Auguste Moses-Nussbaum and Shulmait Jaari/© 2007 Artists Rights Society (ARS), New York/VG Bild-Kunst, Bonn

commandant proclaimed, "The Jewish Quarter of Warsaw is no more!" Polish and Russian Jews accounted for 70 percent of the total Jewish deaths.

Who Knew?   It is impossible that killing on such a scale could have been kept secret. Along with those who ordered extermination operations, the guards and camp personnel involved in carrying out the directives were aware of what was happening. Those who brought internees to the camps, returning always with empty railroad cars, knew it too. People believed for a time that their disappearing neighbors were being resettled in the east. But as news got back to central and western Europe, it was more difficult to sustain belief in the ruse. People who lived near the camps could not ignore the screams and fumes of gas and burning bodies that permeated the environs.

Although it never publicly announced its extermination program, the German government convinced its citizens that the policies of the Nazi state could not be judged by ordinary moral standards. The benefits to the German state were justification enough for the annihilation of 11 million people. Official propaganda successfully convinced millions that the Reich was the supreme good. Admitting the existence of the extermination program carried with it a responsibility on which few acted, perhaps out of fear of reprisals. There were some heroes such as Raoul Wallenberg of Sweden, who interceded for Hungarian Jews and provided Jews in the Budapest ghetto with food and protection. Heroic acts, however, were isolated and rare.

Collaborationist governments and occupied nations often cooperated with Nazi extermination policies. The French government at Vichy introduced and implemented a variety of anti-Jewish measures without German orders and without German pressure. By voluntarily identifying and deporting Jews, the Vichy government sent 75,000 men, women, and children to their deaths.

As the war dragged on for years, internees of the camps hoped and prayed for rescue by the Allies. But such help did not come. The U.S. State Department and the British Foreign Office had early and reliable information on the nature and extent of the atrocities. But they did not act. American Jews were unable to convince President Franklin D. Roosevelt to intercede to prevent the slaughter. Appeals to bomb the gas

---

MANIFESTO OF THE JEWISH RESISTANCE IN VILNA, SEPTEMBER 1943

In May 1943, in spite of the valiant resistance of Jewish fighting groups, the Warsaw ghetto was destroyed by the German SS. In August of the same year, inmates revolted in the concentration camp at Treblinka in the face of insurmountable odds. News of the Warsaw ghetto revolt had spread to the camp, where it inspired Jews to rise up and fight against their captors. Few survived the revolt, although considerable damage was done to the gas chambers, the railway station, and the barracks by the armed inmates. The Jews of the ghetto of Vilna (Vilnius) organized active resistance to the Nazis.

Focus Questions

What is the meaning of the rallying cry, "Jews, we have nothing to lose"? What kind of armed resistance was possible?

Offer armed resistance! Jews, defend yourselves with arms!

The German and Lithuanian executioners are at the gates of the ghetto. They have come to murder us! Soon they will lead you forth in groups through the ghetto door.

Tens of thousands of us were dispatched. But we shall not go! We will not offer our heads to the butcher like sheep.

Jews, defend yourselves with arms!

Do not believe the false promises of the assassins or believe the words of the traitors.

Anyone who passes through the ghetto gate will go to Ponar [death camp]!

And Ponar means death!

Jews, we have nothing to lose. Death will overtake us in any event. And who can still believe in survival when the murderer exterminates us with so much determination? The hand of the executioner will reach each man and woman. Flight and acts of cowardice will not save our lives.

Active resistance alone can save our lives and our honor.

Brothers! It is better to die in battle in the ghetto than to be carried away to Ponar like sheep. And know this: within the walls of the ghetto there are organized Jewish forces who will resist with weapons.

Support the revolt!

Do not take refuge or hide in the bunkers, for then you will fall into the hands of the murderers like rats.

Jewish people, go out into the squares. Anyone who has no weapons should take an ax, and he who has no ax should take a crowbar or a bludgeon!

For our ancestors!

For our murdered children!

Avenge Ponar!

Attack the murderers!

In every street, in every courtyard, in every house within and without the ghetto, attack these dogs!

Jews, we have nothing to lose! We shall save our lives only if we exterminate our assassins.

Long live liberty! Long live armed resistance! Death to the assassins!

Vilna, the Ghetto, 1 September 1943.

chambers at Auschwitz and the railroad lines leading to them were rejected by the United States on strategic grounds. Those trying to survive in the camps and the ghettos despaired at their abandonment.

The handful of survivors found by Allied soldiers who entered the camps after Germany's defeat presented a haunting picture of humanity. A British colonel who entered the camp at Bergen-Belsen in April 1945 gave a restrained account of what he found:

> As we walked down the main road of the camp, we were cheered by the internees, and for the first time we saw their condition. A great number were little more than living skeletons. There were men and women lying in heaps on both sides of the track. Others were walking slowly and aimlessly about, vacant expressions on their starved faces.

The sight of corpses piled on top of one another lining the roads and the piles of shoes, clothing, underwear, and gold teeth extracted from the dead shocked those who came to liberate the camps. One of the two survivors of Chelmno summed it all up: "No one can understand what happened here."

The Final Solution was a perversion of every value of civilization. The achievements of twentieth-century industry, technology, state, and bureaucracy in the West were turned against millions to create, as one German official called it, mur-

■ Internees at Bergen-Belsen upon liberation of the camp by British troops in April 1945.

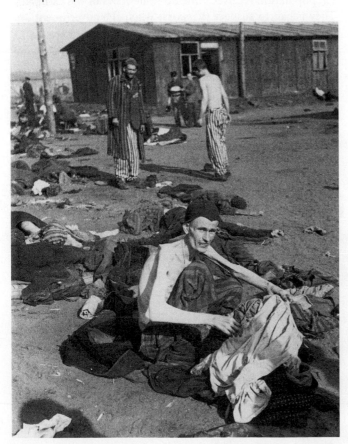

der by assembly line. Mass killing was not prompted by military or security concerns. Nor was the elimination of vital labor power consistent with the needs of the Nazi state. The international tribunal for war crimes that met in 1945 in the German city of Nuremberg attempted to mete out justice to the criminals against humanity responsible for the destruction of 11 million Europeans labeled as demons and racial inferiors. History must record, even if it cannot explain, such inhumanity.

ALLIED VICTORY

The situation at the end of 1941 appeared grim for the British and their dominions and for the Americans who were assisting them with munitions, money, and food. Hitler had achieved control of a vast land empire covering all of continental Europe in the west, north, south, and center. The empire, which Hitler called his "New Order," included territories occupied and directly administered by the German army, satellites, and collaborationist regimes. It was fortified by alliances with Italy, the Soviet Union, and Japan. Hitler commanded the greatest fighting force in the world, one that had knocked France out of the war in a matter of weeks, brought destruction to British cities, and conquered Yugoslavia in 12 days. Much of the world was coming to fear German invincibility.

Then, in June 1941, Hitler's troops invaded the Soviet Union, providing the British with an ally. In December, the naval and air forces of Japan attacked American bases in the Pacific, providing the British and the Russians with still another ally. What was a European war became a world war. It was the war Hitler did not want and that Germany could not win—a long, total war to the finish against three powers with inexhaustible resources: the British Empire, the Soviet Union, and the United States.

The Soviet Union's Great Patriotic War

Hitler had always considered the Soviet Union Germany's primary enemy. His hatred of communism was all-encompassing: Bolshevism was an evil invention of the Jewish people and a dangerous ideological threat to the Third Reich. The 1939 Non-Aggression Pact with Stalin was no more than an expedient for him. Hitler rebuked a Swiss diplomat in 1939 for failing to grasp the central fact of his foreign policy:

> Everything I undertake is directed against Russia. If those in the West are too stupid and too blind to understand this, then I should be forced to come to an understanding with the Russians to beat the West, and then, after its defeat, turn with all my concentrated force against the Soviet Union.

Soviet Unpreparedness. On 22 June 1941, German armies marched into Russia. They found the Soviet army larger but totally unprepared for war. In contrast to German soldiers, who had fought in Spain, Poland, and France, Soviet troops had no firsthand battle experience. Nor were they well led. Stalin's purges in the late 1930s had removed 35,000 officers from their posts by dismissal, imprisonment, or execution. Many of the men who replaced them were unseasoned in the responsibilities of leadership. → result of killing old officers

Russian military leaders were sure they would be ready for a European war against the capitalist nations by 1942, and Stalin refused to believe that Hitler would attack the Soviet Union before then. British agents and Stalin's own spies tried to warn him of German plans for an invasion in the spring of 1941. When the Germans did invade Russian territory, Stalin was so overwhelmed that he fell into a depression and was unable to act for days.

In his first radio address after the attack on 3 July 1941, Stalin identified his nation with the Allied cause: "Our struggle for the freedom of our country will merge with the struggle of the peoples of Europe and America for their independence, for democratic liberties." He accepted offers of support from the United States and Great Britain, the two nations that had worked consistently to exclude the Soviet Union from European power politics since the Bolshevik revolution in 1917. With France defeated and Great Britain crippled, the future of the war depended on the Soviet fighting power and American supplies.

Stalin wto a democratic nations

German Offensive and Reversals.

Hitler's invasion of Russia involved three million soldiers from Germany and Germany's satellites, the largest invasion force in history. It stretched along an immense battlefront from the Baltic to the Black Sea. Instead of exclusively targeting Moscow, the capital, the German army concentrated first on destroying Soviet armed forces and capturing Leningrad in the north and the oil-rich Caucasus in the south. In the beginning, the German forces advanced rapidly in a blitzkrieg across western Russia, where they were greeted as liberators in the Ukraine. The Germans took 290,000 prisoners of war and massacred tens of thousands of others in their path through the Jewish settlements of western Russia.

Within four months, the German army had advanced to the gates of Moscow, but they concentrated their forces too late. The Red Army rallied to defend Moscow as thousands of civilian women set to work digging trenches and antitank ditches around the city. The Soviet people answered Stalin's call for a scorched-earth policy by burning everything that might be useful to the advancing German troops. German troops had also burned much in their path, depriving themselves of essential supplies for the winter months ahead. The German advance was stopped, and the best ally of the Red Army—the Russian winter—settled in. The first snow fell at the beginning of October. By early November, German troops were beginning to suffer the harsh effects of an early and exceptionally bitter Russian winter.

Hitler promised the German people that "final victory" was at hand. So confident was Hitler of a speedy and decisive victory that he sent his soldiers into Russia wearing only light summer uniforms. Hitler's generals knew better and tried repeatedly to explain military realities to the Führer. General Heinz Guderian (1888–1954), commander of the tank units, reported that his men were suffering frostbite, that tanks could not be started, and that automatic weapons were jamming in the subzero temperatures. Back in Germany, the civilian population received little accurate news of the campaign. They began to suspect the worst when the government sent out a plea for woolen blankets and clothing for the troops.

By early December, the German military situation was desperate. The Soviets, benefiting from intelligence information

■ Russian villagers search for loved ones among civilians slain by German troops. Noncombatants were frequent victims of the Nazi policy of enslavement or annihilation.

about German plans and an awareness that Japan was about to declare war on the United States, recalled fresh troops from the Siberian frontier and the border with China and Manchuria and launched a powerful counterattack against the poorly outfitted German army outside Moscow. Under the command of General Gyorgi Zhukov (1896–1974), Russian troops, dressed and trained for winter warfare, pushed the Germans back in retreat across the snow-covered expanses. By February, 200,000 German troops had been killed, 46,000 were missing in action, and 835,000 were wounded in battle and by the weather. Thus the campaign cost the German army more than one million casualties. It probably cost the Soviets twice that number of wounded, missing, captured, and dead soldiers. At the end of the Soviet counterattack in March, the German army and its satellite forces were in a shambles reminiscent of Napoleon's troops, who 130 years earlier had been decimated in the campaign to capture Moscow. An enraged Hitler dismissed his generals for retreating without his permission, and he himself assumed the position of commander in chief of the armed forces.

■ The Battle of Stalingrad was over in the first days of February 1943. Of the original 300,000 members of the German Sixth Army, fewer than 100,000 survived to be taken prisoner by the Soviets. Of those, only 9,000 returned to Germany in 1955, when German prisoners of war were repatriated.

Hitler was not daunted by the devastating costs of his invasion of Russia. In the summer of 1942, he initiated a second major offensive, this time to take the city of Stalingrad. Constant bombardment gutted the city, and the Soviet army was forced into hand-to-hand combat with the German soldiers. But the German troops, once again inadequately supplied and unprepared for the Russian winter, failed to capture the city.

Soviet Patriotism.   The Soviets succeeded by exploiting two great advantages in their war against Germany: the large Soviet population and their knowledge of Russian weather and terrain. There was a third advantage that Hitler ignored: the Soviet people's determination to sacrifice everything for the war effort. In his successive Five-Year Plans, Stalin had mobilized Soviet society with an appeal to fulfill and surpass production quotas. In the summer of 1941, as Hitler's troops threatened Moscow, he used the same rhetoric to appeal to his Soviet "brothers and sisters" to join him in waging "**the Great Patriotic War.**" The Russian people shared a sense of common purpose, sacrifice, and moral commitment in their loyalty to the nation.

The advancing Germans themselves intensified Soviet patriotism by torturing and killing tens of thousands of peasants who might have willingly cooperated against the Stalinist regime. Millions of Soviet peasants joined the Red Army. Young men of high school age were drafted into the armed forces. Three million women became wage earners for the first time as they replaced men in war industries. Women who remained on the land worked to feed the townspeople and the soldiers. Because the Red Army had requisitioned horses and tractors for combat, grain had to be sown and harvested by hand—and that often meant women's hands. Tens of thousands of Russians left their homes in western Russia to work for relocated Soviet industries in the Urals, the Volga region, Siberia, and Central Asia.

More than 20 million Soviet people, soldiers and civilians, men, women, and children, died in the course of World War II. In addition to those killed in battle, millions starved as a direct result of the hardships of war. In 1943, food was so scarce that seed for the next year's crops was eaten. One in every three men born in 1906 died in the war. But Soviet resistance did not flag. The Great Patriotic War had a profound impact on Soviet views of the world and the Soviet Union's place in it. The war left the Soviet people with an enduring fear of invasion. The official falsification of all published maps of the Soviet Union in order to mislead spies and foreign armies was just one indication of the Russian expectation of treachery. (That practice was as recent as 1988.) Today, a visitor to Stalingrad, renamed Volgograd, can still find old tanks in city parks and on streets as reminders of the front line of the Red Army in the Great Patriotic War. Ruins of buildings have been left standing as grim monuments to the need for continued preparedness. The few remaining trees that endured through the war's devastation bear plaques that make their survival a memorial.

The Soviet Union sacrificed 10 percent of its population to the war effort, incurring more than 50 percent of all the

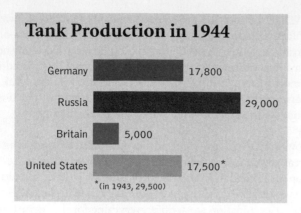

Tank Production in 1944

Germany	17,800
Russia	29,000
Britain	5,000
United States	17,500*

*(in 1943, 29,500)

deaths and casualties of the war. Few families escaped the death of members in the defense of the nation. Soviet citizens correctly considered that they had given more than any other country to defeat Hitler. For the Soviet people, their suffering in battle made World War II the Soviet Union's war, and their sacrifice made possible the Allied victory.

The United States Enters the War

Victory still eluded the Allies in western Europe, where now another nation, the United States, had entered the fray. Although a neutral power, the United States began extending aid to the Allies after the fall of France in 1940. Since neither Britain nor the Soviet Union could afford to pay all the costs

PRESIDENT FRANKLIN ROOSEVELT'S REQUEST FOR A DECLARATION OF WAR ON JAPAN, 8 DECEMBER 1941

On 7 December 1941, the Japanese naval and air forces attacked the American naval base at Pearl Harbor in Hawaii, killing and wounding 3457 military personnel and civilians. Most of the U.S. Pacific fleet was moored in Pearl Harbor, and it sustained severe destruction of its naval vessels, battleships, and aircraft. U.S. military and political leaders were taken completely by surprise by the Japanese attack.

Focus Questions

Why is 7 December 1941 called a "day which will live in infamy"? How does Roosevelt's declaration of war reflect outrage over the "infamy"?

To the Congress of the United States:

Yesterday, December 7, 1941—a date which will live in infamy—the United States of America was suddenly and deliberately attacked by naval and air forces of the Empire of Japan.

The United States was at peace with that Nation and, at the solicitation of Japan, was still in conversation with its Government and its Emperor looking toward the maintenance of peace in the Pacific. Indeed, one hour after Japanese air squadrons had commenced bombing in Oahu, the Japanese Ambassador to the United States and his colleague delivered to the Secretary of State a formal reply to a recent American message. While this reply stated that it seemed useless to continue the existing diplomatic negotiations, it contained no threat or hint of war or armed attack.

It will be recorded that the distance of Hawaii from Japan makes it obvious that the attack was deliberately planned many days or even weeks ago. During the intervening time the Japanese Government has deliberately sought to deceive the United States by false statements and expressions of hope for continued peace.

The attack yesterday on the Hawaiian Islands has caused severe damage to American naval and military forces. Very many American lives have been lost. In addition, American

ships have been reported torpedoed on the high seas between San Francisco and Honolulu.

Yesterday the Japanese Government also launched an attack against Malaya.

Last night Japanese forces attacked Hong Kong.

Last night Japanese forces attacked Guam.

Last night Japanese forces attacked the Philippine Islands.

Last night the Japanese attacked Wake Island.

This morning the Japanese attacked Midway Island.

Japan has, therefore, undertaken a surprise offensive extending throughout the Pacific area. The facts of yesterday speak for themselves. The people of the United States have already formed their opinions and well understand the implications to the very life and safety of our Nation.

As Commander-in-Chief of the Army and Navy I have directed that all measures be taken for our defense.

Always will we remember the character of the onslaught against us.

No matter how long it may take us to overcome this premeditated invasion, the American people in their righteous might will win through to absolute victory. . . .

With confidence in our armed forces—with the unbounded determination of our people—we will gain the inevitable triumph—so help us God.

I ask that the Congress declare that since the unprovoked and dastardly attack by Japan on Sunday, December seventh, a state of war has existed between the United States and the Japanese Empire.

Franklin D. Roosevelt

of defending Europe against Hitler, the U.S. Congress passed the Lend-Lease Act in 1941. The act authorized President Roosevelt to provide armaments to Great Britain and the Soviet Union without payment. America became the "arsenal of democracy." The United States and Britain sent 4100 airplanes and 138,000 motor vehicles, as well as steel and machinery, to the Soviet Union for the campaign of 1943. In all, America pumped $11 billion worth of equipment into the Soviet war effort between 1941 and 1945. Stalin later told Roosevelt that the USSR would have lost the war with Germany without the help of the Americans and the British.

Japan Attacks.   President Roosevelt and his advisers considered Germany, not Japan, to be America's primary target for a future war. Japan nevertheless had been threatening

American trade interests in Asia and had embroiled the United States in disputes over Japanese imperialist expansion in the late 1930s. The United States understood Japan to be an aggressive country determined to expand its control over China and southeast Asia, which it opposed initially through economic embargoes. The presence of the Soviet Union pressing eastward across Asia, coupled with the colonial presences in Asia of Great Britain, France, and the United States, severely constrained Japan's capacity to expand its frontiers and ensure its security. The war in western Europe and the German invasion of the Soviet Union in June 1941 meant that the Japanese could concentrate their attention farther south in China, Indochina, and Thailand. Japan's limited reserves of foreign currency and raw materials made it increasingly vulnerable to economic disruptions. Japanese leaders

JAPAN'S DECLARATION OF WAR ON THE UNITED STATES AND GREAT BRITAIN, 8 DECEMBER 1941

Japan's sense of its mission in East Asia is embodied in Emperor Hirohito's declaration of war against the United States and Great Britain on 8 December 1941, the day after Japanese forces attacked the American fleet in Hawaii. Interestingly, the Japanese declaration speaks of "world peace" and "friendship among nations." In spite of marked cultural differences in the form of the two declarations, both the Japanese and the American leaders make clear their country's dependence on the total support of their people to win the war.

Focus Questions

Why in a declaration of war against the United States and the British Empire does the Emperor talk about China? What are "the true intentions of Our Empire" to which Emperor Hirohito is referring?

We, by grace of heaven, Emperor of Japan, seated on the Throne of the line unbroken for ages eternal, enjoin upon ye. Our loyal and brave subjects.

We hereby declare war on the United States of America and the British Empire. The men and officers of Our Army and Navy shall do their utmost in prosecuting the war, Our public servants of various departments shall perform faithfully and diligently their appointed tasks, and all other subjects of Ours shall pursue their respective duties; the entire nation with a united will shall mobilize their total strength so that nothing will miscarry in the attainment of our war aims.

To insure the stability of East Asia and to contribute to world peace is the far-sighted policy which was formulated by Our Great Illustrious Imperial Grandsire and Our Great Imperial Sire succeeding Him, and which We have constantly to heart. To cultivate friendship among nations and to employ prosperity in common with all nations has always been the guiding principle of Our Empire's foreign policy. It has been truly unavoidable and far from Our

wishes that Our Empire has now been brought to cross swords with America and Britain. More than four years have passed since the government of the Chinese Republic, failing to comprehend the true intentions of Our Empire, and recklessly courting trouble, disturbed the peace of east Asia and compelled Our Empire to take up arms. . . .

Patiently have We waited and long have We endured, in the hope that Our Government might retrieve the situation in peace. But our adversaries, showing not the least spirit of conciliation, have unduly delayed a settlement; and in the meantime, they have intensified the economic and military pressure to compel thereby Our Empire to submission. This trend of affairs would, if left unchecked, not only nullify Our Empire's efforts of many years for the sake of the stabilization of east Asia, but also endanger the very existence of Our nation. The situation being such as it is, Our Empire for its existence and self-defense has no other recourse but to appeal to arms and to crush every obstacle in its path.

The hallowed spirits of Our Imperial Ancestors guarding Us from above, We rely upon the loyalty and courage of Our subjects in Our confident expectation that the task bequeathed by Our Forefathers will be carried forward, and that the sources of evil will be speedily eradicated and an enduring peace immutably established in East Asia, preserving thereby the glory of Our Empire.

The 8th day of the 12th month of the 16th year of Showa.
Hirohito

accepted the necessity of grasping oil and raw materials in southeast Asia.

In September 1940, Japan joined forces with the Axis Powers of Germany and Italy in the **Tripartite Pact**, in which the signatories, promising mutual support against aggression, acknowledged the legitimacy of each other's expansionist efforts in Europe and Asia. Japanese–American relations deteriorated following the Japanese invasion of southern Indochina in July 1941. The United States insisted that Japan vacate China and Indochina and reestablish the open door for trade in Asia. The United States knew, however, that it was only a matter of time until Japan attacked U.S. interests but was uncertain about where that attack would take place.

On Sunday morning, 7 December 1941, Japan struck at the heart of the American Pacific Fleet stationed at Pearl Harbor, Hawaii. The fleet was literally caught asleep at the switch: 2300 people were killed, and eight battleships and numerous cruisers and destroyers were sunk or severely damaged. The attack crippled American naval power in the Pacific as the American navy suffered its worst loss in history in a single engagement. The attack on Pearl Harbor led to the United States' immediate declaration of war against Japan. In President Roosevelt's words, 7 December 1941 was "a date which will live in infamy."

In the next three months, Japan captured Hong Kong, Malaya, and the important naval base at Singapore from the British, taking 60,000 prisoners. Like its earlier march into China, the Japanese invasion of southeast Asia moved swiftly to establish control, outstripping the Japanese military's own timetables for advance. In December 1941, the Japanese landed in Thailand and secured immediate agreement for Japanese occupation of strategic spots in the country. They then turned to the Malayan peninsula, decisively defeating the British fleet off Malaya and pushing on the ground toward Singapore, which they conquered in February 1942. They conquered British Borneo in January, drove the Dutch from all of Indonesia but New Guinea, pushed American forces in the Philippines into the Bataan Peninsula, occupied Burma, and inflicted severe defeats on British, Dutch, and American naval power in East Asia. U.S. General Douglas MacArthur (1880–1964) surrendered the Philippines to the Japanese on 2 January 1942 with the promise to return. With the armies of Germany deep in Russian territory, Australia had little hope of Allied help against a Japanese invasion.

Germany Declares War on the United States. Hitler praised the Japanese government for its action against the British Empire and against the United States and its "millionaire and Jewish backers." Germany, with its armies retreating from Moscow, nevertheless declared war against the United States on 11 December 1941. Hitler, in fact, considered that the United States was already at war with Germany because of its policy of supplying the Allies. Within days, the United States, a nation with an army smaller than Belgium's, had gone from neutrality to a war in two theaters. Although militarily weak, the United States was an economic giant, commanding a vast industrial capacity and access to resources. America grew even stronger under the stimulus of war, increasing its production by 400 percent in two years. It devoted itself to the demands of a total war and the unconditional surrender of Germany and then Japan.

■ The battleship USS *West Virginia* in flames at Pearl Harbor. The attack was carried out entirely by carrier-based aircraft—a sign of things to come in naval warfare.

Winning the War in Europe

The Allies did not always share the same strategies or concerns. President Roosevelt and Prime Minister Churchill had already discussed common goals in the summer of 1941 before the U.S. entry into the war. The United States embraced the priority of the European war and the postponement of war in the Pacific. Stalin pleaded for the Anglo-Americans to open up a second front against Germany in western Europe to give his troops some relief and save Soviet lives. Anglo-American resources were committed to the Pacific to stop the Japanese advance, and the Americans and the British disagreed as to where a second front in Europe might be opened.

Because of British interests in the Mediterranean, Churchill insisted on a move from North Africa into Sicily and Italy. That strategy was put into effect in 1942. The Italian government withdrew from the war in September, but German troops carried on the fight in Italy. The Anglo-American invasion of Italy did little to alleviate Russian losses, and the Soviet Union absorbed almost the entire force of German military power until 1944. Stalin's distrust of his allies increased. Churchill, Roosevelt, and Stalin met for the first time in late November 1943 at Teheran, Iran. Roosevelt and Churchill made a commitment to Stalin to open a second front in France within six months. Stalin, in turn, promised to attack Japan to aid the United States in the Pacific. The great showdown of the global war was at hand.

On 6 June 1944, D-Day, Allied troops under the command of American General Dwight D. Eisenhower (1890–1969) came ashore on the beaches of Normandy in the largest amphibious landing in history. In a daring operation identified by the code name Operation Overlord, 2.2 million American, British, and

■ Soldiers raise the hammer-and-sickle flag over the ruins of the Reichstag as Soviet troops occupy Berlin in May 1945. At war's end, the Soviets occupied most of eastern Europe, which gave Stalin an advantage at the Yalta Conference.

■ A United States Army unit joins Allied forces at the beachheads of Normandy during Operation Overlord in 1944. The invasion began the opening of the second front that Stalin had been urging on the Allies since the German armies thrust into Russia in 1941.

Free French forces, 450,000 vehicles, and 4 million tons of supplies poured into northern France. Allied forces broke through German lines to liberate Paris in late August. The Germans launched a last-ditch counterattack in late December 1944 in Luxembourg and Belgium. The Battle of the Bulge only slowed the Allied advance; in March 1945, American forces crossed the Rhine into Germany. Hitler, meanwhile, refused to surrender and insisted on a fight to the death of the last German soldier. Members of his own High Command had attempted unsuccessfully to assassinate Hitler in July 1944. The final German defeat came in April 1945, when the Russians stormed the German capital of Berlin. Hitler, living in an underground bunker near the Chancellery building, committed suicide on 30 April 1945.

Japanese War Aims and Assumptions

Japan and the United States entered the Pacific War with very different understandings of what was at stake. The Japanese appealed to southeast Asian leaders, presenting themselves as the liberators of Asian peoples from Western colonialism and imperialism.

Japanese Hegemony in Asia. The approach struck a responsive chord as the Japanese established what they called the Greater East Asia Co-Prosperity Sphere. Ba Maw, Burma's leader, said at the Assembly of the Greater East Asiatic Nations held in Tokyo in November 1943, "My Asiatic blood has always called to other Asiatics. . . . This is not the time to think with our minds; this is the time to think with our blood, and it is thinking with the blood that has brought me all the way from Burma to Japan." But the passionate and positive welcome Ba Maw extended to the Japanese liberators did not last long. As he bluntly explained in his memoirs, "The brutality, arrogance, and racial pretensions of the Japanese militarists in Burma remain among the deepest Burmese memories of the war years; for a great many people in southeast Asia these are all they remember of the war."

The Greater East Asia Co-Prosperity Sphere began in 1940 and lasted until the summer of 1945. The reorganization of east and southeast Asia under Japanese hegemony constituted a redefinition of world geography, with Japan at the center. The Japanese fashioned a romanticized vision of the family living in harmony, each member knowing his place and enjoying the complementary division of responsibilities and reciprocities that made family life work smoothly. Behind the pleasant image lurked the reality of a brutal power structure forcing subject peoples to accept massively inferior positions in a world fashioned exclusively for Japanese desires and needs. The Japanese viewed southeast Asia principally as a market for Japanese manufactured goods, a source of raw materials, and a source of profits for Japanese capital invested in mining, rubber, and raw cotton. Plans were made for hydroelectric power and aluminum refining facilities.

Wartime Japanese nakedly displayed their disdain for the people they conquered in southeast Asia. All subject peoples were to bow on meeting a Japanese. At public assemblies a ritual bow in the direction of the Japanese emperor was required, to the dismay of southeast Asians such as Indies Muslims or Philippine Catholics, who regarded Japanese emperor worship as pagan and presumptuous. Japanese holidays, such as the emperor's birthday, were enforced as Co-Prosperity Sphere holidays, and the calendar was reset to the mythical founding of the Japanese state in 660 B.C.E.

The Japanese were less brazen toward the Chinese in their rhetoric, in part because so much of east Asian civilization had its roots in China. But even if more temperate in their pronouncements, the realities of Japanese aggression in China included one of the worst periods of destruction in modern warfare. When they took over the Nationalist capital of Nanjing in December 1937, 20,000 women were raped, 30,000 soldiers killed, and another 12,000 civilians died in the more than six weeks of wanton terror inflicted by Japanese soldiers.

Japan's View of the West. With regard to Westerners, Japanese propaganda avoided labeling them as inferior. In part this reflected Japan's economic and political emulation of the West since the late nineteenth century. Rather than denigrating Western people, the Japanese chose to elevate themselves as a people descended from divine origins. Stressing their unique mythical history gave the Japanese a strong sense of superiority neither intellectual nor physical, but moral. They believed that virtue was on their side in their mission to stop Western expansion in Asia and to take their "proper place" as the leading people in Asia by tyrannizing the Co-Prosperity Sphere.

To achieve their moral superiority, the Japanese government urged their people to "purify" themselves. For the average wartime Japanese citizen, purification meant accepting extreme material poverty and scarcity, rejecting foreign influences, and if called upon, dying for the emperor. The Japanese elevation of patriotism to the level of human sacrifice lay outside Western sensibilities of the time; to expect the spirit to become more purified made little sense to large numbers of Westerners. A bit more comprehensible, perhaps, were Japanese wartime views of Americans as beasts because of the atrocities that American soldiers committed. The grotesque quality of the American soldier's desire for war trophies was captured by a *Life* magazine photograph of a blond young American woman holding a Japanese skull sent to her by her GI sweetheart. What *Life* magazine considered "human interest" the Japanese found racist. However reasonable that assessment may have been, Japanese impressions of Westerners definitely proved fatally false in another matter. The Japanese assumed that individual selfishness and egoism would make Americans and Europeans incapable of mobilizing for a long fight.

Winning the War in the Pacific

The tide in the Pacific War began to turn when the planned Japanese invasion of Australia was thwarted. Fighting in the jungles of New Guinea, Australian and American troops under the command of General Douglas MacArthur turned

MAP DISCOVERY

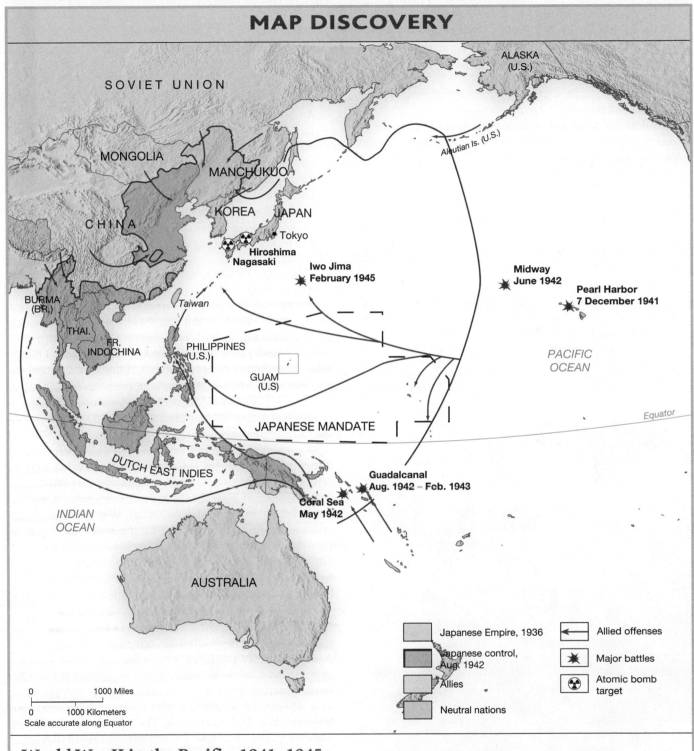

Japanese Empire, 1936

Japanese control, Aug. 1942

Allies

Neutral nations

Allied offenses

Major battles

Atomic bomb target

World War II in the Pacific, 1941–1945

Japan extended control throughout east and southeast Asia until the Japanese Empire reached its pinnacle in August 1942. Note the direction of major Allied offensives and the necessity of coordinated land, sea, and air offensives. Why were Hiroshima and Nagasaki chosen as atomic bomb targets?

"GLITTERING FRAGMENTS"

Hara Tamiki (1905–1951) was a Japanese poet who was living in Hiroshima when the atomic bomb exploded there on 6 August 1945. His poem "Glittering Fragments" tells about what he saw. A victim of the bomb's radioactivity, he committed suicide in 1951.

Focus Questions

How does the economy of words in this poem convey the horror of the atomic bomb for its victims? Why does the title seem to convey a pleasing image?

Glittering fragments
Ashen embers
Like a rippling panorama,
Burning red then dulled.
Strange rhythm of human corpses.
All existence, all that could exist
Laid bare in a flash. The rest of the world
The swelling of a horse's corpse
At the side of an upturned train,
The smell of smoldering electric wires.

■ Photographer Yosuke Yamahata was one of three men sent by the Japanese Army to document the effects of the atomic bomb dropped on Nagasaki on 9 August 1945. The three arrived in Nagasaki just before dawn on August 10, and as the sun rose Yamahata immediately began to take pictures. One of his first was this photo of a young boy and his mother holding riceballs, the only emergency rations available to survivors of the atomic blast.

back the Japanese army. U.S. Marines did likewise with a bold landing at Guadalcanal and months of bloody fighting in the Solomon Islands. In June 1942, within six months of the attack at Pearl Harbor, American naval forces commanded by Admiral Chester Nimitz (1885–1966) inflicted a defeat on the Japanese navy from which it could not recover. In the battle of Midway (3–6 June 1942), Japan lost 4 aircraft carriers, a heavy cruiser, more than 300 airplanes, and 5,000 men. Midway was the Pacific equivalent of the Battle of Stalingrad.

In the summer of 1943, as the Soviet Union launched the offensive that was to defeat Germany, America began to move across the Pacific toward Japan. Nimitz and MacArthur conceived a brilliant plan in which American land, sea, and air forces fought in a coordinated effort. With a series of amphibious landings, they hopped from island to island. Some Japanese island fortresses, such as Tarawa, were taken; others, such as Truk, were bypassed and cut off from Japanese home bases. With the conquest of Saipan in November 1944 and Iwo Jima in March 1945, the U.S. Air Force acquired bases from which B-29 bombers could strike at the Japanese home islands. In the summer of 1945, in the greatest air offensive in history, American planes destroyed what remained of the Japanese navy, crippled Japanese industry, and mercilessly firebombed major population centers. The attack ended with the dropping of atomic bombs on the cities of Hiroshima and Nagasaki. (See "A Closer Look: The Atomic Wasteland," pp. 864–865.) The Japanese government accepted American terms for peace and surrendered unconditionally on 2 September 1945 on the battleship *Missouri* in Tokyo Bay. Four months after the defeat of Germany, the war in Asia was over.

DOCUMENT

An Eyewitness to Hiroshima

The Fate of Allied Cooperation: 1945

The costs of World War II in terms of death and destruction were the highest in history. Fifty million lives were lost. Most of the dead were Europeans, and most of the Europeans were Russians and Poles. The high incidence of civilian deaths distinguished World War II from previous wars—more than 50 percent of the dead were noncombatants. Deliberate military targeting of cities explains that phenomenon only in part. The majority of civilian deaths were the result of starvation, enslavement, massacre, and deliberate extermination.

Civilian Populations. The psychological devastation of continual violence, deprivation, injury, and rape of survivors

---

CHRONOLOGY

World War II

1937	Japan begins undeclared war on China
March 1938	Germany annexes Austria to the German Reich
29 September 1938	Chamberlain, Daladier, Mussolini, and Hitler meet at Munich conference
May 1939	Pact of Steel: military alliance between Italy and Germany
1939	Non-Aggression Pact between Germany and the Soviet Union
1 September 1939	Germany attacks Poland
3 September 1939	Great Britain and France declare war on Germany
April 1940	Germany attacks Denmark and Norway
May 1940	Germany invades the Netherlands, Belgium, Luxembourg, and then France
June 1940	Italy enters the war on the side of Germany
17 June 1940	French Marshal Pétain petitions Germany for an armistice and creates a collaborationist government at Vichy
September 1940	Japan, Germany, and Italy sign Tripartite Pact
September–November 1940	The Battle of Britain
22 June 1941	Germany invades the Soviet Union
1941	First extermination camp created in Chelmno, Poland
7 December 1941	Japan attacks Pearl Harbor; the following day, the United States declares war on Japan
11 December 1941	Germany declares war on the United States
January 1942	Wannsee Conference, at which the Final Solution is planned
June 1942	Battle of Midway
September 1942	Italian government withdraws from the war
April 1943	Unsuccessful uprising in the Warsaw ghetto
November 1943	Churchill, Roosevelt, and Stalin meet at Teheran conference
6 June 1944	Allied forces land in northern France—D-Day
February 1945	Churchill, Roosevelt, and Stalin meet at Yalta
March 1945	American forces march into Germany
30 April 1945	Hitler commits suicide
July and August 1945	Churchill, Truman, and Stalin meet at Potsdam
6 August 1945	United States drops atomic bomb on Hiroshima
2 September 1945	Japan surrenders

THE ATOMIC WASTELAND

The sixth of August 1945 was a typical summer day in southwestern Japan. In the city of Hiroshima at 8:15 A.M., people were walking to work, sitting down at office desks, riding buses, weeding gardens, and clearing away breakfast dishes. Suddenly a noiseless flash lit the sky over the city and its environs for miles. A mammoth column of smoke in the shape of a mushroom cloud ballooned up. The United States had dropped history's first atomic bomb.

The explosion had the intensity of a huge blast furnace. In some areas, the brilliant light created by the explosion bleached everything it touched. Near the epicenter of the blast, human bodies were charred to cinders or turned into frightening statues. Flesh melted and bones fused.

A CLOSER LOOK

Buildings were reduced to ashes. Stones bled. Hiroshima, a city renowned in prewar Japan for its relaxed and agreeable atmosphere, was leveled in an instant by the terrifying force of a single atomic bomb.

There were 78,000 dead in Hiroshima on 6 August. By December, the number had reached 140,000 as the sickness caused by radioactive poisoning continued to take its toll. Rescue workers inhaled the dense dust and became contaminated by radioactivity. Surviving victims often lost their hair and eyebrows and experienced nausea, vomiting, diarrhea, and bleeding. Others suffered from internal hemorrhaging, blindness, chronic weakness,

and fatigue. Many developed cancers such as leukemia, sometimes years later. The bomb scarred and disfigured. Atomic radiation released by the bomb caused unseen damage by attacking the lungs, heart, bone marrow, and internal organs. It poisoned the lymph glands. It worked unobserved to alter genetic structure, deforming unborn babies and those not yet conceived.

Harry Truman, who became president of the United States on 12 April 1945 following the death of Franklin D. Roosevelt, later spoke of his decision to drop the atomic bomb to bring the war to a speedy end. In July 1945, Truman issued an ultimatum to Japan to surrender immediately or face dire consequences. The Japanese ignored the warning. Hiroshima was targeted, according to Truman, to make a point to the Japanese, to demonstrate the unimaginable force of the new American weapon. The city was a military center, a major storage and assembly point that supplied the armed forces. Nagasaki, bombed three days after Hiroshima with an experimental plutonium bomb, was targeted as an industrial center and the place where the torpedoes that had destroyed American ships were manufactured.

It is undoubtedly true that the bombings were responsible for the Japanese surrender a few days later. The atomic bomb did bring the Asian war to an immediate end. But critics of the bombings pointed out that Japan was already close to defeat. Secret U.S. intelligence studies that came to light in the 1980s indicate that American leaders knew in 1945 that Japan had been weakened by intense American

incendiary bombing of its cities. Twenty-six square miles of the working-class and industrial section of Tokyo had been burned at the cost of more than 100,000 lives. Many refugees from other Japanese cities had fled to Hiroshima to live with relatives. The Sea of Japan had been heavily mined, cutting off Japan from its armies on the Asian mainland. Some radical young officers of the Japanese army, however, were preparing to kidnap Emperor Hirohito to keep him from capitulating, and the planned American landing on Japan was expected to be costly. U.S. forces had already suffered more than 100,000 casualties in the conquest of the Japanese island of Okinawa in April. Truman and his advisers were now prepared to use any means possible to prevent further American casualties. Defenders of the decision have argued that any responsible American leader would have made the same decision to use the atomic bomb. Modern total wars acquire a life of their own, and desperate nations use the science, technology, and weapons available to them.

In the summer of 1945, General Dwight D. Eisenhower, then the victorious Supreme Allied Commander in the European theater of war, was informed by U.S. Secretary of War Henry L. Stimson of what was about to take place in Hiroshima. Eisenhower voiced "grave misgivings" based on his "belief that Japan was already defeated and that the dropping of the bomb was completely unnecessary" to end the war. He was not alone among military men in questioning the use of nuclear force on strategic and moral grounds.

■ Hiroshima after the bombing.

Strong opposition to nuclear weapons began to surface among scientists working on the bomb. In opposition to many of their colleagues, they warned that the atomic bomb was an undiscriminating weapon that could not pinpoint supply depots and military targets but would destroy entire civilian populations. The peace movement based on banning nuclear weapons actually began among horrified scientists who were aware, before the rest of the world could know, of the terrible force that they had helped to create.

At the Potsdam Conference in July 1945, Stalin had informed President Truman and Prime Minister Winston Churchill that the Soviet Union was about to invade Manchuria, honoring the promise Stalin had made at Teheran in 1943 to join the war against Japan after Germany was defeated. The Soviet Union would now play a role in determining the future of Asia. Truman told Stalin of the powerful new weapon America had developed. Stalin seemed unimpressed. Secretary of War Stimson was aware that the atomic bomb would be an important weapon to have in the American arsenal when the time came to negotiate a postwar world settlement with the Russians. Truman and his advisers, however, never deviated from their insistence that saving the lives of thousands of American and Japanese soldiers was their only consideration in dropping the bomb.

An American observer called the bombing of Hiroshima "the immersion in death." Survivors repeatedly described Hiroshima after the "flash" as what hell must be like. Photographs of the city record the total destruction of buildings and vegetation. Japanese photographers avoided taking pictures of the devastation the bomb had done to human bodies, believing that what they saw was too horrible to record. Yet the brutality of nuclear war could not be ignored and nuclear weapons continue to be a central issue of international politics in the twenty-first century. The decision to drop the atomic bomb has had enduring moral and political consequences. On that August morning in 1945, the world had its first terrifying glimpse of the power of total annihilation. In an instant—0.3 second—Hiroshima became an atomic wasteland. The world now lived with the knowledge that it could happen again.

cannot be measured. Terrorizing citizens became an established means of warfare in the modern age. Another phenomenon not matched in World War I emerged in 1945: mass rape. The Russians, brutally treated by Hitler's army, returned the savagery in their advance through eastern and central Europe. The Soviet officer corps encouraged the advancing Russian army to use sexual violence against German women and girls. Collective rape became a means of direct retaliation. Victorious Japanese soldiers raped Chinese women as part of the spoils of war. Regardless of which country was involved, victorious armies practiced rape against civilian populations as one of the unspoken aspects of conquest.

Material destruction was great. Axis and Allied cities, centers of civilization and culture, were turned into wastelands by aerial bombing. The Germans bombed Rotterdam and Coventry. The British engineered the firebombing of Dresden. Warsaw and Stalingrad were destroyed by the German army. Hiroshima and Nagasaki were leveled by the United States. The nations of Europe were weakened after World War I; after World War II, they were crippled. Europe was completely displaced from the position of world dominance it had held for centuries. The United States alone was undamaged and stronger after the war than before, with its industrial capacity and production greatly improved by the war.

The Big Three.   What would be the future of Europe? The leaders of the United States, Great Britain, and the Soviet Union—the **Big Three**, as they were called—met three times between 1943 and 1945: first at Teheran; then in February 1945 at Yalta, a Russian Black Sea resort; and finally in July and August 1945 at Potsdam, a suburb of Berlin. They coordinated their attacks on Germany and Japan and discussed their plans for postwar Europe. After Allied victory, the governments of both Germany and Japan would be totally abolished and completely reconstructed. No deals would be made with Hitler or his successors; no peace would be negotiated with the enemy; surrender would be unconditional. Germany would be disarmed and denazified, and its leaders would be tried as war criminals. The armies of the Big Three occupied Germany, each with a separate zone, but the country would be governed as a single economic unit. The Soviet Union, it was agreed, could collect reparations from Germany. With Germany and Japan defeated, a United Nations organization would provide the structure for a lasting peace in the world.

Stalin expected that the Soviet Union would decide the future of the territories of eastern Europe that the Soviet army had liberated from Germany. This area was vital to the security of the war-devastated Soviet Union; Stalin saw it as a protective barrier against another attack from the west. Romania, Bulgaria, Hungary, Czechoslovakia, and Poland, the Big Three decided, would have pro-Soviet governments. Since Soviet troops occupied these countries in 1945, there was little that the Anglo-Americans could do to prevent Russian control unless they wanted to go to war against the USSR. Churchill real-

■ Churchill, Roosevelt, and Stalin—the Big Three—at the Yalta Conference. Stalin invoked the Yalta agreements to justify the Soviet Union's control over eastern Europe after the war.

istically accepted this. But for Americans who took seriously the proclamations of President Roosevelt that their country had fought to restore freedom and self-determination to peoples oppressed by tyranny, Soviet power in eastern Europe proved to be a bitter disappointment.

CONCLUSION

The war that broke out in 1939 was caused by German aggression, which the appeasement policies of the British failed to contain. Within two years Hitler ruled continental western Europe by either occupation or collaboration. Although pockets of resistance existed, the activities of the resisters had little impact on the course of the war. Hitler undertook the destruction of Europe's Jewish population and the elimination of other minorities deemed inferior by Nazi racial policies.

The year 1941 was a critical turning point in the war because of the German attack on its former ally, which brought Russia to the Allied cause. And in December of that same year, the Japanese attack on an American naval base in Hawaii brought the United States into the war. The war became a truly global conflagration. The Allies were able to coordinate the war effort on several fronts. American technology and resources proved critical in the Allied success. The dropping of two atom bombs also set the tone for determining the peace, and the ideological divide between East and West would sow the seeds of future dissension. Meanwhile the Allies celebrated their victory in a war in which 50 million people died. With the defeat of Germany and Japan, the United States and the Soviet Union stood as the undisputed giants in world politics.

QUESTIONS FOR REVIEW

1. What factors made possible Hitler's diplomatic and military successes between 1933 and 1941?
2. Why did the Nazi regime believe that it needed to destroy the Jews, gypsies, and other outsiders?
3. How did Hitler's invasion of the Soviet Union and the entry of the United States into the war transform the military situation?
4. How did the Allies coordinate their efforts, and what factors strained relations between them?
5. How did the three Allied victors envision the future of Europe, and what steps did they take to ensure the peace?

KEY TERMS

appeasement, *p. 843*	Great Patriotic War, *p. 855*
Axis Powers, *p. 842*	holocaust, *p. 850*
Big Three, *p. 866*	Pact of Steel, *p. 843*
blitzkrieg, p. 844	phony war, *p. 844*
Final Solution, *p. 849*	Tripartite Pact, *p. 858*

DISCOVERING WESTERN CIVILIZATION ONLINE

You can obtain more information about World War II at the Websites listed below. See also the Companion Website that accompanies this text, www.ablongman.com/kishlansky, which contains an online study guide and additional resources.

Aggression and Conquest

The Avalon Project: Munich Pact 9/29/38
www.yale.edu/lawweb/avalon/imt/munich1.htm
Electronic text of the Munich agreements.

The Avalon Project: World War II Documents
http://www.yale.edu/lawweb/avalon/wwii/wwii.htm
An important collection of documents from the pre-war years, the war years, and the subsequent peace settlements.

Racism and Destruction

United States Holocaust Memorial Museum
www.ushmm.org
Home page of the United States Holocaust Museum. The site contains a searchable online catalog of both documentary and photographic sources.

Simon Wiesenthal Center
www.wiesenthal.com
Home page of the Simon Wiesenthal Center and the Museum of Tolerance. It has an extensive collection of materials related to the Holocaust and anti-Semitism.

The Vidal Sassoon International Center for the Study of Antisemitism (SICSA)
sicsa.huji.ac.il/
The site of the Vidal Sassoon International Center for Anti-Semitism that contains an extensive bibliography on the Holocaust.

Allied Victory

Internet Modern History Sourcebook: World War II
www.fordham.edu/halsall/mod/modsbook45.html
A collection of primary source documents and links to materials on World War II.

World War II
www.archives.gov/digital_classroom/teaching_with_documents.html#great_depression
War documents from the U.S. National Archives and Research Administration.

Russian Photography Collection—War Photography
www.schicklerart.com/auto_exh/RPCWar
Images of World War II from the Soviet perspective.

Women Come to the Front
www.loc.gov/exhibits/wcf/wcf0001.html
A virtual exhibit by the Library of Congress on women journalists, photographers, and broadcasters during World War II.

SUGGESTIONS FOR FURTHER READING

Aggression and Conquest

Volker R. Berghahn, *Europe in the Era of Two World Wars: From Militarism and Genocide to Civil Society, 1900–1950* (Princeton: Princeton University Press, 2005). The author examines the twentieth-century history of dictatorships and violence in Europe and considers them within the context of the violence of colonial empires and relations with the United States.

Ian Kershaw, *The Nazi Dictatorship* (London: Edward Arnold, 1985). A fine synthesis of key problems of interpretation regarding the Third Reich. Special attention is paid to the interdependence of domestic and foreign policy and the inevitability of war in Hitler's ideology.

Donald Cameron Watt, *How War Came: The Immediate Origins of the Second World War* (London: Heinemann, 1989). An international historian chronicles the events leading to the outbreak of the war.

Racism and Destruction

Renate Bridenthal, Atina Grossmann, and Marion Kaplan, eds., *When Biology Became Destiny: Women in Weimar and Nazi Germany* (New York: Monthly Review Press, 1984). A volume of essays pursuing common themes on the relation between sexism and racism in interwar and wartime Germany.

Raul Hilberg, *The Destruction of the European Jews,* 3 vols. (New York: Holmes and Meier, 1985). An exhaustive study of the annihilation of European Jews beginning with cultural precedents and antecedents. Examines step-by-step developments that led to extermination policies and contains valuable appendixes on statistics and a discussion of sources.

Charles S. Maier, *The Unmasterable Past: History, Holocaust, and German National Identity* (Cambridge, MA: Harvard University Press, 1988). A thoughtful discussion of the historical debate over the Holocaust and the comparative dimensions of the event. Especially valuable in placing the Holocaust within German history.

Michael R. Marrus, *The Holocaust in History* (New York: New American Library, 1987). A comprehensive survey of all aspects of the Holocaust, including the policies of the Third Reich, the living conditions in the camps, and the prospects for resistance and opposition.

Donald L. Niewyk and Francis R. Nicosia, *The Columbia Guide to the Holocaust* (New York: Columbia University Press: 2000). An impressive reference tool with both historiographic and analytic treatment.

Allied Victory

William L. Bird and Harry Rubenstein, *Design for Victory: World War II Posters on the American Homefront* (Princeton: Princeton Architectural Press, 1998). Examines how advertising promoted support of World War II and includes 150 posters.

John Campbell, ed., *The Experience of World War II* (New York: Oxford University Press, 1989). This richly illustrated work provides an overview of World War II in both the Asian and European theaters in terms of origins, events, and consequences.

Akira Iriye, *The Origins of the Second World War in Asia and the Pacific* (London: Longman, 1987). Examines the events of the 1930s leading up to hostilities in the Pacific theater, with a special focus on Japanese isolation and aggression.

John Keegan, *The Second World War* (New York: Viking, 1990). Provides a panoramic sweep of "the largest single event in human history," with special attention to warfare in all its forms and the importance of leadership.

Geoffrey Roberts, *Stalin's Wars: From World War to Cold War, 1939–1953* (New Haven, CT: Yale University Press, 2007). Based on new Russian archival materials, this work integrates military, diplomatic, and political analyses to show Stalin as a great military leader who sought to avoid the Cold War.

Gerhard L. Weinberg, *A World at Arms: A Global History of World War II* (New York: Cambridge University Press, 1994). An overview of the interactions among Germany, the Soviet Union, and Japan, which provides an integrated history of World War II with a helpful bibliographic essay.

For a list of additional titles related to this chapter's topics, please see http://www.ablongman.com/kishlansky.

CHAPTER 29

THE COLD WAR AND POSTWAR ECONOMIC RECOVERY: 1945–1970

EUROPE IN RUINS

WARSAW, 1946

When the dust from the last bombs settled over Europe's cities, the balance sheets of destruction were tallied. Great cities including London, Cologne, Berlin, Stalingrad, and Warsaw incurred serious damage and human loss. Millions of refugees on the Continent found themselves homeless, having lost their loved ones, often all of their personal belongings, and the roofs over their heads. Millions more returned home from battlefronts and concentration camps to rubble, with wounds beyond healing. There were no jobs; there was nothing to eat. Peacetime rationing dipped below wartime levels. What was not measured in the statistics on physical and human destruction, at least not immediately, was the psychological devastation that succeeded such loss. There could be no returning to life as normal. For many, the war was far gentler than the peace. For the combatants of peacetime, often women and children, digging out and surviving were the greatest battles of all.

THE VISUAL RECORD

Warsaw in 1946 stands as a stark example of extreme destruction and of startling renewal. At the close of the war, Warsaw was an almost completely destroyed city, consisting of little more than dust, ashes, and the charred hulks of destroyed buildings, with no inhabitants and no water, electricity, or sanitation. The scene here, captured by a photographer in early 1946, is not an isolated perspective but rather a landscape typical of Poland's capital after the war. By contrast with this image, Warsaw was recognized in the interwar period of the 1920s and 1930s as a metropolitan center of charm and culture, known for its artists and intellectuals and vibrant urban life.

Warsaw's devastation was not achieved in the same way that Hiroshima and Nagasaki were each destroyed by a single atomic bomb. Instead, Warsaw was annihilated in stages over a five-year period by conventional weapons like flamethrowers, tanks, and dynamite. Unrelenting aerial attacks by German planes against the city and its population began first on 1 September 1939. The Nazi occupiers systematically destroyed people and buildings in order to bring the civilian population to its knees. The Jewish ghetto was completely eliminated in 1943. The destruction, building by building, was premeditated and methodical. By the end of 1944, Warsaw was no more than a heap of rubble with almost 90 percent of its buildings destroyed. A large portion of its population was wiped out, and those who survived were in detention camps or in flight. Warsaw became known as "the vanished city."

But that is where the postwar story of recovery begins. With the liberation by the Red Army of what was left of the city, the Polish people almost immediately planned for the rebuilding of their capital, helped raise the necessary funds, and volunteered their labor to the great task. Women and children joined the men in clearing the rubble and sweeping the path for recovery. Aid in the form of food, clothing, and shelter from organizations such as the United Nations Relief and Rehabilitation Administration supported the healing and rebuilding of Warsaw. Civilians returned to the city. By 1951 the population reached 815,000, although still below its 1.3 million inhabitants in 1939.

In rebuilding Warsaw, the Polish people did not ignore the city's historic past by building a modern, postwar metropolis, as the people of Frankfurt, for example, did. Instead they sought to reconstruct Warsaw as it had been in 1939 by recreating monuments and historic buildings in their original form. Often that required architects to consult unconventional sources, including paintings and postcards, in the absence of blueprints and plans. Palaces and castles were reborn, baroque buildings rose up, ornamental gardens were replanted, and ancient vistas and panoramas were brought back to life. The achievement of historical preservation was astounding. By 1951 a large part of the city had been rebuilt, perhaps one of the best examples of how Europeans met the postwar challenge of urban reconstruction and economic revival.

■ Street scene in Warsaw, 1946.

LOOKING AHEAD

In this chapter, we shall see how, under the tutelage of the two superpowers, the United States and the Soviet Union, Europe diverged on two separate paths of reconstruction and economic integration after 1945. Europe dismantled its global empires. Cold war replaced the hot war of global conflagration. In the West and in the Eastern Bloc, different welfare state models emerged for the

regulation and social distribution of economic expansion. Slowed prosperity in the late 1960s, combined with the growth of an independent youth culture, helped fuel protests in the East and the West. Dissent, prosperity, and rising and unmet consumer expectations characterized Western societies within twenty-five years— the span of a generation—after the end of World War II.

THE ORIGINS OF THE COLD WAR

For victors and vanquished alike, the situation in Europe at the end of World War II was dire. Economies geared totally toward war efforts were incapable of the kind of reorientation needed to reconstruct markets and eliminate economic distress. Governments faced political crises as they attempted to restore or establish democratic principles. Moreover, Europe did not have the capital necessary to begin the process of rebuilding. Political disorganization reigned in Berlin, which was divided into sectors, in Germany, which was divided into zones, and in the former European empires, which were in the process of being dismantled. Even the winners were losers as survivors faced a level of human and material destruction unknown in the history of warfare. As one American military observer reported to his superiors in 1947, "Millions of people

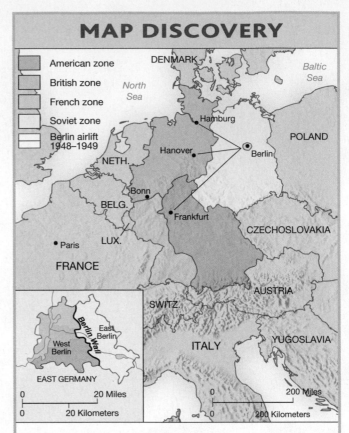

MAP DISCOVERY

American zone
British zone
French zone
Soviet zone
Berlin airlift 1948–1949

The Division of Germany

Examine the division of Germany after World War II. Why did the four victor nations divide Germany into zones at the end of the war? How did Berlin come to be divided into two zones? What was the Soviet goal in blockading West Berlin, and why did the blockade fail?

■ The Berlin airlift of 1948–1949 broke through the Soviet blockade of the city. Called "Operation Vittles," the airlift provided food and fuel for the beleaguered West Berliners. Here children wait for the candy American pilots dropped in tiny parachute handkerchiefs. The Soviets ended the blockade in the spring of 1949.

in the cities are slowly starving." Could Europe rise from these ashes and, if so, in what form?

Tensions initially developed because of differing Russian and American notions regarding the economic reconstruction of Europe. The Soviet Union realized that American aid to Europe was not primarily a humanitarian program; it was part of an economic offensive in Europe that would contribute to the dominance of American capital in world markets. The United States recognized that the Soviet Union hoped to achieve its own recovery through outright control of eastern Europe.

The World in Two Blocs

With the cessation of the "hot" war that had ripped Europe apart from 1939 to 1945, the armies of the United States and the Soviet Union met on the banks of the Elbe River in 1945. Greeting each other as victors and allies, the occupying armies waited for direction on how to conduct the peace. Europe and Japan had been destroyed, leaving the United States and the Soviet Union as indisputably the two richest and strongest nations in the world.

THE IRON CURTAIN

Winston Churchill (1874–1965), prime minister of England during World War II, captured the drama of the post-war international order in a speech he delivered in Missouri in 1946. Churchill had long been suspicious of the political motives of the Soviet Union, though he welcomed Stalin as an ally in defeating Hitler. The term that he coined, "iron curtain," described graphically the fate of Europe that many feared: a Europe rigidly divided between East and West, no more than a pawn in the struggle of the superpowers.

Focus Questions

What are "the Communist fifth columns" in countries such as France and Italy to which Churchill refers? What does Churchill mean by the "grand pacification of Europe," and how does he hope it will be achieved?

From Stettin in the Baltic to Trieste in the Adriatic, an iron curtain has descended across the Continent. Behind that line lie all the capitals of the ancient states of Central and Eastern Europe. Warsaw, Berlin, Prague, Vienna, Budapest, Belgrade, Bucharest and Sofia, all these famous cities and the populations around them lie in what I must call the Soviet sphere, and all are subject in one form or another, not only to Soviet influence but to a very high and, in many cases, increasing measure of control from Moscow. Athens alone—Greece with its immortal glories—is free to decide its future at an election under British, American, and French observation. The Russian-dominated Polish Government has been encouraged to make enormous and wrongful inroads upon Germany, and mass expulsions of millions of Germans on a scale grievous and undreamed-of are now taking place. The Communist parties, which were very small in all these Eastern States of Europe, have been raised to preeminence and power far beyond their numbers and are seeking everywhere to obtain totalitarian control. Police governments are prevailing in nearly every case, and so far, except in Czechoslovakia, there is no true democracy.

The safety of the world requires a new unity in Europe, from which no nation should be permanently outcast. It is from the quarrels of the strong parent races in Europe that the world wars we have witnessed, or which occurred in former times, have sprung. Twice in our own lifetime we have seen the United States, against their wishes and their traditions, against arguments, the force of which it is impossible not to comprehend, drawn by irresistible forces, into these wars in time to secure the victory of the good cause, but only after frightful slaughter and devastation had occurred. Twice the United States has had to send several millions of its young men across the Atlantic to find the war; but now war can find any nation, wherever it may dwell between dusk and dawn. Surely we should work with conscious purpose for a grand pacification of Europe, within the structure of the United Nations and in accordance with its Charter. That I feel is an open cause of policy of very great importance.

In front of the iron curtain which lies across Europe are other causes for anxiety. In Italy the Communist Party is seriously hampered by having to support the Communist-trained Marshal Tito's claims to former Italian territory at the head of the Adriatic. Nevertheless the future of Italy hangs in the balance. Again one cannot imagine a regenerated Europe without a strong France. All my public life I have worked for a strong France and I never lost faith in her destiny, even in the darkest hours. I will not lose faith now. However, in a great number of countries, far from the Russian frontiers and throughout the world, Communist fifth columns are established and work in complete unity and absolute obedience to the directions they receive from the Communist centre. Except in the British Commonwealth and in the United States where Communism is in its infancy, the Communist parties or fifth columns constitute a growing challenge and peril to Christian civilization. These are somber facts for anyone to have to recite on the morrow of a victory gained by so much splendid comradeship in arms and in the cause of freedom and democracy; but we should be most unwise not to face them squarely while time remains.

The Soviets understood that they ran a sorry second to American military superiority—the United States was alone in possessing the atomic bomb—and to American wealth, which, measured in Gross National Product (GNP), was 400 percent greater than that of the Soviet Union. Stalin, nevertheless, committed the Soviet Union to an arms race in which he refused to accept American dominance. War had made the two superpowers wary allies; peace promised to make them once again active foes. In the three years that followed the war, a new kind of conflict emerged between the two superpower victors, a war deemed "cold" because of its lack of military violence, but a bitter war nonetheless.

The **Cold War** was rooted in the ideological opposition between communism and capitalist democracies, dominated by the two superpowers, the Soviet Union and the United States. It affected the entire world. Drawing on three decades of distrust between the East and the West, the Cold War was related to the economic and foreign policy goals of both superpowers.

Winston Churchill captured the drama of the new international order in a speech he delivered in Missouri in 1946: "From Stettin in the Baltic to Trieste in the Adriatic, an iron curtain has descended across the continent." The term **iron curtain** described graphically for many the new fate of Europe rigidly divided between East and West, a pawn in the struggle of the superpowers.

The Division of Germany. In central Europe, Cold War tensions first surfaced over the question of how to treat Germany. The United States and the Soviet Union had very different ideas about the future of their former enemy. In fostering economic reconstruction in Europe, the United States counted on a German economy transfused with American funds that would be self-supporting and stable. To the contrary, the Soviet Union, blaming Germany for its extreme destruction, was explicit in its demands: German resources must be siphoned off for Soviet reconstruction. Stricken as the Soviets were with 20 million dead, millions of homeless refugees in dire poverty, and 1700 cities in ruins, commandeering German labor and stripping Germany of its industrial plant seemed to them only fair.

MAP DISCOVERY

- Soviet Union in 1939
- Lands gained by the Soviet Union
- Iron Curtain

The Soviet Union and the Soviet Bloc

Notice the boundary of the Soviet Union before 1939 and the territory it gained after World War II. Which countries in eastern Europe did the Soviet Union annex after the war and why? In other countries of eastern Europe the Soviet Union established economic and political control without annexation. Which countries constituted the Soviet bloc?

With Germany's defeat, its territory had been divided into four zones, occupied by American, Soviet, British, and French troops. An Allied Control Commission consisting of representatives of the four powers was to govern Germany as a whole in keeping with the decisions made at Yalta before the end of the war. As Soviet and American antagonisms over Germany's future deepened, however, Allied rule polarized between the East and the West, with the internal politics of each area determined by the ideological conflicts between communism and capitalist free enterprise.

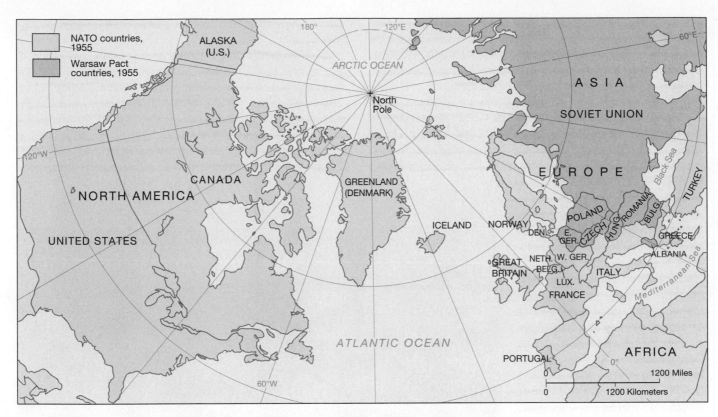

NATO countries, 1955

Warsaw Pact countries, 1955

ALASKA (U.S.)

ARCTIC OCEAN

North Pole

CANADA

NORTH AMERICA

UNITED STATES

GREENLAND (DENMARK)

ICELAND

ASIA

SOVIET UNION

EUROPE

Black Sea

TURKEY

POLAND   ROMANIA

NORWAY   HUNG.   BULG.

DEN.   E. GER.   CZECH.

GREECE

GREAT BRITAIN   NETH.   W. GER.   ALBANIA

BELG.   ITALY

LUX.

FRANCE   Mediterranean Sea

ATLANTIC OCEAN

PORTUGAL   AFRICA

0°

1200 Miles

1200 Kilometers

60°W   0°

■ The Cold War: U.S. and Soviet Alliances. The U.S. and Soviet blocs (NATO countries and Warsaw Pact countries, respectively) constituted a balance of power in global politics.

Allied attempts to administer Germany as a whole faltered and failed in 1948 over a question of economic policy. The zones of the Western occupying forces (the United States, Great Britain, and France), now administered as a single unit, issued a uniform and stable currency that the Russians accurately saw as a threat to their own economic policies in Germany. The Soviets blockaded the city of Berlin, which, though behind the frontier of the Russian sector, was being administered in sectors by the four powers and whose western sector promised to become a successful enclave of Western capitalism. With the support of the people of West Berlin, the Allies responded by airlifting food and supplies into West Berlin for almost a year, defending it as an outpost that had to be preserved from the advance of communism. The Russians were forced to withdraw the blockade in the spring of 1949. The Berlin blockade hardened the commitment on both sides to two Germanys.

The two new states came into existence in 1949, their founding separated by less than a month. The Federal Republic of Germany (West Germany), within the American orbit, was established as a democratic parliamentary regime. Free elections brought the Christian Democrat Konrad Adenauer to power as chancellor. The German Democratic Republic (East Germany) was ruled as a single-party state under Walter Ulbricht, who took his direction from the Soviet Union. The division of Germany became a microcosm of the division of the world into two armed camps.

Eastern Europe and the Soviet Bloc.   With the support of local Communist parties, Soviet-dominated governments were established in Poland, Hungary, Bulgaria, and Romania in 1947. The following year, Czechoslovakia was pulled into the Soviet orbit. Czechoslovakia served as a significant marker in the development of Cold War confrontation. The tactics of the Communists in Czechoslovakia taught the West that coalition governments were unacceptable and undoubtedly hardened the resolve of U.S. policy makers in support of two Germanys. Needing the stability of peace, the Soviets saw in eastern Europe, hostile as the area may have been to forced integration, a necessary buffer against Western competition. The Soviet Union feared U.S. intentions to establish liberal governments and capitalist markets in the states bordering its own frontiers and viewed such attempts as a threat to Soviet interests. For those reasons, Stalin refused to allow free elections in Poland and, by force of occupying armies, annexed neighboring territories that included eastern Finland, the Baltic states, East Prussia, eastern Poland, Ruthenia, and Bessarabia. With the exception of East Prussia, the annexations were limited to territories that had once been part of tsarist Russia.

NATO and Other Treaty Alliances.   With the aim of containing the USSR, a policy known as **containment,** the United States entered into a series of military alliances around the world. In order to provide mutual assistance should any member be attacked, the United States joined with Belgium, Britain, Canada, Denmark, France, Iceland, Italy, the Netherlands, Norway, and Portugal in 1949 to form the **North Atlantic Treaty Organization (NATO).** Greece and Turkey became members in 1952, West Germany in 1955, and Spain in 1982.

A challenge to Cold War power politics came from within the NATO alliance. General Charles de Gaulle, as president of the French Fifth Republic, rejected the straitjacket of American dominance in Western Europe and asserted his country's independent status by exploding the first French atomic bomb in 1960. Refusing to place the French military under an American general who served as Supreme Allied Commander for NATO, de Gaulle completely withdrew France from participation in NATO in 1966. He forged an independent French foreign policy, taking advantage of the loosening of bloc politics in the mid-1960s.

The Southeast Asia Treaty Organization (SEATO) in 1954 and the Baghdad Pact of 1955 (known as the Central Treaty Organization after 1959) followed. The United States strengthened its military presence throughout the period by acquiring 1400 military bases in foreign countries for its own forces.

In 1955, Albania, Bulgaria, Romania, Czechoslovakia, Hungary, Poland, and East Germany joined with the Soviet Union to form a defensive alliance organization known as the **Warsaw Pact.** The USSR intended its Eastern European allies to serve as a strategic buffer zone against the NATO forces.

The Nuclear Club

The nuclear arms race began in earnest during World War II, well before the first atomic bomb was dropped in August 1945. The Germans, the Russians, and the British all had teams exploring the destructive possibilities of nuclear fission during the war, but the Americans had the edge in the development of the bomb. Stalin understood the political significance of the weapon and committed the

Soviet Union to a breakneck program of development following the war.

The USSR ended the American monopoly and tested its first atomic bomb in 1949. Both countries developed the hydrogen bomb almost simultaneously in 1953. Space exploration by satellite was also deemed important in terms of the detection and deployment of bombs, and the Soviets pulled ahead in this area with the launching of the first satellite, *Sputnik I,* in 1957. Intercontinental ballistic missiles (ICBMs) followed, further accelerating the pace of nuclear armament.

IMAGE DISCOVERY

Living with the Bomb

This photo from the early 1950s shows an American family installed in their fallout shelter, intended to protect them from a nuclear blast. These shelters were built below ground or in basements. Note the supplies on hand. From your knowledge of the effects of atomic bombs on Japan, how realistic were people's hopes that radioactive fallout could be avoided? Why were photos like this one common in the 1950s in the United States? Why is this family smiling?

The atomic bomb and thermonuclear weapons contributed greatly to the shape of Cold War politics. The incineration of Hiroshima and Nagasaki sent a clear message to the world about the power of total annihilation available to those who controlled the bombs. The threat of such total destruction made full and direct confrontation with an equally armed enemy impossible. Both the United States and the Soviet Union, the first two members of the **"nuclear club,"** knew that they had the capability of obliterating their enemy, but not before the enemy could retaliate. They also knew that the technology necessary for nuclear arms was available to any industrial power. By 1974, the nuclear club included Great Britain, France, the People's Republic of China, and India. Those countries joined the United States and the Soviet Union in spending the billions of dollars necessary every year to expand nuclear arsenals and to develop more sophisticated weaponry and delivery systems.

The Nuclear Test Ban Treaty of 1963, the first of its kind, banned tests in the atmosphere and inaugurated a period of lessening tensions between the Eastern and Western blocs. Arms limitation and nonproliferation were the subjects of a series of conferences between the United States and the Soviet Union in the late 1960s and pointed the way to limitations eventually agreed on in the next decade. The United Nations (UN), an organization created by the Allies immediately following World War II to take the place of the defunct League of Nations, established international agencies for the purpose of harnessing nuclear power for peaceful uses. By the early 1970s, both the United States and the Soviet Union recognized the importance of closer relations between the superpowers. The USSR and the United States had achieved nuclear parity. On the whole, however, the arms race persisted as a continuing threat in Cold War politics. The race required the dedication of huge national resources to maintain a competitive stance. Conventional forces, too, were expanded to protect Eastern and Western bloc interests.

DOCUMENT

Krushchev Challenges the West to Disarm

Decolonization and the Cold War

No part of the globe escaped the tensions generated by the Cold War. By the end of World War II, European colonial empires had been weakened or destroyed by the ravages of battle, occupation, and neglect. Nationalist movements had been growing in power in the 1930s, and many nationalist leaders saw the war as a catalyst for independence. Former colonies were no longer directly controlled but as newly independent countries, they had to contend with Cold War pressures to belong in one or the other superpower camp. Hence, **decolonization** often meant continued dependence.

Soviet leader Joseph Stalin limited the Soviet Union's foreign involvement following World War II to Communist regimes that shared borders with the USSR in Eastern Europe and Asia. But after Stalin's death in 1953, the Soviet Union turned to the **third world.** Former colonies played an impor-

tant new role in the Cold War strategies with the accession to power of Nikita Khrushchev (1894–1971) in the mid-1950s. The Soviet Union abandoned its previous caution and assumed a global role in offering "friendship treaties," military advice, trade credits, and general support for attempts at national liberation in Asia, Africa, and Latin America. Both East and West took advantage of tribalism and regionalism, which worked against the establishment of strong central governments. Military rule and fragmentation often resulted. Instability and acute poverty continued to characterize former colonies after emancipation, regardless of whether the new leaders joined the communist or democratic camps.

Asia. Great Britain knew that it no longer commanded the resources to control India, historically its richest colony, which under the leadership of Mohandas Gandhi (1869–1948) had been agitating for independence since 1920. (See "The West and the Wider World," pp. 878–879.) The British granted self-government to India in 1946 with the proviso that if the bitter conflict between Hindus and Muslims was not settled by mutual agreement, Great Britain would decide on the division of power. As a result, Muslim and Hindu representatives agreed to the division of British India into the independent states of India and Pakistan in 1947. Ceylon (now Sri Lanka) and Burma (now Myanmar) achieved full independence in 1948.

In its march through Asia during the war, Japan had smashed colonial empires. Japan's defeat created a power vacuum that nationalist leaders were eager to fill. Civil wars erupted in China, Burma, Korea, and Indochina. In 1950, the United States and the United Nations intervened when North Korea attacked South Korea. Korea, formerly controlled by Japan, had been divided following the war as a result of the presence of Russian and American troops. Communist-dominated North Korea refused to accept the artificial boundary between it and Western-dominated South Korea. China, a Communist state following the victory of Mao Zedong (1893–1976) in 1949, intervened in the Korean conflict when American troops advanced on Chinese frontiers in October 1950. After three years of military stalemate, Korea was partitioned on the 38th parallel in 1953. The Soviet Union was not party to the conflict in Korea, but the United States considered China to be in the Soviet camp rather than an independent contender for power.

DOCUMENT

Gandhi on Civil Disobedience

The United States was heavily committed as a military presence in Southeast Asia after the French withdrawal from Indochina following the French defeat at Dien Bien Phu in 1954. The North Vietnamese state was established under the French-educated leader Ho Chi Minh. South Vietnam was declared a republic, and the United States sponsored a regime that was considered favorable to Western interests. Arguing the domino theory—that one Southeast Asian country after another would fall like a row of dominoes to Communist takeover—the United States also intervened in Laos and Cambodia. Between 1961 and 1973, the United States

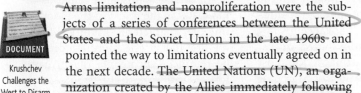

MAHATMA GANDHI'S LEGACY

It may be apocryphal, but when asked by a reporter in 1930 what he thought of Western civilization, Mohandas Gandhi (1869–1948) responded, "It would be a good idea." The exchange captures an essential aspect of Gandhi's critique of the West. Born in colonial India and educated in England, where he was trained as a lawyer and passed the bar, Gandhi received his first real political education in South Africa where he practiced law for 20 years and encountered racism firsthand. In 1905, at the age of 36, Gandhi renounced the trappings of "civilization" in favor of a life of asceticism and service to others. His own particular philosophy was embodied in *Satyagraha*, a term he coined that in Hindi means "holding to the truth." He explained the term further in his writings:

THE WEST AND THE WIDER WORLD

I have also called it love force or soul force. In the application of *Satyagraha*, I discovered in the earliest stages that pursuit of truth did not permit violence being inflicted on one's opponent, but that he must be weaned from error by patience and sympathy. For what appears to be truth to the one may appear to be error to the other. And patience means self-suffering. So the doctrine came to mean vindication of truth, not by the infliction of suffering on the opponent, but on one's self.

Such a philosophy, grounded in Hinduism and influenced by the *Bhagavad-Gita*, expressed itself in nonviolent resistance and civil disobedience as a means of political action. With this "soul force" Gandhi led India to national independence and was hailed as the father of his country because he faced down British rule by nonviolent means. As a vegetarian who made his own clothes, thereby reviving the cottage industries of spinning and weaving stamped out in India by British imperialism, Gandhi was a unique leader indeed in the company of heads of state in the mid-twentieth century. To advance his political agenda, Gandhi fasted or led peaceful protest pilgrimages, the most famous being the 1930 Salt March of 248 miles to overthrow unfair taxation. He also argued for sustainable economies and against the rampant consumerism and materialistic excess of his time.

Gandhi came to be known as "Mahatma," a Hindi term meaning "great soul." His unique contribution was to bring a spiritual sensibility grounded in the Hinduism of south Asia to the world political arena, and he has left an enduring mark on the West. By combining spirituality with politics, he influenced the American civil rights leader and Nobel Peace Prize recipient Martin Luther King, Jr. (1929–1968), who was explicit about his debt to Gandhi's philosophy and tactics. Gandhi's works and deeds have also shaped Aung San Suu Kyi (1945–), a nonviolent, pro-democracy activist in Myanmar, who is also a winner of the Nobel Peace Prize. A prisoner in her own country, she was unable to travel to accept the prize in 1991; but her son, in accepting for her, spoke of her "basically spiritual quest" grounded in her Buddhist faith.

Gandhi sought to promote a dialogue among Hindu, Islamic, and Christian followers and among members of all faiths. He met his own death at the hands of a religious fanatic. But in the midst of the bloodletting that characterized political life in the first half of the twentieth century, he reminded all people that "An eye for an eye makes the whole world blind." King described Gandhi's role in modern history: "Gandhi was inevitable. If humanity is to progress, Gandhi is inescapable. . . . We may ignore him at our own risk."

QUESTIONS FOR DISCUSSION

What methods did Gandhi use to force the British out of India? Why was Gandhi's peaceful philosophy so successful against the considerable power of the British Empire? How do you explain Gandhi's influence throughout the world?

■ By his example, Mohandas Gandhi, in spinning and weaving his own clothes, sought to reintroduce cottage industries and promote political independence for India.

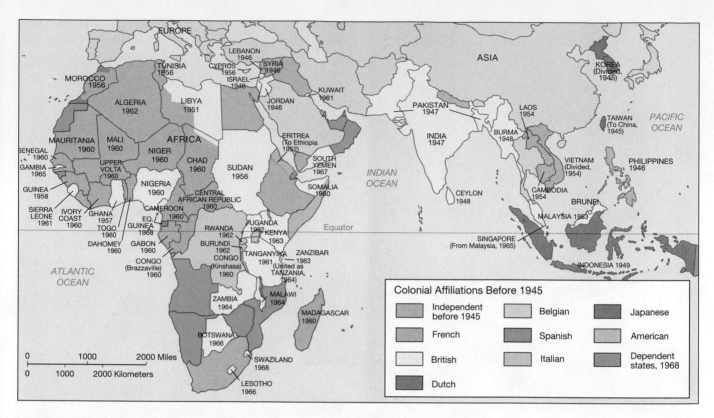

■ Decolonization. Few nations in Africa and south and southeast Asia were independent before 1945. Few remained dependent after 1968.

Kwame Nkrumah on African Unity

committed American troops to a full-scale war—though officially termed only a military action—against Communist guerrilla forces throughout the region. After almost two decades of escalating involvement, in 1973 American troops were finally withdrawn from a war in Vietnam that they could not win.

Africa. The first wave of decolonization after 1945 had been in Asia, but it wasn't until the late 1950s and early 1960s that a second wave crested and crashed in Africa. Wartime experiences and rapid economic development fed existing nationalist aspirations and encouraged the emergence of mass political demands for liberation. A new generation of leaders, many of them educated in European institutions, moved from cooperation with home rule to demands for independence by the early 1960s. British Prime Minister Harold MacMillan (1894–1986) spoke of "the winds of change" in 1960, the year that proved to be a turning point in African politics. Britain and Belgium yielded their colonies. In 1960, Patrice Lumumba (1925–1961) became the first prime minister of the Republic of the Congo (present-day Democratic Republic of the Congo). White European rule continued in Rhodesia (now Zimbabwe) and South Africa, despite continued world pressure. African leader Kwame Nkrumah (1909–1972) of Ghana denounced the situation of African dependence as "neocolonialism" and called for a united Africa as the only

means of resistance. He led Ghana in a policy of nonalignment in the Cold War. With Jomo Kenyatta (1894–1978) of Kenya, Nkrumah founded the Pan-African Federation, which promoted African nationalism.

The French, having faced what its officer corps considered a humiliating defeat in Indochina, held on against the winds of change in North Africa. France's problems in Algeria began in earnest in 1954 when Muslims seeking independence and self-rule revolted. Although the Algerian rebels successfully employed terrorist and guerrilla tactics, European settlers and the French army in Algeria refused to accept defeat. Facing political collapse at home, the French, under the leadership of General Charles de Gaulle, ended the war and agreed to Algeria's independence, which was achieved in 1962.

The Middle East. The United States and the Soviet Union used aid to win support of "client" states in the Middle East. The withdrawal, sometimes under duress, of British and French rule in the Middle East and North Africa and the creation of the state of Israel in 1948 destabilized the area and created opportunities for new alliances. Egypt and Syria, for example, sought Soviet support against the new Israeli state, which had been formed out of the part of Palestine under British mandate since 1920 and which was dependent on U.S. aid.

Oil, an essential resource for rapid industrialization, was the object of Soviet politicking in Iran after World War II. Western oil companies, long active in the area, had won oil concessions in Iran in 1946, but such rights eluded the Soviets. In 1951, a nationalist Iranian government sought to evict Westerners by nationalizing the oil fields. The British blockaded Iranian trade in the Persian Gulf, and the newly formed American espionage organization, the Central Intelligence Agency (CIA), subverted the nationalist government and placed in power the shah of Iran, a leader favorable to American interests.

In 1956, a crisis came in Egypt. Egyptian President Gamal Abdel Nasser (1918–1970), a nationalist in power by virtue of a military coup d'état in 1952, oversaw the nationalization of the Suez Canal. British and French military forces attacked and were forced to withdraw by pressure from both the Soviet Union and the United States, which cooperated in seeking to avert a disaster. The Middle East, however, remained a Cold War powder keg, with Israeli and Arab nationalist interests and Soviet and American aid running on a collision course. The expansion of the Israeli state at the expense of its Arab neighbors further exacerbated tensions.

Latin America. The United States was also experiencing Cold War problems closer to home. In 1954, the CIA plotted the overthrow of Guatemala's leftist regime to keep Soviet influence out of the Western Hemisphere. In 1958, President Dwight D. Eisenhower sent his vice president, Richard M. Nixon, on a tour of Latin American countries. Crowds everywhere jeered the American vice president and hurled stones and eggs at his motorcade in response to U.S. policies. In 1959, a revolution in Cuba, an island nation only 90 miles off the American coast, resulted in the ejection of U.S. interests and the establishment of a Communist regime under the leadership of a young lawyer, Fidel Castro. In 1962, a direct and frightening confrontation occurred between the United States and the USSR over Soviet missile installations in Cuba. Following the Russian withdrawal from the island, both U.S. President John F. Kennedy and Soviet leader Nikita Khrushchev pursued a policy of *peaceful coexistence,* intent on averting nuclear confrontation. Both sides recognized how close they had come to mutual annihilation in the showdown over Cuba.

DOCUMENT

John F. Kennedy and Cuba

POSTWAR ECONOMIC RECOVERY IN EUROPE, JAPAN, AND THE SOVIET UNION

In contrast to the Soviet Union, the United States had incurred relatively light casualties in World War II. Because the fighting had not taken place on the North American continent, U.S. cities, farmlands, and factories were intact. As the chief producer and supplier for the Allied war effort, even before its entry into the conflict, the United States had benefited from the conflict in Europe and actually expanded its economic productivity during the war. In 1945, the United States was producing a full 50 percent of the world's GNP—a staggering fact to a displaced Great Britain, whose former trade networks were permanently destroyed. Furthermore, the United States held two-thirds of the world's gold. A United States bursting with energy and prosperity was a real threat to the Soviet Union viewing the rubble of its destroyed cities and counting the bodies of its dead. However, the United States knew that it lacked one important guarantee to secure its growth and its future prosperity: adequate international markets for its goods. After World War I, American officials and businessmen understood that America's productive capacity was outpacing its ability to export goods. In the 1920s, the United States had exported capital to Europe in the form of private loans with the hope that trade would flourish as a result. The decade following the Great Depression of 1929 witnessed the search for a policy to expand U.S. markets. Both Europe and Japan were recognized as potential buyers for American goods, but both areas parried with protectionism to foster their own post-depression recovery.

The Economic Challenge

Economists judged that Europe would need at least 25 years to regain its prewar economic capacity. The worst was also feared: that Europe would never recover as a world economic power. Large-scale population movements made matters worse. Displaced persons by the millions moved across Europe. Just as the war had caused dislocation, so too did the peace create millions of refugees seeking asylum and a better life. The release of prisoners of war and slave workers imprisoned during the Third Reich strained already weak economies. Germans were expelled from territories that Germany had controlled before the war. Soviet expansionist policies forced others to flee Estonia, Latvia, and Lithuania. Jews who survived the concentration camps resettled outside Europe, primarily in Palestine and the United States.

European industrial production in 1945 was one-third of its level in 1938. Housing shortages existed everywhere. France had lost one-fifth of its housing during the war years; Germany's 50 largest cities had seen two-fifths of their buildings reduced to rubble. Frankfurt, Düsseldorf, Dresden, Warsaw (see "The Visual Record," pp. 870–871), and Berlin were virtually destroyed. The transportation infrastructure was severely damaged: railways, roads, and bridges were in shambles all over Europe. Communications networks were in disarray. In some cases, industrial plants had not been as adversely affected as urban centers. Yet machinery everywhere had been worn out in wartime production, and replacement parts were nonexistent. German equipment was dismantled and seized by Soviet soldiers to be used in Russia in place of what the Germans had destroyed.

Agriculture, too, suffered severe reversals in wartime economies and was unable to resume prewar production in 1945. In general, European agriculture was producing at 50 percent of its prewar capacity. Livestock had been decimated during the war years—in France, for example, 50 percent of all farm animals had been killed—and it was estimated that restoring herds would take decades. Italy suffered greatly, with one-third of its overall assets destroyed. The scarcity of goods converged with ballooning inflation. Black markets with astronomical prices for necessities flourished, while currency rates plummeted. Everywhere the outlook was bleak. Yet in less than a decade, the situation was reversed. The solution came from outside of Europe.

The Economic Solution: The Marshall Plan

World War II facilitated the success of an international economic policy consistent with international economic goals identified by U.S. policy makers as early as 1920. In both Europe and Japan, the United States intervened to aid reconstruction and recovery of war-torn nations. Those economies, hungry for capital, no longer opposed U.S. intervention or erected trade barriers against American goods. The prospect of a Europe in chaos economically, socially, and politically and on the verge of collapse justified immediate action by the United States.

By the spring of 1947 it was clear to American policy makers that initial postwar attempts to stabilize European economies and promote world recovery were simply not working. The United States had, earlier in the same year, engineered emergency aid to Turkey and Greece, both objects of Soviet aspira-

tions for control. President Truman articulated a doctrine bearing his name: "I believe that it must be the policy of the United States to support free people who are resisting attempted subjugation by armed minorities or by outside pressures." The aid emerged in an atmosphere of opposition between the United States and the Soviet Union over issues of territorial control in eastern and southern Europe. The Cold War coincided with and reinforced the U.S. need to reconstruct western Europe.

On 5 June 1947, Secretary of State George C. Marshall (1880–1959) delivered the commencement address at Harvard University. In his speech, Marshall introduced the European Recovery Act, popularly known as the **Marshall Plan,** through which billions of dollars in aid would be made available to European states, both in the East and in the West, provided that two conditions were met: (1) the recipient states had to cooperate with one another in aligning national economic policies and improving the international monetary system, and (2) they had to work toward breaking down trade barriers.

Participating countries included Austria, Belgium, Denmark, France, West Germany, Great Britain, Greece, Iceland, Italy, Luxembourg, the Netherlands, Norway, Sweden, Switzerland, and Turkey. The Soviet Union and eastern European countries were also eligible for aid under the original formulation. But the Soviets opposed the plan from the first, wary of U.S. intentions

DOCUMENT

Truman Doctrine

■ Here General George Marshall, the architect of the Marshall Plan, is shown at the United Nations conferring with Eleanor Roosevelt, former First Lady and widow of Franklin D. Roosevelt, and, on the left, John Foster Dulles, U.S. delegate to the UN and later Secretary of State. Marshall was awarded the Nobel Peace Prize in 1953, a rare distinction for a military officer.

THE MARSHALL PLAN

In the rituals that are part of graduation ceremonies, guest speakers often address the challenges of the future awaiting graduates. Not many commencement addresses change the world. The speech given by U.S. Secretary of State George C. Marshall at Harvard University in June 1947 was different. By pledging gifts in aid, the United States helped rebuild war-torn Europe and transform the world's economy.

Focus Questions

What does Marshall mean when he states that this policy is "directed not against any country or doctrine"? How does Marshall explain that the plan for economic recovery is not intended as charity?

The truth of the matter is that Europe's requirements for the next three or four years of foreign food and other essential products—principally from America—are so much greater than her present ability to pay that she must have substantial additional help or face economic, social, and political deterioration of a very grave character.

The remedy lies in breaking the vicious circle and restoring the confidence of the European people in the economic future of their own countries and of Europe as a whole. The manufacturer and the farmer throughout wide areas must be able and willing to exchange their products for currencies the continuing value of which is not open to question.

Aside from the demoralizing effect on the world at large and the possibilities of disturbances arising as a result of the desperation of the people concerned, the consequences to the economy of the United States should be apparent to all. It is logical that the United States should do whatever it is able to do to assist in the return of normal economic health in the world, without which there can be no political stability and no assured peace. Our policy is directed not against any country or doctrine but against hunger, poverty, desperation, and chaos. Its purpose should be the revival of a working economy in the world so as to permit the emergence of political and social conditions in which free institutions can exist. Such assistance, I am convinced, must not be on a piecemeal basis as various crises develop. Any assistance that this Government may render in the future should provide a cure rather than a mere palliative. Any government that is willing to assist in the task of recovery will find full cooperation, I am sure, on the part of the United States Government. Any government which maneuvers to block the recovery of other countries cannot expect help from us. Furthermore, governments, political parties, or groups which seek to perpetuate human misery in order to profit therefrom politically or otherwise will encounter the opposition of the United States.

From Department of State Bulletin, 15 June 1947.

to extend the influence of Western capitalism. Soviet opposition encouraged members of the U.S. Congress, afraid of a Communist takeover in Europe, to support the plan.

The amount of U.S. aid to Europe was massive. More than $23 billion was pumped into western Europe between 1947 and 1952. By every measure, the Marshall Plan was judged a success in the West. American foreign aid restored western European trade and production while at the same time controlling inflation. Dean Acheson (1893–1971), Marshall's successor as secretary of state, described the plan in terms of "our duty as human beings" but nevertheless considered it "chiefly as a matter of national self-interest." Soviet critics and Western observers differed dramatically in describing selfinterest and domination as the primary motives for the plan.

Western European Economic Integration

As significant as the gift of funds to European states undoubtedly was, no less important was the whole administrative apparatus that American aid brought in its wake. In order to expend available monies most effectively and comply with stipulations for cooperation and regulation, the states of western Europe resorted to intensified planning and limited nationalization.

Planning for Recovery.   The ideas of intensified planning and limited nationalization were not new in the experience of European states: Vichy France, for example, had emphasized the importance of planning and specialization in its corporatist approach to economic development and social welfare policies. Regulation and state intervention dominated the formulation of economic policy. Special attention was given to workers' welfare through unemployment insurance, retirement benefits, public health, and housing policies. European states recognized the need to provide a safety net for their citizens in order to avoid reexperiencing the disastrous depression and stagnation of the 1930s while attempting to rebuild their shattered economies. Those were lessons that had been learned as much from the attempts at recovery before 1939 as from the experiences of running wartime economies.

It was the economic theory of John Maynard Keynes that influenced the planning process. His economic concepts had been applied successfully by neutral Sweden to its economic policies during the war, came into vogue throughout Europe in 1945, and triumphed in the postwar era. Keynes favored macroeconomic policies to increase productivity and argued for an active role for government in "priming the pump" of economic growth. The government should be responsible, according to Keynes, for the control and regulation of the economy, with the goal of ensuring full employment for its people. Governments could and should check inflation and eliminate boom-and-bust cycles, incurring deficits by spending beyond revenues if necessary.

European Economic Cooperation.   Money alone could not have accomplished the recovery that took place. The chief mechanism for administering Marshall Plan aid was the Office of European Economic Cooperation (OEEC). That master coordinating agency made the requirements for recovery clear. European states had to stabilize their own economies. Cooperation between the public and private sectors was intended to free market forces, modernize production, and raise productivity. Planning mechanisms, including transnational organizations and networks, resulted in the modernization of production and the assimilation of new techniques, new styles of management, and innovative business practices from the United States. The modernization of economies through centrally coordinated planning made Europe once again a major contender in the international economic arena.

The major exception to the establishment of central planning agencies and the nationalization of key industries was West Germany. Deciding against the British and French models of planned growth, the West Germans endorsed a free market policy that encouraged private enterprise while providing state insurance for all workers. What has been described as "a free enterprise economy with a social conscience" produced the richest economy in western Europe by the mid-1950s. Some West German industries had been dismantled, but much of West Germany's productive capacity remained intact in the late 1940s. The wealth of great industrialists who were serving prison sentences as war criminals had not been expropriated, and their commercial empires stood ready to direct the economic revival. The Krupp munitions and I. G. Farben chemical empires were successfully broken up into smaller units. Industries forced to start afresh benefited from the latest technology.

European integration, discussed before and during the war, received added impetus in the postwar period. The Marshall Plan reconciled western Europe with West Germany through economic cooperation, although that was by no means its original purpose.

Realizing that Europe as a region needed the cooperation of its member states if it was to contend in world markets, associations dedicated to integration began to emerge alongside

■ A train carrying iron ore crosses the France-Luxembourg border, celebrating the joint community in coal and steel that became effective in 1953. The European Coal and Steel Community was the first step in the economic integration of Europe.

economic planning mechanisms. The Council of Europe dealt with the "discussion of questions of common concern and by agreements and common action in economic, social, cultural, scientific, legal, and administrative matters and in the maintenance and further realization of human rights and fundamental freedoms." Although not itself a supranational institution with its own authority, the Council of Europe urged a federation among European states. Britain alone rejected all attempts to develop structures of loose intergovernmental cooperation.

Belgium, the Netherlands, and Luxembourg were the first European states to establish themselves as an economic unit—Benelux. Internal customs duties among the three states were removed, and a common external tariff barrier was erected. The **Schuman Plan** joined France and West Germany in economic cooperation by pooling all coal and steel resources, beginning in 1950. The creators of the plan, Jean Monnet (1888–1979) and Robert Schuman (1886–1963) of France, saw it as the first step toward the removal of all economic barriers among European states and as a move toward eventual political integration. In 1951, the Netherlands, Belgium, Luxembourg, France, Italy, and West Germany formed the European Coal and Steel Community (ECSC). While constantly confronting domestic opposition on nationalist grounds, the ECSC succeeded in establishing a "common market" in coal and steel among its member states. In 1957, the same six members created the **European Economic Community (EEC)** and committed themselves to broadening the integration of markets. It was the beginning of what became known as the Common Market.

DOCUMENT

A Common Market and European Integration

The Common Market aimed to establish among its member states a free movement of labor and capital, the elimination of restrictions on trade, common investment practices, and coordinated social welfare programs. National agricultural interests were to be protected. Great Britain was initially a vocal opponent of the Common Market and continued to defend its own trading relationship with its Commonwealth countries, eventually founding its own free trade association in 1959. In 1973, Great Britain became a member of the Common Market and joined with other European nations in defining common economic policies. The EEC meanwhile achieved the support of the United States in its transitional period, in which it had 15 years to accomplish its aims.

European union was a phenomenon of exclusion as much as inclusion. It sharpened antagonisms between the West and the East by its very success. While promoting prosperity, European economic unification favored concentration and the emergence of large corporations. Vast individual fortunes flourished under state sponsorship and the rule of the experts. National parliaments were sometimes eclipsed by new economic decision-making organizations that aimed to make western Europe into a single free trade area.

Japan's Recovery → U.S. AID

Japanese economic challenges in the postwar era were similar to those of western Europe. As a defeated and occupied nation in 1945, Japan faced a grim future. U.S. aims for Asia were similar to those for Europe: American policy makers sought to create a multilateral system of world trade and preserve America's sphere of influence against Communist encroachment. The American general Douglas MacArthur was appointed the Supreme Commander for the Allied Powers and the head of occupation forces in Japan. His mission in Japan was to impose rapid economic change from above. The occupation government set out to erect institutions to promote political democratization and to eliminate militaristic institutions, official patronage, and censorship. Planning, both formal and informal, reshaped the economy as U.S. aid flowed into Japan during the late forties and early fifties. The changes

in Japan, as in western Europe, took place alongside growing American fears of communism in the region.

Japan turned its wartime devastation into an advantage by replacing destroyed factories with the latest technology, obtained by license from foreign firms. Through a combination of bureaucracy and patronage devoted to planned growth, Japan's GNP reached prewar levels by 1956. By 1968, Japan had turned defeat into triumph and stood as the third largest industrial nation in the world. Japanese growth paralleled the "economic miracle" of West Germany, with the Japanese economy growing at a rate three times faster than that of the United States between 1954 and 1967.

The abolition of the army and navy was a boon for the Japanese economy, since 16 percent of prewar GNP had been devoted to support of the military. Postwar demilitarization freed Japan of the financial exigencies of the arms race. Funds formerly used for arms now flowed into investment and new technology. Slowed population growth after 1948 and an increased volume of foreign trade contributed to Japanese prosperity. In the 1960s, Japan emerged as an affluent society undergoing a revolution in consumer durables, including televisions, washing machines, refrigerators, and automobiles.

DOCUMENT

The Constitution of Japan

Recipients of American aid surpassed U.S. goals. A multilateral system of world trade emerged out of the ashes of war. The effects of the Great Depression, which the world had been unable to shake throughout the 1930s, had been laid to rest by global war and its consequences.

The Soviet Path to Economic Recovery

Sets up the Comecon to satellite states

The Soviet Union countered economic integration in the West with its own alliances and organizations. In 1949, the USSR established the Council for Mutual Economic Assistance, or **Comecon,** with bilateral agreements between the Soviet Union and eastern European states. Comecon was Stalin's response to the U.S. Marshall Plan in western Europe. Rather than providing aid, however, Comecon benefited the Soviet Union at the expense of its partners, seeking to integrate and control the economies of eastern Europe for Soviet gain. The Soviet Union implemented an expansion of its territorial boundaries as a way of reversing some of its drastic losses in the war. Above all, it wanted a protective ring of satellite states as security from attack from the West. Stalin also was eager to see the Soviet Union surrounded by "friendly" governments in eastern Europe to replace the hostile regimes with which the Soviets had had to contend in the period between the wars. Picking up territory from Finland, Poland, and parts of East Prussia and eastern Czechoslovakia; forcibly reincorporating the Baltic states of Estonia, Latvia, and Lithuania; and recovering Bessarabia, the Soviet Union succeeded in acquiring sizable territories. The Soviet state then began to dedicate itself to economic reconstruction behind a protective buffer of satellite states—Poland, East Germany, Czechoslovakia, Hungary, Romania,

REPORT TO THE TWENTIETH PARTY CONGRESS

Like Stalin before him, the Soviet leader Nikita Khrushchev perceived that the Soviet Union was locked in a worldwide struggle with the United States and Western capitalist nations. The experiences of the Korean War and the escalation of the nuclear arms race prompted him to proceed with wariness in foreign policy. In his now-famous speech before the Twentieth Party Congress in February 1956, Khrushchev, as first secretary of the Communist party, accused the United States, England, and France of imperialism and pleaded for the peaceful coexistence of communism and capitalism, confident that, in the end, communism would win the day.

Focus Questions

How does Khrushchev portray the Soviet Union as a victim? How does he describe the origins and the purposes of the Cold War?

Soon after the Second World War ended, the influence of reactionary and militarist groups began to be increasingly evident in the policy of the United States of America, Britain, and France. Their desire to enforce their will on other countries by economic and political pressure, threats, and military provocation prevailed. This became known as the "positions of strength" policy. It reflects the aspiration of the most aggressive sections of present-day imperialism to win world supremacy, to suppress the working class and democratic and nation-liberation movements; it reflects their plans for military adventures against the socialist camp.

The international atmosphere was poisoned by war hysteria. The arms race began to assume more and more monstrous dimensions. Many big U.S. military bases designed for use against the USSR and the People's Democracies [East European countries under Soviet control] were built in countries thousands of miles from the borders of the United States. "Cold war" was begun against the socialist camp. International distrust was artificially kindled, and nations set against one another. A bloody war was launched in Korea; the war in Indochina dragged on for years.

... The Leninist principle of peaceful coexistence of states with different social systems has always been and remains the general line of our country's foreign policy.... To this day the enemies of peace allege that the Soviet Union is out to overthrow capitalism in other countries by "exporting" revolution. It goes without saying that among us Communists there are no supporters of capitalism. But this does not mean that we have interfered or plan to interfere in the internal affairs of countries where capitalism still exists.

When we say that the socialist system will win in the competition between the two systems—the capitalist and the socialist—this by no means signifies that its victory will be achieved through armed interference by the socialist countries in the internal affairs of the capitalist countries. Our certainty of the victory of communism is based on the fact that the socialist mode of production possesses decisive advantages over the capitalist mode of production. Precisely because of this, the ideas of Marxism-Leninism are more and more capturing the minds of the broad masses of the working people in the capitalist countries, just as they have captured the minds of millions of men and women in our country and the People's Democracies. [*Prolonged applause.*] We believe that all working men in the world, once they have become convinced of the advantages communism brings, will sooner or later take the road of struggle for the construction of socialist society.

and Bulgaria—over which Soviet leaders exercised strong control. Yugoslavia and Albania chose to follow a more independent Communist path. Lacking the capital necessary to finance recovery, the Soviets sought compensation from eastern and central European territories.

Under Stalin's direction, the Soviet Union concentrated all its efforts on reconstructing its devastated economy and, to that end, sought integration with eastern European states, whose technology and resources were needed for the rebuilding of the Soviet state. U.S. dominance threatened the vital connection with eastern Europe that the Soviet Union was determinedly solidifying in the postwar years. In the years before his death in 1953, Joseph Stalin succeeded in making the Soviet Union a vital industrial giant second only to the United States. In addition, the postwar Soviet economy assumed the new burdens of the development of a nuclear arsenal and an expensive program for the exploration of space. Stalin maintained the Soviet Union on the footing of a war economy, restricting occupational mobility and continuing to rely on forced-labor camps.

De-Stalinization. In 1953, Stalin, who had ruled the Soviet Union for almost three decades, died. The vacuum that he left provoked a struggle for power among the Communist party leadership. It also initiated almost immediately a process of **de-Stalinization** and the beginnings of a thaw in censorship and repression. A growing urban and professional class expected improvements in the quality of life and greater freedoms after years of war and hardship. In 1956, at the Twentieth Party Congress, Nikita Khrushchev (1894–1971), as head of the Communist party, denounced Stalin as incompetent and cruel. After five years of jockeying for power among Stalin's former lieutenants, Khrushchev emerged victorious and assumed the office of premier in 1958.

De-Stalinization also took place in eastern Europe. Discontent over collectivization, low wages, and the lack of consumer goods fueled a latent nationalism among eastern European populations resentful of Soviet control and influence. Violence erupted in 1953 in East Berlin as workers revolted over conditions in the workplace, but it was quickly and effectively suppressed. Demands for reforms and liberalization in Poland also produced riots and changes in Communist party leadership. Wladislaw Gomulka (1905–1982), a Communist with a nationalist point of view who had survived Stalin's purges, aimed to take advantage of the power vacuum created by the departure of Stalinist leaders. Gomulka refused to back down in the face of severe Soviet pressure and the threat of a Soviet invasion to keep him from power. Elected as the first secretary of the Communist party in Poland, Gomulka sought to steer his nation on a more liberal course.

Hungarians followed suit with their demands for the withdrawal of Hungary from the Warsaw Pact. On 23 October 1956, inspired by the events in Poland, Hungarians rose up in anger against their old-guard Stalinist rulers. Imre Nagy (1896–1958), a liberal Communist, took control of the government, attempted to introduce democratic reforms, and relaxed economic controls. The Soviets, however, were unwilling to lose control of their sphere of influence in Eastern Bloc nations and to jeopardize their system of defense in the Warsaw Pact. Moscow responded to liberal experimentation in Hungary by sending tanks and troops into Budapest. Brutal repression and purges followed. The Hungarian experience in 1956 made clear that too much change too quickly would not be tolerated by the Soviet rulers. The thaw following Stalin's death had promoted expectations among eastern Europeans that a new era was dawning. The violent crushing of the Hungarian revolution was a reminder of the realities of Soviet control and the Soviet Union's defense priorities in eastern Europe.

The Soviet Standard of Living.

The Soviet Union's standard of living remained relatively low in the years when western Europe was undergoing a consumer revolution. Soviet consumption was necessarily stagnant, since profits were plowed back as investments in future heavy industrial expansion. In the Soviet Union and throughout the Eastern Bloc countries, women's full participation in the labor force was essential for recovery. In spite of their presence in large numbers in highly skilled sectors such as medicine, Soviet and Eastern Bloc women remained poorly paid, as did women in the West. Soviet men received higher salaries for the same work on the grounds that they had to support families.

The Soviet population was growing rapidly, from 170 million in 1939 to 234 million in 1967. Nikita Khrushchev promised the people lower prices and a shorter workweek, but in 1964, when he fell from power, Soviets were paying higher prices for their food than before. With a declining rate of development, the Soviet economy lacked the necessary capital to advance the plans for growth in all sectors. Defense spending nearly doubled in the short period between 1960 and 1968.

■ A West Berlin bride waves her wedding bouquet over the Berlin Wall to friends and family isolated on the other side.

■ Soviet tanks rumbled through Prague as troops from the Warsaw Pact countries invaded the Czechoslovakian capital in 1968, bringing an end to Alexander Dubcek's reform movement. Dubcek was rehabilitated in the liberalization of 1989 and elected chairman of the parliament.

Eastern Bloc Economies and Dissent. The nature of planned Soviet growth exacted heavy costs in the Eastern Bloc countries. Adhering to the Soviet pattern of heavy industrial expansion at the expense of agriculture and consumer goods, East Germany nearly doubled its industrial output by 1955, despite having been stripped of its industrial plants by the Soviet Union before 1948. Czechoslovakia, Bulgaria, Romania, and Yugoslavia all reported significant industrial growth in this period. Yet dislocations caused by collectivization and heavy defense expenditures stirred up social unrest in East Germany, Czechoslovakia, Poland, and Hungary. The Soviet Union responded with some economic concessions but on the whole stressed common industrial and defense pursuits, employing ideological persuasion and military pressure to keep its reluctant partners in line.

East Berlin in the late 1950s and early 1960s posed a particular problem for Communist rule. Unable to compete successfully in wages and standard of living with the capitalist western sector of the city, East Berlin saw increasing numbers of its population, especially the educated and professional classes, crossing the line to a more prosperous life. In 1961, the Soviet Union responded to the problem by building a wall that cordoned off the part of the city that it controlled. The **Berlin Wall** eventually stretched for 103 miles, with heavily policed crossing points, turrets, and troops and tanks facing each other across the divide that came to symbolize the Cold War.

The process of liberalization that had begun after Stalin's death and continued under Khrushchev certainly experienced its setbacks and reversals in the case of Budapest and Berlin. But in 1968 the policy of de-Stalinization reached a critical juncture in Czechoslovakia. Early in 1968, Alexander Dubcek, Czech party secretary and a member of the educated younger genera-

tion of technocrats, had supported liberal reforms in Czechoslovakia that included decentralization of planning and economic decision making, market pricing, and market incentives for higher productivity and innovation. He acted on popular desire for nationalism, the end of censorship, and better working conditions. Above all, he called for democratic reforms in the political process that would restore rule to the people. Dubcek spoke of "socialism with a human face," although, unlike the Hungarians in 1956, he made no move to withdraw his country from the Warsaw Pact or to defy Soviet leadership. Moscow nevertheless feared the erosion of obedience within the Eastern Bloc and the collapse of one-party rule in the Czech state and sent in thousands of tanks and hundreds of thousands of Warsaw Pact troops to Prague and other Czech cities to reestablish control. The Czechs responded with passive resistance in what became known as the **Prague Spring** uprising. The Soviet invasion made clear that popular nationalism was intolerable in an Eastern Bloc nation.

Alone among eastern European leaders, Marshal Tito of Yugoslavia resisted Soviet encroachment. As a partisan leader of the Communist resistance during World War II, Tito had earned the reputation as a war hero for his opposition to the Germans. Ruling Yugoslavia as a dictator after 1945, he refused to accede to Soviet directives to collectivize agriculture and to participate in joint economic ventures. For its defiance of Soviet supremacy, in 1948 Yugoslavia was expelled from the Cominform, the Soviet-controlled information agency that replaced the Comintern after 1943.

The slowed growth of the 1960s, the delay in development of consumer durables, and the inadequacy of basic foodstuffs, housing, and clothing were the costs that Eastern Bloc citizens paid for their inefficient and rigid planned economies dedicated to the development of heavy industry. In eastern Europe and the Soviet Union, poverty was virtually eliminated, however, as the state subsidized housing, health care, and higher education, which were available to all.

THE WELFARE STATE AND SOCIAL TRANSFORMATION

The **welfare state,** a creation of the post–World War II era throughout Europe, aimed to protect citizens through the establishment of a decent standard of living available for everyone. The experiences of the Great Depression had done much to foster concern for economic security. In France, the primary concern of the welfare state was the protection of children and the issue of family allowances. In Great Britain, as in Germany, emphasis was placed on unemployment insurance and health care benefits. Everywhere, however, the welfare state developed a related set of social programs and policies whereby the state intervened in the cycles of individual lives to provide economic support for the challenges of birth, sickness, old age, and unemployment.

Protection of the citizenry took varied forms according to Cold War politics. In the Warsaw Pact countries, the need to industrialize rapidly and to dedicate productive wealth to armament and military protection resulted in a nonexistent consumer economy in which the issues of quality of life and protection took a very different direction. Based on a concept of equal access to a minimum standard of living, welfare states did not treat all their members equally. Women were often disadvantaged in social welfare programs as family needs, men's rights, and the protection of children led to different national configurations.

Prosperity and Consumption in the West

Despite the different paths toward reconstruction following World War II, every western European nation experienced dramatic increases in total wealth. Per capita income was clearly on the rise through the mid-1960s, and there was more disposable wealth than ever before. Prosperity encouraged new patterns of spending based on confidence in the economy. That new consumerism, in turn, was essential to economic growth and future productivity.

The New Consumption.   The social programs of the welfare state played an important role in promoting postwar consumption. People began to relax about their economic futures, more secure because of the provisions of unemployment insurance, old-age pensions, and health and accident insurance. The state alleviated the necessity of saving for a rainy day by providing protection that had formerly been covered by the savings of workers. In the mid-1950s, all over western Europe, people began to spend their earnings, knowing that accidents, disasters, and sicknesses would be taken care of by the state.

The main items in the new consumption were consumer durables, above all televisions and automobiles. Refrigerators and washing machines also developed mass markets, as did the increased consumption of liquor and cigarettes. Increased leisure resulted in a boom in vacation travel. In addition to spending their salaries, western Europeans began to buy on credit, spending money they had not yet earned. That, too,

■ A traffic jam on the Place de la Concorde in Paris in 1962. Western Europeans learned that prosperity had its price as nineteenth-century cities were thrust into the automobile age.

was an innovation in postwar markets. People sought immediate gratification through consumption by means of delayed payment against future earnings.

Welfare programs could be sustained only in an era of prosperity and economic growth, since they depended on taxation of income for their funds. Such taxation did not, however, result in a redistribution of wealth. Wealth remained in the hands of a few and became even more concentrated as a result of phenomenal postwar economic growth. In West Germany, for example, 1.7 percent of the population owned 35 percent of the society's total wealth.

Women's Wages. Just as the welfare state did not redistribute wealth, it did not provide equal pay for equal work. In France, women who performed the same jobs as men received less pay. In typesetting, for example, women, who on average set 15,000 keystrokes per hour at the keyboards compared to 10,000 by men, earned 50 percent of men's salaries and held different titles for their jobs. Separate wage scales for women drawn up during the Nazi period remained in effect in West Germany until 1956. The skills associated with occupations performed by women were downgraded, as were their salaries. Women earned two-thirds or less of what men earned throughout western Europe. Welfare state revenues were a direct result of pay-scale inequities. Lower salaries for women meant higher profits and helped make economic recovery possible.

Family Strategies

The pressures on European women and their families in 1945 were often greater than in wartime. Severe scarcity of food, clothes, and housing required careful management. Women who during the war held jobs in industry and munitions plants earned their own money and established their own independence. After the war, in victorious and defeated nations alike, women were moved out of the work force to make room for returning men. Changing social policies affected women's lives in the home and in the workplace and contributed to the politicization of women within the context of the welfare state.

Demography and Birth Control. Prewar concerns with a declining birthrate intensified after World War II. In some European countries, the birthrate climbed in the years immediately following the war, an encouraging sign to observers who saw in the trend an optimistic commitment to the future after the cessation of the horrors of war. The situation was more complicated in France and the United States, where the birthrates began to climb even before the war was over. Nearly everywhere throughout Europe, however, the rise in the birthrate was momentary, with the United States standing alone in experiencing a genuine and sustained **"baby boom"** until about 1960. In Germany and in eastern Europe (Poland and Yugoslavia, for example), the costs of the war exacted heavy tolls on families long after the hostilities ended. On average, women everywhere were having fewer children by choice.

Technology had expanded the range of choices in family planning. In the early 1960s, the birth control pill became available on the European and American markets, primarily to middle-class women. Europeans were choosing to have smaller families. The drop in the birthrate had clearly preceded the new technological interventions that included intrauterine devices (IUDs), improved diaphragms, sponges, and more effective spermicidal creams and jellies. The condom, invented a century earlier, was now sold to a mass market. Information about their reproductive lives became more accessible to young women. Illegal abortions continued to be an alternative for women. Abortion was probably the primary form of birth control in the Soviet Union in the years following the war. Controversies, however, surrounded unhealthy side effects of the pill and the dangerous Dalkon shield, an IUD that had not been adequately tested before marketing and that resulted in the death or sterilization of thousands of women. Religious leaders also spoke out on the moral issues surrounding sexuality without reproduction. And in France and Italy, birth control information was often withheld from the public.

The Family and Welfare. Concurrent with a low birthrate was a new valuing of family life and domestic virtues in the years after the war. Those who had lived through the previous

■ Many basic needs are provided for under Britain's cradle-to-grave social welfare system. Here mothers and children line up to receive orange juice. Vitamins and milk are also provided for growing children.

20 years were haunted by the memories of the Great Depression, severe economic hardships, destructive war, and the loss of loved ones. Women and men throughout western Europe and the United States embraced the centrality of the family to society, even if they did not opt for large families. Expectations for improved family life placed new demands on welfare state programs. They also placed increased demands on mothers, whose presence in the home was now seen as all-important for the proper development of the child. Handbooks for mothers proliferated, instructing them in the "science" of child rearing. The best-seller *Baby and Child Care* by Dr. Benjamin Spock was typical of such guides.

European states implemented official programs to encourage women to have more children and to be better mothers. **Pronatalism,** as the policy was known, resulted from an official concern over low birthrates and a decline in family size. It is unlikely that pronatalism was caused by a fear of a decline in the labor force, since the influx of foreign workers, refugees from eastern Europe, and migrant laborers from poorer southern European nations provided an expanding labor pool. Other considerations about racial dominance and women's proper role seem to have affected the development of policies. In 1945, Lord Beveridge (1879–1960), the architect of the British welfare state, emphasized the importance of women's role "in ensuring the adequate continuance of the British race" and argued that women's place was in the home: "During marriage most women will not be gainfully employed. The small minority of women who undertake paid employment or other gainful employment or other gainful occupations after marriage require special treatment differing from that of single women."

Welfare state programs differed from country to country as the result of a series of different expectations of women as workers and women as mothers. Konrad Adenauer, chancellor of West Germany, spoke of "a will to children" as essential for his country's continued economic growth and prosperity. In Great Britain, the welfare system was built on the ideal of the mother at home with her children. With the emphasis on the need for larger families—four children was considered desirable in England—English society focused on the importance of the role of the mother. Family allowances determined by the number of children were tied to men's participation in the work force; women were defined according to their husbands' status. The state welfare system strengthened the financial dependence of English wives on their husbands.

In Great Britain, anxiety over the low birthrate was also tied to the debate over equal pay for women. Opponents of the measure argued that equal pay would cause women to forgo marriage and motherhood and should therefore be avoided. There was a consensus about keeping women out of the work force and paying them less in order to achieve that end.

The French system of *sécurité sociale* defined all women, whether married or single, as equal to men; unlike English women, all French women had the same rights of access to welfare programs as men. That may well have reflected the different work history of women in France and the recognition of the importance of women's labor for reconstruction of the economy. As a result, family allowances, pre- and post-natal care, maternity benefits, and child care were provided on the assumption that working mothers were a fact of life. French payments were intended to encourage large families and focused primarily on the needs of children. More and more women entered the paid labor force after 1945, and they were less financially dependent on their husbands than were their British counterparts.

Both forms of welfare state—the British that emphasized women's role as mothers and the French that accepted women's role as workers—were based on different attitudes about the nature of gender difference and equality. Women's political consciousness developed in both societies. The women's liberation movements of the late sixties and early seventies found their roots in the contradictions of differing welfare policies.

The Beginnings of Women's Protest. The 1960s were a period of protest in Western countries as people demonstrated for civil rights and free expression. In Europe and America, protests against U.S. involvement in Vietnam began, emulating patterns of activism established in the movement for black civil rights. Pacifist and antinuclear groups united to "ban the bomb." Women participated in all of the movements, and by the end of the 1960s had begun to question their own place in organizations that did not acknowledge their claims to equal rights, equal pay, and liberation from the oppression of male society. A new critique began to form within the welfare state that indicated there were cracks in the facade.

One book in particular, written after World War II, captured the attention of many women who were aware of the contradictions and limitations placed on them by state and society. *The Second Sex* (1949), written by Simone de Beauvoir (1908–1986), a leading French intellectual, analyzed women's place in the context of Western culture. By examining the assumptions of political theories, including Marxism, in the light of philosophy, biology, history, and psychoanalysis, de Beauvoir uncovered the myths governing the creation of the female self. By showing how the male is the center of culture and the female is "other," de Beauvoir urged women to be independent and to resist male definitions. *The Second Sex* became the handbook of the women's movement in the 1960s.

A very different work, *The Feminine Mystique,* appeared in 1963. In that book, author Betty Friedan voiced the grievances of a previously politically quiescent group of women. Friedan was an American suburban homemaker and the mother of three children when she wrote about what she saw as the schizophrenic split in her own middle-class world between the reality of women's lives and the idealized image of the perfect homemaker. After World War II, women were expected to find personal fulfillment in the domestic sphere. Instead, Friedan found women suffering from the "sickness with no name" and the "nameless desperation" of a profound crisis in identity.

A new politics centering on women's needs and women's rights slowly took root. The feminist critique did not emerge as

■ French novelist and feminist Simone de Beauvoir participated in demonstrations for women's issues such as family planning.

a mass movement until the 1970s. Youth culture and dissent among the young further influenced growing feminist discontent. But the agenda of protest in the sixties, reinforced by social policies, accepted gender differences as normal and natural.

Youth Culture and Dissent

Youth culture was created by outside forces as much as it was self-created. Socialized together in an expanding educational system from primary school through high school, the young came to see themselves as a social force. They were also socialized by marketing efforts that appealed to their particular needs as a group.

The prosperity that characterized the period from the mid-fifties to the mid-sixties throughout the West provided a secure base from which radical dissenters could launch their protests. The young people of the 1960s were the first generation to come of age after World War II. Although they had no memory themselves of the destruction of that war, they were reminded daily of the imminence of nuclear destruction in their own lives. The combination of the security of affluence and the insecurity of Cold War politics created a widening gap between the world of decision-making adults and the idealistic universe of the young. To the criticisms of parents, politicians, and teachers, the new generation responded that no one over 30 could be trusted.

New styles of dress and grooming were a rejection of middle-class culture in Europe and the United States. Anthropologists and sociologists in the 1960s began studying youth as if they were a foreign tribe. The **"generation gap"** appeared as the subject of hundreds of specialized studies. Adolescent behavior was examined across cultures. Sexual freedom and the use of drugs were subjected to special scrutiny. But, above all, it was the politics of the young that baffled and enraged many observers. When the stable base of economic prosperity began to erode as a result of slowed

■ Isle of Wight Festival, England, 1969. Open-air music festivals were a popular feature of the sixties—the era of pacifism, when young people experimented with sexual liberation, the drug culture, and Eastern mysticism.

THE SECOND SEX

Simone de Beauvoir, one of France's leading intellectuals, wrote philosophical treatises, essays, and novels that drew on a wide variety of cultural traditions and synthesized philosophy, history, literary criticism, and Freudian psychoanalysis in her studies of the human condition. The Second Sex, which first appeared in French in 1949, has subsequently been translated into many languages and has appeared in numerous editions throughout the world. It has served as a call to arms for the feminist movement, provoking debate, controversy, and a questioning of the fundamental gender arrangements of modern society.

Focus Questions

What does de Beauvoir mean when she says that men and women occupy separate economic castes? From her analysis, can you tell if de Beauvoir is "very well pleased with [woman's] role as the *Other*"?

A man never begins by presenting himself as an individual of a certain sex; it goes without saying that he is a man. The terms *masculine* and *feminine* are used symmetrically only as a matter of form, as on legal papers. In actuality the relation of the two sexes is not quite like that of two electrical poles, for man represents both the positive and the neutral, as is indicated by the common use of man to designate human beings in general; whereas woman represents only the negative, defining by limiting criteria, without reciprocity. In the midst of an abstract discussion it is vexing to hear a man say: "You think thus and so because you are a woman"; but I know that my only defense is to reply: "I think thus and so because it is true," thereby removing my subjective self from the argument. It would be out of the question to reply: "And you think the contrary because you are a man," for it is understood that the fact of being a man is no peculiarity. A man is in the right in being a man; it is the woman who is in the wrong. It amounts to this: just as for the ancients there was an absolute vertical with reference to which the oblique was defined, so there is an absolute human type, the masculine. Woman has ovaries, a uterus; these peculiarities imprison her in her subjectivity, circumscribe her within the limits of her own nature. It is often said that she thinks with her glands. Man superbly ignores the fact that his anatomy also includes glands, such as the testicles, and that they secrete hormones. He thinks of his body as a direct and normal connection with the world, which he believes he apprehends objectively, whereas he regards the body of woman as a hindrance, a prison, weighed down by everything peculiar to it. "The female is a female by virtue of certain lack of qualities," said Aristotle; "we should regard the female nature as afflicted with a natural defectiveness." And Saint Thomas for his part pronounced woman to be an "imperfect man," an "incidental" being. This is symbolized in Genesis where Eve is depicted as made from what Bossuet called "a supernumerary bone" of Adam.

Now, woman has always been man's dependent, if not his slave; the two sexes have never shared the world in equality. And even today woman is heavily handicapped, though her situation is beginning to change. Almost nowhere is her legal status the same as man's, and frequently it is much to her disadvantage. Even when her rights are legally recognized in the abstract, long-standing custom prevents their full expression in the mores. In the economic sphere men and women can almost be said to make up two castes; other things being equal, the former hold the better jobs, get higher wages, and have more opportunity for success than their new competitors. In industry and politics men have a great many more positions and they monopolize the most important posts. In addition to all this, they enjoy a traditional prestige that the education of children tends in every way to support, for the present enshrines the past—and in the past all history has been made by men. At the present time, when women are beginning to take part in the affairs of the world, it is still a world that belongs to men—they have no doubt of it at all and women have scarcely any. To decline to be the Other, to refuse to be a party to the deal—this would be for women to renounce all the advantages conferred upon them by their alliance with the superior caste. Man-the-sovereign will provide women-the-liege with material protection and will undertake the moral justification of her existence; thus she can evade at once both economic risk and the metaphysical risk of a liberty in which ends and aims must be contrived without assistance. Indeed, along with the ethical urge of each individual to affirm his subjective existence, there is also the temptation to forgo liberty and become a thing. This is an inauspicious road, for he who takes it—passive, lost, ruined—becomes henceforth the creature of another's will, frustrated in his transcendence and deprived of every value. But it is an easy road; on it one avoids the strain involved in undertaking an authentic existence. When man makes of woman the *Other*, he may, then, expect her to manifest deep-seated tendencies toward complicity. Thus, woman may fail to lay claim to the status of subject because she lacks definite resources, because she feels the necessary bond that ties her to man regardless of reciprocity, and because she is often very well pleased with her role as the *Other*.

From Simone de Beauvoir, *The Second Sex* (1949).

growth and inflation in the second half of the sixties—first in western Europe and then in the United States—frustrated expectations and shrinking opportunities for the young served as a further impetus for political action.

The Sexual Revolution.

Increased emphasis on fulfillment through sexual pleasure was one consequence of the technological revolution in birth control devices, and it led to what has been called a revolution in sexual values in Western societies in the 1960s. The sexual revolution drew attention to sexual fulfillment as an end in itself. Women's bodies were displayed more explicitly than ever before in mass advertising in order to sell products from automobiles to soap. Sex magazines, sex shops, and movies were part of an explosion in the marketing of male sexual fantasies in the 1960s.

Sweden experienced the most far-reaching reforms of sexual mores in the 1960s. Sex education became part of every school's curriculum, contraceptive information was widely available, and homosexuality was decriminalized. Technology allowed women and men to separate pleasure from reproduction but did not alter men's and women's domestic roles. Pleasure was also separated from familial responsibilities, yet the domestic ideal of the woman in the home remained. Some women were beginning to question their exploitation in the sexual revolution. In the early 1970s, that issue became part of mass feminist protest.

The Anti-War Movement and Social Protest.

Student protest, which began at the University of California, Berkeley in 1964 as the Free Speech movement, by the spring of 1968 had become an international phenomenon that had spread to other American campuses and throughout Europe and Japan. A common denominator of protest, whether in New York, London, or Tokyo, was opposition to the war in Vietnam. Growing numbers of intellectuals and students throughout the world condemned the U.S. presence in Vietnam as an immoral violation of the rights of the Vietnamese people and violent proof of U.S. imperialism.

Student protesters shared other concerns in addition to opposition to the war in southeast Asia. The growing activism on American campuses was aimed at social reform, student self-governance, and a recognition of the responsibilities of the university in the wider community. In West Germany, highly politicized radical activists, a conspicuous minority among the students at the Free University of Berlin, directed protest out into the wider society. Student demonstrations met with brutal police repression and violence, and rioting was common.

European students, more than their American counterparts, were also experiencing frustration in the classroom. European universities were unprepared to absorb the huge influx of students in the 1960s. The student–teacher ratio at the University of Rome, for example, was 200 to 1. In Italian universities in general, the majority of more than half a million students had no contact with their professors. The University of Paris was similarly overcrowded. The Soviet bloc was not immune from student protests, as youth in Czechoslovakia followed the lead of their western counterparts in speaking out against oppression.

For the most part, student protest was primarily a middle-class phenomenon. In France, for example, only four percent of university students came from below the middle class. Higher education had been developed after World War II to serve the increased needs of a technocratic society. Instead of altering the social structure, which politically committed student protesters thought it should do, mass education served as a certifying mechanism for bureaucratic and technical institutions. Many of the occupations that students could look forward to were in dead-end service jobs or in bureaucratic posts.

■ Czech students distribute underground literature in Wenceslas Square, Prague, in protest against the Soviet occupation of their country.

"SUBTERRANEAN HOMESICK BLUES"

The gap between the generations yawned into a gulf as rock music became political in the mid-1960s. Bob Dylan, an American rock performer, introduced folk music to the genre with songs of social protest such as "Blowin' in the Wind" and "Only a Pawn in Their Game." Rock music was denounced as a communist plot as performers urged their audiences to "make love, not war." Dylan's "Subterranean Homesick Blues" targeted the hypocrisy of his society.

Focus Questions

Can you find examples of social protest against the government and a questioning of law and order in this song? How does Dylan target hypocrisy in these verses?

Subterranean Homesick Blues
Bob Dylan

Johnny's in the basement
Mixing up the medicine
I'm on the pavement
Thinking about the government
The man in the trench coat
Badge out, laid off
Says he's got a bad cough
Wants to get it paid off
Look out kid
It's somethin' you did
God knows when
But you're doin' it again
You better duck down the alley way
Lookin' for a new friend
The man in the coon-skin cap
In the big pen
Wants eleven dollar bills
You only got ten
Maggie comes fleet foot
Face full of black soot
Talkin' that the heat put
Plants in the bed but
Look out kid
You're gonna get hit
But users, cheaters
Six-time losers
Hang around the theaters
Girl by the whirlpool
Lookin' for a new fool
Don't follow leaders
Watch the parkin' meters

Ah get born, keep warm
Short pants, romance, learn to dance
Get dressed, get blessed
Try to be a success
The phone's tapped anyway
Maggie says that many say
They must bust in early May
Orders from the D.A.
Look out kid
Don't matter what you did
Walk on your tip toes
Don't try "No Doz"
Better stay away from those
That carry around a fire hose
Keep a clean nose
Watch the plain clothes
You don't need a weather man
To know which way the wind blows
Get sick, get well
Hang around a ink well
Ring bell, hard to tell
If anything is goin' to sell
Try hard, get barred
Get back, write braille
Get jailed, jump bail
Join the army, if you fail
Please her, please him, buy gifts
Don't steal, don't lift
Twenty years of schoolin'
And they put you on the day shift
Look out kid
They keep it all hid
Better jump down a manhole
Light yourself a candle
Don't wear sandals
Try to avoid the scandals
Don't wanna be a bum
You better chew gum
The pump don't work
`Cause the vandals took the handles

Protest and the Economy.

Student dissent reflected the changing economy of the late 1960s. Inflation, which earlier in the decade had spurred prosperity, was spiraling out of control in the late sixties. In the advanced industrial countries of western Europe and later in the United States, the growth of the postwar period was slowing down. Economic opportunity was evaporating and jobs were being eliminated. One survey estimated that only one in three Italian university graduates in 1967 was able to find a job. The dawning awareness of shrinking opportunities in the workplace for students who had attained their degrees and been properly certified further aggravated student frustration and dissent. Anger about the uncertainties of their future mixed with the realization of the boredom of the careers that awaited them upon graduation.

By the late sixties, universities and colleges provided the students a forum for expressing their discontent with advanced industrial societies. In their protests, student activists rejected the values of consumer society. The programs and politics of the student protesters aimed to transform the world in which they lived. Student protesters in France chanted "*Métro, boulot, dodo,*" a slang condemnation of the treadmilllike existence of those who spent their lives in a repetitive cycle of subway riding (*Métro*), mindless work (*boulot*), and sleep (*dodo*). The spirit of protest was expressed in the graffiti and posters that seemed to appear overnight on the walls of Paris:

"Action must not be a reaction—but a creation"
"Power to the Imagination"
"The revolution will be won when the last bureaucrat is strangled in the entrails of the last cop"
"The state is each one of us"

In May 1968, French protest spread beyond the university when workers and managers joined students in paralyzing the French economy and threatening to topple the Fifth Republic. Between 7 and 10 million people went on strike in support of worker and student demands. White-collar employees and technicians joined blue-collar factory workers in the strike. Student demands, based on a thoroughgoing critique of the whole society, proved to be incompatible with the wage and consumption issues of workers. But the unusual, if short-lived, alliance of students and workers shocked those in power and induced reforms.

CONCLUSION

The division of the world into two camps framed the recovery of combatant nations dealing with the losses of World War II. The Cold War instilled fear in the populations who lived on both sides of the divide. Yet the Cold War also created the terms for stability following the upheaval of war. It promoted prosperity that preserved the long-term policies of both the United States and the Soviet Union in the twentieth century. The Soviet Union had buffered itself from the West by creating a ring of friendly nations on its borders and had continued its race to industrialize. The belief that the USSR had won the war for the Allies and the sense of betrayal that followed the war determined the outlook of grim distrust shared by postwar Soviet leaders who had survived the years from 1939 to 1945.

The United States, on the other hand, found itself playing the role of rich uncle in bankrolling the European recovery. Its long-term commitment to promoting its own economic interests by helping future trading partners led it also into playing the role of police officer throughout the world. The escalating war in Vietnam made America vulnerable to growing world criticism and to growing domestic discontent.

Cold War and Economic Recovery

1947	Marshall Plan starts U.S. aid to European countries; pro-Soviet governments established in Poland, Hungary, Bulgaria, and Romania
1948	Pro-Soviet government established in Czechoslovakia
1949	European states and United States form North Atlantic Treaty Organization (NATO); Federal Republic of Germany and German Democratic Republic established; Soviet Union creates Council for Mutual Economic Assistance (Comecon); Soviet Union tests its first atomic bomb
1950–1953	Korean War, ending with the partition of Korea
1953	United States and Soviet Union develop hydrogen bombs
1955	Formation of Warsaw Pact
1956	Hungarian uprising and subsequent repression by Soviet military forces
1957	The Netherlands, Belgium, Luxembourg, France, Italy, and West Germany form the European Economic Community (EEC), also called the Common Market; Soviet Union launches first satellite, *Sputnik I*
1961	Berlin Wall built
1961–1973	U.S. troops engaged in Vietnam
1962	Cuban missile crisis
1963	Soviet Union and United States sign Nuclear Test Ban Treaty
1968	Prague Spring uprising in Czechoslovakia, quelled by Soviet Union

The gains of economic recovery began to unravel in the mid-1960s. The protests of 1968 were a response to changing economic conditions. In the West, rising expectations of consumer societies came up against the harsh realities of slowed growth. In the East, frustrated nationalism, the lack of consumer goods, and repressive conditions resulted in low morale, demonstrations, and outright conflict. After Stalin's death, resources were diverted to consumer goods, but there was little measurable improvement in the quality of life. By 1970, changing economies in both East and West affected the goals of the Cold War, still very much an organizing reality in the international arena. By 1970 the players in the Cold War now faced a world no longer caught up in the aftermath of war, but one challenged by the prospect of peace.

QUESTIONS FOR REVIEW

1. What did it mean for postwar European politics that the Continent was divided by an "iron curtain"?
2. What factors encouraged decolonization in the decades after World War II?
3. Why did western Europe's economy recover so rapidly, and how did that contribute to a gradual process of European economic integration?
4. How did the Soviet Union's strategy for recovery differ from that of western Europe?
5. What is the welfare state, and how did it transform the lives of ordinary Europeans?
6. What were some of the concerns that provoked protests from women, students, and others in the 1960s?

KEY TERMS

baby boom, *p. 890*

Berlin Wall, *p. 888*

Cold War, *p. 874*

Comecon, *p. 885*

containment, *p. 875*

decolonization, *p. 877*

de-Stalinization, *p. 886*

European Economic Community (EEC), *p. 885*

generation gap, *p. 892*

iron curtain, *p. 874*

Marshall Plan, *p. 882*

North Atlantic Treaty Organization (NATO), *p. 876*

nuclear club, *p. 877*

Prague Spring, *p. 888*

pronatalism, *p. 891*

Schuman Plan, *p. 884*

third world, *p. 877*

Warsaw Pact, *p. 876*

welfare state, *p. 889*

DISCOVERING WESTERN CIVILIZATION ONLINE

You can obtain more information about the Cold War and postwar economic recovery at the Websites listed below. See also the Companion Website that accompanies this text, www.ablongman.com/kishlansky, which contains an online study guide and additional resources.

The Origins of the Cold War

The Berlin Airlift: Documents, Images, History
www.trumanlibrary.org/whistlestop/study_collection/berlin_airlift/large/berlin_airlift.htm
A virtual exhibit with electronic texts on the Berlin Airlift as presented by the Harry S Truman Library and Museum.

Internet Modern History Sourcebook: A Bipolar World
www.fordham.edu/halsall/mod/modsbook46.html

A collection of primary source documents and links to the creation of the United Nations and the outbreak of the Cold War.

Cold War International History Project
wwics.si.edu/index.cfm?topic_id=1409&fuseaction=topics.home
This site, sponsored by the Woodrow Wilson International Center for Scholars, provides a comprehensive list of primary documents and images, secondary sources, bibliographies, and working paper series on all aspects of the Cold War.

Soviet Archives Exhibit
www.ibiblio.org/expo/soviet.exhibit/entrance.html
A Soviet archive exhibit on the Cold War with images and electronic texts by the Library of Congress.

Postwar Economic Recovery in Europe, Japan, and the Soviet Union

Internet Modern History Sourcebook: Eastern Europe Since 1945
www.fordham.edu/halsall/mod/modsbook50.html
Two collections of links to primary sources and other sites on postwar western and eastern Europe.

The European Recovery: The Fiftieth Anniversary of the Marshall Plan
www.loc.gov/exhibits/marshall
A virtual museum exhibit with images and electronic primary and secondary texts on the Marshall Plan.

The Welfare State and Social Transformation

Internet Modern History Sourcebook: Modern Social Movements
www.fordham.edu/halsall/mod/modsbook56.html
A collection of primary source documents and links to sites on modern social movements including feminism, black power, and gay and lesbian rights.

The Sixties Project Home Page
lists.village.virginia.edu/sixties/
Web site of The Sixties Project, which brings together discussion lists, primary documents, bibliographies, museum exhibits, and personal testimonies about the 1960s and the Vietnam War from an exclusively American perspective.

Paris 1968 Posters
burn.ucsd.edu/paris.htm
A collection of posters from the 1968 protest movement in Paris.

SUGGESTIONS FOR FURTHER READING

The Origins of the Cold War

Franz Ansprenger, *The Dissolution of the Colonial Empires* (London: Routledge, 1989). An analysis of Europe's withdrawal from Asia and Africa following World War II, beginning with an examination of post–World War I imperialism.

Aleksandr Fursenko and Timothy Naftali, *Khrushchev's: Cold War: The Inside Story of an American Adversary* (New York: W. W. Norton, 2006). The authors have access to newly available Soviet archives and are able to present the inner workings of Khrushchev's foreign policy and his desire for peaceful coexistence.

John Lewis Gaddis, *The Cold War: A New History* (New York: Penguin Book, 2006). A synthetic update of U.S.–Soviet relations by a leading Cold War historian.

Edward H. Judge and John W. Langdon, eds., *The Cold War: A History Through Documents* (New York: Prentice-Hall, 1998). Includes about 130 edited documents covering the period from 1945 to 1991.

Postwar Economic Recovery in Europe, Japan, and the Soviet Union

Eric Hobsbawm, *The Age of Extremes: A History of the World, 1914–1991* (New York: Vintage Books, 1996). This volume covers what the author calls "the short twentieth century" from the outbreak of World War I to the fall of the Soviet Union. Of particular interest is the section on the 30 years following World War II, which the author sees as a "golden age" of extraordinary economic growth and social transformation.

Michael J. Hogan, *The Marshall Plan: America, Britain, and the Reconstruction of Western Europe* (Cambridge: Cambridge University Press, 1987). A thoroughly researched argument on the continuity of U.S. economic policy in the twentieth century. Hogan counters the belief that the Marshall Plan was merely a response to the Cold War.

Derek W. Urwin, *Western Europe Since 1945: A Political History,* 4th ed. (London: Longman, 1989). A general survey of postwar politics, with a special focus on the problems of reconstruction and the role of the resistance after 1945.

The Welfare State and Social Transformation

David Caute, *The Year of the Barricades: A Journey Through 1968* (New York: Harper & Row, 1988). More than its title suggests, this work is an overview of postwar youth culture on three continents. The politics of 1968 is featured, although other topics regarding the counterculture, lifestyles, and cultural ramifications are considered.

Simone de Beauvoir, *The Second Sex* (New York: Knopf, 1963). The author, one of France's leading intellectuals in the twentieth century, describes the situation of women's lives in the postwar West by placing them within the context of the history and myths governing Western culture.

John R. Gillis, *Youth and History: Tradition and Change in European Age Relations, 1770–Present* (New York: Academic Press, 1981). Connects the history of European youth to broad trends in economic and demographic modernization over the last 200 years.

Jane Jenson, "Both Friend and Foe: Women and State Welfare," in *Becoming Visible: Women in European History,* ed. Renate Bridenthal, Claudia Koonz, and Susan Stuard (Boston: Houghton Mifflin, 1987). This essay illuminates the mixed blessing of the welfare state for women after 1945 by focusing on the experiences of women in Great Britain and France.

Margaret Mead, *Culture and Commitment: The New Relationships Between the Generations in the 1970s* (New York: Columbia University Press, 1978). This series of essays, written by one of America's premier anthropologists, explores the origins and consequences of the generation gap, with special attention to Cold War politics, historical conditions, and technological transformations.

Susan Pederson, *Family, Dependence, and the Origins of the Welfare State: Britain and France, 1914–1945* (Cambridge: Cambridge University Press: 1994). Although this work covers the earlier period, the comparative approach to differing attitudes and policies provides an essential background to understanding family policy in postwar Europe.

Denise Riley, *War in the Nursery: Theories of the Child and Mother* (London: Virago Press, 1983). Treats social policies of postwar pronatalism within the context of the popularization of developmental and child psychologies in Europe, with special attention to Britain and the United States and an emphasis on the postwar period as a turning point in attitudes toward women and the family.

Mary Ruggie, *The State and Working Women: A Comparative Study of Britain and Sweden* (Princeton, NJ: Princeton University Press, 1984). A sociological study comparing the economic status of women in two European welfare states.

Peter A. Swenson, *Capitalists Against Markets: The Making of Labor Markets and Welfare States in the United States and Sweden* (New York: Oxford University Press, 2002). The author convincingly overturns traditional accounts of the origins of the welfare state that credit labor and looks at employers' influence on social reformers in two countries.

For a list of additional titles related to this chapter's topics, please see http://www.ablongman.com/kishlansky.

CHAPTER 30

THE END OF THE COLD WAR AND NEW GLOBAL CHALLENGES, 1970 TO THE PRESENT

THE WALL COMES DOWN: BERLIN, 1989

The American poet Robert Frost captured a basic aspect of human nature when he wrote, "Good fences make good neighbors." The uneasy coexistence of Communist East Germany and liberal and capitalist West Germany reached a confrontation point 16 years after the end of World War II, with the building of a "fence"—the Berlin Wall. In August 1961 the Wall, erected by the East German government under Soviet direction, bifurcated the former German capital and served its intended purpose of keeping East Germans confined behind it.

THE VISUAL RECORD

Why the Wall? East Germany's chief problem in the 1950s was the exodus of over two million East Germans in search of a better life in the West. The flow of emigration throughout the 1950s turned into a torrent in the first eight months of 1961. The Berlin Wall was, more than anything else, erected to keep skilled and professional workers in East Germany. German leaders in the West continued to voice their long-term commitment to reunification, while East German leaders insisted on the independence and autonomy of their state.

Throughout its 28-year life, the Berlin Wall served as a chilling reminder of the great ideological divide between East and West in the Cold War. Cutting through neighborhoods, streets, and railway lines, the Wall also divided families in two. Yet the Wall was porous, if even only slightly so. Passes could be authorized for holidays and special family events, funerals, weddings, and births so that East Berliners could visit their relatives. But long lines through checkpoints with passport and currency controls prevented circulation. Individuals attempting escape from East Berlin to the West were gunned down from watch towers along the Wall. Consisting of over 90 miles of concrete slabs and barbed wire, the Wall stood as a scar through the center of Berlin and around West Berlin. In 1963 President John F. Kennedy visited West Berlin and proclaimed in solidarity with citizens on both sides of the Wall, "Ich bin ein Berliner" (I am a Berliner). In that same speech,

Kennedy stated, "There are some who say that communism is the wave of the future. Let them come to Berlin." President Ronald Reagan used the occasion of his visit to West Berlin in 1987 to highlight the apparently increasing openness of the Soviet bloc.

Applications for authorized immigration to West Germany increased in the 1980s, and in 1984 East Germany allowed 30,000 citizens to emigrate to the West. Throughout the late 1980s, the emigration rate remained high, with an average exodus of 20,000 a year. With Hungary's refusal to continue to block the passage of East Germans into West Germany, the floodgates were opened: 57,000 East Germans migrated via Hungary within a matter of weeks. In the face of angry demonstrations, Erich Honecker, head of the East German state, was forced to resign.

The new government opened the Berlin Wall on November 9, 1989, ending all restrictions on travel between East and West. The toppling of communism, already underway, was captured in that moment. Robert Frost wrote of good fences, but he concluded, "Something there is that doesn't love a wall." With the rise of democratic institutions, open markets, and civil liberties, the Cold War had come to an end.

LOOKING AHEAD

By 1970 the postwar restrictions of a bipolar world were giving way to signs of republicanism, democracy, and self-rule. Some transformations were achieved with violence. Most notably, the history of ethnic differences led to war in the Balkans and the former Soviet republics. The United States was embroiled in conflicts throughout the Middle East. The place of the West in the global community continued to depend on social and gender inequalities. And a new kind of war based on the terrorism of civilian populations emerged as the weapon of choice of dispossessed groups around the globe.

■ In a scene that symbolizes the end of the Cold War, people celebrate atop the Berlin Wall in November 1989.

THE END OF THE COLD WAR AND THE EMERGENCE OF A NEW EUROPE

The Cold War, while it lasted from the post-1945 period to the late 1980s, provided a way of ordering the world. It served to divide friend from foe, to create spheres of economic interest, and to promote market relations among blocs of nations. Also, in a seemingly contradictory sense, it was a conflict that promoted stability and peace between the superpowers, no matter how uneasy. Yet chinks in the façade of Communist unity were already present by the mid-1960s, as we have seen in the previous chapter. As the Soviets faced growing discontent within the Soviet bloc, and as the nuclear threat made cooperation necessary, the bipolar security of the Cold War began to crumble.

The Brezhnev Doctrine and Détente

The use of military intervention to resolve the Czech crisis (Chapter 29) opened a new era governed by what came to be known as the **Brezhnev Doctrine.** Leonid Brezhnev (1906–1982), general secretary of the Communist party and head of the Soviet Union from 1966 to 1982, established a policy whereby the Soviet Union claimed the right to interfere in the internal affairs of its allies in order to prevent counterrevolution. Brezhnev was responsible for the decision to intervene in Czechoslovakia, arguing that a socialist state was obliged to take action in another socialist state if the survival of socialism was at stake. The Brezhnev Doctrine influenced developments in eastern Europe throughout the next decade. After 1968, rigidity and stagnation characterized the Soviet, East German, and Czechoslovakian governments, as well as Communist party rule in other eastern European states.

In the international arena, the Soviet Union had achieved nuclear parity. Now, from positions of equality, both sides expressed a willingness to negotiate. The 1970s became the decade of **détente,** a period of cooperation between the two superpowers. The Strategic Arms Limitation Treaty, known as SALT I, signed in Moscow in 1972, limited defensive antiballistic missile systems.

In the "dangerous decade" of the 1980s, nuclear strategists on both sides were once again talking about nuclear war as possible and winnable. Popular concern over the nuclear arms race intensified in the United States, in the Soviet Union, and throughout Europe as the United States pursued the Strategic Defense Initiative (SDI), popularly called "Stars Wars" because of its futuristic, science-fiction quality of promised superiority of a single power through technology. At the least, the new system threatened an escalation in nuclear defense spending on both sides in an attempt to end the stabilizing parity between the United States and the Soviet Union.

In spite of grandstanding gestures such as the Star Wars initiative, East–West relations after 1983 were characterized by less confrontation and more attempts at cooperation between the Soviet Union and the United States. The world political system itself appeared to have stabilized, with a diminution of conflict in the three main arenas of superpower competition—the third world, China, and western Europe. By the end of 1989, leaders in the East and West declared that the ideological differences that separated them were more apparent than real. They declared an end to the Cold War and sought a new and permanent détente.

The New Direction in Soviet Politics

By the mid-1980s, Soviet leaders were weighing the costs of increasing conflict within the Soviet bloc, which the Brezhnev Doctrine failed to control, and the promise of benefits from improved relations with the West. Growing dissent from intellectuals within the Soviet Union joined the voices of those from abroad who criticized Soviet repression. In response to the same forces of change, a different kind of leader was being forged in the ranks of the Communist party among a generation that favored more open political values and dynamic economic growth.

Soviet Dissent.   With the repression sanctioned by the Brezhnev Doctrine came growing protest within the Soviet Union. In response to state repression in the period from the late 1960s to the early 1980s, dissidence took on a variety of forms. Some dissenters sought an international forum for their cause. At first weak but increasing in volume, dissent from within communist countries commanded international attention in the mid-1970s.

Growing numbers of Soviet Jews, for example, petitioned to emigrate to Israel in order to escape anti-Semitism within the Soviet Union and to embrace their own cultural heritage. Some of the 178,000 who were allowed to emigrate found their way to western Europe and the United States, and stories of persecution were published in the world press. In May 1976, a number of Soviet dissidents, including Jewish protesters, commanded international attention by openly declaring themselves united for the purpose of securing human rights in the Soviet Union. The state retaliated by charging organizers with anti-Soviet propaganda and handing out harsh prison sentences or relegating protesters to mental asylums, drawing the criticism of democratic states.

One vehicle of protest was the self-published, privately circulated manuscripts in either typed or mimeographed form, known as *samizdat*, which became the chief means of dissident communication. For the most part, dissidents were members of a university-trained professional elite. The leading Soviet dissident of the period was Andrei Sakharov (1921–1989), internationally renowned as the father of the Soviet hydrogen bomb and a scientist of great eminence. In 1968 he wrote *Thoughts on Progress, Peaceful Coexistence, and Intellectual Freedom,* a work that opposed Communist party rule in favor of a liberal democratic system. For his dissident activities and criticism of the invasion of Afghanistan, Sakharov was sentenced to a life in exile in Gorky in 1980.

Sakharov was not the only figure of stature to engage in protest. The novelist Alexander Solzhenitsyn denounced the abuses of Soviet bureaucracy in *Cancer Ward, The Gulag Archipelago,* and *One Day in the Life of Ivan Denisovich,* works that were highly respected in the West. The historian Roy Medvedev also criticized Stalinism and continued to speak out in favor of peace and democratic principles in the Gorbachev years.

For almost three decades, dissidents waged a lonely battle within the Soviet Union for civil liberties, democratic rights, and the end of the nuclear arms race. In the 1980s it became clear to Soviet watchers in the West that demands for recognition of nationalities were an important part of the dissident movement in the Soviet Union, echoing similar demands throughout eastern Europe. Cultural, religious, ethnic, and ecological concerns and demands for national autonomy

joined forces with protests for civil liberties and economic freedom. The reinstatement of Sakharov, one of the Soviet Union's most visible dissidents, as a national hero just before his death and after years of persecution was one of the best barometers of the social revolution that was transforming Soviet politics in the 1980s.

Gorbachev's Economic Reforms.   Typical of the new generation of political leaders was Mikhail Gorbachev (1931–), who was, above all, a technocrat, someone who could apply specialized technical knowledge to the problems of a stagnant Soviet economy. In 1985, the accession to power of Mikhail Gorbachev as general secretary ushered in a new age of openness.

As the youngest Soviet leader since Stalin, Gorbachev set in motion in 1985 bold plans for increased openness, which he called *glasnost,* and a program of political and economic restructuring, which he dubbed *perestroika.* The economic challenges that Gorbachev faced were enormous. Soviet citizens were better fed, better educated, and in better health than their parents and grandparents had been. Yet while economic growth continued throughout the postwar years, the rate of growth slowed down in the 1970s. Some planners feared that the Soviet Union could never catch up to the United States, Japan, and West Germany. Soviet citizens were increasingly aware of the sacrifices and suffering that economic development had cost them in the twentieth century and of the disparities in the standards of living between the capitalist and communist worlds. Given outmoded technology, declining older industries, pollution, labor imbalances, critical shortages of foodstuffs and certain raw materials, and a significant amount of hidden unemployment in unproductive industries, discontent became more widespread.

DOCUMENT

Gorbachev on the Need for Economic Reform

The problem was not salaries. Workers were well paid, with more disposable income than ever before. But purchasing power far outstripped supplies. The state system of production, which emphasized quantity over quality, resulted in overproduction of some goods and underproduction of others. The state kept prices low in order to control the cost of living, but low prices were a problem because they did not provide sufficient incentive for the production of better-quality goods.

Gorbachev's programs between 1985 and 1988 promised more than they delivered. The promises were part of the problem since they created unmet expectations. Modest increases in output were achieved, but people's demands for food and consumer goods were rising faster than they could be met. The Soviet Union did not increase imports of consumer durables or food to meet the demand, nor did the quality of Soviet goods improve appreciably. Rising wages only gave workers more money that they could not or would not spend on Soviet products. The black market was a symbol both of the economic failures of the state and of the growing consumerism of Soviet citizens. Rather than purchase poor-quality goods, Soviets chose to purchase foreign products at vastly inflated prices.

■ Mikhail Gorbachev's rule ushered in a new age of openness in the Soviet Union. Here, Gorbachev and his wife, Raisa, are shown making a public appearance before a crowd in September 1988.

Although his economic reforms broke sharply with the centralized economy established by Stalin in the 1930s, Gorbachev candidly warned that he would not implement a consumption revolution in the near future. Many critics, including fellow communist Boris Yeltsin (1931–2007), believed that Gorbachev did not go far or fast enough with his economic reforms. In place of a controlled economy, Gorbachev offered a limited open market free of state controls for manufacturing enterprises organized on a cooperative basis and for light industry. He loosened restrictions on foreign trade, encouraged the development of the private sector, and decentralized economic decision making for agriculture and the service sector.

Reforming the Soviet State.   In contrast to the ingrained conservatism of his predecessors, Gorbachev represented experimentation, innovation, vitality, and a willingness to question old ways. Gorbachev appointed men who shared his vision to key posts, especially in the foreign ministry. And he extended the olive branch of peace to the West, meeting with U.S. President Ronald Reagan in a superpower summit in Geneva.

Furthermore, he argued that economic and political reforms had to be accomplished in concert; the economy, in other words, could only be restructured by "a democratization of our society at all levels." Therefore, Gorbachev's foreign policy also served his economic goals. Military participation in decision making declined as state expenditures on defense were cut. Moscow had always borne larger military costs than Washington. Gorbachev recognized that Cold War defense spending must decline if the Soviet Union was to prosper: consumer durables had to take the place of weapons on the production lines. But there the transformation was bound to be slow.

Gorbachev and Reagan agreed to systematic arms reduction and greater cooperation. In 1988, Soviet troops began the withdrawal from Afghanistan and completed the process by the following year. Also in 1989, in a stunning reversal of the Brezhnev Doctrine, the Soviet state refused to intervene in the upheavals that were sweeping eastern Europe. By 1989, many observers inside and outside the Soviet Union believed that a new age was at hand as the Soviet leader loosened censorship, denounced Stalin, and held the first free elections in the Soviet Union since 1917.

Reform in Eastern Europe

The Soviet example of restructuring and Gorbachev's calls for reforms and openness gave the lead to eastern Europe. In 1988, Gorbachev, speaking before the United Nations, assured the West that he would not prevent eastern European satellites from going their own way: "Freedom of choice is a universal principle," the Soviet head of state declared.

Poland and Grassroots Protest.   Poland's first free elections in 40 years were part of a vast mosaic of protest from which a pattern began to emerge in the spring of 1989. Poland, the most populous nation in eastern Europe, had played an important role in the Soviet bloc because of its strategic location as a corridor for supplies to the Soviet Union's 380,000 troops in East Germany. Yet its economy was never robust, and it had a 20-year history of worker protest and resistance. Throughout the 1970s, the Polish government, based on one-party rule, drew loans from abroad for investment in technology and industrial expansion. The government increased its foreign indebtedness rather than raise prices at home. In 1976, however, price increases were again

■ Strike leader Lech Walesa addresses shipyard workers in Gdansk, Poland, on 30 August 1980.

1. **Poland.** Solidarity party sweeps elections, June 1989.

2. **Czechoslovakia.** Communist leadership ousted, Nov. 1989; Vaclav Havel named president, Dec. 1989.

3. **Germany.** Berlin Wall breached, Nov 1989. Reunification of East and West Germany, Oct. 1990.

4. **Yugoslavia.** Government decides to hold free elections, Dec. 1989.

5. **Romania.** Communist dictator Ceaușescu overthrown and executed, Dec. 1989; Salvation Front led by dissident former Communists wins elections, May 1990.

6. **Albania.** Communist party still retains Leninist orientation, Jan. 1990. Parliament backs liberal reforms, May 1990.

7. **Bulgaria.** Government disavows "dominant role" for Communist party; pledges free elections and new constitution in 1990.

8. **Lithuania** declares independence, March 1990; Moscow calls move illegal.

9. **Hungary.** Free election sweeps non-Communists into power, April 1990.

10. **Latvia and Estonia** begin process of separation from Soviet Union, April 1990.

■ Events in Eastern Europe, 1989–1990. The events of 1989 and 1990 seemed to indicate that peaceful democratic change through free elections and liberal reforms would fill the void left by the collapse of communist rule.

decreed. A new wave of spontaneous strikes erupted, forcing the government to rescind the increases.

Poland's indebtedness to the West rose from $2.5 billion in 1973 to $17 billion in 1980. Poland was sinking into the mire of ever higher interest payments that absorbed the country's export earnings. At the beginning of July 1980, the government was forced yet again to raise food prices. Shipyard workers in Gdansk were ready, solidly organized in a new noncommunist labor union called **Solidarity** under the leadership of a politically astute electrician named Lech Walesa. The union staged a sit-down strike that paralyzed the shipyards. Union committees coordinated their activities from one factory to the next and succeeded in shutting down the entire economy. The government agreed to a series of union-backed reforms known as the Gdansk Accords, which, among other measures, increased civil liberties and acknowledged Solidarity's right to exist.

Within a year, Solidarity had an astounding 8 million members out of a population of 35 million. The Catholic Church lent important support to those who opposed Communist rule. Dissident intellectuals also cast their lot with the organized workers in demanding reforms. General Wojciech Jaruzelski became prime minister in February 1981, but the situation of shortages did not change appreciably. Jaruzelski attempted to

curb the union's demands for democratic government and participation in management by harsh measures: he declared martial law on 13 December 1981. Jaruzelski was trying to save the Polish Communist party by using the Polish military to crack down on the dissidents. The Soviet response was to do nothing. Soviet leaders knew that the size of the Polish protest would require a massive retaliation, which they were unwilling to undertake—especially since to do so would fly in the face of Western opinion that supported the Solidarity movement. In addition, the Soviet Union had other problems in this period: in 1979, it began a war in Afghanistan to secure Communist rule. Moscow feared that the Islamic fundamentalism at its border threatened to stir up the rapidly growing Muslim populations in six Soviet republics—Azerbaijan, Kazakhstan, Uzbekistan, Tadzhikistan, Turkmenistan, and Kirgizia. Poland, as a result, was left to Polish rule.

Martial law in Poland produced military repression. Solidarity was outlawed and Walesa was jailed. The West did not lose sight of him: in 1983, the union leader was awarded the Nobel Peace Prize for his efforts. After years of negotiations and intermittent strikes, Solidarity was legalized once again in 1989. The economy was in dire straits, and Jaruzelski knew that he needed Solidarity's cooperation: he agreed to open elections. At the polls, Solidarity candidates soundly defeated the Communist party. Poland was the first country anywhere to turn a Communist regime out of office peacefully. Yet Poland did not pull out of the Warsaw Pact. As Lech Walesa explained in 1989 on West German television, "Poland cannot forget where it is situated. You know we are in the Warsaw Pact. That cannot be changed."

The great challenge before the Solidarity government, as for the Communist regime that preceded it, was economic recovery. Inflation drove food prices up at the rate of 50 percent a month. The Polish government committed itself to freeing the zloty from state control and making it a convertible currency, one that could be bought and sold for other currencies on the international currency market, so that Polish goods could compete in world markets. Poland faced the task of earning enough foreign trade credits to alleviate its indebtedness and to justify foreign investment. In the mid-1990s, Poland continued its pursuit of a free market economy by attracting Western companies and corporations to open subsidiaries and to do business within its borders. Inflation slowed to a still high 20 to 30 percent, and a prosperous management class began emerging.

Hungary, Czechoslovakia, and Romania. In the same period as the Polish free elections, Hungary dismantled the barbed-wire fences on its Austrian border; all of its borders to the West were opened in September 1989. People wanted freedom of movement and freedom of expression. Everywhere Eastern Europeans demanded democratic institutions mod-

eled on those of Western nations. "People power" swept away Communist leaders and ousted the Communist party, many believed for good. The leader of the New Socialist Party in Hungary, Imre Pozsgay, declared: "Communism does not work. We must start again at zero." Unlike other eastern European countries, Hungary had begun experimenting cautiously with free markets and private control as early as the 1970s. As a result, Hungary was best positioned to engage in serious trade with western Europe and made the most prosperous adjustment to democratic autonomy.

Czechoslovakia's revolution began with angry university students. Singing Czech versions of protest songs such as "We Shall Overcome," student protesters were reminiscent of the student activists of 1968. They tried to give flowers to police, who responded by bludgeoning the protesters. That spark touched off a mass movement that within days drove out the Czech Communist party. Idealism and growing public sympathy were on the side of the protesters. The dissident playwright Václav Havel, released from jail just before the demonstrations began, emerged as the leader of the democratic opposition and was elected president of the new government. He became a powerful spokesperson for democratic institutions and oversaw a relatively peaceful separation of the Czech Republic from Slovakia. All of these countries underwent what were considered **"velvet revolutions,"** characterized by a lack of violence and an apparently smooth passage to a new order and the achievement of independence.

The year 1989 did not end, however, without bloody upheaval. Romania under communist dictator Nicolae Ceaucescu

■ "Nothing Lasts Forever" reads the sign hanging from the battered bust of Communist dictator Joseph Stalin being carried through the streets of Prague by Czech demonstrators celebrating the end of the Communist regime in their country.

PRESIDENT VÁCLAV HAVEL'S ADDRESS TO CZECHOSLOVAKIA, 1 JANUARY 1990

Václav Havel's (1936–) election as president of Czechoslovakia in December 1989 typified many aspects of the velvet revolutions throughout eastern Europe. A dissident under the Soviet-dominated regime, Havel spent time in prison for his political beliefs. Not a politician, he brought the sensibilities of a playwright and intellectual to the task of establishing democracy in his newly liberated country.

Focus Questions

How does Havel's inaugural speech portray the Communist regime that preceded him? What is the nature of the "decayed moral environment" he is describing? What are the principles underlying his idea of democracy? How does he convey his own moral values?

Dear fellow citizens. For the past 40 years on this day you have heard my predecessors utter different variations on the same theme, about how our country is prospering, how many more billion tons of steel we have produced, how happy we all are, how much we trust our government, and what beautiful prospects lie ahead of us. I do not think you proposed me to this office for me, of all people, to lie to you.

Our country is not prospering. The great creative and spiritual potential of our nation is not being used to its full potential. Whole sectors of industry are producing things in which no one is interested, while the things we need are in short supply.

The state, which calls itself a state of the working people, is humiliating and exploiting the workers. Our outdated economy is squandering energy, of which we are in short supply. A country which could once be proud of the standard of education of its people spends so little on education that today it occupies 72nd place in the world. We have laid waste the water and soil, the rivers and the forests that our forefathers bequeathed to us, and we have the worst environment in the whole of Europe today. Adults in our country die earlier than in most other European countries.

• • •

But not even all of that is the most important thing. The worst thing is that we are living in a decayed moral environment. We have become morally ill, because we have become accustomed to saying one thing and thinking another. We have learned not to believe in anything, not to have consideration for one another, and only to look after ourselves. Notions such as love, friendship, compassion, humility, and forgiveness have lost their depth and dimension, and for many of us they merely represent some kind of psychological idiosyncrasy, or appear to be some kind of stray relic from times past, something rather comical in the era of computers and space rockets. Few of us managed to cry out that the powerful should not be all-powerful.

Dear fellow citizens. By your will 3 days ago, as conveyed by Federal Assembly deputies, I became president of this republic. You rightly expect me to mention the tasks which I see as your president lie ahead of us.

The first is to make use of all my powers and my influence to ensure that we all come soon and with dignity to the ballot box in free elections and that this journey of ours to this historic milestone is a decent and peaceful one.

My second task is to watch over to ensure that we come to these elections as two truly sovereign nations which respect each other's interests, national identity, religious traditions, and each other's symbols. . . .

As my third task I regard my support for everything that will lead to a better position for children, the elderly, women, the sick, those involved in heavy manual work, members of ethnic minorities, and in general all citizens who are worse off than others for whatever reason. Better food or hospitals must no longer be the privilege of the powerful but must be offered to those who need them most. . . .

Perhaps you are asking what kind of republic I have in mind. My reply is this: a republic which is independent, free, and democratic, with a prospering economy and also socially just—in short a republic of the people which serves the people, and is therefore entitled to hope that the people will serve it too. I have in mind a republic of people with a well-rounded education, because without such people none of our problems—can be tackled.

One of my most distinguished predecessors began his first speech by quoting Comenius.* Allow me to end my first speech with my own paraphrase of the same statement: people, your government has returned to you!

*Comenius, the Latin name for Johan Amos Komensky (1592–1670), was one of Havel's intellectual heroes. He was a Czech churchman who sought tolerance and understanding among all religions through universal education and the spread of knowledge.

appeared to be pursuing a peaceful path. It had evaded its military responsibilities in the Warsaw Pact; it alone of the member states had refused to participate in the Czechoslovakian intervention of 1968. Yet Romania was a state that could not tolerate internal protest. In December 1989, Ceaucescu ordered his troops to fire on demonstrators. Thousands of men, women, and children were killed and buried unceremoniously in mass graves. The slaughter set off a revolution in which Ceaucescu and his wife and co-ruler, Elena, were captured, tried, and executed by a firing squad. They were charged with genocide—the slaughter of 64,000 people—and the mismanagement of the economy.

The Unification of Germany

The crumbling façade of Communist unity within the Soviet bloc was nowhere more evident than in East Germany. The German Democratic Republic (East Germany) and the German Federal Republic (West Germany), divided by the victorious Allies following World War II, continued to develop after 1968 as two separate countries with different social, economic, and political institutions. On the surface, the differences seemed insurmountable. The erection of the Berlin Wall in 1961 (see The Visual Record, pp. 900–901) cutting the city in two stood as a continual reminder of the ideological divide between East and West.

The two Germanys had been linked economically, if not politically, throughout most of the postwar period. When West Germany entered the European Community in 1957, it insisted that in matters related to trade the two Germanys were to be treated as one country. As a result, East Germany benefited from its free trade relationship with West Germany. That advantage had provided an important part of East Germany's prosperity since the 1960s. West Germany, in turn, achieved much of its prosperity through export-led growth, and it found markets in East Germany.

In the 1980s, West Germany stood as an economic giant, second in foreign trade only to the United States and far ahead of Japan. East Germany also established itself as an important trading nation—fifteenth in the world in 1975. Nevertheless, citizens in East Germany were lured by the greater prosperity of the West. The lure proved too great in the 1980s, and East Germany increasingly allowed its citizens to emigrate. The dismantling of the Berlin Wall in 1989 was

■ Reunified Germany, October 1990. Divided into zones as a consequence of its defeat in World War II, East and West Germany were reunited by peaceful means after 45 years of separate rule.

symbolic of a greater opening of borders as greater numbers of East Germans chose the West.

An East Germany with open borders could no longer survive as its citizens poured into the promised land of the West in record numbers. The West German government intervened

BALANCE SHEET: EAST AND WEST GERMANY ON THE EVE OF UNIFICATION

East Germany built the strongest economy in the Soviet bloc, but its standard of living lagged far behind that of West Germany, creating challenges for the unified German state after 1990.

	Federal Republic of Germany (West)	**German Democratic Republic (East)**
Population	61 million	17 million
Life Expectancy	Men, 71.2 years; women, 78.1 years	Men, 69.5 years; women, 75.4 years
Gross National Product	$1.12 trillion	$207.2 billion
Public Spending on Education	9.4% of all government expenditures	5.5% of all government expenditures
New Books Published	50,903 volumes	5636 volumes

Sources: *Statistical Yearbook,* UNESCO, 1988; *Demographic Yearbook,* United Nations; CIA *World Factbook,* 1988.

to assist East Germany in shoring up its badly faltering economy; the West German deutsche mark was substituted for the East German currency. Monetary union prefigured political unification. In October 1990, Germany became a single, united nation once again.

Germans represent the largest nationality in Europe west of Russia. Other Europeans feared the prospect of a united Germany, although publicly European leaders endorsed the principle of the self-determination of peoples. In addition, western Europeans were troubled by the impact a united Germany might have on plans for European unification in the European Union. Not least of all, Germans themselves feared reunification. Former East Germans were wary about marginalization and second-class citizenship, while West Germans worried that their poor cousins from the east would act as a brake on West Germany's sustained economic expansion.

Russia and the New Republics

As eastern and central European nations were choosing self-rule and greater independence from the Soviet Union, the Soviet Union's own Communist party faced a dilemma. How could party rule and centralization be coordinated with the demands for freedom and autonomy that Gorbachev's own reforms fostered?

To gain credibility and backing, Gorbachev supported the formation of new parliamentary bodies, including a 2250-member Congress of People's Deputies in 1988. Yet the new Congress soon became the forum for attacks on the Communist party and the KGB. In March 1989, in the first free elections held in the Soviet Union since 1917, Communist party officials suffered further reversals. Early in 1990, Gorbachev ended the Party's constitutional monopoly

of power; the Party now no longer played a leading role in Soviet political life. New political parties proliferated, some defending the old order but many demanding a total break with the past and with Communist ideology and programs.

Among Gorbachev's harshest critics was his former ally and supporter, the former Moscow Party leader Boris N. Yeltsin, who began in 1987 to criticize Gorbachev's caution in implementing reforms. Later, as the popularly elected president of the Russian Republic in 1990, Yeltsin called for a true democracy and decisive economic action.

Aware of his precarious political position, Gorbachev appeared to retrench by increasing control over the media and by attempting to consolidate his base of power. As a result of the attempts, many believed that the regime was becoming authoritarian. Gorbachev was clearly walking a fine line in attempting to maintain stability, yet he was making no one happy—neither Communist party hard-liners nor Western-oriented supporters of capitalism.

The shocking end to the Gorbachev experiment came in August 1991. A quasi-military council of Communist hard-liners seized power in order to restore Communist rule and reverse democratic reforms. Gorbachev was taken prisoner in his vacation home in the Crimea. Soviet citizens from the Baltic republics to Siberia protested the takeover, and tens of thousands of Muscovites poured into the streets to defy the tanks and troops of the rebel government. Three people were killed outside Russia's parliament building, which had become a rallying point for the protesters. The timing of the coup was probably determined by the fact that Gorbachev was scheduled to sign a new union treaty with nine of the republics the day following his house arrest, which would have effectively broken up the Soviet Empire.

Boris Yeltsin became a hero overnight, publicly defying the plotters, rallying popular support behind him, and helping

■ The Big Mac comes to Moscow. McDonald's opened its first Soviet fast-food outlet in 1990, just a few blocks from the Kremlin. Muscovites stood in long lines for milkshakes, fries, and the "Bolshoi Mak."

convince Soviet army troops to disobey orders to attack the White House, as the parliament building in Moscow is called. After only two days, the coup d'état failed; Gorbachev returned to Moscow and banned the Communist party. Although Gorbachev retained his title of Soviet president, his prestige had been seriously damaged by the coup and by the challenge of Yeltsin's new dominance as a popular hero. In the national elections for the Congress of People's Deputies that followed, Boris Yeltsin, who had been dismissed as the head of the Moscow party in 1987, garnered 89 percent of the popular vote. As Yeltsin's star was on the rise, the Soviet Union was now in full collapse.

Economic Challenges.

Embarking on a drive toward Westernization and playing catch-up with capitalist nations, liberal reformers in Russia pressed after August 1991 for pri-

■ Economic problems, including high prices and shortages of food and goods, plague post–Soviet Union Russia. Here a woman tries to exchange a used sweater for fish at a flea market in Moscow.

vatization of industry and the lifting of price controls. There was hope inside and outside Russia that the new state would easily enter the capitalist marketplace. The long lines in front of stores disappeared. But inflation ominously galloped to new heights, wiping out savings and pensions overnight. The black market, always in the shadows even in the most repressed of times, emerged boldly as a corrupt "mafia," and its people became the new business leaders of Russia. New markets relied on dollars, and neither banks nor police had the power to stem illegal activities. Visitors to St. Petersburg (the former Leningrad) could ride in taxis whose meters registered the fare in dollars and could eat in restaurants in sections reserved for dollar-paying customers where the service and the food were better—all violations of government policy and law, because dealing in dollars was outlawed. The combined crises of inflation and rule by a gangster elite weakened the barely emergent market economy and undermined the Russian ruble, whose value crashed in October 1994. After 2000, due to soaring export revenues from oil, Russians experienced a rise in real income. The ruble appreciated. By 2005, according to the World Bank, poverty was in steady decline to 12 percent of the population, from 30 percent in 1994.

DOCUMENT

Scientists on Russia's Economy and Environment

The Nationalities Problem.

A crucial element in understanding the end of the Soviet Union was the **nationalities problem** within its borders—the claim to self-determination made by Soviet minorities. The Soviet Union listed 102 separate nationalities in its 1979 census. Twenty-two of those nationalities had populations of one million or more people. That very diversity contributed to the disintegration of the Soviet Union from within.

The three major areas of nationalist conflict—Central Asia, Armenia, and the Baltic states—had been voicing grievances against the Soviet state since the 1920s. The protests of the 1980s differed from earlier outcries because a new and educated urban elite, formed after World War II, were now the protesters. Moscow relied on those groups of university-educated and upwardly mobile professionals to further its economic reforms. The groups also became the driving force behind demands for nationalist reforms.

Ethnic minorities, especially in the Soviet Baltic republics of Latvia, Lithuania, and Estonia, threatened the dominance of Party rule in favor of immediate self-determination. Endorsing diversity of opinion, individual rights, and freedom as the bases of good government, Gorbachev now had to deal with vocal nationalities who took him at his word. Large-scale riots erupted in Lithuania over demands for nationalist rights. In 1988, Estonians demanded the right of veto over any law passed in Moscow. The Russian minority in Estonia protested attacks and prejudicial treatment in the Estonian republic. In the same year, outright violence erupted in Azerbaijan as tens of thousands of Armenians took to the streets to demand the return of the Armenian enclave of Nagorno-Karabakh, incorporated into Azerbaijan in 1921. In the Azerbaijan capital of Baku, the center of Russia's oil-producing region, demonstrators demanded greater autonomy for their republic and the accountability of their deputies in Moscow. Violence between Azerbaijanis and Armenians resulted in 32 deaths and the displacement of tens of thousands. The state upheaval climaxed in December 1988, when an earthquake in Armenia killed 25,000 people. Soviet troops were placed in the area, ostensibly to deal with the aftermath of the natural disaster.

In 1986, university students in the Central Asian republic of Kazakhstan incited two days of demonstrations and rioting over the removal of a corrupt local leader who was replaced with a Russian Party official. The Soviet government's attempts to clean up politics in the area betrayed a clumsy disregard for ethnic issues and seemed at odds with Gorbachev's commitment to decentralization. Crimean Tatars, who had been exiled in Islamic fundamentalist Kazakhstan since World War II, agitated for a return home.

The Breakaway Republics Lead the Way.   One by one, all 15 of the Soviet republics proclaimed their independence, following the lead of the breakaway Baltic republics of Estonia, Lithuania, and Latvia. Having failed to agree on a new plan for union, Gorbachev and the leaders of ten republics transferred authority to an emergency State Council in September 1991 until a plan could be devised. By the end of the year, the Soviet Union was faced with serious food shortages and was bankrupt, unable to pay its employees and dependent on the financial backing provided by Yeltsin as head of the Russian state. Rejecting all Soviet authority, Russia, Belarus, and Ukraine joined together in December 1991 to form the Commonwealth of Independent States (CIS). Eight other republics followed their lead. The Soviet Union thereby came to its end on 21 December 1991 with the resignation of Mikhail Gorbachev, who had become a man without a state to rule. Russian President Yeltsin moved into Gorbachev's Soviet presidential offices at the Kremlin.

In the elections of December 1993, a post-Soviet constitution was approved. Ominously, ultranationalists became a troubling presence in Russian politics as they combined forces with communists and other groups to receive almost 50 percent of

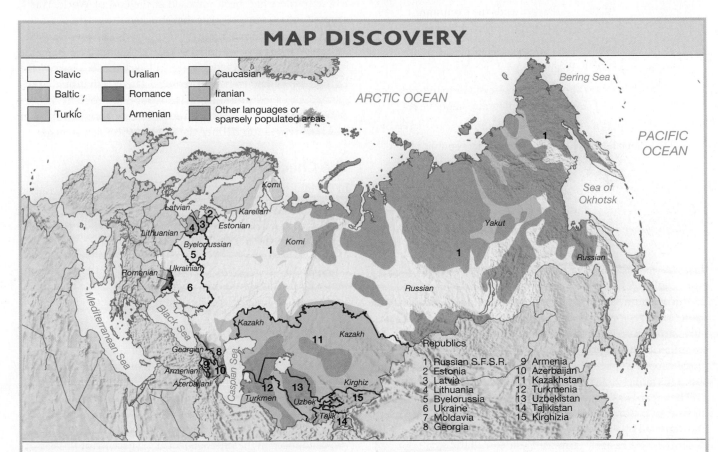

MAP DISCOVERY

Slavic · Baltic · Turkic · Uralian · Romance · Armenian · Caucasian · Iranian · Other languages or sparsely populated areas

Republics

1) Russian S.F.S.R.	9) Armenia
2) Estonia	10) Azerbaijan
3) Latvia	11) Kazakhstan
4) Lithuania	12) Turkmenia
5) Byelorussia	13) Uzbekistan
6) Ukraine	14) Tajikistan
7) Moldavia	15) Kirghizia
8) Georgia	

Republics of the Soviet Union

The Soviet Union broke up into 15 independent nations, which embraced a variety of ethnic groups. Note the correspondence between ethnicity/language and independent nation status. What new republics have only one language? In the nation of Uzbekistan how many ethnicities and languages are there? How many different ethnic groups remained in the new Russian state?

the votes cast. Yeltsin's grasp of the reigns of power slipped as he faced challenges both from inside and outside the government. In the vacuum of power that resulted from the collapse of Soviet rule, regions operated autonomously and local rule was often supreme. After easily winning the national election in the summer of 1996, Yeltsin began his second term in failing health, hidden from public view, and under a heavy cloud of doubt about his ability to lead.

The year 1989 marked a watershed in the history of European politics. The beginnings of transformation were first signaled by the Soviet Union, followed by dramatic events in central and eastern Europe. The democratic tide appeared irreversible as symbols of freedom and cooperation proliferated throughout the former Warsaw Pact countries. One million people joined hands in a widely publicized event to form a 370-mile-long human chain that stretched across the Soviet Baltic republics of Estonia, Latvia, and Lithuania in protest against Soviet annexation in 1940. Other bodies defied borders, as in September 1989, when East Germans began a mass exodus into West Germany, voting with their feet for economic prosperity and democracy. Poland and Hungary opted for democratic regimes, and Bulgarians ended the 35-year reign of the dictator Todor Zhivkov and endorsed parliamentary government. Tens of thousands of Czech demonstrators in the capital city of Prague typified the peaceful "velvet revolution" of the democratic movement that swept through eastern and central Europe as they poured into the streets to sing songs about freedom and cheer their new heroes, dissidents persecuted and jailed under the former communist regimes.

ETHNIC CONFLICT AND NATIONALISM

Yet freedom was not the only force unleashed with the collapse of communism. Ugly battles based on long-standing grievances erupted. Groups intent on autonomy and independence vied with each other over territories and borders. Chechnya struggled to be free of Russian rule. The Balkans, where borders had been imposed at the end of World War I, erupted into genocidal strife that shocked the world.

In Bosnia, where a bloody war dragged on for years in the former Yugoslavia, the term **ethnic cleansing** laid bare the barbarity and genocide that were still very much a part of the Europe of the late twentieth century. The international arena seemed bereft of solutions to the troubling problem of borders at the beginning of the twenty-first century as terrorism and state repression defined the Chechen-Russian struggle.

The Chechen Challenge

In the midst of its own crisis of rule, in December 1994, Russia committed itself and 30,000 Russian troops to a war with one of its ethnic minorities, the secessionist Chechens, who had declared themselves independent of Russia in 1991. Chechnya, a territory of plains and peaks in the Caucasus, had also posed a problem for the former Russian Empire. In the nineteenth century, Muslims of the area waged a series of what they called "holy wars" to fend off the Russian invaders but to no avail.

Russian Invasion, 1994–1996. Following in the footsteps of their forebears and in a long tradition of resistance, secessionist Chechens challenged Russian rule that appeared insensitive to local needs. In December 1994, Russia launched a full-scale invasion, seizing control of the Chechen capital of Grozny. After almost two years of battle, Russian officials estimated that the death toll stood at 80,000, with some 240,000 wounded. The war was denounced in the international arena because of Russian attacks against the civilian population. Reportedly, 60 percent of schools, kindergartens, and nurseries were partly or fully destroyed. An estimated 80 percent of the war dead were civilian. Russian warplanes bombed rebel-occupied villages, and thousands of refugees fled their homes in search of shelter. By the summer of 1996, Russia appeared to have lost the war, despite the fact that it possessed the largest army in Europe deployed

■ Chechen women and Russian soldiers' mothers united in a peace march to try to bring an end to the war in Chechnya. Russian troops halted the women, who were on their way to the village of Samashki in western Chechnya, the site of an alleged massacre by Russian soldiers.

against an enemy estimated to be about 4000. Russian estimates were undoubtedly low, but the disparity in forces was real. Despite the disparity, Chechen rebels forced the withdrawal of Russian troops by the mid-1990s.

The peace agreement proposed in the summer of 1996 called for a referendum in Chechnya in the year 2001 for the purpose of determining the future of the republic. But attempts at implementation of a peace plan demonstrated the fissures in Russian leadership. Kremlin officials expressed dismay that the move toward Chechen autonomy threatened "Russian territorial integrity."

Renewed War and Terrorism.   In the summer of 1999 conflict again escalated into open warfare because of terrorist bombings of apartment buildings and barracks in and around Moscow that killed hundreds. The terrorist deeds were attributed to Chechen rebels. Russia had important economic motives for subduing the runaway republic. Chechnya's location was central to the oil pipeline routes near the Caspian Sea. Several former Soviet states had begun building a new pipeline in the 1990s in order to circumvent the Russian supply and to sell directly to Western buyers.

Violence continued as Chechens protested the presence of Russian troops. Following terrorist attacks in the United States on 11 September 2001, the Russians escalated their war against terrorism in Chechnya. The Chechens responded with more terrorist tactics within the Russian state. Atrocities against Russian civilians escalated in 2004. Plane bombings on two flights leaving Moscow and the killing of 339 hostages held in

a schoolhouse, half of whom were children, provoked global denunciation. Russian president Putin responded to these atrocities by limiting democracy and civil liberties for the Russian population, a move that unleashed popular discontent within Russia and international criticism. By 2007 Russia appeared to have the upper hand against Chechen insurgency.

War in the Balkans

Hopes for social transformation and liberal economic reforms were highest for Yugoslavia in 1989 with the waning of Soviet power and the end of the Cold War. Yugoslavia, after all, was the success story of the Soviet bloc with open borders and its escape from the Stalinist grasp in 1948. Many Europeans believed it was moving toward a market economy with its liberal economic policies and trade agreements.

Yugoslavia was a federation of six people's republics, with Serbia, Croatia, and Bosnia and Herzegovina the three largest in descending order. In 1991 festering differences erupted in civil war between Serbs and Croats, as Serbian nationalists overran multiethnic Bosnia and Herzegovina in a bid for territorial aggrandizement of Serbia. Serbia and Croatia were long-standing rival enemies with a history of hostility that had been masked by their federated status in the Yugoslav state.

The History of Ethnic Differences.   The question of national independence in the Balkans had caused war before in the twentieth century. A Serbian nationalist intent on independence for Serbia from Austria-Hungary assassinated an

■ Bosnian soldiers in 1996 show the solidarity of their cause with the Muslim "holy war" by wearing headbands with Muslim phrases and chanting their readiness to die in Allah's name in pursuit of Bosnian independence.

Austrian archduke in 1914, sparking the outbreak of World War I (See Chapter 26, p. 777). The nation of Yugoslavia had been created in 1918 by consolidating different ethnic groups as part of the peace that settled the war. The divide between the Serbs and Croats was partly identified with religious differences—the Croats were historically Catholic, the Serbs Orthodox—but for the most part, their enmity was based on the competing claims over the South Slavic lands, Bosnia and Herzegovina, that were part of the former Ottoman and Austro-Hungarian empires.

Conflicting territorial claims of the Serbs and Croatians were considerably exacerbated by two facts. First, a large number of Serbs lived in Croatia, and Croatians were present in the Serbian-claimed lands of Bosnia. Under Tito's rule, ethnic differences were held in check. After 1991, land claims were considerably complicated by the mixed population of Bosnia and Herzegovina. Second, another group, neither Catholic nor Orthodox but Muslim, amounting to 9 percent of the population of the former Yugoslavia and a majority of the Bosnian population, got caught in the crossfire of the war between Serbs and Croats and became a target for massacre and atrocities by the Serbs.

In 1992, the Serbian army evicted 750,000 Muslim civilians from their homes in Bosnia. Serb forces also continued to bomb civilians in the Bosnian capital of Sarajevo. It later came to light that in 1992 Serb leaders had authorized a policy of ethnic cleansing—including concentration camps, rape, and starvation—against Muslims. In 1995, the Serb military was also responsible for the mass killings of Muslims from Srebrenica. Such barbarity contributed heavily to forging a strong sense of national identity among Bosnian Muslims, who controlled the Bosnian army and the presidency.

Beginning in 1992, Muslims from other parts of the world, including Afghanistan, Iran, Turkey, Pakistan, and Arab countries such as Egypt, volunteered to fight alongside the soldiers of the Bosnian army as Muslim holy warriors or ***moujahedeen*** against the Serb nationalists. Used as shock troops by Bosnia commanders, they quickly earned a reputation as fierce fighters who inspired religious fervor among the Bosnian army.

In the course of the war, with more than a quarter of a million lives lost and two million people displaced, the Bosnia conflict was recognized as the bloodiest ground war in Europe in 50 years, and Bosnian Serb leaders were indicted as war criminals. The United Nations placed forces in Bosnia on a peace-keeping mission, which allowed it to take neither side in the war. NATO intervened against the Serbian attempt to overrun Bosnia after the outbreak of hostilities, and, in September 1995 NATO stepped up the bombing of Bosnian Serb military installations and Serbian-held positions in Bosnia with the policy of avoiding civilian targets.

The **Dayton Peace Accords** brokered by the United States brought Bosnian, Croat, and Serb leaders together in Ohio in November and December 1995. As part of the commitment to

■ Balkans. New republics, federations, and sectors were carved out of the former Yugoslavia in the 1990s, with conflicts still unresolved at the turn of the new century.

the accord, the Clinton Administration sent 20,000 U.S. troops to join the 60,000 NATO troops already present to help enforce the peace. The aim of the Accords was to create a unified country in Bosnia while recognizing ethnic interests. The settlement called for a shared three-person presidency chosen by free elections. In the judgment of some Western diplomats, such an arrangement offered little hope of a stable and enduring peace. Despite the Accord, Bosnia remained a partitioned country, with Croats, Serbs, and Muslims still struggling for separate rule.

Kosovo and the Ongoing Conflict in Eastern Europe. Yet another arena of bloodshed opened up in 1998. Kosovo, one of the six former Yugoslav republics, had been known as the "autonomous province" of Serbia. With the breakup of Yugoslavia, there had been movement toward an independent Kosovo, and even talk of a "Greater Albania," which would reunify Albanians in Kosovo, western Macedonia, and Albania. Checking attempts at Kosovo independence, Serbia proceeded to strip it of its autonomous status after 1990. In addition, there was overwhelming evidence that the Serb state intended to drive more than one million Kosovo Albanians from the province. The Kosovo Liberation Army responded with guerrilla actions against the Serbs.

Civil rights abuses and atrocities against Kosovo Albanians by Kosovo Serbs shocked the world into action in 1998. On

the night of 24 March 1999, NATO forces began attacking Serbian targets in Kosovo in a massive military campaign of air strikes that lasted for almost 11 weeks. As the lead partner, the United States justified an unpopular war at home by promising not to commit ground troops in battle. The air war succeeded, and United Nations peace-keeping forces, including U.S. troops, entered Kosovo in June 1999. The Serbs were probably responsible for the deaths of at least 10,000 and the expulsion of 800,000 Kosovo Albanians. With the defeat of Serb forces, Kosovo Albanians took the place of their Serb oppressors and committed new atrocities, now under the nose of peace-keeping forces, with the aim of driving non-Albanians out of the province. Intolerance and the desire for revenge boded ill for the future of peace in the region.

The new Serbia remained a tightly controlled state economy. Privatization was unconstitutional in Serbia. Former communist officials continued to run things, as before, as feudal fiefdoms for the profit of a few. Bosnia had no economy at all, and foreign investors, so necessary for economic recovery and trade, avoided putting funds in a country lacking financial institutions and a market orientation. In 2002, Serbia and Montenegro, both part of the former Yugoslavia, began discussions that resulted in the formation of a federation of the two republics, the new state of Serbia and Montenegro, in 2003.

Albania, a tiny nation of 3.5 million people, as Europe's poorest nation, with the highest infant mortality rate and the lowest life expectancy rate in Europe, faced the challenges of the post-communist era with its industrial infrastructure in ruins, its government in shambles, and its environment polluted. Without the authoritarian control of communist rule, Albania disintegrated into a primitive society ruled by bandits, blood feuds, and vendettas.

Other eastern European states also were riddled with ethnic troubles—including Czechs and Slovaks, the Hungarians and Romanians over the border region of Transylvania, and the Bulgarians and Turks in Bulgaria.

THE WEST IN THE GLOBAL COMMUNITY

The phenomenal growth and prosperity of western Europe came up against a new set of harsh realities in the 1970s with skyrocketing oil prices, inflation, and recession. Western European nations saw greater cooperation as the best response in world markets dominated by the American superpower. A key component in achieving growth was not only the U.S. capital that helped fuel recovery, but also the availability to western European economies of a floating labor pool of workers from southern Europe and from former colonies in Asia and Africa. The permanent presence of foreign workers, many of them unemployed or erratically employed during the economic downturns of the 1970s and 1980s, came to be seen as a problem by welfare-state leaders and politicians of the New Right. Europe's new working class became the brunt of racist antagonism.

With the goal of reviving the economy in the 1980s the 12 member states of the European Economic Community devoted themselves to making western Europe competitive as a bloc in world markets. They hoped that by uniting they could serve as a counterweight to American economic hegemony in the West. At the same time that Russian satellites in eastern Europe were breaking free of Soviet control and attempting to strike out on their own, the nations of western Europe were negotiating a new unity based on a single market and centralized policy making.

Yet at the beginning of the twenty-first century, social and economic problems persisted, the costs of the welfare state rose, terrorism tyrannized democratic societies, and a new nationalism vied with cooperation across borders.

European Union and the American Superpower

In 1957, the founders of the European Economic Community, Robert Schuman and Jean Monnet, envisioned the idea of a United States of Europe. Both men perceived that Europe's only hope of competing in a new world system was through unity. The European Community (EC) had been created in 1967 by merging the three transnational European bodies—the European Coal and Steel Community, the European Economic Community, and the European Atomic Energy Community. It operated with its own commission, parliament, and council of ministers, though it had little real power over the operations of member states. In 1974, a European Council was created within the European Community, made up of heads of government who met three times a year. Almost since its inception, the European Community has been committed to European integration.

The Politics of Oil. In 1973, the international politics of oil prices provoked an economic crisis followed by a recession. The Organization of Petroleum Exporting Countries (OPEC) cut back production and forced price increases. Western European countries depended heavily on imported oil, which they used to fuel their prosperity through the early 1970s. As the crisis abated, competition and efficiency reemerged as priorities within the EC. Europeans were well aware that the United States and Japan had surged ahead after the 1973 crisis. The Common Market had been successful in promoting European growth and integration since 1958. Western European leaders realized that integration was the only defense against the permanent loss of markets and dwindling profits. In unity there was strength.

Toward a Single Europe. In 1985, the EC negotiated the Single European Act. The 12 members of the EC intended to eliminate internal barriers and to create a huge open market among the member states with common external tariff policies. In addition, the elimination of internal frontier controls with a single-format passport was intended to make travel easier and to avoid shipping delays at frontiers, thereby lowering costs. An international labor market based on standardized requirements for certification and interchangeable job qualifications would result. The easier movement of capital to areas where profitability was greatest was encouraged. All aspects of trade and communication, down to electrical plugs and sockets, had to be standardized. The goal behind the planning was to make the EC think and act as a single country. Supporters compared it to the 50 individual American states participating in one nation.

In 1989, there were 320 million European citizens of the 12 countries of the EC: the original Common Market six of France, West Germany, Belgium, the Netherlands, Luxembourg, and Italy were joined by Britain, Denmark, and Ireland in 1973, Greece in 1981, and Portugal and Spain in 1986.

Plans for European economic integration moved dramatically forward in October 1991 when the 12-nation European Community and the 7 nations of the European Free Trade Association (EFTA) joined forces to form a new common market to be known as the European Economic Area. The EFTA countries that joined forces with the EC included

Austria, Finland, Iceland, Liechtenstein, Norway, Sweden, and Switzerland. Several of the EFTA nations announced plans to join the EC as well. The European Economic Area constituted the world's largest trading bloc, stretching from the Arctic Circle to the Mediterranean and consisting of about 380 million consumers. The nations of the EFTA agreed to abide by the EC's plans for economic integration and adopted the vast array of laws and regulations that governed the EC.

The European Union. Meeting in Maastricht, the Netherlands, in December 1991, the heads of the 12 EC countries ratified a treaty momentous for the European Union. They agreed that a common currency, the **euro,** would replace the national currencies of eligible nations, and that a single central banking system, known as the European Monetary Institute, would guide member nations in reducing inflation rates and budget deficits. Economic union would be reinforced by political union, with member states sharing a common European defense system and common social policies regulating immigration and labor practices. In that sense, the new **European Union (EU)** was intended as something more than the European Community (EC), which had been primarily an economic entity to promote free trade. In the words of French President François Mitterrand the goals of the European Union were: "One currency, one culture, one social area, one environment."

On 1 January 2002, Europeans in 12 of 15 member nations began using the euro. The new hard currency replaced national monetary units including the French franc, the German mark, the Spanish peseta, the Greek drachma, and the Dutch guilder. Hailed as the European Union's boldest achievement, the new currency was intended to solidify the basis of integrated European markets and be competitive in international markets against the dollar. Within two months of the introduction of the euro, at the end of February 2002, the member nations of the European Union held a convention for the purpose of considering the creation of a Europe-wide constitution.

DOCUMENT

European Money
Before the Euro

Britain was the most reluctant of the member states at the prospect of European integration. British negotiators strongly resisted plans for monetary union because they feared losing national sovereignty rights. Nonetheless, Prime Minister Margaret Thatcher and her successor, John Major, solidly committed Great Britain to the EU. As Thatcher explained it: "Our destiny is in Europe." In addition to resisting monetary union, British public opinion polls reflected cynicism over the 1991 Maastricht negotiations and a social policy affecting working hours, minimum wages, and conditions of employment throughout Europe. Prime Minister Tony Blair continued to be committed to the European Union, although the British pursued a separate path to full membership.

By 2007, the inclusion of eastern European nations brought EU membership to 27. Some planners were wary

■ A young boy in Nicosia, Cyprus, waves a European Union flag to celebrate entrance of Cyprus into the EU on 1 May 2004.

about the prospect of including eastern European nations whose troubled economies, they feared, would dilute the economic strength of the EU. Most controversial of all was the bid by Turkey begun in earnest in 2005 to become a full member by 2013. As a predominantly Muslim nation, its attempt was met with criticism and concern. In its English-language homepage, the European Union explained its enlargement in this way: "In taking this decision, the European Union was not simply increasing its surface area and its population. It was putting an end to the split in our continent—the rift that, from 1945 onwards, separated the free world from the Communist world."

The plan for European unity affected more than just economics. Education, too, faced standardization of curricula and requirements for degrees. There were proposals for a common European history textbook that, in place of national perspectives, would emphasize the values of a single political entity in its discussion of battles, wars, social change, and culture. The EU also had its own flag—a circle of twelve gold stars on a field of blue—and its own anthem, Beethoven's "Ode to Joy."

Original EU member in 1992

Became member in 1995

Became member in 2004

■ European Union. The most stable and prosperous European nations formed the 12 original member states of the European Union in 1992, soon joined by 3 additional members. These members agreed to share a common currency, economic and social policies, and planning. In 2004, 10 new nations joined the EU. By 2007 there were 27 member nations and 3 candidate countries (Croatia, Macedonia, and Turkey).

Export-producing nations, including Japan and the United States, expressed concerns over "Fortress Europe," that is, Europe as a global trading bloc with a common external tariff policy that would exclude them. A united Europe, with the world's largest volume of trade and the highest productivity, would constitute a formidable presence in the world arena. In fact, the EU became the largest customer for American products. In addition, Ford, IBM, Digital, Boeing, Unisys, Otis,

General Electric, Pratt & Whitney, McDonnell Douglas, and Pacific Telesis were just a few of the American companies that entered into partnerships and joint ventures with EU firms. The possibility of the emergence of a truly global marketplace seemed, paradoxically, more likely with the creation of the EU and other regional associations throughout the world. By fostering market economies, economic competition, political stability of democratic institutions, as well as common political, economic, and social policies, the EU offered a counterbalance to the void filled by the end of the Cold War and the promise of peace based on productivity and trade.

A New Working Class: Foreign Workers

Foreign workers played an important role in the industrial expansion of western Europe beginning in the 1950s. Western European nations needed cheap, unskilled laborers. Great Britain, France, and West Germany were the chief labor-importing countries; their economic growth in the fifties and sixties had been made possible by readily available pools of cheap foreign labor. The chief labor-exporting countries included Portugal, Turkey, Algeria, Italy, and Spain, whose sluggish economic performance spurred workers to seek employment opportunities beyond national borders. Great Britain also imported workers from the West Indies, Ireland, India, Pakistan, Africa, and southern Europe.

Migrant employment was by definition poorly paid, unskilled or semiskilled manual work. Italian workers in West Germany, for example, commonly worked factory night shifts that German workers refused. France employed a large number of foreign laborers in agriculture, public works, commerce, and engineering. Foreign male workers found employment on construction sites all over western Europe. Foreign women worked in domestic service, personal care, and factories.

Commonly, married men migrated without their families, with the goal of earning cash to send home to those left behind. Most immigrants who came looking for jobs carried with them the "myth of return," the belief that they would someday go back home. For the most part, however, foreign workers stayed in the host country. Irish workers were alone in returning to their home country.

Working Conditions and Rights. The lot of foreign workers was difficult and sometimes dangerous. Foreign workers were often herded together in crowded living quarters, socially marginalized, and identified with the degrading work they performed. Street cleaning and refuse collection in France were jobs typically performed by black Africans. Foreign workers were frequently denied the rights of citizenship and subjected to the vagaries of legislation. In economic downturns they were the first to be laid off. Yet the obligations of foreign workers to send money back home to aged parents, spouses, children, and siblings persisted. Children who resided in the host country with their foreign-worker parents suffered from severe identity problems, experiencing discrimination in schools in the countries in which they were born and with which they identified. A rising incidence of violence among second-generation Algerian adolescents in France, for example, indicated tensions and a new kind of rebellion among migrant populations in the 1970s and 1980s. Third and fourth generations of foreign workers born on West German soil were refused the rights of citizenship and denied the possibility of naturalization.

Women endured special problems within the foreign work force. Between 1964 and 1974, the majority of Portuguese immigrants to France came with families, but there were few social services to support them on their arrival. Dependable child care was either too expensive or unavailable to female workers with children. Increasing numbers of single women began migrating to western Europe independently of their households. Like men, they worked in order to send money back home. Often housed

■ Indian immigrants in France sewing in a sweatshop. Immigrant workers in European countries took low-paying, menial jobs. They faced resentment from xenophobic native Europeans.

MADE IN JAPAN

In the years following World War II a revolution was taking shape in manufacturing and marketing that would change the world. The revolution began in an unlikely place—war-crippled Japan—and it was all the more startling because, with the rise of Japanese industry, American and European producers were left behind in key electronics markets that came to symbolize the new consumption.

Japan's economic competitiveness commanded notice beginning in the late nineteenth century because it combined the new industrialization techniques of the West with traditional values of family and nation. The Japanese were influenced certainly by modes of production in the West and rapidly advanced their own productivity through the 1930s and the wartime economy.

The rise of the Sony Corporation provides a good case study of the Japanese transformation. Sony's founders, according to the company's own history, were committed from the very beginning to capturing a mass consumer market and appropriating whatever tools available to do so. Working in less than optimum surroundings in an abandoned department store, Sony's founders stressed the importance of the team in production. After failed beginnings in rice cookers and heating pads but greater success with tape recorders, Sony struck on the radio and its potential in a mass market. Sony was the first to develop transistor radios for the home by applying a technology developed in the West and available to but not utilized by American and European producers. The Japanese company developed technical superiority and soon became a leader in the world market. The great success of Japanese industry resided in its ability to mass produce quality products at cheap prices.

How were the Japanese able to achieve such resounding success in the second half of the twentieth century? One way, of course, was by the appropriation of lessons learned in the West. Japanese industrial leaders visited the United States regularly, met with American business leaders, visited assembly lines, and studied management as a science. One American in particular, W. Edwards Deming, became a Japanese hero because of his seminars taught in Japan during the occupation on "statistical quality control." In 1960 the Japanese government created a prize in Deming's honor which is awarded annually to industries for their use of consumer research in improving the design of products and production. Sony, Matsushita, and Toyota are just a few of the industries

THE
WEST
AND
THE
WIDER
WORLD

■ Sony TR-55 from ca. 1955, Japan's first all-transistor radio.

■ Toyota automobile construction at the Motomachi factory, Japan, ca. 1960s.

that employed Deming's methods and those of other Western consultants who favored "total quality management." Such a total approach to the production process was not utilized by Western competitors until it was rediscovered in the West in the 1980s, thanks to Japan's success story.

In its unique culture of the workplace, the Japanese method put emphasis on the values of the individual worker and the importance of working in small teams. Management fully participated in production and respected employees' opinions and insights. The founders of Sony launched their enterprise immediately after the war by treating their employees like family, providing daily rice to them for their lunch breaks, and organizing joint recreation and vacations. Such emphasis on family and the values of caring

and responsibility for employees resonated strongly with Japanese culture and traditions. The emphasis in this new workplace culture was on the participation of the employees and the needs of the customers. Explicitly rejected was the Ford assembly-line model of mass-production as dehumanizing and destructive of quality in the goods produced. The Japanese innovators appropriated selectively from Western industrial theory and models and applied this knowledge to their own strategies.

So successful were the management innovations of the Japanese producers that Western industries began sending observers to study Japanese methods. Japanese auto producers in the United States at the present time use their own production methods based on Japanese cultural values with their

American employees. And industrialists from the European Union continue to send their business leaders to learn "the Japanese way." Perhaps no industry better demonstrates the two-way cultural exchange of ideas, institutions, and practices than consumer electronics in the global economy. Japan succeeded in dominating world markets because it understood that production and success must be rooted in the culture and values of its own people.

QUESTIONS FOR DISCUSSION

How did Japan develop new goods and new markets in the 1950s? Why was the mass-marketing of small electronics so well suited to postwar Japan? In what ways did the United States and western Europe learn lessons from innovations in Japanese production?

in dormitories provided by their employers, Spanish and Portuguese women factory workers in Germany and France were isolated from the communities of their compatriots.

Opposition and Restrictions.

Opposition to the presence of foreign workers was often expressed in ultranationalist rhetoric and usually flared up in periods of economic reversals. Right-wing politicians sometimes complained that foreign workers deprived native workers of jobs. That argument seemed baseless, since many of the jobs filled by migrants were spurned by native workers as too menial, too poorly paid, or too physically demanding. Opposition to foreign workers nonetheless became virulent. In 1986 in France, the xenophobic National Front campaigned on a platform of "France for the French" and captured 10 percent of the vote in national elections. Racism was out in the open in Western countries that had depended on a foreign labor force for their prosperity. Arab and black African workers in France resorted to work

stoppages to protest police discrimination and identity controls that they likened to the yellow Stars of David that Jews had been required to wear in Nazi Germany. In 1996, the French government chartered planes to return undocumented Africans to Africa. Riots in Great Britain in 1980 and 1981, particularly in the London ghetto of Brixton, were motivated by racial discrimination against blacks, severe cuts in social welfare spending, and deteriorating working conditions.

Before 1973, most countries in western Europe, including Great Britain, had actively encouraged foreign labor. After that date, restrictions became the order of the day. It is no coincidence that restrictions on foreign labor followed the 1973 oil crisis. Western governments enforced new conservative policies throughout the 1970s and 1980s aimed at keeping out third-world refugees. Exceptions were made for political refugees from eastern Europe. Racial considerations lay beneath the surface of discussions about political asylum. In 1989, the British government sent back to Vietnam the "boat

IMAGE DISCOVERY

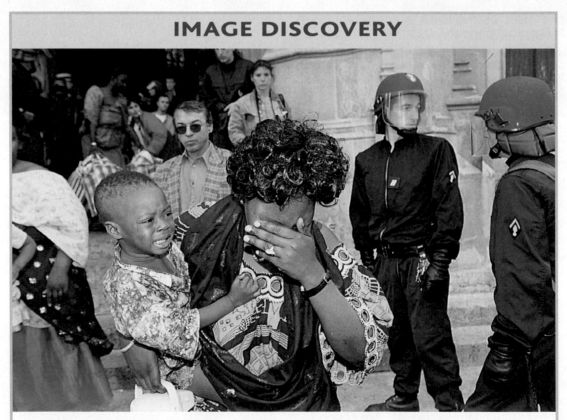

Immigrant Rights

A weeping African woman and her child leave St. Bernard Church after riot police stormed the church to disperse the 300 African immigrants who had gathered there to protest French treatment of immigrants. Many of those arrested in this 1996 encounter were found to be "without papers" and deported. Note in this photograph the contrast between riot police and civilians. For what reason were the police dressed in full protective gear? This photograph, widely published with others, showed the police invading the church. Does the photograph succeed in depicting the crisis for immigrants as a family issue?

people" who had escaped to Hong Kong in search of a better life. Britain earned the condemnation of other Western governments and humanitarian groups for its refusal to provide a haven for Asian refugees, many of whom were children.

The European Union attempted to impose uniform standards and quotas on immigration but these were often resisted by member nations. One reason they resisted was the lack of skilled workers to do certain jobs. For instance, at the beginning of the new century, Spain's economy was one of the fastest growing in western Europe. Yet Spain suffered labor shortages in the construction and agricultural sectors. Spanish employers relied heavily on illegal immigrants in spite of the fact that Spain had the highest unemployment rate in the European Union in the year 2000. Germany likewise suffered from high unemployment, yet sought increased numbers of professional workers from abroad because of the limited skills in the available pool of workers. A declining birth rate in western European countries also contributed to labor shortages and reliance on imported labor. On the whole, restrictions failed to achieve what they set out to do—remove foreign workers from Western countries by repatriation—in spite of numerous policies to restrict and police illegal immigration.

The issue of immigration became a prominent one in electoral campaigns throughout Europe in the 1990s. Opposition to the presence of foreign workers and concerns about protecting small business interests fueled ballot-box victories for the far right in Austria, the Netherlands, and France. In the first presidential election of the twenty-first century in France, the National Front candidate Jean-Marie Le Pen ran on the party's "France for the French" platform and garnered an unprecedented 18 percent of the electorate, giving pause to the democratic leadership of many European countries. Debate raged in the industrialized countries about how to deal with the apparently contradictory demands of high rates of endemic unemployment and labor shortages.

French Laws on Secularity.   The presence of populations from north Africa and southern and eastern Europe in western Europe resulted in a clash of cultures, values, and religious beliefs. In France these issues came together around a particular item of clothing prohibited for school children at the primary and secondary levels. Muslim girls wore veils and head scarves in school in growing numbers beginning in the late 1980s. A long national debate in France ensued following the expulsion of two young girls for wearing head scarves. An amendment to the law in 2004 raised enforcement to the national level. The public debate about assimilation and citizenship reinforced the idea that citizenship required adherence to a common code and common cultural values. This situation highlights the challenges that cultural diversity presented to all European nations with growing minority populations. Although in the first week of school in September 2004 only 240 girls out of nearly 12 million students came to school wearing head scarves, the issue captured the attention of the world by exposing the tensions within Western societies caused by the influx of new, often foreign-born Muslim, minorities.

Women's Changing Lives

During the last quarter of the twentieth century, the lives of Western women reflected dramatic social changes. Access to institutions of higher learning and professional schools allowed women to participate in the work force in education, law, medicine, and business throughout the world, whether in France, the United States, or the Soviet Union. Women had been active in calling for the liberation of oppressed groups in the 1960s. Those activities served to heighten women's collective awareness of the disparities between their own situations and those of men in Western societies: women worked at home without pay; in the workplace, women received less pay than men for the same work.

■ French Muslim schoolgirls wearing head scarves outside of Lille High School, France. French laws on separation of church and state resulted in a ban in public schools of all accessories and clothing that indicate religious affiliation, including head scarves, crosses, and yarmulkes.

In that period of increased educational and work opportunities, an international women's movement emerged. International conferences about issues related to women were media events in the 1970s. In 1975, the United Nations Conference on the Decade for Women was convened in Mexico City. Women activists believed that something more was needed than the conference, which was accused of seeking only to integrate women into existing social structures dominated by men. On 8 March 1976—International Women's Day—the International Tribunal of Crimes Against Women was convened in Brussels.

Modeling the conference on tribunals such as the Nüremberg Commission, which dealt with Nazi atrocities in World War II, the feminists who convened in Brussels concentrated on crimes against women for the purpose of promoting greater political awareness and action. Fertility and sexuality were at the center of the new politics of the women's movement, justified in the slogan "The personal is political." Rape and abortion were problems of international concern. "Sisterhood is powerful!" gave way to a new organizing slogan, "International sisterhood is *more* powerful!"

■ French women demonstrate for the right to choose. The sign says, "A baby, no baby, ten babies if I wish."

Reforms and Political Action.   In Italy, political action by women yielded a new law in 1970 that allowed divorce under very restricted circumstances. In France, the sale of contraceptives was legalized in 1968. French feminists, like their Italian counterparts, worked through the courts to make abortion legal: they achieved their goal in 1975. With the increasing integration of Europe in the 1990s, differing national practices in child care, health care, and gender parity were reviewed by the deliberative bodies of the European Union. Yet national differences still prevailed among European countries, including differences in education, healthcare, and reproductive rights.

The feminist movement created a new feminist scholarship that sought to incorporate women's experiences and perspectives into the disciplines of the humanities and the social sciences. Women's studies courses, which emphasized the history of women and their contributions to civilization, became part of university and college curricula throughout Europe and the United States. Reformers also attempted to transform language, which, they argued, had served as a tool of oppression.

Western feminists continued to be politically active in the 1970s and 1980s in the peace movement, in antinuclear protests, and in the 1990s in ecological groups concerned with protecting the environment. As Petra Kelly, the West German leader of the Green party, an ecological and pacifist coalition, described it: "Women all over the world are rising up, infusing the antinuclear, peace, and alternative movements with a vitality and creativity never seen before." At the turn of the new century feminists, student activists, environmentalists, and internationalists found common ground in the concerns of exploitation of a global work force, sweatshops, ecological devastation, and the pollution and exploitation of the environment.

Soviet Women's Experiences.   In the last quarter of the twentieth century, women in socialist countries were also engaged in the process of redefining women's social roles and political participation. The Soviet Union provides an interesting case study of comparison and contrast. Increasingly, well-educated Soviet women demanded reforms, and the beginnings of a women's protest literature in the 1970s indicated an awakening concern for women's issues. Soviet women enjoyed more representation in parliamentary bodies than women in the West. More than half of the 2.3 million deputies to the local Soviets in the 1980s were women. One-third of the 1500 members of the Supreme Soviet were women. Gorbachev appointed a woman as one of the 12 Central Committee secretaries—the most politically influential people in the country. In spite of greater participation, however, women enjoyed little real authority in the higher echelons of political life, and most Soviet women rejected feminism as a political movement.

The same pattern held true for women in the work force. More than 85 percent of Soviet women worked, compared to about 60 percent of women in the West. Although 70 percent of doctors and 73 percent of teachers were women, women held few positions of authority. Both their pay and their status were lower than men's, as the example of primary school teaching reveals: 80 percent of primary school teachers were women, but two out of three head teachers were men, a phenomenon similar to that in other Western countries.

Unlike western European women, many Soviet women—two out of three on average, according to censuses in the 1970s—performed heavy manual labor. Older women, for example, still chopped ice from Soviet streets. The practice had begun 40 years earlier because of the heavy losses of men in World War II—20 million had died in the war. In her doctoral dissertation on the sociology of the rural village of Stavropol, Raisa Gorbachev, wife of the Soviet leader, argued that while men were trained to run machines and tractors, women were expected more and more to perform the heavy physical labor associated with farm work.

Birthrates fell in the Soviet Union as in Western countries; women were bearing fewer children. Technology had made controlled fertility possible in safer, more dependable ways, but most birth control devices remained unavailable to Soviet women, and what was available was often unreliable. Abortion continued to be a common form of birth control in the Soviet Union, with two abortions for every live birth. Women were also choosing to have their children later, often because of work and financial considerations, with a growing percentage delaying childbearing until their thirties. Women complained of lack of quality in maternity hospital care. As one young mother explained, "The only experience worse than an abortion is having a baby in a Soviet hospital."

In the late 1980s, Soviet President Mikhail Gorbachev made direct appeals for women's support by promising preschool nurseries and kindergartens for every child. Gorbachev also committed himself to supporting increased sick leave for mothers of sick children, paid maternity leave for a period of 18 months, increased child-care allowances, and shorter workdays for women who worked at home. In support of women's voice in the workplace, women's councils were to be revived.

Women's work experience in the East and the West varied in degree, but a startlingly similar pattern of home and work life prevailed at the beginning of the twenty-first century. Neither state institutions nor the law met the needs of women.

Terrorism: The "New Kind of War"

A new kind of warfare emerged globally as disfranchised groups rejected the avenues of cooperation and reform and instead chose violence as the sole means of achieving their political ends. The history of contemporary terrorism began after World War II. The creation of the state of Israel in part of the land of Palestine in 1948 led to conflict between the Israelis and the Palestinian Arabs, who refused to accept the new Jewish state. Israel's Arab neighbors went to war to support the Palestinians but were defeated by Israel in late 1948. Hundreds of thousands of Palestinians became refugees in neighboring Arab states, and Palestinian guerrillas decided that the best way to attack Israel and its protectors was with a global strategy of terrorist violence. The first Palestinian hijacking took place in the summer of 1968. Ejected from Jordan, Palestinian guerrillas set up their headquarters in Syria and Lebanon in order to continue their terrorist activities.

Another influence figured prominently in terrorism of the late twentieth century: Islamic fundamentalism. Muslim militants intent on waging a "holy war" for the oppressed could be found throughout the world in areas as different as Algeria, Bosnia and Herzegovina, France, the Philippines, and Great Britain. Muslim radicals in those and other countries shared a truly global commitment and were often heavily influenced by their formative volunteer experiences in the Afghan war of the 1980s. Conceiving of their mission as a holy one, they were able to form a series of loose connections with Muslims from other countries for the purposes of recruitment, training, and deployment of dedicated fighters. A taxi driver from Egypt, for example, who fought in the Afghan war was convicted for the 1993 bombing of New York's World Trade Center. Conspirators led by the convicted Egyptian cleric Omar Abdel Rahman plotted to bomb the United Nations building, FBI headquarters in lower Manhattan, and the Lincoln and Holland tunnels linking Manhattan with New Jersey. The French blamed Afghan-trained Algerian Muslims for the 1994 Christmas Eve hijacking of an Air France airbus in which three passengers were killed in the initial shoot-out in Algiers.

Terrorists came from many nations and religious backgrounds. Peace-loving Muslims were maligned in Europe and the United States because of fundamentalists' actions. Following the 1995 bombing of the federal building in Oklahoma City, Arabs and Muslims across the United States were singled out for reprisals and intimidation until it was discovered that the Oklahoma City bombing was the act of domestic terrorists protesting U.S. government policies. The Oklahoma City attack, which terrorized the United States, fit the essential definition of the new terrorism as a violent act against innocent civilians for the purpose of undermining the power of the government.

Terrorism in the New Century. By the late 1970s, political killings became a tactic of choice for terrorists throughout the world. Victims were targeted by terrorists not because they merited any punishment themselves but as a means of attracting international attention to the terrorists' cause. Although motivated by different political agenda, terrorist groups often formed cooperative networks on an international basis, sharing training, weapons, and information. A small group of West German left-wing radicals known as the Red Army Faction executed key industrial, financial, and judicial leaders in the 1970s. The Red Army Faction was also responsible for a number of bombings, including that of the West German embassy in Stockholm in 1975. In Italy, a small group known as the Red Brigades was responsible for violent incidents, including the "kneecapping"—permanent crippling of people by shooting them in the knees—of leading Italian businessmen and the kidnapping and murder of the former Italian prime minister Aldo Moro in 1978. In 1981, the Red Brigades targeted the United States for their terrorist reprisals when they abducted an American general, James Dozier.

Western Europe served as an important arena for terrorist acts by non-European groups. To succeed—that is, to terrify mass populations—terrorists needed publicity. Terrorists relied on media exposure and claimed responsibility for acts only after they had been successfully completed. In September 1972, members of the Palestinian Black September movement kidnapped 11 Israeli athletes at the Olympic Games in Munich. An estimated 500 million people watched their televisions in horror as all 11 were slaughtered. In a dramatic shoot-out, also televised, five of the terrorists died as well. Incidents such as the taking hostage of the OPEC oil ministers later in the decade in Vienna made urban populations aware of their vulnerability to gratuitous acts of violence. In 1979, 52 Americans were kidnapped from the American Embassy in Teheran and were held hostage for 444 days by a group of young Iranian revolutionaries who claimed to be battling against the "great Satan."

A recurrent pattern of terrorism prevailed throughout the 1980s with Israel and the United States often the targets of attacks. Incidents highlighted by international media coverage included the attempted assassination of the pope in 1981 by a Turkish fascist; the blowing up of the U.S. Marine garrison in Beirut in 1983 by a Lebanese Shi'ite, whose act took the lives of 241 American soldiers as well as his own; the 1985 hijacking of a cruise ship, the *Achille Lauro,* by Palestinian ultranationalists, who killed one aged Jewish American passenger; and the bombing of TWA and El Al registration counters at two of Europe's busiest airports, in Rome and Vienna, in 1985. In December 1988, hundreds of people died when a Pan American plane on which a bomb had been planted exploded

■ A hooded Arab terrorist stands on a balcony during the attack on the Israeli Olympic team headquarters at the Munich Olympics in 1972.

in flight over Lockerbie, Scotland. The bombing was probably in retaliation for the downing of an Iranian passenger airliner by the U.S. Navy in the Persian Gulf.

Terrorist activities against the United States escalated following the U.S. military action against Iraq in 1991 known as the Persian Gulf War. In February 1993, the explosion of a bomb planted in a small truck parked in the basement garage of the World Trade Center in New York killed six people, wounded a thousand, and did limited damage to the structure. Two terrorist attacks in Saudi Arabia in 1995 and 1996 killed 24 Americans. In August 1998, two major assaults against American embassies, one in Tanzania and the other in Kenya, killed 224 people and injured hundreds of others. In October 2000, a suicide attack against the USS *Cole* in the port of Aden took the lives of 17 sailors.

All of these attacks were attributed to the network of a single man, Osama bin Laden, a Saudi Arabian millionaire, who had been trained by the U.S. Central Intelligence Agency and who, between 1980 and 1989, had fought against the Russians in Afghanistan. In June 2001, bin Laden called on the Muslims of the world to mobilize themselves into a general **jihad,** or holy war, against their enemies. Three months after this call-to-arms, terrorists dealt their most extreme blow against the United States.

Terrorism in the New Century.   On 11 September 2001, four U.S. passenger planes were hijacked and used as flying bombs in a coordinated action that targeted the World Trade Center in New York City and the Pentagon just outside of Washington, DC. Two of the four hijacked planes slammed into the twin towers of the World Trade Center, and a third plane hit its mark by diving into the Pentagon. The fourth plane crashed in a field in Pennsylvania, its suicide attack foiled by passengers who opposed their captors. More than 3,000 people were killed, thousands more were wounded, and the loss of property was unprecedented in the worst terrorist attack in history. The events horrified people around the world who understood that two symbols of American global financial and military dominance had been singled out in a carefully planned and executed mission of destruction. Once again, Osama bin Laden was identified as the mastermind of terrorist devastation. President George W. Bush declared, in the wake of the terrorist attacks, that the United States was entering "a new kind of war," one not waged between nations but one whose stateless enemy would be sought out and hunted down. Terrorism had long plagued Europe and the Middle East, but the September 11 attacks marked the first time in history that an act of terrorist warfare by an external enemy took place on American soil.

In October 2001, less than a month after the attacks, the United States and Great Britain undertook war in Afghanistan in pursuit of bin Laden, who was believed to have been harbored there by the **Taliban,** the fundamentalist Muslim ruling group. Though bin Laden was not captured, the Taliban was removed from power. In the fall of 2004, free elections were conducted throughout Afghanistan under the eyes of military

■ This photograph captures the massive explosion caused when a second hijacked plane crashed into the World Trade Center in New York on 11 September 2001. The landmark twin towers were destroyed in the attack, and thousands of people were killed.

observers for the nation's first elected president, although peace proved elusive, and the U.S. military presence continued. In 2007 observers feared a Taliban resurgence.

Stringent security measures in airports and public places were instituted worldwide as nations faced harsh new political realities, including incidents of bioterrorism—germ warfare against civilians—in the months following the September terrorist attacks. When the European Union and the United States passed new laws and directives to combat terrorism, critics feared the curtailment of civil liberties. Such a curtailment in fact took place in Russia following terrorist incidents in the summer of 2004. Racist incidents against Muslims and Arabs mounted, even as European and American leaders stressed that bin Laden and his network were a non-representative and fanatical fringe within the Muslim world.

The Iraq War.   Throughout the post-9/11 era, Iraq and its leader Saddam Hussein (1937–2006) were singled out by the U.S. government as sympathetic to the terrorist cause and committed to developing "weapons of mass destruction." As a consequence of a United Nations resolution, UN inspection teams entered Iraq in mid-November 2002 in a search for such weapons. None was found. In further pursuit of such weapons and with the intention of removing Hussein from power, President Bush ordered U.S. troops in coalition with British forces to lead an attack against Iraq in March 2003. Saddam Hussein was captured, but insurgent forces resisted the military occupation. Terrorist actions continued to take American and Iraqi lives as the American government attempted to rebuild the Iraqi economy during the peace. The American military presence was met with Iraqi insurgency and outright civil

war between Iraqi Sunni and Shia opposing sects of Islam. Saddam Hussein was captured in 2003, brought to trial, and executed in 2006 for atrocities against 148 Shiites. His trial and the manner of his execution by public hanging provoked further violence. In early 2007 U.S. President George W. Bush increased American troop presence. With rising death tolls weighing heavily on Iraq's civilian population, a majority of Iraq's parliament voted in May 2007 against the ongoing occupation of their country by U.S. forces. American involvement in this war was greatly unpopular and resulted in undermining Western alliances and increasing criticism of American foreign policy throughout the world.

Terrorism and Counterterrorism.   Terrorism in the last quarter of the twentieth century was not a single movement but a wide variety of groups and organizations on both the left and right. Some organizations were Marxist; some were nationalist; some were Islamic fundamentalists. All defined the enemy as an imperialist and a colonizer. Industrial nations, especially the United States and Israel, were common targets of terrorist attacks. Terrorists all shared a vision of the world based on the commonly held belief that destruction of the existing order was the only way to bring about a more equitable system. Palestinian terrorists were willing to sacrifice their lives to ensure the establishment of an independent Palestinian state. In the case of bin Laden's fundamentalist Muslim terrorists, holy war was perceived as the only way to create an Islamic state free of Western influence and the corruption of a U.S.-dominated global economy.

By the mid-1990s it was clear that terrorism was an effective challenge to the tranquility of industrial nations. Modern

CITIES AS ENVIRONMENTAL LEADERS, 2005

In 2005, 169 countries began to enforce the directives of the Kyoto Protocol, an amendment to a United Nations treaty on climate change. The goal of the protocol was to reduce emissions from greenhouse gases, considered a primary cause of global warming. The United States was not a signator of the Protocol, and progress has been slow. In 2005, mayors of 22 of the world's largest cities joined together to address the problem. What follows is a press release by Ken Livingstone (1945–), a leader of the cities group and the Mayor of London, explaining their collective commitment "to change the world." With financial support from the Clinton Climate Initiative, a private philanthropic foundation, these cities have undertaken concrete steps.

Focus Questions

What are the practical steps these cities plan to take to reduce greenhouse gas emissions? What is the value of such urban partnerships strung across the globe? How are such partnerships possible after 2005? What is the value of cities working together?

Last October [2005] London convened a meeting of large cities to discuss cooperation on addressing global warming. The Large Cities Climate Leadership Group recognized the need for action and cooperation on reducing greenhouse gas emissions and pledged to work together towards that end.

Mayor of London, Ken Livingstone said: "There is no bigger task for humanity than to avert catastrophic climate change. The world's largest cities can have a major impact on this. Already they are at the centre of developing the technologies and innovative new practices that provide hope that we can radically reduce carbon emissions.

"Former President Clinton and his Foundation have proved that they can intervene decisively to make a real impact on one of the world's biggest problems, AIDS. On behalf of the Large Cities Climate Leadership Group, I am delighted to be able to enter into this new partnership to rapidly accelerate cities' response to global warming. Our aim is simple—to change the world."

To enable partner cities [of the Large Cities Climate Leadership Group] to reduce energy use and greenhouse gas emissions [the Clinton Climate Initiative (CCI)] will:

1. Create a purchasing consortium that will pool the purchasing power of the cities to lower the prices of energy saving products and accelerate the development and deployment of new energy saving and greenhouse gas reducing technologies and products. . . .
2. Mobilize the best experts in the world to provide technical assistance to cities to develop and implement plans that will result in greater energy efficiency and lower greenhouse gas emissions.

3. Create and deploy common measurement tools and internet based communications systems that will allow cities to establish a baseline on their greenhouse gas emissions, measure the effectiveness of the program in reducing these emissions and to share what works and does not work with each other.

Many cities have worked individually to reduce energy use and greenhouse gas emissions but most of these practices are not in widespread, systematic or coordinated use, thus greatly reducing their effectiveness. CCI will engage the largest cities in the world and allow them to be leaders for all cities by making the direct benefits from the purchasing consortium, technical assistance, and measurement and communication tools available to other cities throughout the world.

There are a number of practical steps cities can take to increase efficiency and reduce emissions including:

- More energy efficient lighting for traffic and street lights
- Building codes and practices that make use of more effective insulation, more energy efficient windows, more energy efficient heating and ventilation systems and more energy efficient lighting
- More energy efficient municipal water and sanitation systems
- Localized, cleaner electric generation systems
- Use of bio-fuels or hybrid technologies for city buses, garbage trucks and other vehicles
- Schemes to reduce traffic congestion
- Reduction of emissions from city garbage dumps and the use of biomass to generate electricity
- More intelligent design of electric grids both across the city and within office and municipal buildings

The CCI—Large Cities partnership begins with 22 of the largest cities in the world participating—Berlin, Buenos Aires, Cairo, Caracas, Chicago, Delhi, Dhaka, Istanbul, Johannesburg, London, Los Angeles, Madrid, Melbourne, Mexico City, New York, Paris, Philadelphia, Rome, Sao Paulo, Seoul, Toronto, Warsaw and the partnership anticipates that many more cities will join over the next four to six months.

terrorists were often able to evade policing and detection. Surveillance had not prevented terrorists from striking at airplanes and cruise ships. Yet terrorists accomplished little in the way of bringing about political change or solutions to problems.

West European governments often refused on principle to bargain with terrorists. Yet at times, European nations and the United States have been willing to negotiate for the release of kidnapped citizens. They have also been willing to use violence themselves against terrorists. Israel led the way in creating antiterror squads. In 1976, Israeli commandos succeeded in freeing captives held by pro-Palestinian hijackers of an Air France plane in Entebbe, Uganda. The following year, specially trained West German troops freed Lufthansa passengers and crew held hostage at Mogadishu, Somalia, on the east coast of Africa. The Arab kidnappers had hoped to bargain for the release of the imprisoned leaders of the Red Army Faction; the West German government refused. In 1986, the United States bombed Libya, long recognized as a training ground for international terrorist recruits, in retaliation for the bombing of a discotheque frequented by U.S. service personnel in West Germany. Israel bombed refugee camps to retaliate against Palestinian nationalists. The greatest mobilization in counterterrorist efforts came with U.S. leadership following the events of 11 September 2001. The goal of the "counterterrorism" was to undermine support for terrorists among their own people; its tactics and ends opened counterterrorism to the criticism that it was very similar to the terrorism it was opposing. In fact, torture of prisoners and interrogations in violation of the Geneva conventions at the hands of American soldiers and civilian personnel came to light in an Iraqi prison in the summer of 2004.

In spite of tactics of meeting violence with violence, the advanced industrial states of western Europe and the United States remained vulnerable to an invisible terrorist enemy. That elusive enemy could terrorize populations and incapacitate the smooth functioning of the modern industrial state. With the dawn of a new century, terrorism continued to threaten peace and paralyze security, at the very moment when people all over the globe celebrated the hope for a better world. After the large-scale terrorist attacks of 2001, the promise of a new and better world seemed, for many, to move further out of reach.

CONCLUSION

In 1970 Western nations had managed to put the destruction, hardship, and sacrifice of World War II behind them in the space of a single generation. Yet economic downturn and rising expectations of a better life continued to fuel protest and discontent. The escalating costs of nuclear parity were in conflict with the growing demands of consumer societies, and this conflict helped to end the Cold War. With the collapse of the Soviet Union, a period of new hope and international cooperation dawned.

The world of 1989 was now a world dominated by one superpower, the United States. It was also a world characterized by the rise of new political entities and the search for integration and stability in Europe. The Western world was undoubtedly a different place in the last quarter of the twentieth century from all that had gone before. But was the world really so transformed that one could speak of its being ordered in a different way? The iceberg of communism had melted. As democrats replaced dictators, some observers wondered if counterrevolution was waiting in the wings should the new capitalist experiments fail. In other countries, the dictators did not leave; they only changed their political allegiances. Proto-fascist and anti-Semitic groups became more vocal in the early 1990s amid the economic chaos.

One potentially unifying force was the marketplace. Democratic institutions seemed most stable in those countries with developed market economies. In the former Yugoslavia, for example, little had changed for the better since the fall of the communist regime. Russia itself suffered from a similar problem of economic readjustment and restructuring. Even where political reforms had been accomplished, economic reforms lagged behind or were nonexistent.

Western Europe and the United States realized the devastation that industrialization had wrought in their own countries after a century and a half of development, and were taking steps to control pollution and to clean up the air and the environment. Yet in eastern Europe, ecological concerns were considered a luxury as industries struggled uncontrolled to establish footholds in competitive markets. In spite of the emergence of a new world order of democratic states, many Europeans, both in the East and in the West, saw an uncertain future of misery and repression as long as virulent nationalism remained unchecked.

Problems that plagued Western states in the modern era persisted. The triumph of the nation-state in the nineteenth century had carried the seeds of violence and destruction, as two world wars and countless local conflicts had proven. Democracy, likewise viewed as the best hope for a better world, struggled in new settings that lacked the institutions, the culture, and the experience of democratic values. Elected elites from Russia to Romania used positions of power for aggrandizement, both political and economic.

As the benefits of the welfare state in the West dwindled with slowed economic growth, the gap between the rich and the poor widened. The widening gulf characterized the new capitalist economies of the former Soviet bloc as well as those of the West. In the United States, the richest 1 percent of households controlled about 40 percent of the nation's wealth. In Germany, high-wage-earning families earned about two and a half times as much as low-wage workers. And the gap between rich and poor on a global scale yawned even wider.

What lay ahead for Western societies? Would the third millennium be so different? Arthur Miller, the renowned American playwright, commented in the aftermath of the terrorist attacks of 11 September 2001, "It is so simple to destroy a city." Citizens of Western industrial societies had a new and shocking sense of their own vulnerability. Yet leaders of 22 of the world's largest cities banded together in 2005 to change the world by improving the environment. The authors began this book by pointing out that the West is an idea, not a place.

To understand the past frees us to create a better tomorrow. The challenges of civilization at the beginning of the twenty-first century require understanding of our commitment to the creativity of devising a better future. What was best in civilization at the beginning of the third millennium—selflessness, self-sacrifice, and willingness to help others in spite of personal cost—came face to face with mindless destruction and attacks on civilian populations.

QUESTIONS FOR REVIEW

1. What caused the end of the Cold War?
2. What was the nature of dissent in the Soviet Union?
3. How did the ideas of *glasnost* and *perestroika* help bring about the end of the Soviet Union?
4. How did the collapse of communist regimes in Russia and eastern Europe promote national and ethnic conflict?
5. What social, economic, and political forces contributed to German reunification?
6. How did the treaty signed by the nations of the European Community at Maastricht in 1991 create both hopes and fears of European unity?
7. In what ways have women's lives in eastern and western Europe been similar and in what ways have their experiences differed since the 1960s?
8. What is the difference between the European Community and the European Union?
9. How have democracy and nationalism come into conflict since 1989?
10. What nations and populations experienced terrorism in the late twentieth and early twenty-first centuries? What were the causes of terrorism and from what did terrorism derive its power?

KEY TERMS

Brezhnev Doctrine, *p. 902*	*moujahedeen, p. 914*
Dayton Peace Accords, *p. 914*	nationalities problem, *p. 910*
détente, *p. 902*	*perestroika, p. 903*
ethnic cleansing, *p. 912*	*samizdat, p. 903*
euro, *p. 917*	Solidarity, *p. 905*
European Union (EU), *p. 917*	Taliban, *p. 926*
glasnost, p. 903	velvet revolutions, *p. 906*
jihad, *p. 926*	

DISCOVERING WESTERN CIVILIZATION ONLINE

You can obtain more information about the end of the Cold War and new global challenges at the Websites listed below. See also the Companion Website that accompanies this text, www.ablongman.com/kishlansky, which contains an online study guide and additional resources.

The End of the Cold War and the Emergence of a New Europe

Mikhail Sergeyevich Gorbachev
www.almaz.com/nobel/peace/1990a.html
A biography of Mikhail Gorbachev with electronic texts compiled by the Nobel Prize Internet Archive.

A Research Guide to Soviet History
www.unc.edu/depts/slavlib/html/guides/history_0.htm
A research guide to Soviet history sponsored by the University of North Carolina libraries.

Chronology of Russian History: Post-Soviet Period
www.departments.bucknell.edu/russian/chrono4.html
A chronology of Russian history since 1991 with links to additional resources.

Boris Yeltsin
www.cs.indiana.edu/hyplan/dmiguse/Russian/bybio.html
A chronology of Yeltsin's presidency with links to further materials on key events and personalities.

The Fall of the Berlin Wall 1989
www.remote.org/frederik/culture/berlin
A photo tour of the fall of the Berlin Wall supplemented by text from several German newspapers (in English).

A Concrete Curtain: The Life and Death of the Berlin Wall
www.wall-berlin.org/gb/berlin.htm
A virtual exhibit to commemorate the tenth anniversary of the fall of the Berlin Wall with links to further readings.

Post-Soviet Russia: Library and Internet Resources
www.libraries.wright.edu/libnet/subj/pol/pls460.html
A research guide to post–Soviet Russian library and Internet resources sponsored by the Wright State University libraries.

Ethnic Conflict and Nationalism

International Helsinki Federation for Human Rights
www.ihf-hr.org/
Official Website of the International Helsinki Federation for Human Rights, a nonprofit organization. This site is useful as a resource for the latest developments in the Balkans and in Chechnya from a human rights activist perspective.

Physicians for Human Rights: Chechnya Resources
www.phrusa.org/research/chechnya/chech_resources.html
Part of the Physicians for Human Rights official Web page with links devoted to the conflict on Chechnya, including current newspaper and journal articles.

Bosnia HomePage at Caltech
www.its.caltech.edu/~bosnia/
This site provides links to essays and documents on the history of the disintegration of Yugoslavia and subsequent developments in the region.

Bosnia and Herzegovina Web Links

www.usip.org/library/regions/bosnia.html

The United States Institute of Peace provides links to Web resources on the Balkan conflict and its resolution.

The West in the Global Community

History of European Integration Site

www.let.leidenuniv.nl/history/rtg/res1

This site provides primary source materials and bibliographies of the history of European integration. It also includes links to statistical data relating to the European Union and its organizations. It provides annotated links to the broader theme of Cold War history.

The New Europe@nationalgeographic.com

magma.nationalgeographic.com/ngm/0201/feature3/

This National Geographic feature on the New Europe includes articles, multimedia resources, and a downloadable map, as well as links to related sites.

The Terrorism Research Center

www.terrorism.com/index.shtml

The home page of the Terrorism Research Center. The site provides essays, documents, and links to additional materials on terrorism and political violence.

SUGGESTIONS FOR FURTHER READING

The End of the Cold War and the Emergence of a New Europe

Timothy Garton Ash, *In Europe's Name: Germany and the Divided Continent* (London: Jonathan Cape, 1993). An original and complex thesis that looks at German reunification from its origins in the 1970s.

Richard K. Betts, *Conflict After the Cold War: Arguments on Causes of War and Peace* (New York: Longman, 2004). An updated edition that examines twenty-first century warfare, terrorism, and violence and considers the future of war.

Archie Brown, *The Gorbachev Factor* (New York: Oxford University Press, 1996). Traces Gorbachev's career and examines in detail his attempts to convert the Soviet Union into a social democratic variant of socialism.

Geoffrey Hosking, *The Awakening of the Soviet Union* (Cambridge, MA: Harvard University Press, 1990). Published in the midst of the dramatic changes taking place in the Soviet Union, this study emphasizes the social bases of reform and the challenges to Soviet leadership.

Michael Ignatieff, *Blood and Belonging: Journeys into the New Nationalism* (Toronto: Viking Press, 1993). A companion to a BBC television series, the volume provides a sophisticated exploration of expressions of nationalism throughout Europe.

Walter Laqueur, *The Dream That Failed: Reflections on the Soviet Union* (New York: Oxford University Press, 1994). This work recognizes the tenuous hold of capitalism in Russia and the possibility of a Communist party return.

Martin Malia, *The Soviet Tragedy: A History of Socialism in Russia, 1917–1991* (New York: Maxwell Macmillan International, 1994). A reevaluation of the failure of communism by a leading Russian historian.

Adam Michnik, *Letters from Freedom: Post–Cold War Realities and Perspectives* (Berkeley: University of California Press, 1998). Michnik, a journalist, politician, and writer imprisoned for his political views in the 1980s, is widely regarded as a hero in Poland today. This volume includes his articles, speeches, and interviews with leading European political figures and addresses the political realities of Europe after the end of the Cold War.

Henry Ashby Turner, Jr., *The Two Germanies Since 1945* (New Haven, CT: Yale University Press, 1987). A political history of the postwar division of Germany until 1987 that bridges a period the author contends was one of increasing involvement and underlying mutual interests between the two nations.

Ethnic Conflict and Nationalism

Richard Holbrooke, *To End a War* (New York: The Modern Library, 1998). The author offers a firsthand account of the intense diplomatic negotiations surrounding the Dayton Accords and a clear understanding of the problems plaguing Bosnia.

Tim Judah, *Kosovo: War and Revenge* (New Haven, CT: Yale University Press, 2000). Based on careful research, the author analyzes "the last great European war of the twentieth century."

Noel Malcolm, *Kosovo: A Short History* (New York: Harper Collins, 1999). The author is a historian who traces Kosovo's history to medieval times and challenges myths and debates about national origins.

Julie A. Mertus, *Kosovo: How Myths and Truths Started a War* (Berkeley: University of California Press, 1999). Having spent two years in Kosovo interviewing people affected by the conflict, the author is able to offer an understanding from the perspective of the victims of what has happened there.

Michael A. Sells, *The Bridge Betrayed* (Berkeley: The University of California Press, 1996). The author stresses the role of religious nationalists, Serbian Orthodox and Croatian Roman Catholic, in waging a holy war resulting in genocide and destruction.

Susan L. Woodward, *Balkan Tragedy: Chaos and Dissolution After the Cold War* (Washington, DC: The Brookings Institution, 1995). This important study explains, in terms of the breakdown of political and civil order, why Yugoslavia disintegrated into ethnic hatreds so rapidly after 1989.

The West in the Global Community

Mark Juergensmeyer, *The New Cold War? Religious Nationalism Confronts the Secular State* (Berkeley: The

University of California Press, 1994). The author examines the growing significance of religious nationalism from a global perspective.

Geir Lundestad, *"Empire" by Integration* (New York: Oxford University Press, 1998). Provides a comprehensive overview of U.S. policy toward European integration.

Wolfgang Mommsen and Gerhard Hirschfeld, eds., *Social Protest, Violence and Terror in Nineteenth- and Twentieth-Century Europe* (London: Macmillan, 1982). Places terrorism within a historical context in Europe over the last century and a half in a series of articles that takes a national case-history approach.

Richard E. Rubenstein, *Alchemists of Revolution: Terrorism in the Modern World* (New York: Basic Books, 1987). Examines the local root causes of terrorism in historical perspective and argues that terrorism is the social and moral crisis of a disaffected intelligentsia.

For a list of additional titles related to this chapter's topics, please see http://www.ablongman.com/kishlansky.

GLOSSARY

absolutism   Government in which power was consolidated in the hands of a divinely ordained monarch; typified by reverence for the monarch, weakening of representative institutions, and expansion of military.

agricultural revolution   Changes in the traditional agricultural system during the eighteenth century that included enclosure, introduction of fodder crops, intensified animal husbandry, and commercial market orientation.

alchemy   Study of metals in an effort to find their essence through purification. Medieval alchemists attempted to find precious metals such as silver and gold as the essence of base metals such as lead and iron.

Allies   In World War I, the United States, Great Britain, France, and Russia—the alliance that opposed and defeated the Central Powers of Germany and Austria-Hungary and their allies.

Anabaptists   Part of the radical Reformation, Protestant groups that varied in belief but agreed on the principle of adult baptism.

anarchism   A political movement based on rejection of extant political systems; most prominent in less industrialized Western nations.

Anarcho-syndicalists   Craft workers in France combined local trade union organization with anarchist principles to oppose capitalism and maintain worker solidarity from the end of the nineteenth-century to World War I.

anti-Semitism   Hostility toward and discrimination against Jews.

appeasement   British policy of making concessions to Germany in the 1930s in order to avoid war. It allowed Hitler to militarize the Sudetenland and eventually take all of Czechoslovakia.

April Theses   Lenin's promise to the Russian people and challenge to the Provisional Government to provide peace, land, and bread. These three issues became the rallying cries for the second Russian revolution and for the withdrawal of Soviet Russia from World War I.

Arians   During the early Christological controversies, followers of the Alexandrine theologian, Arius, who believed that Jesus was not equal to God the Father.

Axis Powers   In World War II, the alliance of Germany, Italy, and later Japan.

Baby boom   The dramatic and sustained growth in the birth rate in the United States and western Europe immediately following World War II and lasting until about 1960.

Baghdad Railway   Railway Construction began at the end of the nineteenth-century to link Constantinople with Baghdad, ad was undertaken by the Ottoman abd German Empires. The railway had geopolitical goals for Germany in the Persian Gulf and the Ottoman Empire in Arabia.

balance of power   Distribution of power among nations in alliances so that any one nation is prevented from dominating the others.

Balfour Declaration   The commitment by the British government issued in 1917 to support a Jewish homeland in Palestine.

Berlin Wall   Barrier built by East Germany in 1961 to halt an exodus of skilled professionals to the West; opened in 1989 as a prelude to the reunification of East and West Germany.

Big Three   The British, Soviet, and U.S. leaders who coordinated defeat of Germany and Japan in World War II and negotiated postwar settlements. Referred to Churchill, Stalin, and Roosevelt until 1945; Attlee, Stalin, and Truman by summer 1945.

Black Death   The virulent combination of bubonic, septicemic, and pneumonic plagues that destroyed between one third and one half of the population of Europe between 1347 and 1352.

blitzkrieg   "Lightning war"; the rapid advance accompanied by armored vehicles that typified the German military during World War II.

Bolsheviks   Radical faction of Marxist Social Democrats following a political theory based on necessity of violent revolution. The Bolsheviks came to power with Lenin in November 1917.

bourgeoisie   A French term referring to the commercial classes of Europe after the seventeenth century; primarily an urban class.

Brezhnev Doctrine   Policy of Soviet leader Leonid Brezhnev that approved the use of military intervention in the internal affairs of Soviet allies to prevent counterrevolution.

broad-spectrum gathering   A technique of subsistence common in the Neolithic era that preceded permanent settlement in one place and relied on the exploitation of many seasonal sources of food over a limited area.

cahiers de doléances   Lists of grievances sent with representatives to the French Estates-General in 1789; demonstrated the existence of a widespread public political culture in France.

caliph   The successors of Muhammad who served as political and religious leaders of the Islamic world (see Umma).

capitularies   The written instructions for the implementation of royal directives at the local level produced by the clerics of the Carolingian court.

caravels   Small Portuguese ships developed in the fifteenth-century that were ideal for ocean travel.

Carnival   One of the traditional sixteenth-century festivals, the feasts and carousing of which preceded the onset of Lent.

Carolingian Renaissance   The cultural revival of classical learning sponsored by the emperor Charlemagne. New schools and the copying of manuscripts were among its important achievements.

cartels   Combinations of firms in a given industry to fix prices and establish production quotas.

Cartesianism   Philosophy of René Descartes that rested on the dual existence of mind and matter, a principle that enabled the use of skepticism to create certainty.

Central Powers   Germany and Austria-Hungary during World War I.

chartism   An English working-class reform movement that flourished in the 1830s and 1840s and that demanded universal male suffrage (right to vote), payment for parliamentary service, equal electoral districts, and secret ballots.

chivalry   The ideals of knighthood, most notably fighting, that spread from northern France across Europe in the High Middle Ages.

Christian humanism   The application of the principles of humanistic education, particularly philology, to the documents of Christianity. It resulted in a program of reform through better education.

Christological controversies   The debate about the Christian Trinity (Father, Son, and Holy Spirit) and the relationship between humanity and divinity within it. It caused great division and conflict in the Church and society from the third to the fifth centuries.

city-states   Self-governing political units centered upon an urban area. During the fifteenth and sixteenth centuries, city-states took on various forms of government, including republics such as Venice and oligarchies such as Milan.

civic humanism   The use of humanistic training and education in the service of the state. Many humanists became advisors to princes or republican governments, holding high office and helping to establish policy.

Cold War   The diplomatic and ideological confrontation between the Soviet Union and the United States that began in the aftermath of World War II, dividing the world into two armed camps.

collectivization   Soviet plan under Stalin to create large communal state farms to replace private farms owned by peasants.

coloni   Tenant farmers who worked on the estates of wealthy land owners in the Roman Empire.

colonization   Process by which colonies, or new settlements with links to a parent state, are established.

Columbian Exchange   The transfer of microbes, animals, and plants in the encounters between Europeans and Native Americans during the age of exploration.

Comecon   The Council for Mutual Economic Assistance established in 1949 with bilateral agreements between the Soviet Union and eastern European states. Comecon was Stalin's response to the U.S. Marshall Plan in western Europe, but rather than providing aid it sought to integrate and control the economies of eastern Europe for Soviet gain.

Communist Manifesto, The   A call to arms written in 1848 by Karl Marx and Frederich Engels in which they defined in general terms the class struggle in industrializing Europe.

conciliarism   The movement proposed by church lawyers in which only a general council of bishops could end the Great Schism.

condottiere   A mercenary military leader who sold his services and that of his private army to the highest bidder; used in the wars between the Italian city-states.

Congress of Vienna   A meeting of European powers after the Napoleonic wars in 1815; established a balance of power to preserve the status quo in post-revolutionary Europe.

conquistadores   "Conquerors." Spanish adventurers who led the conquests in the Americas in the sixteenth century.

conscription   Compulsory service of citizens in the army. France was the first modern state to enforce conscription. The ability to draft all able-bodied men was a key component in the Revolutionary and Napoleonic wars.

conservatism   Nineteenth-century ideology that favored tradition and stability and only gradual, or "organic," growth and change.

containment   Cold War policy of resisting the spread of Soviet communism.

Continental System   The economic boycott of England by Napoleon during the wars beginning in 1803.

Counter-Reformation   Catholic response to repel Protestantism.

Crusades   Religious wars of conquest directed against non-Christians and heretics in the eleventh through the thirteenth centuries.

Crystal Palace Exhibition   This international exhibition, held in London in 1851 in a specially built see-through exhibition hall, featured the greatest technological advances of the day and served as a spur for further industrialization.

culture   Those shared beliefs, values, customs, and practices that humans transmit from generation to generation through learning.

cuneiform   A form of writing from Mesopotamia characterized by wedge-shaped symbols pressed into wet clay tablets to record words.

Cycladic culture   The artistically and economically sophisticated culture which flourished on islands in the Aegean Sea during the early and middle Greek Bronze Age (3000–1500 bce).

Cynics   Followers of a Hellenistic Greek philosophy that rejected the world as the source of evil and unhappiness and advocated the reduction of possessions, connections, and pleasures to the absolute minimum.

Dawes Plan   The plan crafted by international financial experts in 1924 under the leadership of the American banker Charles Dawes whose aim was to end inflation and restore economic prosperity to Germany by a reform of the reparations repayment schedule.

Dayton Peace Accords   The peace agreement brokered at the end of 1995 among Bosnians, Croats and Serbs by the United States, which provided U.S. troops to support the peace. The aim was to create a unified country in Bosnia, while recognizing ethnic differences.

Declaratory Act   A statute enacted in England in 1766 that stated that Parliament held sovereign jurisdiction over the North American colonies.

decolonization   Withdrawal of Western nations from colonies in Africa and Asia after World War II.

decurions   Members of the city councils in the Roman Empire. Initially, they were the backbone of the provincial elite but by the third and fourth centuries were crippled by their personal responsibility for provincial taxes.

deists   Those who believed that God created the universe but then did not intervene in its operation.

Delian League   League of Greek cities formed to drive out the Persian invaders. Its leader, Athens, turned it into its own empire.

demesne   Land kept by a medieval lord for his direct profit and worked a specified number of days each week by his peasants.

democracy   Form of government in which the citizens choose their leaders; began in Athens, Greece, in the fifth century b.c.e.

de-Stalinization   Process initiated by Nikita Khrushchev beginning in 1956 that reversed many of Stalin's repressive policies in the Soviet Union.

détente   From the French word meaning a relaxation in tension, cooperation between the two superpowers, the Soviet Union and the United States. This policy was characterized by improved U.S.-Soviet diplomatic relationships in the 1970s to lessen the possibility of nuclear war.

dictator   In the Roman Republic, an official who was granted unlimited power to rule the state for a period up to six months in a time of emergency. Sulla and Caesar both used the dictatorship for political ends.

diplomas   The records of royal grants and decisions produced by clerics in medieval courts.

divine rights of kings   Political theory that held that the institution of monarchy had divine origin and that the monarch functioned as God's representative on earth.

doge   Chief magistrate of the Venetian Republic who served for life.

Eastern Question   The "question" posed by the Great Powers about the future of the Ottoman territories.

Edict of Nantes   The proclamation by Henry IV of France granting limited toleration to Huguenots.

ekklesia   The assembly of all free male Athenian citizens.

emirs   Local military commanders who took control of provincial administration in the Islamic world at the expense of the caliphs by the tenth century.

empiricism   The philosophy propounded by Aristotle which rejected Plato's idea of abstract Forms in favor of practical observation and explanation, building general theories from particular data.

enclosure   In the eighteenth century, the closing off of common and public land within the open field system to foster private landholding.

Enlightenment   Philosophical and intellectual movement that began in Europe during the eighteenth century. The movement was characterized by a wave of new learning, especially in the sciences and mathematics, and the application of reason to solve society's problems.

entrepôt   A place where goods were brought for storage before being exchanged; a commercial concept originated by the Dutch.

Epicureans   Those who adhered to a Hellenistic Greek philosophy that the world was a random collection of atoms (atheistic and materialistic), and that one must pursue pleasure, but only in moderation as excess causes pain.

equestrians   In the early Roman Republic, the equestrians were one of the richest classes in the Roman army, those who could afford to maintain a horse. By the late republic, their role expanded into banking and commerce.

Estates-General   An official body assembled periodically by the medieval French state, consisting of representatives from three separate groups or "estates": those who prayed (the Church), those who fought (the aristocracy), and those who worked (commoners). Long in disuse by the monarch, it was convened by Louis XVI in 1789.

ethnic cleansing   Term introduced in the Balkan war of the 1990s to describe the systematic killing and forcible removal of one ethnic group by another.

ethnos   Large rural territorial units in the Dark Age and Archaic Greece focused around a central religious sanctuary and dominated by a local oligarchy, such as in Aetolia.

Etruscans   Peoples native to Italy who influenced the formation of the Roman state.

eugenics   An ersatz scientific theory that promoted the improvement of the human race through selective breeding.

eunomia   The good order and obedience to the law which was the ideal of Sparta's militaristic society.

euro   Common currency of the European Union; accepted as common currency by all members of the European Union except the United Kingdom.

European Economic Community (EEC)   Formed in 1957 by Belgium, the Netherlands, Luxembourg, Italy, France, and West Germany to provide a single, integrated European market. Also known as the Common Market.

European Union (EU) Formed in 1992 to succeed the European Community in terms of economic integration; members share defensive, social, and economic policies as well.

extraterritoriality Exempted all foreigners in China from Chinese legal jurisdiction; practiced within foreign "spheres of influence" in China.

Fabians Members of a late nineteenth-century socialist movement in Britain who advocated gradual reform rather than revolution and supported the Labour party.

Factory Act (1833) British Parliamentary legislation that prohibited factory work by children under age nine, provided two hours of daily education for factory children, and limited labor for adults to twelve hours each day.

fascism Rooted in mass politics of the late-nineteenth century, a totalitarian political system that glorifies the state and subordinates the individual to the state's needs. First emerging in Italy after World War I, fascism appeared in virtually all European countries, but particularly Germany.

feudalism Anachronistic term used by early modern lawyers to describe medieval relations of vassalage.

fief A parcel of productive land along with the serfs and privileges attached to it granted by a lord to a knightly follower (vassal) in return for loyalty and military service.

Final Solution The term used by the Third Reich to refer to the extermination of all people deemed unfit; resulted in the execution of 11 million men, women, and children, 6 million of them Jews.

first triumvirate Political alliance between Pompey, Crassus, and Caesar to share power in the Roman Republic.

fodder crops Crops that were grown not for human consumption but to improve the nutrients in the soil. Some, such as turnips, were also used as animal feed.

Forms In Plato's philosophy, the perfect ideal that underlies all worldly objects. In recollecting them from one's previous existence one communes with all that is good, true, and beautiful.

Fourteen Points U.S. President Woodrow Wilson's idealistic set of guidelines drawn up as part of the peace process whose goal was to create a lasting peace after World War I.

French wars of religion Violent clashes between French Catholics and Calvinists (Huguenots) from 1562–1598.

Fronde An aristocratic revolution in France beginning in 1648 during the minority of Louis XIV, which was initiated by the tax policies of the minority government under Cardinal Mazarin.

futurists Artists and intellectuals of the late nineteenth and early twentieth century who wished to create a new culture free from traditional Western civilization. Futurists lionized technology, the masses, violence, and upheaval.

general strike a central concept for anarcho-syndicalism, this strike action had as a primary purpose the symbolic promotion of worker solidarity by means of a mass protest of limited duration which could mobilize workers from a variety of sectors. Unlike a strike called by a union, general strikes were of a short and defined period of time and were not aimed at improved wages or better working conditions, but were intended to signal the end of capitalism.

generation gap The baby boom following World War II resulted in a generation that came of age in the 1960s. The gap refers to the divergence in values between a large cohort of adolescents and young adults and their parents that resulted in more liberal values and socio-cultural mores.

Geopolitics Geopolitics, or the politics of geography, is based on the recognition that certain areas of the world are valuable for political reasons—for example the Suez canal was important to Great Britain because of its economic interests in India.

Girondins French revolutionary faction that was more moderate than the Jacobins.

glasnost A Russian term meaning openness; one of the programs of reform initiated by Mikhail Gorbachev in the 1980s.

Glorious Revolution Change of government in England in 1688–1689 when the Catholic monarch James II was replaced by the Dutch ruler William of Orange. Called "glorious" because it supposedly was accomplished without bloodshed.

Gnostics An early Christian group that interpreted scripture as gnosis, or secret wisdom, and believed that Jesus had no human element. They were opposed by many bishops.

Golden Bull The edict of emperor Charles IV in 1356 recognizing that German princes and kings were autonomous rulers.

Great Chain of Being A hierarchic model of social organization common in the fifteenth and sixteenth centuries in which all parts of creation held a specific place in a divinely ordered universe.

Great Depression Devastation of the global economy that began in 1929 with the U.S. stock market crash and lasted through the 1930s.

Great Fear The term refers to that period in the summer of 1789 when French peasants, gripped by fear, revolted, attacked the chateaux of French nobility and burned documents that legally bound peasants to taxes and service.

Great Patriotic War The term by which the Russian people referred to World War II, reflecting their sense of dedication, nationalism and sacrifice in waging the war.

Great Purge A series of executions between 1934 and 1938 in the Soviet Union that removed all of Joseph Stalin's political enemies.

Great Reform Bill of 1832 An extension of the right to vote in England to men of the middle class that resulted in a 50 percent increase in those eligible to vote.

Great Schism The conflict (1378–1415) between two sets of rival popes based in Rome and Avignon that divided the loyalties of states and individuals across Europe.

guilds Professional associations of merchants or artisans that offer protection of members and regulation of a particular trade or craft.

hadith The written form of the Sunnah, practices established by the prophet Muhammad that guide the interpretation of the Qur'an.

Hanseatic League A commercial and political alliance of northern German towns established in the late fourteenth century to monopolize the grain and fish trade of the Baltic Sea.

Haussmannization The radical rebuilding of the city of Paris during the Second Empire directed by the Prefect of the Seine Baron Haussmann. Wide avenues, public parks and elegant apartment buildings defined the transformation of the city of Paris from narrow medieval streets into one of the world's most beautiful cities.

Hijra In early Islam, the journey undertaken by Muhammad from Mecca to Medina in 622 in order to govern Medina and calm its internal political dissension.

Holocaust During World War II, mass extermination of Jews by the Nazis under Adolph Hitler.

Holy Alliance Prussia, Austria, and Russia, under the leadership of tsar Alexander I, agreed to protect the peace and the Christian religion following the Congress of Vienna.

honestiores The privileged classes of the later Roman Empire: senators, municipal gentry, and the military.

hoplites In Archaic Greece, armed infantry soldiers.

Huguenots French Calvinists led by Henry of Navarre. Huguenots were victims of the St. Bartholomew's Day Massacre, a slaughter of numerous Protestants in Paris in 1572 during the French wars of religion.

Humanists Scholars who studied and taught the humanities, the skills of disciplines like philology—the art of language—and rhetoric—the art of expression; concentrated on ancient texts.

humiliores The lower classes of the later Roman Empire whose status declined from the period of the *Pax Romana* and who suffered disproportionately from the tax increases of the period.

Hundred Years' War A series of military engagements between England and France (1337–1452) over territorial and dynastic rivalries.

Hussites Followers of Jan Hus who attacked the sale of indulgences and German political dominance in the kingdom of Bohemia. After his execution, they led a partially successful revolt.

iconoclasts Breakers of icons; opponents of the mediating use of icons (religious images) in worship. Most emperors supported this faction in eighth- and early ninth-century Byzantium.

iconodules Venerators of icons; the ecclesiastical faction that resisted the iconoclasts. Most of the people and lesser clergy were iconodules.

icons   Sacred images.

imperium   The powers conferred on magistrates by the Roman people: the supreme power to command, to execute the law, and to impose the death penalty.

indulgences   Remission of temporal punishment in Purgatory due to one's sins. Originally granted for performing pious acts, but later acquired through a grant to the church treasury. In the sixteenth century, indulgences were sold to raise money for the papacy; a critical issue in the Lutheran reform.

industrialization   Process by which production becomes mechanized.

Industrial Revolution   Sustained period of economic growth and change brought on by technological innovations in the process of manufacturing; began in Britain in the mid-eighteenth century.

intendants   Officials appointed by the central government in France to oversee the local administration of the regional aristocracy; a critical component of the centralization of the French state.

Irish Great Hunger   The famine of 1845 was caused by a potato blight that resulted in the decline by 25 percent of the Irish population within five years.

iron curtain   The term coined by former British Prime Minister Winston Churchill to describe the ideological divide between western and eastern Europe after World War II.

Jacobins   One of the political factions of the French National Convention that seized the initiative provided by the sans-culottes to take control of the radical revolution in the late eighteenth century; led by Maximilien Robespierre.

Jacquerie   The revolt of French peasants against the aristocracy and crown in 1358. It was part of the struggle for rights caused by the labor shortage after the Black Death.

jihads   Holy wars waged by Muslims against their religious enemies.

jingoism   Use of public opinion to stir support for one's own nation and hatred for another nation; used extensively by political leaders to justify imperial expansion.

joint-stock companies   Business enterprises that raise capital by selling shares to individuals who receive dividends on their investments.

Kellogg-Briand Pact   An agreement, named for the two men who devised it—the U.S. Secretary of State Frank B. Kellogg and the French Foreign Minister Aristide Briand, signed by 23 nations in 1928 whose purpose was an idealistic renunciation of war.

kouros   Nude statues of young men that were a common subject in Archaic art. The stiff posture demonstrates the influence of Egyptian sculpture.

Kristallnacht   "Crystal night" in German; refers to the night of 9 November 1938 when mobs directed by the Nazis destroyed the homes, businesses, and synagogues of German Jews.

Kulturkampf   "Struggle for civilization"; legislation of the German Empire against the Catholic Church in the 1870s.

laissez-faire   An economic theory that required government to cease interference with private economic activity; Adam Smith and the Physiocrats were its leading proponents.

latifundia   The vast rural estates of the Roman patricians which were worked by slaves or free but dependent tenant farmers.

lay investiture   The practice by which kings and emperors appointed bishops and invested them with the symbols of their office. It led to conflict between the Papacy and the emperors in the eleventh century.

League of Nations   A global, supra-national organization formed following World War I (1919) for the purpose of promoting the peaceful resolution of disputes among member nations. Even though Germany in 1926 and the Soviet Union in 1934 were permitted to join, the failure of the United States to become a member of the League undermined its effectiveness.

Lebensraum   "Living room"; one of Hitler's foreign policy objectives to extend the borders of Germany in eastern and central Europe.

lectio divina   In monastic life, the process of reading and studying the Old and New Testaments that formed an important part of each day's activities.

liberalism   A political philosophy based on freedom of the individual and the corruptibility of authority; associated with constitutional reform in the first half of the nineteenth century.

Linear B   A syllabic form of writing from the late Greek Bronze Age which preserves the earliest known form of Greek. It was used by Mycenaean elites almost entirely for record-keeping.

linear perspective   A technique developed in painting to give a flat surface the appearance of depth and dimension.

Long Parliament   An English Parliament that officially met from 1640 to 1653. It forced reforms under Charles I, defeated the royal armies during the English Civil War, and tried and executed the king.

Luddites   Workers who attacked machines in order to protest the loss of their skilled jobs.

Ludendorff Offensive   The final German offensive of World War I, named after the general who devised it, launched against the Allies on the Western Front in March 1918. The offensive ultimately failed.

maat   In Egyptian thought, the ideal state of the universe and of society which the pharaoh was supposed to uphold.

Maginot Line   A system of defensive fortifications built by France along its German border in the 1920s and 1930s.

Magna Carta   The "great charter" limiting royal power that King John was forced to sign in 1215.

manses   Farms worked by slaves, serfs, and freemen in the Middle Ages.

March on Rome   The takeover of political power in Rome by the fascists in Italy on 28 October 1922, followed by similar takeovers in Milan and Bologna.

Marchfield   The assembly of all free warriors in the early Germanic kingdoms in which the king's authority was all-powerful.

Marshall Plan   The U.S. economic aid program for European countries after World War II; intended to establish U.S. economic influence in European markets.

mercantilism   A popular state economy of the seventeenth century; involved bullionism, protective tariffs, and monopolies.

metics   The non-Athenian residents of Athens who comprised about half of the free population of the city. They were active in commerce and banking.

Minoan civilization   The culture of Crete in the Middle Bronze Age (2000–1550 b.c.e.) in which elites based at great palaces, such as Knossos, dominated the island politically, economically, and religiously.

minuscule   New style of handwriting developed in the Carolingian Renaissance to preserve texts; later adopted as standard script.

Mishnah   In Jewish law, the oral interpretation of the Torah (scripture) which was developed by the Pharisees and later developed into an extensive written body of legal interpretation.

missi dominici   Teams of counts and bishops that examined the state of each county in the Carolingian Empire on behalf of the king.

monasticism   The life of monks devoted to God, from the fourth century onwards, either as part of communal organization or in solitary life. Monasticism began in Egypt as a rejection of the worldliness of civilization.

monopoly   Exclusive control of a market or industry; a form of economic regulation in which special privileges are granted in return for financial considerations and an agreement to abide by the rules set out by the state.

Moujahedeen   An Arabic word referring to Muslim holy warriors fighting for Islam in various countries, including the Balkans and Chechnya, in the late 20th and 21st century.

Museum   The shrine to the Muses in Hellenistic Alexandria to which was added the Library containing all the great works of Greek literature and learning.

Mycenaean   Late Greek Bronze Age civilization that arose ca. 1600 b.c.e. at Mycenae and that encompassed the Greek mainland and parts of Asia Minor. Mycenaeans developed the Linear B script.

mystery cults   Religions that promised immediate, personal contact with a deity that would bring immortality.

Napoleonic Code   The recodification of French law carried out during Napoleon's reign.

National Assembly   That body formed on 17 June 1789 by the French Third Estate when it changed its name to the National Assembly, laying claim to being the true representatives of the French nation.

nationalities problem   The existence of numerous ethnic minorities within the borders of the Soviet Union leading to demands for self-determination and political independence.

natural selection   A theory advanced by Charles Darwin that accounted for evolution of species; a realist scientific approach.

Navigation Acts   English economic legislation providing that colonial goods could only be shipped in English ships.

Nazism   National Socialism; German variant of fascism.

Neolithic era   The New Stone Age (8000–6500 b.c.e.) in which modern man developed agriculture and the first villages.

Neoplatonism   Use of the writings of Plato to advance modern ideas about science, particularly mathematics and the health sciences.

New Economic Policy (NEP)   A state-planned economic policy in the Soviet Union between 1921 and 1928; based on agricultural productivity, it required set payments from peasants; surpluses could be sold on the free market.

new imperialism   Imperialism practiced by European countries after 1870 that was, in essence, the domination by industrial powers over the non-industrial world. Distinguished from the earlier acquisition of territory, new imperialism took a variety of forms including territorial occupations, colonization, exploitation of labor and raw materials, and development of economic spheres of influence.

New Monarchies   The more centralized European governments of western Europe created in the fifteenth and sixteenth centuries.

New Piety   An aspect of the Roman Catholic reform movement; originated among the Brethren of the Common Life with an emphasis on simplicity and more personalized religious practice.

nominalism   The doctrine of William of Ockham that argued that human reason could not aspire to certain truth.

North Atlantic Treaty Organization (NATO)   An organization founded in 1949 the members of which signed a defense pact to protect those countries bordering the North Atlantic.

nuclear club   The group of nations in possession of atomic weapons, originally consisting of the United States and the Soviet Union. By 1974, the nuclear club included Great Britain, France, the People's Republic of China, and India.

Old Regime   The old order; political and social system of France in the eighteenth century before the French Revolution.

oligarchy   Government by an elite few.

optimates   The traditionalist Roman political faction that succeeded the Gracchi and sought to preserve the senatorial oligarchy against the populares.

Orthodox Christianity   The official "right-teaching" faith of Constantinople as opposed to the heterodox peoples on the margins of the Byzantine Empire.

ostracism   A practice in Athenian democracy by which anyone deemed to threaten the constitution could, by popular vote, be exiled for ten years without the loss of property.

Pact of Steel   A military alliance formed between Hilter's Germany and Mussolini's Italy in May 1939 pledging cooperation and military and economic coordination.

Paleolithic era   The Old Stone Age (600,000–10,000 b.c.e.) in which advanced primates developed into Neanderthals and also modern man. They hunted food or collected it by gathering.

Paris Commune   Created in 1871 in the aftermath of the Franco-Prussian War; crushed by the national army after a brief struggle; symbol of revolution for radical politicians, including Marxists.

parlements   Provincial courts in France; the Parlement of Paris, the main law court of the state, was the most powerful of these.

parties   A form of political organization in which members of the British parliament divided into groups with identifiable interests. Whigs and Tories were the first political parties.

Patent of Toleration   An edict of Joseph II of Austria in 1781 that granted freedom of worship to Protestants and members of the Greek Orthodox Church, in addition to Roman Catholics.

paterfamilias   The male head of household in the Roman family. His power was absolute, including the power of life and death.

patricians   Leaders of the gentes, or clans, in early Roman society.

Pax Romana   The two centuries of peace and stability in the early Roman Empire inaugurated by the emperor Augustus.

Peace of Paris of 1856   The peace treaty that ended the Crimean War whereby Russia relinquished its claim as protector of Christians in Turkey and ceased interference in the Ottoman Empire; the British gained the neutralization of the Black Sea; Turkish control was reestablished over the mouth of the Danube; Russia gave up a portion of Bessarabia; and the Danubian Principalities were placed under guarantee of Great Britain and France.

perestroika   A Russian term meaning restructuring; part of Mikhail Gorbachev's attempts to reform the Soviet government and economy in the 1980s.

Peterloo Massacre   In August 1819, the English army troops policing a political crowd gathered near Manchester, England, lost control resulting in the deaths of 11 and the injury of hundreds of others.

phalanx   A tightly ordered and well-disciplined body of elite Greek warriors in heavy armor that attacked in close formation with long spears.

philology   The art of language; one of the most important aspects of humanist studies, based on models of ancient texts.

philosophes   A French term for the intellectuals of the eighteenth-century Enlightenment. Voltaire, Diderot, and Condorcet were leading philosophes.

phony war   The period between 3 September 1939, when Great Britain and France declared war on Germany, and the spring of 1940, when the German offensive against France commenced armed combat between France and Germany. In this strange interlude, while civilian populations waited for attack, an attitude of defeatism grew in France.

Physiocrats   A group of French thinkers who subscribed to the view that land was wealth and thus argued that improvements in agricultural activity should take first priority in state reforms.

pictograms   The earliest form of writing in Mesopotamia, ca. 3500 b.c.e., in which pictures represented particular objects, such as animals.

Pietà   A painting or sculpture of Mary mourning the dead Jesus. The most famous was carved by Michelangelo and is in St. Peter's Basilica.

plebs   Families not organized into gentes, or clans, in early Roman society. The lower classes.

pogroms   State-organized massacres of Jews.

polis   The city-state of Archaic and Classical Greece, particularly found on the shores of the Aegean. A city formed the center of government (tyranny, oligarchy, or democracy) and of religious life with temples on its citadel (Acropolis).

politiques   During the sixteenth-century French wars of religion, a group of Catholics who joined with Huguenots to demand a practical settlement of the wars.

populares   The Roman political faction that succeeded the Gracchi whose leaders appealed to the masses as a source of power.

Popular Front   Socialist governments established in both France and Spain in the 1930s; the French version failed to solve the Depression and was voted out of office; the creation of a socialist republic in Spain initiated a civil war.

Pragmatic Sanction   The document that attempted to secure the recognition of Maria Theresa as heiress to the Habsburg possessions of Charles VI.

Prague Spring   Popular uprising and reform movement in 1968 Czechoslovakia, ended by Soviet invasion in August 1968.

predestination   A fundamental principle of Calvin's theology: the belief that all Christians are predestined to either heaven or hell from the act of creation.

presbyters   The priests of the early Christian tradition who were subordinated to bishops as hierarchy developed in the Church.

Price Revolution   The dramatic price inflation of the fifteenth and sixteenth centuries; caused by monetary debasement and the influx of bullion from the New World.

princeps   "First citizen"; the title assumed by the emperor Augustus to reassure public opinion by preserving the traditional constitutional forms.

Proclamation of the German Empire   The creation in 1871 of the nation-state of Germany by uniting the 38 German states into a single national entity.

proletariat   The industrial working class.

pronatalism   State programs implemented after the Second World War to encourage women to have larger families.

Puritans   English Protestants who sought to purify the Church of England of all traces of Catholicism.

putting-out system   Mobilization of the rural labor force for commercial production of large quantities of manufactured goods; raw materials put out to homes of workers where manufacture took place.

quadrivium   Part of a medieval liberal arts education that included arithmetic, geometry, astronomy, and music.

Quadruple Alliance   Pact signed in 1815 by the four powers who defeated Napoleon—Great Britain, Austria, Russia, and Prussia—for the purpose of protecting Europe against future French aggression.

quinine   An important nineteenth-century medical advance derived from cinchona that was an effective treatment for malaria; it permitted large numbers of Europeans to travel without risking death and disease.

raison d'état   Reason of state; placing the needs of the nation above the privileges of its most important groups.

realism   An artistic and literary style that criticized industrialized society and rejected bourgeois concepts of morality.

Realpolitik   Pragmatic political theory advanced by Otto von Bismarck; ruthless pursuit by any means, including illegal and violent ones, in the interests of the state.

reconquista   The Christian reconquest of the Iberian peninsula from the Spanish Muslims or Moors; completed in 1492 under Ferdinand and Isabella.

Reformation   A movement to reform and purify the Catholic Church that resulted in the creation of new religious denominations in Europe collectively known as Protestants.

Reichstag   The national legislative body of the German Empire; elected by universal male suffrage.

Reign of Terror   The period from 1793 to 1794 when Maximilien Robespierre assumed leadership of the Committee of Public Safety and oversaw the revolutionary tribunals that sentenced about 40,000 people to execution.

Renaissance   A "rebirth" of classical learning and emphasis on humanity that characterized the period between 1350 and 1550.

revisionism   A German socialist school that favored gradual reform through the parliamentary system; led by Edouard Bernstein.

rhetoric   The art of expression and persuasion.

Risorgimento   The nineteenth-century movement to reunite Italy.

robot   Labor service that peasants owed to their lord; more typical in eastern Europe after the fifteenth century.

romanticism   An artistic and literary tradition based on emotions rather than the intellect; rejection of classical traditions in favor of "nature"; often associated with nationalism.

salons   Informal social gatherings during the Enlightenment, frequently organized by women, in which topics of intellectual interest were discussed.

samizdat   Self-published, privately circulated manuscripts; chief vehicle for circulating information among dissidents in the Soviet Union.

sans-culottes   Literally "those without knee-breeches"; working-class revolutionaries who initiated the radical stage of the French revolution in 1792.

Schlieffen Plan   The strategy of the German high command at the outset of World War I, predicated on knocking France out of the war.

Scholastic method   The combination of legal analysis from the new university at Bologna with Aristotelian logic; established by Peter Abelard in the twelfth century.

Schuman Plan   In 1950 France and West Germany joined together to pool all their coal and steel resources. The plan is named for the French Foreign Minister Robert Schuman who was influenced by the economic vision of Jean Monney. The following year the European Coal and Steel Community, predecessor to the European Union, was formed.

scientific revolution   In the sixteenth and seventeenth centuries, a period of new scientific inquiry, experimentation, and discovery that resulted in a new understanding of the universe based on mathematical principles and led to the creation of the modern sciences, particularly astronomy and physics.

scramble for Africa   The colonization of Africa as part of the new imperialism. This domination of Africa by Germany, Britain, and France ended with the crisis at Fashoda.

second triumvirate   Alliance of Octavian, Mark Anthony, and Lepidus following the assassination of Julius Caesar to defeat the assassins and control the Roman Empire.

seigneur   Manor lord responsible for maintaining order, administering justice, and arbitrating disputes among tenants.

Semi-nomadic south   A society that remains at fixed locations for extended periods but also remains migratory.

serfs   Peasants of degraded status and very limited legal rights who were dependent on the lords in the High Middle Ages. They formed the great bulk of the population.

**Shi`ites**   Muslims who follow the tradition that legitimate leadership of Islam can only come through the descendants of `Ali, whom they regard as the last orthodox caliph.

social Darwinists   Those who applied the theory of evolutionary biology, particularly the concept of "survival of the fittest," to human society.

social question   The question of how to treat poverty became a pressing issue for European societies between 1830 and 1850. The social question revolved around what the role of government and the role of private individuals should be in addressing social misery.

sola fide   A fundamental principle of Luther's theology: justification of Christians by faith alone.

"Socialism in one country"   The slogan employed by Joseph Stalin in the 1920s to justify his plans for rapid industrialization as a means of preserving socialism in the Soviet Union.

sola scriptura   By the word alone; emphasis on scriptural authority in preference to the canons of the Church, a fundamental element of Luther's theology.

Solidarity   A non-communist Polish labor organization founded by Lech Walesa in the Gdansk shipbuilding yards; legalized in 1989 as a political movement, it won a victory in the first Polish democratic elections.

Sophists   Professional teachers in fifth-century Greece who traveled from city to city instructing students, for a fee, in rhetoric, the art of persuasion.

Soviets   Councils of workers in Russia formed after 1905 that became one center of power after the overthrow of the tsar; source of power for Lenin and Bolsheviks.

Spanish Armada   The Spanish fleet sent in 1588 to transport troops from the Low Countries for an invasion of England; defeated by the English fleets of Elizabeth I.

Spanish Inquisition   An ecclesiastical tribunal utilized to combat heresy and non-Christians; used by Ferdinand and Isabella against the conversos, or converted Jews of Spain.

spheres of influence   Diplomatic term used to connote territorial influence or control of weaker nations not necessarily occupied by the more powerful ones. The term was first used to explain one kind of control of western European powers in the 1800s during African imperialism, and was later used to describe European and Japanese territorial control and influence over markets in China at the end of the nineteenth century.

"Spirit of Locarno"   A series of treaties, signed in Locarno, Switzerland in 1925 by Germany, France, Great Britain, Belgium and Italy, and intended to promote cooperation and respect for borders, promoted an atmosphere of good will in the international arena known as the "spirit of Locarno."

Stoics   Followers of the Hellenistic Greek philosophy propounded by Zeno, which teaches that orderliness is proper to the universe and that happiness derives from embracing one's divinely ordained role and unhappiness from rejecting it.

strategoi   Generals, the military commanders of themes in the Byzantine Empire. They were responsible for civil and military administration.

suffragettes   Militant members of the English feminist movement led by Emmeline Pankhurst who engaged in acts of violence against private property in order to secure the vote.

sunnah   In Islamic theology, the practices established by the prophet Muhammad. They were initially preserved by oral tradition.

Sunnis The majority tradition of Islam that accepts that political succession should be based on consensus, the existing political order, and a leader's merits.

synod A meeting of bishops called to debate Church policy, such as that at Whitby in 664, which established the customs of the Roman Church among Angles and Saxons.

Talmud Rabbinic discussions of the Mishna and its interpretation complied around 500 C.E.

Table of Ranks Official state hierarchy in Russia under Peter the Great that established the social position or rank of individuals according to categories of military service, civil service, and ownership of landed estates.

tetrarchy Rule by four; Diocletian's attempt to regulate the suggestion of the Roman Empire by dividing the empire into eastern and western parts, with both an augustus and a junior emperor, or caesar, ruling each part.

Taliban The fundamentalist Muslim ruling group that controlled Afghanistan for the period between 1996 to 2001, and currently waging guerilla actions against Afghanistan's democratic government. A rigid sect, the Taliban follows strict observance, denying rights to women.

Thermidorian Reaction Revolt beginning in July 1794 (the month of Thermidor) against the radicalism of the French Revolution, leading to the downfall and execution of Robespierre and the end of the Reign of Terror.

Third Estate Branch of the French Estates-General consisting of the bourgeoisie and the working classes; separated from the other estates to form the National Assembly in 1789.

Third Reich "The Third Empire"; Hitler's government, established after 1933.

third world The former colonies of European and Asian imperialism; sought to separate themselves from European economic control after independence; operated in the United Nations as a non-aligned bloc.

Thirty Years' War War lasting from 1618–1648.

three-field system An efficient agricultural system in which one-third of the land was planted in autumn with wheat or rye, one-third remained fallow, and one-third was planted in spring with a crop that added nutrients to the soil.

Time of Troubles The period of disruption within Russia following the death of Ivan the Terrible; only ended with the Polish invasion of Russia.

Torah The body of law in Hebrew scripture.

Tories Members of a political party in England that in the seventeenth century defended the principle of hereditary succession to the crown; in opposition to the Whigs. The Tories sought to preserve the traditional political structure and supported the authority of the Anglican church.

total war War that requires mobilization of the civilian population in addition to the military; typified by centralized governments with limits on economy and civil rights.

Treaty of Brest-Litovsk The Treaty between Russia and Germany signed in March 1918 whereby Soviet Russia withdrew from World War I.

Treaty of Rapallo An economic treaty signed between Weimar Germany and Soviet Russia in 1922 intended to promote economic recovery and trade.

Treaty of Tordesillas A 1494 agreement that recognized Portugal's claims to Brazil, but gave all of the remainder of the New World to Spain.

Treaty of Versailles Peace settlement with Germany at the end of World War I; included the War Guilt Clause fixing blame on Germany for the war and requiring massive reparations.

triangular trade A three-way trade system during the seventeenth century involving the shipment of calicoes to Africa for slaves who were transported to the East Indies in exchange for sugar, which was shipped to Europe.

Tripartite Pact In September 1940 Japan, Germany and Italy promised mutual support against aggression and endorsed each other's expansionist aims in Europe and Asia.

Triple Alliance An alliance founded in 1882 between Germany, Austria-Hungary, and Italy at Germany's instigation for the purpose of securing mutual support on the European continent.

Triple Entente Alliance founded in 1907 between France, Britain, and Russia. With the defection of Russia from the Three Emperors' League, it hemmed in Germany on both eastern and western borders.

trivium The basic education in cathedral schools of the Middle Ages: grammar, rhetoric, and logic.

tyrants Rulers who had seized power illegally. Tyrannies replaced oligarchies in many *poleis* in Archaic Greece, such as at Corinth and Athens. The term did not have the negative connotations it does today, as many tyrants were popular leaders welcomed by their subjects.

Umma The community of all believers in the Islamic faith. Initially, it was both a political and religious supertribe of Arabs.

universitas The guilds of students that formed the first true universities from the twelfth century onwards.

utilitarianism Jeremy Bentham's philosophical plan to ensure social harmony through measurement of pleasure and pain or the greatest happiness of the greatest number; a liberal philosophy.

vassals Knights sworn to fealty or loyalty to a lord; in return the lord granted the vassal a means of support, or fief.

Velvet revolutions the term refers to the peaceful transformations from communist rule to democratic governments that occurred in 1989 in Poland, Hungary and Czechoslovakia.

Victorian Compromise The balance between freedom and protectionism achieved by liberal parliamentary reform during the reign of Queen Victoria.

Villanovans Peoples of the first Iron Age culture in Italy (1000–800 b.c.e.), which was based in the north. They made iron tools and weapons and placed the ashes of their dead in large urns.

War Guilt Clause As part of the Treaty of Versailles of 1919, the Clause assigned sole responsibility for World War I to Germany and stated that Germany must be made to pay: "Compensation will be made by Germany for all damage done to the civilian population of the Allies and their property by the aggression of Germany by land, by sea and from the air." Reparations resulted from this assignment of guilt, which the German people considered punitive.

Warsaw Pact Defensive alliance organization formed in 1955 by Albania, Bulgaria, Romania, Czechoslovakia, Hungary, Poland, East Germany, and the Soviet Union. The alliance served as a strategic buffer zone against NATO forces.

Weimar Republic German government founded at the end of the First World War; used by German general staff as scapegoat for German defeat and harsh peace terms; overthrown in 1933.

welfare state The tendency of post–World War II states to establish safety nets for citizens in areas of birth, sickness, old age, and unemployment.

wergeld In Germanic society, the payment in reparation for crimes in place of blood vengeance. Tribal leaders used it to reduce internal hostilities.

Whigs Members of a political party in England that in the seventeenth century supported the Protestant succession and a broad-based Protestantism and advocated a constitutional monarchy that limited royal power; in opposition to the Tories. The Whigs were later identified with social and parliamentary reform.

Young Plan The plan devised by the American businessman Owen Young in 1929 that replaced the Dawes Plan and transferred $100 million to Germany to assist in reparations repayments.

zemstvos Local elected assemblies in Russia during the reign of Alexander II; representatives elected by landowners, townspeople, and peasants.

ziggurat Babylonian tiered towers (or step-pyramids) from ca. 2000 b.c.e. that were dedicated to gods and stood near temples. They were among the most important buildings of Babylonian cities.

Zimmermann note Arthur Zimmermann, the German foreign minister during World War I sent a telegram, or "note," in support of Mexico's territorial claims against the United States in New Mexico, Arizona and Texas in exchange for Mexico's support of Germany in the war. As a result of the interception and publication of this note, the United States declared war against Germany in April 1917.

Zionism A program initiated by Theodor Herzl to establish an independent Jewish state in Palestine.

Zollverein A unified trading zone created by Prussia in which member states adopted the liberal Prussian customs regulations; an attempt to overcome the fragmented nature of the German economy.

Zoroastrianism A monotheistic religion founded by Zoroaster in sixth-century b.c.e. Persia that emphasized the personal choice between good (light) and evil (darkness).

CREDITS

DOCUMENT CREDITS

Chapter 20

"What Is the Third Estate?": Abbe Emmanuel Joseph Sieyes "What is the Third Estate?" in *A Documentary Survey of the French Revolution* by John Hall Stewart. Copyright © 1951. Reprinted by permission of Pearson Education, Upper Saddle River, NJ.

"The Civil Code of the Code Napoléon": "Code Napoleon, 1804" from *The French Civil Code*, trans. Henry Cachard.

Chapter 22

"Young Italy": G. Mazzine, "Young Italy" in *Metternich's Europe*, edited and translated by Mack Walker, 1968.

"Flora Tristan and the Rights of Working Women": Giselle Pincetl, "Flora Tristan" from *L'Union Ouvriere*, 3rd edition, as translated in *Harvest Quarterly*, 7 (Fall 1977). Copyright © 1977 Giselle Pincetl.

Chapter 23

"The Russian Emancipation Proclamation, 1861": Excerpt from *The Diary of a Russian Censor: Aleksandr Nikitenko*, abridged edition, edited and translated by Helen Saltz Jacobson, p. 222. Copyright © 1975 by The University of Massachusetts Press. Reprinted by permission.

Chapter 24

"J'Accuse": *From The Affair: The Case of Alfred Dreyfus* by Jean Denis Bredin, translated by Jeffrey Mehlman, pp. 248–249. Copyright © 1986 by George Braziller, Inc. Reprinted by permission.

Chapter 25

"Leopold II of Belgium": From *French Colonialism, 1871–1914: Myths and Realities* by Henri Brunschwig. Reprinted by permission of Armand Colin, Editeur.

Chapter 27

"The Depression for Women": From *Women and a Changing Civilization* by Winifred Holtby. Copyright © 1934 by The Bodley Head Ltd. Selections reprinted by permission of Paul Berry and Marion Shaw, literary executors for Winifred Holtby.

"The Results of the First Five-Year Plan": From *Selected Writings* by Joseph Stalin. Copyright © 1942 by International Publishers. Reprinted by permission.

"The Law on the Abolition of Legal Abortion": Rudolph Schlesinger, *The Family in the USSR: Documents and Readings*, pp. 251–254. Copyright © 1949 Routledge & Kegan Paul. Reprinted by permission.

"Adolf Hitler on Racial Purity": From "Racial Purity: Hitler Reverts to the Dominant Theme of the National Socialist Program, January 30, 1937" from *Hitler's Third Reich*, edited by Louis L. Snyder. Copyright © 1981 by Louis L. Snyder. Reprinted by permission of Nelson-Hall, Inc.

Chapter 28

"Manifesto of the Jewish Resistance": From *An Anthology of Holocaust Literature*, edited by J. Glatstein, I. Knox, and S. Margoshes, pp. 332–333. Reprinted by permission of the Jewish Publication Society.

"President Franklin Roosevelt's Request for a Declaration of War on Japan, 8 December 1941": From *World War II: Policy and Strategy* by H. Jacobsen and A. Smith, pp. 182–185. Reprinted by permission.

"Japan's Declaration of War on the United States and Great Britain, 8 December 1941": From *World War II: Policy and Strategy* by H. Jacobsen and A. Smith, pp. 182–185. Reprinted by permission.

"Glittering Fragments": "Glittering Fragments" by Hara Tamiki from *The Penguin Book of Japanese Verse*, translated by Geoffrey Bownas and Anthony Thwaite, p. 221. Copyright © Geoffrey Bownas and Anthony Thwaite. Used by permission.

Chapter 29

"The Iron Curtain": From "The Sinews of Peace" by Winston Churchill in *Winston Churchill: His Complete Speeches 1897–1963*, (Vol. VII; 1943–1949), edited by Robert Rhodes James. Copyright © 1974. Reprinted by permission of Chelsea House Publishers, LLC.

"Report to the Twentieth Party Congress": Nikita S. Khrushchev, from *Current Soviet Policies II: The Documentary Record of the Twentieth Party Congress and Its Aftermath*, translation copyright by The Current Digest of the Soviet Press, Columbus, Ohio. Used by permission.

"The Second Sex": Simone De Beauvoir, *The Second Sex*, translated by H. M. Parshley. Copyright © 1952 and renewed 1980 by Alfred A. Knopf. Reprinted by permission of Alfred A. Knopf, a Division of Random House, Inc.

"Subterranean Homesick Blues": Copyright © 1965 by Warner Bros. Music. Copyright renewed 1993 by Special Rider Music. All rights reserved.

Chapter 30

"Career Advancement, Communist-Style": Tony Parker, *Russian Voices*, pp. 210, 213, 214. Copyright © 1991 by Tony Parker. Reproduced by permission of Henry Holt and Co., LLC.

"Cities as Environmental Leaders, 2005 press release": Press Release issued by The Clinton Foundation.

PHOTO CREDITS

Unless otherwise acknowledged, all photographs are the property of Pearson Education, Inc. Page abbreviations are as follows: (T) top, (B) bottom, (L) left, (R) right.

Chapter 20

591 Erich Lessing/Art Resource, NY **593** Bridgeman-Giraudon/Art Resource, NY **594** "Abus à Suprimé" ("Abuses to Suppress"), engraving by Dessal, Musée de la Révolution Française (MRF 88–133) **596** Réunion des Musées Nationaux/Art Resource, NY **598** Bridgeman-Giraudon/Art Resource, NY **602** Library of Congress **604** Bridgeman-Giraudon/Art Resource, NY **605** University of Maryland Libraries (DC 187.7 C655 [1794]) **607** Musées Royaux des Beaux-Arts de Belgique, Bruxelles **610** Goya, Francisco. Spanish, 1746-1828, *Y No Hai Remedio (And there is no remedy),* from Los *Desastres de la Guerra.* Etching, fourth state. The Metropolitan Museum of Art, Schiff Fund, 1992 (22.60.25[15]). Photo © 2002 The Metropolitan Museum of Art **614** Olin Library, Rare Books, Cornell University (Cornell nap. 31)

Chapter 21

619 Claude Monet, French, 1840–1926, Arrival of the Normandy Train, Gare Saint-Lazare, oil on canvas, 1877, 59.6 x 80.2 cm, Mr. and Mrs. Martin A. Ryerson Collection, 1933. 1158, The Art Institute of Chicago.photography © The Art Institute of Chicago **624** Yale Center for British Art/Paul Mellon Collection USA/Bridgeman Art Library **625** Bedfordshire & Luton Archives & Records Service **627** © British Library Board, All Rights Reserved (966.g.4-7) **630** (T) The Board of Trustees of the National Museums and Galleries of Merseyside (Walker Art Gallery, Liverpool [WAG 659]) (B) akg-images **631** The Granger Collection, NY **635** Daumier, Honore (1808–1879) *The Third Class Carriage.* Oil on canvas. H. 25 3/4 in. W. 35 1/2 in. (65.4 3 90.2 cm.) The Metropolitan Museum of Art, H. 0. Havemeyer Collection, Bequest of Mrs. H. 0. Havemeyer, 1929. (29.100.129) Photograph by Malcolm Varon. Photograph © 1984 The Metropolitan Museum of Art **636** Victoria & Albert Museum, London/Art Resource, NY **641** John R. Freeman/Fotomas, London/Bridgeman Art Library **642** Mansell Collection/Time Life Pictures/Getty Images **645** Bridgeman-Giraudon/Art Resource, NY **649** Print and Picture Collection, The Free Library of Philadelphia

Chapter 22

653 Potato Planters, about 1861; Jean-François Millet, French (1814–1875), oil on canvas; 82.5 x 101.3 cm (32 1/2 x 39 7/8 in.) Gift of Quincy Adams Shaw through Quincy Adam Shaw, Jr. and Mrs. Marian Shaw Haughton (17.1505). Museum of Fine Arts, Boston. Reproduced with permission. © 2007 Museum of Fine Arts, Boston. All Rights Reserved. **657** Bibliothèque Nationale de France, Paris **660** By courtesy of the Wedgwood Museum Trust, Barlaston, Staffordshire, England **663** akg-images **664** Bridgeman-Giraudon/Art Resource, NY **665** The Granger Collection, NY **669** Hulton Archive/Getty Images **671** FA/Roger Viollet/The Image Works **672** Erich Lessing/Art Resource, NY **677** Hulton Archive/Getty Images **678** bpk/Art Resource, NY

Chapter 23

685 © Oxford Science Archive/Heritage-Images/The Image Works **689** © Stapleton Collection/Corbis **690** © Hulton-Deutsch Collection/Corbis **692** bpk/Art Resource, NY **696** Bibliothèque Nationale de France, Paris **697** Erich Lessing/Art Resource, NY **698** Bridgeman Art Library **699** Mary Evans Picture Library **703** By courtesy of the Board of Trustees of the Victoria & Albert Museum **705** Mary Evans Picture Library **707** Galerie Neue Meister, Dresden, Germany, © Staatliche Kunstsammlungen Dresden/ Bridgeman Art Library **708** National Portrait Gallery, London (NPG153) **709** Down House, Kent, UK/Bridgeman Art Library

Chapter 24

717 Bridgeman Art Library **718** Stadtmuseum Berlin (PC9890) **723** akg-images **726** Hulton Archive/Getty Images **727** Mary Evans Picture Library **728** Bridgeman Art Library **731** Jewish Museum, NY/Art Resource, NY **733** AP/Wide World Photos **737** Erich Lessing/Art Resource, NY **738** Digital Image © The Museum of Modern Art/Licensed by Scala/Art Resource, NY © 2007 Estate of Pablo Picasso/Artists Rights Society (ARS), New York **739** (L) Staff finial, Kongo peoples, Democratic Republic of the Congo, Congo, Angola, 16th-19th century, Ivory, ceramic, camwood, resin. 6.5 x 5.1 x 6 cm (6 1/2 x 2 x 2 3/8 in.), Museum purchase (85-15-4) National Museum of African Art, Smithsonian Institution, Washington, D.C. (R) Face mask, Guro peoples, Côte d'Ivoire, Mid 20th century, wood, paint, 54 x 28.6 x 17 cm (21 1/4 x 11 1/4 x 6 1 1/16 in.). Bequest of Eliot Elisofon (73-7-167) National Museum of African Art, Smithsonian Institution, Washington, D.C. **740** Mary Evans Picture Library **741** © Roger-Viollet/Carnavalet/The Image Works

Chapter 25

745 Corbis **748** © Nico Tondini/Robert Harding World Imagery/Corbis **749** © Scherl/SV-Bilderdienst/The Image Works **750** © Albert Harlingue/Roger-Viollet/The Image Works **753** The Granger Collection, NY **763** Eileen Tweedy/The Art Archive **764** The Granger Collection, NY **767** © The British Library Board, All Rights Reserved (154 f. 31d, neg. B6140)

Chapter 26

772, 773 From the copy in the Bowman Gray Collection, Rare Book Collection, University of North Carolina at Chapel Hill **776** Private Collection, Archives Charmet/Bridgeman Art Library **778** Bettmann/Corbis **779** Imperial War Museum, London (Q3990) **781** National Archives **785**Imperial War Museum, London (Q3995) **786***We Are Making a New World,* 1918 (oil on canvas) by Paul Nash (1889–1946) Imperial War Museum, London, UK/Bridgeman Art Library **787** Imperial War Museum, London (Q20220) **789** Mansell Collection/Time Life Pictures/Getty Images **792** Illustrated London News **795** Sovfoto **797** Imperial War Museum, London (Q11586) **798** Brown Brothers **802** Mary Evans Picture Library

Chapter 27

806 Hulton Archive/Getty Images **807** bpk /Art Resource, NY. © Estate of George Grosz/Licensed by VAGA, New York, NY **813** Reprinted, with permission, from The Columbus (Ohio) Dispatch **814** (T) Stock Montage (B) Michael Holford Photographs **817** Getty Images **820** Novosti/Sovfoto **821** Sovfoto **824** Erich Lessing/Art Resource, NY **826** Bettmann/Corbis **828** Corbis **829** German Propaganda Archive **831** Bibliothèque Nationale de France, Paris **833** AP/Wide World Photos **835** Museo del Prado, Madrid © 2007 Estate of Pablo Picasso/Artists Rights Society (ARS), New York **837** Private Collection, Archives Charmet/Bridgeman Art Library

INDEX

A boldface entry indicates a key term and the page number where its definition can be found. Terms and definitions also appear in the Glossary on pages G-1–G-7.